Twelve Notables in W

MW00904317

Mini-biographies featuring compelling life journeys, as told to author Jack J. Prather

- **Rev. Dr. Dan Matthews, OBE —Waynesville**
  Priest at Ground Zero on 9-11 / Recipient Order of the British Empire / Chair, Friends of the Smokies

- **Musician David Holt —Fairview**
  Multi-Instrumentalist, Storyteller / Four Grammy Awards, Eight Nominations / PBS-TV, NPR-Radio Host

- **Captain Ray F. West, Jr., USNR, Ret. —Flat Rock**
  Founder-President Moldova World Children's Fund / UNCA 2006 Taylor Distinguished Alumnus Award

- **Judge Harry C. Martin —Biltmore Forest**
  Former NC and Cherokee Supreme Court Justice / Honorary Cherokee / 2010 Liberty Bell Honoree

- **Olson Huff, MD, FAAP —Black Mountain**
  Founding Medical Director Mission Children's Hospital, Asheville / Former President NC Pediatric Society

- **Glenis Redmond —Asheville**
  Mountain Xpress Hall of Fame Poet / Third in National Poetry Slam / Kennedy Center Teaching Artist

- **Douglas M. Orr, Ph.D. —Black Mountain**
  President Emeritus Warren Wilson College / Author / Musician / Order of the Long Leaf Pine Award

- **Billie Ruth Sudduth —Bakersville**
  Basket Artist / Smithsonian Collection / 1st Woman NC Living Treasure / Order of Long Leaf Pine Award

- **Matthew J. Hayes, M.D., Ph.D., FACEP —Hendersonville**
  Pioneer National Emergency Medical Services / Co-Founder American College of Emergency Physicians

- **Joe Epley, APR —Tryon**
  Global PR Leader / UNC Journalism School Hall of Fame / Order of Long Leaf Pine Award

- **Richard Ritter —Bakersville**
  Studio Glass Art Master / NC Living Treasure 2011 / Governor's Award for Volunteer Service as Fire Chief

- **Julyan Davis —Asheville**
  Nationally Recognized Oil Painter of Southern Art / Gallery Shows on East-West Coasts and Europe

Future Now Publishing—est. 1986

Portion of Proceeds Support Warren Wilson College Young Writers Scholarship

Excerpts from Testimonials about the Twelve Notables

- **Former NC Supreme Court Chief Justice-Ret. James B. Exum—**
  Justice Harry C. Martin was 'the conscience of the court' for ten years, from 1982-to-1992.

- **Former North Carolina Governor Jim Hunt—**
  I had the distinct honor of working with and counting on many of the Notables in Jack Prather's fine book, including founding Medical Director of Mission Children's Hospital Dr. Olson Huff, Warren Wilson College President Emeritus Dr. Doug Orr, former Supreme Court Justice Harry C. Martin, and Global Public Relations leader Joe Epley. I applaud these twelve exemplars from such diverse fields as medicine, education, the military, faith, charity, business, entertainment and the arts. All Tar Heels should be grateful for their contributions to our state!
  (*Note:* James B. Hunt, Jr. is the only four-term governor in State history, serving from 1977-1985 and 1993-2001.)

- **Katie Couric, ABC-TV—**
  Rev. Dr. Dan Matthews is one of the most empathetic and smartest people I've ever met. I enjoy discussing everything under the sun with Dan, from the events of the day to philosophical questions about life, to the mysteries of human behavior, to the latest pop culture phenomenon. Dan has a wisdom and depth that is unusual even for a man of the cloth. He has been a constant and steadfast source of support for me during times of gut-wrenching loss, career challenges and romantic travails. I appreciate his tolerance in embracing all faiths at a time when religion has become more divisive than uniting. He's a mixture of Spencer Tracy and Jack Lemmon, and I love his ebullience, mischievous grin, and the gleam in his eye when he talks about something he's passionate about.

- **NC Arts Council Literature Director David Potorti—**
  Representing a diverse range of artistry, basket-maker Billie Ruth Sudduth, studio glass art master Richard Ritter and traditional musician David Holt are celebrated examples of the creative 'Notables' found throughout our Western Carolina Mountains. Their dedication to their craft and to our state is legendary, and their stories told to Jack Prather will inspire and delight you.

- **North Carolina Secretary of State Elaine F. Marshall—**
  In my mind, Navy Captain Ray West is a giant for his legacy of giving to others. Ray is leading by example to help deserving people in a very poor land become self-reliant, and providing them with a few of the basic good things in life that we in America sometimes take for granted. We need more like him!

- **Traditional Music Legend Doc Watson—**
  David Holt and I have a lot of fun when we play music. He loves music and it shows. He is one of the best old-time banjo pickers you'll ever hear.

- **Author/Professor Ron Partin—**
  I was moved by the life stories that capture the essence of the Notables. Along with the nine cited above, I salute Hall of Fame Poet Glenis Redmond for her amazing performances that I have enjoyed, contributions of emergency physician pioneer Dr. Matt Hayes, and the incredible realism in the Southern art oil-paintings of Julyan Davis.

- **Charleen Bertolini, Educational Book & Journal editor—**
  Fabulous! It was a welcome treat to learn how you chose your subjects and your motivation in writing the book. I was really moved as I read each chapter and inspired to reach higher in life. Thanks.

Meet the Twelve Notables

Rev. Dr. Dan Matthews and wife Deener with ABC-TV's Katie Couric.

Captain Ray West in his Navy Attire.

David Holt (l) and traditional music legend Doc Watson - with Grammys.

Pioneer Emergency Physician Matt Hayes dressed in familiar garb.

Judge Harry C. Martin chats with Court bailiff Isaac.

Billie Ruth Sudduth nestled in a bunch of her famed baskets.

Dr. Olson Huff (r) greets Rev. Billy Graham.

Julyan Davis painting a Southern art scene.

Dr. Doug Orr with NPR host and co-author Fiona Ritchie.

Studio Glass Artist Richard Ritter hard at work.

Poet Glenis Redmond on stage during a performance.

Joe Epley (l) chats with Arthur Chiliangarov of the Russian State Duma.

Dedication

This book is sincerely dedicated to the twelve Notables from Western North Carolina who trusted the author with their remarkable life and career stories so they could be shared with you, the reader, and to their families, friends and associates who helped forge each of them into the exemplars they are today. The Tar Heel state is richer for their presence! — **Jack J. Prather**

How to Order *Twelve Notables in Western North Carolina*
@2012 Author Jack J. Prather. *From Future Now Publishing (FNP) - est. 1986*

Cost for Single or Multiple Books
Hardcover: $29.95 + s-h/NC tax. Softcover: $19.95 + s-h/NC tax.

Discount Program :
10% discount for students, AARP members, organizations, multiple book orders.
Indicate status in the order and the discount will be applied to the PayPal invoice.

Ordering Guidelines
Visit our online store at: www.futurenowpublishing.com/order.html
Tel. Orders: 828-808-0660

Standard Bookstore Discounts
e-Mail detailed orders to: info@futurenowpublishing.
ISBN-10: 14662766222.
ISBN-13: 978-1466276222
Library-of-Congress No. pending.

Mail Order details with check to
Future Now Publishing
c/o The Prather Group
828 Sandburg Terrace
Hendersonville NC 28791

Delivery of ordered books guaranteed by FNP.

AVAILABILITY SUMMER 2012:
Softcover book available at all bookstores by request;
Hardcover or softcover books available from Future Now Publishing;
e-Book available at online outlets.

Young Writers Scholarship fund

To donate by mail:
Make checks payable to: Warren Wilson College.
Write on check memo line: "Young Writers Scholarship"

Mail to:
Office of Advancement
Warren Wilson College
PO Box 9000
Asheville NC 28815-9000

To donate by credit-card:
Go to website: https://a.warren-wilson.edu/give
Go to Designation: Young Writers Scholarship
e-Mail confirmation of your pledge to: prathergroup@aol.com

Be sure to "like" us on Facebook at: www.facebook.com/TwelveNotablesInWesternNorthCarolina

Table of Contents

Acknowledgments

Gratitude for the nurturing assistance of others as I visualized then wrote *Twelve Notables in Western North Carolina* cannot be overstated. The commitment to the book and trust in me by each Notable helped light my path through the complexities of gathering the factual history of their lives and careers, and more importantly helped me capture their core essences.

Special thanks go to the Editorial Board Chairman of Future Now Publishing books E.M. 'Rick' Rickerson, Professor *Emeritus* College of Charleston and co-author of *The Five-Minute Linguist.* Rick's unerring editorial eye was of enormous help, and he graced this book by penning the Foreword. Thanks also to Editorial Board members James Charles Rogers, a former IBM executive, and Pam Prather, my wife and the editor of four of my six books.

Appreciation goes to Barbara Gregory of Blue Ridge Community College in Flat Rock for assigning intern Christopher Condrey to take on the difficult task of transcribing into coherent form my multiple in-depth taped interviews with each of the twelve Notables. Chris then became my professional technical assistant and designed both the cover and interior of the book. He has since been working as a Virtual Office Assistant, helping individuals and businesses become successful, doing business as 'Alternative Imperative Solutions' I wish him good luck.

I'm grateful for editorial input from education book and magazine editor Charleen Bertolini, from biographer and former New York Daily News columnist Professor Bruce Chadwick, and for comments about the book from former TV and radio station owner Peter Bardach, and former Chamber of Commerce President Doug Laird.

The process of selecting twelve Western North Carolina residents who have made significant contributions to the region, state, nation or world during their remarkable careers was aided by:

David Portorti, Literature Director of the North Carolina Arts Council, who suggested crafts masters Billie Ruth Sudduth and Richard Ritter, and noted musician and storyteller David Holt; and Billie Ruth for recommending iconic 9/11 Priest Ground Zero, Rev. Dr. Dan Matthews;

The Unitarian Universalist Church of Hendersonville, where I first enjoyed hearing Hall-of-Fame Performance Poet Glenis Redmond;

Russell Rawlings, Communications Director of the North Carolina Bar Association, who recommended former North Carolina and Cherokee Supreme Court Justice Harry C. Martin;

Barbara Hipwell and Connie Vlahoulis of Conn-Artist Studios in Hendersonville, who brought to my attention the immense talent of Southern art painter Julyan Davis;

David Johnson of the Western North Carolina Yale University Alumni Association, who recommended Warren Wilson College President *Emeritus* and author Doug Orr;

Notable global public relations professional Joe Epley, who recommended renowned pediatrician and founder of Mission Children's Hospital in Asheville, Dr. Olson Huff;

And to Ron Partin, author and Bowling Green University Professor *Emeritus* who introduced me to Captain Ray West, USNR-ret., founder of the Moldova World Children's Fund.

Foreword

As the 'nose' of North Carolina that pokes its way into mountains shared with Georgia and Tennessee, Western North Carolina (WNC) is sometimes overlooked in a state with its center of gravity in Raleigh/Durham and Charlotte. It is a largely rural place of winding roads and little towns in the valleys of the Southern Appalachians. Other than Asheville, famous for an opulent summer home of the Vanderbilts, WNC has neither well-known cities nor the brand-name tourist attractions that turn a region into a household name. What it does have is endless woods, a hospitable climate, an abundance of inviting trails and streams, and tranquility that lures – and *holds* – people who want a healthy and rational life style. It is an extraordinary place that has both birthed and attracted, and continues to attract, some very exceptional people. *Twelve Notables* is a book about some of those people, men and women in Western North Carolina whose lives and achievements richly deserve to be recognized.

Focus on living Notables -

One of author Jack Prather's first decisions for this book was whether to include personalities from the past who once made their homes in WNC, such as Asheville's Thomas Wolfe, or poet Carl Sandburg who did much of his writing in the tiny village of Flat Rock. Prather's choice was to focus on living individuals, to raise the profile of a group of talented people who fly under the radar of what we call fame. Many of his "Notables" have been honored through awards or national acclaim, but this is the first time their life stories have been written.

Other than living in Western North Carolina what the twelve Notables have in common is that they are at or near the top of their professions and recognized as such by their peers; that they have made significant and *positive* contributions to the rest of us; and that, in addition to their accomplishments, they have 'given back' to the community through their work and charitable acts, or perhaps as teachers or mentors in their field. In short, there is more to admire in them than whatever makes them high-achievers. They are a diverse group, including two physicians, a painter, a musician, a glass artist, a basket maker, a performance poet, an educator, a priest, a businessman, a state Supreme Court justice, and a military officer. Politicians, the reader may note, are conspicuously absent.

Not your usual biography -

Although the book offers a well-rounded picture of who these individuals are and why they deserve attention, it is not a collection of biographies in the usual sense of the word. Most biographies are a detailed account of someone's life told by a narrator who has researched the personality and experiences of his subject, with a description of the times he or she lived in. Such a book might normally run three or four hundred pages or more. Following that model, the life stories of Prather's Notables taken together could have been over 4,000 pages long.

His approach was to create what he calls "mini-biographies," each consisting of 30-to-45 pages. The twelve chapters are really cameos; brief portraits supplemented by biographic data, rather than full-scale biographies. Since the subjects are living and the time is the present, there is little need for historical or sociological background. Because the author does not take the role of narrator, he does not spend time on exploration of his subjects' personalities. Their character and values emerge mostly in their own words, through interviews that are the centerpiece of the book.

Their life stories are expanded through an excellent array of photographs, a detailed summary of the highlights of their careers, and comments about them by contemporaries, who in many cases are themselves 'notable'. The author remains almost entirely in the background, collecting, collating, organizing and editing the material. His voice is heard mainly as a scene-setter for the interviews, and as the gentle questioner who conducts them.

While it is an unusual format for biography, the non-narrative structure allows Prather to keep his own point of view out of the book. As he is fond of saying, "This is not about me; it's about them."

How the book evolved -

Like many successful books, *Twelve Notables* started with nothing more than a bit of table talk and a gleam in the eye of a creative writer in search of a project. When Prather and his wife Pam moved to the WNC area in late 2005, they were intrigued by the number and variety of gifted people they met, and Pam encouraged her husband to write about them. Jack wasn't sure where his research for such a project would take him or how the book would evolve. But in a sense – even though it took a great deal of intensive work - the book wrote itself as he talked with his subjects and their stories emerged. There was no particular reason for choosing *twelve* as the number of biographies, although six might have seemed too few and more than a dozen too ambitious. There were times during the writing of the book, I'm sure, when the author passionately wished he had settled for ten, or maybe even eight!

Not your usual biographer -

It should be pointed out that *Twelve Notables* is a radical departure from Prather's usual fare. While he limits his role as narrator here, in earlier writings he made his mark primarily as a story teller. In the 1970's he wrote sports and editorial columns for a New Jersey newspaper and in later years a pair of thriller novels, *The Day of the Knights* (2009) and *Investigative Reporter* (2011). As a journalist he received prizes for magazine articles and a number of New Jersey Press Association writing awards, including Best Column in All Divisions. Prather writes with some wonder in his Prologue at the "serendipities" that came up as he worked on this project, but it is no coincidence that the author of a book on Notables is himself a person worthy of note.

Beyond his achievements as a writer, however, I would especially highlight one of Prather's strengths that made the book possible: his ability to put people at ease. It takes a particular personality to persuade someone to let you probe both the positive and negative details of his or her life. It is not unusual in times of 'tell-all' biographies for writers to highlight the negative side of a life story. How did Prather's subjects know he wouldn't write a book with a hidden agenda? I suspect that some of them signed onto the book with a certain level of wariness: who is this man and what are his motives? But it took only a short time for a trust relationship to build.

Peering over the author's shoulder as the book evolved, I had a chance to see some of the e-mail exchanges between him and his subjects. It was clear that even though he entered their lives as a stranger, they all came to like and trust him. He showed himself to be a talented listener: posing questions that were penetrating, but kind and tactful in how they were phrased. Far from feeling wary, the Notables developed a close rapport with the author, and applauded the way he brought their professional and personal stories to light.

Something happened along the way -

That of course was a hoped-for result. But something else happened along the way. Although born of intellectual curiosity and at first seen chiefly as a literary project, the writing of the book evoked in Prather something more emotional: a deep admiration for his subjects and a strong desire to do them justice through his skill as a writer. As he worked on the biographies, the book morphed slowly from a "project" to a tribute, honoring twelve people who changed from being his "subjects" into people he came to see as heroes.

While it is unlikely that any of the twelve would think of themselves as heroic, their ability and achievements clearly warrant the admiration they are given in this book. They are indeed Notables, and they make Western North Carolina proud.

    — **E.M. Rickerson, Ph.D.** Professor Emeritus, College of Charleston, Charleston, SC

Prologue

By Author Jack J. Prather

The Idea— The initial idea was to identify a suitable subject for a biography, a natural writing progression after penning two strategic public relations guidebooks, an issue-based book of poetry & prose, and two mystery-thriller novels over the past quarter-century. But as the well-known saying goes: "The best laid plans of mice and men oft go astray." Well not really, the plan for one biography grew into a collection of twelve about Notables who reside in Western North Carolina and, despite the inherent complexities, it was a joy.

The Vision— The vision was to try to capture the core essences of the twelve Notables in comprehensive condensed biographies with photo arrays that would serve as indelible legacies for their families, friends and associates, as well as readers throughout the state and beyond.

The Theory— The theory of the book was to first inform readers about each Notable through testimonials, highlights from their lives and careers, and excerpts from writings by and about them, and then to present their life-journeys as told to the author in multiple taped interviews. Each biography ends with factual chronologies of their lives; for the artists, examples of their crafts and paintings captured in vivid photos; and for the poet, samples of her original poetry writings. Websites are included for those wishing further information.

Selecting the Twelve Notables— Intensive research revealed that Western North Carolina is home to a virtual treasure-trove of living Notables! That search, plus recommendations from credible sources, led to the twelve exemplars selected for this book. In fact, so many deserving subjects were uncovered that this unique collection of biographies may serve as the template for a sequel.

Serendipity— As the project unfolded, the universe seemed to connect in mind-bending ways. I attribute this to serendipitous coincidences rather than mythical explanations ('serendipity' is carved on the wooden sign by our home). This book is not about me, except in this Prologue, so please sit back and ponder the serendipitous occurrences that unfolded during the writing of this book that are worth the telling:

I first met global public relations leader **Joe Epley** at a Roanoke PRSA meeting in 2004 when we lived at Smith Mountain Lake, Virginia and he in Tryon, North Carolina. *Joe* became my first Notable, and fortuitously for me recommended Founding Medical Director of Mission Children's Hospital **Dr. Olson Huff** . . . After contacting college alumni associations in Western North Carolina I discovered **Dr. Doug Orr**, president *emeritus* of Warren Wilson College via Yale University alumnus David Johnson, who happens to live in Biltmore Forest across the street from former Supreme Court and Cherokee Supreme Court Justice **Harry C. Martin,** a venerable jurist recommended by Russell Rawlings, communications director of the NC Bar Association . . . *Orr* and *Martin* belong to the storied century-old 37-member Pen & Plate Club in Asheville, and *Orr* and *Huff* can almost see each other's homes tucked on neighboring Black Mountain hillsides . . . *Note:* Johnson's daughter Elizabeth, a best-selling author, is on my short-list for a potential second book tentatively titled *Young Notables in WNC* . . .and the beat goes on, pun intended >

I researched the entertainment industry and selected Grammy-winner PBS-TV host and storyteller **David Holt** of Fairview, who is featured as a 'Song-Catcher' in the upcoming book on Celtic-Appalachian music co-authored by *Orr* and NPR Radio host Fiona Ritchie . . . David Potorti, NC Arts Council Literature Director, led me to Smithsonian Collection basket artist **Billie Ruth Sudduth** and studio glass artist and honored volunteer fireman ***Richard Ritter***, both of Bakersville. *Billie Ruth* was selected as the first female NC Living Treasure in 2006, and *Ritter* was named a Treasure in 2011.

Friend Cookie Lyday (Jackson) later told me that she and *Billie Ruth* delivered babies on the same day in the same hospital four decades ago . . . *Billie Ruth* guided me to the **Rev. Dr. Dan Matthews**, the iconic priest at 'Ground Zero' on 9/11 who owns The Swag Country Inn in Waynesville. *Dan,* as he prefers to be called, preached at Kanuga Conference Center in Hendersonville a decade ago where another Notable, **USNR Captain Ray West** of Flat Rock who founded the Moldova World Children's Fund, was administrator. I later learned that *Holt* had performed at both Kanuga and the Swag Inn . . . FNP Editorial Board Chairman and friend Rick Rickerson introduced me to his Hendersonville neighbor, emergency physician pioneer **Dr. Matt Hayes** . . . Two other friends, Connie Valhoulis and Barbara Hipwell of Conn-Artists studio in Hendersonville, suggested painter **Julyan Davis** of Asheville, the master of Southern art whose work is featured in galleries in America and abroad.

And finally this serendipitous vignette: During a taped interview with Performance Poet and Kennedy Center Teaching Artist **Glenis Redmond** at a café sidewalk table in Asheville, a woman spotted *Glenis* then rushed up and raved about her talent and originality. The woman, who had sold *Glenis* her Asheville home, was en route to a board meeting at nearby Diana Wortham Theatre to also be attended by *Orr,* who I had interviewed just that morning – go figure! One last note: the omnipresent *Orr, Sudduth, Epley* and *Huff* all received one of the top honors presented by the State of North Carolina to a citizen: The Order of the Long Leaf Pine.

Heroes, Past and Present: It has been my honor and good fortune to have connected with all but one of five personal heroes: President John F. Kennedy, who was the subject of one of my cherished newspapers columns. Both JFK, who inspired my career as a political consultant, and my father Ted, named after president, Theodore Roosevelt, were good and kind men taken too soon.

My hero as a Brooklyn boy was Dodger first-baseman Gil Hodges, whose photo adorned my bedroom wall and number 14 was on my uniform during amateur baseball days. As a young sports editor of the New Jersey Herald I interviewed Gil during his recovery from surgery. Brother Bob and I went to the rustic cabin where Gil was recuperating, and when the massive man emerged from his bedroom clad in robe and slippers and extended an enormous hand in greeting, he was not only warm and friendly, but very human. I captured those spine-tingling moments in a column titled *The Quiet Man,* and we were invited to be Gil's guests at a night in his honor at the Polo Grounds, the first Mets home. We spent most of the ceremony and game looking at the back of Gil's head while pinching ourselves to see if we were awake. Sadly, Gil also died young.

Senator Hubert H. Humphrey became my hero after I learned that in 1948 he had stood up for civil rights, the first national elected official to so do. I wrote an endorsement of the then vice-president during his presidential run in 1968 in my editorial page column *The Observer,* and gave him a copy at a campaign stop, just in case he had not read it. Three days later I received a personal letter of thanks.

Perhaps my most unusual hero was Charles 'Sparky' Schultz, author of the funny yet poignant 'Peanuts' cartoons. I wrote a column telling how his insightful messages both amused and stirred me. My reward was a tiny canary-yellow envelope bearing the return address 'One Snoopy Lane', with a sketch of the lovable beagle sprawled atop a mailbox. The personal note of thanks inside was beyond generous.

And now, thanks to this book, I have twelve more personal heroes. How fortunate am I? Very!

Western North Carolina demographics and geography >

Western North Carolina Demographics and Geography

Many residents of Western North Carolina, including the author, have an almost poetic feeling about the primarily mountainous region that seems so idyllic and welcoming. A refresher course in the geographic and demographic profiles of the region follows so readers can gain more in-depth and comprehensive knowledge about the beautiful WNC area where the twelve Notables reside:

- **Geographic Boundaries / Population—**
Western North Carolina covers approximately 11,000-square-miles, roughly the size of Massachusetts, with a population of 1.3 million. Its various regions are defined as -

- *Appalachian Mountains - 'The Mountain Region'—*
'Land of the Sky' is the original nickname for this mountainous region that later became known as 'The Asheville Area'. The northwest portion of the region includes Boone and Blowing Rock, referred to as 'The High Country'.

- *'The Foothills'—*
Situated along WNC's eastern boundary, this area consists of a transitional terrain of hills between the Appalachians and the Piedmont Plateau of central NC. The westernmost part of WNC is in the Tennessee Valley.

- *23 Counties in WNC—*
There are 23 counties in WNC: Alleghany, Ashe, Avery, Buncombe, Burke, Caldwell, Cherokee, Clay, Graham, Haywood, Henderson, Jackson, Madison, McDowell, Mitchell, Polk, Rutherford, Swain, Transylvania, Watauga, Wilkes, Yancey.

- *Seven Cities and Towns with Populations Over 10,000—*
The seven cities and towns with populations over 10,000: Asheville, Morganton, Lenoir, Hendersonville, Boone, Waynesville, North Wilkesboro. Western North Carolina towns with fewer than 10,000 residents are listed on the next page.

- *Important Unincorporated Communities—*
- Cherokee – headquarters for the Eastern Band of the Cherokee Nation (ECBN);
- Cullowhee – site of Western Carolina University main campus;
- Deal's Gap – site of a nationally famous motorcycle and sports car resort;
- Lake Junaluska – headquarters of World Methodist Council, site of United Methodist Camp & Conference Center.

- *WNC Higher Education—*
Western Carolina University has three campuses in the region, and Appalachian State University in Boone and UNCA in Asheville. Warren Wilson College in Swannanoa is noted for strong pro-environment policies, social liberalism and activism. Liberal arts colleges include Mars Hill north of Asheville, affiliated with the North Carolina Baptist Convention and the oldest in the state, founded in 1856; Montreat College east of Asheville, affiliated with the Presbyterian Church, as is Lees-McRae College near Banner Elk. Brevard College is affiliated with United Methodist Church.

- *WNC Economic Overview—*
Tourism is a major part of the economy of the area which contains half of the Great Smoky Mountains National Park, as well as the Nantaha and Pisgah National Forests. There are several lakes and dams scattered through the region, including Lake Lure and dam.

Towns with Fewer than 10,000 Population-

Andrews
Bakersville
Balsam Grove
Banner Elk
Beech Mountain
Belwood
Biltmore Forest
Black Mountain
Blowing Rock
Bostic
Brevard
Bryson City
Burnsville
Cajah's Mountain
Canton
Casar
Catawba
Cedar Rock
Chimney Rock
Cliffside
Clyde
Collettsville
Columbus
Connellys Springs
Conover
Crossnore
Dillsboro
Drexel
Elk Park
Elkin
Ellenboro

Fallston
Flat Rock
Fletcher
Forest City
Franklin
Gamewell
Glen Alpine
Grandfather
Granite Falls
Hayesville
Highlands
Hildebran
Hot Springs
Hudson
Jefferson
Kings Mountain
Lake Lure
Lake Santeetlah
Lansing
Lattimore
Laurel Park
Lawndale
Linville
Maggie Valley
Marion
Mars Hill
Marshall
Mills River
Mooresboro
Murphy
Newland

Newton
North Wilkesboro
Old Fort
Polkville
Rhodhiss
Robbinsville
Ronda
Rosman
Ruth
Rutherford College
Rutherfordton
Saluda
Sawmills
Seven Devils
Shelby
Sparta
Spindale
Spruce Pine
Sugar Mountain
Sylva
Taylorsville
Toluca
Tryon
Valdese
Vale
Weaverville
West Jefferson
Wilkesboro
Woodfin

Source: Wikipedia

● ● ●

Rev. Dr. Dan Matthews, OBE
Episcopal Priest at 'Ground Zero' on 9/11/01

Reverend Doctor Dan Matthews shakes the hand of former President Jimmy Carter.

I asked "Who opened that basement door and let us out? I'd like to thank the person who saved our lives on 9/11." Silence. So I thought that the person who had opened the door was sick, or not back to work yet. For weeks I kept asking "Who opened the door?" but nobody ever answered. One day this bossy woman from the accounting division said "Doctor Matthews, you keep asking who opened the door." I said "Yes, tell me so I can thank them." She replied "Everybody in this room knows who opened the door except for you, it was . . ."
— **Dan Matthews**

Sections about Reverend Dan Matthews:

1) What Others Say about the Episcopal Priest

2) Highlights of his Life and Career

3) **Dan's Life Journey, in His Own Words**

4) Photos

5) Nuggets of Wisdom from his Writings and Prayers

6) Chronology

Section 1: **What Others Say about the Episcopal Priest**

- **Famed Newswoman reflects about Rev. Dr. Matthews—**

Dan is one of the kindest, smartest, most empathetic people I've ever met. I can't tell you how much I enjoy sitting with Dan and his wonderful wife, Deener, and discussing everything under the sun, from the news events of the day to philosophical questions about life, to the mysteries of human behavior, to the latest pop culture phenomenon. Dan has a wisdom and depth that is unusual even for "a man of the cloth." He has been a constant and steadfast source of support for me during times of gut-wrenching loss, career challenges and romantic travails. I appreciate his open-mindedness and not just tolerance, but embrace of all faiths at a time when religion has become more divisive than uniting. He's a mixture of Spencer Tracy and Jack Lemmon, and I love his ebullience, mischievous grin and gleam in his eye when he talks about something he's passionate about.
     — **Katie Couric,** ABC-TV

- **Iconic Status in the Episcopal Church—**

I am pleased to comment on Dan Matthews' career and his unique contributions. Known as Father Dan to many of his friends and followers, Rev. Dan Matthews has achieved iconic status within the Episcopal Church. With deep roots in the mountains of Western North Carolina, he is not only devoted to the preservation of our national parks but a master story teller of the first order, always mindful of the guiding hand of God in all things good and glorious.
     — **Justice Gary Wade,** Tennessee Supreme Court Justice

- **Remarkable Rector of Trinity Church in New York—**

Dan Matthews, Canton, North Carolina native, has returned to his roots in the Western Mountains and is beginning to have the kind of impact he had while Rector of Trinity Church on Wall Street in New York. For a mountain boy from Haywood County to have become Rector of Trinity Church is remarkable. Proof that if one has energy, intelligence, honesty and drive, all virtues we like to associate with mountain people, then one can go far. Dan Matthews did go far and he remains revered among parishioners in Trinity Church.

Now Dan has returned to the Swag on its mountaintop in Haywood County and is directing those energies that made him such a success in New York to the needs of preservation of our precious Western North Carolina Mountains. As the new chair of the Friends of the Smokies board, Dan brings that same energy, intelligence, honesty and drive in making the Friends organization a success.

A final word, no matter how good Dan is, and he really is good, he is supported by his wonderful wife, Deener, every bit as great as Dan!
     — **John S. Stevens,** Attorney, Roberts & Stevens, P.A., Asheville, N.C.

- **A personal letter from his longtime secretary—**

I was a church secretary in 1972 at St. John's Episcopal Church in downtown Knoxville, Tennessee when my boss, the Reverend Frank Cerveny, accepted a call to the Cathedral in Jacksonville, Florida. I assumed I would lose my job, but when new Rector Dan Matthews arrived from Nashville I thought we could work together.

The first few months were difficult for me, since Rev. Dr. Matthews' way of operating was much freer. At times I felt I couldn't keep up, as I am pragmatic, practical and structured. But his free spirit and my more structured world made a good match, and we have worked together since October of 1972 in Knoxville, Atlanta and New York City.

Dr. Matthews loves creative thinking and imaginative exploring. It is as if every day he could come up with some new idea. Thank goodness he didn't implement all of them, because every time he did, it meant more work for the staff and for me.

The church staff dreaded when he attended a conference because we were certain he would come home full of new proposals that we would find overwhelming to implement. One of my associates, Lavada Rigsbee, remarked to me one day, "Oh Lord, he's not going to another conference!"

An extra benefit for me personally was to have a rich and ongoing relationship with his children. Gail, Dan, Jr. and Laurin knew that no matter where he was or what he was doing, they could always reach me and I would contact their father.

I was at times for the Matthews a house-sitter, a baby-sitter, a spell checker, a chaperone, a car-pooler, and a vacation companion. These personal occasions bonded me with his children, and I have been blessed to be Godparent to several of his grandchildren. My son and his son are the same age, and through the years have shared skiing, out-door adventures, and love of storytelling and guitar playing.

Dr. Matthews' wife Deener has long been for me a sterling example of hospitality in action, with amazing energy and personal charm.

Each changing church job for me turned into an extremely steep learning curve. Each church has its own culture and social patterns that impinge significantly upon the rector's secretary. This meant daily sorting for him the important issues from the trivial.

Needless-to-say, my seventeen years as the rector's secretary at Trinity Wall Street was over the top with challenges, rewards, meeting famous people, and sharing in Trinity's rich and diverse worship community. I have been transformed into a New Yorker from having grown up in Chattanooga, Tennessee, a long way geographically, and even a longer way culturally when immersed in the intense world of the Wall Street community.

My retirement from Trinity allowed me to volunteer with Dr. Matthews at the Cathedral Church of St. John the Divine, assisting him in development efforts. The city I initially found intimidating has not only turned into my home but the place I have chosen to retire.
    — **Carol Stevenson,** Secretary to Rev. Dr. Mathews since 1972

Section 2: **Highlights of His Life and Career**

- **Honored with the Order of the British Empire—**

This Order of the British Empire (OBE) Citation signed by the Queen was presented to the Rev. Dr. Dan Matthews by Sir David Manning at an Investiture Ceremony in the British Embassy in Washington D.C. on March 2, 2006:

The award of an honorary OBE to the Reverend Daniel P. Matthews is in recognition of his services to the Anglican Communion, and for his remarkable leadership following the terrorist attacks 11 September 2001. Dan Matthews served as Rector of Trinity Church, Wall Street, New York, from 1987 until May 2004. One of the oldest churches in New York, Trinity Church has a long and historic link with the United Kingdom and with the Royal Family. In 1697, Queen Anne gave the church a parcel of land; it has prospered and played a significant role in Lower Manhattan ever since. In 1997, on the 300th anniversary of Queen Anne's gift, The Queen and Prince Philip received Dan Matthews, his wife Diane and the entire vestry of Trinity Church for tea at Windsor Castle.

In the terrible aftermath of the terrorist attack of 11 September 2001, Trinity Church and its daughter church, St. Paul's, became centers of ministry to the rescue workers at the World Trade Centers; they gave hope and help to all those who worked in the Trade Center and lived in Lower Manhattan. From his parish office Dan Matthews saw the second plane fly into the south tower of the World Trade Center and experienced first-hand the devastation that followed. In the difficult days after 11 September, he showed extraordinary leadership, vision, and compassion. He helped to turn St. Paul's, situated on the edge of Ground Zero, into an emergency centre, spiritual refuge and, subsequently a place of pilgrimage.

Trinity Church became a rallying point. His work and his ministry helped New York begin the healing and rebuilding process after the horrors of the terrorist atrocities.

On the first anniversary of 11 September 2001, the Archbishop of Canterbury, together with the Lord Mayor of London, and Britain's Foreign Secretary, Jack Straw, presented a bell from the citizens of London to the citizens of New York. The bell, a symbol of solidarity between the people of Britain and the United States, is now housed at Trinity Church. 11 September 2001 was a defining moment, but there are many other aspects of Dan Matthews' work that contribute to this award. Under his ministry, Trinity Church has made significant contributions and grants to Third World countries many of which are part of the Commonwealth. Several million dollars were given to the Anglican Communion and some of the poorest countries around the world.

Dan Matthews has also established excellent relations with successive Archbishops of Canterbury and offered them great support. Lord Carey, the Archbishop of Canterbury from 1991 to 2002 has said that he "found Dan's support quite outstanding" and that "honouring him would send a ripple of pleasure around the Anglican Community".

Having served as Rector of Trinity Church, Wall Street, Dan Matthews is now its Rector Emeritus. He is also Trustee of New York's Cathedral Church of St. John the Divine and co-chairs its Development Committee. He has been active in developing interdenominational projects, and helped to develop the Hallmark Television Channel which has brought together many people from different faiths. He has played a significant role in the development of the Clergy Leadership Project, a renewal programme for clergy throughout the United States, in the publication of a national magazine, Spirituality & Health; and in the creation of the award winning drop-in shelter, John Heuss House near the New York Stock Exchange.

In short, Dan Matthews has been a tireless champion of the poor, a steadfast supporter of the

Anglican Communion around the world, and provided New York with outstanding leadership and support after the events of 11 September, 2001. It is in recognition of this contribution that I am commanded by her Majesty, The Queen, in accordance with the powers vested in me as Her Ambassador, to confer on the Reverend Daniel P. Matthews the insignia of Honorary Officer of the Most Excellent Order of the British Empire.

- **Serving the Episcopal Church—**

Daniel Paul Matthews, rector *emeritus* of historic Trinity Episcopal Church on Wall Street in New York City, was born in Chicago, moved to Western North Carolina while in grade school, and graduated from high school in the small mill town of Canton.

The Rev. Dr. Matthews spent the first twenty years of his ministry as a priest in Tennessee parishes. Since 1972 the hallmark of his work has been concentrated in large inner-city parishes. This phase of his service began when he moved to St. John's in Knoxville, where the parish focused on the broad needs of the city within and outside the church. In 1980 he was called to serve at St. Luke's in downtown Atlanta.

In 1987 he received the call to minister to the landmark global and urban parish of 300-year-old Trinity Church, which he faithfully served for seventeen years, and was a leader in inter-faith television, founding the VISN-TV religious network.

During an extensive conversation between Senior Minister Lillian Daniel, Emmy-winning religious broadcaster Lydia Talbot and Dr. Matthews there was this exchange about his emphasis on televised ministries that appears in full on his website:

Daniel: *It's interesting that God can use a medium like television to proclaim a message like this, but television is also where so many of us find our temptation. It's where so many of these ideas about scarcity and needing more are propagated.*

Dr. Matthews: *Touché! Absolutely.*

Talbot: *The twin Gods of money and image.*

Dr. Matthews: *That's right. We're having a hard time with this, but we know in our hearts we're beginning to turn that corner . . . and that's allowing us to say 'I'm grateful for what I have, I don't have to have more'.*

- **The Bishop's Cross—**

Dr. Matthews was honored in 2001 with the Bishop's Cross of the Diocese of New York. The Diocese described him as "A gift to our city and diocese from wide-ranging experience in Tennessee and Georgia."

The citation continued: "His gifts of creativity and imagination have been expressed in many forms, from the establishment of what is now called the Hallmark Television Channel, where he brought together over fifty faith groups that include Jews, Roman Catholics, Mormons, mainline churches and historic black churches in joint ownership of the cable channel, to the Clergy Leadership Project, an intense renewal program open to clergy throughout the nation, to the publication of a national magazine, *Spirituality and Health,* and to the creation of the award-winning drop-in shelter John Heuss House near the New York Stock Exchange.

"His leadership has been recognized by four honorary doctorates; his preaching has been heard throughout the nation as well as in Canterbury Cathedral in England and Nanjing Seminary in China.

His magnetism and charm have been evident by his television appearances for the Chicago Series *Thirty Good Minutes* and *The Protestant Hour;* and most recently he was selected as chaplain at the historic Chautauqua Institution."

- ## Witness to the 9/ll Tragedy—

On September 11, 2001, Dr. Matthews saw the second plane fly into the south tower of the World Trade Center from his Parish offices and was forced to evacuate lower Manhattan with his staff and the children of the Parish pre-school. Trinity's Chapel, St. Paul's, located across the street from the World Trade Center served as a twenty-four-hour center of refuge and relief for eight months after the attack.

An Apostle of Hope: Dr. Mathews became an 'apostle of hope and healing' for lower Manhattan as the district sought to rebuild, appearing on all three network TV evening news shows and many others overseas and locally, both as an advocate for and commentator on the church's post-9/11 mission. He is currently chairman of the National Interfaith Cable Coalition Inc. in New York City

- ## Chairman 'Friends of the Smokies' and Other Organizations—

In March of 2011 Dr. Matthews was elected Chairman of the Board of the 'Friends of Great Smoky Mountains National Park', the first chairman from North Carolina since the regional organization was established in 1993 to help preserve the treasured National Park.

His other current religious and secular memberships include being on Advisory Boards of the Church Divinity School of the Pacific in Berkeley, CA, and the Vanderbilt Divinity School in Nashville TN. He is a board member of the Seamen's Church Institute in New York City; and on the Presidents Leadership Council for Rollins College in Winter Park FL

Both Dr. Matthews and wife Deener serve on the Foundation Board of the Haywood Regional Medical Center in Waynesville.

- ## The Swag Country Inn in Waynesville, N.C.—

'Deener' Matthews is the innkeeper during the summer season at their 'Swag Mountaintop Inn' situated on edge of the Smoky Mountain Park at 5,000 feet above the nearby Haywood County town of Waynesville, N.C.

Our State magazine writer Jeri Rowe captured the magic of the inn in its January 2010 edition:

It's just so beautiful. It's so foggy it looks like an ocean, and the sky is just so red it looks like a dreamland. Rowe went on to write: *Since 1982 guests have struggled to describe this place. You see in the room journals and thank-you notes that call it a 'sanctuary', a 'North American Shangri-La', and 'my place of peace'.*

Comfortable and cozy accommodations and delectable dishes, created with fare from local farms, are all part of Dan and Deener Matthews' mission to help guests feel 'in touch with the awesomeness of creation'.

In retirement, Dr. Matthews lives in Manhattan, where he continues to serve the Cathedral Church of Saint John the Divine where he maintains his office. During the summer the Matthews live at their log country inn.

Section 3: **Dan's Life Journey, in His Own Words**

When the tragedy of the 9/ll terrorist attacks ravaged lower Manhattan in 20001, The Rev. Dr. Dan Matthews was at Trinity Episcopal Church on nearby Wall Street where he was rector. St. Paul's, Trinity's chapel across the street from 'Ground Zero', was miraculously spared, and for eight months was the spiritual and medical triage center for hundreds of firefighters and other responders. The iconic and richly honored priest retired in 2004 after serving Trinity Church for seventeen years, but continues to serve his fellow human beings in both religious and secular capacities.

Multiple interviews with the personable and impressive priest took place at 'The Swag Country Inn' where his wife Diane 'Deener' Matthews is the innkeeper. The majestic yet quaint inn, perched more than 5,000 feet above the nearby Western North Carolina town of Waynesville, is a monument to warm Southern hospitality. We begin the initial interview by asking Dr. Matthews about the inn's name:

Dr. Matthews, please explain why your inn is called The Swag.

We didn't invent the word swag; it's been used in the Appalachian Mountains for a long time to describe the dip between two knobs. You would say the back of a horse has a swag, or that a swag in a drapery is too deep or not deep enough. If you stand way down in the valley and look up to the Cataloochee Ridge, you'll see one.

When we decided to open the log structures to the public in 1982, our hospitality consultant insisted: "You can't call your inn The Swag; you've got to name it 'Laurel Ridge' or 'Windy Gap' or something like that. But our kids said, "No, you're not going to change the name!" So we kept it.

It's quite a leap from being a priest to being an innkeeper.

I am not really the innkeeper; technically my wife Deener runs it, so when I'm not here it doesn't matter very much. My contribution is that I designed the road and all of the buildings.

We tried to use an architect in the earliest days, but he wanted to put the logs upright with black glass and other modern things. We wanted to build a place that closely resembled what the early mountain people had here. If they built a log house or a hunting lodge, this is what it would have been like.

The Swag is intended to resemble the natural beauty of what the early settlers' architecture was like, and we tried to maintain that pretty closely. For example, the room we're in now is structurally authentic because back in the days of the frontier a fireplace at one end of the living room heated everything. The entire Appalachian family would sleep on a balcony like ours because heat goes up during the night while somebody would tend the fire.

The Swag is authentically mountain. The logs are hand-hewn because the early settlers didn't have saws and had to chop the log flat on each side to make it look sawed. No self-respecting mountain man would build a cabin out of round logs since that is the way he would construct his barn. We had fun finding the logs and putting them up and making the floors, the wood trim, and the chairs as authentic as we could, all in keeping with early Appalachian life.

I see the stuffed bear over our heads on a beam stretched across the rafter. There must be a story connected with that.

The bear is sleeping up on our rafter to tell the story that if a bear came inside this inn he would climb straight up the post, stretch out on the beam where he could be safe and see the world below. If he was scared in the woods he would climb a tree.

- **First home becomes an inn—**

What inspired you to become innkeepers?

My parents lived in Canton, North Carolina in a paper-mill town at the bottom of our mountain, fourteen miles from here and halfway to Asheville. When my parents died suddenly in 1967 just six-weeks apart, we sold their house in town, but we wanted to stay connected with the mountains.

Deener and I had always lived in a church-owned rectory. Early on, it wasn't very popular to buy your own home, so you lived in whatever house the church provided.

Deener's uncle died and remembered us in his will. We put our two inheritances together from each side of our families and built this log lodge in the mountains. In the beginning, Deener would entertain small church groups for a retreat on the weekends and by doing the cooking and household chores, she felt like she was creating her own mission project. That was a beginning toward being used as an inn. We felt as if the money we inherited from our family was really not ours, having not earned it, we considered ourselves as trustees. So we decided to do something that would help other people. It was clearly a surprise that the inheritance came our way, because a clergyman could never earn enough income to build something like this.

- **The early years—**

Please tell me about your early years.

I was born in Chicago. We moved to Canton, when I was about twelve-years-old. My parents were Robert and Martha Matthews, and my father's father was a Presbyterian minister. My father graduated from Lake Forest College on the North Shore of Chicago. He became a newspaperman in a number of places. He wound up at the Chicago Tribune where he felt he found his true calling.

That vocational calling was interrupted long before I was born, by Reverend Billy Sunday, who was as famous an evangelist in the early twentieth Century as Reverend Billy Graham is today. Billy Sunday was having great difficulty with the press,. In that ear there were no such professionals as PR or press agents.

Billy Sunday went to Mr. Cyrus McCormick, owner of the Chicago Tribune, to seek help and relief from the heavy- handed press, and Mr. McCormick asked my father, one of his reporters, if he would be willing to spend a year with the famous evangelist to straighten out his press relations. My father traveled the nation with Billy Sunday, and the intended one-year commitment turned into eighteen. He was both secretary to Mr. Sunday and the tabernacle pianist until he retired during the early days of the depression.

What happened to your family then?

There were no jobs in Chicago but my father eventually found a position as a high school band director in Canton. The huge Champion paper mill at that time subsidized the band in order to have them play at special retirement ceremonies for the champion employees and the Labor Day Parade.

I went into seventh-grade at Pennsylvania Avenue Grammar School in Canton, the only new student in the school. My brother four years older was the only new student in the high school. Canton naturally had a mill town mentality, and during recess kids would tease me and call me 'Yankee boy' because I had a Chicago accent. Sixty five years ago Canton was a self-contained Appalachian mountain community.

How long did it take before you felt accepted, if ever?

Back then it was hard to move into the mountains and find peer group acceptance. I was obviously an outsider. I remember when the grammar school principal, Turner Cathy, who also taught us in the seventh grade, said "You are going to graduate and next fall go to the high school, and you ought to think about things like college and what you are going to do when you grow up." Then for some reason he asked our class, "How many of you have a mother and a father who both graduated from college?"

I suddenly felt embarrassed feeling mine was the only hand up.

That was the new world I had moved into, and I had no idea as a kid how to appreciate it. Through the years I have come to love it and am completely dedicated to these spectacular mountains and their transcendent awe. I would like to think of myself today as an 'almost' native.

• The College years—

Tell me about your college experiences?

I wanted to major in theater and to be an actor, so I went to a Rollins College in Winter Park, Florida, which was well known for its great drama department. There were only 600 students, but it had two full-time theaters, so I thought it was ideal. But after a couple of highly competitive years I discovered I didn't have any talent.

One student actor in my major became world famous, Tony Perkins, who starred in the movie 'Psycho.' In fact, he dated Deener before I did. I knew Tony as a brilliant actor but a bit strange and not easy to get to know.

On one afternoon date, Deener was walking with him to a movie in Winter Park when a car pulled up beside them and Tony said "See you later" jumped in the car with some friends and it drove away leaving Deener stranded alone on the sidewalk.

After you discovered you didn't have the talent for acting, what direction did you turn?

A woman professor of business, Dr. Florence Peterson, took me under her wing and urged me to go to graduate school to earn an MBA. She suggested I apply to the Amos Tuck School of Business at Dartmouth College for its two-year MBA program, and I did.

She and I had many challenging moments in our private tutoring. I remember one time her asking, "What do you think of labor unions?" and my answer, "They are all bad." When she asked why, I said, "Because my dad thinks they are." She had me immediately read *The 10 Great Strikes in American History* about the devastation in America caused by labor-management conflict. The historical reflection today suggests that the labor movement might have saved capitalism as we know it. We could have become a more socialistic country but as labor got its vote and voice, it balanced capital's power.

Dr Peterson kept up the philosophical discussions and challenges to my way of thinking, determined that I was going to grow out of my intellectually narrow world. During one tutorial she said, "You used the word pantheism and I'm not sure you know what that means." I was told to write a ten-page paper on pantheism and I did.

I always wondered if she even liked me as a person because she never once smiled in my presence. She was known by all of the students to be a demanding professor, not very feminine, and never married. Then years later after my parents died we found a box stored in the basement of our home with all my college report cards. This professor who had taken me under her wing had written in long hand: "This young man is going through an intellectual awakening."

• From Dartmouth to Divinity School—

I found fellow Dartmouth students to be amazingly attractive, bright, and charming; but they rarely talked about ideas; the topics were about future success, money and accomplishments. We didn't have discussion groups like those I remembered from college: "Is there life after death?" or "Do you believe in capital punishment?" and other topics kids discuss into the early mornings that help form the building blocks for integrity, morality, and character.

Many of the graduate students I went to school with at Amos Tuck wound up working on Wall Street where strangely enough I also ended up, but at a church.

How did you handle your dissatisfaction?

I discussed it with Dean Carl Hill, a wonderful man. I remember saying, "These guys are going to be running American capitalism. They will become the most powerful men in their towns. We at this school ought to be talking more about leadership values, integrity, honesty, and what a business executive can do to create a good community." He agreed.

Here I was in the finest and oldest MBA program in America, in fact the Harvard MBA program we were told patterned itself after Dartmouth's Tuck School, but it seemed to me nobody was talking about the real purpose of responsible leadership. Running the company and making money is the real purpose, while at the same time, leading that work environment into the highest standards for performance and integrity. I couldn't seem to get my points across. I eventually got discouraged and left the MBA program.

Where did you go?

I went to Vanderbilt University in Nashville, Tennessee. The dean of the Divinity School decided to treat me as if I were a "Danforth Scholar." That meant I could "test" my vocational call to the ministry by taking any course I wanted for one year. It was an ideal track for those of us who had some misgivings about ordination, yet serious interest. It was an exciting plunge into a dramatically different kind of graduate school.

• Joining the Episcopal Church—

When did you begin your journey as an Episcopalian?

While I was a student in Hanover, New Hampshire, I discovered there was no Presbyterian church in the village. So even after being up late most Saturday nights, on Sunday mornings I was up early and drove all alone to a nearby town called White River Junction ten or so miles south to go to church.

When the snows came and driving became difficult, I walked across the campus to an Episcopal Church and remember thinking, "I like the fact that they kneel during prayer." It was a simple thing, but nice and it became a comfortable new ritual for me.

During Divinity School in Nashville, I joined the downtown Episcopal Church, Christ Church, and it was there that the bishop of Tennessee said, "I want you to go to an Episcopal Seminary and not finish your degree at Vanderbilt. I'd like you to go to Berkley California to our seminary." And so I did. I spent three wonderful and exciting educational years at the Church Divinity School of the Pacific on the edge of the University of California campus in Berkeley. It was a very academic world, and I enjoyed its rich stimulation.

Was the seminary connected with the university?

No, but the semesters were the same and we as theological students could take courses at both. Toward the end of my three-year program, I wrote my mother that I wanted to stay on the west coast because I had a girlfriend and a job offer. My mother wrote back, totally unlike her, and used her affectionate nickname for me: "Dearest Toots, You will come home! Love, Mother." That was the whole letter, and it was like a bombshell! However I knew my parents were getting older, so it was not difficult to realize I had to go back east to be closer to them.

- **Then to a tiny Mission—**

Then I received in the mail my assignment from Bishop Barth of Tennessee, "I want you to go to Monteagle on the Cumberland Plateau and take charge of the Holy Comforter Mission." I would then become the first full-time Episcopal priest to ever live in the tiny town of 800 people. My second mission was in Midway, TN a rural area a few miles outside of Sewanee, sometimes referred to as 'Tickbush'.

Coming to the Tennessee hills directly from Berkeley presented interesting experiences. Members asked me to go coon huntin.' Well, I really didn't have any desire to go. I heard from a wife that it meant going to the edge of the Plateau and let the dogs run. Nobody did real hunting; they'd just sit by the fire, drink white-lightning and tell stories while listening to the sounds of the barking dogs in the woods all night long.

I also remember as a single young priest it was hard to find someone to date. A church member lined me up for a date with a girl in Chattanooga who was an Episcopalian, a lovely girl just out of college. I drove there in my little Volkswagen and knocked on the door and her attractive mother opened it and said, "So, you're Dan, the new priest who has driven fifty miles down that mountain to date our daughter. We've heard about . . ." but before she could finish the father came out, a gracious man who ran his own insurance company, and they invited me in. I felt fortunate and warmly welcomed.

After the movie and on my fifty mile, before Interstates, drive home, I felt we were just marginally compatible. I pondered my loneliness on top of a mountain and realized I faced a hundred mile roundtrip drive just for a blind date; Oh, for Berkeley!

When does Deener enter the picture?

We had been a bit in touch over the years since college through Christmas cards. Deener had gotten married to a graduate of the Naval Academy, had a daughter, and was living in a different world. I read in the *Rollins Alumni Magazine* that her husband, Lieutenant Commander John Sangster, had been killed in a plane crash, so I wrote that I was coming through Washington where she lived on my way to Europe and would like to stop to see her.

She asked a neighbor to put me up for a night, farmed out her daughter Gail, fixed me dinner, and we sat up and talked all night long. We were catching up on our event-filled nine years since we had seen each other. When the sun began coming up Deener said, "You better go over there and get into bed for a little while."

Deener likes to tell people we went through that whole evening and didn't even hold hands. We had previously enjoyed each other's company in college, but she was three and a half years older and mostly dating veterans from WW II, men in their late twenties. I was just eighteen. I couldn't compete for her with them, but we'd occasionally have coffee, and maybe see a play or movie. When we got back together I was making only $2,800 a year from my two tiny missions, so we had about six inexpensive dates, and then decided to get married.

- **The next 51 years—**

I found a clergy position in Memphis as an assistant in a big suburban church that had an interesting and gifted priest, Eric Greenwood, from whom I felt I could learn much. We were there for five years then went to Nashville, St. David's, for seven, Knoxville's St John's for seven and Atlanta's St. Luke's for seven more years before going to New York for twenty-five. That gives you an overview.

I'll say it does; that's more than fifty years of service to the church. Tell me about your ministries.

In Memphis we had a wonderful suburban ministry at the Church of the Holy Communion that had a lot of young people, maybe fifty or sixty kids who would attend youth group every Sunday night.

The church was also home to Saint Mary's, a girl's school of 400 students. I preached short chapel sermons each morning. I loved the kids and developed rich relationships with many of them. The diocesan youth camp in those days wasn't exciting enough for the privileged and affluent kids in our East Memphis neighborhood.

We tried a summer youth camp experiment and went to Wyoming where we took over two dude ranches. It was a non-stop trip on two Greyhound buses. For five years Deener and I ran it as a Christian summer camp for teenagers. We would have seventy boys and girls who were entering the eleventh, twelfth, or first year of college. Each teenager had his/her own horse. One whole day was spent in rock climbing with the Exum School. There were all day float trips through rapids down the Snake River. The camping experience was called 'Westward Ho for Senior Highs.' The two dude ranches we took over were White Grass and R Lazy S ranches in Moose, Wyoming.

Did you hire local experts for the activities?

The riding, mountaineering, floating all were led by seasoned instructors. I also had an OBGYN physician on the trip who did an all-day session on human sexuality. That doctor, Walter Ruch, was asked every conceivable question by the kids who were hungry for healthy and trustworthy answers.

I wanted the teaching program to be honest and open about sexuality. I also wanted open conversation about race so we decided we needed more black kids. It was expensive, but some supporters believed in what we were doing and gave scholarships for African American kids from poor neighborhood churches to also attend. It was all intended to be on the Christian cutting-edge. We had in-depth Bible and religious studies. About two-thirds of the campers were Episcopalians who had come from area Episcopal churches where I presented slide-shows to their youth groups.

• Next to Nashville—

What was your next priestly venture?

After five years in Memphis with Dr Greenwood, I wanted my own church and answered a call to St David's in a suburban area of Nashville called West Meade. The area consisted of 400 to 500 homes developed after World War II. The church was a mission of St. George's, Bell Meade, with about 120 members. We built it into the fastest-growing Episcopal Church in Tennessee.

There are lots of similar suburban churches where everybody attends the same high school, shops at the same mall, and attends the same clubs. It was very communal because everybody knew everybody. That was contributing factor to our rapid growth.

How long were you there, how big did it get, and to what do you attribute the growth?

During my seven years there the congregation grew to 550. The members and their children were most interested in going to church, and it was central to their family life. I was energized, had a young wife and three young children, and for me it was kind of like . . .

Pardon the interruption—like the life of 'A Man Called Peter'?

Perhaps a little bit. You know his story?

I read a biography of Peter Marshall, father of the son who preaches today. You remind me of him.

I felt I was at the right place at the right time with the right gifts of the Holy Spirit.

Back then Deener and I were about thirty-five, and three-quarters of the congregation that lived in our neighborhood were around our age. I remember one man of seventy-five who seemed ancient to me at the time and now I'm older than that.

I learned to realize that churches that grow rapidly are homogenous: most of the people tend to look like you, smell like you, think like you, and they're all the same. I decided I didn't want that for the rest of my ministry. I wanted to be in a downtown situation that was urban and rich with diversity and perhaps would not grow very fast.

Now when I got that call to the inner city and I could hardly wait to move on.

- **Downtown Knoxville is next—**

Our family moved to St John's, a downtown church in Knoxville, Tennessee. An interesting thing happened my first Sunday night when I asked the youth group of eleven kids where they went to high school, since that is the center of their lives. I learned to my surprise they all went to different high schools with competitive sports teams against each other, maybe even a dislike for each other.

I remember thinking back to St David's in suburban Nashville where almost every kid in our church went to Hillwood High School. It's hard to make a downtown church youth program exciting for kids with such diversity.

How did you make it grow?

We worked hard. We installed the local origination cable tv channel, staffed by young people, and carried live every Sunday service as well as the city council, board of education and other city gatherings. St. John's was known as the 'old-mother church of East Tennessee', a big stone building right downtown in a beautiful urban setting. It was a parish church then but has now become Saint John's Cathedral. The word 'Cathedra' means the chair where the Bishop sits.

Speaking of Cathedrals, the Cathedral Church of Saint John the Divine in New York where I now work, is the largest cathedral structure in the world. It is not the largest church structure, that is the Basilica in Rome, but it's not a cathedral.

- **On prejudice in America—**

Your Knoxville church was downtown; did it have a diverse congregation?

Saint John's was a wonderful church with great diversity. It opened up the world of worship to all ages. Some wealthy, some poor, some academic, some black, some business, some gay, and many singles; all driving past other churches to join the diversity.

Unfortunately, there were not many black people, maybe five or six and one in the choir; and this was the era when most in the clergy worked hard on that issue. If you went to Memphis or Nashville today and asked, "How can you make your church open enough so that a black family will feel welcome?" you'd find it is still tough to get an easy answer.

That wasn't easy to do for the best clergy, but I'm still not certain why we haven't been able to do it better. It is a serious failing that Christian churches in America are not able to racially unite all brothers and sisters.

Do you feel this is a failing of intention, or of not knowing how to act on an intention?

Very well put; both. There is still much more prejudice in America than most of us want to admit. It is deep; it is denied; it is profound. For those of us who have gone through the wrenching struggle of owning our prejudice and releasing that bias, the new peace does in fact "pass understanding."

Much work must be done on purging oneself from subtle but deep and unidentified prejudice. When you can get through that, then you realize our nation is still in the mode of very slowly accepting diversity.

Let me give you an example. We moved to New York after living in the South for my entire ministry. The New York church owned an apartment. We were to live in their co-operative, not a condominium. We discovered that in a cooperative the apartment dweller owns a piece of the whole; therefore the whole building is not unlike a private club. Whoever bought an apartment in our building had to be approved by the board, having a secret vote.

The board of course asks questions, looks at your financials, and even looks at your tax returns. Just one vote can blackball you. It's like in a fraternity. Of course, there was not one black person in our building. I remember thinking, "In terms of race, this building makes the South look pretty advanced."

President Nixon, after leaving the White House, tried to buy an apartment in a nearby building on Park Avenue but was turned down.

To find such prejudice in New York City, of all places, must have been discouraging.

Yes. My predecessor, Bob Parks, who was rector of Trinity Wall Street for fifteen years, found an apartment he and his wife Nancy wanted to buy in his retirement but he too was turned down, and they didn't even need to say why.

Do you know why?

No, and he never knew why, but maybe it was because his church, Trinity, had previously supported Bishop Desmond Tutu and divestment of stocks in South Africa. Prejudice in America is still very deep, and if you are African American, you can spot it in a second.

Racism is rampant all over our country, and of course I believe we are experiencing it now in fresh and subtle ways with a black president.

For the record Father Matthews, we are on the same wavelength.

- **Dealing with bias and prejudice—**

Thank you! Now please explain how introspection and confession helped you deal with and heal from your own biases and prejudices.

Yes, absolutely. In 1957 I gave a sermon in my seminary chapel in Berkeley CA to the whole student body and faculty. Giving a sermon was an academic requirement and I worked hard on it, especially since I was one of the few students from the South. The sermon title was "Why the Civil Rights Movements is Moving too Fast," and in it I said although the movement is doing great things, it needs to slow down. I almost weep now even thinking about that sermon.

When leaving the chapel, one of the several black students came up to me and I honestly expected him to say it was a great sermon, but he said the opposite and I was crushed. That was my first recognition that when it came to race, I had no idea what I was talking about, I mean zero! I had preached a twenty-minute sermon on a subject about which I later realized I knew nothing. Over the next several weeks, that fellow student straightened me out, and it was wrenching for me to hear what he said.

Do you remember what he told you?

First he told me that I didn't really know what I was talking about then said, "I wish you could be black for a month or two then you'd begin to understand."

I thought that was the silliest thing I'd ever heard, I couldn't be black, but it was also very, very painful. And with that I began to realize, "I'm afraid he's right, I really don't know what I am talking about." So, I began to make friends, not only with him but with other blacks, and I began to challenge my entire southern white frame of reference.

I began to see that it was an epistemology, a way of knowing, a way of not even seeing black people. It didn't matter where you grew up, you could not be free of prejudice unless perhaps you lived in Northern Montana, almost absent of African Americans.

Right now in New York City the prejudice is still so strong that getting acceptance into one of those cooperative apartment buildings on Park Avenue is not likely to happen. In a cooperative, unlike a condo, every tenant is voted in. It doesn't matter how much money you have, it doesn't matter if you went to Harvard, an acceptance vote is very difficult if your skin is black. So this was the dominant issue during my first twenty-five years in the ministry.

So you saw the ugliness that is racism early in your career.

When I was a young priest In Memphis, the Second Presbyterian Church placed their deacons across the front steps so no blacks could enter, and that was just fifty years ago!

For the five years we were there, we often went to dinner parties in lovely homes and it always seemed I ended up with an argument over race. It was the dominant issue of the day for everyone especially churches and every clergyman I knew.

We would struggle to get our church members to move forward just a little bit and these were otherwise wonderful people. I had a lawyer who was a graduate of Princeton and Harvard Law School, a good man, but he was blind about this issue. He said to me, "You don't realize it, Dan, but you're a fellow-traveler of the communist party." He meant I was contributing to the communist cause by advocating equality for blacks.

- **Dealing with who is in and who is not—**

In Monteagle, Tennessee I discovered the beautiful and historic assembly grounds. It is a Chautauqua type summer campus that has been there for more than a century and it contains 150 beautiful vacation homes, tennis courts, and the first swimming pool in the South. It was founded primarily by several Protestant denominations: Methodist, Presbyterian, Episcopalian, and Baptist.

In 1962 Deener and I bought one of those summer cottages and named it "The Lion's Den."

After a few summers, the board voted me in as president of the organization, so of necessity I had to deal with those who could own a home and who could not. When a Roman Catholic woman, whose Protestant husband had died, inherited his family home, the board voted that she couldn't retain her husband's membership because of her Catholic religion, and suggested she sell it.

Of course, here I was having in mind sometime bringing to the board our first black, but you can just imagine any person of color trying to acquire home ownership when a Roman Catholic could not.

That is when I said to myself, "I can't do this" and resigned. We sold our Lion's Den and started the process of building The Swag in the NC mountains.

Tell me more about your ministries in Knoxville and Atlanta.

Knoxville was a wonderful experience, and I was committed to the downtown ministry, the urban life, the urban ministry, and the real complexity of pulling people together to create a community. That is hard work. But in 1980 I left there and got even more 'downtown', on Peachtree Street in Atlanta, Georgia, which was booming.

We moved to St. Luke's Episcopal Church, which at the time was one of the most exciting churches in America because it had developed what we call a 'street ministry'. The Rev. Tom Bowers, the man who preceded me, had done the leadership. The church fed lunch to 500-to-800 people five days a week. We called it our 'soup kitchen.' The street people called it "Luke's Place."

Were they mostly minority?

Yes, maybe two-thirds. Then we discovered a group of people trying to do inner-city school youth work and we dedicated a part of our building for that. It was The Street Academy, made up of 150 high school kids, mostly black with a few exceptions. They all had been in trouble or kicked out of school or had babies or drug problems. We had fulltime truant officers, and the minute a kid was late they would search for him or her, pick them up and take them to school.

I instituted a space called a 'drop-in shelter' with counselors in the large basement of one of our buildings, where street people could spend the day. It was closed at night, but buses would take them to a suburban church where they would sleep in fellowship halls on cots. We weren't supposed to have more than 100 at a time but always had more. In the soup kitchen line some days we served food to 1000 people. It was at that time the largest soup kitchen in the country.

• Mrs. Bush Visits the 'Soup Kitchen' —

Barbara Bush, President George H. W. Bush's wife, came to Atlanta see our Street Academy, having heard it was well known for saving kids off the streets and putting them into a high school that worked. Mrs. Bush is herself a devout Episcopalian, so her interest in our youth program touched a personal chord. I recently preached at their church, St Martin's, and saw them in Houston.

The Secret Service had lined up her total Atlanta itinerary so the Street Academy was safe for her to tour, but they informed her she could not go to the soup kitchen. But she insisted and marched into the large parish hall where several hundred people were eating. Our street clients didn't even look up, didn't know this was the President's wife, and proceeded to eat their soup and sandwich.

What did she say?

She was dumbfounded and didn't say much, except "My goodness, who are all of these people and where did they come from?"

That gave me a chance to say, "Some of them were released from mental institutions when Jimmy Carter was president." The big state hospitals were shut down because they were not well run and the patients were to be placed in small residential neighborhood units of ten or twelve. Since the small units were never created, all of those released patients became 'street people,' as we refer to them today.

What were you able to do for these street people besides feeding and counseling them?

We started a program that took a few people out of the soup kitchen line who we thought were promising, and who had potential to break with the street tradition in which they were mired. Georgia Power and Light Company provided free insulation for any homes that needed it, and gave St. Luke's grants to train these street folks how to insulate a home.

We asked the Reverend Dr. Raynelle Parkins, my number one assistant, to create the program. He was our full-time black priest, one of seven clergy on the staff. He had been a full professor teaching law in the School of Architecture at the University of Tennessee at Knoxville and had tenure. Some years earlier I said, "If I accept the call to be rector of St. Luke's Church in Atlanta, you are going with me." But when he learned what his salary would be, he said "No, I can't afford it, that's a $10,000 cut a year!"

He finally said, "Okay, I'll go with you," and the two of us moved to Atlanta. It turned out later, that I had hired the first fulltime black priest of a major Episcopal church in the South! He helped organize Saint Luke's Economic Development Corporation, a non-profit corporation we designed to work with the poor. Parkins had grown up in Panama and spoke fluent Spanish, so with his help we also developed one of the first Spanish-speaking congregations in our area.

- **And then New York—**

In 1987 after seven exciting years in Atlanta, we received a call to New York. In Episcopal Church tradition and polity, we clergy are free-agents. The Bishop does not assign us to a church. I can't call the bishop and say, "Assign me a church." The Methodists can do that, but not Episcopalians. The 300-year- old Trinity Church Wall Street in New York City had an opening for rector, and after it searched around the country and England, selected me.

For the United States, Trinity Church is not only old but very unusual in that every other Episcopal Church in our country is managed by a vestry or board consisting of regular active members of the congregation. Trinity is the only Episcopal Church with an incorporated outside board made up of Episcopalians who are actually members of parishes in New Jersey, Connecticut and New York.

When we arrived at the parish, twenty-two outstanding people from the greater New York community were on the board (vestry), Membership on the Trinity Vestry has such esteem it is often the number-one listing in an obituary. The most exciting part of my seventeen years at Trinity was working with these extraordinarily gifted people who were not there for themselves, but to offer their skills in human resources, accounting, real estate, the law, finance, grant making and the like. But they rarely attended Trinity on Sunday, they went to their own churches, and that was also where they made their tithes and pledges. I didn't need to play golf with them or socialize since it was for them a board of expertise, and they always said, "Just tell us what you want us to do."

What positions did you hold over those seventeen years?

My Amos Tuck School experience led the vestry to think, "Here is a man who has been to business school and likes that kind of world," so that's probably why I was hired. I held one position for all those years: as rector in charge of Trinity Church and St. Paul's Chapel up the street. We had about 300 employees, with most of them serving our real estate because Trinity owns six-million-square-feet of commercial office space in New York. That is almost the size of all of Asheville.

Trinity Wall Street is a relatively small congregation with about 600 members; no one can belong to our nearby St. Paul's Chapel. It is an historic church that had members for many years before it became mainly a museum. By the way in its early years George Washington was a member and came to pray there after his inauguration on Wall St. Although I was rector of both of the churches on Broadway, I rarely did baptisms, weddings, or burials. Those pastoral roles were taken by the vicar and his /her staff.

Though it is certainly not a church term, in some ways as rector I was CEO, with a COO and staff for the real estate, grants, school and other divisions. I was in church every Sunday and usually preached every other Sunday. The vicar and staff did pastoral work at hospitals, counseling, and wherever else was needed.

Please jump ahead to when you retired.

When I retired in 2004 the dean of the New York Episcopal cathedral asked, "If you are willing to come here one or two days a week to help with development, I'll give you an office." And that is what I have been doing ever since.

My wife Pam has been silently listening and now makes an observation: Dr. Matthews, you drew on your dreams and education and experience, including acting where you didn't think you had talent, and the MBA program where you didn't think you belonged because of a disconnect with core values, then you created the essence and persona you needed to be authentic in your career.

Beautifully said, Pam, you ought to be writing this book *(thankfully, laughter all around)*. The interesting thing about life is that you often don't recognize what's going on when you are doing whatever you are doing. But when you are sincere, dedicated, and committed to the task, your life will take focus.

- ## And then 9/11—

Before we hear your painful account about the terrorist strike of September 11, 2001, please explain exactly where the church and chapel are located in relation to Ground Zero.

Trinity Church is located on Broadway at the head of Wall Street just five blocks from the East River. From anywhere on Wall Street you can see the spectacular church spire rise between the even taller banking towers. It was known as the tallest structure in New York for almost forty years, 265-feet high, about the same as a twenty-five story building. It used to cost one penny to go up the tower steps and see the entire harbor.

The back door of Trinity Church is 250 yards from where the World Trade Center stood, and St. Paul's Chapel was just 100 yards away and directly across the street.

Where were you when the terrorists struck?

I was in the church office building at 74 Trinity Place for an eight a.m. executive meeting of our Grants Board, which gives millions of dollars away each year. I was with Cathy McFarland vestry member and professionally in charge of the Victoria Foundation for Chubb Insurance Company in New Jersey, and Father Jamie Callaway, our deputy for Grants.

Suddenly at about eight-thirty we heard a loud boom, a huge explosion, and Cathy said, "Wow, that was a huge gas main!" as if something massive underneath the street had exploded. We didn't even get up!

Did the building rattle?

Tremendously, it was like it came from right outside on Broadway and the building shook for four or five seconds. Then our door was suddenly opened and Joe Palombi the head of real estate, whose office windows faced the World Trade Center Towers, shouted, "A plane just hit the World Trade Center!"

We ran down the hall and into his office but couldn't see the north side of the North Tower where the plane actually hit because we were a little south. We did see billows of smoke coming from around the tower and I gasped, "Oh my Lord." Then one of our anxious staff people said, "That is where the Aon offices are," and another exclaimed, "That's where Mary and Sue and Fred work!" Aon is the brokerage firm that helps Trinity select insurance companies.

Within about fifteen minutes we heard a whistling sound like a German rocket aimed at England in an old World War II movie, and the South Tower was suddenly hit. A huge mushroom cloud of fire engulfed the side of the tower right in front of us and my friend from Chubb screamed, "War!" and dove under a table scarring her face.

One young man said, "Oh wait, wait, wait, Steven Spielberg must be making a movie!"

Can you remember your initial reaction?

Yes, that this couldn't be happening; this just can't be real. We couldn't assimilate it; it was beyond comprehension for all of us. I thought if this is really war, with whom would we be at war; who would attack the United States of America? Why would the war be in New York?

Quickly everybody began yelling, "Don't use the elevators." At that point with electricity we were ok and could have used the elevators for another hour or two, but everybody in the building went down our narrow little stairs. And after nine or ten floors of stairs some people's legs were becoming unstable.

- ## The building shook again—

After a lapse of disorienting time, suddenly the building shook again even harder and someone screamed, "They are hitting the exchanges now!" The American Stock Exchange is right next door and if true it would have meant a bomb hit the building immediately against our adjacent wall.

In seconds our space began to fill with smoke. We discovered much later that it was at that moment the South Tower fell straight down and the thundering impact shook our building like an earthquake. As it fell, sheetrock and concrete turned into fine white dust. Our air-conditioning unit on roof of the building sucked the white powdery dust in and our duck work distributed it throughout the entire building. Thinking the dust to be actual smoke, everybody began screaming, "We're on fire!"

Very quickly the dust thickened and we could only see about ten or fifteen feet in front of ourselves, as people used handkerchiefs to cover their noses and mouths. We felt we might burn up and decided to exit out the big iron fire door to the back street sidewalk, but it wouldn't unlock. We had just installed a sophisticated magnetic card system needed to unlock all doors and I had the master card, but the tiny electronic light kept flashing red and wouldn't stay green long enough for us to open the outside door.

Other staff members tried my card but it still wouldn't work, so we began banging on the metal fire door in case there was somebody on the other side. We kept banging and became afraid we were trapped and doomed to die in that smoke-filled basement.

- **Ready to die—**

Did you seriously believe you were doomed?

My CFO John McKegney, a devout Roman Catholic, with sons at Notre Dame and Georgetown University, whispered in my ear, "I'm ready because I just made my confession." I said "Great John, we're going to Heaven together."

Thirty seconds later he said "I just made my confession again" and I asked "Why did you make it a second time?" He answered "The Lord is very busy right now; I don't want him to miss my confession."

Then a young woman from our accounting division said "Doctor Matthews, if you live and I die, please tell my husband I love him very much. You see this morning we had a horrible fight." And with that she was gone. There was an overwhelming intensity.

Trinity had planned for months to produce a Spirituality series of TV programs in our studio. We had the Archbishop of Wales, Roan Williams, who is currently the Archbishop of Canterbury, come to keynote the series along with a dozen more spiritual authors and teachers. September 11 was the day of production. When Archbishop Williams returned to England he wrote a book about what it felt like to know you were about to die. That night he had dinner with my wife Deener at our New York apartment while I was still stranded on Staten Island.

- **Taking care of the kids—**

Early on before the towers fell, we realized, "We've got to take care of the kids!" There were 140 registered from infants to age four, in the pre-school, and we had practiced what to do in the event of a fire or other emergency. We took them down to the 'jump-jump room' in the basement, where they would play whenever it rained or snowed. So there we were in the jump-jump room, and the children had sensed that something big was happening. They seemed almost frozen.

- **Suddenly the door swung open—**

Suddenly the heavy iron fire door flew open, and we ran outside on to the street. The dust was five or six inches deep and like snow. It was similar to when the astronauts walked on the moon and put their feet down; there was a puff of a powdery substance with every step. Then I saw a tire from the plane and a portion of a woman's leg with a high heel shoe still on her foot.

We tried to run holding hands, while tripping over shoes people had lost as they ran or had intentionally kicked off. We really couldn't run because of the 'snow' like dust, and it was difficult to tell where the curb began and the street stopped.

I couldn't see much and was holding onto the arm of Joe Palumbi, the man in charge of Trinity Real Estate. He barked, "Close your eyes Dan and just follow me!" I didn't want to do that, I didn't trust that his eyes were less encrusted, but we just kept trying to run until a police officer shouted, "Go this way!" But when we went his way another police officer later yelled, "Go that way!" It was absolute chaos.

What happened to the children?

I remember thinking, "If we take these kid's outside we're going to be killed out there; if we stay in this building we are going to burn up; what do we do?"

We left a phone message for the parents on our preschool answering machine. We had to make sure the children got taken care of amid the chaos and the noise and the confusion. They were taken to another nearby pre-school on the Lower East Side described on our answering machine. Parents were told that their child was safe and could be picked up there. By 6:00p.m. every child had been picked up by an overwhelmingly grateful parent. That was one of the miracles of 9/11.

We naturally assumed that some of the parents who worked in the World Trade Towers might have been dead, but we didn't know for sure. Fortunately, many of the pre-school parents and children saw the devastation from the first plane when they came up out of the subway and immediately turned around and headed back home.

• 'Beats the hell out'a me'—

Amid all this confusion and anxiety staff members continued to ask, "Doctor Matthews, what should we do?"

A strange reaction, but at that moment I remembered when I was about fourteen I saw a war movie that had a swear word in it, the first of such language I had heard in a movie. During a chaotic battle scene a buck private shouted to his sergeant, "Sarge, what should we do, what should we do?" and frustrated, the sergeant shouted back, "Beats the hell outta me." Though I was the rector in this crucial time, all I wanted to say was, "Beats the hell outta me" because I had no idea what to do. I asked and answered myself: do we run outside? No, we'll be killed! Do we stay inside? No we'll be burned up!

During this utter confusion somebody had a little transistor radio and on it we heard that the Pentagon had been bombed. The Pentagon! And then a short time later we learned that a plane had gone down in Pennsylvania. And we wondered if San Francisco was next? Los Angeles? Chicago?

This is probably more than you wish to know.

No, please go on.

Rushing through the dust and debris, we finally got down to the Staten Island Ferry in Battery Park and jumped on board. We were the last people to get on board as they pulled the chain across the stern and started out. We stood right against the chain since the ferry was packed with people escaping over to Staten Island.

All we wanted was to get out of the intense dust filling our eyes. When the packed ferry got us out into the harbor, we looked back and saw the entire end of Manhattan Island engulfed in dust-filled smoke.

How dire was your situation?

Joe kept dialing on his cell phone. I said, "If you can get through to Deener, please tell her I'm all right." Joe reached a friend in Fort Lauderdale who was watching the entire tragedy on television and said, "The Towers are both down!" That was beyond our imagination.

The United States Government in its wisdom had brought in military fighter jets, and they were flying over our heads at about 300 feet and making tremendous noise. Of course they were there to protect us, but instead they were adding to our terror since we had no idea but what they were part of the original attack.

As we got off on Staten Island we realized that the broken wooden slats above our head had contained hundreds of life preservers, and that the people wearing life jackets were filled with the same terror of the boat being struck as were we. They no doubt feared, "They are going to sink the ferry!"

We got to a phone booth when we landed and called one of the Staten Island parishioners Leff LaHuta who said, "I'll come and get you. You can sleep on my floor tonight." And so six of us piled into his car and spent the night at his house. The next morning we got on a Brooklyn subway that was still running into the city uptown; none of the downtown trains were operational. It took us up to Queens, and from there we headed back to the city.

The area around Trinity was quarantined by the FBI, crime-scene tape blocked it, and we were not allowed to go to the church for a number of days.

- **The effects of violence—**

That violent day resonates with every American, but you were at Ground Zero, so please continue your story. What were, or are, the lingering effects on you from that terrible tragedy?

Everything about it was total disorientation. I find now I can't watch a war movie, I dislike watching violence on television shows; I am even disturbed by violence in commercials. The sense of being disoriented didn't so much cause feelings of anger or fear, but rather the belief that "everything is coming apart!"

We respect ourselves for the control that we have over our lives and the world around us. You want whatever you do to be in your control, but when you totally lose that control you don't know who you are anymore, and you feel helpless, lost.

We were all utterly helpless. There seemed to be nothing we could do to understand what was happening to us or why it was happening and what was actually going on. And for those of us in leadership positions, and I've understood this from some of the people who are Wall Street executives, it was horrible, horrible.

Everybody holds in awe the idea of war. In the 'The Greatest Generation' by Tom Brokaw, we learn that those returned veterans never talk about their war experiences, even with their families. I now know why; it's because they don't have the language to explain it to somebody who wasn't there.

- **Sacred Ground—**

You mentioned earlier that you love photography. Did you take photos at Ground Zero?

I am a camera buff, I own several cameras, and I've taken countless pictures since I was a boy. I'd love to be a photographer if I weren't a clergyman. But I've never taken my camera to the site, I've never taken one picture, and our Trinity windows looked out on the whole disaster.

It seemed to me that taking pictures would be intruding into a sacred space, so I didn't. It is still repulsive to think I would have even dared to take pictures. And to this day I would rather not talk about what I saw, even with Deener.

Ground Zero was already sacred to you.

It turned into sacred ground for all of us.

• No fear of dying—

Great thanks for speaking so eloquently and poignantly about a major tragedy that deeply affected us all. If it's all right to ask, please describe your feelings when you thought you were going to die?

I had no fear of dying, I was certain I was going to Heaven, and I was telling other people that we were going to heaven together. In fact, when John told me of his two confessions to the Lord I said, "You and I are going to join your daddy today, and that will be a joyous moment for both of us." The expectation that Heaven is a doorway to something else was why I had no fear. It was more about consoling the people in my presence, and telling them that we were all going to be all right.

There was no alternative to the oppressive smoke choking us, the coughing, our eyes burning, and we sensed it would not take us long to die.

• Who opened the door?—

Now let me tell you the rest of the story about when we thought we were dying but that locked basement door suddenly flew open and we were able to escape the smoke-filled building.

About ten days after 9/11 the entire Trinity staff found space in one of our own buildings, in an advertising agency that had just gone bankrupt. The desks and the potted plants were still there, and we moved in *en masse*. Once a week we met with the entire staff to talk about how we were doing. At the end of the first meeting I asked "By the way, who opened the door and let us out? I'd like to thank the person who saved our lives."

Silence. So I thought that the person who had opened the door was sick, or not back to work that day. For weeks I kept asking who opened the door, but nobody ever answered.

One day a woman in the accounting division walked up front to me after our gathering and said "Doctor Matthews, you keep asking who opened the door." "Yes, tell me," I said, "I'd like to thank that person."

She replied "Everybody here knows who opened the door except for you," to which I said "Well tell me so I can thank that person." "It was an Angel" she said, then turned around and walked away.

Oh ye of little faith.

Apparently the whole staff accepted the fact that a miracle happened in that basement that day. But there were many miracles going on in our midst during that terrible tragedy, and it was like trying to sort out what was real and what was not. It is still hard to sort out.

• Aftermath of the terrorist strike—

Please go back and relate more of what happened in the aftermath of the terrorist strikes.

When the attacks happened, Trinity Church was immediately cordoned off by the FBI as I have said because the whole area was considered a crime scene.

Almost immediately, Seaman's Church Institute Director the Rev. Peter Larom and some of his staff rushed to St. Paul's Chapel five blocks away to set up outdoor grills on the porch and cook hamburgers and hot dogs. All the restaurants in the area were closed, so there was no other available food.

After a few days the Waldorf Astoria Hotel chefs brought prepared food on trucks. It was fabulous food. The hotel had been forced to close, along with many other area businesses.

Those were wonderful things to do.

Yes. And what started out with a few hamburgers and hot dogs grew and grew, so we opened up St. Paul's and moved everything inside. And it suddenly became the famous 'recovery center' for firefighters, police officers, construction workers and other responders.

The St Paul's Chapel soon had volunteer massage therapists, podiatrists to treat feet, boots, all kinds of medication being dispensed, little Teddy-bears for firefighters and others to hug when they lay down on the pews, music playing, and dozens of people serving food twenty-four hours a day.

It evolved into an exclusive place only for people wearing FEMA badges; even if you were a multi-millionaire from Wall Street, you needed a badge to get inside St. Paul's.

- **The chaos outside—**

What was going on outside the chapel?

The recovery began in a spontaneous way out of the chaos. Fred Burnham, a Ph.D. in the philosophy of science and a proponent of the theory that chaos self-organizes itself into a system, was a priest on the staff at Trinity Church. He has spoken around the country about how he believes the chaos of 9/ll impacted St. Paul's, and what ensued is well-described by that theory.

The big iron fence that wrapped around the chapel and its cemetery began to be covered with signs, memorabilia, photographs, hats, Tee-shirts and scrawled messages of all sorts.

People from all over the country drove or flew to New York and volunteered to work twelve-hour day or night shifts at St Paul's. Those working on 'the pile', as it was called, were warmly welcomed into the chapel if they needed a bandage, a meal, free counseling, or to spend a few hours sleeping in a pew or cot on the balcony.

Our rich and wonderful ministry became quite well-known, and the Chapel continued as the busy recovery center for eight months. Trinity Church itself remained closed for several weeks and after extensive cleaning, re-opened.

What kind of workday did you put in?

I re-introduced our staff to the building. The dust was everywhere and it had become filthy. We brought in outside commercial teams to clean everything, and learned how complicated it was to clean all the air ducts in a 25-story building. The organ was destroyed and had to be removed.

A lot of people were anxious about going back to work in the Wall Street area. One young man announced "I'm through!" then took his family and moved to Ireland. There were many people who couldn't imagine returning to the area, so we were carefully nurturing the process with counseling, slowly bringing the staff back into the buildings.

We also dealt with questions like: is this going to happen again and when is the next shoe going to fall? Whenever there was a subsequent emergency or the fire alarm sounded, everybody worried that this could be the "next one."

How many priests did your church have at that time?

Perhaps seven. The priest assigned to St. Paul's Chapel five blocks north, Linden Harris, was there to create a new worship community in the Chapel. He was a young man working on his doctorate at

General Seminary who just happened to be hired a few months before 9/ll. He spent day and night as the staff manager of the recovery process. When our eight months of recovery ended, Trinity gave him a grant to help in finishing his Ph.D.

- **Shutting down the Chapel—**

Closing the chapel became very difficult, because while we were in the midst of the busy recovery effort we were told by the city health department to clean up our buildings. It seemed obvious to me, we couldn't clean up St. Paul's because we were in the midst of using it 24/7. That caused a conflict for me as rector. The city was asking us to shut down St. Paul's for health reasons, but the volunteers and people being helped were pleading with us stay open. Those were difficult leadership challenges.

Did the city finally force you to shut down St. Paul's?

We did eventually shut down, in part because the local merchants had opened their restaurants and complained, "You're taking our paying customers. We're trying to reopen and you're serving free food."

Lots of soul searching counseling was going on. People would sit in a pew together, such as a firefighter who had just discovered his buddy's body and wanted to talk. We had many well trained clergy of various denominations from all around the country, and some New York folks having been trained for this. They were all there day and night.

Years later we learned that some workers developed lung illnesses from the dust and other particles that floated for weeks in the air at Ground Zero.

- **Handling the grief—**

You were the spiritual adviser for many people, including employees, congregants and others injured in the attacks, and I wonder how you handled your own grief, if you don't mind the question?

That is a good question. There is, I know, much denial in my grief. It's slow to heal. Real grief is difficult to admit in this American culture where "Get over it," is our dominant way to handle trauma.

I have thought hundreds of times about what I wish I had done or what I didn't do or what would have been sensible to do, but of course that is only with hindsight. At those excruciating moments I had absolutely no idea where to go or what to do or how to do it, and that struggle continued for weeks. I couldn't seem to get my bearing, I couldn't get my center.

I think at times I have some wisdom but it was hard to center down on it. It was near impossible to find common sense; or "This is the logical next step." In my grief it was hard to know what to do, or what the Lord wanted me to do in this situation. After some time passed, I realized that any church or synagogue anywhere across the street from an absolute disaster would automatically do what St. Paul's did. As a church, it is just in our DNA.

In 2011 the nation came together to observe the tenth anniversary of the attacks. What did you do?

Grief work is complicated and difficult and as I have said is not handled well by our dominant culture. A lot of the Nation's enormous energy that went into the tenth-anniversary of 9/ll was really delayed grief work. The anniversary happened to fall on a Sunday, and I preached at St. Paul's, a downtown church in Winston-Salem, simultaneous with thousands of pastors all over the country.

We are still struggling with what 9/11 was really all about, so perhaps it's about time for our arts culture to produce plays and poetry and movies and those kinds of expressions to help us focus on our deepest feelings, and what we haven't as yet worked through.

You are humble about your pastoral work during the difficult months on and after 9/ll, but I just learned that you were honored with the Order of the British Empire from Queen Elizabeth for your fine service.

I received a letter from the British Embassy in Washington DC to come there to receive the OBE from the Queen of England. Since she was not there, the British Ambassador to the US made the presentation.

- **Changes—**

How long did it take to return to who you were before, to get your feet to get back on the ground?

Don't think I've done that yet. Something deeply affected me, but I am not sure exactly how to describe it.

That was to be my next question: how did 9/ll change you?

I am different. I don't have the same kind of pride. I don't have much stomach for risk. I used to be more adventurous and liked to test and try and do new things, but those desires have diminished. It cut off some of my energy, imagination, and definitely my tolerance for violence.

Are these irreparable wounds? How much do those tragic events still live within you?

I think it is all there in a subtle way all the time. There are countless moments when I stop and say to myself, "I wish I had …, why didn't I …, what prevented me from …?"

I guess after any disaster one could say "if only," and I say that a lot. We were, on 9/11, subjected to something we couldn't comprehend, and then the shocking word of additional attacks in Washington and Pennsylvania made it seem our whole world was collapsing around us, that this was no less than war, and we were utterly lost in what to do if in fact this was war.

- **Perspective on evil—**

As a priest, how do you reconcile the evil that happened on 9/ll?

The number one issue for all religions in all the world for the entire history of humankind is: the problem of evil.

What is Father Dan Matthews' perspective on evil?

God does not cause evil, rather God is involved in redeeming evil. There are lots of ways of trying to describe the place of evil, and the most popular concept is to conceive of evil as a person: the devil. And that is very helpful for many people because it personifies it, makes it manageable, identifiable; and we can understand wickedness that takes on flesh. We can point at it. There are many religions of the world that are helped by making evil visual and personal.

I don't believe in an evil being, that the devil is a fallen angel. Free will for humans, however, is the double-edged sword God chose for us. Since God is love, our free choice to love was an essential element in the building blocks of the creation story in Genesis. We are free to choose and those nineteen terrorists were free to choose evil. I believe that God, the Creator, or however you might wish to describe what controls the whole universe, as the power, the source, the energy, the creative authenticity of all of creation, is not yet finished. Creation is in process right now.

There are lots of creation struggles going on as we speak. God limits God's self and is therefore from our perspective not omnipotent. God allows us the free will to reject him and reject our brothers and sisters. As Genesis suggests, we are our brother's keeper. The Creator still creating right now says to us "Come help me create a better world." Some of us respond, "No I am not interested in that." So God looks as did Jesus for co-creators, disciples who will help God in the long process of making the world whole.

- ## The Muslim Community Center—

Certain political and religious factions oppose the proposed Muslim Community Center that will include a small mosque 1500 feet from Ground Zero. What are your thoughts about this?

When it suddenly hit the press that the Islamic community was planning to "build a mosque at Ground Zero," many thought they were thumbing their noses at the Nation. I contacted some clergy friends and learned that the truth about the issue had not gotten out to the broad press.

For example, before 9/11 there had been for years an Islamic Prayer Center on the seventeenth-floor of the South Tower of the World Trade Center. As the *New York Times* described it, "the prayer room might include financial analysts, carpenters, receptionists, secretaries, and ironworkers. There were American natives, immigrants who had earned citizenship, visitors conducting international business — the whole Muslim spectrum of nationality and race." The terrorists destroyed one of their own worship centers, but that never came out in the media. The proposed Islamic Center was seeking to expand through proper neighborhood procedures and permission was already granted from the city and county.

But some people later exploited the proposed new center by labeling it 'the World Trade Center Mosque', which was never to be the case. That concept got its legs, as you might say, from what was really a publicity stunt to make us angry and resentful, and make the Islamic religion the enemy. It was extremely successful and very soon everywhere I went there were questions. I would answer: "There was always a mosque worship center in the World Trade Center." That helped dilute the anger, and then the Christian clergy in lower Manhattan got together and circulated petitions in favor of the proposed worship center.

What should Americans do about this, regardless of which side they are on?

We should study Islam. The Trinity Center said that this is a major issue facing the United States, not just next month, not just next year, but for decades to come. We must figure out how to live in peace with this world-wide religion that seems to include huge masses who are against the west, against our way of life, against the way we interpret 'good'.

What would your advice be to someone who is unsure of his/her feelings toward Islam?

Obviously, first we should have deep respect for the people whose lives were lost, and deep sympathy for those who were innocently going to work that morning and suddenly were confronted with fire, terror, and death. We need to understand more about Islam. There seems to be a part of Islamic tradition that says nonbelievers are infidels, enemies not be tolerated and who can be, under certain conditions, justifiably killed. We must be deeply concerned about finding solutions to such theological extremism. Christianity also has a few of its own theological radicals who are belligerent and interested in defeating people who don't agree with them.

One final question about religion: as a Christian and an Episcopal priest, how do you look at other religions around the world and the gods they worship?

Well, that is the big question. I ultimately believe that since I've spent my entire life trying to understand different theological perspectives and how they speak about the nature of the one we call God, that there are endless ways to approach whatever is the source of our Creation. To that end I have spent the last 25 years to help create an interfaith cable television channel, 56 different faith groups involved including Christians, Jews, Muslims, Hindus, and we still thrive a quarter of a century after our founding.

My word is God, but there are other words used for God. Our tradition is based on the New Testament thesis that God revealed God's self in a human man, and that of course was Jesus. And that person Himself came out of the very ancient tradition of Judaism, and we continue to build on that Hebrew tradition. It appears that many other traditions aren't far from ours.

I don't know what they all believe, so I will just say that some beliefs are close to what I believe to be the truth and others are not as close. Only God knows. For me personally Jesus is the standard by which I measure all religious truth. But in the next 100 years or so I sense there will be little tolerance in the world for religions that deem themselves as exclusive holders of the truth. That is our prevalent epistemology today.

- **An open mind—**

You have a very open mind, Father Matthews, both spiritually and intellectually.

I would like to try to be honest. I would like to remain open. I created a national magazine, *Spirituality & Health* to help people search and struggle with the mystery of the Creation and the mystery of God, from every theological perspective.

And by the way there are some fascinating things going on in physics in what is called the sub-atomic world of particles, which move in unpredictable ways and do strange things.

Like being in two places at once?

Yes, two places at once; the sub-atomic world is a one of mystery. Georgia Tech professor Gary Zukav wrote a book, *The Dancing WU LI Masters,* and in it says, "In order to be a physicist today you have to first become a poet, because you are explaining that which we do not really know."

The best way to explain the Bible is that it has in itself vast elements of poetry, though there are also many historical and theological writings. So, even the Bible uses many different approaches to unpackage and describe what 'force' created all this magical and ever-expanding universe of ours.

I think there is increasing tolerance of different religions of the world. Islamists theology is not growing intellectually using what we in the west call the rational mind. They are not religiously moving into what we know as 'the ability to analyze.'

There is no place for critical scriptural analysis of the Koran as we in the west have had for over 100 years with all sorts of critical analyses in our Biblical scholarship. As Sir Isaac Newton might say, they do not allow rational exploration to enter their religious belief system. Our own world of scholars even challenge such ideas as which letters were actually written by St. Paul. Some even ask, "Did Jesus really live? Was Mary really a virgin?" We find it is perfectly common place for doubters to critique our own Holy Bible that way.

But it is not all right for Muslims and that is why the book *Satanic Verses* is not allowed to be read by followers of Islam; they absolutely reject the notion of critiquing their own Koran. Author Salman Rushdie is still on a death watch for writing his book. This stands as a huge barrier in our ability to understand Islam.

- **Post 9/11 insights—**

Kindly share some more of your post-9/ll memories and insights.

Two days after the attack, President Bush asked all churches and synagogues in the country to ring their bells at noon on Friday for those who lost their lives.

On Friday I called Mike Borraro of the Trinity Buildings Department and asked him to ring the Trinity Church bells, but he couldn't because Trinity was within a crime scene; cordoned off by the authorities.

I realized that the most appropriate bell to ring was at St. Paul's Chapel right across the street from the World Trade Center that had been saved from destruction. I told Mike to ring the St Paul's bell there, but he reminded me that it was powered by a solenoid and all the electricity was cut off.

You must have been mightily disappointed.

At first yes, but on Friday at five minutes after twelve Mike called me and boldly announced, "Doctor Matthews, I took a flashlight and an old piece of pipe and crawled up that old tower, and right at twelve noon I took that pipe and beat the hell out of that bell!"

I said, "Praise the Lord, Mike, praise the Lord." And he yelled "That's not the best part Dr. Matthews" and I shouted back, "What is the best part?"

Mike barked back, "When I came halfway down I looked through the shutters and saw that firefighters and construction workers and police officers had all taken their hats off and placed them over their hearts, and there were tears coming down their cheeks."

"May God's Name be praised," I said, "that was a wonderful thing to do Mike, thank you, thank you."

That must have been comforting to all concerned. What came next?

We began the process of figuring out how we were going to find workspace. We had a vacant rentable full-floor in the Trinity office portfolio. We moved in there about twenty blocks away.

During that time psychological counselors helped us every day with an open-door policy where anybody could walk in, whether it was for two minutes or an hour. The response to grief is complicated, as different people respond to tragedy in different ways. Our culture as I have said does not give us much permission to grieve.

Many older cultures on earth are very sensitive to and respectful of the grief process. It isn't unusual for a widow to grieve for a year, by wearing black for that entire year. In contrast, we have this strange idea that we should move on. Make the changes necessary for a new life, start afresh.

As a pastor I've visited widows and witnessed great grief, sorrow and sobbing. I would hear a knock on the door and see her pull herself together to greet a neighbor who would ask, "How are you doing?" and she would fabricate an answer "I'm doing very well." After faking it for the neighbor, she would sob again.

Then two American leaders said to all of us on television, "Go Shop," when what they were really saying was, "Let's not have the economy hurt by this." But that was just like saying to that widow whose husband had just dropped dead on the golf course, "go shopping." That is the last thing that widow would want to do; she only wants to grieve, to be quiet, to reflect, and to hurt.

The same was true for the whole nation. The dust that fell that day all over Lower Manhattan, also fell all over the world. We were all covered in 9/11 dust. We are still deciding what to dust off and keep and what to discard.

• A priest and a human being—

You suffer because you thought you should have done more on 9/11 and afterwards. So it is with the utmost respect and at the risk of being presumptuous that I encourage you to cut yourself some slack. Dan Matthews is a priest but also a human being who I dare say did his best and more than his share!

Thank you, thank you. So many innocent people died, and it is almost impossible to deal with the massive tragedy of their deaths that day. The loyalty, dedication and commitment of those firefighters who kept walking into that burning building becomes too much to think about.

I know it was their job, but they just walked into buildings that were about to collapse.

They just kept walking in and they are gone.

The priest in the pulpit of the General Theological Seminary in New York City at its convocation and dedication of the Daniel P. Matthews Conference Room in 2004.

Mayor Rudolph Giuliani requested the use of historic St. Paul's Chapel, the location of George Washington's pew, for his farewell speech in 2002 as mayor to the city, and ultimately to the world, following 9/11.

Singer Dolly Parton served as ambassador-at-large for the 75th anniversary of Great Smoky Mountains National Park celebration while Dan Matthews was its chaplain - high atop the 5000-foot TN/NC border at Newfound Gap in 2009.

This view of historic Trinity Church Wall Street built in 1846 shows the World Trade Center Twin Towers only a few hundred yards away before the 9/11 terrorists struck.

Trinity Wall Street Episcopal Church stands nestled among towering structures on Broadway with front doors that open straight down Wall Street post 9/ll - without the Twin Towers .

Archbishop Desmond Tutu, recipient of numerous Trinity grants, chats with the priest during the celebration party of their friend Bishop Hays Rockwell's 50th wedding anniversary in Narragansett, Rhode Island.

ROYALTY — On the 300th anniversary of the founding of New York's Trinity Church in 1977, England's Queen Elizabeth and Prince Philip invited the vestry to England for tea at Windsor Castle.

The late ABC-TV news anchor Peter Jennings inspects some of the thousands of items of memorabilia that hang on the iron fence surrounding St. Paul's Chapel across from City Hall in New York. The chapel became a center for rest and renewal serving the recovery workers after 9/11.

Section 5: Nuggets of Wisdom from his Writings and Prayers

- **From the Closing Prayer at the 75th Anniversary Rededication of the Great Smoky Mountains National Park at Newfound Gap, September 2, 2009—**

We thank You for the thousands of Your stewards, many who lived before our time, who shared their resources, their work and the talents that made this national park a lasting reality . . .
  —For our Cherokee brothers and sisters, whose reverence for this ancient land has never waned;
  —For the generous gifts of the nearby schoolchildren in North Carolina and Tennessee, and the generous faraway gifts of the Rockefellers in New York;
  —For the young people of the Civilian Conservation Corps – their trails, their fences, their roads, their bridges;
  —For authors and writers and photographers who with their creative skills captured our imaginations of grandeur and awe with their vision for a national park;
  —For scientists and researchers who probe the mysteries of your creation and continue to unfold for us today the majesty of our treasured environment.
  —And now let our loud AMEN ring through these hills.

- **An article written October 6, 1985—**

It is hard to see where we stand right now as Holy ground. We are a people so caught up in the process of living that we find it nearly impossible to live in the present moment. Almost everything in our society lures us to dream of the future. Everything will be better, we think, when things are different than they are right now.

The very best God can do is what He is giving us today. Not only is the ground we stand on Holy, but each day is a gift. Look where you sit as you read this and honor that spot as Holy and give thanks to God for the present moment just as it is.

- **Excerpts from his writing in the *St. John's Record*, Knoxville TN—**

- January 30, 1977— *A Vice President of Walt Disney Productions came up with the answer when it rains – 'Have a rain parade and turn what seems to be a natural disaster into something creative and fun'. We Christians believe in rain parades, and our theology teaches us that times of disappointment can be, by the Grace of God, turned into times of celebration.*

- February 6, 1977— *A small black child saw a yellow balloon escape from a clown's hand and soar up to the sky and asked, "Would a black balloon go up that high?" Realizing the boy's insight, the clown answered, It's not the color that counts, but what's inside." . . . We are all like balloons. We vary in size, in color and shape. We move in different directions blown by different winds. We must be free to soar to our heights, but we are very fragile and need to have that which is inside be the measure of our worth.*

- March 6, 1977— *It is a constant problem for us religious folk to keep our priorities straight . . . It has always been our problem from the time of the golden calf to the present. We need to be reminded of the basics . . . I know what the Lord wants me to do. Love God, love my neighbor, love myself . . . Use this time to purge idols if they are more important to you than they should be.*

- May 15, 1977, Easter Season— *A baked potato has about the same number of calories as an apple and less than a pear. Who would have thought that the commonplace potato might be the single most important contribution in solving the food problems of the world . . . How often it seems that the problems of life can be solved with something commonplace. We search and dream without taking the time to discover the resources right at our own disposal . . . God is so commonplace, so available that we have lost sight of His full meaning in our lives . . . With a lack of seriousness, we have talked about 'spuds'. They well may save us in our fight against world hunger. With that same lack of seriousness we have talked about God. He is always available. He can save us from our most deadly enemy – ourselves.*

- *December 4, 1977— Most of us have to work very hard at knowing we are lovable and acceptable. We spend a portion of every day proving our worth, and at the same time wondering if we truly have the value we pretend we have. The Church speaks forth in every voice available to it – you, are accepted. We need to work at hearing these words and claim them for our own. Jesus proclaimed through his ministry the love the Father had for such as you and me.*

- *March 5, 1978— . . . We believe in our rights and our privileges to the detriment of authentic humility. We tend to think of ourselves as the center of the universe. Our pride is always warring with grace, but during Lent we try to live graceful lives.*

- *October 1, 1978— . . . Most of us claim church membership in the same way we claim familiarity with well-known persons. Our church affiliation is another trophy. We like to have it pointed out at special times when others are watching. We might say we use Jesus as one who can enhance our own respectability . . . Be no longer a stranger needing His esteem, become a disciple loving His friendship.*

- *October 8, 1978— If a parish church is anything at all, it is a place of hope . . . Life without hope is cruel. We need all the hope we can get . . . His light colors our darkness, and we are again able to be buoyed by His words.*

- *January 28, 1979— . . . Most of us try to cover up all of our blemishes. We think it is 'pretty' to have a flawless countenance. We paint, and spray, and powder, and color that which God has given us naturally in order to cover every flaw. We sometimes wind up looking plastic. Nature's flaws enhance beauty. They denote life and growth . . . If only we could admit that faults mean life and life means growth . . . Remember, you might be covering up that which makes you real to others.*

- *February 4, 1979— . . . Our Lord has forgotten not only the Bishop's sins but ours as well. We can let things go. They are not remembered in Heaven. What freedom our souls would know if we only believed in the forgiveness of our sins.*

Section 6: **Chronology**

- **Personal—**
- Daniel Paul Matthews
- Born January 14, 1933 in Chicago, IL
- Married October 4, 1960 to Diane 'Deener' Kendrick Vigeant
- Children, Dr. Gail Matthews DeNatale, The Rev. Daniel P Matthews, Jr., Ms Laurin Matthews Baldwin

- **Employment History—**
- Currently: Rector Emeritus Trinity Church Wall Street
- Co-chair Development Committee, Cathedral Church of St. John the Divine, New York
- Trustee and Co-chair of the Development
- April 1987–May 2004, Rector Trinity Church Wall Street, New York City
- 1980-1987, Rector St. Luke's Episcopal Church, Atlanta, GA
- 1972-1980, Rector St. John's Episcopal Church, Knoxville, TN
- 1965 - 1972, Rector of St. David's Episcopal Church, Nashville, TN
- 1961 - 1965, Assistant Church of the Holy Communion, Memphis, TN
- 1959 - 1961, Deacon/Priest St. James Mission, Midway, TN and Church of the Holy Comforter, Monteagle, TN

- **Education—**
- Rollins College, Winter Park, FL, 1955, B.A.
- President, Student Body
- President, ODK
- Dartmouth College, Hanover, NH, 1955
- Amos Tuck Graduate School of Business
- Vanderbilt Divinity School Nashville, TN 1956
- Church Divinity School of the Pacific, Berkeley, CA, B.D., 1959

- **Honorary—**
- General Theological Seminary, New York City, Doctor of Divinity, *honoris causa*, May 1987
- Church Divinity School of the Pacific, Berkeley, CA, Doctor of Divinity, *honoris causa*, May 1984
- University of the South, Sewanee, Tennessee, Doctor of Divinity, *honoris causa*, May 1992
- Rollins College, Winter Park, FL, Doctor of Humane Letters, *honoris causa*, May 1986

- **Valuable Service—**
- Order of the British Empire, March 2, 2006

- **Ordination Dates—**
- June, 1959 - Diaconate
- February, 1960 - Priesthood

- **Former Board Membership—**

Educational
- Rollins College, Winter Park, FL
- General Theological Seminary, New York City
- National Story Telling International, Jonesboro, Tennessee
- Forward Movement Publications, Cincinnati, Ohio
- Trinity Prep School, New York City

Low-Income Housing

- St. Margaret's House (retirement housing) New York City Chairman
- Frederick Fleming House, Homeless, Recovery, New York City, Chairman
- John Heuss House Drop in Center, New York City, Chairman

Marine

- Sailor's Snug Harbor (merchant marine retirement) Sea Level, N.C., Chairman

- **Current Board Memberships—**
- Chairman, National Interfaith Cable Coalition Inc., New York City
- St. John the Divine Cathedral Trustees, New York City
- Church Divinity School of the Pacific, Advisory Board, Berkeley, CA
- The Seamen's Church Institute, New York City
- Chairman, Friends of Great Smoky Mountains National Park, Kodak TN
- Vanderbilt Divinity School, Advisory Board, Nashville TN
- Haywood Regional Medical Center, Foundation Board, Waynesville, N.C.
- Rollins College Presidents Leadership Council, Winter Park FL

David Holt

Musician, Singer, Storyteller, Folklorist, and Historian

"David and I have a lot of fun when we play music. He loves music and it shows. He is one of the best old-time banjo pickers you'll ever hear."
— **Doc Watson.**

Sections about David Holt:

1) Reviews about David Holt, Performer

2) From Those Who Know David, the Man and the Musician

3) Some Important Life and Career Highlights

4) **David's Life Journey, in His Own Words**

5) Photos

6) Chronology

Section 1: **Reviews about David Holt, Performer**

- **Esquire: David Holt, One of the People Changing America—**

The 'Proud Performers', feature section of the 516-page Register edition of *Esquire* magazine in 1984 cited David Holt as "One of the Best of the New Generation - Men and Women Under Forty Who Are Changing America." More than 5,000 people were nominated in several categories, and 272 were selected on the criteria of courage, originality, initiative, vision and selfless service.

David was among luminaries who went on to even greater fame like actors Meryl Streep, Whoopie Goldberg and Will Smith, director Steven Spielberg, Hall-of-Fame basketball player Julius 'Dr. J' Irving, Olympic champion diver Greg Louganis, trumpeter Wynton Marsalis, and musician-singer Ricky Skaggs.

Esquire said of David in 1984: "When Holt was a child, his father played a set of bones and spoons that had been passed down for generations. Later Holt sought out Carl Sprague, the first of the recorded singing cowboys, who taught him the harmonica. After studying biology and art at the University of California, he became a student and collector of traditional music. He would go to fiddle conventions, or simply stop in hidden mountain towns and ask who could play music.

Before long Holt had amassed a small library of on-site recordings and learned how to play a dozen instruments, including the claw-hammer banjo, the hammered dulcimer, and the paper bag. Holt began the Appalachian Music Program (the only one of its kind) at Warren Wilson College, and expanded his archival work with the help of his students. He also matured as a performer and took State Department tours to Nepal, Thailand and South America. Holt has subsequently recorded two LPs, hosted a rural culture series on PBS called *Folkways,* and is currently seen on the Nashville Network's *Fire on the Mountain.* "I almost feel like it's a calling," says Holt, proud of his potential corniness, "and I feel the spirit of the old musicians helping me out."

From a later review in ***VOGUE:*** "David Holt's work is marked not only by vigor and charm, but by particular craftsmanship. He is one of the best of the new generation changing America."

- **Media Reviews of David Holt—**

"He performs up a storm." — ***Boston Globe.***

"The best minstrel-storyteller is David Holt." — ***VOGUE.***

"I think he could ring music out of a stump." — **Bob Terrill, *Asheville Citizen-Times.***

"A dazzling array of music and stories." — ***Entertainment Weekly.***

"David Holt and his music are American originals." — ***Columbus Dispatch.***

"David Holt is a gifted performer." — ***Sing Out!***

Section 2: **From Those Who Know David, the Man and the Musician**

- **'The Legendary' Doc Watson—**

David has been a big help in keeping me on the road doing concerts all these years. He has worked hard on learning my songs. He learned a lot of Merle's slide work, too. David knows how to put together a show and talk to the audience. I tell the audience that I am just myself on stage. I talk to them just like they were sitting in my front room. David does the same thing. He knows how to tell a good story. People like that and so do I. I really enjoy playing with David.

- **Pete Wernick, 'Dr. Banjo', former President, International Bluegrass Music Association—**

David is one of the most versatile, amiable, and knowledgeable performers I've ever met. He really knows how to dig into the meat of why people like traditional music, and help make it alive in the moment for everyone he's with, both his co-performers and the audience.

Having been on stage with him quite a few times, and having watched him in action from the audience, I marvel at how well he uses his quick mind and ample resources to help everyone have a good and meaningful time.

- **Dr. Doug Orr, President *Emeritus* of Warren Wilson College, Author and Musician—**

David Holt's talents and achievements are many: multi-instrumentalist, singer, storyteller, song collector, Doc Watson's musical partner, radio and television host, and Grammy Award winner. But to me, perhaps his finest attribute is the manner in which he honors and remembers those many black and white artists, some well-known and some not, upon whose shoulders we stand, and without whom we would have a much lesser tradition.

David also is our teacher, historian and keeper of the flame for a family tree of music that stretches over the generations and cultures.

- **Wayne Martin, Folklife Director, North Carolina Arts Council—**

David Holt has taken on the legacy of Bascom Lamar Lunsford, as he is both a wonderful musician and a great advocate for traditional musicians. No one has worked harder than David Holt, or enjoyed greater success in bringing national and international acclaim to the music traditions and history of western North Carolina.

And from a longtime employee >

- **Betty Nichols, after twelve-plus years working for David—**

Over the past twelve years I have been truly blessed to work for David Holt. I have come to know one of the most generous, considerate and thoughtful professionals that I have ever worked with or for, or for that matter, ever known.

David's schedule involves travel all over the world, which means much business is conducted by phone or e-mail, and he always takes the time to ask how my family and I are doing because he genuinely cares.

He understands the importance of relationships and teaches others that importance through his actions. This is a quality deeply rooted inside David, and part of why he loves speaking with his mentors, trying to understand their world, lives, and who they really are. Plainly, David realizes that 'people' are what matter in life.

His attributes are never more evident than his closest relationship; he and wife Ginny have a dedication and long-lasting love that is seldom seen in this age. It is a love that has endured with strength and grace from two who are committed to one another. I can't think of David's generosity, considerateness and thoughtfulness without praising his wife for the exact same qualities.

Not only does David care about people, but people care about David. They are drawn to his character. He isn't flat or predicable. He has many sides that contribute to his well-roundedness. His attitude and demeanor have been influenced and slowly molded by life experience and learning from others.

Now, at this point in his life, he embodies a warm and relaxed spirit that is comforting to his friends and inviting to strangers.

David's many sides make him interesting, enlightening, and just plain fun.

  — **Betty Nichols**

Section 3: **Some Important Life and Career Highlights**

- David Holt is well-known for his television show *Folkways,* a North Carolina program on PBS-TV that takes viewers through the Southern Mountains to visits with traditional craftsmen and musicians. He also hosts the PBS series *Great Scenic Railway Journeys,* and has hosted The Nashville Network's *Fire on the Mountain. Celebration Express* and *American Music Shop.* And he was a frequent guest on *Hee-Haw* and *The Grand Ole Opry.*

- David hosts the long-running show *Riverwalk Jazz* for Public Radio International broadcasted nationally from San Antonio, Texas. The show combines the stories of jazz greats told by David with traditional jazz music from the Jim Cullum Jazz Band, featuring guests such as the late Lionel Hampton and Benny Carter.

- David played the role of a musician in the popular Coen Brothers movie, *O Brother, Where Art Thou.*

- He has won four Grammy Awards in eight nominations. In 1996, *Stellaluna* garnered David both the artist and producer Grammy awards in the Children's Spoke Word category. In 2002, David won two Grammys in Best Traditional Music for *Legacy,* a three-CD collection of stories and songs about legendary Doc Watson's inspiring life story. Grammy Nominees are: *Live and Kickin' at the National Storytelling Festival, Cutting Loose, Grandfather's Greatest Hits, Spiders in the Hairdo: Modern Urban Legends, Why the Dog Chases the Cat: Great Animal Stories,* and *Mostly Ghostly Stories.*

- David won the *Frets* magazine's poll for the 'Best Old-time Banjoist' three times.

- A native of Garland, Texas and long-time resident of Asheville, North Carolina, David graduated *magna cum laude* in biology and art from the College of Creative Studies at the University of California, Santa Barbara.

- From 1975-1981, David founded and directed the Appalachian Music Program at Warren Wilson College in Swannanoa, N.C., then the only program in the country for students to collect, study and learn traditional music and dance.

- The songs and tales David collected over a four-decade span have become part of the permanent collection of the Library of Congress in Washington, D.C and the Southern Folklore Archive at UNC Chapel Hill.

- David was awarded a grant from the National Endowment for the Arts to learn the unique music of the South's last traditional hammered dulcimer player, Virgil Craven.

- The U.S. State Department has sponsored David Holt performances in many parts of the world as a Musical Ambassador, bringing the sounds of American Folk music to such diverse lands as Nepal, Thailand, South America and Africa.

- **The Holt Discography—**

Music
- ***Legacy* with Doc Watson and David Holt** Grammy Award winner. 3 CD set of interviews with Doc including a live concert with Doc & David. (High Windy Audio, 2002)
- ***Grandfather's Greatest Hits*** with Doc Watson, Chet Atkins, Duane Eddy, Jerry Douglas & Mark O'Connor. Grammy Nominee for Best Traditional Folk Recording; PARENTS Magazine's First "PARENTS PRIZE" (High Windy Audio,1992)

- ***Reel & Rock*** with Doc and Merle Watson and Jerry Douglas. 25th anniversary expanded re-issue (2010) INDIE Award winner (High Windy Audio,1985)
- ***Let It Slide*** with featuring Sam Bush and Doc Watson. (High Windy Audio, 2005)
- ***Live & Kickin' at the National Storytelling Festival*** with Zeb Holt. Grammy Nominee. (High Windy Audio, 2003)
- ***Cutting Loose*** with Josh Goforth. Grammy Nominee (High Windy Audio, 2009)
- ***David Holt & the Lightning Bolts*** with Josh Goforth, Laura Boosinger, David Cohen and Zeb Holt. (High Windy Audio, 2006)
- ***I Got A Bullfrog: Folksongs for the Fun of It*** with Sam Bush. American Library Association's Notable Recording (High Windy Audio, 1994)
- ***When the Train Comes Along*** David Holt and Friends. (High Windy Audio, 2011)
- ***Play The Jaw Harp Now!*** David Holt. CD & Jaw Harp (High Windy Audio, 2009)

Storytelling
- ***Stellaluna*** Grammy Award winner. (High Windy Audio, 1996)
- ***Hairyman Meets Tailybone.*** (High Windy Audio, 2006)
- ***Mostly Ghostly Stories.*** Grammy Nominee (High Windy Audio, 2006)
- ***Spiders in The Hairdo: Modern Urban Legends*** with Bill Mooney. Grammy Nominee (High Windy Audio, 1997)
- ***Why the Dog Chases the Cat: Great Animal Stories*** with Bill Mooney. Grammy Nominee (High Windy Audio, 1995)

Instructional DVDs
- *Folk Rhythms* taught by David Holt (Homespun 1996, 2004)
- *Get Started on 5-String Banjo* taught by David Holt (Homespun 1996)
- *Clawhammer Banjo 1* taught by David Holt (Homespun 1996)
- *Clawhammer Banjo 2* taught by David Holt (Homespun 1996)

Television Specials hosted by David Holt
- *The Blue Ridge Parkway* (UNC-TV and Wide Eye Productions)
- *The Outer Banks of North Carolina* (UNC-TV)
- *Highway 64: North Carolina's Heritage Highway* (UNC-TV)
- *North Carolina's Mountain Treasures* (UNC-TV)
- *Pottery in North Carolina* (UNC-TV)

Wide Eye Productions:
- *Great Scenic Railway Journeys: Eastern Railroads*
- *Great Scenic Railway Journeys: Western Railroads*
- *Great Scenic Railway Journeys: the Great Smoky Mountain's Railways*
- *Great Scenic Railway Journeys: Celebrating 175 Years of the American Railroad*
- *Great Scenic Railway Journeys: North American Steam Railways*
- *Great Scenic Railway Journeys: Australia Railroads*
- *Great Scenic Railway Journeys: New Zealand Railroads*

Books by David Holt
- *Spiders in the Hairdo: Modern Urban Legends,* co-written by David Holt and Bill Mooney, illustrated by Kevin Pope (August House, 1999)
- *Exploding Toilet: Modern Urban Legends,* collected and retold by David Holt and Bill Mooney (August House, 1994)
- *The Storyteller's Guide,* co-written by David Holt and Bill Mooney (August House, 1996)
- *Ready-to-Tell Tales,* edited by David Holt and Bill Mooney (August House, 1994)
- *More Ready-to-Tell Tales from Around the World* edited by David Holt and Bill Mooney (August House, 2000)

Section 4: David's Life Journey, in His Own Words

David Holt dreamed about a life of adventure while harboring a passion to become an old-time banjo player. In 1969, David began his journey to fulfillment by traveling into the heart of remote Appalachian Mountain communities like Kingdom Come in Kentucky and Sodom Laurel in North Carolina, where he found hundreds of old-time mountaineers to share their wealth of folk music, stories and wisdom. He was particularly impressed by banjoist Wade Mainer, ballad singer Dellie Norton, singing coal miner Nimrod Workman, and believe it or not, 122-year-old Susie Brunson.

David learned to play the banjo and many other unusual instruments, like the mouth bow, the bottleneck slide guitar, and even the paper bag. For more than four decades, David's penchant for traditional music and culture has fueled a successful performing and recording career that earned him four Grammy awards in eight nominations.

He takes great pride in having performed and recorded with many mentors, including Doc Watson, Grandpa Jones, Bill Monroe, Earl Scruggs, Roy Acuff and Chet Atkins. As recently as last year, the Watson-Holt performance played to a sold out audience at the famed Ryman Auditorium in Nashville, home of the Grand Ole Opry. That year David also performed in Ireland. He tours the country as a solo performer and with his band 'David Holt and the Lightning Bolts.'

Interviewing David Holt would prove to be intriguing, complex and thoroughly enjoyable. The hilltop home in Fairview he shares with his wife Ginny is concealed from the hub-bub of nearby Asheville, and is where the master of ten acoustic instruments revealed his life story, of course while wearing his trademark hat.

David, welcome to the book. People who know you and follow your career speak of your diverse talents, so I will begin our first interview with one simple question: how would you describe yourself?

I would say I play and perform traditional music from the mountains of North Carolina where I spent most of my life learning from old-time mountain musicians; that I am the father of Zebulon Holt, who heads Internet Development at NBC; that I lost a daughter, Sara Jane, when she was only ten; that I am the husband of Ginny Callaway and that we've been together for thirty-eight years, and that it is amazing we made it this long considering what we've been through. I would say I have had a rich and varied life full of good fortune and heartbreaking loss.

What was your early motivation and who are some of your heroes in the world of music?

I started playing music as a drummer when I was fourteen in Pacific Palisades, California. In those early days, my musical heroes were other drummers: Joe Morello, Philly Joe Jones, Gene Krupa, Lionel Hampton, Baby Dodds, Sandy Nelson and Buddy Rich.

When I think about the people who have been most influential to me in mountain music, I would put Doc Watson at the top of the list. Other good friends who helped and encouraged me were Roy Acuff, Grandpa Jones, John Hartford and Sam Bush. But most of my heroes were not famous "stars." They were regular people with extraordinary talent.

Etta Baker was a huge influence on me. She lived to be ninety-three, and I knew her for forty years. Most of these people I knew that long. But most of my mentors are people you've never heard of such as Dellie Norton. She was a traditional ballad singer from a little mountain community called Sodom Laurel and was a very important influence for me. She was like a grandmother. Byard Ray from the same community of Sodom Laurel spent many hours playing and showing me tunes with his fiddle and banjo. There are so many, like Wade Mainer and Walt Davis. Both were professional musicians in the 1920s and 30s and taught me a good bit about performing old-time music.

You had or still have relationships with some of them.

Yes, the ones that are still living. I started many of these relationships when I was in my twenties so many of my mentors have passed away in the last few years. We had friendships that lasted many years. It was kind of unusual for a guy of twenty-two to have mentors who were ninety. And that just keeps going on today. Doc Watson turned eighty-nine-years-old in March, 2012.

I was very lucky to have been influenced by so many great people. Sadly, I've also watched a lot of these people get old and die. But it taught me a lot about growing old with style.

What was most interesting to me was that people born in the late 1800s were a different kind of folk, who had a certain wisdom that I don't think exists anymore.

• The early years—

Tell me about your early years.

I was born in Texas on October 15, 1946. My ancestors moved from North Carolina to Texas in 1850s. We had been in Texas for about five generations when I was born. Gatesville, Texas is where I was born and where my mother grew up. Her brothers were the town doctors. Most of my extended family is still in Texas.

The Sputnik satellite was launched in 1957. My dad was an electronics engineer and an inventor and wanted to start a company of his own. We moved to California where the aerospace industry was really starting to boom. He figured that was the place to be.

I feel a very close connection to both Texas and North Carolina. My great, great grandfather John Oscar Holt lived near Burlington, North Carolina and moved to Texas in 1858.

I like to say it took me 130 years to get back to North Carolina, but I got back as quick as I could!

Let's regress for a moment to your early childhood. What is your first memory?

I was six-months old and my parents were trying to stop me from sucking my thumb. They put a blue knit wool glove on my hand.

Are you, David Holt, telling me with a straight face that you remember that?

I remembered it, then asked my mother if it actually happened or had I just imagined it. She said, "Yes, it did happen and the glove was wool and blue." I think that it was so traumatic that it was embedded in my memory.

When did you first think "I am going to be a musician" and what were your feelings?

I didn't ever consider being a full time professional musician until I was in my late twenties. You see, I was expected be a doctor or lawyer like other family members. As a kid I was not encouraged to play music. In fact, when I was fourteen, my parents were away on vacation and I took all the money out of my piggy-bank and started taking drum lessons. My parents didn't want me to take drum lessons because they knew it would be noisy and we lived in a quiet neighborhood in the Palisades.

After a year of taking lessons I started "The Persuaders," a rock and roll band with my friend Byron Case and later Chris Gordon. We played jobs all over Southern California. We even had a "hit" 45-rpm instrumental single called "Ski Storm" produced by Kim Fowley and featured my drum solo. You can even find it on youtube! By the time I was fifteen I was having fun playing on weekends and making money while my other friends were bagging groceries after school.

After I finished college with degrees in biology and art and a teaching credential, I finally said, "I've done my duty, now I am doing to do what I want to do!" That's when I moved to North Carolina to really absorb mountain music. I wasn't thinking I was going to make a living playing, but that I was just going to learn how to play and whatever happened, happened.

- ### The sound of tapping—

Tell me about how drumming led to your lifelong interest in music.

I just naturally loved rhythm...something innate.

My parents were not musicians, they hardly played the radio. But oddly, my father and grandfather played the bones. The bones are a rhythm instrument consisting of two seven inch long sections of cow ribs clicked together as percussion. It is an ancient musical instrument.

My great, great grandfather, the one from North Carolina, made several pairs of wooden bones that have been handed down in the family. They were carved during the Civil War. Something about the sound of the rhythm bones caught my ear as a child. The bones also made me aware that there were other kinds of music besides what you hear on popular radio.

I just naturally loved rhythm and was the kid always beating or tapping on the desk. I wasn't a trouble maker, but I just had this rhythm in me, and I loved the sound of drumming on a cardboard box or wooden crate, anything.

What came next for you?

I graduated from high school in Pacific Palisades in 1965 then went to college at San Francisco State.

This was the very beginning of the hippie era, before they were even called hippies. I just stumbled into this new world. We could see it brewing in LA, but it wasn't anything like San Francisco. When I got there I found this world of new music.

The Grateful Dead was a local band. I saw their very first concert. The Jefferson Airplane and Jimi Hendrix were also local bands. Janis Joplin lived down the block. They were not nationally famous yet. My drum set was still in LA. I was living in a dorm and so I didn't play while I was living in San Francisco.

This was 1966, a year before the "Summer of Love" and a wonderful time to be in the City. The mood of the day was peace and love and togetherness.

I went to San Francisco State College for two years as an art major. I realized I was going to need to do something more practical. I thought I might enjoy being an elementary or middle school teacher.

There was a private elementary school in Martinez, California called Pinel. It was very progressive and patterned after Summerhill School in the UK. I decided to drop out of college, get a job at Pinel and see if I really did like teaching. My girlfriend Linda and I were going to live there and teach. I was hoping for a life changing experience that would help me decide what I wanted to do with my life. I got more than I bargained for.

- ### A near-death experience—

The school was way out in the country with no street lights or houses nearby. On the very first night out there I was standing in the parking lot looking up at the stars, thinking: "That light coming from those stars is probably fifty-million years old."

At that moment, three guys pulled up in a car, headlights blaring. They jumped out of the car, ran at me, and two fists hit me in the face at the same time. I felt my jaw brake in two places. I tried to yell out through the blood, "Stop, there must be some mistake, you have the wrong person!" I knew they couldn't possibly know me. They kicked me when I was on the ground, and I passed out. My mind filled with the most intense orange light, the near-death experience people talk about.

Then they went into the school and tore it up. Broke out the windows, smashed the TV. Luckily they didn't find Linda. She was hiding in a small room with no lock on the door. The police came but never found those guys. It was a random act of violence. Evil sweeping across my path.

When you saw that light what did you think was happening?

There was no thinking involved. It was as though my mind exploded or "expanded." The orange light just filled my mind. The amazing thing is that it was a very loving peaceful feeling with no anger or fear, just this incredible peace and a feeling of oneness, an understanding that everything is interconnected. These were not thoughts but rather a knowing. It is difficult to put into words since it was not a thought, but a complete mind and body experience.

Looking back, how did the assault affect you?

It changed me forever. I realized that life is short. We think of the veil of death being out there, far from us, but actually it's right here next to us. We can step through it in a heartbeat and be gone. It also made me realize death is probably going to be a peaceful experience; even if the death is full of great violence, you will leave this world gently.

So there I was at twenty-one, recovering from this brutal physical and mental trauma. It was like coming out of a terrible dream. I was angry and fearful, but most of all I was in shock about how quickly one's life can change. I continued to teach through a jaw that was wired shut. Then I found some solace in music.

During that year, one of the teachers at Pinel let me listen to his 78-rpm record collection. He had some Carl Sandburg recordings that included an old cowboy song called, *I Ride an Old Paint.* The verse goes:

> *Old Bill Jones had two daughters and a song,*
> *One went to Denver, and the other went wrong.*
> *His wife, she died in a pool room fight,*
> *And still he sings from morning to night.*
> *Ride around little doggies, Ride around 'em slow,*
> *They're fiery and snuffy and rarin' to go.*

The cowboys sang in such a raw, real way I said to myself, "I can sing like that, I need to learn to sing like that!" I had never sung before in my life. But, like the cowboy song said after all that trouble Old Bill Jones was still able to sing "from morning 'til night." I realized I could easily be dead. I needed to get on with my life and learn to "sing from morning 'til night." I needed to figure out what I wanted to do and do it. Life is short.

- **Wrangling roses and cowboy songs—**

And what did you do?

I got a guitar from my dad and moved to Santa Barbara, California.

I was hired to tend roses for a couple in the Santa Barbara hills. The lady of the house had about 200 different roses in the garden. Roses take a lot of tending so I became the rose wrangler. They didn't want any sprays. I had to pick all the bugs off each rose by hand. I have probably handled more Japanese beetles than anyone you have ever met!

It was very healing to be around all those prize roses. After working in the garden most of the day, I would sit alone among the roses in the evening as they opened up and perfumed the air and watch the Santa Barbara sunsets. It was just what I needed. Very, very healing.

The husband was a psychologist and I lived in a one-room apartment with a kitchen attached to his home office. There was nothing dividing his office and my kitchen but a thin door. In the evenings I would sit in my kitchen with the lights off and listen to his client's problems and the doctor giving them advice. I could hear every word they said. Of course, I never saw them and didn't know who they were. When you're only twenty-one and hear the problems adults have, it is an eye-opener. I thought, "Wow, if this is what is ahead in life, I definitely need to do what I want to do...now!" The doctor had one aphorism he used quite often: "There are two ways to get to the top of an oak tree, you can climb the branches or sit on an acorn and wait." I realized I needed to start climbing the branches.

And what branches did you climb?

I was inspired to look for other folk songs; particularly cowboy songs. The Santa Barbara Public Library had two recordings that set me on the path I am still on today. One was the "Anthology of American Folk Music" edited by Harry Smith and the other was "Authentic Cowboys and Their Western Songs." Both were collections of 78-rpm recordings that had been made in the 1920s and 1930s. I had a three-dollar record player that had two speeds: too fast and too slow. I would tape a pile of pennies to the vinyl records to slow them down to the proper speed. I must have listened to those albums a hundred times.

I heard that UCLA had a one of the largest collections of 78-rpm folk recordings in the world called the John Edwards Memorial Collection. I made a trip to UCLA. As luck would have it, I met Archie Green there. He was one of the country's most important folklorists. We got to talking about cowboy songs and Archie told me that Carl Sprague, the first cowboy singer to record back in 1927, was still alive in Bryan, Texas. Archie encouraged me to go find him.

Sprague had recorded "When All the Work is Done This Fall" and "Bury Me Not on the Lone Prairie" back in the 1920s. He really was the one who started the Western part of country music. My folks lived close to Bryan, so I went to Texas and looked him up. Carl Sprague was about eighty-years-old at the time and still played. I also found out that he was also a retired baseball coach for Texas A&M.

Carl Sprague showed me how to play the harmonica cowboy-style, and the basic lick of cowboy guitar. I spent the whole day with him and came away thinking, "If you have mentors that are accessible, you can actually go see them, get to know then and learn from them." This was a revelation to me. I tried to find other cowboy singers, but I really didn't know how to go about it and most of the great early ones were dead.

- **Old-time Banjo—**

In 1968, I enrolled at the University of California at Santa Barbara where I met a young banjo player named Steve Keith. We both were interested in going back to the southern mountains because we heard that traditional mountain music was very much alive and could be found in every community. You wouldn't have to search for it.

Ralph Stanley happened to come to UCSB and do a concert that spring. Very few people were in the audience, so I talked to him after the show. I asked him where I should go to learn the old-time clawhammer banjo style that he learned from his mother. Ralph said, "You need to go back to Clinch Mountain where I'm from or Asheville, NC or Roanoke, VA or maybe Galax, VA. There is lots of old-time music in each of those places."

Steve and I decided to go to the Blue Ridge Mountains that summer of 1969. We drove all the way across country in my '52 Chevy pickup truck with this old dog, Jezebel. We traveled from California to Georgia. We explored the entire Appalachian chain that summer, visiting musicians during the week and going to fiddlers conventions on the weekends.

We met hundreds of mountain musicians. The oldest were born in the late 1800s. They were a different breed and the last of the pioneer generation. I felt like I had found what I was looking for... something real. Here was a treasure trove of music and lore. I was really excited by it.

Steve Keith was very charismatic and a good clawhammer banjo player. We would go to mountain communities like Hazard and Kingdom Come, Kentucky, looking for musicians. These old mountain folks knew what old-time banjo was, but most had not seen that style in a generation. It was the style their fathers and grandparents played. So, when Steve would pull out his banjo and play a rousing old-time song, folks just loved it and would invite us in to visit. It was like magic.

I was playing guitar, not very well I might add, but our music was the key to opening up the southern mountains for us. Everybody was very friendly. They were so happy to see young people playing old music, especially young people all the way from California! This was very unusual in 1969.

• Back to college—

I went back to college in California that fall and started learning to play banjo myself. I thought, "I want that magic key."

I loved the sound of the banjo because it was kind of a drum blended with strings, strong rhythm and melody together in one instrument.

I had tapes of the people I'd heard in the mountains. I worked really hard on learning to play.

So you were self-taught.

Well, there was nobody teaching old-time music in those days; there were no DVDs or teaching tapes or anything like that. Yeah, I was pretty much self-taught, but learned a lot by watching people very closely. There was one musician in Santa Barbara, Peter Feldman, who showed me some of the finer points. We are still friends today.

So, you learned by observing other musicians?

Exactly! You watch what their hands are doing and try to do the same thing yourself. You keep working until you get it right. You listen for the tone and rhythm they are getting and you try and make that same sound.

I returned to the mountains in the summer of 1972 with my girlfriend, now my wife, Ginny. By this time I had learned to play, so I could join in jam sessions. It was inspiring musically.

I was tempted to just stay in the North Carolina mountains, but decided to go back and finish college at UCSB to get a teaching credential.

What was your degree?

I earned two BA degrees, one in biology, one in art, then took a fifth year, which you had to do in

California if you wanted a teaching credential. One of my master teachers was Stan Tysell. Stan is an excellent musician who had become an elementary school teacher instead of a full time musician.

When I graduated and was offered a job at the highest paying elementary school in the United States, in Montecito, California, Stan said, "If you take that job, you're going to be sitting right here at my age" and asked, "Is that what you want to do?" He urged me to go to the southern mountains, take a chance while I was young.

Growing up in Texas, I understood and enjoyed southern culture. I wanted to go deeper into the old-time mountain culture. After coming south in 1972, I was absolutely sure I wanted to live here.

- **A sign from Nanny—**

I graduated from college and at that same time my grandmother, Nanny (Kate Lowrey), who was an old-time Texas character, died and left me a ten-year-old Chevy with just 10,000 miles on it and $2,000 cash. I thought, "This is a sign. I'm leaving".

I left California and moved to Asheville, NC in 1973. Lynn McKinney and her husband gave me a room for free in their house and I got a job as a sign maker. Asheville was a town full of traditional music. The Mountain Dance and Folk Festival was started in Asheville in 1927 by Bascomb Lamar Lunsford. The festival added excitement to the music scene in town. Every night after the festival people would gather at the Westgate shopping center and play music in the parking lot all night. Thousands of people would show up. There was also a wonderful event every weekend during the summer called Shindig on the Green. Folks would come from all around the area to play music. Shindig is going strong to this day.

You became a sign maker to get by, but what about your music?

I became a sign maker because I didn't want to be thinking about anything but music in the evenings. I wanted to just work on learning to play better.

I was able to give music my full attention. In the evenings after work I would get together with old musicians like Byard Ray or Tommy Bell. Byard was particularly good to me. He would come over in the evening and teach me tunes and songs with his fiddle, and I'd play them on the banjo. He taught me how to 'shade a tune', as he called it. "Shading" meant playing all of the little embellishments that you can add to a simple tune to make it interesting and deep. Byard was a great mentor.

By the end of a year of intense practicing I had become a good banjo player.

- **Publicity pays dividends—**

Martha Abshire, a newspaper reporter for the Asheville Citizen-Times, did a story on me. At the time, it was so unusual for someone to come from out west to learn traditional mountain music around Asheville that it was worthy of a feature story. It was a full page with a large photo. That seems funny now, but in 1973 it was news.

Do you still have the article?

I've given all of my materials to the archive at UNC Chapel Hill. I'm sure it's there.

After the article came out people started calling and asking me to perform. I had not performed since my days as a drummer. I asked John Bridges at the Asheville Library if I could do a concert in the old library in Asheville. A lot of people came. I had a great time and realized that I really liked to entertain. It seemed like an interesting challenge to try to get an audience excited about an older form of music. It has been an interesting challenge to this day.

Organizations started asking me to do little gigs, schools called, churches called, and I realized I could possibly make a living doing this. And I also realized I had a knack for it. I worked hard on my music and started learning other instruments besides banjo and guitar. I was very interested in the odd instruments mountain people played like the mouth bow, the bottle, the washboard, the hammered dulcimer. Leonard Hollifield, a musician here in Asheville, told me years ago, "Most people don't really hear the individual notes and don't know what a chord is. They do hear fast and slow, and complex and simple, but what they mainly hear is different sounds. They like to hear different instruments."

He was right. Most people do respond to different sounds. I found that in order to entertain an audience as a solo performer playing a bunch of old songs, I needed various sounds to keep their attention.

What musical instruments did you play?

In those days banjo was my main instrument. I worked hard learning the odd instruments I found in the mountains like the mouth bow, the autoharp, the dulcimer, the spoons and bones that had been handed down in my family. The Jew's harp, the harmonica, hambone (body slapping rhythms), all kept the audience interested with the variety of sounds.

I worked all of those instruments into my show. I didn't want these odd instruments to be merely schtick. I really tried to play them as musically as possible, even something as simple as the paper bag which I learned from old man Morris Norton in Sodom, NC. I tried to get the rhythm just right so it would be entertaining and musical.

And singing?

I had been the kid in church who mouthed the words but never sang out loud. I found out later that hymns are in terrible keys for young men; we really couldn't get them because they are pitched for women.

But as a performer, I tried to sing as best as I could, inspired by those old cowboy singers. And of course, the more I sang the more I enjoyed it. I love to sing now.

• Teaching Appalachian Music—

What came next for you?

A really wonderful thing happened in 1975 when the Dean of Warren Wilson College, Sam Scoville, asked me to start an Appalachian Music Program at the college. It would be the only program of its kind in the country.

It wasn't just an academic program, but an actual applied music program, where the students could learn how to play the instruments as well as learn the history of the music. I wrote grants and hired traditional musicians to give lessons.

We had ballad singing, fiddle, banjo, guitar, mandolin, string band classes as well as history of country music classes. It was an exciting time. Now, mind you, these old-time mountain people had never given lessons before. So, it was tricky, but the students realized they were getting a rare opportunity to be with "the real thing" and they understood the value of that.

We also put on a series of concerts highlighting the different styles of banjo, fiddle, guitar and mandolin in Western NC. In the 1970s the Asheville area had a vibrant community of traditional musicians playing a wide variety of styles.

Was there a good turnout of students for your classes?

Yes, the Appalachian Music Program was very popular at Warren Wilson College. Folks came from all over the country. Laura Boosinger, Suzie Gott, Jerry Reed Smith, Jeff Robbins and Tom Fellenbaum are just a few of the people who came through the program and became professional musicians. David Wilcox, a great singer and songwriter, came to the program just as I was leaving, but we claim him anyway.

As with many small colleges, I was paid for half time but was working full time. I continued performing on the side and realized that I could make more money and have more fun doing concerts. After teaching at the college for six years, I decided to leave Warren Wilson and try to make a living performing full time.

- **A fulltime performer—**

How did it work out when you became a full-time performer?

I went out solo because I realized that was the only way I could make any money. I figured out right away that if you are paid very little, you better keep it all. At this point I had a wife, Ginny, two children, Zeb and Sara Jane, and that really gave me impetus to work hard.

A solo performer really has two choices starting out: you can either play for schools or in bars, but they are mutually exclusive. Bars keep you up late at night, while schools start early in the morning and you are finished by 3 pm. You couldn't do both.

As my old friend John McCutcheon said, "Playing for school kids is a lot like playing for a bunch of drunks anyway."

That's a good line. You obviously have a great sense of humor. Do you interject that into your act?

Always, humor is very important. It makes everybody feel connected.

I already knew the answer but wanted to hear it. What is the relative importance of humor to audience?

It's huge. Audiences come to be entertained, and a sense of humor is probably the most entertaining thing that we share as humans. It is the best "social lubricant" there is.

I like humor with a twist. I think humor has been important for me from the very beginning, for setting up songs and stories and putting them in context. Today most people do not know anything about mountain music so you have to set it up for them.

Back in the 1970s you could say to an audience, "This is a tune from Tommy Jarrell who lived in Surry County, North Carolina," and the audience would already know all about him. But these days nobody knows what you are talking about. So, I bring large photographs I have taken of musicians and tell stories about them. I might say, "My friend Chet Akins gave me some good advice. He said, 'David, figure out where the bad notes are on the guitar and stay off of them.' Or I might tell the story about how Uncle Dave Macon rode on top of all the money in the Woodbury, TN bank when they moved the cash by wagon to a new location. He sat on top of the money pile and played his banjo so it would attract a big crowd and no one would be bold enough to steal it.

So, you are not only a performer but a historian.

Definitely! I try to set things up in context and give some historical background…in an entertaining way. Mountain music doesn't just come out of the blue; it comes from a long tradition. I have always loved history. If you find the right stories to tell, history really comes alive.

Basically, I try to make the music palatable to a modern audience, bend it a little but not break it. Doc Watson has been a great influence on me. He blends the old and the new so beautifully.

I notice you often call the music 'mountain music' instead of 'bluegrass' or 'old-time music'.

I do. Mountain music is an inclusive term. Older traditional music has a lot of variety. In the 1970s, there were no precise divisions. I think the term mountain music encompasses bluegrass, old-time music, unaccompanied ballads, blues and a lot more...basically all the styles of traditional music played in the mountains. I am sorry the music genres have become so segmented today. Over the last thirty years people have forgotten about the variety of music, rhythms, instruments and styles that existed in the early 1900s.

- **The Grand Ole Opry and Hee-Haw—**

Where did you take your special brand of music?

A big turning point for me was when I was teaching and took my Appalachian Music Program students down to the Grand Ole Opry in Nashville in 1980. After the show I thought, "The Opry is really missing something; they don't have any old-time mountain music anymore. The only thing that was the least bit old-timey was a great western swing group called Riders in the Sky."

When I got back home I called the Opry and talked to Hal Durham, the manager at that time. This was in 1980. I told him he ought to have more old-time music, because that is what the Opry was founded on, people like Uncle Dave Macon, Uncle Jimmy Thompson, Stringbean, the Crook Brothers, Deford Bailey, all these great old-time musicians.

He said, "Well, I'd like to have old-time music, but I don't know anybody that plays that style of music." I said, "I do!" He invited me down the following week to play for him.

A friend of mine named Anne Romaine told me: "If you go down there to meet Hal Durham, don't go in jeans looking grubby. Dress up in a sequin suit or whatever you plan to wear on the Opry. Go there in full regalia, even if it is just to play for him in his office."

I always loved Mark Twain's white suits, so I bought a white suit and white hat and planned to show him my beautiful tree of life banjo. I brought all my instruments and played for him, and at the end of the interview he said, "Great, I'll put you on in a couple of weeks."

The very first time I played the Opry I played the paper bag. Something I learned from Morris Norton up in Sodom, NC. It sounds like a snare drum and when you play the harmonica at the same time it is very powerful. I was taking a chance doing something that odd but it brought the house down. I played the Opry for a number of years after that and tried to always sing something from Uncle Dave Macon or other early Opry stars.

From that I was booked on Hee Haw. That was a huge thing because in the 1980s, it was one of the most popular shows on television. There were some great people in the cast and it was fun. Hee Haw was like a big family; it was great.

How many times did you play the Grand Ole Opry?

Maybe twenty times. I loved playing it, but the problem with the Opry was you'd call them on Wednesday, and they wouldn't tell you until Friday morning whether you were going to be on that weekend. So, you might cancel a whole weekend of concerts then learn they couldn't use you because they had a full house of Opry members that wanted to play. You had to wait around to find out if you would be called.

It sure was fun being backstage, though. Roy Acuff held court in his dressing room, Grandpa Jones would be roaming the halls and Bill Monroe would be jamming with his band. It was a thrill.

How about Hee Haw?

The producers of Hee Haw heard me on the Opry and asked me to be on the show some time in 1980. At first I was a featured guest. I would perform two songs on the show, songs like "John Henry" and "Bound to Ride." Then they asked me to open the second half of the show and lead the entire cast in an old-time song. Roy Clark and Grandpa Jones, everybody, would all be singing along. It was big fun.

They invited me to do the four harmonica players and the four banjo players segments. In one segment I taught Roy Acuff how to play the paper bag and he showed me an old body slapping rhythm he knew as a child. Roy was a real booster for me. He always suggested songs that I should learn. He knew I wore 1940s style ties, and sent me some hand painted ones from his vast collection.

But I didn't want to do any of the silly comedy or act like a rube. I wanted the old music to be treated respectfully. I was on Hee Haw from 1980 until it went off the air in 1987. I was on maybe twenty-six times and with repeats, more than fifty times.

I asked a friend recently if he knew of David Holt. He answered, "You mean the guy with the hat?" How did your trademark hat come about?

The hat became a logo before I was actually bald. The first time I was on Hee Haw in 1980 is when I decided to wear a hat. On Hee Haw they made you up like you had just come from the undertaker, with tons of makeup. So, I'm sitting there in a chair, and I had hair at that time, just a receding hairline. The makeup artist takes out an eyebrow pencil and starts drawing in hair.

I said, "Hey, wait a minute, what are you doing?"

She answered, "Well, I'll have to do this every time you are on the show, or you have to get a toupee, or you have to wear a hat." I said, "I've got a hat in the car." I went and got it. Once I was on that first show, a hat became my logo. I realized people recognize a hat much sooner than they recognize a face.

You have a young face, so the hat keeps you looking younger, I think.

With a hat you don't have to worry about your hair. And you can always buy a new hat, but you can't buy a new face.

Do you write songs?

I've always written songs. There are original pieces on all my CDs. But I didn't want to become known as a singer-songwriter. I really loved the traditional music and wanted that to be seen as my focus. It was obvious to me that what often happens to performers is if they get too diversified nobody can identify what they do. I was clear about what I did, what I loved to do, and that was helpful in building a music career.

- **Folkways PBS TV series—**

Also in 1980 North Carolina Public Television asked me to host FOLKWAYS. It has been on the air the last thirty-five years. I was thirty-years-old when I started doing the show I am still hosting it today. Jim Bramlett was the producer/director over most of those years and he was a jewel to work with.

In the show we would feature different North Carolina folk artists: potters, weavers, musicians, blacksmiths, toy makers, mountain dancers, black gospel singers, you name it, we did it.

Most of the people we featured on FOLKWAYS have passed away. I am so glad we were able to get them on videotape. And now, the shows can be downloaded for free on iTunes or from UNC-TV.org. So they should be around long after I am gone.

Because FOLKWAYS is only shown in North Carolina, it has allowed me to make a good living in the state. We only made thirty-five of those shows, but they still play all the time on PBS in North Carolina.

You've been hosting Folkways since 1980 and it's still on the air. To what do you attribute its long history?

I think because it's so down home and real. The show always has a loyal following. It has obviously had an impact, and people still like it. I am very proud of that.

- ## Nashville TV Network and *Esquire*—

It sounds like you followed your instincts and did very well.

I enjoyed my work in TV during the early '80s and wanted to do more. Cable television was new in the 1980s. I wanted to be part of it. The Nashville Network (TNN) was a new country music cable channel. I was asked to host *Fire on the Mountain* in 1984 when the Nashville Network started. It was a live concert show.

For the next four years we taped ninety-five half-hour shows featuring the very best in bluegrass and old-time music. Everybody from Doc Watson to Bill Monroe, from Mike Seeger to Tommy Jarrell.

We had a wide and dedicated audience around the country. It got old-time and bluegrass music out to a much larger public. It also gave me national exposure for the first time. But more important *Fire On the Mountain* allowed me to meet and work with all the best people in mountain music. It was the first time I worked with Doc Watson, Sam Bush, John Hartford, Bill Monroe and so many more.

It is probably the best documentation of traditional folk music in America in the years 1984 to 1989.

In 1984 Esquire magazine chose you to be in their first annual 'The Best of the New Generation – Men and Women Under Forty Who Are Changing America' edition. I cite that article in a previous section that disclosed you were honored alongside such greats as Steven Spielberg, Meryl Streep, Wynton Marsalis, Julius Erving, Whoopie Goldberg, Ricky Skaggs and Greg Louganis, to name just a few. All that major exposure must have helped your career.

I certainly was surprised and honored to be chosen. It was a very big deal for a time but as I have found over the years, a career builds slowly. Everything helps but no one thing takes you to the top.

The Esquire recognition was amazing though. I remember thinking that it wasn't clear what my limits were. Cable was just beginning, the Nashville Network was new. There were no precedents. To give you an example, I was at a big cable meeting in Las Vegas representing the Nashville Network. Nina Blackwood was there for MTV, anchorman Bernard Shaw was representing CNN and Jerry Mathers (from Leave It to Beaver) was there for Nickelodeon. We were all equal. No one knew which cable networks were going to be successful. That was how new it was. It was so unusual to have traditional music on television so I got a lot of attention from the press.

The Nashville Network sent me to LA to do interviews with some of the major news writers. The big interview was with Jerry Buck, who had an entertainment column in most newspapers in America. We met in the Beverly Hills Hotel and had a great interview. I thought, "Once this interview appears in every newspaper in the country with a photo I'm going to be instantly well known. This is going to be great!"

The article and photo appeared but nothing happened except I got a few calls from high school friends I hadn't seen in years and that was it. That was an interesting taste of publicity, but as you know from being a publicist once yourself, it all builds up slowly. But all in all the publicity was great because it took me from being a local musician here in Asheville to having a national TV show even if it was on cable.

- **Play for pay—**

How did that work out for you financially?

It paid pretty well, but it wasn't great, probably a thousand dollars per show, which was pretty good in those days. But I was at the career building stage, money wasn't very important. The best thing was working with all the great musicians.

An interesting story about the money they offered to host *Fire On the Mountain* involves John Hartford, who wrote 'Gentle on my Mind.' The producers of *Fire on the Mountain* auditioned John, Mike Cross and me. Luckily, they chose me to host the show. I was really excited. But they were offering very low pay to host the show. I felt they were not being fair.

Hartford called me and said, "The producers told me they are going to let me host the show instead of you if you don't come down to their price. I'd like to do it and I don't need the money. I can live off 'Gentle on my Mind.' So, if you want to do the show, go ahead and take what they are offering. I think it would be a really great thing for you. If you don't, I will take their offer."

I did take it, and my hat is forever off to John Hartford for being so generous. And I didn't even know him that well at the time; he was ten years older and was just looking out for me. He helped me many times over the years. I loved the man.

Was television your main thing during that period?

No, just a few weeks out of the year. We'd tape thirteen shows twice a year and they would be on the air every week. I was still making my living performing, mostly in schools and family concerts, but about that time I wanted to do more adult venues and less family shows. It can be a difficult transition to make, but I was determined.

The TV exposure took me to the next level. When *Fire On the Mountain* went off the air, TNN asked me to host a new show called *American Music Shop*. This show didn't concentrate on mountain music, but featured all sorts of performers from Steve Earle to Earl Scruggs. The house band was the best in the business and included Mark O' Connor, Jerry Douglas and Brent Rowan.

After *American Music Shop,* TNN asked me to host *Celebration Express*, which sent me around the country to seventy-nine different cities doing a Charles Kuralt "on the road" type show. We did a story on an interesting personality in each city like Buck Owens at home in Bakersfield or the alligator hunter in Florida or the man in Houston who completely covered his house in fifty thousand flattened beer cans.

Thanks to the Nashville Network I had gained a lot of television experience by this point, after hosting several hundred TV shows.

Do you receive residuals from those TV programs?

No. Public Television doesn't pay residuals and TNN is defunct. People think there is money in television, but I have never seen it. The real residual effect is that these shows put me before a larger public and helped me make a living playing music. Doing concerts and workshops is how I have always paid the bills.

Have you ever considered doing a documentary about all that?

I would love to have done it, but I didn't want to produce it. I want to focus on playing music. Music is first and foremost to me.

- **Featuring black performers—**

In our pre-interview you said that you tried to feature black performers and craftsmen. Tell me more.

As a historian of mountain music I feel the contributions of black Americans are often overlooked. In my live shows and on the television shows I always try to highlight how important black influences are on the music. I had a grand opportunity to do that when we were taping The Nashville Network's *Celebration Express* since we had to find interesting characters in seventy-nine different cities. For example we did shows on black cowboys, musicians and craftsmen like Phillip Simmons, the great Black wrought iron artist in Charleston, SC.

Were your TV shows shot before live audiences?

Yes, both *Fire on the Mountain* and the *American Music Shop*. But *Folkways* and *Celebration Express* were shot on location.

Did you find yourself relating to your audiences, or did you play mostly to the camera?

Both, it's important to connect to the live audience and to the camera. From the very beginning of doing television I made up my mind that I would try to be myself and not create a persona. I got better at it as time went along and really enjoyed doing TV.

What happened when the Nashville Network was sold; did that get you down?

I was really sorry because I thought TNN was going to be around a long time. I knew if I could stay with *Fire on the Mountain* for twenty years or so, it could become a cultural phenomenon, something like the Grand Old Opry or Prairie Home Companion. But that didn't happen.

The way the show ended must have been disappointing.

Yes, that was a disappointment, but I have always been able to make a good living anyway. I had never become dependent on television work to make a living. And the Nashville scene was not that comfortable to me. Everybody was too eager. At one point I wondered if I should move to Nashville since it was the center of country music. But I realized that Nashville likes to pigeon-hole people, and it is difficult to break out of the pigeon hole they put you in. I was an odd act anyway.

I said to myself: "The mountains are my home, it is where my music is, it is where I learned to play music, and it is where I'm going to stay." I never regretted my decision to stay in North Carolina.

The other big disappointment was that CBS bought the Nashville Network and just locked all the tapes of the shows away. I am really sorry they have not been re-released. There was so much great music on the shows we did. The good news is lots of folks taped it and now you can see *Fire on the Mountain* clips on YouTube.

Are you doing much television now?

Yes, I often do specials for UNC-TV. We recently made some new *Folkways* segments. And I host another national PBS show called *Great Scenic Railway Journeys* produced by Rob Van Camp. We travel around the country visiting historic railroads. I have really learned to love steam engines. Each one has its own personality, quirks and strengths. They are almost like living beings. I have always said that musical instruments are as close to being alive as an inanimate object can be, but I think trains also have this 'living' quality about them.

- **A love of instruments—**

Tell me about the instruments you play.

I love instruments! They all have very distinct personalities. A good one will encourage you to play better and continue to get better. They have a voice of their own, so you put your musical voice into their body and try to make them come alive. I love instruments, and I've collected a bunch of them.

I've heard you say that instruments are like your children. Explain.

Yeah, they are like my children. When I am playing solo, life on the road can get pretty lonely. They are like family; they entertain you, inspire you, keep depression from your door. You put a lot of your soul into an instrument during the time you play it, so it really becomes your friend, and your meditation, too.

Can you expand on that?

The meditation? Well, you have to find that place in yourself where you enjoy practicing, where it is not a chore, and then you have to focus. The best kind of practice is concentrated focused attention. Nobody ever calls it this, but it is a kind of mindfulness training. That is key to learning an instrument.

You talk about your instruments like they have personalities, and what you put in is what you get out.

I do. First of all is the tone of the instrument. The tone is something you look for, but everybody is not always looking for the same tone, and you need one that fits you.

It takes years to find what kind of tone you are looking for: do you want it loud, do you want it brash, do you want it quiet, do you want it subtle, do you want a lot of sustain or no sustain, those kinds of considerations. Also does the instrument fit your body and is it easy and fun to play? Does the way it looks inspire you to play it?

When you finally figure out what you want, getting that instrument can take half your life going through hundreds of instruments that don't quite fit. Well, that may be exaggerated, but I bet I've been through twenty banjos and fifty guitars to find ones that I really, really like.

Is there a comfort level you reach each time you develop a relationship with your instrument?

I think the longer you play the same instrument, the better you get to know it. That is one of the things I learned from Doc Watson. I have a lot of instruments, but he has just a few. He really knows how each one feels. Of course, he is blind so he has to really know the feel of his guitar.

I play a lot of different ones and I think that is a disadvantage, but I just love the different sounds of them. I am willing to put up with having to learn the idiosyncrasies of each one.

It seems like there is always a new one that is calling to me. A friend of mine said he is part of the

Eleven-Step Guitar program – one more and he'll be cured!

- **Wisdom of Appalachian music culture—**

You often talk about the unique wisdom of the Appalachian music culture and the musicians and the music and all the history. How would you capsulize your relationship with all of that?

The old-time mountain people I first met were born in the late 1800s. They were relatively uninfluenced by mass media. Radio didn't really come in until 1922 and records didn't come until 1923, so people who were adults by that time already had learned much of their music repertoire and had established who they were as people.

They came of age before self-doubt was invented. They were incredibly centered people. That doesn't mean they knew everything, but that they did know a lot about nature, about natural ways, about the seasons of life. That's powerful information, and it helps one realize what is important. They had very little artificiality.

I think the media has led us astray. We have forgotten what is important. Today it is easy to get distracted. There is almost too much information. We are bombarded by a culture where celebrity is king, where money is the master, and we get jealous and envious, and side-tracked. The old mountain people didn't have to deal with that. Of course, not every old-timer is full of wisdom, but many were. Moreover a person who has spent a life-time learning to be a good musician has accomplished something and it made them more profound people.

The Appalachian people were very solid within themselves. They knew they could survive just about anything you could name, floods, fires, love, hate, deaths, accidents and poverty. They knew how to persevere.

- **And then, tragedy—**

My life was turned upside down in 1989. My daughter was killed in a car accident, and the grief from that loss almost took me out. Sara Jane was only ten, and the apple of my eye. We had just moved into this house that week. Ginny was driving our daughter to school on a very stormy day. The car hydroplaned and was hit by another car. That changed everything for me and for us.

Over the next few years Ginny, our son Zeb and I were just trying to survive. Going through grief is exhausting and all consuming. You are on a runaway train and can't get off. Ginny and I did every kind of grief counseling you could imagine. That probably saved our lives.

I lost my sister, Gina, to drowning when I was a little boy. I was ten and she was seven. That changed me as a child. It was unbelievable that this kind of tragedy could happen twice in my life. For ten years after Sara Jane died I was out on the road and never really let up, but that was very hard to do. There were times when the grief seemed insurmountable.

Looking back, did tragedy change your music?

Oh yeah, it sure did change my music. It put me in the center of the blues.

My mother's plumber gave me what is called a National Steel Guitar, a resophonic guitar that has a certain far-away, soulful sound. I didn't know exactly how to play the blues on it, but I knew that is what it was meant for. You are supposed to play it with an open tuning and use a broken bottleneck on your finger.

So, I would get up at sunrise every day and play the saddest tunes I could come up with. The sunrises in the mountains that November of 1989 were intense oranges and reds, brooding.

Somehow that slide guitar sound went way down deep inside me and help bring the pain to the surface. It literally saved my life. I had no real intention of learning to play slide blues guitar but after a couple of years of playing just to keep my emotional head above water, I realized I actually might be able to learn to play the instrument well. I added blues to my concert programs and found the sound of the slide guitar could take a whole audience to a deeper level.

When you play really soulful wailing music down low, do you find yourself descending with it, and then coming back up into the light?

You know, I think that is what the blues does. It doesn't depress you, it goes down with you. You can get down in that bluesy part of yourself. Then it lifts you back up.

People ask me, "How did you survive after losing a child?" Well, you survive because you don't kill yourself. It is that simple. There are times when you feel like leaving this world, but you survive by just keeping on, being with your family and finding something like the blues. I found the music to be therapeutic. Things would have been even harder for me if I didn't have music.

I did all of the other kinds of therapy, too, but the music helped me as much as anything, and also performing. If you are a performer you can be getting the flu and still go on and do a great show. By the end of the evening your flu is gone. It heals you because somehow you've blown it out of your system during the performance. So it was the same with the grief, performing was a way of healing. It helped me get my strength back.

Do you think that helped mature you for your musical life, and as a man and husband?

Oh, goodness yes. When someone as dear as Sara Jane dies you feel like you are standing on the edge of an infinitely deep black hole of sadness and grief. And at the same time you know that everyone in the history of mankind who has lost a child has felt the same thing. It makes everything artificial just melt away. Money, success, prestige, recognition all lose their meaning.

I was forty-three when Sara Jane died. It took about twelve years for Ginny and me to get to a "new normal." By that time I was fifty-five-years-old. Then you realize that your own life is going to end in the next 30 or 40 years if you are lucky. So, there is nothing left to do but to live your life and enjoy what you can. Get the most out of the time you have left. And Sara would want Ginny, Zeb and me to do that. She wouldn't want me to be depressed all the time, or kill myself. Sara Jane was a very loving and positive person. She would have wanted us to go on with life and enjoy it.

I heard that eighty-six percent of people who lose a child get cancer or have a heart-attack or die within six years, and something like fifty percent of couples who lose a child break-up. We really worked hard not to allow that to happen. Unless you lose a child yourself there is no way to imagine it; there is no reason to even bother trying to imagine it, you cannot even get close.

- **Then—*Riverwalk Jazz*—**

What happened with your career after the tragedy?

Around the time of the accident, 1989, I was starting a show for public radio called *Riverwalk Jazz* out of San Antonio. The show is still on the radio after twenty five years. I host it, and tell the story of classic jazz and interview some of the jazz greats like Lionel Hampton, Benny Carter, Clark Terry. I don't play music on the show.

I flew to Texas for the show many, many times to do hundreds of hour-long shows. It is a first-class production. Margaret Moos Pick writes and produces the shows. She started Prairie Home Companion with Garrison Keillor. She is one of the best in the public radio business, and made this a great show.

In 1989 Margaret was looking for a host who could tell a story, could interview old musicians and didn't sound like Garrison Keillor. Luckily I fit the bill. It has been a wonderful experience because I have been able to meet all the living jazz greats from the 1920s-1940s.

Now you can hear online more than 400 shows at RiverwalkJazz.org.

And the other thing that happened was I started taking my son Zeb on gigs to play bass with me. That was a wonderful thing we shared. He was just 12 years old and we would have great fun out on the road. It also taught him how to be professional when a job had to be done. It brought us closer together.

- **Playing with Doc Watson—**

What happened during the next phase of your career?

I was on the road about 220 days a year, playing solo or with Zeb, or with my old friend bass player Will McIntyre. I was traveling and playing all over the world.

When I was almost fifty-three I started playing with Doc Watson. In 1998 UNC-TV asked me to do a concert with him for Public Television. We did the TV show *An Evening with Doc Watson* and within months people started asking us to perform shows together.

It just took off. I have been playing with Doc for the last fourteen years. It has been the highlight in my career, because Doc had been my greatest mentor. I didn't want to copy him. I just wanted to be close enough to absorb some of his amazing musicality. It is great fun to play together because when the rhythm is right it feels like you are riding on a train roaring down the tracks.

Doc's great skill is taking a new song like 'Ready for the Times to Get Better' and making it sound old. He can take a old folk song, like 'Way Downtown' and make it sound new to a modern audience. It is a wonderful way to bring older music into the present, and that is something I have always tried to do as well.

Doc is one of the greatest musicians of all time, so it is a challenge to play with him. He is always doing these quirky little things musically that keep you on your toes. You can't just think it is going to be the same old way every time, because it never is. He never plays it the same way once! There is no award, no compliment from anybody, nothing that could be more important to me musically than playing with Doc.

When did you make your discs with Doc?

In 2002 my buddy Steve Heller and I produced a live concert at the Diana Wortham Theatre in Asheville called 'An Evening with Doc Watson and David Holt'.

That concert became the basis for the three CD set, LEGACY. It was Steve's idea to interview Doc about his early life and his life in music and put it on CD. Doc never allowed an authorized biography so I said to him, "What if you spoke your biography? Tell your life the way you want to tell it."

Those interviews were recorded in a studio near Doc's home in Deep Gap and to me they are the heart of the three-CD set. Doc almost speaks in poetry. I wrote a seventy-two page book to accompany the recording that was a real labor of love. It was fun talking to family members and old friends to put together stories and photos from Doc's life.

We really caught the moment; Doc was in his eighties and quite sharp. LEGACY was another personal career high and became another turning point. In 2002, I won two Grammys for LEGACY as producer and artist. I received a Grammy several years earlier for a children's book STELLAUNA that I narrated.

In all, I've had four wins and eight Grammy nominations. But to win with Doc was very meaningful. The rest was icing on the cake, after playing together with Doc.

Did the four Grammys help your career much?

Well, at first the Grammys helped sell CDs and get some notoriety, but the real value they give you is credibility. It is hard to be nominated but almost impossible to win.

It's amazing that you and Doc are still performing together.

Fourteen years later Doc and I are still performing together. We just recently did a very special concert. Doc and I along with T. Michael Coleman and Sam Bush played in Nashville at the Ryman Auditorium, home of the Grand Ole Opry, and sold out the twenty-three hundred seats. It was an exciting show with many stars in the audience. The audience realized they were probably not going to get to see Doc again since he was eighty-eight. We were in a zone and played wonderfully. What a magic night that was. There are not many people in the history of the music business that kept going and did such a good job at Doc's age. He may drop a chord or a word or two now, but he still is remarkable.

How many band members in the Lightning Bolts?

Five members, including Josh Goforth, Laura Boosinger, Byron Hedgepeth and Jeff Hersk. A great bunch of musicians.

How did you meet Josh?

I played at his middle school up in Madison County and his teacher came to me and said, "I have this young man and wonder if he could play with you. He's just twelve."

I said, "You know I am about to go in front of eight hundred middle-schoolers. Are you sure he can do this?" She said "Yeah, he's pretty good." So I said, "Well, get him up here and let us run through something."

Josh did great, so we stayed in contact. And when he was nineteen, I put together *David Holt and the Lightning Bolts* because we had this big gig at the largest country music festival in Europe, in Gstaad, Switzerland. I wanted to take a band made up of musicians from Western NC.

I took Josh and Laura Boosinger and my son Zeb, who plays bass, and David Cohen on percussion. We just tore it up in Switzerland. It was a huge success. Josh and I have played together ever since. The band is still going strong with a few replacements. Zeb moved to New York to work for NBC and Byron Hedgepeth came on board as percussionist.

Josh and I also perform as a duo. It is very important to me that a guy sixty-five years old can play with someone only thirty who is an incredibly good musician. I try to mentor him in terms of how to entertain a crowd and the business end of music, but I really can't mentor him musically. We work together and have a great time sharing musical ideas.

Laura was my student when she was only nineteen at Warren Wilson College in those early days. She continued as a professional musician and is head of the Madison County Arts Council. I am really proud of her.

- **Storytelling and 'The Hanged Elephant'—**

When did you start your journey into storytelling?

I didn't know there were professional storytellers until 1976 when I was invited to the National

Storytelling Festival in Jonesboro, Tennessee. There really wasn't much of a movement up to that point.

I started telling stories on my own because I was coming across stories as I was collecting songs in the mountains. One of the first ones I came across really stuck in my mind, about an elephant that was hanged in Erwin, Tennessee in 1916. This old mountaineer Stanley Hicks told a version of it. I checked old newspapers in Erwin, Johnson City and Kingsport, then assembled what happened and created a story out of it.

When I told the story to an audience, they were stunned. They hated it because, as I later found out, no one wants to hear about an animal being hurt.

This was a true story that I thought was fascinating. But I quickly learned that if a story can be that powerful and stun the audience negatively, then the right story could do the same thing positively. I had always added little bits of humor to my concerts and started to tell complete stories.

In 1976, I was still making my living doing schools and began to find that kids would listen to a story, sit completely still, riveted, for fifteen minutes, while I could just barely hold them with a three-minute song. It was amazing to discover how stories really gripped an audience.

Gwenda Ledbetter was 'The Storylady' in Asheville. Every Saturday morning she told stories on a local TV program, 'The Mr. Bill Show'. She was tired of doing it every Saturday and asked me if I would do it. That was my first TV experience. It made me learn a lot of new stories.

Then Connie Reagan-Blake heard about me and told Jimmy Neil Smith at the National Storytelling Festival that he ought to invite me, so in 1976 I performed at the National Storytelling Festival. There were about 150 people in the audience. I also met Ray Hicks and Katherine Windham, two people that became major mentors for me. The stage was a truck bed. Now thirty-five years later, the festival has grown so much that there are 11,000 to 12,000 people there.

I was very lucky because rarely in life do you get in on the beginning of a movement and watch it grow. I did get to ride the wave of storytelling to the point of the peak. The storytelling movement has spread out to festivals in every state, and in countries all over the world.

I grew up in Texas where there are lots of stories because it was such a hostile environment, and tough times made for good stories. I had plenty of rough and tumble ancestors that my family told stories about, frontier doctors, cowboys, even Jesse James.

I continue to incorporate storytelling with my music and music with my storytelling.

How often have you played the National Storytelling Festival?

Many, many times; I'm there every two or three years.

Do you use your guitar and sing?

Oh yeah, I am known as one of the tellers who incorporates music in his stories. And that has been useful to me because there weren't many people in the early days that did that. There are more now.

I think the human mind loves that combination of story and song. I've noticed in situations where I sit around with old ballad singers and mountain musicians that they would play for a little while then stop to tell informal stories about something they heard about or about somebody who got killed or other gossip. I find that stories and music go together as naturally as can be.

- **Three talents in one package—**

You can be described as a storyteller, a musician and a singer in one package.

I really consider myself a musician first, but storytelling has been a wonderful addition, something I will always do because it adds richness and meaning to a concert of music. You have to give people a reason to care about what you are telling them, and stories are perfect for that.

How do the audiences differ at a standard concert and at a storytelling event?

I would say a storytelling event attracts people who are very good listeners. They know they are going to be sitting listening to stories, and nobody is going to be shooting off cannons, and cars won't be crashing or anything like that. In general they are an intelligent and curious crowd.

You've been a performer for a long time, have you noticed your audiences aging along with you?

Yes. In the early part of my career I was playing schools, and many of the kids from those days come up to me now as adults. I started when I was in my twenties, so I meet people now fifty who saw me when they were only ten. That is amazing to me.

Something I've noticed for almost every performer is the bulk of the audience is about the same generation as the performer. Look at Lady Gaga or Tony Bennett or anybody, and their audiences are about their same age.

Do you have a fan club?

Not a formal one, but I have a great website, Davidholt.com, and a Facebook page.

In the LEGACY CD I loved what Doc said when you asked what it was like to be blind, especially when he talked about dreams. You got inside of his mind, like I'm trying to get inside yours now. Doc seems like a gentle soul.

He certainly can be. We took out some of that conversation that might make it seem otherwise.

Salty stuff?

No, no, no. Doc had nine brothers and sisters who were tough on him, rough mountain people, so he had a lot of anger when he was younger, but he is not that way anymore.

I'm particularly interested in Doc because of his influence on you, and that you produced the Legacy CDs and the bio-booklet. Share more about his innate wisdom, his persona, and how the world views him?

Doc used to be fierce and some people were afraid of him because he is a strong willed and a very commanding presence. He is intelligent and powerful, but can be very stubborn. He realized that some years ago and has become much more tender. He is thoughtful and very smart. Being blind, he has a good bit of time to think about things and his thoughts run deep.

One of the interesting things about Doc is when he went into the wider world, this blind mountain boy created a public persona, but not a fake one at all. He is very genuine. His wonderful persona is evident in the *Legacy* CDs. He can sound real country when he talks, but never sounds ignorant. He took away the twang in his voice and made it very mellow and pleasant to listen to. I think he created that because he is so auditory oriented. He is beloved by the public because they sense his depth and his innate soulfulness.

- **Preserving the old-time music—**

Now I want to know how you think the world sees David Holt; answer optional.

I never think about it, but I am very aware about what I am trying to do. In music you have to be totally self-motivated. There is nobody saying you have to do this or learn that or make this CD.

I really don't know what others think, but hopefully they would see me as somebody who has worked very hard and is very honest. I don't think you'll find anybody that would say, "That guy screwed me" or "stepped on me." That is very important to me.

My wife, Ginny, has been a huge help to me in every way. We are a team. I often go to her to get an opinion. We bounce ideas off each other and try and come up with the best solution. I couldn't have done all this without Ginny.

Betty Nichols, my assistant, keeps the business running smoothly. She oversees the office and the bookings, something I just couldn't keep up with. Betty is so level headed and wise. Working with good people is very important. Friends Steven Heller and Will and Deni McIntyre have been a huge help to me...talking out possibilities and developing ideas.

I hope that I am seen as somebody who has helped preserve the music, who has been a good musician and a really good performer, and who can help carry this older music forward one more century. Hopefully I've led a useful life that has been valuable to others. I sure have enjoyed it.

You always go back to the value of music and musical history, and you try to preserve that and pass it on. I assume that's the legacy you'd like to leave behind. It's important to have a mission in life.

Is that ever true! I knew as a young man that to work for something bigger than myself is invaluable. I have decided that what everybody really wants is respect, more than money or fame. And if you give 100% and treat people fairly, everything is probably going to work out fine. Respect will come naturally.

What do you see as the future of mountain music?

There are so many great young players. It is in good hands. Of course, it will always be changing, evolving. But that is the way it works if the music is a living music. Bluegrass with its emphasis on difficult technique is very attractive to young people. It has an athletic quality that young people can really dig into. The old-time music is doing quite well, too. There is a thriving old-time music scene here is Asheville and around the country. As long as people are interested in roots music and soulful music, there will be a place for all the forms of mountain music.

When you go on stage with Doc and 5,000 people are in the audience, what are your feelings? Do you go into a different zone, or is it a comfortable extension of who you are?

It's different with Doc because I feel my main goal is to serve Doc. The first things I think are: "How's Doc doing? Does he need the microphone moved? What should be our first song? What would be the most interesting questions to ask him in this concert?" Then I check to see what I need to do. At a concert in Golden Gate Park we played in front of 250,000 people...that will get your attention!

So, performing with Doc is a different situation than when I go on by myself.

When you walk out on the stage on your own to perform before a big audience, what emotions come into play, and do they change when you finish and walk off the stage?

My goal is to bring this audience together for an evening. So, I step out there and try to immediately open myself to what is going on with the people in the room and what I am feeling. I think about what I want to play, and then start focusing on how to play as good as I can. You can practice songs at home, but then get out on a stage and totally screw it up. It is a completely different process from playing perfectly at home and playing perfectly on stage.

I try to get settled and greet the audience, add a bit of humor. That always opens people up. Then I play a song that includes them in some way, some little thing they can sing back to me just to get them immediately involved.

Did you feel nervousness and a heightened state of awareness through the early years when you stepped on stage, and when did performing become second nature to you?

Energy definitely races through my body when I perform, but I am not nervous. I don't usually get very nervous, but I have been in situations that make me nervous, like when I performed with the North Carolina Symphony and sang a James Taylor song I wasn't used to singing. That made me nervous, but generally I am not.

You have to learn how to entertain a crowd. It is a skill like anything else. So much of it has to do with feeling the energy of the crowd at any given moment. If the audience is not giving back much energy, if they are really tight-lipped, it makes it more difficult. But I can usually find a way to open up a group of folks. That's my job.

Sounds like you are really in your element when you perform.

Yes, I know what I am doing, and I know what I want from it: for the audience to have a good time, to bring a room full of strangers together. I realize after these many years that they're there to have a good time, not to criticize, so we work together.

It must be exciting when you hear laughter and the audience sings along and the chemistry builds.

It is. I can tell where the audience is on that first song, what kind of energy they have. Then if it goes well, I take them through a range of emotions and lots of humor.

I don't look at any one individual person; I just get this feeling from an audience as to what they need. If their energy is dropping, it's weird how you can feel that. I have a number of stories or instruments that will reel them in again. I'm wrangling them in a nice way. I'm trying to make the concert an experience for them and for me.

- **An Appalachian music and song repository—**

As the personal repository for Appalachian music and song are you collecting old records and materials, doing interviews with other musicians, and planning a museum for all this?

All of the material I have collected will be at the Southern Folklore Archive at UNC in Chapel Hill. I have amassed quite a collection of audio and video recordings. The photographs I have taken may end up being the most important part of my collection.

Is that collection on display there?

No, it is not on display, but somebody could go look at it. I've also kept all of my own career materials. If I do a gig and there is a newspaper article about it, I put it in a box. There are many video tapes from the TV shows, hundreds of cassette tapes. It isn't as organized as I would like, and if I had been a highly trained folklorist, I would have known how to do a better job of that.

I figured there were plenty of people videotaping and trained folklorists collecting, but my mistake was to not learn how to do that in an organized way. But it is pretty good; I have a terabyte of video a friend of mine has been taking off of VHS tapes and putting on a hard-drive. Luckily he is organized and is listing what everything is, and that is very helpful.

What I really want is for my grandchildren, if I ever have them, to be able to see it, and for any type of scholar of music to be able to look through it and learn from it.

- **Mentoring—**

What is one piece of important mentoring advice you would offer?

It is important to keep yourself entertained over a long career so that you don't burn out.

How do you entertain yourself?

I like learning, so I'm constantly pressuring myself to find new stuff. I'd be damn lucky to remember all of what I already know, but I constantly search for new material that is fascinating to me. And I am always reading, and doing research and practicing.

Music is constantly changing and expanding into new genres; how has Appalachian music changed?

Appalachian music is not static and never has been. New styles are always being absorbed in the mix. In the 1850s, the minstrel shows where a huge influence, then the Civil War, then the blues in the early 1900s, then radio and recordings in the 1920s. It is always changing but slowly. People who are fans of traditional music don't appreciate radical change. So, it changes slowly, but I can tell you how it has changed since I became involved in the late 1960s. Do you want to hear it?

Yes, very much, please continue.

Okay. When I got here in the late sixties there weren't many young people playing this music. The folks who were raised in the Southern Mountains were trying to get away from the old ways and there weren't many young people coming from outside the region.

Then in about the mid-1970s there was a migration of musicians that came from all over the United States, but mainly from the Northeast. They brought their own sensibilities to it, which were different from the southern sensibilities. Many young folks latched onto a great old fiddler and banjo player named Tommy Jarrell from Surrey County, North Carolina. In Mount Airy, near where he lived, there were several other musicians that played this very distinctive style, Fred Cockerham, Kyle Creed and Benton Flippin, to name a few.

This very distinct style in this little county of Surrey was quite different stylistically from the music around Asheville. In this part of the state fiddle tunes are very melodic with a lot of notes, and down in Surry County the music was more rhythmic, with not as many notes.

- **Spreading in the world—**

Was that when old-time music really began to catch on?

People who came to Tommy Jarrell's place learned what they could, went back home, and the Surry County style began to spread all over the world. This style is what most post call 'old-time music'.

The Surry County style is great, but there was a time when mountain music was much more inclusive of various styles and even instruments. There were old-time piano players and harmonica players. There was even a family that lived in Black Mountain, NC that played pan pipes in harmony. They made them out of river cane and would play gospel tunes in four-part harmony! That was old-time music, too.

Now all of that is pretty much gone. Today the music concentrates on the banjo and fiddle, and mostly fiddle tunes, not even much singing. That is where it stands now, but it's constantly changing, and has never stayed the same. That is just one thing I've seen in my lifetime.

Great description and an eye-opening analysis; I think music fans would like to learn how you see it. Do Appalachian musicians get together and kind of jam like jazz musicians, and do you participate?

Yeah, I still do. There are different kinds of jam sessions. Some happen on a certain night every week and go on for years. Chub Parham used to have one at his house out in Leicester. The place would be full of musicians of all ages jamming together. His wife, Thelma, would always have food and coffee out for anyone who came. There are sessions like this all over the Southern Mountains, all year long. Some are public, and then there are ones where you just call your friends and get together and jam.

I assume you learned a lot from other musicians at the sessions.

You bet. I don't care how good you are, you've always just scratched the surface of music. There is so much, especially if you are a folk musician. Because I wasn't trained in music, which was a definite mistake on my part, I learned it by ear.

How adept are you at reading music?

I read music slowly. But the nuances of traditional music must be learned by ear. There is no way to write the subtleties down. You just try to figure them out by ear. It's a fun way to learn.

- **Loyalties and Legacies—**

You obviously respect and maintain relationships. I managed a few singers and groups, and learned that many in the entertainment industry tend to break ties with people after they succeed.

Some people have no loyalty, but loyalty is very important to me. I am loyal to people, and most have been that way toward me. I haven't been let down at all. Roy Acuff told me years ago to always treat everyone well and pay other musicians fairly. He was right about that.

Life is just like a chess game. You have to choose your moves. I visualize creating my life like making a sculpture. You do your best to form it into something meaningful knowing full well you can't really control the material it is made from.

We are going to get old and die, and it all comes down to the present moment, which is the only one you really have. Reaching a goal is only satisfying for a short time. You have to enjoy the journey.

What do you hope will be your legacy?

A legacy is important, but I feel like if I am honest and good at what I do, that is going to take care of itself. I'm getting just old enough to find that to be true.

For example, the weekend before the concert with Doc Watson at the Ryman, I was given the 'Uncle Dave Macon Heritage Award', which doesn't mean anything to anybody except for people who knew that Uncle Dave Macon was the first star of the Grand Ole Opry. People who previously won include Roy Acuff, Grandpa Jones and the Delmore Brothers.

To me the award was meaningful because I appreciate someone noticing the devotion I have put into playing traditional music.

When you swim against the tide your whole career, you appreciate the appreciation.

So you live moment-to-moment and appreciate where you are now.

I certainly always try to do that.

Do you feel like you are still at the top of your game?

Pretty close. When I was younger I might have been able to do more physical things, but aside from that I am at the top of my game. I am wiser now.

We have covered most of your life and career journey, give me some final thoughts.

When I started digging deeply into mountain music, my only goal was to learn about it. Later my goal was just to make a living doing what I wanted to do, and to support my family.

Doc always said the same thing many times: "I never really wanted to be in commercial country music 'cause I was just there to support my family. That's all I really wanted to do." I agree with him. Support your family and have fun along the way.

As I got further into it preservation became more important. It became almost a calling to get young people interested and involved and to help create an audience for other musicians trying to make a living playing traditional music.

My greatest love and reward has been spending time with my mentors. To have spent so much time in the presence of people like Doc Watson, Etta Baker, Dellie Norton and Wade Mainer has meant so much to me.

Luckily, I realized pretty early on that fame was nothing worth going after. I had a wonderful taste of a little corner of fame with the *Fire on the Mountain* television show. Of course, most people didn't know who I was, but in certain situations I would be quite famous. So I got to occasionally see what fame felt like. Every year at Fan Fair in Nashville thousands of fans gather. Most of these folks watched me on the Nashville Network and to them I was quite famous. I found it very uncomfortable. It becomes difficult to know who is a friend and who wants to use you. I didn't enjoy it at all.

You hear famous people say all the time: "It's worth nothing, except for notoriety which brings in more money." I have found what I want is respect, as do most people. That is all you need. Fame is a hollow illusion.

You have to motivate yourself because nobody sees your vision of what you want, not your wife, your friends or anybody else. You have to envision it strongly, and then figure out the steps to get there, because usually you are your worst enemy. And I found out if you are self-employed, your boss is the biggest jerk you've ever seen because he is you.

I say that all the time, too. But you can give yourself employee of the month, free parking, and 'Atta-Boys' whenever you want them.

You have to critique yourself, but be careful not to hurt yourself with criticism. You just have to constantly ask yourself, "Hmm, was that really good enough?"

I call that positive-negative criticism.

Humans naturally tend to hear the bad stuff about themselves and obsess about it. But when people say, "That was great!" you just want to say, "Yeah, yeah, yeah, now tell me what was wrong." But you need to find the balance because there is always something good that you need to acknowledge and keep in the show!"

I always say that word-of-mouth is the best and the worst form of advertising.

It is true, and it is the longest lasting, the one that will not fade away quickly. But you have to have it, and you have to be aware of it.

- **Documenting a career—**

Do you have plans to use your personal career documentation for historical purposes?

Documenting my career with pictures and video has always been important and useful. In the last few years I have been using the photos I took of my mentors in concerts. The audience really appreciates this. It helps them see the kind of folks I am talking about. I certainly wasn't thinking about that when I took the photos thirty years ago. And now with the Internet it is always useful to have photos to illustrate your history. I have a lot of them posted on the "Mentors" section of my website.

Something that is very important to me is to give credit where credit is due. Many people are very stingy about giving credit; they think it takes away from their accomplishments. But the fact of the matter is it doesn't take away from you at all, it only enhances you. It lets people know about this other person in a good way, and since word-of-mouth is the most important thing in this business, that helps them and doesn't hurt you. It is an important way of paying respect.

I'm sure it is the other way around when people give you credit.

Yes, it is. I appreciate being given credit for something I did. I worked with a wonderful producer that taught me this, Margaret Moos Pick, who produced *Prairie Home Companion* and *Riverwalk Jazz*. She is great at listening to your idea. Everybody gets to speak his or her mind, and then she gives credit where credit is due. It keeps the good ideas flying and everybody is happy.

You create real synergism when you do that.

You do. And people like working for you and with you.

What final advice would you give to young musicians?

You have to start out slowly and locally, and then build up from there, especially if you are doing something odd like traditional mountain music where you are swimming against the tide.

Many people I meet in the entertainment business are quite bitter. Early on I decided to never let anyone have total control over what I do. It's better to not let your money come from one source because there is always the threat of having the rug pulled out from under you. Keep a wide stance so that nobody can really hurt you.

If somebody is threatening you, you can say, "See ya', I won't be back." It has been very important to me to never have all my eggs in one basket.

I would also advise young musicians to be easy to work with. A lot of people become prima donnas, and that is a great way to kill a career.

And of course you have to be dependable and honest. That is a given.

- **Future Goals—**

That brings us to the present. Tell me what the future may hold for you, and your immediate goals.

My goals continue to be the same as they have always been: be good and get better. I want to keep learning new tunes and add new songs to my repertoire. I love to play with other people so I am eager to keep my band, *David Holt and the Lightning Bolts* together. Josh Goforth is a phenomenal young musician and we have a duo that performs quite often. It is a total joy to make music with him. I still do a number of shows with Will McIntyre on bass.

I'm excited about a new trio we are putting together with Bryan Sutton and T. Michael Coleman called *Deep River Rising.* Bryan is one of the best acoustic guitarists in the world and he loves the traditional music from North Carolina. Michael played bass with Doc for fifteen years from 1970s and is not only a great bass player, but good harmony singer, too. It is going to be a great group.

And I want to support Doc in every way as he winds down an amazing career.

In the future I wouldn't mind having a more normal life. For the last thirty-five years I've been traveling on tour. Exotic to me is to stay home, have friends over for a meal, cook my own food and never eat in a restaurant again!

What is important to David Holt at this juncture in life?

The things most important to me are my family and friends, music and being in nature. Staying healthy is right up there, too; I walk and do yoga every day.

My motto is, "Be good, and get better."

Now that I am sixty-five, I hope I can keep this up. I love to be learning new things. There is a time in everyone's life where nature just slows you down, but I use Doc and many of my old mentors as guiding lights. They have been great inspirations to me on how to live a long productive life.

Do you consider yourself fortunate?

Overall, yes. I've had an incredible life of amazing good luck and unbelievably misfortune. I've had really horrible things happen, but I just continually put one foot in front of the other and keep on moving forward. It has been a wonderful journey.

I think it was Einstein who said, "There are only two ways to live your life. One is as though nothing is a miracle. The other is as though everything is a miracle." I am from the "everything is a miracle" school.

Section 5: **Photos**

David Holt and the Lightning Bolts 2011:
Laura Boosinger, Jeff Hersk, David Holt, Byron
Hedgepeth and Josh Goforth.

David Holt hosting "Great
Scenic Railway Journeys."

On the Riverwalk Jazz radio show
with Benny Carter and the Jim
Cullum Jazz Band, 1998.

David Holt's first appearance on the Grand Ole Opry playing the paper bag, 1980.

Deep River Rising—
T. Michael Coleman, David,
Bryan Sutton.

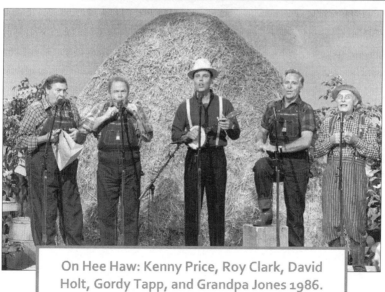

On Hee Haw: Kenny Price, Roy Clark, David Holt, Gordy Tapp, and Grandpa Jones 1986.

David and Doc Watson have been performing together since 1998.

. . . with wife, Ginny Callaway, Towersy, England.

Zeb and Sara Jane Holt, 1987.

Section 6: **Chronology**

- **Personal—**
- Date of birth: October 15, 1946, Gatesville, Texas, has resided in Western North Carolina near Asheville since 1973 with wife Ginny.

- **Education—**
- University of California at Santa Barbara, College of Creative Studies; BS and Arts degrees, *magna cum laude* – Biology and Art. Advanced degree in Education.

- **Work History—**
- Performs full-time throughout the world since 1981.
- Founded and directed the Appalachian Music Program at Warren Wilson College in Swannanoa, N.C. 1975 — 1981.
- Tours for US State Department as musical ambassador - Nepal/India/Thailand (1971); South America (1980-1985); Africa (1986); Venezuela (1997); Chile (2000)

- **Instruments—**
- Banjo, Slide Guitar, Guitar, Washboard, Spoons, Bones, Jaw Harp, Harmonica, Paper Bag, Tune Bow and more.

- **Awards—**
- Winner of Four Grammy AWARDS. Two for 'LEGACY' (artist & producer) with Doc Watson—Best Folk Recording, 2003; two for Stellaluna (artist & producer)—Best Children's Spoken Word Recording, 1997
- Eight Grammy nominations.
- Named "The Best of the New Generation" by *Esquire* magazine in its first annual Register of Men and Women Who Are Changing America, 1984.
- Presented the Brown-Hudson Folklore Award by the North Carolina Folklore Society as a person who has in special ways contributed to the appreciation, continuation, or study of North Carolina folk traditions, 2007.
- Inducted into the National Storytelling Association's "Hall of Fame" Circle of Excellence, 1987.
- Inducted into the Blue Ridge Hall of Fame for contributions to culture of the Blue Ridge region, 2011.
- Three-time winner of *FRETS* magazine readers' poll: "Best old-time banjoist".
- University of North Carolina "Razor Walker Award" (1993) "Presented to individuals in the service of youth who have demonstrated vision, tenacity, sacrifice and courage to those who walk the razor's edge."

- **Television—**
- Host of PBS-TV Folkways series, 1980–present;
- Great Scenic Railway Journeys, 2004–present, PBS series;
- For North Carolina PBS-TV: An Evening with Doc Watson, 1998; The Blue Ridge Parkway, 2000; The Outer Banks, 2002; NC Mountain Treasures, 2005; Highway 64: North Carolina's Heritage Highway, 2011;
- TNN: Fire on the Mountain (1984-1987), Celebration Express (1988-1989), American Music Shop (1989 – 1991); Regular Guest appearances on TNN's Nashville Now
- Guest appearances on Hee Haw (50-plus, 1985-1994)

- **Radio—**
- Host of Public Radio's Riverwalk: Classic Jazz from the Landing (1989-present)
- Guest appearances on Grand Ole Opry (1982-present)

- **Recordings—**
- Music (on High Windy Audio):
- Cutting Loose with David Holt & Josh Goforth; 2007 Grammy Nominee
- David Holt & the Lightning Bolts with Josh Goforth, Laura Boosinger, David Cohen and Zeb Holt 2006
- Let It Slide with Sam Bush & Doc Watson 2005
- Live And Kickin' at the National Storytelling Festival with Zeb Holt 2003 Grammy nominee
- Legacy with Doc Watson 3 CD set 2003 Grammy Award winner
- I Got A Bullfrog: Folksongs For The Fun Of It 1994 American Library Association's "Notable Recordings"
- Grandfather's Greatest Hits, 1992 Grammy nominee for Best Traditional Folk Recording, PARENT magazine, First prize.
- Reel & Rock with Doc and Merle Watson, 1985 INDIE award 'Best Folk Recording', 25th anniversary re-issue 2010
- It Just Suits Me 1981 (June Appal Records)
- Instructional Videos – Folk Rhythms, Old-time Banjo - Levels I, II, III (Homespun)

- **Story Recordings—**
- Audio (on High Windy Audio):
- Hairyman Meets Tailybone 2006
- Spiders In the Hairdo with Bill Mooney 2001 Grammy nominee
- Stellaluna 1997 Grammy Award winner, American Booksellers Assn."Pick of the List", A.L.A. Notable Recording
- Why The Dog Chases The Cat: Great Animal Stories 1995 Grammy nominee, A.L.A. Notable Recording, NAIRD Award winner
- Mostly Ghostly Stories 1995 INDIE Award winner
- Tailybone 1985 A.L.A. Notable Recording, INDIE Award winner
- Hairyman 1981 A.L.A. Notable Recording
- The Hogaphone and Other Stories (video) 1991

- **Books—**
- The Exploding Toilet: Modern Urban Legends with Bill Mooney (August House Publishers, (2004)
- Spiders In the Hairdo: Modern Urban Legends with Bill Mooney (August House Publishers)
- More Ready-To-Tell Tales: Stories from Around the World with Bill Mooney (August House Publishers) (2000)
- Ready-To-Tell Tales: Collection of Sure-fire Stories with Bill Mooney (August House Publishers) (1994)
- The Storytellers Guide: Complete "How-to" for Storytellers with Bill Mooney (August House Publishers) (1997)

Visit www.davidholt.com for more information, or contact David at office@davidholt.com.

Ray F. West, Jr.
Captain USNR –Ret

Navy Captain Ray West hugs a Moldovan youngster.

"After spending 22 of my 34-year career in the U.S. Navy squaring off against the Soviets, I was anxious to take this opportunity to help the innocent children of Europe's poorest county, Moldova. It was been a blessing beyond measure."
— Captain West in UNC Asheville AlumniView, Winter 2003

Sections about Ray West Jr:

1) From Those Who Served with Captain West

2) Highlights from His Life and Career

3) **Ray's Life Journey, in His Own Words**

4) Photos

5) Oaths of Office by Father and Son

6) Chronology

Section 1: **From Those Who Served with Captain West**

- **From the North Carolina Secretary of State—**

My Thoughts on Ray West: Margaret Mead once cautioned skeptics to "never doubt that a small group of thoughtful, committed citizens can change the world. Indeed, it is the only thing that ever has." To validate Margaret Mead's sage wisdom, one only needs to know Ray West and to feel the energy, passion and commitment he brings to his work in helping others. Ray West lives a life where making a difference every day is his standard operating procedure.

I first met Ray in the late 1990s, when I was asked as North Carolina's Secretary of State to become active in what was then North Carolina's newly created official relationship with the Republic of Moldova. The new relationship was an outgrowth of a federal government program known as the Partnership for Peace, wherein the Eastern European states of the former Soviet Union were given special priority for assistance by the United States Department of State and Department of Defense. It was widely believed that building formal friendships and assistance efforts would help these former Soviet states come to see and understand democracy through person-to-person interactions and to also promote peace and stability.

Ray began his interest in Moldova, Europe's poorest country, through his U.S. Navy activities. He positively answered the call to build personal relationships like few others. One thing I quickly learned: Ray is truly an "idea" man. When he sees a worthy project, he formulates an idea, develops a plan, and diligently works to implement that plan. One of the first things Ray achieved was to focus the Western North Carolina Episcopal Conference (Kanuga) on Moldova, its people, and their needs.

Since retirement, Ray founded the Moldova World Children's Fund and continues his interest in Moldova through that organization. He has an absolutely amazing talent for bringing people, resources, and lots of energy together to benefit others. One of the signature aspects of his projects is that they do not solve problems just for a moment, but rather they contribute to long-term solutions for the people they are helping.

I am not sure that anyone can accurately count the exact number of projects Ray West has either accomplished directly or used his great motivational skills to set into motion. For example, Ray worked with United States Embassy personnel, leaders of other countries, and other Moldovan leadership to establish a tuberculosis hospital in northern Moldova.

Other examples of such activities by Ray include providing leadership in constructing greenhouse operations affiliated with an orphanage in Moldova so that the children can have purposeful projects and also learn skills that will serve them for a lifetime. Ray has also worked to provide hot water at other orphanages and foster care homes. He almost single-handedly built a dormitory-style bathroom for a foster care home for the Fortuna family, a well-known Moldovan couple with a long history of providing shelter, safety, nourishment, and loving guidance for needy children. He has also been instrumental in obtaining first rate medical care and treatments for children with serious injuries or illnesses.

In my mind, Ray is a giant for his legacy of giving to others. Ray is leading by example to help deserving people in a very poor land become self-reliant and providing them with a few of the basic good things in life that we in America sometimes take for granted. We need more like him!
    — Elaine F. Marshall, NC Secretary of State

- **From a former United States Ambassador to Moldova—**

During my assignment as the U.S. Ambassador to Moldova, I was often asked: what is the best thing about the United States of America? I consistently replied that it is the spirit of our people to give and share with anyone who is in need anywhere around the globe. Captain Ray West and the Moldova World Children's Fund that he leads have done more to represent what is the best part of America than any other individual or organization.

If a burn victim needed urgent help, Ray West was there to take on the challenge to literally transform the life of that young person by arranging treatment by the best medical facilities in the State of North Carolina. If a project needed funds to rebuild a crumbling living facility for a group of children exposed to tuberculosis and no hope for the future, Ray was ready to take on a second mortgage on his home to make sure these children did not suffer through another winter with holes in the roofs of their rooms.

During the last few years, I cannot recall any major charitable project in Moldova that Ray has not been a part of. He has inspired so many Americans, and Moldovans, to get involved and make caring for the orphans and the underprivileged a part of their everyday lives. I believe that the most important part of our foreign policy is to show the world who we are; and we certainly cannot ask for a better example than Ray to show what makes America the greatest nation in the history of mankind. Ray West is a great American, and it has been my privilege to have known him over the last few years.
    — Ambassador Asif J. Chaudhry

- **From a Moldova World Children's Fund Board Member who visited Moldova—**

Ray West has been outstanding in every endeavor he has attempted. For many years he was employed as second in command at Kanuga Conference Center in Hendersonville, NC. Since then, during and since his service in the Naval Reserve he has befriended and enhanced the lives of children of former Soviet Union country Moldova, now in poverty and without adequate resources to keep its children healthy or provide for their future and success as contributing citizens.

Ray began Moldova World Children's Fund in 2005 after his service in the Navy, where he was sent to Moldova to find ways to help orphaned children. He is well known in Moldova and when they speak of him, citizens smile. He has provided help to orphanages, schools and individuals, in at least one case saving a child from starvation. I am proud to serve on the MWCF board and have been to Moldova to see the results of his leadership and ability to attract help in meeting needs there, and bring together different groups of church, military and government resources to work together on projects.

The most recent task he has undertaken is to 'honcho' the blending of several counties and religious groups, plus secular help, in turning a boarding school for children with tuberculosis, or whose parents are afflicted and unable to care for them, from a heatless, hot water-less, dirty place with leaking roofs, rotting window sills, inadequate plumbing and bathroom facilities - a horrible and unhealthy place - into a viable, attractive and healing place with warm water and heat, as well as caring doctors who were already there trying to care for the children without funds to do it. This man's energy matches his passion for helping these children, and it is a pleasure to see him crawl up on a roof to examine it and check over details before he pays for work done, and to see how the children respond to 'Mr. Ray'.
    — Nancy Rice Duvall, Vice Chairman, MWCF Board of Directors (Mrs. Charles Farmer Duvall, Columbia, SC}

- **From the Senior International Advisor, J5, Joint Improvised Explosive Device Defeat Organization, Washington, DC—**

Captain Ray West, Naval Officer and patriot, put the Cold War behind us and started the viable, effective MWCF. He represents America and North Carolina as an ambassador for our people. And the Ambassadors and statesmen he works with know him as an equal. Captain West is committed, sincere, and has a record of making changes to lives. He is an inspirational leader, a humble person who thinks of others first, and maintains disarming humor which makes everybody laugh. I guess we call people like him a Great American. By my association with him he has made me a better person.
  — **Chuck Brady, Lt. Col. USMC, Ret.**

- **From a Longtime Colleague and Friend—**

Ray West and I have been colleagues since April 1983 when I became president of Kanuga Conferences. His job description was business and personnel manager. Not long after arriving, I asked the Board of Directors to approve the title Vice President for Administration for him. We worked well as a team. He managed the budget, recommended persons for employment, handled difficult personnel matters, was responsible for the majority of our bookings, and was a valued confidant. During our 23 years together, Kanuga generated an operating surplus each year. Those surpluses, added to unrestricted annual gift income, enabled us to practically rebuild a campus neglected for many years. He proved to be a superb businessman. Additionally, he was a loyal, trusted, and respected colleague who was not hesitant to offer a differing opinion when he thought one necessary. He saved me occasionally from mistakes.

Ray began to come into his own with his U.S. Navy Reserve assignment to the Republic of Moldova. Sent to the town of Drochia to determine the advisability of US Department of Defense humanitarian assistance for a reported orphanage, he found that it was instead a private home. A retired Soviet officer, Peter Fortuna and his wife Anna, childless, had adopted eight older children. Shortly after bringing the children home, the Soviet Union collapsed, Peter lost his pension, and the family huddled in an unfinished house, enduring a bitter Moldova winter. Since it was not an official orphanage, the U.S. government could not provide assistance. Ray and his mother planned to give a significant amount to finish the home. The Kanuga Board of Directors, hearing the story, provided $20,000 to supplement the West gift. We still support the Fortuna family, now with their third generation of children, 23 in all.

That was 1998. Seven years later, after trying to balance Kanuga work with his continuing and growing interests in Moldova, Ray resigned his position at Kanuga to found the Moldova World Children's Fund (MWCF) , a 501 (c) (3) corporation committed to humanitarian work for Moldova's children. Our work is of two kinds: 1) assistance for village and boarding schools which includes new heating systems, windows, doors, and roofs, rebuilt sewage systems, fresh water, and 2) medical attention for individuals, and college and technical school education for promising youngsters. We have done work from Tirnova in the northwest of Moldova to Manta in the far south and in towns and villages along the way.

He has been honored by the government of the Republic of Moldova, his college the UNC-Asheville, and by the U.S. Department of Defense, and has worked with the last six US Ambassadors to Moldova. I count myself fortunate that he has asked me to work with him for Moldova's children.

I knew Ray initially as a committed and hard-working business man. Ray is a compassionate, caring person. I respect him for the first quality and I admire him for the second.
  — **Albert S. Gooch, Jr., Ph.D., former President of Kanuga Conferences, Inc., Hendersonville, N.C.**

Section 2: **Highlights from His Life and Career**

- The son of Navy Senior Chief and Nabisco manager Ray F. West, (Sr.) and Mission Hospital social services director Evelyn Kennard West, Captain West was born December 22, 1950 in Asheville, North Carolina. He grew up with two older sisters, Sarah Marjorie Powell, current resident of Greensboro, NC and Lillian Reeves Alverson, now living in Reidsville, NC. After graduation from Lee H. Edwards High School in 1968, he enlisted as a Seaman Recruit in a Naval Reserve program which allowed him to enroll at Asheville-Biltmore College.

- The B.A. in Social Science, with a concentration in Economics, from the University of North Carolina-Asheville that he earned in 1972 included studies in philosophy at Oxford University, England. He worked his way through UNCA living and working at Morris Funeral Home, played varsity soccer, was Secretary of his Senior Class, and was President of the Huns athletic fraternity.

- West was commissioned Ensign after completion of Naval Officer Candidate School, Newport, Rhode Island. His active duty began during the Vietnam War serving Commander, Allied Naval Forces Korea; including duties as communications security advisor to the Republic of Korea Navy and Marine Corps, 1972-1974.

- In 1973, Ensign West met dental assistant Kyungmi "Mia" Chang in Chinhae, Korea, and they married 20 months later in Norfolk, Virginia. The Wests have two sons, Bryan, a Naval Flight Officer, and Andrew, a teacher and rock climbing instructor...both UNC-Chapel Hill graduates.

- Immediately following his tour in Korea, he served two years aboard submarine rescue ship USS Kittiwake (ASR-13) attached to Submarine Squadron Six and home ported in Norfolk, VA. He remained in the Naval Reserve following active duty and was attached to destroyers, billeted aboard nine. He was the Commanding Officer of four successful units, with one receiving the honor of "Best Afloat" on guided missile destroyer USS William V. Pratt (DDG-44).

- Individual accomplishments included earning the designation of Surface Warfare Officer and qualifying as a small arms weapons expert. While in Korea he began studying the martial art Tae Kwon Do, later earning a first degree black belt.

- After reaching a rank essentially too high for service aboard surface combatants, he retooled and moved on to special assignments at naval headquarters outside the United States and American embassies in Greece and the former Soviet Republic of Moldova. He spent the final five years of his reserve career running U.S. European Command (EUCOM) humanitarian assistance projects; renovating hospitals, schools, and orphanages.

- West transitioned from fulltime military life in 1975 managing budget motels and restaurants. In early 1977, he joined the staff of Kanuga Episcopal Camp and Conference Center in Hendersonville, NC. He served as president of the Western North Carolina Association of Conference Center Administrators and president of the Hendersonville Lions Club. An after work passion included years as a volunteer coach for youth sports. After a thirty-year civilian career in hospitality, he retired as Kanuga's Vice President for Administration in 2005 and created the Moldova World Children's Fund, Inc. (MWCF).

- In 2006, MWCF incorporated in North Carolina as an IRS Section 501(c)(3) non-profit charity. MWCF provides medical, educational, vocational, and life support for individuals in addition to its hallmark work of renovating hospitals, orphanages, traditional schools, and boarding schools for abandoned children throughout Moldova.

- Captain West was the recipient of University of North Carolina – Asheville's highest alumni honor for 2006, the Roy A. Taylor Distinguished Alumnus Award. The accolade cited his significant humanitarian work in the struggling Republic of Moldova, and in the words of

University Chancellor Dr. Anne Ponder: *"Ray West exemplifies Liberal Arts education in action as a true citizen of the world."*

- **Presidential Certificate of Appreciation—**

A presidential Certificate of Appreciation for Outstanding Meritorious Service from October 1994 to December 2002 was awarded on December 6, 2002 to Captain Ray Ferris West, Jr., USN-Ret.

I extend to you my personal thanks and the sincere appreciation of a grateful nation for your contribution of honorable service to our country. You have helped maintain the security of the nation during a critical time in its history with a devotion to duty and a spirit of sacrifice in keeping with the proud traditions of military service. Your commitment and dedication have been an inspiration for those who will follow in your footsteps, and for all Americans who join me today in saluting you for a job 'extremely well done'. Best wishes to you for your continued future happiness and success.
  - **Bill Clinton, Commander-in-Chief**

The following citation accompanied the medal:

For outstanding meritorious service as Commanding Officer, Naval Reserve Voluntary Training Unit 0707, Greenville, South Carolina, from October 1994 to December 2002. Demonstrating exceptional dedication, organizational ability and leadership skills, Captain West personally provided extraordinary humanitarian assistance to the former Soviet Republic of Moldova.

His efforts were instrumental in providing relief of suffering, and helped to enhance regional stability through construction of an orphanage; renovating five schools, including a boarding school for 460 abandoned children; and the construction of a children's tuberculosis hospital.

Through his keen insight and astute management skills, he secured funding for the humanitarian assistance efforts from private sources when the scope of government funds was extremely limited.

Personally recognized by the United States Ambassador to Moldova, his selection as 'Hero of Moldova' was featured on Moldovan Public Television and his accomplishments were a regular feature in the news media of that country.

The exceptional professional ability, steadfast initiative, and selfless dedication to duty exhibited by Captain West reflected great credit upon him and upheld the highest traditions of the United States Naval Service.
  - **K.C. Belisle, Rear Admiral, US Naval Reserve; Commander, Readiness Command Southeast**

- **Information about Moldova and Moldova World Children's Fund*—**

- The Republic of Moldova is a landlocked country in Eastern Europe situated between Romania to its West and Ukraine to the North, East and South. It has one small deep-water port to the Black Sea at the junction of the Danube and Prut Rivers. Its capital is Chisinau. The republic declared itself an independent state in 1991, immediately following the dissolution of the Soviet Union. Moldova operates as a parliamentary republic, with a president as the head of state and a prime minister as head of the government. It is a member state of the United Nations and the Council of Europe, and hopes to join the European Union in the future.

- Its landmass occupies just over 13,000-square-miles, slightly smaller than New Jersey. It has a population of 4.3 million, 123rd among nations; is 78 percent Romanian and 8.4 percent Ukrainian; 98 percent Eastern Orthodox Christian and 1.5 percent Jewish. Largely rural, its rich soil produces grapes for superior wine to the South, with varied vegetable farming to the

North. There are no gas, oil or coal deposits so imports contribute significantly to the national debt. Per-capita GDP is just $2,500 per year, 176th among nations, with 30 percent of people below the poverty line. Education expenditure is 9.6% of the national GDP, 7th among nations. The literacy rate is 99.1 percent, and an astonishing number of Moldovans are bi-lingual.

- Little was known outside of Eastern Europe about Moldova, the poorest country in Europe, when Captain West began work there in 1998. Now the tiny Eastern European nation is being helped by a wide diversity of organizations and individuals.

- Since incorporation in 2006, Moldova World Children's Fund has participated in millions of dollars in contributions that help with the daily care, medical and dental treatment, housing, hygiene, education, and vocational start up for many thousands of needy children.

- MWCF demonstrates its organizational ability to build and lead coalitions, and to manage projects. Cooperation with other entities has been crucial to its success. The result is that each donation to MWCF serves the children far more than the dollar value of the gift, a good investment by all standards.

- The wide range of partners includes: the past seven U.S. Ambassadors to Moldova, Wide Horizons for Children: A Better Life-Moldova; U.S. Department of Defense Humanitarian Assistance, U.S. Department of State, Wake Forest University Children's Hospital and Pitt County Memorial Hospital and associated physicians, International Women's Club of Moldova, Lions International, Little Samaritan Mission, North Carolina National Guard, Kanuga Conferences, Sun Communications of Moldova, Rotary Clubs, Latter Day Saints Charities in Moldova, North Carolina-Moldova Bilateral Partnership, and the Republic of Moldova Ministries of Social Welfare, Education, Health and Foreign Affairs.

- Impressed by the widespread concern for children, Sun Communications contributed to the Leova School for Abandoned Children, helped construct a playground in a low-income Chisinau neighborhood, and partnered in donating a computer lab at the Tirnova Children's TB Rehab Center and School. CEO John Maxemchuk said:

> *"My first contact came when we supplied internet service to orphanages*
> *and schools for 400 computers donated by North Carolina State*
> *University and shipped by MWCF. Moldova World Children's Fund*
> *operates with efficiency and economy, and Sun Communications is proud*
> *to be a partner."*

(*All information as of 2011.)

- ### A Few of the Children Helped by MWCF—

Natalia Bolea: An infant burn victim from Yaloveni who had the fused parts of her fingers separated by surgery in North Carolina. After completing surgery and rigorous therapy, she became a tailoring and clothes design student at a vocational college using a special donated sewing machine.

Elena Gulina: After losing both parents to cancer, penniless and alone, this young woman was found semi-conscious and near death on an apartment floor. She was then cared for by MWCF through the rest of her high school years, and eventually won a highly competitive academic scholarship to Moscow State University. After finishing in the top of her class in International Business Relations and Languages, the piano prodigy Elena was invited to stay on for graduate work, financially assisted by MWCF.

Gheorghe and Marica Ungureanu: Gheorghe is in his final year as a wine industry major at a Technical University of Moldova in the capital city of Chisinau, and Marica finished in the top of her class at the State University of Moldova, with tuition provided both by MWCF. They had enjoyed warm primary and secondary school years in Lapsuna, thanks to heating systems provided by MWCF and its partners in 2001.

Julius Vasilchenco: Now in his early twenties, at age five began stuttering at a progressive rate. Successfully tested for a 'Speech-Easy' device developed along the pioneer concept of hearing one's own voice as portrayed in the Oscar-winning movie The King's Speech, MWCF and friends have financed a trip to the U.S. for custom-fitting of his device.

Veronica: This pretty nine-year old was born with a badly crossed eye, but thanks to a visiting MWCF donor, underwent successful surgery and received corrective glasses. MWCF provided for other expenses, the physician performed the surgery on her and another girl at no charge.

Mother and Sons: In Manta in indescribably wretched conditions lived a deaf mute mother with two mildly retarded sons. MWCF friends from the Carolinas to California rebuilt their home and gave renewed purpose to three human beings. MWCF support continues.

Adriana Verejan: Two-year old girl with Crouzon's Syndrome, an impounded brain condition, flown to Winston-Salem, N.C. for three life-and-sight-saving skull and brain surgeries.

- ## Chronology of selected MWCF action—

- 1998: Captain Ray West assumes management of U.S. European Command (EUCOM) Humanitarian Assistance projects in Moldova; contributions from American friends help build the Fortuna Family Home for orphans.

- 1999: Moldovan children selected for American summer camps, vocational and university scholarships begin; students study in Moldova, Russia and the U.S. with privately funded educational aid.

- 2000: Ceadyr-Lunga Hospital reopens after two-year EUCOM funded reconstruction managed by Moldova World Children's Fund founder, Captain West.

- 2001: Central heating systems installed and other improvements made in Lapusna, Ungheni, Inesti public schools with U.S. Department of Defense and private gift funding.

- 2002: Roof at Ivanca's public school collapses under heavy snow, replaced quickly by private gifts. Captain West retires from the Naval Reserve.

- 2003: Municipal sewer lines regularly flooding secondary school in Straseni replaced and re-routed with private donations.

- 2004: Over 300 mentally-challenged children living at the Crihana Veche Boarding School move into a new dormitory constructed from an abandoned Soviet building, a major DOD project supplemented by private donations; a home built and support provided for a deaf mute mother and two sons.

- 2005: Ray West resigns his civilian career to found MWCF as a 501(c)(3) charity governed by a Board of Directors, all of whom are required to travel to Moldova at their own expense to tour hospitals, schools, and orphanages. Roofs replaced and construction begun for a hospital-living care facility for severely handicapped children in Orehi.

- 2006: First of 400 computers shipped by MWCF from North Carolina State University installed in 48 schools and orphanages by Moldova Sun TV; Peace Corps volunteers and MWCF collaborate to replace the heating system in Zirnesti secondary school. Three intricate life-saving surgeries reconstruct a child's skull at a Wake Forest University hospital.

- 2007: Central heating system, insulated windows and doors installed in 400-student boarding school for abandoned children in Leova with private funding from MWCF and partner Wide Horizons for Children: A Better Life-Moldova. Nap room beds and furniture provided for a village kindergarten.

- 2008: Parents travel to Germany with their infant daughter to reconstruct her upper lip following an acute infection. Playground for abandoned children constructed in Leova; hot water heaters added to Ialoveni boarding school for handicapped children. Severe burn victim Natalia begins six months of reconstructive surgery in Greenville, NC.

- 2009: Greenhouse and horticultural vocational building built at Leova Boarding School for Abandoned Children. Sea-Land containers ship medical books and journals in bulk from North Carolina universities to Moldova medical schools and libraries. Elementary school aged Veronica and Violeta undergo successful corrective eye surgeries.

- 2010: Windows and doors replaced, exterior hot water heating pipes insulated at Cazanesti boarding school for abandoned children. Hot water provided to Leova school dormitories. Playground equipment installed for low-income Chisinau neighborhood. Student university, technical, and vocational studies provided financial aid. MWCF and International Women's Club Moldova build six dormitory hot water shower rooms for the 185 children residing at the Tirnova Children's Tuberculosis Center in the far north of Moldova.

- 2011: MWCF facilitates construction of student and faculty restrooms at the Tirnova School utilizing a new fresh water system constructed by Latter-Day Saints Charities and sewer lines reworked by U.S. Department of State. MWCF prepares architectural design and public bid details for three major building roof repairs and replacement of hundreds of exterior windows and doors to hold heat from a new hot water central heating system provided by Swedish International Development Cooperation Agency (SIDA). Fortuna Family Home has its bathroom totally renovated, laundry machine installed, and new sewer system built.

- 2012: MWCF coordination of the Tirnova renovation project concludes with U.S. DOD, Rotary, LDS Charities and MWCF provided funds. Final projects included construction of a new laundry building, installation of laundry machines, dormitory exteriors insulated and finished, and a sewage treatment plant built. A Moldovan student inflicted with a severe stuttering problem has state-of-the-art Speech Easy device custom fitted by a manufacturer in North Carolina.

Note: Projects assisting orphans in Moldova that offer medical treatment and provide educational support continue unabated.

- **Media Coverage—**

Media coverage of Ray West and MWCF in North Carolina and Moldova have included numerous features on both radio and television outlets, and in newspapers, magazines, and other publications. The long list of covered stories includes a Christmas Day 2008 Greenville Daily Reflector article about burn-victim Natalia Bolea, a feature on Easter Sunday 2009 in the Hendersonville Times-News about her surgeries and therapy, and one in UNC Asheville's AlumniView Winter 2003 edition that featured Captain West with numerous Moldovan children. 'Rebuilding Moldova' quoted Captain West: *"After spending 22 of my 34-year career in the Navy squaring off against the Soviets, I was anxious to take this opportunity to help the innocent children of Europe's poorest county. It has been a blessing beyond measure."*

Note: To join in the effort to help the children of Moldova, visit the website: www.moldovawcf.org. Introductory brochures and documentary DVDs are available. To contact Moldova World Children's Fund or Captain Ray West by e-mail: ray.west@moldovawcf.org and moldovaworld@yahoo.com; by U.S. Postal Service: P.O. Box 548, Hendersonville, NC 28793-0548; by telephone: 828-551-8209 (office) when he is in the USA or 828-697-0583 (home).

Section 3: Ray's Life Journey, in His Own Words

The first time I met Captain Ray West was on a warm Western North Carolina morning over coffee in a popular restaurant in the charming little town of Flat Rock. Still the ideal picture of a military man: ramrod straight with buzz-cut hair and a direct manner, he almost immediately eased into witty humor peppered with wry comments. I've enjoyed our many conversations ever since.

We had previously spoken over the telephone and I had asked him to bring to our meeting any personal background information that he felt might be helpful in my drafting a story about his life. He came prepared: I left carrying a thick bundle of printed material that included a chronology of his stellar military career, virtually all of it telling the story of his passion, the Moldova World Children's Fund he founded and presides over.

I knew right away that Ray West has a life journey worth telling, and that I would enjoy retelling it.

Ray, start telling your story any way you would like.

Always found it interesting to hear stories about my father. Ray West, Sr. had polio as a child, and doctors told him he would never walk without crutches. But he was a very strong minded man, a Forrest Gump of his time. He proved the doctors wrong, and eventually got an appointment to the United States Naval Academy in order to play linebacker on the football team.

It played into my father's childhood dream to design and build ships. Just days after hearing from the Academy, he also got accepted at MIT, which at the time was the best school in this country for studying ship design. The Naval Academy may have been rated number two, but MIT was number one, at least in his mind. My grandfather, told him: "Son, if you want to go to MIT, then we will figure out a way to get you there."

So he turned down the appointment to the Naval Academy and its offer of a free education; but before his first class at MIT, the financial crisis of the Great Depression hit.

What happened then?

Actually what I think happened was my grandfather became very ill, and my grandmother had to stay home and take care of him; so neither parent could work. As the oldest child, Dad had to go out and support the family. He ended up working two eight-hour jobs a day, six-days a week. He never made it to MIT and the Naval Academy opportunity was long lost.

Dad ended up with two years of night courses at the University of Florida. He enlisted in the Navy during World War II. He was determined to do well, was smart, a good mathematician, an engineer and an architect in his own right.

After graduation from boot camp he went to electronics school, while his classmates went off to fight the Japanese. He did so well in electronics school he was asked to remain and be the instructor of the class. He put in for repeated transfers so he could go fight, join his comrades in the war, until he finally got a request approved. Story goes Dad was literally walking across the quarterdeck of a warship, docked in California and headed for the far Pacific, when the Captain's voice came on the loudspeaker announcing that Japan had surrendered. He had been so determined to get over and join the fight, but now it was all over. He felt guilty for never being in the middle of battle. In his mind the war had been won without him.

That entire frustrating process deeply affected him. I think my father had more disdain for the Japanese than those who fought them in hand-to-hand combat, mainly because he kept being refused an opportunity to fully defend his country. He continued to be denied because he did so well every step of the way, always placed in a more-needed position.

After the war ended, because he was married with a child, he was quickly released from active duty. But he stayed in the Reserve and became a Senior Chief Petty Officer. Dad's intense lifelong involvement with the Navy was a major influence on me.

Your father was Ray, and you were Ray Jr. Did you end up with any nicknames?

I was the youngest of my parents' three children and shared a cramped bedroom with my two older sisters, Margie and Lillian. Had our bathroom been any smaller, it would have required the tub to be moved to the side yard. The house was small. When I was old enough to recognize my name called and to come running, something had to be done about there being two Rays in our little home. Otherwise, the secrecy called for at Christmas gift wrapping times would continue to present awkward moments.

It was decided that my father would remain Ray, and I would become Jay. It made sense, utilizing the "J" in "Jr." and rhyming with Ray. It was close enough, but sufficiently different. Some folks expanded Jay to Jaybird. I've been called everything in the book since.

- **Involvement in business and non-profit worlds—**

Captain, I understand you also have business experience.

Long before I entertained the notion of one day joining the Navy myself, I tried my hand in business as a four or five year old entrepreneur. My initial entrée into the for-profit arena was selling earthworms to fishermen who lived in the neighborhood. My father liked my idea and helped me build a large wooden container in the backyard to house the worms which I would collect after it rained. I fed the slimy critters coffee grinds and corn meal, and they grew fat and sassy. My thinking was that the coffee would keep the worms alert and wiggly, while the corn meal would make them big and juicy.

Having developed a number of regular clients, I was soon claiming to have available of sale the best fish bait in town. I ran into an inflated inventory problem upon discovering that I liked catching night crawlers more than I did soliciting new customers. Soon the crowded box of well-fed worms began reproducing at a staggering rate. Things began to get somewhat messy, and smelly; to the point that my two sisters successfully conspired to redirect my interests into the academic wonders of kindergarten and first grade.

When did you enter the non-profit community?

My failure to stay in business was disheartening; but it was nothing compared to the disaster that lay ahead of me in the non-profit sector.

The boys in the neighborhood played ball every day. While still in elementary school and with baseball season approaching early one spring, us guys decided we needed to build a backstop to prevent missed balls from rolling far down the steep hill of the vacant lot we played in on Vandalia Avenue. Construction would require sturdy posts and a bunch of chicken wire. A fine ballpark was envisioned. Some new gear would be good too, as we were making do with ancient ball gloves, tapped-up broken wooden bats, worn out waterlogged baseballs, and no catcher's equipment. There was the problem of not having any money.

So I hatched a plan to establish my first charitable institution, the Vandalia Street Boys Club. Such an organization was needed to obtain candy for door-to-door sales from Mrs. Leland's Candy Company, who sold wholesale only to schools, churches, services clubs, and the like. I elected myself President, Secretary, and Treasurer of our newly formed club, and all the other guys agreed to help sell the candy to fit out our team. Left over profits would be spent on footballs and basketballs which were sorely needed during other times of the year.

The application to Mrs. Leland, with me as authorizing club President, was approved. I placed our order for both boxes and canisters of Easter chocolates and everyday peanut butter crunchies. As club Treasurer, I screwed up the order form unit-of-measure, inadvertently checking the "gross" option, as in 144 or twelve dozen, instead of the single "dozen" choice for the number of cases requested of each type of candy.

Late one afternoon a week or so later, with both of my parents at work, an enormous delivery truck rolled up out front. As club Secretary, I signed the acceptance invoice, and the driver unloaded with his hand truck several hundred cases of candy into every room of the house, onto the side porch, spilling over into the yard. Surprised was a mild way of putting it, my father was furious.

My buddies sold candy for a day or two, got discouraged, and then all of them quit; rightfully leaving me with total responsibility for the fiasco. My mother, God bless her, helped me sell candy for the next three years. By the time we moved the last of the Easter chocolates, wouldn't you know it, a multitude of little brown worms had taken up residency in the remaining cases of peanut butter crunchies. In the eloquent words of Baseball's Hall of Fame catcher Yogi Berra, it was *déjà vu* all over again.

- **Overcoming a handicap—**

Early in elementary school, it was discovered that I had a reading handicap. Some years ago a candidate for political office was informed by his opponent that he was no John Kennedy. Well neither am I. It was said that President Kennedy could read an entire page of a book with a single glance. At best, I read one word at a time; making me one of the slowest readers in the educated world. Special speed reading courses were of no help. My high school counselor told me to forget about going to college; that I would be unable to pass any of my courses, except for maybe math.

A colossal habit of procrastination has also plagued me since day one. A mantra of U.S. Army Four Star General George S. Patton during WWII was "A good plan today is better than a perfect plan tomorrow". Well, I am no George Patton either. The combination of procrastinating and reading very slow has forever held me back.

For my entire life, I have created ways to compensate for these shortcomings. By the time I took Latin One in high school, for the second time, I was already inventing ways to cope. Only a year removed from struggling with my first attempt at Latin in Junior High, having a different teacher and moving up to the next school both helped, as I devised my own approach to dealing with this particular academic challenge.

Sandlot ball took up much of my time after getting home from school and there was little time for study. For first year Latin homework we had to translate a page or two of *Caesar's Conquests* almost every night. I would carefully translate the first two sentences of the nighty assignment, but that would be it.

Years before, I had fallen in love with *Classics Illustrated*. Our family did not have a television, much less a color one. The meticulously researched and beautifully illustrated comic book sized publications were perfect for me. I could eagerly digest the pictures with only the greatly condensed text to read. I literally memorized the stories of *Ulysses*, *The Iliad*, and *Caesar's Conquests*.

In class, our teacher would begin by calling for volunteers to go first in translating the previous night's homework. To the delight of my teacher and, even more so, my equally unprepared classmates, I would quickly throw my hand up.

An honored tradition soon developed. Allowed to start things off and under the admiring eye of my teacher, I would flawlessly translate the first line. Halfway through the second sentence, I would stop cold in obvious exasperation and say: "It is so difficult to accurately translate ancient Latin into a modern Germanic based language like English. Let me tell you what Caesar is really saying here." Given a green light, I would proceed to tell the story comprised in the remainder of the assigned pages; throwing in scenery details and related commentary not covered in the textbook.

I later learned that my Latin teacher believed in reincarnation, and she was convinced that I was Julius Caesar reincarnated. How could there be any other explanation for my intimate knowledge of Caesar's exploits in Gaul some two-thousand years ago? She brought in an internationally renowned archeologist to examine a *papier-mâché* and plaster of Paris layout that I had constructed reminiscent of Caesar's 54 B.C. successful invasion of Britain. As many a wise consultant does, he confirmed the belief of the person paying his bill, agreeing with my teacher that the layout's builder, in order to get everything displayed so accurately, really had to have been there.

This labor of love with varied landscape, more than a hundred individually painted soldiers, ships, and weapons went on display in Asheville's City Hall; remaining four months, nearly ten times longer than the normal allotted time for student projects.

I was never delusional about the Julius Caesar thing. I suspected that I could not possibly have been reincarnated from the time of Imperial Rome since I had been required to repeat Latin One. Surely Caesar would have been able to better handle first grade Latin. I was lucky the Jr. and Sr. high Latin teachers were not talking to each other at the time.

In my senior year at Lee H. Edwards High School, the class of 1968 graduated 528 students. When time came for the school's Spring Musical, of all people, I was appointed the principal role and leading vocalist in *The Lamentable Tragedy of Julius Caesar*; a comical distortion of a Shakespearean play reformatted with the tunes of familiar modern day songs. The musical was a big hit, and this time around I made an A in Latin.

- **Considering military options—**

When did you first think about a military career?

At age sixteen, I was a high school senior, and proud that I had just gotten my driver's license. My father told me: "Son, you're a man now, from here on out, all decisions are your own." The literal meaning of this pronouncement was that Dad was declaring my financial independence, and nothing more. In any event, I thought "Wow," I'm all grown up". So when I turned seventeen, I brought home papers for my parents' signature allowing me to join the Marine Corps. It was 1967 and the Vietnam War was in high gear. This was for me my first real big independent decision, an opening door to manhood, and my father would have none of it.

Being in the Navy, he had great respect for the Marine Corps, but thought the Marines were being terribly misused and overused in Vietnam. At the time the readiness of our draft-fed Army was such that the more highly trained and highly motivated Marines were much better prepared to fight the Viet Kong and North Vietnamese regulars. So, when the Marines would arrive in combat areas and figuratively secure a beachhead, contrary to historical protocol, they weren't allowed to leave the jungle. My father was really upset. He thought that the Marines were being slaughtered. That was supposed to be the privileged role of the Army.

Did you understand his philosophy at the time?

Enough so I imagine. I remember his emphatic words even today. Here it is 2012 and I can recall him saying to me in 1967, forty-five years ago: "Anything but the Marine Corps!" The next day I brought home papers for him to sign for me to join the Army Infantry; and oh boy, did I ever get it, again. I'd already gotten my butt kicked once when I had confidently suggested the Marines. My father was a big man, and he really lit into me. I remember that after a few hours of deliberate thought in my room, licking my wounds, I decided that the Navy was for me.

And what was his problem with the Army back then?

Hurried training, limited equipment, and overall lack of 'want-to'. Far removed from today's well trained, adequately equipped, fit and ready all-volunteer Army.

So you finally made him happy.

Yes. After hammering me hard on my first two choices, my father said, "Good decision son, I've always admired your wisdom beyond your years." He applauded me and said he would sign the papers allowing me to join the Navy.

Your father was pleased you joined the Navy, but why did you want to join the military in the first place?

Somehow I survived most of my grade school years without the benefit of television at home. Video games, movie rentals and the internet were inventions still waiting to ripen. Enticing billboards that adorned the roadsides of thoroughfares were a big part of my visual connection to the world outside the mountains of western North Carolina. Hands down, the best billboard messages of the day, or any era, belonged to the Navy: "Join the Navy and See the World.", "It's not just a Job, it's an Adventure!" And later: "Join Our Frequent Flyer Program!" From an early age, I knew my soul belonged to reaches far beyond my current places.

I also had an inflated sense of duty, along with a distain for cruel bullies who threatened and harmed the weak, or people who simply assumed that they could get away with being rude. I probably got this from my dad. I felt that someone needed to stand up and do the protecting, and who better than me? Always figured it was my responsibility to defend, if for no other reason than I knew I was up to the task.

My careers in the military and business have taught me that if you torture statistics long enough, you can get them to admit to anything. With that said, a shocking seventy-five percent of seventeen to twenty-four-year-old American men and women are ineligible for military service recruitment due to lack of education, obesity, prescription as well as non-prescription drug use, other physical problems, or criminal history. This is a mere three percent of the nation's total population. Of this small percent of eligible prospects left for military recruiters to track down and enlist, how many actually have the necessary aforementioned "want to" for the job?

As a side, can you imagine the bind the armed forces would be in if the female half of these numbers were not included? Furthermore, the Defense Department shutters to think how it would handle the three out of four ineligible youth if the mandatory military service draft was to be reinstated today.

I believed it was my duty to be a guardian for my country and that it was a foregone conclusion that I would join a branch of the armed forces as soon as I was old enough.

To get her two cents in and provide some balance to my servant mindset, my mother pulled me aside saying: "Think not what you can do for the Navy, but what the Navy can do for you." She quickly apologized for paraphrasing, make that butchering, the stirring words of John Kennedy. Her point was that if I was going to end up in a position of leadership, then there would be those counting on me to have a purposeful plan. If I was not in control of myself and where I was heading, then how could I portray whatever sense of competence was needed to guide others through times of peril?

Mom continued by revealing that she knew me better than anyone else could; for after all, she was my mother. She asserted that I had always been one who had carried my share of the load, and then some. And that the Navy would be receiving more than their money's worth from me, getting the better end of the deal, regardless of where I was placed. So, I should always let the Navy know exactly what I wanted and to go after it with conviction, never feeling guilty for obtaining preferred jobs or getting promoted ahead of my peers. Obviously, she was blowing smoke up my butt; and I understood that she was even then. Nevertheless, it was sound advice and provided me a general road map to obtaining my share of success and for enjoying my thirty-four years of requested and fascinating assignments in the Navy.

So with all this worldly guidance, I decided to join the Navy in a special program, and flew from Asheville to Marietta, Georgia, as the only passenger on a Navy plane to meet with recruiters. I went for my interview on a Friday afternoon, but the interviewing Chiefs were anxious to get to the Chief's club for a little gathering. They asked, "What do you want to do?" I answered with a question of my own, "Well what do you have specifically?" Irritated, they handed me a thick book of seventy-something enlisted aviation professions, to carefully read of course, each one described in lengthy detail, and left the room.

They came back in five minutes and asked if I'd made up my mind. I said, "You've only given me enough time to skim the surface of this book and to decide that I don't want to be stuck in a paper-pushing job, and I'll certainly need more time to decide what I'd like to do for the next four or so years of my life". I didn't realize at the time that they were both paper-pushers, and my comments didn't endear me to them in the least.

They wasted no time in saying, "We don't have more time! We need someone in this program who can make quick decisions, and obviously you aren't the person."

Were your hopes dashed at this point?

Didn't get in the enlisted program that I wanted, but had no problem soon after being selected elsewhere in the Navy for an officer program. Go figure.

Did your father live to see you promoted to Captain?

Yes. I was thrilled with my selection because I knew my father was going to be thrilled. He was in Thom's Rehabilitation Hospital after suffering his second stroke. He was in no condition to jump for joy, but was extremely proud. I was happier for him than I was for myself. He died at age eighty-four.

The promotion ceremony was a big to-do at the Reserve Center in Greenville, SC. Only two unrestricted line officers in the Readiness Command were picked up for Captain that year.

Felt that reaching the rank sounded pretty good, but to be quite honest, my first reaction was that whoever sat on the Captain Selection Board probably never knew me.

- **Mother and best friend—**

Growing up, my mother was my best friend, my confidant, a great gal. She was a career social worker. As early as my elementary school years, she would have me tag along with her when she delivered food baskets to needy families around Thanksgiving and Christmas. On more than one occasion after dropping off the holiday provisions, she would drive a short distance away from the home and park around a corner. We would watch for a brief time until one of the adults would bolt from the house with the large canned ham or whole turkey and head directly to a neighborhood store to exchange it for booze. She would always have me think of the children who would never get a bite, not even a sniff, of the centerpiece of the package we had delivered with such care. It was the sort of thing that one never forgets. Her name was Evelyn.

That was my mother's name, too.

Get out of here! I loved my mother dearly.

Being painfully aware that from day one I had kept busy the emergency medical profession, in Asheville and around the globe, Mom began an annual ritual. She told me that she was convinced that she was going to outlive me. The unpublished odds might have been in her favor. She began telephoning me early on her birthday without fail for the remaining thirty plus years of her life, to congratulate me for having survived another twelve months. She would thank me, on her birthday, always saying that it was the nicest present she would receive that day. For someone who never smoked, Mom could sure blow some smoke.

Let me tell you a story about her, and my father. I played a bunch of sports from the time I was old enough to walk, though I wasn't very big and had small hands. I was in Little League when you had to try out to be selected to play for a team. I was a good outfielder, but back then wasn't much at hitting the ball.

My father was operations director and office manager for Nabisco in Asheville. He worked long hours, but he got off at around five o'clock in the afternoon and could have made most every practice and game I ever played. For whatever reasons, he chose not to.

In my next to last year of Little League, I overheard my mother one night in tears telling Dad that if he did not attend my next baseball game she was going to leave him. Well that scared the hell out of me. I suddenly thought that I was going to be the reason of my parents breaking up and my mother leaving. I didn't sleep that night, and we had a game the next day.

But Dad came to that game! I was beyond excited, very much aware of exactly where he was seated in the stands, worried because I wasn't a very good hitter.

On the mound for the opposing team was David Cheadle, the league's best pitcher, who later became a first-round draft pick of the New York Yankees, and for the next forty years remained the highest Major League Baseball drafted player ever from Western North Carolina. We had been on the same Matthews Motors team for a short while until I was traded to West Asheville Lions. My brief baseball career had one thing in common with Pete Rose, the all-time MLB hits leader with 4256: We were both struck out by the same guy. But I have it all over Pete; he only struck out once against David, I struck out every time I faced him.

My father hadn't been following my team's schedule, much less anything about our opponents, and didn't know that for our level, a Sandy Koufax-like player was on the mound pitching against us. I was very conscious of my father's presence, worried about his reaction when I would swing and surely miss, and how disappointed he would be when he saw his son strike out at the only game he had ever attended.

So, my initial time up as a batter, I took a mighty swing at David's first pitch and the bat slipped out of my sweaty hands, and, focused as I was, you know where it went – yep, straight at my father's head. Had he not ducked, it probably would have killed him. As the saying goes, "No good deed ever goes unpunished." And whereas I was a little bitter about my father never having come to any of the games before, I certainly understood why he never came to another. My mother heard the story in dramatic detail later that evening. She did not leave home and never pressured Dad to risk life and limb again by appearing at any more of my games.

- **A window to the future—**

I grew up in a lower middle class neighborhood in West Asheville. The boys were a rough lot; we all understood that we had to be tough; any sign of softness was not acceptable. With this as a backdrop, you can imagine that I kept things under my cap when I found myself joining my elderly high school English Literature teacher in her love for poetry. I wonder if some of Ms. Middleton's poetry favorites in any way foretold my life; or better yet, is it possible for a song, a piece of art or a poem, once read and heard, to affect the selected paths one takes as the years unfold? I was drawn to Samuel Taylor Coleridge's *The Rime of the Ancient Mariner*. Even more so, Thomas Gray's *Elegy Written in a Country Churchyard* seems to have accompanied me my entire life. I remember its opening verse well:

> The curfew tolls the knell of parting day,
> The lowing herd wind slowly o'er the lea,
> The ploughman homeward plods his weary way,
> And leaves the world to darkness and to me.

That poem resonates with me, as does the stillness of Taps played in the evening aboard ships, throughout the military, at church conference centers and summer camps, toward the conclusion of burial ceremonies, reminding us that it is time to call it a day.

Over the years how did your life's journey further bear resemblance to Gray's poem?

As a boy I had a morning newspaper route, waking up every day of the year at O-dark-thirty, make that 3:30 a.m. and much earlier than my two sisters and all of my friends in the neighborhood, to deliver the Asheville Citizen.

Worked my way through college living and working weekends and nights at a funeral home. I came on duty to look after things, alone, right when most folks in town were getting off and heading home, tired from a normal eight or nine hours. I participated in many burial services.

Countless different times over thirty-four years in the Naval Reserve, I recall being on the bridge and in the pilot house aboard ships at sea off the coast as the sun set, watching fishing boats and commercial ships heading into port at day's end, standing watch well into the night as other seaman returned home, and most of our crew slept.

My brief bout with budget motel management in the mid-seventies was an exercise in late night drama. During my twenty-eight years at Kanuga camp and conference center I would work late, often past midnight, sometimes well into the next day.

Presently my months each year spent in the former Soviet Republic of Moldova, where many farmers still plow their fields by oxen, horse, and hand, are hauntingly consistent with my past. The little agrarian country is in a time zone seven hours different than North Carolina; often night-time there while it is daylight here. Even today I am a night owl; saving the late hours for my best work.

- **Enlisting in the Navy and college—**

I was very fortunate the day that I enlisted in the Navy. Entrance into the officer program of interest was contingent upon being accepted into a college or university; so I went across the street from the Merrimon Avenue located Naval and Marine Corps Reserve Center and applied to Asheville-Biltmore College, which became the University of North Carolina-Asheville one year later.

Applied to attend college in the morning, got accepted after lunch, took my school acceptance back across the street to the Reserve Center, and enlisted into their officer program, all in the same day. I was seventeen years old, the Vietnam War was raging, the mandatory military draft would soon be introduced, and I basically had a free pass to go to college for four years before being required to go on active duty. I was expected to spend most of my summers with the Navy doing boot camp and shipboard training cruises as an enlisted sailor.

How did that affect the way you felt about life in general? Was it a good experience, positive?

Things happened fast. It had not been my intention to go to college, and not in my home town if I did go, so I wasn't exactly a happy camper my first semester and ended up on academic probation. After the first two terms of my freshman year, things started to turn around for me. It was confidence, pure and simple, and a developing sense of belonging. I was recruited by an athletic fraternity to play for their intramural flag football team, and found myself being welcomed into a group. Started having a good time. Grades improved. It was pretty much a rowdy, rebellious fraternity nicknamed the 'Huns'. We were quite proud that our club did not have a Greek name.

Did you play linebacker, like your father?

No, was recruited to be a cornerback, a defensive back to cover wide receivers because I was fast and scrappy enough. I loved flag football, and eventually became team captain and principle running back. Played a little basketball, softball and, uh, a lot of 'fraternity'.

Tried out for the junior varsity basketball team. I was not quite 5'11", same as now, and needed to play guard; but my hands were really too small to be very competitive. Played varsity soccer briefly, started in a game or two; but fared little better at this than I had in my one unspectacular year as a 119-pound high school wrestler.

Okay so you were in this rebel group. How did that work out?

Asheville-Biltmore College was progressing into UNC-Asheville, a new campus, relatively speaking, and fraternities were not well established. Greek frats struggled in the sixties and seventies because so many students didn't buy into the traditional fraternity scene. Most in our group were former Western North Carolina high school athletes who had not gone on to the next level of college athletics. It was the Vietnam War era; many had been in the military and were now going back to school on the G.I. Bill. It was a pretty rough group.

You don't strike me as a rebellious person, and your upbringing was strict. Did you feel rebellious?

Well, I did have quite a bit in common with my fellow Huns. Loved sports and an occasional tussle. Was a member of the Naval Reserve. Think I was rebellious in the sense that most kids are, but not rebellious from the standpoint of the social revolution. I was not a hippie.

What was your major?

Political Science, International Relations to begin with. I switched majors my junior year, and got a degree in the epitome of indecision and the path of least resistance, a B.A. in Social Science, with a concentration in Economics. I would have graduated with honors had it not been for that disastrous first semester.

In my senior year at UNCA I hurt a leg on the last play of the last game of the flag football season. Had quite a struggle with a large hematoma in one of my thighs, and it delayed my return to Naval Officer Candidate School, OCS, which had been split up between two summers. Had gone through the first half of OCS after my junior year, then after receiving my university degree returned to Newport, Rhode Island to complete training.

- **Active-Duty and OCS—**

How did you do in OCS?

Okay, but not in class standing because of one thing that kept me from finishing high academically: a navigation quiz. Was always a slow reader and usually the last to finish an exam. It was the first big navigation test and it counted a lot. I finished long before the end of class, and even though we were very well disciplined to not let our eyes wander to other students' exams, noticed that they were all still working away.

I wanted to believe that I had gotten every answer correct, and was confident in assuming: "I'm really good at this." A few days later the grades were posted and I couldn't believe I had failed the exam terribly. I had taken enough exams along the way to figure that this wasn't possible. So, when the class started reviewing the exam question by question, I found that I was getting all the answers right. I'm thinking "I should've gotten a 100." Then I discovered that I had been given an exam that was missing the last several pages, that it had not been properly collated.

When you get a failing score on a major exam that counts a heavy percentage, it ruins your grade. And the Navy has this thing of expecting its officers to know something about navigation.

Surely they gave you a chance to retake the test.

Nope. And not only did they not allow that, but I was sent to a performance review board. I was at risk of being kicked out, so I quietly stood at attention as a junior officer berated me for my lack of performance. Finally got a chance to tell the board my side of the story; only to have this prosecuting officer cut into me and say: "You know the Navy is looking for officers who perform at a high level and do not give excuses for their failures." Then the senior-most officer heading up the review board stopped him and said, "Lieutenant, I think we all know what has happened here, and that will be enough." Even still, I was not permitted to retake the exam. They let me stay in Officer Candidate School, despite having the worst navigation score in the entire battalion, which was a full twenty-five percent of the grade point for class standing.

What were your feelings about the unfairness, how did you deal with it?

Like most people when they choke on a piece of bureaucratic chicken crap; not good. However, there are some things you just choose to swallow. My mother had taught me that I alone was responsible for my feelings.

Local WNC writer Lewis Green was a mentor of mine for forty years. A combat seasoned veteran of the Korean War, he was uncompromising and aggressive. Pampered, timid people were intuitively frightened by him. Hypocrites hated him. Lewis was to be admired for uniqueness and talent as a very good and creative writer. I embraced his magnetism, his spirit, and his tortured soul. Lewis gave license and shelter to my 'poly-phrenic' nature.

Lewis was a tuning fork, enabling me to discover hidden strengths whenever defeat came knocking. He had pointed out to me that there are two kinds in the military, warriors and bureaucrats. They take turns on center stage depending upon the severity of conflict. Consequently, the self-absorbed pettiness of a desk jockey junior officer or two did not come as a total surprise and was not about to derail me.

- **Aquatics taken seriously—**

But that wasn't the only stumbling block. Here I am in the Navy, but due to my unusually solid bone density I'm not buoyant, I don't float in fresh water. Understandably, swimming and aquatics in general are taken more seriously in the Navy than in the other services.

That makes sense. How did you cope with that?

Not always so well. We had a classic Marine drill sergeant as our aquatics instructor, and we were at the pool for one of our first classes when he bellowed: "Gentlemen, what happens to you when you are in the water and you stop flapping your arms and legs?" One of the officer candidates replied, "You sink."

The Sergeant barked, "No, wrong answer, you don't sink, you float, and for that wrong answer the entire company will swim additional laps until I'm convinced you're thinking more clearly. Don't make that mistake again." And so we swim, and we swim, finally permitted to drag ourselves out of the pool exhausted. Again: "Gentlemen, what happens to you in the water when you stop flapping your arms and legs?"

Crisis addicted as ever, I piped up with two simple words I would soon regret, "I sink." Didn't say, "You sink." The Sergeant turned on me, beet red. "Oh, you sink! Well, get in the water and show us?" I went to the shallow end and started walking upright on the bottom of the pool toward deeper water until totally submerged; continued walking in the same direction flatfooted on the bottom of the pool for a reasonable distance to prove my point, and then came up for air.

Proof positive that I was right - I sink. Make that, this smart ass sinks when he stops flapping his arms and legs. There was hell to pay. Swimming had always been very difficult for me, but now it became much more grueling, cause the Sergeant was embarrassed and from there forward took it out on me every day of swim training.

Spent most of the rest of my time at school physically exhausted, extra laps in the pool on top of the strenuous routine that goes with officer candidate training. That, plus having the lowest navigation grade in the entire battalion, makes it a wonder I made it through to graduation. A smile pops up whenever I'm reminded that my best kept secret for over thirty years in the Navy was that I was never good in and around the water. Winston Churchill's productive brilliance also came in handy for me. While rallying some of England's weary coastal defense units during World War II, he was quoted as saying something along the lines of: "It is no use saying 'We are doing our best.' You have to succeed in doing what is necessary."

• Commissioned Navy Ensign—

I was commissioned Ensign in 1972. You get one stripe on your shoulder - one gold bar as a collar device. Felt pretty good about it, overcoming the debacle with the navigation exam and handling the challenge of the added swimming. My father was proud, having retired himself as a Senior Chief. He was far smarter than I ever was, knew more about ships, but had lost his opportunity to go to the Naval Academy and become a Naval Officer.

What happens first for a new officer?

Officer detailers conduct interviews and then decide where to put green Ensigns. If you don't go on to Nuclear Power, Supply or Aviation schools, you are most likely commissioned as an Unrestricted Line Officer in the Surface community, with command of a ship at sea as the ultimate career goal. They ask a bunch of questions, similar to our conversation here, trying to get a feel for where you might best fit. Told them about my college days and they became intrigued by my recount of the large house I had leased in my name, sub-leased bedrooms to my fraternity brothers, and generated revenue by making it party-central for students. We christened the castle the *Huns House*, installed gaming machines, bowling machines, vending machines, and made additional money in a variety of other ways. We held dances and parties, things like that, and terrorized the neighborhood with noise.

The detailers were drawn to all this because one of the roles glorified in the military is that of the 'cumshaw' artist. Almost every outfit had a self-appointed one, normally a senior enlisted guy who could acquire, outside of official channels, just about anything. Nothing was ever out of reach, be it a case of bourbon, scotch, or whatever, for the most serious of unofficial occasions.

This sounds like what James Garner did in the 1960s movie titled The Americanization of Emily.

I suppose. And like in the television sitcom 'McHale's Navy', every military unit worth its salt has a Sergeant, Petty Officer or Chief that does that. So my experience led the detailers to think that I was industrious and someone who would be of value in remote areas having to deal with limited resources.

I was an Ensign, an entry-level-one officer, but was handed an O-3, or level three, billet. Before being shipped off to the Pacific, I was pushed through three communications and cryptology courses.

Parts of my new job involved being Communications Material Security Custodian for Commander, Allied Naval Forces Korea and the Admiral's Top Secret Control Officer. Duties included being the issuer of the South Korean Navy & Marine Corps offline cryptographic equipment and key lists that enabled them to communicate securely with other Allied Forces. Stood watch as a duty officer in the Korean Navy's operations control center and served as communications security advisor to the Republic of Korea's Navy and Marine Corps. With the ROK Marines being one of our staunchest partners in the Vietnam War, this was considered a serious posting.

My immediate supervisor Lieutenant Commander Jake Reed was a legend in the Navy and Korea long before I arrived in the charming port city of Chinhae. Big Jake looked like John Wayne, walked like John Wayne, and talked like John Wayne. Many people feared him, I found him captivating. We both worked for Admiral Henry "Hank" Morgan. Admiral Morgan was part of the J.P. Morgan family.

An interesting thing is if you run a ship aground, even if only onto a soft sand bar, then it probably will be the kiss of death for your naval career. Well, Admiral Morgan had not always been an Admiral. At one point of his Navy career, he was skipper of a diesel submarine. He had been enthralled early on by Italian frigates that would come into the port of Naples at a high rate of speed, reverse screws, rapidly slowing and sharply turning, perfectly sliding to a stop up against the pier bumper guards. Italians seem to love flamboyant ship drivers who show off more than they should. It's a formula for eventual disaster.

So, one time with his submarine entering the port of New London, Connecticut at an unusually high rate of speed, Hank ordered the lee helmsman "all stop" and immediately followed with "back full emergency." But the lee helmsman got so excited and confused that he mistakenly went to flank speed ahead. The racing sub hit the cement sea wall, actually jumped up out of the water, and landed on top of a row of telephone booths and parked cars. Fortunately none were occupied.

There was a big stink, but the Morgan family offered to buy the Navy a new submarine, and as you know, that is a pretty expensive piece of equipment! It was surprising how far up the chain of command the family's offer went before somebody came to their senses and said, "That's not the way the government does things". The Morgans ended up not buying the Navy a new submarine, and Hank's career was not really hurt. He rose to the rank of Admiral and Commander of Naval Allied Forces Korea. Can you imagine the owner of one of the parked vehicles that got flattened having to file testimony with his automobile insurance company, claiming that his car had been squashed by a submarine?

- **Enchanting Korea, Land of the Morning Calm—**

Chinhae is home to the South Korean Navy; its main operating base and command center in case of all-out war. It is South Korea's equivalent of our Norfolk, San Diego, Great Lakes and Annapolis; nearly their entire Navy wrapped up in one town on the southern end of the peninsula. Chinhae is a relatively secure place; walled by impressive mountains on three sides and with numerous steep rocky islands standing guard over its seaward approach. Views from high elevations surrounding the port are splendidly panoramic. I found the locale unescapably romantic.

Fortunately, Chinhae had been within the hard-fought protected boundaries of the Pusan Perimeter during the Korean War against the ruthlessly destructive Communists. Its complementary make-up of Korean, Chinese, Russian, Japanese, and Western architecture has survived hundreds of years of violent conflict. Chinhae's annual spring cherry blossom spectacle is one of the country's most popular attractions.

Piloting a Cessna 150 single engine airplane provided spectacular views of Chinhae's mountainous coastline. But after no more than sixteen successful landings and one disconcerting intentional mid-air engine stall, I informed my flight instructor that flying was not my cup of tea. Since then, I have been content to sit in economy coach and leave the piloting of aircraft to those so inclined. It's a good thing because I spend a lot of time on airplanes.

- **Moving on after Korea—**

It was a bit unusual for a Ensign line officer's first tour to not be aboard a ship for the explicit purpose of cutting his teeth by going to sea. I was not bounding the waves of the deep blue, but loving things all the same, and doing well enough to be given an opportunity to extend my stay. I realized that by the time I finished a second tour ashore I'd be a Lieutenant Junior Grade or a full Lieutenant before ever getting aboard a ship as an officer, and so far behind the seamanship learning curve that a senior Ensign would have to hold my hand and show me around the ship, even though I would outrank him by one or two grades. This is definitely not how the Navy is set up to work. Breaking in Ensigns is normally done early in their careers and is a job generally entrusted to the Executive Officer and the salty Chiefs aboard.

Figuring that if I was going to consider the Navy as a career, I needed to go to sea without further delay. Taking advice to get on board a small ship to maximize my opportunities for ship-handling, I received orders to USS Kittiwake (ASR-13), a submarine rescue ship attached to Submarine Squadron Six out of Norfolk. The ship was named after a seagull, and for the life of me, don't know why all submarine rescue ships in the U.S. Navy are named for seagulls. Incidentally, the Kittiwake was recently decommissioned, towed down to the Cayman Islands then sunk to be an artificial reef for fish and to help the local diving industry. On the day she was retired, Kittiwake was the oldest active ship in the U.S. Navy.

A submarine rescue ship is a surface ship. Back then, its main features were a diving bell and the ability to lie out on the deep ocean in what's called a four-point moor. Its supply of long heavy chains, controlled by powerful wenches, is used to position the ship above a submarine in distress. Booms lower the diving bell, or recovery chamber, onto the submarine and a water tight seal is created around the sub's escape hatch. The hatches on the bell and submarine are then opened and several submariners are brought up at a time.

Except for training exercises did you ever have to do that?

No, never found myself in an actual submarine rescue situation. Of particular note, in 1986 Kittiwake recovered the black box from the Space Shuttle Challenger disaster. I was several things:

Communications Officer, an Underway Officer of the Deck and Conning Officer, and public relations officer. But my primary day job was Supply Department Head, responsible for keeping the ship in needed repair parts and supplies, and more importantly, feeding the crew.

I was not a trained Supply Corps Officer with proper insignia, credentials and diploma from the Navy Supply School in Athens, Georgia. Navy ships needed a wartime complement of one-hundred sailors to warrant having a professional Supply Corps Officer aboard, and Kittiwake had been conveniently assigned a maximum of ninety-nine to save money on personnel.

How long did you have that job?

Two years. Since I was the junior guy coming in, not rank-wise because there were warrant officers in the wardroom, but being the most inexperienced officer, I became the supply guy. This was a risky decision on someone's part.

At the U.S. Naval Prison in Portsmouth, New Hampshire, a saying went that it was filled with Supply Corps Officers and Communications Officers. Now here was a guy doing both jobs, at the same time, and with no supply school education or training whatsoever.

We were the last U.S. Navy ship to have a crew's rum ration. The official reasoning was to help divers with decompression, the bends, and the like. I stretched my assignment as commissary officer a bit, and put one beer in the ship's vending machines for every case of soft drinks. A sailor couldn't get drunk on one beer while chasing it with twenty-four Cokes; sick but not drunk.

That really helped morale, because every time an exhausted, sweaty sailor went to a vending machine, it was like a lottery: he knew there was one chance in twenty-five that he was going to get a cold beer. That wasn't exactly in keeping with naval regulations, but it was fun.

- **Arduous duty assignments—**

Due to its operating schedule, type of work, and rough seas we always had to deal with, submarine rescue ship tours are considered arduous duty for career rotation purposes. The assignment in Korea was also considered to be unique, remote, risky, and challenging in its own right. So after these first two billets I was due for rotation to one or two relatively calm shore stations, but had yet to serve as an officer aboard a surface combatant. My class, or year group, was advancing and I realized that if I did not go back to sea and get on a destroyer this time, then my Navy career would be shot; no pun intended.

Up to that point I had spent most of my married time on the ocean and away from home. Didn't think it was fair to my wife, and to be quite honest with you, figured the marriage wouldn't last, if I did back-to-back tours aboard ship. So the decision to get off active duty. Really didn't want to, but my career just sort of fell that way. There was a decision to be made and I was actually tired of going to sea. I had spent long spells underway on the Kittiwake just bobbing around waiting for higher priority nuclear submarines to rendezvous with us.

- **The Family—**

Tell me about your wife and children.

My wife's family name is Chang, and her full maiden name is Chang Kyungmi, but she mostly goes by Mia. She was working as a dental assistant at the dispensary in Chinhae when I met her. I was sitting in the dentist chair when a soft voice asked me to lay my head back. Leaning backward, I looked up, spotted her and just kept on falling. Smitten is the word. A year and a half later we got married in Norfolk. Mia was graduated from Warren Wilson College, Swannanoa, NC, Class of 1981, with a B.A. in Business Administration and Economics. She worked in Korea and North Carolina dental clinics before joining the staff of Kanuga conference center where she has worked in a variety of jobs for the past thirty-five years.

We have two sons; both Bachelor-degreed from the University of North Carolina at Chapel Hill. Bryan is a Navy Flight Officer, Lieutenant at last count. He is single and has been stationed in the Arabian Gulf, Okinawa, Hawaii and the Mediterranean region. If not Djibouti on Africa's east coast near the mouth of the Red Sea, then San Diego, California is next for him. Andrew, who is hopefully heading off to law school soon, is an occasional substitute school teacher and seasonal counselor and climbing instructor at camps primarily in Western North Carolina. In 2006, he attended a spring semester at Yonsei University in Korea, before continuing around the world, rock climbing on all four hemispheres. He actually made it to North Korea that year; something neither his mother nor I have done. Andrew has a wedding coming up in a few months.

Thinking of my clan, I am drawn to Jimmy Buffet's 1978 song *Son of a Son of a Sailor*. Traveling the globe seems to run in the family.

• Entering the motel business—

I got off active duty and went into the budget motel business for a couple of years as a manager and troubleshooter for Scottish Inns of America. My job was to relieve managers on vacation and to help properties that were losing money; which was almost impossible because the economy was going so well, and the company had strategically built at numerous exits of the then fairly new interstate highway system.

Back then, it was highly unusual for budget motels to lose money for their parent companies. That is unless the local managers embezzled funds or got involved in drugs or prostitution to the point where they would lose focus on doing their jobs. Accompanying a corporate district manager, we would go to mismanaged properties and fire the general manager. From there I would take over and do my best to figure out which other staff were involved in any funny business and get rid of them too. This led to more than a few angry confrontations with terminated employees and their stunned or unknowing spouses. New staff would be hired and trained for every department as first steps in getting the motel and restaurant operations out of the red, and turning a good profit.

But you left. Why?

I was running a 100-room motel and restaurant on Cox Road in Gastonia, North Carolina, a town just outside of Charlotte, a three-time winner of the All-American City award. If my memory serves me correct, in the mid-seventies it had the highest capital crime rate in the country two years running and was featured on CBS's *60-Minutes* for that reputation. The inn hosted major events most weekend nights, like vice-squad busts of street level drug trafficking, assaults with deadly weapons, the capture of an escaped prison convict, things like that. Found myself toting a pistol; kept it with me and put it to use more often than the ones I occasionally carried when I was in the military; mainly to show force, never had to actually fire it at anyone.

My home office got wind of the weapon, and sent my district manager Joe Crowley to my unit to show me that a gun was not needed in our line of work, and how to properly work the premises without one. He failed. Joe began his hands-on course of instruction by demonstrating to me how to approach cars that didn't belong in the parking lot, and to effectively ask their drivers to leave. The first car we went up to was a red convertible, and Joe said, "Let me show you how to do this." As soon as Joe began his authoritative spill, the tough looking driver pulled a monster pistol of his own then drove away laughing. Joe slowly turned to me and said, "Carry the gun!"

Later on I was at Joe's house for Thanksgiving while my wife was visiting her parents in Korea for several months. Dinner was interrupted when the desk clerk telephoned and apologetically said, "Mr. West I hate to bother you on Thanksgiving, but there's a man in Sambo's parking lot, a restaurant beside the Inn, with a rifle, and he's got this couple pinned down in room 128. I think the woman is his wife." I asked the clerk if she had followed our standard operation procedure and phoned the police. She calmly replied that she had. Then I inquired: "What did they allow?" She said that they asked only if the guy was still shooting. When she answered yes, they said to call back when it appeared that the dude had run out of ammunition. The main problem in Gastonia was domestic violence, which was extremely dangerous for the police.

I jumped in my car, but by the time I got to the Inn, the police had already taken the shooter into custody. Having a sense of humor is essential in law enforcement.

That's an interesting anecdote, tell me another.

Late one evening at the Gastonia motel, David Baity, our night clerk and auditor, a newspaper writer during the day, was tied up and robbed with a pistol to his head. The two robbers got furious because they couldn't get the safe open, even with the proper key. They started shooting at the safe with a .45 automatic, a blue steel piece, intimidating. Scared half to death, Dave just knew he was going to be next.

One of the bullets ricocheted off of the safe and powered through the wall to my office, across the room right above my chair, in which fortunately I wasn't sitting, then through the next wall into the parking lot and right into the radiator of their escape vehicle. There was over a thousand dollars in the safe, but they took off with only $114.95 from the cash register. My favorite saying of all time is derived from Sir Isaac Newton's Third Law of Motion: "For every action there is an opposite and equal reaction." Due to the damaged radiator, their car overheated on the interstate and the law nabbed them. Dave identified the crooks in a police lineup in Charlotte. Turns out they had shot and killed an owner of a jewelry store in a neighboring town earlier that same day.

- **Re-affiliating with the Navy in 1976—**

While in Gastonia, I picked things back up with the Naval Reserve at a center in Charlotte. I was recruited to be commanding officer of a food service unit whose mobilization site was in Little Creek, Virginia and had been established to feed 3,000 Marines in the event of the next big war. Because of my supply and food service experience on the Kittiwake, the powers at be figured I was the ideal person to fill this billet; since for some obscure reason it didn't call for a Supply Corps officer, but a line officer.

It was a small Reserve unit, just ten of us. If I recall correctly, I became the youngest and most junior commissioned commanding officer of a Reserve unit in the country. These guys had been cooks while on active duty, but they weren't cooks now. One owned an auto repair shop, one was a postal deliveryman, and one was a chewing tobacco salesman. But we successfully operated a highly mechanized kitchen where we loaded our bake ovens with a forklift, and had large conveyer belts that ran food over grills and through massive deep-fat fryers. It was made to order for just a handful of sailors to feed thousands of hungry Marines. That was an interesting tour.

You mentioned earlier to me that you organized and baked things from scratch, and used intuition, creativity and hard work to get things done. Is that an accurate summation?

Well yeah, and we did a lot of things differently. We didn't have a full kitchen at the supporting Reserve Center in Charlotte. We weren't allowed to cook regular lunch meals for the Reservists; that would have made too much sense. However, we would come in early and bake sourdough cinnamon rolls and things like that to sell, using the money for ship's parties. The enticing smells of baking pastries would fill the drill hall, eliminating any need for us to advertise our goods. We drilled one weekend a month and headed off for two weeks of training each year. We got our share of credit, and had more than our share of fun.

What were you doing during most days, and what was your career change at that point?

I was still working for Scottish Inns at the Gastonia motel, and I was also the lead officer of the Reserve unit. One evening, the Training Center was hosting a reception for some Admiral from Charleston at the home of a senior officer in Charlotte.

Went to the affair and ended up in a conversation about careers, mentioning that I might be agreeable to going back on active duty after listening to some friends sing the praises of the Supply community. Only a few drinks into the party, they had pretty much talked me into going to Naval Supply School.

Then somebody's wife came up to us and said, "Now wait a minute, you guys are all pressuring Ray to jump into the Supply Corps. Have you asked him if he's applied for any other jobs, that is, other than cowboys and Indians at budget motels?" Responding, "There is this conference center that has shown interest in me up in Western North Carolina. The wife quickly asked, "Which one?" Didn't so much as get the word Kanuga out of my mouth when she screamed, "Oh, that's the greatest place in the world; we go there every chance we get!"

I went to the party as a motel manager, half-way through was headed for Athens, Georgia for Naval Supply School, and by the time the gathering broke up, was on my way to work at a conference center near Hendersonville. I came back to the mountains in January of 1977.

How long did your new career here last?

Twenty-eight years.

- **Progression in the Navy Reserve—**

What happened in your Navy career?

During a full time civilian career at Kanuga, I had one Reserve assignment after another, including three more command tours. Ultimately settled in as Commanding Officer of the Volunteer Training Unit at the Naval & Marine Corps Reserve Center in Greenville, South Carolina.

Now a Captain and to be competitive for further promotion, I needed to fill one of the few paying billets available, but for most of those positions, would have had to travel at my own expense to Norfolk or Washington at least one weekend per month.

My father was seriously ill and I was the closest family caregiver. Chose not to travel any further than necessary to train. By remaining affiliated in Greenville, I could continue to visit my father in the hospital in Asheville by driving back from the Reserve Center Saturday evenings, then turning around and heading back the same night for Sunday's drill.

Was your mother still alive then?

Yes, but by then her health was not good either, and she was staying in Greensboro with the older of my two sisters Marge. My other sister Lil was not far away in Reidsville.

That was pretty much the end of my Reserve advancement, in that I had decided not to leave my father to pursue the type of billet it would take for me to continue to be paid and have even so much as a remote chance of getting picked up for admiral. It was now convenient for me to remain in Greenville and continue drilling in a non-pay status. Had plenty of points to retire, but it was in my blood to be associated with the Navy.

- **Humanitarian Assistance Project—**

So, you were at a crossroads. What did you decide to do next?

Entering the thirtieth year of my Navy career, I stopped to realize that it was down to my final four years of seeing the world on Uncle Sam's nickel. The Navy had indeed been more than just a job, but an adventure. During a December 1997 Naval Reserve drill weekend, I asked my Executive Officer, Captain Charlie Medd, who coincidently was also from Hendersonville, North Carolina, to search for particularly interesting special work assignments for the personnel of our Volunteer Training Unit located in Greenville. Charlie was a public school teacher and normally had extended periods of time during the summer vacation months to take off and train with the Navy. He had acquired a reputation as quite the guru in the arena of available overseas duty assignments.

That Sunday afternoon, Charlie ran me down and said: "Hey Skipper, U.S. European Command is looking for Guard and Reserve units from any and all of the military branches to manage humanitarian assistance projects inside its area of responsibility...including several in the former Soviet Union." That sounded like an exotic enough way to finish up my Navy years...so we went straight to work on the opportunity.

EUCOM's Humanitarian Assistance plan, hatched in part to win friends and in a positive way to influence people, had slowly marched up the priority scale of underfunded programs following the collapse of the Soviet Union. However, the subsequent down-sizing of militaries, especially in the European theater, resulted in there not being enough 'in-country operatives' to do the needed work in the field. Thus the call for experienced volunteers, one of the purposes and justifications for the existence of the Guard and Reserve and a perfect fit for me. The Republic of Moldova was one of the countries in EUCOM's new Partnership for Peace program.

Historically, it seems that naval officers are universally expected to know everything about the globe. Scurrying off to find an encyclopedia, locating the tiny country in Eastern Europe, I then pretended having known all there was to know about Moldova since boot camp. A few weeks later we 'rogered-up' by agreeing to manage one modestly presented project...the final construction phases of a small orphanage in the town of Drochia, Republic of Moldova. We were told we were the only Guard or Reserve unit from any of the services to step up. Consequently, we were awarded the job and advised that we would be in and out of Moldova in no more than two weeks.

How did that work out?

A U.S. Army officer at EUCOM telephoned while I was in my civilian office at Kanuga and said: "You are going to finish building this orphanage in northern Moldova, correct?" After responding affirmatively, he went on to say that things in general were beginning to heat up in Moldova, and that the number one priority in EUCOM's HA program, encompassing seventeen different countries, was now a children's tuberculosis hospital in southern Moldova. He said that since my unit was already planning on going to Moldova, it was extremely important for us to take on this tuberculosis hospital project instead of the orphanage. He said that admittedly it was a complicated project, but it would take only one more week, three in total to complete.

I bounced this slightly longer commitment off my boss at Kanuga, Albert Gooch. He responded by saying that it sounded like a wonderful thing to do for the children of Moldova and that he would cover for me at work, seeing that only one more week of my being away would be involved.

Informing the officer at EUCOM that my unit would switch to the hospital project, he said: "Great, so now, since you are going to Moldova for the more demanding TB hospital, then you might as well do the little orphanage as well while over there."

As I sorted through this escalating recruiting game, I was reminded how the Army had long ago mastered the art of blatant manipulation. This moving target of a few weeks turned into more than a decade of involvement in Moldova.

• Off to Moldova—

So in April 1998 it was off to Moldova with two projects to tackle. Charlie Medd and I showed up at the Fortuna Family Home unannounced, a rude thing to do, but we wanted to see conditions at the orphanage without allowing our hosts advance notice and time to prepare anything out of the ordinary. We quickly learned far more than our investigative minds could have imagined. The husband and wife running the home, along with their collection of diverse looking children, had a personal story far more compelling than their dilapidated house.

Peter and Anna Fortuna married soon after Peter had begun his career as a Soviet Army policeman. They lost a child in their first attempt due to an extremely difficult and dangerous pregnancy. An emergency operation to save Anna's life resulted in her losing the ability to bear children. The couple was relatively young when Peter retired from the military; and still desiring a family, they decided to adopt. The Fortunas chose to settle in the small town of Drochia in northern Moldova. Like couples with similar circumstances all over the world, they headed off to the nearest orphanage in search of the brightest-eyed infant available.

Peter and Anna were entering unfamiliar territory as they were about to experience firsthand the plight of orphan children. Since I am not an orphan myself, and I have never been able to muster the strength to adopt, I am not an authority in this arena by any stretch of the imagination. What I have witnessed is something I understand to be a disheartening stigma which many, if not most, orphans endure: the feeling that they are orphaned because it is somehow their fault, that they are not worthy or loveable enough to have parents.

Is the adoption process in Moldova any different from anywhere else?

The process at orphanages is often the same everywhere. Prospective parents look over available children on display and select the 'pick-of-the-litter'; leaving all the other children behind to be reminded that they are indeed not good enough. With each subsequent failure to be chosen, the probability of ever being picked becomes slimmer. Over time the passed-over children become old enough to understand what is going on. Their sense of self-worth plummets.

There are those who find the term 'children at risk' distasteful. Believe me, when it becomes obvious to a child that he or she is unwanted, confidence and self-esteem hit rock bottom. Why should they continue trying to please when they realize that their best is not enough? Children burdened with similar circumstance are not playing on a level field, and chances of a prosperous life become severely handicapped. Their lives are at risk.

In such a setting Peter and Anna enthusiastically arrived at the nearby orphanage planning to find that one pretty infant to complete their family. But their eyes and hearts discovered something unexpected; so many children ages five to eight years, too old to have any realistic chance of ever being adopted. The couple was overcome by the sad faces and prevailing sense of hopelessness. Tossing practicality aside, they chose not one young baby, but five of the older children. While packing up to leave with this herd of truly shocked and excited youngsters, the word leaked throughout the dormitories. They were rushed upon by other children, begging to be chosen too, grasping Peter's and Anna's hands and coat sleeves, promising to be good, to work hard, to make their parents proud. Peter and Anna left with eight new members to their family.

Back at home, the small neighborhood was not all together thrilled with the arrival of such a motley crew. But Moldovan hospitality prevailed and they were allowed to build a house at the end of a road beside a garbage dump. Peter obtained building blocks and other materials on credit, using his military pension as collateral. The initial shell of the house was constructed. Then things literally began to fall apart.

Peter's pension vanished with the collapse of the Soviet Union. The national economy faltered as the free market failed to produce enough decent paying jobs for those without political or family connections. Then a severe winter storm barreling down from Russia took off the roof and blew out all of the windows, leaving the home exposed to the elements. At least the family was blessed to be living by the local dump; there were scraps to be found, enough to survive the short term. Word of their desperate situation reached U.S. military humanitarian assistance personnel stationed at the American Embassy in Chisinau, Moldova's capital.

- **European Command—**

What were some of the geo-political issues you had to address?

After a half century of the Cold War, the years that immediately followed were an awkward time for many of us. United States European Command was the Western strength that faced off against the advance of Communism, the Soviet Union, Stalin, and all that followed. With rapidly advancing technologies and escalating nuclear capabilities, the U.S. and USSR had grown into the most powerful military forces the world had ever seen.

When the Soviet Union dissolved there were concerns about a vacuum that might result, knowing that some of its Republics would fare well, like the ones in the Baltic States of Lithuania, Latvia, Estonia, but that some others which had little if any energy resources would struggle. Moldova was recognized as a country that was going to have a hard time because it had no deposits of oil, natural gas or coal. Additionally, Moldova, a historically agrarian country, for the previous fifty years had been hauling their exceptional farm products by train to Russia to feed the Communist Party elite. Now their only substantial export market had literally disappeared overnight.

During the years of Soviet expansion, many Russians had been relocated from cities to labor in Siberian mines and work the fertile farm lands of Ukraine and Moldova. Many of the people forced to move ended up as preferred Soviet administrators for controlling and managing the local populations. A Russian speaking minority became a ruling minority in Moldova. With the collapse of the USSR, the Russians in Moldova suddenly found themselves as a real minority, and not very happy about it. When the ethnic Romanian majority grabbed political control, there was a lot to be learned overnight about governing a country.

- **Showing up unannounced—**

Tell me more about your first meeting with Peter and Anna.

One wonderful and time-honored Moldovan custom is if you visit a home in peace and good will, the people that own the home are expected to invite you in for a meal and be genuinely hospitable. So Anna Fortuna, stunned to discover that help may be on the way, was happy to invite us in to share whatever she could drum up to serve on short notice.

Did you have a translator with you?

Yes, two. Dorin Trestianu, a great story Dorin, a Moldovan who worked for the U.S. Department of Defense at the Embassy, and a young Moldovan woman learning to become a translator. Anna invited us into the kitchen, it was bleak, bare-bones, with only the basic essentials including a small table and a few chairs. For sure our visit was a surprise and Anna didn't have much food to offer, but she gave us some sort of a meal, not mamaliga the national staple similar to thick grits, but some sort of barley like grain. I thought at the time that it might have been from the seeds of weeds that grew around the nearby dump. The highlight of the meal was pickled watermelon, which to be quite honest with you, was one of the least appealing things I have eaten in my life. It ranked right there for me with the first time I was given, with no heads up, spicy hot Korean kimchee without rice and beer to help it down.

But you didn't let them know that.

No of course not. Told them we were in a hurry due to another appointment. While still sitting at the table, some of the children came home from school and began peeking their heads around the corner of the kitchen door. Two of us were in uniform, the children were curious, wondering why military people were in their home. On top of that, there was a lot of talk in a language they could not comprehend. I looked across the table at Peter and realized that he was taking care of these kids against seemingly impossible odds, a greater undertaking than anything I had attempted in my entire life, or probably would ever try.

- **'Come to Jesus Moment'—**

I had a *'Come to Jesus'* moment when I realized that here was a guy, who for a career had been in the Soviet military police, in a manner of sorts my adversary since I joined the Navy in 1968, now doing something pretty dad-gum humbling to me. I said to myself, maybe this is where I was destined to be and truly supposed to be doing. I had a real sense of that, and left determined to do what I could.

Soon after that we sat down with U.S. Ambassador John Todd Stewart. During the course of conversation, we concluded that because the Fortuna home was not a public orphanage, but more like a large foster home by American definition, we couldn't use U.S. taxpayer money to finish building a privately owned residence. Adhering to the insistence of the Ambassador, I had to cancel the Fortuna Home project completely and jerk the rug out from that family one more time. It was a dreadful feeling.

The Ambassador, Captain Medd and I were sitting together in the Embassy office when I became noticeably upset about the situation. Charlie kicked me in the shin under the table, reminding me that the Ambassador was just doing his job. The long flight back to the States was agonizing as I pondered the dilemma of the Fortuna family.

- **The Universe conspires for the cause—**

Got home and down to Greensboro to see my mother. She was always insistent on getting a blow-by-blow report of my escapades whenever I went off with the military, and she required nothing short of a full report.

"Mom, I can't just walk away from this and abandon that family over there; to be the one who once again pulled the plug on them." Officially I was the one who on legal grounds had cancelled everything that was finally falling into place for these people. "This string of bad luck must be stopped. When we go back over to work on the Children's Tuberculosis Hospital, I am going to find time to slip up north and see what can be done to help them."

In response, my mother said, "Son, you are not going back over to Moldova to help that family; that is, not without some help from your mother."

Did you know where she was going with that?

That was my mother. She was good at it. She meant she'd be tossing in some money to help.

So I said, "Yes ma'am," and we started looking at it all. We had to come up with the money ourselves, as now there was no Department of Defense funding to help the Fortunas. We realized that we could actually do more than initially calculated if we could get tax deductions. Drove back home to Hendersonville with a plan, confident that my boss Albert Gooch would be receptive. In his office, I told Albert that my mom and I needed a vehicle for treating our involvement as charitable giving. Kanuga was a 501(c)(3) non-profit organization.

Being the chief financial officer and vice president for administration and Albert the president, we were able to create Kanuga's first very own international outreach program: the Kanuga-Moldova Children's Fund. Income and expense line-items were soon established within Kanuga Conferences, Inc. allowing restricted gifts for Moldova to be handled. That was in 1998.

Plans were to go back to repair the asbestos tile roof on the children tuberculosis hospital, as stupid as that sounds, and to carry subsistence money to help the Fortunas. Less than two weeks prior to taking off for Moldova, Kanuga's Board of Directors held its Annual Fall meeting. For the first time ever the board was running ahead of schedule and we found ourselves waiting for the next presenter to arrive. Albert slipped me a note asking, "Why don't you tell the board about your trip to Moldova?" Over the years he had learned that I never used one word when two would do… and we needed to kill some time.

I had not prepared to make a presentation on the subject, but dug deep to tell the story, got choked up in the process, and had a hard time finishing. Leaving the podium and returning to my seat beside an Episcopal clergyman, Doug Remer from Atlanta, he proceeded to elbow me in the ribs. I thought he was firmly suggesting "get a grip sailor; what do you mean by coming unglued in front of all these people?" Or so I thought. As I turned around in defense, he handed me a check, and said "take this with you." straightening back in my seat, I glanced down the rows of chairs, and here they came, check after check after check; over twenty-thousand dollars!

It sounds like the universe was conspiring for you.

It really was.

- **Back to Moldova—**

Ten days after that board meeting I headed back to Moldova accompanied by trusted colleague Commander David Laughter. I was carrying two-hundred $100 Travelers Cheques, almost enough to finish the Fortuna home. The military was paying us to run their other project of fixing up the children's hospital, designated as the number one humanitarian assistance priority in EUCOM. I didn't totally understand why, but I would find out.

When our flight from Atlanta was delayed, I remembered that I needed to talk with Annette Cullipher who was conducting a conference at Kanuga, trying to reconcile Jungian psychology with Christianity. Some people believe that is impossible, but I think she and her husband Jim did a pretty good job of it.

Called her from an airport pay phone. Had our airplane been on time, I wouldn't have called. As we spoke about a number of things, I mentioned that most of the money needed for the Fortuna home was in hand, but not quite enough. Then Annette told me that her group had taken up a collection that morning to help, and she would hold it for the time being, unless I needed it to be wired over right away to Moldova. It was just enough to close the deal on construction of the Fortuna Family Home. While traveling I reflected a bit more about what Peter and Anna were doing, and felt good about helping them. The more I thought about it, the more pumped I got.

The Fortunas were to some degree overwhelmed. They were simple people who adopted a mob of children, despite tremendously hard circumstances. They were courageous and good people committed to each other, and to their new family. I can't say that they had any other reaction to our visits other than gratitude and hope, but what could be finer than that? They had left it in our hands, to see to it that whatever was needed got done.

So you felt a personal responsibility to give them some hope?

Yes. Many times in life you jump into a situation responding to the call of duty, feeling a sense of responsibility toward the task at hand. As you get further into things, human interaction kicks in giving rise to a next generation of feelings. Reckon if you are not helping someone in need, then you should be supporting someone who is. One of Steven Spielberg's movies, *Schindler's List,* echoes in my mind.

A routine job assignment grew into something more personal as I felt that something would conjure itself up to help this very deserving bunch of people. The Fortunas met all this with considerable skepticism, owning to so many unfulfilled promises throughout their life. They weren't going to allow themselves to get too excited about it. Culturally, Peter and Anna were conditioned not to be optimistic.

But things did get better for them and they took in even more children, twenty-three in all. Then six months ago, Peter died unexpectedly from a sudden brain hemorrhage. Anna is alone now with a house full of children. I am so thankful that Moldova World Children's Fund has a loving volunteer within a three hour's drive of their home.

- **Helping a special child in need—**

Give me an example of a Moldovan child in need that you helped.

A winter storm was dumping heavy snow one night on the village of Bacioi. Little Natalia Bolea, only five months old, was sound asleep in her makeshift crib beside the kitchen stove heating the home when it exploded and set her bedding ablaze. The flames burned off much of her face and all ten fingers. Her mother, who was in an adjacent shed tending to farm animals, raced back to the house and tossed her daughter through the open front door into the deep snow outside. Natalia, her life saved, was terribly disfigured. To compound matters, the scar tissue that formed over much of her body, especially her face, was tough and lacked elasticity. She could still see out of both eyes, but her eyelids were stuck in place and could not close.

Making things worse, her father walked away from the fire gutted home, leaving her mother alone to raise severely handicapped Natalia and two other children. The hardships the victimized family faced simply to survive stretches the imagination.

And you stepped in to help.

Yes, but years later. While stationed in Moldova, Major Robert Carver of the North Carolina National Guard (NGNC) met Natalia at a boarding school for handicapped children. NGNC conducts numerous humanitarian projects each year, like furnishing support for a number of dentists from North Carolina who make periodic trips to Moldova. The dentists provide volunteer dental treatment for needy youngsters like Natalia, many of whom are abandoned to some degree. Determined to help Natalia, Major Carver got up with me in Moldova hoping that our newly formed children's fund would help.

We paid the airfare for a couple of reconstructive surgeons from Wake Forest University Medical Center to travel to Moldova, and they released her locked eyelids. When the bandages were removed, Natalia was able to close her eyes for the first time in fourteen years. Along the way, Moldovan surgeons transplanted her two big toes, attaching them to the stubs of her hands, giving

Natalia the equivalent of thumbs with which to clinch objects. One toe transfer was barely successful and is not very functional, but the other works quite well as a thumb.

Do you stay in contact with Natalia and follow her progress?

Absolutely. Natalia deserves any good thing that comes her way, not just because of the horrors she has endured, but for the kind of person she has become. Asked once what she would like for Christmas, she replied that she had everything she needed. When pressed to be less modest, she relented and asked for a doctor's help; not for herself, but for her sister who had a problem with her eyes. Can you imagine a desperately poor fifteen-year-old having one wish and all she could think about was helping her sister?

A few years after Natalia's eyelid release procedure, MWCF flew her to the United States for six months of donated surgery. Along with the generosity of Pitt County Memorial Hospital in Greenville, NC, Dr. Richard Zeri improved the closing of her eyes. Doctor Jasper Lewis and his son, both pediatric dentists, performed extensive dental work through the taut, narrow-opening of Natalia's mouth. The two joints at the tip of all of Natalia's fingers had been burned off, while the remaining joint of each finger closest to the palm on both hands had fused together from the extreme heat. Admittedly, the damage to her left hand remains beyond repair. On the right hand, Dr. Zeri separated joints where possible, giving her three half fingers to use with a transferred big toe to grasp things.

Natalia is home in Moldova now, attending vocational college and learning to be a tailor. A seamstress, can you believe it? We have given her a personal sewing machine that is equipped with large dials and controls which are easier for her to handle. She is getting quite good at crochet. This child, who is overcoming so much, is an inspiration to her fellow students, the school's faculty, everyone. She is working hard to help herself and to provide her own support for the rest of her life, a self-made craftsman despite unbelievable obstacles.

After all you've been through, what are your feelings toward Natalia and other children like her?

I am extremely proud of Natalia. I want nothing but the best for her; she is such a sweet girl and doesn't seem to be sour about anything. It pleases me that she is grateful and has worked to maximize the investment others have made in her. The burden carried by every brutalized child is different from all others. A hurting child is a hurting child, wherever they may be.

> From the *Rime of the Ancient Mariner*;
> *He prayeth best, who loveth best*
> *All things both great and small;*
> *For the dear God who loveth us,*
> *He made and loveth all.*

When you become involved in tragedy, when you experience it up close, you are driven forward to help when you don't think that you could possibly have time. You find energy when your body is telling you to slow down. You refocus and go out and recruit others to assist and find new donor gifts when the economy suggests there is nowhere to turn. It seems that for many people, nobody of any significance exists, other than themselves and their own families; and for them the world ends at the county line. There are many of us who have never had to seriously worry about our own physical and financial security. We have been relatively healthy and have had our freedom handed to us by others. In many ways we are spoiled and naïve. We have never been really hungry or thirsty, and never have had to truly fear for our lives. Reaching out to someone like Natalia is first and foremost a blessed opportunity, a chance to turn tears into smiles, a challenge well worth every minute, every penny, every long airline flight, every risk, every bead of sweat.

- **Thirty visits—**

So you have continued your commitment to the children of Moldova.

My whole involvement in Moldova has been a work in progress. I was told my first trip would be the only one necessary, then a second trip was needed, then a third trip would surely be my last. To date, I've traveled to Moldova thirty times. The average stay the first few years was two and a half weeks. Then it moved to six weeks at a shot, two or three times a year. Let's see, thirty visits, an average of four weeks each, plus or minus some each trip; that's about 120 weeks. So we're moving toward three years of actual time over there.

But the value of the time spent there is the main thing. The most gratifying part of the Moldovan experience is that kids are being helped. The initial project of helping the Fortunas did not take all that much time. The Fortuna home was completed in short order. However, when we arrived at the children's hospital in the southern town of Ceadyr-Lunga with $120,000 of EUCOM humanitarian assistance to repair a big roof, we found the entire facility totally gutted; no running water, no electricity, no functioning sewage system, no heat. General consensus was that the situation there was hopeless and at best it would take years, not weeks to complete.

The venture ended up costing about a million dollars. Back then you could get an awful lot of construction work done in Moldova for a small amount of money. Today it is a functioning 120-bed hospital. This second ordeal grew into a huge investment of time, money, and energy and was a formative time that served as preparation for eventually finishing a similar project this year, another TB center, but in the country's far north.

- **Prison-Bred TB—**

What was the tuberculosis situation in Moldova?

Over the years, the Communists put an awful lot of innocent folk in prison, and that alone killed a lot of their own people. Prisons are cold, damp, moldy places, definitely breeding ground for tuberculosis.

Two major drugs are used around the world to effectively treat TB, and not all that expensive. Still the money simply ran out and many inmates being treated did not get complete doses. With the supply of needed drugs exhausted, hybrid strains of tuberculosis evolved which are immune to standard treatment.

When the Soviet Union collapsed there was no money to keep the many prisons operating, so inmates were simply released. Former prisoners are often not welcomed home, or so they fear, and they scatter instead. These ex-inmates carried drug-immune forms of tuberculosis to the far reaches of the former Soviet Union, which is a big part of the globe.

When a husband and wife both have to work the fields every day, they don't have the luxury of going into a TB sanatorium for eight months of closely monitored treatment. To do so would cut into plowing, planting, tilling, harvesting, and everything else they do. And if they carry tuberculosis into their small homes, their children become exposed. Frequently what we find in Moldova are safe-haven facilities for children so their parents can continue to work the fields and not expose them to TB.

Tell me about the hospital you built.

The hospital is a pretty big facility that has evolved as the TB epidemic has lessened. It is now the Moldova National Children's Rehabilitation Hospital. It serves children from all over the country. By Moldovan standards it's construction and current state of repair is state-of-the-art. The rebuilt facility soon attracted other foreign supporters. A number of countries saw that the facility was now a worthy platform for donating equipment to, and a good supporting venue for doctors and other medical people to visit on humanitarian assistance trips. The facility's director came up with the splendid idea to open it up for adults as well, but on a paying basis. That helped considerably because the Moldovan government had no money to keep it up and running.

I met a policeman there who had been severely crippled in a work accident and was completing nine months of rehabilitation. He was one happy camper, overflowing with praise for the effective treatment he had received. Foreign children with more affluent parents and paying adults from Moldova and abroad are charged enough for therapy to cover the operating expenses for the hundreds of Moldovan children who receive care at no charge.

- **No money for new projects—**

A couple of years ago, Albert Gooch, the rest of our Board and I found ourselves yet again in a typical situation where Moldova World Children's Fund had spent every dime it had raised for the tasks at hand. With a crippling downturn of the economy and little money on the horizon for new projects, it was concluded that it was time to scale back the budget.

It was then, with no money in our bank account, when a friend, John Maxemchuk, CEO of Sun Communications and founder of the Moldovan-American Chamber of Commerce, called to say he had spoken with the United States Ambassador to Moldova and his wife, Asif and Charla Chaudhry. Charla, president of the International Women's Club in Moldova, and several other ambassadors' wives had visited the Tirnova Children's Tuberculosis Center and School in the north, were horrified at the conditions at the facility, and felt they had to do something. So, they committed almost all of their organization's funds to help the children there.

Charla forwarded to me a stirring report and photographs that were absolutely awful. They showed children living at latitude equal to that of southern Canada trying to recuperate from TB. The youngsters where having to walk 100 yards in ice and snow out of their dormitories that had no showers to a Gestapo-looking windowless and unheated shower building. There they undressed in a freezing changing room to take cold showers because there was no hot water. Then they would get dressed again in the cold, and with wet hair, trek back to their poorly heated dormitories. And there was the chilling matter of outdoor latrines.

Charla turned her determination to help the children at Tirnova into an obsession. She was passionate and spread the word to whoever would listen. Ignoring my pleas to the contrary, she appointed me to manage the collaborative efforts of a growing list of international players interested in lending a hand. With her husband's enthusiastic consent, Charla opened up the Ambassadorial residence and their dining room table as a meeting place for renovation team coordination. Ambassador Chaudhry kicked in a hundred percent of his, for a lack of a better term, discretionary fund, two years running. He was allotted only $12,000 a year in this account; but all was available for humanitarian relief.

How many children were housed at this facility, at any one time?

The Tirnova center was built for 400, but only about 185 were there at the time. I asked a Moldovan architect friend of ours to go there, and he did in late December 2009, driving with his son for hours through the deep snow. They took a lot of pictures and studied the situation, reporting that what they had seen was just unbelievable. He said that the cost of fixing up the dormitories would probably be out of our reach, and that redoing the commercial laundry building might be a more practical place to start; but it alone might cost $180,000. We now only had a grand total of $39,000 to work with, $10,000 from the International Women's Club-Moldova, the Ambassador's $24,000 from the Department of State, and another $5,000 commitment from John Maxemchuk. MWCF had no other unspoken for money in its budget, so I just put everything off until my visit in the spring of 2010, and saw the awful conditions first hand.

Albert Gooch has been Chairman of Moldova World Children's Fund, Inc. ever since it spun off from Kanuga in 2005. With his prodding, again, he said this was an opportunity beyond measure, and one which was right down our alley. We presented the challenge to the MWCF Board. New members Janet Miller of Victoria, Texas and Nancy Duvall, along with her Episcopal Bishop husband Charles, packed their bags and headed off to join Albert and me in Moldova. Our visit to Tirnova was alarming, we found the conditions appalling, the prospects of funding refurbishment daunting. Nevertheless, everyone felt we had to do something; just didn't know where the money would come from. Our group was called to proceed on faith, bringing to mind a Bruce Wilkinson published inspirational "The Prayer of Jabez". For sure there was hope aplenty, but only a glimmer of light emanating from the end of the tunnel.

At around that time Ambassador Chaudhry talked with the ranking admiral at U.S. European Command who at the time was holding a humanitarian assistance conference in Chisinau. The annual event is held in different countries on a rotating basis, and they were meeting, by sheer coincidence, in Moldova while I was there. The conference head invited me to attend.

Again the universe was working for you.

For sure. Ambassador Chaudhry encouraged the Admiral to have his people take a look at the facility, and I ended up escorting a team of Army, Navy, Air force and civilian DOD folks to Tirnova. I am not an architect, engineer, or physician, but at least had been to the facility the week before.

As it turned out, U.S. European Command chipped in around $450,000 to help with the renovation of the facility. I discovered that Sweden was in the process of investing between $700,000-to-$800,000 in the central-heating and hot-water. But the center wouldn't be able to afford operating the new systems because the roofs were in terrible condition and much of the heat would go right out the top. Added to this were problems of dozens of broken windows, rotting window seals, and doors that no longer fit worn out frames.

How old was the facility?

It was about sixty years old, Soviet construction not meant to last, and definitely not maintained. The international Church of Latter Day Saints, LDS Charities, offered $20,000 to rebuild the fresh-water system. Things were beginning to look up. Then I put together a meeting of all of the people who had expressed any interest in the renovation of the facility. Unlike most of the other players who were permanently stationed in Moldova, I was in-country for never more than fifteen weeks in any given year. Nevertheless, I had agreed to coordinate things, comforted by the reminder that I had done this sort of thing before. But when we got a proposal for the fresh water supply system, instead of $20,000, it was going to cost $60,000, a huge jump.

- **Needed money comes in—**

The Mormon officials talked to their European bosses in Germany, and LDS Charities upped their commitment to cover the higher $60,000 figure for the clean water. Albert put together a package with the Hendersonville Rotary Club and the Western North Carolina Rotary District to get a matching grant from Rotary International. All together Rotary contributed another $60,000. We recruited as project partners a Rotary club in Iasi, Romania and the Rotary District of Romania and Moldova. The group of donors was growing at a good pace, and the next thing we knew MWCF was itself committed for another $100,000, which we didn't have. The heating and hot-water systems were done, and then MWCF and the International Women's Club of Moldova put in shower rooms on each floor of both dormitories.

MWCF arranged a project ceremony in May of 2011 at the partially finished property. Much of the work, in particular the large Swedish piece, had been completed. Some of the people participating in the effort were nearing the end of their assigned stays in Moldova and I felt they needed to be recognized before their departure. Four principals keynoted the event: Moldova's Prime Minister Vald Filat, U.S. Ambassador Chaudhry, the head of LDS Charities from Germany, and Albert Gooch, representative of Rotary and MWCF. I spoke on behalf of the absent Swedes and Irina Rusanovschi, our representative in Moldova, ran the show with the center's director and staff. My longtime friend Dorin Trestianu translated the endless speeches.

After a delightful program presented by the children resident at the center, I gathered together participants of the major sponsors for a property tour, knowing full well that we had a sewage problem. A treatment plant was sorely needed as raw sewage was seeping out of the ground at the center's edge and flowing into the neighboring fields. LDS Charities were so moved, that they chipped in yet another $ 65,000 to complete things. The projects the Department of Defense committed to were in the first stages of being completed; new roofs, windows, doors, indoor toilet facilities, a laundry and pharmacy building. Frugal management of the project's funding allowed DOD to insulate and finish the exterior walls of both dormitories.

How would you characterize MWCF and your role as project manager?

Moldova World Children's Fund became the engine for putting together the diverse collaborative efforts and added a number of missing links. But it's important to note that when we got started, the Swedish International Development Cooperation Agency (SIDA) had already committed to it.

SIDA's investment was roughly half the cost of total renovation of the facility. But the center could not take advantage of the Swedish investment if the facility and the buildings could not hold the heat, and there were no shower rooms in the dormitories for the children to use the hot water. The Swedes did their part. All the rest of us took it to the next level. In June 2011, U.S. Secretary of State Hillary Clinton recognizing the work at the Tirnova Children's Center presented Charla with the Department's global humanitarian project award of the year.

Someday I'd like to see the fruits of your labor and dedication.

A couple who had wanted to accompany me for years ended up going in 2011 on their own. Moldovan colleagues showed them around the region. My friends are already planning a return trip. All members of the MWCF Board of Directors are expected to visit Moldova at least once at their own expense.

We normally have a small team going over twice a year, once in the spring and again in the fall. You are definitely welcome and encouraged to join us any time.

Severe burn victim Natalia Bolea had surgery to allow her to close her eyes for the first time in fourteen years.

Ensign West at his 1972 commissioning from U.S. Naval Officer Candidate School, Newport, R.I.

Driving a guided missile destroyer.

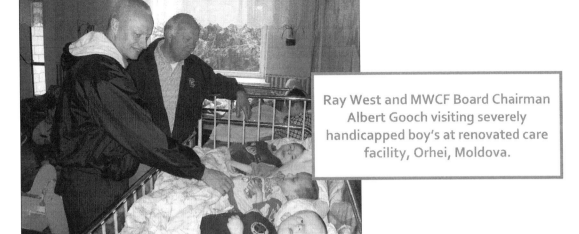

Ray West and MWCF Board Chairman Albert Gooch visiting severely handicapped boy's at renovated care facility, Orhei, Moldova.

Captain West congratulates his son Bryan at commissioning; Officer Candidate School, Pensacola, Florida.

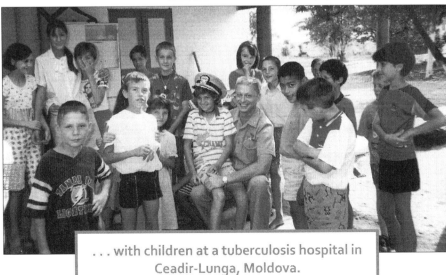

. . . with children at a tuberculosis hospital in Ceadir-Lunga, Moldova.

Newly constructed children's hospital in Ceadir-Lunga, Moldova.

Ray West as a novice preparing for a deep-sea dive off the Florida Keys.

Captain Ray West, wife Mia and sons Bryan and Andrew.

Section 5: Oaths of Office by Father and Son

- **Oath of Office—**

Following is the Oath of Office sworn four decades ago by Surface Warfare Officer to be Ray F. West, Jr. at his commissioning from Naval Officer Candidate School (OCS) in Newport, RI. Then in 2007, five years after his retirement from the Navy, Captain West was honored to be the field parade reviewing officer and guest speaker for another graduation ceremony, this one involving the commissioning of his eldest son at OCS in Pensacola, Florida. The *Hendersonville Times-News* reported CAPT West as saying that the personal swearing in of his son Bryan as a Naval Flight Officer was the proudest moment of his Naval career.

The Oath: *Having been appointed an Ensign in the United States Navy, I do accept such an appointment and do solemnly swear that I will support and defend the Constitution of the United States of America against all enemies, foreign and domestic; that I will bear true faith and allegiance to the same; that I take this obligation freely, without any mental purpose of evasion; and I will well and faithfully discharge the duties of office on which I am about to enter, so help me God.*

- **Anchors Aweigh—**
  Composed by Charles A. Zimmerman and original lyrics by Alfred Hart Miles

> *Anchors Aweigh, my boys, Anchors Aweigh.*
> *Farewell to foreign shores, We sail at break of day–ay–ay–ay.*
> *Through our last night on shore, Drink to the foam,*
> *Until we meet once more. Here's wishing you a happy voyage home!*

- **Eternal Father, Strong to Save: The Navy Hymn—**
  Original Lyrics by William Whiting and Music by John B. Dyke

> *Eternal Father, strong to save, Whose arm hath bound the restless wave,*
> *Who bidd'st the mighty ocean deep Its own appointed limits keep.*
> *O hear us when we cry to Thee, For those in peril on the sea!*

> *Lord, guard and guide all them who fly And those who on the ocean ply;*
> *Be with our troops upon the land And all who for their country stand:*
> *Be with these guardians day and night Do keep them ever in Thy sight.*

> *O Gracious God of love and power! Our brethren shield in danger's hour;*
> *From rock and tempest, fire, and foe, Protect them whereso'er they go.*
> *Thus fore'ermore shall rise to Thee, Glad praise from air, and land, and sea.*

> *God, who dost still the restless foam, Protect the ones we love at home.*
> *Provide that they should always be By Thine own grace both safe and free.*
> *O Father, hear us when we pray For those we love so far away.*

> *Amen.*

Section 6: **Chronology**

- **Personal—**
- Born: Ray F. West, Jr. Dec, 22, 1950, Asheville, North Carolina
- Parents: Ray Ferris West and Evelyn Frances Kennard West
- Sisters: Sarah Marjorie West Powell, Lillian Reeves West Alverson
- Married: to the former Kyungmi "Mia" Chang of Chinhae, Republic of Korea
- Children: Bryan Chang West, born July 5, 1983; Andrew Chang West, Aug. 28, 1986

- **Education—**
- St. Joan of Arc School, Catholic Kindergarten and First Grade, Asheville
- Aycock Elementary, Second through Sixth Grades
- Hall Fletcher Junior High School, Seventh through Ninth Grades
- Lee H. Edwards High School, graduating class of 1968
- University of North Carolina at Asheville, graduating class of 1972
- Degree: B.A. in Social Science, with an Economics concentration
- Oxford University, Oxford, England, summer of 1970, studies in Philosophy
- Postgraduate studies in Computer Programing, Western Carolina University

- **Military—**
- Enlisted in the Navy as a Seaman Recruit (E-1) 20 Aug 1968
- Commissioned Ensign (O-1), Naval Officer Candidate School, Newport, RI, Nov. 1972
- Active Duty with Allied Naval Forces, Korea, Nov 1972-Jan 1974
- Active Duty aboard submarine rescue ship USS Kittiwake (ASR-13), Jan 1974-Nov 1975
- Naval Reserve Assignments 1968-2002, including four as commanding officer

- **Civilian Employment—**
- Morris Funeral Home, Asheville, 1968-1972; Night and Weekend Manager
- Scottish Inns of America, NC and TN, Nov 1975-Jan 1977; General Manager
- Kanuga Conferences, Inc., Hendersonville, NC, 1977-2005; Vice President for Administration
- Moldova World Children's Fund, Inc., NC and Republic of Moldova, 2005-Present; President

- **Awards / Qualifications / Elected Positions—**
- Secretary, Senior Class, University of North Carolina-Asheville
- President, Huns athletic fraternity, UNC-A
- Surface Warfare Officer, U.S. Navy
- Pistol and Rifle Expert, U.S. Navy
- Meritorious Service Medal, U.S. Navy
- Commanding Officer of Readiness Command's Best Unit Afloat, FY-86, on USS William V. Pratt (DDG-44)
- Black Belt, 1st Dan degree, Kukkiwon, Tae Kwon Do, Chung Do Kwan
- President, Lions Club, Hendersonville, NC, 1995-1996
- Lions Club's International Foundation Melvin Jones Fellowship for Humanitarian Assistance
- Lions International President's Everyday Hero Award, 2009
- Rotary International Paul Harris Fellow, 2012
- President, International Association of Conference Center Administrators South East 1985-1987
- Roy A. Taylor Distinguished Alumnus Award, University of North Carolina-Asheville, 2006
- Graduation Parade Reviewing Officer and Commissioning Ceremony Guest Speaker, Officer Candidate School Class 13-07, Naval Air Station, Pensacola

Judge Harry C. Martin

Former North Carolina and Cherokee Supreme Court Justice

*Justice Harry C. Martin was
'the conscience of the court'
for ten years, from 1982-1992.*
— North Carolina Supreme Court Chief Justice James B. Exum, Jr.

Sections about Judge Harry C. Martin:

1) Son Matthew and Chief Justice Exum About Judge Martin

2) Harry Martin's 64-year Law Career Remembered

3) **The Judge's Life Journey, in His Own Words**

4) Photos

5) Significant Highlights Involving Justice Martin

6) Chronology

Section 1: **Testimonials About Justice Martin**

- **Privileged to spend time with father and fellow lawyer—**

It is difficult to quantify my father, Judge Harry C. Martin. I am privileged to have spent a great deal of fun time with him as a lawyer and fellow Judge over the last two decades, so we relate as colleagues as well as parent and child. He is a man who loves being in the bosom of his family, but sometimes seems most at home in a black robe.

He views the world with an almost 'Einsteinian' childlike quality, but, can also make an extremely quick and cold political calculation. His knowledge of the law, even at age 92, is encyclopedic. His body of work is groundbreaking. Either he or Judge Stanley Peele has served longer than any other current Judge within the geographical confines of North Carolina as of the moment.

He has taken great pleasure in teaching law students, and in helping young people become admitted to and navigate law school. Because of this, his friendships span many generations from those in 'the greatest generation' down to the 'millennials'.
   — **J. Matthew Martin, Esq., son.**

- **Former Chief Justice Exum about his Fellow Judge and Friend—**

James G. 'Jim' Exum, Jr., who served as an Associate Justice (1974-1986) and Chief Justice (1986-1996) of the North Carolina Supreme Court and is a law teacher at Elon University, spoke about his colleague on the court and friend, Associate Justice Harry C. Martin, at his portrait unveiling in 2000. After Justice Martin's grand-daughter Clarke unveiled his official portrait Justice Exum said:

The North Carolina Constitution occupied a special place in Justice Martin's legal universe, and he understood its primary role in protecting individual rights and liberties. Justice Martin's remarkably productive life began in the horse and buggy days of the early part of the twentieth century and continues with considerable vigor into the space and cyberspace age of the twenty-first century . . . Judge Martin had his own brand of mountain humor and sagacity, spoke with the calm voice of reason, and his colleagues usually listened and were guided accordingly.

- **A case about dogs cited with fact and whimsy—**

The former Chief Justice went on to cite with fact and whimsy a case that involved his fellow jurist:

As a member of the Court of Appeals from 1978-to-1982, appointed by Governor Jim Hunt, Judge Martin's wit did not desert him. In State v. Wallace, the defendant was accused of violating a statute prohibiting hunting deer with dogs. The Court did not reach the constitutional issue, concluding the case should be dismissed because the charge failed to adequately allege a crime.

Judge Martin, author of the panel's opinion, wrote eloquently on the social and legal history of the dog: 'This is a case about dogs. As dogs do not often appear in the courts, it is perhaps not inappropriate to write a few words about them'. Judge Hedrick noted his 'opposition to using the Court of Appeals Reports to publish my colleague's totally irrelevant, however learned, dissertation on dogs'.

(Capsules of significant Supreme Court cases and opinions involving Judge Martin are in Section 5.)

Section 2: Judge Harry Martin's 64 Year Law Career

- ## Began Practice of Law in 1948—

Harry C. Martin began a solo law practice in Asheville in 1948. Then he was a partner in Gudger, Elmore & Martin until 1962 when he was appointed to the Superior Court by Governor Terry Sanford. He was reappointed by Governor Dan Moore and then elected by the people. His unprecedented sixty-four-year career as lawyer, judge and educator in North Carolina includes service as Associate Justice of the Supreme Court from 1982-1992, as Supreme Court Justice for the Eastern Band of Cherokee Nations from 2000-2006, as Chief Mediator for the Fourth U.S. Circuit of Appeals from 1994-1999, as Judge in the North Carolina Superior Court in Buncombe County from 1962-1978, and as Judge of the North Carolina Court of Appeals from 1978-1982.

- ## The 'Conscience of the Court'—

Judge Martin became known as the 'Conscience of the Court' due to multiple significant opinions that included *Corum v. UNC* and *State v. Carter*. He unsuccessfully sued to overturn North Carolina's mandatory retirement law that forced him to retire from the North Carolina Supreme Court despite a decade of service. He has stated that he would still be on the court if he had won the case.

He also was well known for several dissents in Workers Comp. cases that later became law. As a lawyer, he primarily represented human beings rather than corporations. Notably, Harry Martin and fellow attorney Bruce Elmore succeeded in obtaining an acquittal for defendant Dorothy Mae Gosnell on first-degree murder charges in Madison County, and along with son Matthew of Martin & Martin, P.A. and John D. Loftin, winning a case in Orange County that resulted in a $2.75 million award to their client, a little girl molested by her neighbor. It was the largest civil award in the history of Orange County.

- ## Harry Martin, innovator—

Harry Martin became known as an innovator who invented and implemented the 'Firecracker' a one-day, one-case jury system that is still used in Buncombe County and other Districts. As Chief Circuit Mediator of the United States Court of Appeals for the Fourth Circuit, he designed and implemented the Appellate Mediation Program. He was an early advocate of using computers to compile and organize Judicial Branch data.

- ## Supervised creation of Cherokee Tribal Court—

Judge Martin became Chief Justice of the Supreme Court of the Eastern Band of Cherokee Indians, and supervised creation of the Tribal Court System on the Qualla Indian Boundary in Western North Carolina. The Cherokee Court is now a leader among Indian Nations, and is the Tribal Court that has the most jurisdictions within Indian Country.

- ## Made an 'Honorary Cherokee'—

In 2007 Harry C. Martin was made an Honorary Member of the Eastern Band of Cherokee Indians. He is now a Temporary Judge for the Cherokee Court, after being recalled from retirement by the Eastern Band and sitting by designation by the Chief Justice.

- ## Continuing as an attorney and educator—

The nonagenarian Biltmore Forest resident continues his career as a practicing attorney, as Temporary Judge for the Cherokee Court, as an adjunct law professor at the UNC School of Law, and at Elon University School of Law as a lecturer at continuing legal education seminars.

- **Service by appointments—**

Judge Martin has a long and distinguished record of service to organizations that include being: a delegate to the National Conference of State Trial Judges for 1966-to-1972; Vice President of the North Carolina Bar Association; President of the North Carolina Conference of Superior Court Judges from 1972 -1973; and Founder and Chair of the North Carolina Judges Bench Book Committee from 1977-1995.

He also was on Governor's Brown Lung Study Committee in 1979, the North Carolina Fair Sentencing Procedures Committee as Chairman in 1980, the Governor's Commission on Appellate Court Facilities in 1984, the North Carolina State Judicial Center Commission as Chairman from 1985 -1987, and the North Carolina State Bar, Client Security Fund, Chair from 1996-1998.

- **Keeping busy and fit—**

Now the judge also keeps busy and fit by jogging or walking a mile-and-a-half and working out most days, playing bridge, enjoying the thirty-seven member Pen & Plate Club meetings that have been continuous since 1904, and singing when the mood strikes him with a voice that Colby Dunn described in the a 2011 *Smokey Mountain News* as 'mid-tenor with a slight Southern lilt'.

- **Honors continue to Flow—**

Honors continue to flow to venerable Judge Harry C. Martin. As recently as 2011, he received the North Carolina Bar Association's John McMillan Distinguished Service Award, and in 2010 was honored with the University of North Carolina's Distinguished Alumni Award. He had received Harvard University's Traphagen Distinguished Alumna Award in 2006. The UNC award was presented on October 12 of 2010 when the judge participated in the University Day Commemoration of the Laying of the Cornerstone of Old East on that same date in 1793.

- *The Liberty Bell Award—*

On Law Day, May 21 of 2010, the judge was awarded the Liberty Bell from the NC Bar Association Young Lawyers 'in recognition of an individual who has strengthened the American System of Freedom under law'. Presenting the award was his son, Judge Matthew Martin of the Cherokee Tribal Court, and Cindy Hanson Holman, who serves on the executive committee of the 28th Judicial District Bar which nominated him.

A May 21st article about Judge Martin contained a slice of his sense-of-humor: *For everyone else, it was Law Day. For Harry Martin, it was homecoming. The former justice slipped into the courtroom as if slipping into the kitchen for a late-night snack. Linda Stephens of the N.C. Court of Appeals acknowledged his presence. Chief Justice Sarah Parker welcomed Martin back to the place where he devoted ten years of his remarkable career.*

"Governor Hunt made the same mistake twice," Martin quipped, *"first when he appointed me to the Court of Appeals, second when he appointed me to the Supreme Court."*

- *The John J. Parker Award—*

In 2001 when the Hon. Harry Martin became the sixth recipient of the Liberty Bell, he joined a select group that had won that honor and the NCBA's John J. Parker Award, all fellow jurists during their careers: Sam Ervin Jr., Susie Sharp, Joseph Branch, Frank Dupree, Jr. and J. Dickson Phillips, Jr.

- *Order of the Long Leaf Pine—*

In 2000, Governor James B. Hunt awarded Judge Martin the Order of the Long Leaf Pine, one of the state's top awards given to a citizen.

- ### *A National Award—*

In 2007, Judge Martin was awarded the American Bar Association Judicial Division's Franklin N. Flaschner Award as the Nation's Outstanding Specialized Court Judge.

- ### Offices Held—

Among the numerous offices held by Harry Martin were President of the North Carolina Conference of Superior Court Judges and Vice President of the North Carolina Bar Association in 1973. He founded and chaired the NC Judges Bench Book Committee (1977-1995), and was on the Governor's Brown Lung Study Committee in 1979.

- ### Honor of Playing for FDR—

In 1937 when Harry Martin was seventeen and playing the trombone and baritone horn for Lenoir High School under Band Leader James Harper, an independently wealthy volunteer, the band had the honor of performing in front of President Franklin Delano Roosevelt. The teenaged Martin went on to win a music scholarship to Davidson College and the University of North Carolina at Chapel Hill, which he chose and graduated from with an AB in 1942. He later earned an LLB at Harvard Law School in 1948, and an LLM at the University of Virginia Law School in 1982.

- ### Serving in World War II—

After graduating from UNC, this brave member of 'The Greatest Generation' was a combat photographer in World War II from 1942-through-1945, serving in the 13th Jungle Air Force that saw action in Guadalcanal, the Solomon Islands and Saipan.

Harry C. Martin, 92, gets a hug from wife Nancy on May 10, 2012, after the NC Department of Transportation named the bridge on I-26 that spans Long Shoals Road in Bucombe County the "Justice Harry C. Martin Bridge." Judge Robert Collier (l), Chairman of the Board of the NC DOT, spoke about his friend and colleague's six-plus decades of practicing law to the Martin family and area officials at UNC-Asheville. Judge Martin thanked the women and men who served with and for him then concluded: "The State has done more for me than I have done for the State, and I'm proud to be a Tar Heel!"
Photo courtesy of NC DOT

Section 3: The Judge's Life Journey, in His Own Words

Could the elderly but fit gentleman in the jogging suit scurrying up the tree-lined driveway of this ranch home in Biltmore Forest really be nonagenarian former North Carolina and Cherokee Supreme Court Justice Harry C. Martin? Yes. Friendly, courteous, witty, the man who spent sixty-four years in a remarkable law career announced he was ready to share his life journey, and so we began our first interview in the comfort of his living room:

- **Family reflections—**

Where did you grow up, Judge?

I was born in Caldwell County in North Carolina at two p.m. on January 13 of 1920 in my grandmother's house, which is still standing and occupied but no longer in our family.

They told me that my three-year-old sister wanted to stay for the birthing but they wanted her out of the house. Bear in mind this was in January, so my grandfather packed a picnic lunch, got his horse 'Old Dixie' from the barn and hitched her up then put a blanket over my sister and they went off someplace. When they came back that afternoon there I was.

I remember hearing about Old Dixie, but I don't ever remember seeing that horse.

I had an older brother who was at the other grandmother's house at the time, so I was the third child. Then there was another boy and a fifth child, a girl who died when she was only five-years-old. Then they had another daughter. The only ones still living are me and the sixth child, Lida, who lives here in Asheville and is married to a lawyer. My father was Hal Martin, and I was named for my grandfather, Harry C. Martin. My daddy was a newspaper person and worked in Charlotte, Gastonia and Lenoir.

Please share some lore about the Martin family roots.

Philetus Augustus Martin was one of several Martins that came over in the early 1700s to Virginia, then went down to Wilkes County, and were active in the Revolutionary War. Philetus got into a fuss with another boy over a girl and killed him then was arrested for manslaughter and served a year and a day in prison. He was only seventeen-years-old when he got out.

Philetus' brother came to Asheville to practice law. In those days he was known as GTT, 'Gone to Texas', because he went to Fort Worth and got a job as a sheep-herder for the owner of a farm, a lawyer who took an interest in him. Back then you just read the law and studied under a lawyer, so he did that and passed the Bar exam and became a lawyer, a judge, and then a Supreme Court Justice. When he died, not one word was written about him killing that boy back in North Carolina, because in Texas, everything was forgiven. I still have a bunch of cousins in Texas who are lawyers.

How many members of your family have been or are lawyers and judges?

Well, not very many. Philetus' son is a lawyer, my brother was a lawyer with two children that are lawyers, and my two sons are lawyers. So, counting me, that makes eight. Philetus, my son Matthew and I make three judges in the family.

Tell me about your school years, and about deciding to study law.

I went to high school in Lenoir. My grandparents had a place in Blowing Rock, about nineteen miles from Lenoir. I went to the Lenoir Courthouse once in a while, but I didn't really make up my mind to study law until I got in college at the University of North Carolina in Chapel Hill.

- **Special memories—**

At Lenoir High School we were fortunate to have James Harper, who was independently wealthy and didn't have to teach to make a living, but who did teach music and was the band director. Almost everybody played in the band. I studied and played the trombone and the baritone horn, I still have the mouth piece I used, and was offered music scholarships by Davidson College near Charlotte and UNC.

Are there other special memories you recall from those years?

In addition to playing in the school band, we played in a local dance band for a guy named Stubby because he was only five-feet tall. The Stubby Taylor band played at dances in the area, especially during the summer, and at the two hotels in Blowing Rock, the Green Park Inn that is still there, and Mayview Manor, which was torn down. Saturday night was a big deal and we got paid five or six dollars, which was a lot of money in those days, or so it seemed to us.

From the time I was twelve-years-old until I was twenty-two, music earned me a lot of money.

And the scholarships I was offered by Davidson and UNC were for music, so it was really helpful to me until I graduated in 1942.

- **A Fork in the Road—**

What do you remember about leaving Lenoir and heading off to college?

I have a little vignette about when I left home: I was hitch-hiking to go to Davidson and UNC to decide which one I wanted to attend, carrying a suitcase with a North Carolina sticker on the side. Before you could get to the big highways you had to go through every little town, and in Statesville the road forked east to Chapel Hill and South to Davidson.

As I was walking across the street to look at directional signs in Statesville, a car with two or three boys inside pulled up and they hollered toward me, "Are you going to Chapel Hill?" I said "Yeah" and got in.

Then and there I made the decision I was going to go to UNC at Chapel Hill, not Davidson.

Life is a game of inches sometimes, isn't it?

Yes.

What were your first impressions of UNC?

I had been down there every fall with the high school band to play at University of Virginia against North Carolina football games. We were the band for the visiting team every other year.

When I got to Chapel Hill I think I had forty-six dollars in my pocket and a tuition grant, so I went to see what we called the Self-Help Officer, a fine man who got me jobs. I worked in the cafeteria, the library, cut grass, stuff like that, and was able to get along. I went to UNC year-round, including summers.

How were your grades?

Well, I was not the top student in high school; there were two or three others that made better grades. But in college I made very good grades in political science and courses of that sort, but not in mathematics.

I remember in my last semester telling the professor that I needed to graduate because we were going to get into WWII. I had gotten a six-month deferment from the draft so I could finish college. The professor said, "Don't worry, you are going to graduate." I don't know if he just decided to pass me or what, but it turned out all right.

The war was on and the boys were volunteering. One friend who left school in October gave his dog to me, and we lived together above the university laundry where I got my room and laundry done for free. And they paid me two dollars a month on top of that.

I graduated with an AB Degree, with majors in Political Science and History because I thought I was going to go to law school one day. My mother and daddy came to graduation because I told them I would not be going home because I was going right into the service.

• Military Service—

And after you graduated from UNC?

I took the dog and went to Blowing Rock for a couple of days then volunteered for the Army Air Corps. I went overseas in December of that year until June of 1945 when I came home on a forty-five day leave.

I had been in combat situations for two-and-a-half years, in the Solomon Islands, Guadalcanal and Saipan.

At that time the Air Corps was not a separate unit like it is today. I was in a photography outfit, and about ten of us were selected to what they called 'detached service'. In other words, we were with the squadron occasionally but most of the time we were ahead of them doing different things.

Was that for reconnaissance photography?

Yes. The ten of us would take photographs, develop and print them then take them to the United States Navy officer in control of the South Pacific.

Just before the end of my leave in Blowing Rock was when the atomic bomb was dropped, and I thought, 'this war is over'. So, instead of going back overseas, I was ordered to Fort Bragg. But a lieutenant there said I was ordered back to Saipan.

As I was leaving a sergeant who had overheard everything told me to come back and see him at one o'clock. I went back, and he had gotten a new set of orders cut for me to go to Fort Bragg, signed by a major.

But after a fifteen-day leave I went to Fort Bragg and was told, "Your orders have changed; you are going to be discharged." So I went to Chapel Hill and just hung around for a day or two.

I had been admitted to Harvard Law School, and fortunately met a blind fellow who was also going there, and he asked me to ride along when his parents took him to Cambridge in October.

• Off to Harvard Law School—

I went to Law School year-round, graduated with an LLB in 1948, but when I came back home wasn't sure what I was going to do.

Philetus, the relative called 'GTT' I spoke about earlier, had a brother who was a lawyer for the United States Attorney General's office in Washington D.C., and I went there and asked for help in getting a job.

He said, "I could put you to work but you would be making a big mistake because in five years you wouldn't be making much money at all, and that won't increase very rapidly then suggested I go to Asheville and practice law, as he had practiced there for thirty years until the war began.

He said, "I've got a building there, and I'll give you my law books and furniture and everything."

In June of forty-eight, I opened up my own general practice law office in downtown Asheville in the Jackson Building, the old high-rise on Pack Square. I made fifteen dollars the first month and my rent was thirty, but then things picked up.

Was there much competition in those days?

Today there are about six-hundred lawyers in this county, but when I started in 1948 there were only about sixty. Two who were also starting to practice law after military service, Bruce Elmore and Lamar Gudger, and I formed a partnership. Bruce had been elected to the legislature while in law school and had an office in Raleigh, as did Lamar, so we rented an office for three, but I was the only one there.

- **Practicing Law, Becoming a Judge—**

How and when did you become a judge?

After eight years Lamar went with another firm. Bruce and I practiced until 1962 when I was appointed by Governor Terry Sanford to be a Special Judge. A Special Judge follows a schedule and knows what district he will be working in for three years, subject to assignment by the Chief Justice to any county in the state. I had met Terry as an undergraduate at UNC when he was in Law School and going with a girl in my class that I was friends with. He later married her.

The war came and I never saw or heard of Terry again until after it ended and he got into politics and decided to run for governor. He called me to ask for help in the west, as he was living and practicing law in Scotland County.

My wife Nancy and I were living off of Charlotte Street in Asheville, and Terry stayed with us for two or three days and we took him around the mountain counties and introduced him to the sheriffs and clerks and other key people. He won the election.

When my four-year appointment as Special Judge ended, Terry was no longer governor. In those days you could only serve one term.

On June 30th when my term ran out, I took the family to the beach for a week but paid someone to answer my phone. When I came home back I was told Governor Hunt had called.

I called back and the governor asked, "How was the beach?" I said, "It was very good, how may I serve you?" He said, "I want you to be the second Resident Judge in the Asheville District." The legislature had passed a statute for a second judge here, and I was appointed. That was in 1966.

How long were you a Resident Judge?

In 1978 Governor Jim Hunt appointed me to be a judge on the Court of Appeals, the intermediate Appellate Court. I traveled back-and-forth to Raleigh for a year or so, and then we moved there.

In the Governor's second term I thought I would get an appointment to the Supreme Court, but he gave it to another guy. Then he called and we chatted for a while before he announced, "I'm going to give you the next appointment on the Supreme Court."

- **The Supreme Court—**

Five months later there was a vacancy and Governor Hunt appointed me, and then I was elected. The North Carolina Constitution has a provision that nobody can be a judge after he is seventy-two-years-old, which I think is absolutely silly, so I was forced to retire.

If a judge becomes too old and gets to a place where he can't be a judge, there are ways to get him off the court without making him retire at seventy-two. I'd still be on the court if it didn't have that provision.

That sounds like age discrimination.

I brought a lawsuit to have that provision declared unconstitutional while I was still on the Supreme Court and Jim Exum was Chief Justice. When the case came on the docket I went out just like everybody else and sat on the bench, and Exum leaned over and whispered, "Are you going to sit on a case you brought?"

I said, "No, I just want to listen in."

They voted against me six-zip, but later on some of the justices said, "We made a great mistake."

Is the age restriction still in force?

Yes. If it wasn't I'd be running for court.

- **Family—**

Tell me how you met Nancy, and about your children.

Nancy is from Dallas but was living in Georgia when her first husband, who was in the military, was killed in an airplane crash.

On a Saturday night in November of 1954 our crowd went to see a program in the Civic Center in Asheville, and that's when I first met Nancy. I called the next day to ask if I could come by her house, she said yes, and it just kept going. Nancy's sister had married a Navy man from Asheville.

How long did you go together before you proposed?

I met her in November and we got married in April of 1955.

Did she say yes right away?

No, but said we could talk about it. I know she talked to her sister, I don't know who else, but I passed the test.

Nancy had a son John by her first marriage, who I later adopted, and we have another son, Matthew. Both sons are lawyers. And we have a daughter Mary, an architect, and one grand-daughter, Clarke.

- **Judicial Philosophy—**

Let's go back to your lengthy law career; tell me your judicial philosophy and how it evolved.

Well, I really don't know the answer to that question. I suppose people who look at my product would say that I was a liberal, whatever that means, rather than a conservative, whatever that means.

Judges can only eat the food that is on the plate given to them, they can't reach out and get another roll or banana or whatever; they've got to decide the case on what is before them.

A lot of this talk about conservative judges and liberal judges really doesn't mean anything, because somebody who thought women should have the right to vote would hear, "Well, he's a liberal." But as a judge, he could not give them the right to vote, that had to be done by the Legislature, or by the vote of the people as a whole.

So I think if a question came up of whether a legal fee was too large, for example, I would decide that after who would get the money: is it a poor person or is it a wealthy person, or is it a big corporation? And, who is going to pay it? Is it an insurance company, is there a business to pay it, or is it a poor person? I would consider all those things.

What about your judicial philosophy still resonates, and does it match your personal philosophy?

I always looked out for black people because they were picked on for so long.

I remember when I was a boy one of my very best friends was Vincent Dixon, a black guy about my age. He used to come to my house in the summer time every Monday and Tuesday because his grandmother, who raised him, came to our house to do the laundry. She would go to the back yard and build a fire under a big black pot full of water, then heat the water and put in sheets and stuff in that needed to be washed and punch it around with a stick.

I went to his house once or twice on the weekends but not a lot, because back in those days in Lenoir black people lived in the black area and the white people lived in the white area. We didn't think about why Vincent lives over there and we live over here; it just didn't enter our minds.

Did you and Vincent remain friends?

Oh yeah, but sadly he was killed in WWII.

Good enough to fight for our country but not good enough for equality.

Fortunately, things have changed since then.

You must have presided over some interesting cases.

Well, I was holding court down east and the defendant was a black guy charged with murder. We had been trying the case all week, and on Friday when I got back from lunch there were ashes scattered all over the bench and the judge's chair.

The bailiff who was with the defendant said, "I'll clean that up judge." I asked, "Why are those ashes there?" He answered, "There's a sect of black folks here that think there's something special about the ashes they put there."

I told the bailiff to leave the ashes right there, and that I'd go ahead and sentence the man, and that they would find out spreading ashes doesn't work. There was a sort of moaning in the audience, but they came to realize this was not the way to change things; you know, spreading ashes.

- **The Death Penalty—**

How many capital cases did you judge?

I sentenced six people to be executed in the gas chamber. That was not an easy thing for me or any judge to do, but the law back then sentenced you to be executed if you were convicted of murder in the first-degree.

It just so happened that the ones I sentenced to be executed were still in prison when the United States Supreme Court decided that method was unconstitutional, and everybody that had been sentenced to execution instead got life-imprisonment.

So, my six all died in prison, and that kind of made me feel better.

How do you feel about the death penalty now?

I think in some cases the death penalty is justified. Difficulties arise when prosecutors and judges are unable to differentiate those particular cases from others.

I'll give an example, a case down in Winston-Salem that I didn't try but presided over in post-verdict proceedings. I heard the lawyers representing the defendant claim that he should have a new trial.

The facts in the case were that this black guy, a forty-something-year-old family friend of a four-year-old black girl, took her to get an ice cream cone, as he had done before. She left her home pulling a little red wagon. On the way back the man took the child through a wooded section, raped and killed her, and placed the wagon over her body.

If anybody deserved the death penalty, he did. I didn't try or sentence him, but during the post-conviction hearing of three days all this testimony came out, and he never said he was sorry, or anything of that sort.

This killing was the worst, as most are done quickly and spontaneously, bang-bang and the victim is dead, and then the killer asks himself, "Did I really do this?"

• Thousands of Cases Tried —

How many total cases would you say you presided over in your career?

I really don't know exactly how many, but thousands. There were usually ten sessions of the Supreme Court each year, with three or four cases during each session. So, we had roughly thirty-five cases a year, and in my ten years that would be 350 opinions. The court had two months off in the summer, July and August.

Attorney Alan Dershowitz says that the court system and judges follow procedure and the law, but it is not about truth and justice. Can you explain that to a layman?

Truth and justice is the goal you try to reach, and you can attain it through the facts of the case and the law applicable to those facts. That is what gives you truth and justice.

Can you recall a Eureka moment or an epiphany when you were a judge?

I don't know that I ever had that feeling in those words, but while I was on the bench I was very satisfied. Some judges have told me that they didn't like being a judge, but I liked it so much that if court was going to start at nine-thirty, I'd be there at eight-thirty to talk to people.

I had the feeling, probably wrong, that I could decide cases better than anybody else. But when you get reversed by the Supreme Court, you find out you didn't have all the ability you thought.

Who were your heroes in law and who inspired you?

I thought Supreme Court Justice Oliver Wendell Holmes was a great guy, and that Justice William Brennan was a good guy. President Kennedy appointed Byron 'Whizzer' White to the Supreme Court, which was a fatal mistake. He was a great football player, but he was 'way out there'.

Before Felix Frankfurter went on the Supreme Court he was a law professor at Harvard Law School.

After he got on he thought he was still a law professor, and they had a bad time with him because of it.

I remember Joe Branch, who was Chief Justice when I went on the North Carolina Supreme Court. He was from way down east and had been campaign manager for the same man that appointed me to the court.

There was a woman appointed to the court by the republican governor, a teacher at Wake Forest law school and a smart lady, but in conference she would talk to the other six like they were students in law school, and would go into long lectures.

Joe Branch was a real east Carolina gentleman. After a conference one day he said, "If that woman doesn't stop talking, I don't know what I am going to do." He was too much the gentleman to interrupt.

- **'Firecracker Jury System'—**

When I was on the bench I started what we called the 'firecracker jury system'. The way that it had been, thirty jurors would stay for the whole week, or until court was over on Thursday or Friday. A lot of the time twelve jurors would be in the box for maybe three days, and the rest would be in the jury room looking at last year's magazines.

I decided that instead of having thirty jurors come for five days, thirty would come on Monday then a different thirty on Tuesday, and a total of 150 different people could serve on a jury in one week's time.

The jurors loved that because if they got on a case on Monday they had to stay until that case was over, but the other eighteen got to go home and not have to come back on Tuesday.

The system had flexibility because if a case was going to last two or three days you could send word to the thirty jurors scheduled for Tuesday and Wednesday to not come. This also saved money for the county, as jurors were paid whether they were working or not.

What would you say was the peak moment in your life?

Well, I really don't think I've come to the peak point yet. But there have been several good things, of course, like being appointed to the Supreme Court.

I'll tell you that one of the greatest moments a lawyer can have is trying a case for two or three days, and the jury deliberates and comes back to the jury box and says, "Your Honor we find the defendant not guilty."

- **Wisdom of the Years—**

Switching gears for a moment, tell me how the wisdom of the years helps with your life's ups and downs.

There are sometimes sad times where things may happen to you, like if something happened to my dog Jake that would be a bad time. But you get through those all right.

I've had a lot of good moments, more good than bad, I am sure of that.

I remember an election before I was appointed to the Court of Appeals when I ran as a candidate for the court and lost to Fred Hedrick, who was blind. He put up billboards, and I don't blame him, showing him with his seeing-eye dog.

Later at a trial judge event I was introduced, "We are very fortunate today to have with us Judge Harry Martin because he is still recovering from being bitten by a seeing-eye dog."

What is your opinion about television portrayals of lawyers?

I think that with TV lawyers and court scenes they need to rub it all out and start over. Very seldom do I see anything on television about courts that is real, and the public is in danger of getting the wrong ideas as to what the court does and what lawyers do, and so on.

When I started practicing law you went to the courtroom on the fifth floor of the court house and there would be a sizable group of people there to see what is going on. They had no interest, no involvement in the case, but they just came.

If you go there today, there aren't more than two or three people, and that includes lawyers. We used to go to court even if we didn't have a case to watch, especially young lawyers.

That is one of the best things, to go to the court and observe what is going on.

How do you feel about television in the courtroom?

When local television station WLOS started, they came to see me in the courthouse. I was the senior resident judge then, and they asked if they could cover a case coming up.

I told them, "I have nothing against television if you will do it as I think it should be done. If you want to televise this case, televise it from the beginning to the end and do not pick out certain places you think are important for whatever reason you have." When they said, "Oh, we can't do that," I responded, "Come to court, but not with your cameras." I wouldn't let them televise it, and I followed that in whatever county I went into.

In Charlotte one time the sheriff came to me as I was beginning a criminal case of some public interest down there and said, "There is a man here from the TV and he's got a camera and says he wants to televise." I said "Sheriff, bring him in and sit him in a front row, but tell him to leave his camera outside."

What amazed me about the O. J. trial was that the 'dream team won by jury nullification, not evidence, and most of the public disagreed with their verdict.

Ordinarily when the public hears the whole case they usually reach the right verdict.

- **Amusing Stories—**

You obviously relish memories of your days on the bench. Tell me more about that.

Back in the days when I first started practicing, judges didn't wear robes, just a blue shirt suit, or whatever. I remember a judge from Greensboro who smoked a pipe. He would enter the courtroom from chambers and when the jury was being selected would sit in the hall and smoke. But he could see and hear everything going on inside the courtroom.

One day I happened to be there and heard a juror say to a lawyer "I'm not going to answer that question." The judge was watching and said, "Answer the question," and the juror snapped, "Who the hell are you? You're sitting over there smoking a pipe."

The judge didn't say it but I am sure he thought "I'll show you who I am" as he walked up and sat on the bench. The juror said, "I didn't know you were the judge because you were sitting out there. I wouldn't have said that if I knew you were the judge."

The judge didn't do anything to him but was upset, and he quit sitting outside the courtroom smoking his pipe.

The funniest things happen in the courtroom, and this just popped in my mind. I was sitting on the bench when my former law partner, Bruce Elmore, was trying a case for a little chap charged with shoplifting a pair of tennis shoes from a store. The shoes were introduced as evidence; he had been caught going out of the store with them. But Bruce pled him as not-guilty at the jury trial.

I charged the jury and they came back in and the foreman said, "We find the defendant not guilty." You could have heard a pin drop in the courtroom as the little guy leaned over to Bruce and said, "Mr. Lawyer, does this mean I get to keep the shoes?"

What happened after you left the Supreme Court?

Sam Erwin, who I call Judge Sam, was my friend on the Fourth Circuit Court of Appeals. His daddy was former Supreme Court Justice Sam Erwin, a U.S. Senator on the Watergate Committee, and then there is a third Sam Erwin, who sits on the Court of Appeals in North Carolina.

Judge Sam wanted to start a mediation program to get rid of some cases coming up for the Fourth Circuit to alleviate the load, and asked me if to develop it. I had just gotten off the Supreme Court and didn't have anything to do, though I was practicing law with my son John in Hillsborough.

So I went to Richmond and talked to the Court about it. I knew of a judge in Cincinnati who was doing mediation for the Sixth Circuit Court of Appeals, and I went there and stayed with him, and watched what he was doing for three or four days.

When I came back I drafted a Mediation Program and schedule, and worked with two other mediators. I ran all that for six years.

What is the main premise and function of the mediation?

When Sam first approached me I said, "We're not going to be able to settle many cases because they have already been tried and are on appeal. But it turned out that lawyers who won cases were willing to talk about settling.

What I had to avoid was indicating that the trial judge didn't know what he was doing. Somebody once said, "Notice of appeal is entered for some reason, and perfection of it is something else."

The program operated from a federal government building in Durham and we settled a lot of cases. After six years I retired.

• A Call from the Cherokee—

Did you stay retired?

In 2000 I got a call from the Principal Chief of the Eastern Band of Cherokee Indians to talk about starting a Tribal Court. The Bureau of Indian Affairs Court had judges and employees employed by the federal government, but there was no connection between the BIA and the Tribal Government.

The Chief convinced me to do it and I drove from Asheville to Cherokee and back, about fifty miles each way, every Monday through Friday to get the Tribal Court started.

There were two Indians, not Cherokees, who had been judges on the BIA court. They had been to law school but never passed the Bar exam in North Carolina so couldn't practice law here. They agreed to stay on until I recruited one or two licensed lawyers.

I put a lawyer from a nearby town on an hourly basis, and told the Chief my goal of everybody else on the court to be from The Eastern Band.

One of the first BIA Judges was Kirk Saunooke, a Cherokee of about twenty-five. When we first met I said, "Kirk you've got a great future, you've graduated from Western Carolina, and after law school you can come back here and be a judge, or a lawyer making a fortune practicing law in front of this court."

But Kirk said, "I don't want to go to law school."

Then I remembered what Terry Sanford had done for me and got Kirk in the car one day and the same thing happened for him. Kirk asked me where we were going, and about ten miles down the road I said, "We're going to Chapel Hill and the law school to see if I can get you in."

The Law School dean was a former football player, a big guy who's still there but no longer dean. He told Kirk to send his application to UNC and copy him so he could help him get admitted."

Kirk was admitted that fall, and we rented our house in Chapel Hill to him. He went through law school without any problems. At graduation the dean said, "Kirk Saunooke is the only person I know who was a judge before he went to law school." And Kirk is still a judge for the Tribal Court.

Tell me more about the Eastern Band of Cherokee Indians.

There are about fifteen thousand Cherokee in the EBCI, about 8,500 who live here on what I call a reservation, though technically it is not, and another 7,000 who live all over the world. The land of about 58,000 acres here belongs to the tribe but was conveyed to the United States government so they won't have to fool with taxes and all that sort of stuff. They are descendants of the Cherokee that hid out in the mountains here and would not go to Oklahoma when President Jackson ordered the army to take all of the Cherokee to the west.

Was that the infamous 'Trail of Tears'?

Yes. And the reason was to get the land that the Cherokee had found gold on, so Jackson was a bad president as far as the Indians are concerned.

What would you say was the highlight of your establishing and running the Tribal Court?

The highlight was to get that Court going, and in a proper fashion, and then I became Chief Justice of the Supreme Court. In 2000 there were maybe two or three lawyers living around the reservation, so I started a lawyer's list and charged twenty-five dollars for a lifetime certificate to practice law in the Cherokee Nation. I bet we have 150 lawyers from all over the state that try cases there. There is always somebody slipping and falling in the casino and bringing a lawsuit.

Now we have a great court, including three trial judges.

My son Matthew has been a judge in Cherokee for about eight years, but I had nothing to do with hiring him. He didn't even tell me that he was applying to be a judge until they took him.

I was retired for about six or eight months when they asked me to come back to help. I did, and they pay me on an hourly basis to work one day a week. Matthew and I travel to the Tribal Court together.

There aren't many Indians east of the Mississippi River, just one tribe in North Carolina that is recognized by the Federal Government as an American Indian Tribe, the Eastern Band.

They have to help the Eastern Band by law, but it is not like it used to be since the Cherokee now have the Casino and jobs and other things.

I know that you are revered by the EBCN.

In 2008 I told the Principal Chief I was going to retire. He didn't say anything to me about it, but he went before the Tribal Council with a motion to issue a proclamation for me as an Honorary Member of the tribe.

I am one of only two people that have been made honorary members of the Tribe.

That is quite an honor. What is your role there now?

I am a Temporary Judge but not Chief Justice any more. I tell them in advance what day I am coming or the chief justice will call to ask if I can be there on a specific day, and that system works out all right. I'm lucky to ride to the court there and back home with Mathew.

I had nothing to do with getting it, but we received a twenty-million-dollar grant to build a new Court House in Cherokee, and we are working on the architectural plan now.

- **Still teaching law—**

Judge, if you could influence the curriculum at law schools what would you suggest?

It has changed so much since I went to law school, but as you know I still teach at UNC Law School in Chapel Hill that starts in September and runs through November, three hours per day for fifteen weeks. Matthew teaches there too, and we commute together.

I started teaching one course every year or every other year for seventeen years, including during the ten years I sat on the Supreme Court.

What courses do you teach?

Mostly Constitutional Law, but I have also taught about the Federal Constitution and the State Constitution, two separate courses about two different documents.

For the Cherokee I taught American Indian law, and that is now taught out West in Nevada and other places where there are a lot of Indians.

Are you still going strong, or are you getting tired of teaching and judging?

No, I am not getting tired of it; I look forward to it for a whole lot of reasons. For one, it puts you in a whole different area when you go into the teaching arena.

Now we teach at UNC one year then teach at Elon the next.

I also taught at Duke a time or two but didn't much like that.

Did any of your clerks turn out to be legal stars?

Yes, they were all very bright. One teaches at UNC Law School now.

What are your feelings about the current United States Supreme Court, if you care to comment?

There are three women on the court now, and that is the biggest change. The court is split with four conservatives and four liberals and one centrist.

At different times you get certain people on there that have strange ways. Clarence Thomas is the strangest guy on there because he never talks to his brothers and sisters unless he absolutely has to say something, and thinks the world is against him. He was voted in by the Senate with just a two vote majority.

But there are some good justices too, like Ruth Bader Ginsburg.

Did you ever appear before the U.S. Supreme Court?

I appeared one time but did not argue the case but Matthew did. We lost, but we wanted the law to be changed and it was. When the court ruled, "It just applies to future cases, not your case" it didn't help our client. That appearance was concerning a criminal case.

What is your opinion about the litigious society we live in now?

I don't know that we are more litigious, but I suspect there are more cases being tried and more laws. I do think that the best way to decide things is in the courtroom, that it's better for the court to decide than the legislature.

There is a Bar Association education meeting tomorrow in Asheville and I am going on a panel that will talk about how the law profession has changed dramatically since I came here in 1948.

It used to be that when court was in session, there were a from six to fourteen or so lawyers in the courtroom watching a trial, even though they had no real interest in that specific case. Now there may be two or four people trying a law suit, but no lawyers just watch the thing.

When I came here there were maybe as many as seventy-five lawyers in Buncombe County, and now there are as many as 600.

I still think law is a good field for young people to think about entering. I would still rather be in the law profession than any other. Next I'd be a teacher, or maybe a farmer.

- **Other Interests—**

What are some of your interests these days?

I like to play bridge. We have a crowd of ten that plays on Mondays and Tuesdays at the Biltmore Club, but sometimes just four to seven show up. We have a good time playing bridge.

Almost every day I spend from forty-five minutes to as much as an hour on lifting weights and doing floor exercises. I walk and run, not very fast, maybe jog would be a better word, about a mile-and-a-half five times a week.

I also read a lot. I'm reading a book now about the U.S. Supreme Court called *The Center Holds.* It's about the center of the court and the far-out conservatives and the far-out liberals.

What would you say your plan is now, to just keep on truckin'?

You mean for the future? Well I'm ninety-one-years-old and my birthday is in January, so I don't plan too far ahead. Right now I plan through the fall of the year, do the teaching, get that taken care of, then do whatever has to be done, and going to see the football games while we're down there, and all that stuff.

I basically hope that my physical condition will be sufficient that I can continue to work on occasion in Cherokee. Matthew and I go there on a Wednesday or Thursday, and it gives us the opportunity to talk for an hour and fifteen minutes each way. This is a very valuable thing for me, and I think for him too.

We got one case last week that they gave notice of appeal on, so it may be coming to the Cherokee Supreme Court or may be settled in the meantime. This sort of thing continues to come along.

My wife's health is good and we get along good, and now our son John is back. Our daughter just sold her house in Miami and is coming back to North Carolina. And we've got a little place down in Lake Summit near Flat Rock, had it since 1956. All the kids grew up there and keep going back there, which is good.

Judge, you've covered a lot of ground and shared a lot of interesting stuff. You have obviously been a straight arrow all of your adult life - were you like that as a child?

Well, I got into the usual mischief that little kids get into; sometimes you would get into fights at the school grounds during recess.

Did you win?

Nobody wins a fight, and the teacher grabs you both.

• The importance of practicing law—

The final question: after sixty-four years of practicing law, what emerges as the most important personal element to you?

I like the law. When there is something about a case in the newspaper, I automatically start to defend it in my head. It is a good profession. I've got one grandchild and would be pleased if she studied law.

If you want to be a business lawyer, or a lawyer that stays in his office all the time, that is all right. But I think the most important and best thing he or she can do is to help people. A lawyer should be in a position where people can come into a law office and talk about a problem, whatever it might be. The lawyer can listen and give advice, and if he earns money, well, that is a bonus.

I guess the best feeling I ever had as a lawyer was when I tried a case and the jury came back in and said, "Our Verdict is not guilty".

That is about the best feeling that you can get, knowing you won against the state of North Carolina with all its power on behalf of this little guy sitting at the table next to you.

On the Golden Wedding Anniversary of Harry and Nancy outside of St. Mary's Church in Asheville.

Former NC Supreme Justice Harry C. Martin with Attorney sons John (left) and Matthew Martin in the early 1990's.

Harry (right) As a young law student at UNC Chapel Hill.

. . . in Military service at Guadalcanal.

The Cherokee Court with Chief Justice Bill Boyum (seated), and Matthew Martin (left), Kirk Saunooke, and Harry Martin in 2008.

Harry with O.E. Starnes (left) and N.C. Lieutenant Governor Walter Dalton (center) in 2010.

... with son Matthew and wife Catherine, and grand-daughter Clarke on Harry's 90th birthday.

... and with wife Nancy D. Martin, 2000's.

... celebrating his 90th birthday in 2010 with daughter Mary D. Martin.

Section 5: **Significant Highlights Involving Justice Martin**

- **Capsules from Chief Justice Comments and Citations—**

- *Examples of significant cases and opinions involving Associate Justice Harry C. Martin during his service from 1982-to-1992 on the North Carolina Supreme Court were cited by former Chief Justice Jim Exum at his friend and colleague's portrait unveiling ceremony in 2000. Following are excerpts from Chief Justice Exum's presentation:*

- **Energizing State Constitutional Law—**

- In 1992, as part of the *North Carolina Law Review* Symposium on the Constitution, Justice Martin published a scholarly piece titled 'Font of Individual Liberties: North Carolina Accepts the Challenge'. He wrote: *During the past decade North Carolina has been at the head of the movement to energize State Constitutional law.*

- **No exclusion of evidence in State Constitution—**

- In *State v. Carter,* Justice Martin led a majority of a closely divided Court to conclude there is no 'good faith exception' to the exclusion of evidence obtained illegally under the State Constitutional prohibition against unreasonable searches, notwithstanding that such an exception had been recognized in the U.S. Supreme Court' Fourth-Amendment jurisprudence. This case is now under attack by the North Carolina General Assembly.

- **Two Memorable Dissents—**

Justice Martin was not prone to dissent, but two of his dissenting opinions are memorable, one for its passion, and the other for its persuasive force which ultimately gained the support of a majority.

- He dissented with great vigor in *State v. Norman,* where the issue was: if a woman long physically and mentally abused by her husband, and who suffered from battered-wife syndrome, was entitled to an instruction of self-defense when she shot her husband in the head while he was sleeping.

  The Court thought not and reversed a contrary decision of the North Carolina Court of Appeals. Justice Martin, standing alone but with his blood up, noted his disagreement with eloquent conviction. He wrote, "Where torture appears interminable and escape impossible, the believe that only the death of the oppressor can provide relief is reasonable in the mind for a person of ordinary firmness, let alone in the mind of the defendant, who like a prisoner of war of some years, has been deprived of her humanity and is held hostage by fear."

  Later Justice Martin drove home his point: "By his barbaric conduct over the course of twenty years, J.T. Norman reduced the quality of the defendant's life to such an abysmal state that, given the opportunity to do so, the jury might well have found that she was justified in acting in self-defense for the preservation of her tragic life."

- *Alfred v. Shaw* was one of the Court's more significant cases in the area of corporate law. The question was the limitation on judicial review of a special litigation committee's decision regarding the pursuit of a minority shareholder derivative claim against members of the corporate board for alleged fraud and self-dealing. The Court's first decision concluded that judicial review was significantly limited by the so-called 'business judgment rule' to inquiring only whether the committee was in fact disinterested, independent and acted in good faith, and whether its investigative procedures were sufficient.

Justices Martin and Frye filed separate dissents, arguing that North Carolina's Business Corporation Act required more extensive Court review. Justice Martin accused the majority of having placed "the corporate fox in charge of the shareholders' henhouse". On rehearing, the Court withdrew its prior decision and decided that courts should not be so limited.

This time Justice Martin found himself writing for the majority: "The Court must make a fair assessment of the report of the Special Committee, along with all the other facts and circumstances in the case, in order to determine whether the defendants will be able to show that the transaction complained of was just and reasonable to the corporation."

- **Named 'Hero of the Law'**

- The Court's second *Alford* decision caused Duke University Corporate Law Professor James D. Cox to add Justice Martin and the Court itself to his short list of "Heroes in the Law". He wrote in the *North Carolina Law Review*: *"Alford-II* is a significant decision. It has already generated national interest because it shows so clearly the way for others to follow."

- **A lawsuit against the State**

- Justice Martin enjoyed himself so much that, as he approached the mandatory retirement age of seventy-two, he filed a lawsuit to have the statute mandating retirement declared unconstitutional: *Martin v. State of North Carolina.* It gave the Court no pleasure to do it but after Martin recused himself, the other six justices unanimously disagreed with his position.

I am sure Justice Martin will recall that I happened to write that opinion.

Note: Additional historical records of North Carolina Supreme Court decisions are available online, or by request from the North Carolina Bar Association.

Section 6: **Chronology**

- **Personal—**
- Born January 13, 1920.
- Raised in Lenoir and Blowing Rock, N.C.
- Married to Nancy D. (Dallam) Martin, 1955.
- Children: attorneys Matthew and John, architect daughter Mary; grand-daughter Clarke.

- **Military—**
- 1942-1945, Combat Veteran, WWII, 13th Jungle Air Force, Guadalcanal, Solomon Islands, Saipan.

- **Education—**
- 1942, AB, University of North Carolina at Chapel Hill.
- 1948, LLB, Harvard Law School.
- 1982, L.L.M., the University of Virginia School of Law.

- **Career as Lawyer and Judge—**
- 1948-1962, Private Practice, Asheville; general solo practice, and with Gudger, Elmore & Martin. Primarily represented human beings rather than corporations. With Bruce Elmore, successful in obtaining acquittal for Dorothy Mae Gosnell on first-degree murder charge in Madison County.
- 1962-1978, Superior Court Judge, Buncombe County. Appointed by Governor Terry Sanford, re-appointed by Governor Dan K. Moore, and elected. Became known as an innovator; implemented the 'Firecracker, or one day/one case jury system still in use in Buncombe County, other Districts; early advocate of computers to compile Judicial Branch data.
- 1978-1982, Associate Judge, North Carolina Court of Appeals. Appointed by Governor James B. Hunt, Jr.. Known for several dissents in Workers Compensation cases which later became law, and a case on dogs that is still cited today: *State v. Wallace*.
- 1982-1992, Associate Justice, Supreme Court of North Carolina. Appointed by Governor Hunt, elected. Known as 'The Conscience of the Court'. Multiple significant opinions include *Corum v. UNC* and *State v. Carter*. Unsuccessfully sued to overturn NC's mandatory retirement law for Judges and retired.
- 1992-2003, Private practice in Orange County with Martin & Martin, P.A. Still holds with son Matthew and John D. Loftin the largest verdict in Orange County history, $2.75 million on behalf of a little girl molested by her next door neighbor.
- 1994-1999, Chief Circuit Mediator, United States Court of Appeals for the Fourth Circuit. Designed and implemented the appellate mediation program for the Fourth Circuit.
- 2000-2006, Chief Justice of the Cherokee Supreme Court, Eastern Band of Cherokee Indians. Supervised creation of Tribal Court system on Qualla Indian Boundary in Western NC; established Cherokee Court as a leader among Indian Nations and the Tribal Court, and with the most jurisdiction in Indian Country.
- 2007, Made an Honorary Member of the Eastern Band of Cherokee Indians.
- 2003-present, Private practice in Buncombe County with The Martin Law Firm, P.A. representing individuals primarily in appellate matters.
- 2008-present, Temporary Judge Cherokee Court, recalled from retirement, designated by the sitting Chief Justice.

- **Awards and Recognitions—**
- *Raleigh News & Observer* Tar Heel of the Week - 1978

- North Carolina Academy of Trial Lawyers, Outstanding Appellate Judge of the Year - 1988
- Phi Alpha Delta Law Fraternity, Certificate of Outstanding Service - 1995
- Order of the Long Leaf Pine, awarded by Governor Hunt - 2000
- North Carolina Bar Association, John J. Parker Award - 2002
- Harvard Law School, Traphagen Distinguished Alumni Award – 2006\
- American Bar Association, Judicial Division, Franklin N. Flaschner Award - 2007. Awarded by the ABA's National Conference of Specialized Court Judges as 'the nation's outstanding specialized Court Judge'.
- North Carolina Bar Association, Liberty Bell Award – 2010
- University of North Carolina at Chapel Hill, Distinguished Alumni Award - 2010
- North Carolina State Bar, John McMillan Distinguished Service Award - 2011

- **Teaching and Lecturing—**
- Visiting Lecturer in Law, University of North Carolina School of Law - 1984-1992
- Visiting Lecturer, Duke University Institute of Policy Sciences and Public Policy - 1990-1991
- Distinguished Governor Dan K. Moore Visiting Professor of Law, UNC School of Law - 1992-1995
- Adjunct Professor of Law, UNC School of Law - 2003-present
- Lecturer at numerous continuing legal education seminars – 1980-current.

- **Published Articles:**
- Campen & Martin, *Justice and Efficiency: Computer-Aided Jury Selection in Buncombe County*, Popular Government-spring, 1979
- Campen & Martin, *North Carolina's Judicial Rotation System*, Popular Government - spring 1981
- Martin, *Freedom of Speech in North Carolina Prior to Gitlow v. New York, with a Forward Glance Thereafter*, 4 Campbell Law Review, 243 -1982
- Martin & Slawson, *Freedom of Speech Without a Constitutional Guarantee: A State Case History*, Free Speech Yearbook, Vol. 29 - 1987
- Martin, *The State as a "Font of Individual Liberties"; North Carolina Accepts the Challenge*, 70 North Carolina Law Review, Number 6 – 1992; Martin, *Statistical Compilation of the Opinions of the Supreme Court of North Carolina Terms 1993-94 through 1994-95*, 74 North Carolina Law Review, No. 6 – 1996

- **Appointments—**
- Delegate to the National Conference of State Trial Judges, 1966-1972
- Vice President, North Carolina Bar Association, 1972-1973
- President, North Carolina Conference of Superior Court Judges, 1972-1973
- Founder and Chair, North Carolina Judges Bench Book Committee, 1977-1995
- Governor's Brown Lung Study Committee, 1979
- North Carolina Fair Sentencing Procedures Committee, Chair, 1980
- Governor's Commission on Appellate Court Facilities, 1984
- North Carolina State Judicial Center Commission, Chair, 1985-1987
- North Carolina State Bar, Client Security Fund, Chair, 1996-1998

Olson Huff

M.D., FAAP

Being a pediatrician did not make me a better father, but being a father made me a better pediatrician.
— **Dr. Olson Huff.**

Sections about Dr. Olson Huff:

1) Testimonials about the Notable Physician

2) Significant Career Achievements and Highlights

3) **Dr. Huff's Life Journey, in His Own Words**

4) Photos

5) Excerpts from Dr. Huff's extensive writings

6) Chronology

Section 1: **Testimonials about the Notable Physician**

- **From the President of the American Academy of Pediatrics—**

Dr. Olson Huff is the consummate child advocate and everyone's role model community pediatrician. Anchored by a lifetime of stellar, highly regarded pediatric practice, he has chaired the American Academy of Pediatrics Committee on Federal Government Affairs through a challenging period that brought affordable health care to almost all of America's children.

Dr. Huff has been a national voice for their health insurance coverage, a clinical benefits package that promotes optimal growth and development, and reasonable payments for pediatricians and other physicians who care for them. While reaching out to governments with one hand, he has reached back into the community at large with the other.

Specifically, he is instrumental in linking community assets and resources to clinical pediatric practice in order to promote optimal health, wellbeing, growth, development and life success for current and future generations. On a personal level, Dr. Huff walks humbly among us, America's 85,000-plus pediatricians, but is indeed without equal.
  — **O. Marion Burton, M.D., President, American Academy of Pediatrics**

- **From the President of Presbyterian Graduate School—**

Olson Huff is an extraordinary man. His brilliant mind coupled with his creativity combined to make a difference in the lives of people from Western North Carolina and beyond. Even more significant than his list of accomplishments and remarkable ability to network is his genuine compassion and love for people. Olson gives of himself in ways that are only known by the individuals and families he has assisted. His quiet demeanor is more than matched by his passion to serve others.

When he speaks to a group of people, this quiet doctor from Western North Carolina becomes an enthusiastic and articulate advocate for his concerns. Whether he is dealing with a president or governor, or a young mother who has no resources to care for her sick baby, he is consistent in expressing his concern and love. No bias or prejudice enters into his belief that all people have the right to be treated with dignity and respect. His faith is paramount to who he is, but it is never imposed on others. Olson has a way of making all people feel they are his best friends. I am proud to be one of those people.
  — **Dr. Heath Rada, former president, Presbyterian Graduate School of Christian Education, Senior Executive, American Red Cross**

- **President *Emeritus*, University of North Carolina—**

Olson Huff is one of those exemplary North Carolinians who successfully serves as pediatrician, child advocate, leader in all matters concerning children, and he does so with courage, grace and good will. His splendid career of public service inspires us all."
  — **William Friday, President *Emeritus*, UNC**

- **From Dean *Emeritus*, College of Education, UNC—**

Few people have contributed so much to their profession, to their community, and to children as has Dr. Olson Huff. A fine pediatrician, a wise mentor, and a strong and positive leader, Dr. Huff has done more than most to make North Carolina a healthier and safer place for children.
  — **Don Stedman, Dean *Emeritus*, College of Education, UNC at Chapel Hill.**

Section 2: **Significant Career Achievements and Highlights**

Author's Note: Before reading the life journey far of notable Dr. Olson Huff as told to the author, it is instructive to review the distinguished career of the renowned pediatrician, and how his commitment, dedication and talent served children in Western North Carolina, and their grateful parents.

- **45 years+ of service to children's healthcare—**

Beginning with a two-year residency in pediatrics at Charlotte Memorial Hospital in 1966, Dr. Huff has spent more than forty-five years serving healthcare needs of North Carolina children in a wide variety of positions. Dr. Huff retired in 2001 but continues to serve in various capacities through the present. As recently as 2011 Dr. Huff was presented with two significant honors: the Glaxo-Smith Kline Lifetime Achievement Award, and the Jim Bernstein Community Health Achievement Award. A list of his numerous career awards appears in the chronology section.

After operating a private practice in Charlotte through 1982 that concentrated on development disabilities in children, Dr. Huff and wife Marylyn moved to Asheville where he joined the Development Evaluation Center (DEC), and served the Mountain Area Education Center (MAHEC) as assistant clinical professor of pediatrics.

In 1987, following his work with the DEC, Dr. Huff was recruited by Chat Norvell, CEO of Thoms Rehabilitation Hospital in Asheville, to be medical director for the newly established Center for Childhood Development and Rehabilitation (CCDR). The program became a successful means of providing evaluation, treatment and community resources to hundreds of children with disorders of development and learning. Genetic evaluation was added with cooperation of Wake Forest University Medical Center and a program (grant funded) to aid children with significant motor dysfunction, called 'The Free Wheelers' was begun. Therapies in all areas including psychological, social, occupation and physical, as well as speech and language, rounded out the comprehensive nature of the Center as it expanded to serve the region. In 1995, with the encouragement of Mr. Norvell, the Thoms Hospital Board of Directors re-named the center 'The Olson Huff Center for Child Development'. Although Dr. Huff was recruited to become the Medical Director for the Ruth and Billy Graham Children's Health Center at Mission Hospital in 1994, he continued to see patients at the Olson Huff Center, both at Thoms and after the Center was moved to Mission Children's Hospital

His role as medical director of the Ruth and Billy Graham Children's Health Center was to oversee program development that offered three components:

- *Inpatient Services:* the neonatal internal care unit, pediatrics, and a general inpatient floor;
- *Outpatient Services:* he raised funds that built the major new facility called the Reuter Pediatric Outpatient Center that houses offices for pediatric specialists employed by Mission Children's Hospital;
- *Outreach Programs:* he initiated mobile 'Tooth Bus' dental units, the Safe Kids program, the Family Support Network, and summer camps for children with special illnesses.

Dr. Huff currently serves on the Adjunct Faculty for the Center for Healthy Aging at the Mountain Area Health Education Center (MAHEC) that is part of the statewide health education system called AHEC, acronym for Area Health Education Centers. He has served on several committees and boards that support the AHEC and MAHEC concepts. Dr. Huff's primary role in MAHEC's Center for Healthy Aging is to search for ways to provide information on preventative health care for people in the latter part of their lives.

- **Governor's Appointment—**

In 2003 then North Carolina Lt. Governor Beverly Purdue appointed Dr. Huff as chair of the Task Force on Obesity and Nutrition of the Health and Wellness Trust Fund Commission. The work of this group led to changes of policy in North Carolina that improved nutritional options for school-aged children, and increased the opportunity for physical activity during the school day. These important steps addressed the fact that 25 percent of children and youth in the state are overweight.

- **Instrumental in Key Tobacco Vote—**

As a member of the North Carolina Health and Wellness Trust Fund Commission, Dr. Huff was instrumental in a key 2002 legislative vote to set aside $6.2 million per year for three years to deal with tobacco use, especially among teen-agers, the largest amount ever designated for a single program by the Commission. At the time he said: *"Now there will be money for media messages, for school-based cessation programs, for enforcement efforts to reduce sales to minors, and we'll place a great deal of emphasis on rural areas and pregnant teens."*

- **The 'Tooth Bus' Triumph—**

Another of Dr. Huff's major accomplishments is the mobile 'Tooth Bus' program that has served many thousands of children. It treats low-income children with necessary dental care that helps to improve their self-esteem and performance in school. As Medical Director at Mission Children's Hospital that serves Western North Carolina, the pediatrician was instrumental in developing Tooth Bus units that dispatch dental care and preventive care and education in the most poverty-stricken areas within more than 20 counties. The program also offers operating room services for children in need of more intensive dental care.

- **Helping to Change the Law—**

To accomplish the advances in dental care for children, Dr. Huff worked with state legislators to change the law so that dentists could be employed by a hospital, and then worked with them and the North Carolina Dental Society to improve the Medicaid reimbursement rate. For this he was honored with the NCDS 'Special Recognition Award', and has been recognized nationally by both dental and pediatric organizations for his work on this important program.

- **Philosophical Focus—**

One of Dr. Huff's major philosophical focuses is to improve the health and well-being of children in the often overlooked southern Appalachians. His vision was and is to break the cycle of poor health and hopelessness often found in children who call the hills, coves and hollows of Appalachia their home. Dr. Huff's efforts to improve health care for the rural poor gave him statewide re0cognition as an effective advocate for children's issues. The following quote from the renowned pediatrician speaks to the core essence of his career: *"My specific focus is on Appalachian children because my heart is here, but I recognize that wherever children in need are, they are the same as Appalachian children!"*

- **Newspaper Recognitions—**

An *Asheville Citizen-Times* editorial entitled 'Huff A Credit to Medical Profession-And to Humanity' was published during a pivotal point in his career: he had just been honored with the 'Children-First Leslie Anderson Leadership Award' for his dedication to improving the lives of children and their families through advocacy, policy development, education and collaboration, and had just announced his retirement as Medical Director of Mission St. Joseph's Hospital's Children Center.

That prominent Western North Carolina newspaper also proclaimed Dr. Huff as one of 'The 50 Most Influential People in Western North Carolina in the 20th Century'.

- **An Effective Negotiator—**

Dr. Huff personally negotiated to break the stalemate between the North Carolina House and Senate when the State Child Health Insurance Plan (SCHIP), the health plan for the working poor, was being introduced but facing stiff opposition.

His successful solution was to tie SCHIP to the State Employees Health Plan, and to add speech, dental and vision services, and that led North Carolina to soon becoming recognized for having the best plan for poor children in the entire United States!

- **Dr. Huff, Teacher—**

Throughout his prolific career, Dr. Huff has been a teacher, influencing others with his eloquence and stellar example. He used his passion to fuel development of programs to teach resident physicians and medical students through community hospitals, office-based practices, and local public agencies that serve children.

He has also worked with public schools to provide cooperative educational and service experiences for students, staff, and physicians in training.

Perhaps his most impressive achievement was recognizing that the well-being of families and children must be on both the societal level and the personal level.

He counted on others, too, as demonstrated by his statement:

"A leader must be surrounded by people who share a vision while maintaining independence of thought."

- **Support for His Work—**

Dr. Huff's work is largely supported through grants to the many significant advocacy organizations he works on behalf of. A commitment to and belief in his efforts is amply demonstrated by Mission Hospitals. His ongoing fundraising efforts helped construct the Reuters outpatient facility of the Children's Hospital, and fulfilled his vision.

It has been said of Dr. Olson Huff that he cares so deeply about children he puts their needs above his own, and has done so throughout his distinguished career.

- **An Early Lesson—**

Dr. Huff learned early in his career that children born with disabilities were treated as less than whole, with no potential. They were often institutionalized and cut off from society. But he saw their potential, their 'special gifts', and knew they had a right to be in school, part of a community, part of their family, and had a right to health care. He worked with school systems and made the point that a productive life depends on how it is defined, and encouraged medical providers to care for these children.

He also recognized that they require resources beyond the ability of a family to pay, including equipment, day care, respite care, specialized treatment, medications, and some semblance of family joy. So, he devised and recommended programs and plans to help them.

- **Passion to Make a Difference—**

Following and fulfilling his passion, and realizing his vision to become a developmental pediatrician and make a positive difference in children's lives, Dr. Huff dedicated his career to provide direct care, and to date has served many thousands of children.

Dr. Huff listened to each one of them with respect, and provided the kind of professional health care they required and deserved! He has been instrumental in breaking down barriers, and adding resources that help to ensure a high quality of healthcare for all children. His influence greatly helped North Carolina children to have access to health care, and will have a lasting positive impact on their social environment, intellectual understanding and education.

- **The Sixty-Second Parent Program and Three Books—**

Ongoing programs and writings of Dr. Huff have provided vast healthcare benefits to the greater Western North Carolina community. In 2007, Dr. Huff established *The Sixty-Second Parent* program to provide a means of giving quality, affordable, accurate and timely information on health, behavior and development of children. He also initiated its website, developed and published three books on children, and launched a magazine distributed free for parents throughout the region.

The books are: *The Window of Childhood: Glimpses of Wonder and Courage,* Westminster John Knox Press 1990/2001; *Practical Guide to Parenting Two, Three and Four Year Olds,* Book One of *The Triumphant Child Series* from 'The Sixty-Second Parent', and *The First 60 Days of Life: How to Enjoy Your Newborn Baby,* also a part of *The Triumphant Child Series.* The books were dedicated to specific audiences: people with two, three and four-year-olds, and those with newborn babies. The newborn book won the Internet Parenting Award and the Independent Publishers Gold Medal, and is considered to be so comprehensive and well done that it is a must-buy for parents of a new baby.

- **And Then Retirement—**

Upon his retirement in 2001, a ceremony honoring Dr. Huff was held at The Renaissance Hotel in Asheville, featuring tributes from David T. Tayloe, Jr., M.D., Chair of District Four of the AAP, and Robert F. Burgin, Chief Executive Officer of Mission Healthcare Systems. The final line spoken during the program summed up the career and life of the renowned pediatrician: *Olson's deep faith has given him his perspective on life and his call to service, as well as his respect and care for all people.*

Section 3: Dr. Huff's Life Journey, in His Own Words

Author's note: I'm pacing a bit, anxiously waiting to meet and record the life journey of renowned pediatrician Olson Huff, and chatting with a pleasant receptionist in the lobby of one of the buildings in the new MAHEC Center complex cleverly positioned on a picturesque hilltop just east of downtown Asheville. Suddenly striding my way is a spry septuagenarian with Carl Sandburg-like white hair and bright smiling eyes. He escorts me to an efficient second-floor office that awaits a decorator's touch where we will begin our first interview. No better place to start than with my first impression, so I ask:

Doctor Huff, please share with me how you stay so trim and fit?

Thanks! My oldest son David and I left at about eleven last Saturday morning and drove to the Davidson River area and hiked for five hours in the Pisgah National Forest. I seem to be in pretty good health, and plan on running in a 5-K race on Saturday.

I run with my dog religiously every other morning, a 'labra-doodle', wonderful animal named Strider, from the Lord of the Rings. We run about a mile and a half together most days; that's about all his bones will tolerate now, or mine.

One of your co-notables is retired Supreme Court Judge Harry C. Martin who lives in Biltmore Forest next to Asheville. He's ninety-one and jogs and walks a mile and a half four days a week.

Good for him. That's what we all should be doing as we get older: just keep on going.

Tell me about the rest of your immediate family.

My wife of forty-eight years Marylyn and I have three sons, David, Stephen and Daniel. David is a creative photographer, and does videography for a Charlotte insurance company, did his doctoral studies in mythology and psychology, and was executive producer our theatrical film titled *Country Remedy*. David lives in Charlotte and has not yet married he never found the right one.

Stephen is 42, CEO of our *Sixty-Second Parent* multi-media parenting network, and lives in Australia. He develops companies, started a successful software firm, and has been described as a 'serial entrepreneur'.

Daniel is 40 and was a teaching Fellow and taught high school science in Brevard before moving to Minneapolis, where his now supervisor of the environmental program. He earned a Master's Degree in Public Affairs from the Hubert H. Humphrey School of Public Affairs at the University of Minneapolis. His children are Benji, 10, and Lydia, 6, as of today.

Stephen is father to Katie, 10 and Riley, 7, and they live in an area called the Sunshine Coast north of Brisbane, Australia. They were here this summer for three weeks, and we've been to Australia eight times. I like it when I get there, but I don't enjoy the long plane ride.

Where did you meet Marylyn, and was it love at first sight, if you don't my asking?

We met right across the valley from where we now live in Black Mountain, at the Blue Ridge Assembly. We were both on the summer staff of the YMCA there. She was finishing her sophomore year at Florida State University and I was finishing my first year in medical school at the University of Louisville.

I think it was love at first sight, although it took us three years to finally get around to getting married. We had gone our separate ways but came back together. We've lived in Black Mountain for over twenty-three years now, it's a wonderful town.

Marylyn owns her own business, Huff Associates, in organization development and leadership training, primarily working with churches to organize and develop staffs and searches for pastors. She was a member of the Charlotte-Mecklenburg School Board during the major crisis in school desegregation.

She currently operates her company, Huff Associates, and is writing a series of assessment guides for clergy, elders and church staff.

• Childhood Memories—

Can you go back to your childhood and your first memories?

The first thing I remember was playing with a youngster by the name of Douglas Huff. We might have been distant relatives, with possible family ties because we were born and lived in the very isolated area of Eastern Kentucky in Krypton. It wasn't a real town, just a railroad stop on a road that forked into the Kentucky River, with a depot, post office and community store. Most of us lived in ramshackle houses built on hillsides along one of the tributaries to Campbell's Creek where I and five siblings were born. Only three of us are still alive.

We lived on a hardscrabble farm in London, Kentucky, during the war years. Dad was a laborer for the railroad, and my mother tried to grow whatever vegetables she could.

I was ten when we moved to near Salem, Indiana. I remember the trip because we stopped in Louisville, where the truck driver bought me an ice cream stick.

I remember an epiphany moment occurred during the first night in the new house when I could not sleep because there was an electric light! I was only eleven but thought I had died and went to heaven. That light was the greatest thing to me, and I often compare it to moving from black-and-white to color.

It was monumental to realize that we were suddenly in a different situation economically, and there was a different atmosphere about everything. These were my formative years, but I understood what it meant to have limited resources. I have bits and pieces of memories about how tough rationing was during those early years, and that my parents were very creative in raising sheep and farming. And that they were always kind.

The farm was not in the hills but was rolling. You could see nice green fields and trees, and there was a paved highway in front of the house. It was the nicest house, though by today's standards it was pretty pitiful. But it had electricity! It was a totally new environment.

My mom and dad bought that house in 1947, and my oldest brother continued to live there until he died three years ago; sixty years later. Two older brothers and sisters had gone on to Berea College, which was tuition free, and still is. I technically moved out when I went to college in 1954, but I continue to go back on a regular basis.

Do you have fond memories of your childhood?

Mixed. The first several years of my life were pretty bleak because we were economically restrained. This was during the war years, and my oldest sister married a boy who was immediately drafted then severely wounded in Sicily. We didn't think he was going to live, and she went through a lot of emotional stuff. She and her daughter were living with us, meaning me, my youngest brother, my sister, our niece, and mom and dad.

We were isolated at the end of a road. In winter it became so muddy that you couldn't get a car through, and the only way to get to school was to walk. The winters were pretty bad, and there was always a lot of snow. I remember many times coming home with my overall legs so frozen they could stand on their own.

Dad could only come on weekends because he worked on the Eastern Kentucky Division of the Louisville and Nashville Railroad. He lived in camp-cars during the week.

Then when all of us kids went off to school, our family became really disconnected.

Those were not very memorable years

- **Choosing a Medical Career—**

When did you first become interested in a career in medicine?

That is a very good story and one that I think reflects the value of teachers in a young person's life as well as the determination and dedication of parents who wish only the best for their children.

My parents were barely educated with only about a third or fourth grade education, yet they knew the value of a good education and they worked very hard to see that all six of their children had opportunities to learn that were denied to them.

In my junior year there was a so-called 'honors chemistry class'. In those days, the fifties, I'm not sure what qualified it as honors, but my chemistry teacher chose me for it one spring day. I remember when the teacher asked the class one day: "Well, what are ya'll going to do when you finish high school? Next year is your last, so what do you plan to do afterward?"

When he came around to me, most of the kids had already said they were going to college to become teachers, since that was the basic model we were all expected to follow, so I said: "I guess I'd kind of like to be a teacher, or maybe a doctor."

To this day I still do not know where that doctor part came from; I think from the Universe.

It must have been the universe, because the very next week I got a call from the guidance counselor to come see him and he said: "Mr. Willis told me what you said in class Olson, and now you have an appointment to go downtown to see the family doctor to talk about going to medical school."

That was a powerful thing in my life. That one teacher, Donald Willis, touched an incredible number of children, and I will forever owe him gratitude for pointing me in a direction that, once I met with the doctor, became a foregone conclusion.

Then it was off to college.

- **The College Years—**

Please share some of your college experiences.

I went on to the University of Kentucky, and I'm not exactly sure how this came about, but I got a full scholarship! Then in my senior year the university let me live free in a house normally reserved for pre-med students, and I had a job that paid my other expenses. I graduated in just three years in 1957.

After my free ride through college guess where I send a check every year.

Later I continued my education at the University of Louisville Medical School, but not before there was·an interesting hiatus. I had been admitted to several medical schools and chose Indiana University, since that was my home state at the time.

But right before I was supposed to enter I had a clash with the dean, who said I could not be admitted because I had not taken this one course in college. I was left hanging high and dry, and then all of the classes I needed to take became filled.

So I taught high school for a year, which was probably one of the best things I have ever done, since that was my other choice for a profession anyway. I had a wonderful year of teaching, and then went to the University of Louisville without having to re-apply because I had already been accepted.

I probably could have done a little bit better academically if I had applied myself more, but I was more interested in medical politics and some of the other stuff. I'd always been interested in advocacy, so I spent a fair amount of time doing that. But I still graduated okay.

Why and when did you choose pediatrics as your discipline?

My senior year in medical school I started leaning towards pediatrics. I discovered there was a pediatric externship for a certain number of students interested in actually living in the children's hospital and working on-call for the pediatric staff. I was chosen as one of those students and spent my senior year, in addition to class activities and other regular rotations, doing extra work in the children's hospital. That's where I got my teeth into pediatrics.

I had also joined the Air Force medical program and got paid as a second Lieutenant in my senior year, a Godsend because I was out of money. I served my medical internship at the US Air Force Hospital in San Antonio, Texas, on a rotating internship that gave me good experience in all of the disciplines in medicine.

• Air Force Experiences—

You were well-educated and became a valuable service member. Please share some military experiences.

I went to the Air Force Flight Training School in San Antonio, Texas and was labeled as a Flight Surgeon. I spent a year in Southeast Asia during the Vietnam War, mainly stationed in Thailand, with some time in Vietnam. Later I spent two years at an Air Force base in New Hampshire.

The time served in Southeast Asia was extremely interesting. I was a captain stationed in a remote area of Thailand in an old Japanese WWII camp. We lived in barracks close to the River Kwai that the Japanese had built, with the help of POW's. It was kind of quiet for the first part of the tour there. A squadron of fighter planes would come on rotation from New Mexico every three months, and I was the flight surgeon for them, as well as for base operations.

Though it was a fairly quiet base at first, we did serve all of the Armed Forces in Vietnam. Most of the air strikes from the fighter squadrons went out of Thailand into Vietnam just a short hop away. I flew many times for training sessions in the second seat of F-100 planes along the borders of Cambodia, Laos and adjacent areas. It was exciting fun to fly with those fighter pilots!

But then, after the Gulf of Tonkin incident, we became a busy base, with a plane landing about every ninety seconds. It was amazing that I was the only doctor caring for a massive influx of troops. The biggest maladies I had to treat were tropical illnesses, and I had to manage injuries.

Your being so far away and in danger must have been tough on your new bride.

We had been married less than three months before I got shipped out to active duty. Fortunately though, I did get time to go to Bangkok on occasion, and Marylyn came there on her own. So I was able to have an affair with this beautiful young woman, my wife! It was wonderful. She got a job as director of education for a non-denominational church in Bangkok.

• Settling in Charlotte—

And when your Air Force service ended?

After the Air Force service we moved to Charlotte, North Carolina, where I did my residency in pediatrics and set up practice in 1968. Marylyn became a member of the school board. We were both deeply involved with education there. I was a member of the usual medical societies, and we both remained active in the Presbyterian Church.

We thought we were going to stay in Charlotte permanently, and in 1976 built the home we planned to live in for the rest of our lives. But five years later, in 1982, we left there to come here.

It's interesting how opportunity and desire seem to meet in time. Frederick Buechner, a Presbyterian minister and a great author, wrote something that I think is very telling in one of his books: "When your greatest passion meets the world's greatest need, then that's where your call is." I think he was absolutely correct.

What organizations are you involved in here?

I have been either a part of the beginning or tagged along with many things. 'Children First' is a child-advocacy organization that I was instrumental in getting off the ground, and I serve on the advisory board. I initiated a local program called 'Kids and Parks' along the Blue Ridge Parkway, which has become a national model for getting kids into the woods safely, and I'm chair of that advisory board. I'm also on the board of directors for The Pavilion Drug rehab program, and the board of the Black Mountain Pastoral Care Center that provides counseling for people in need.

And of course I'm active in our church here. I'm an ordained elder.

You are too modest: you also served as president of the North Carolina Pediatrics Association!

Yes, I was president from 1994 to 1997. Currently there are approximately sixteen-hundred pediatricians in the association. In fact, our state meeting is in Asheville next week, with the annual dinner for past-presidents, and that is always fun.

Shifting gears and modesty aside, how would you describe yourself, and how would others describe you?

Everyone who does any reflection about me believes I am a visionary leader who always thinks about what can be, that the essence of what we ought to be thinking is to make the future better for everyone, and that inherent skills and desires in every human soul and spirit make them want to move forward.

What I see as our job in terms of pediatric medicine is to help children grow healthy bodies, encourage development of healthy minds, and inspire expression of wonderful spirit. I think those are the three main opportunities for people in the pediatric world to do in the children's world.

Pediatrics is not really a job, it's an opportunity!

- **Producing and Writing—**

Tell me about the movie you produced, and your books.

The movie is now called *Country Remedy*. It was picked up by a distributing company and renamed from our original film titled *Simple Things*. The story is about a fictional pediatrician from Chicago who finds himself in the mountains of western North Carolina for what he assumes will be a short summer stint. There he finds not only healing for himself, but healing for the people who live there. The film was inspired by the book I wrote called *The Window of Childhood*.

Country Remedy is a 102-minute feature film, not a documentary, and all of the actors are known entities. Bellamy Young, the lead actress, is from Asheville, a Yale graduate. She appeared in many *CSI* segments on television and several films. Cameron Bancroft, the male lead, was in many *24* TV segments, the hockey film *Mystery Alaska with Russell Crowe,* and the remake of *The Little House on the Prairie* Disney Film. Supporting roles were played by Edie McClurg, a character actress and one of the voices in the *Cars* movie, and Mickey Jones, who is recognizable from many biker movies and *Sling Blade* with Billy Bob Thornton.

Marylyn and I both made cameo appearances, and that was a lot of fun. We rehearsed together for about a month. And as you know, David and I co-produced it in 2008. It was mostly filmed in Transylvania County, and partly in Brevard. The summer weather had been wet, but from the day we started filming and for that entire month the weather was incredibly cooperative. They shot the film from early morning to late night every day, and wrapped it up in less than a month, which was exceptional. It's available on Netflix, and for purchase from Amazon.com. It's been shown on the Starz TV Network a number of times, and is still 'out there' making the rounds.

When and why did you decide to become an author?

When we moved from Charlotte to Asheville in 1982 I got a great deal of relief from the strenuous schedule that I had been operating on. I had shifted the kinds of work I was doing, so I had the time to begin to put down some of my thoughts about children I had worked with, and the results of that. The books contain fact-based fictionalized accounts of events involving some of those children.

It was also a way of letting go of that particular part of my professional life. I had practiced general pediatrics for fourteen years, and the shift I was making was considerable because I had moved into more administrative and teaching duties, and was working strictly with children with developmental disabilities. The book project gave me an opportunity to make the emotional shift from the intensity of dealing with acute patient situations to those that became chronic.

How did the 'Window of Childhood, Glimpses of Wonder and Courage' go over with the reading public?

It did so well that the publishers came out with a second printing. Then we used it as the focus as part of the campaign to build and expand the Children's hospital here and it went into a third printing. So the book gained a fair amount of 'legs', and has been picked up by many bookstores around the country. It can still be found on Amazon, but is no longer in general circulation.

- **'Sixty-Second Parent'—**

Explain more about the significance and impact of the Sixty-Second Parent program.

I'm happy to talk about *The Sixty-Second Parent* because I share that project with Stephen as the CEO, and with David, who handles North American development. Both sons also have careers as entrepreneurs, and other interests.
I established this program a little over three years ago to provide a means of giving quality, affordable, accurate and timely information on health, behavior and development of children. We also initiated *The Sixty-Second Parent* website, and from there developed and published two books on children.

The first book in what we call 'the triumphant child series' is titled *Raising Two, Three, and Four-Year-Olds,* and the second is titled *The First 60 Days of Life,* which I edited and helped write. The two books are dedicated to specific audiences: people with two, three and four-year-olds, and those with newborn babies.

The newborn book won the Internet Parenting Award, and also the Independent Publishers Gold Medal Award. The Internet Parenting Award was from the Internet Parenting Association, an International organization. The International Publishers Gold Medal was in the parenting niche from an organization that consists of university presses and independent publishers.

The way we did the newborn book was to co-edit it, meaning co-brand it, with the hospitals. That means that each hospital can request its cover or logo on the book then purchase it from us to give to the parent of a baby born in their hospital as a going-home gift. It is now widely judged to be so comprehensive and well done that it is a 'must-buy' for parents.

Next we developed *Sixty-Second Parent* magazine that we can distribute free thanks to the ads. We have a memorandum of understanding with 'Reach out and Read', the national literacy program, for us to publish the magazines and they will place them in pediatricians' offices for parents to take home. We also developed a relationship with two radio stations in Western North Carolina that broadcast our daily tips on behavior development, and what have you.

The main thrust of the *Sixty-Second Parent* is that we are a multi-media company focused on parenting.

You speak and write insightfully and with great skill. Do you plan to write another book?

Thank you. Yes, there are lots of books I want to write. I have written several short stories that I haven't submitted for publication yet. And of course I've done a lot of pieces and articles and things that relate to work. Now I want to get back to the creative part of writing.

I did a story on mountain lore, and one that is kind of a mystery. Now I'm writing a novella based on experiences from early childhood called *Christmas Candy* that I've been revising for some time. I'd love to get to the point where I feel comfortable enough to get it published, and I do think it will be publishable.

Do you have other hobbies or avocations?

Of course reading is one, and I enjoy being around people who tell stories. I like to putter in the ground, and love to be outside running or hiking. It's not so much gardening that I do but planting flowers and hoping they will grow, and digging in dirt and collecting things. I often pick up nice rocks to pile into a rock border, or whatever.

- **Reading Level of Today's Children—**

As a pediatrician, writer and avid reader, how concerned are you about the reading levels of today's children?

Very! The written word and reading greatly helped our growth as human beings from the beginning of civilization. Our brains have been engineered to learn by reading, and if we lose the ability to read then we lose some of the capacity to learn.
A recent study concluded that mothers who read to their small children, even to their babies, are in a real sense the champions of that child's life because they are giving an opportunity for that child's brain to fully develop an ability to learn.

If we go back and try to understand the significance of the written word we will be able to engage in better development of our brains, and that would be good for our whole society.

I've often thought about and dealt with childhood reading disability; it's been a major area of interest throughout my career. Kids of today play too many video-games and watch too much TV, and are only flat-learning. The term 'flat-learning' means simply sitting and watching something without being engaged in it.

Reading is engaging in the subject in a fashion that gives it depth, and rounds it into completeness that is the basis of learning. We miss that if we rely too much on the eye to see without the brain engaging.

- **The 'Smart Start' Program—**

You mentioned the 'Smart Start' Program, which is no doubt a smart investment in our children.

In the spring of 2011 I was asked by Governor Perdue to chair the board for the North Carolina Partnership for Children, an agency that oversees 'Smart Start', a hundred-twenty million dollar program that provides early childhood intervention in education, day care, development and more. Preschool children in this state who want to participate are eligible. Unfortunately that program was also cut by twenty percent this year, which is a real blow to parents who need quality day care for their children. Finding funding for that program occupies a significant amount of my time.

We are trying desperately to get everyone to understand, particularly our legislators, that investment in this would help the development of young children's minds, and provide a key to their ability to learn, socialize and lead in the future. Unless we invest in early childhood now, we are going to have a future with people who just sit and vacantly stare at a screen, and not understand a thing about what they are watching.

So you see this syndrome as an imminent and real danger to American children?

I see it as a danger to the entire world, as well as our country! Too much of the economy is based on technology that children engage in. Though In medicine, technology has driven us far forward, some of that technology zealously used can create rather than solve problems.

Technology for entertainment impacts one's ability to actually read. But I think Kindle and things like that are good, as long as it's a printed page that people get on it. I think that the loss of people's desire to read is a great tragedy.

Can I assume that Smart Start is confronting this dangerous syndrome?

Yes. Smart Start was started in 1993 in North Carolina, the initiative of a group of early childhood developmental specialists who saw a significant absence of programs to aid the development of young children, resulting in poor school performance and social-skill development. And the day care system then was inadequate.

Jim Hunt, governor at that time, saw this as an opportunity, and so was born Smart Start. The mission of Smart Start was to help every child enter school healthy and ready to learn. The concept was based on the idea of a public-private partnership, with a significant state grant and funds raised from the private sector.

Counties or groups banded in non-profit partnerships in each area of the state, and then contracted providers of a variety of things in education, arts and crafts, anything that aided in the development of children. This was based on the area's own particular need and ability to provide for those needs.

Significant amounts of the money went to developing better day care programs, and educating their employees. To them this was an opportunity to become educated, and many went ahead to earn college degrees in early childhood development.

At its height, roughly $221 million was distributed annually by the state to all 100 counties. But funding was cut in the last decade by $80 million dollars, and in 2011 the legislature cut it by another twenty percent.

These cuts seriously hurt our program, which was the model for this nation and countries around the world, and affected our early childhood development, education, safety and health programs, virtually every aspect of a child's health, with the family at the epicenter.

It has been clearly demonstrated that this type of early intervention leads to better performance by the third grade, with performance in math, reading and social skills being elevated over those without that experience.

What was your involvement with the program?

I was on the original board of directors for thirteen years, chaired the committee of planning and oversight which looked at how we allocated funding and developed standards for the partnerships to adhere to, and provide for the early childhood development resources.

By then I felt thirteen years on the board was enough, so I retired to focus on many other things. But Governor Perdue asked me to return as chair of the North Carolina Partnership (NCPC), so I did.

Are there qualitative or quantitative analyses of the effects of early intervention?

A report from Duke University this year analyzed data from third-grade performance levels of children who had been through Smart Start, and also the More at Four Program, compared with children who had not. It made clear that children with these experiences were statistically much better off than those without.

A study initiated almost forty years ago looked at children from disadvantaged homes and in a progressive kind of day care, and then tracked them to the present time, and they're remarkable findings. Children from disadvantaged homes and largely minorities who were in a quality day care program had fewer divorces, completed college more times, got involved less with the legal trouble, used less drugs and alcohol, and the like.

By every marker that we judge people, social and developmental skills of children with those experiences did better than those who did not. The question then is: what must it take for legislators who make the rules to learn this lesson?

Sounds like you're saying that to some people, facts don't matter.

Yes.

- **Healthcare Funding Cut Impacts—**

How are across-the-board cuts in spending at this critical moment affecting health care?

Funds previously available for training primary care physicians have dried up, so we must figure out more creative ways to raise money. But everybody is after the same dollar, and grants and other programs across the country are down from five-to-twenty percent.
Our state of North Carolina has slashed funding up to twenty percent across the board for early childhood education, intervention programs, higher education, and child development, almost a death-blow for some of those programs.

I think elected leaders who sacrifice the health and well-being of residents are acting unconscionably, but this is about you and what you think, so please summarize the political situation as you see it.

I think you are right, and that we are singing the same song. Not only is it harmful and wrong to cut programs that help people, I believe that we are in trouble as a nation because too many politicians are far off base when they are mainly guided by personal agendas for their decisions as elected officials.

The whole political debacle in Washington over recent years is a tragedy upon the face of the human existence. But this is where the human genome is going if we keep on cultivating the way we are doing now. It's time to reorganize our human DNA, I think.

You are an accomplished medical person who just might be able to help accomplish that.

I doubt I will have that many years left to try, but I am not going to give up. My hours are flexible, but I must admit since I have a brand new office that I may be spending a little too much time in it. I also work with the foundation at the hospital, and there are several other areas in which I am quite heavily involved that occupy a good deal of my time. I still work forty-plus hours a week, counting at MAHEC.

My former workload during active times was from sixty-to-seventy hours a week, which was fairly much on par with most other physicians.

- **Programs at MAHEC—**

When will programs you head at MAHEC be fully operational, and with how many resident physicians?

The programs have all been in operation for some time. In terms of the number of residencies, including a connected program in Hendersonville, we have about fifteen-to-eighteen Family Practice physicians, and six in OBGYN who start training every year. We also have a Dental residency program.

The center is now affiliated with UNC in Chapel Hill for the expansion of a medical school in this region. So there is a tremendous amount happening in relationship to medical education to help confront the increasing need for primary care doctors in this region, and throughout the country.

The residency program is for three years for the full scope of family medicine. A graduate from medical school works in the Family Health Center and the hospital to become fully trained as a family physician that can manage medical problems across the spectrum. It is the same for the OBGYN residency: they come out of medical school and are registered in the program here for three or four years, and then are qualified as an OBGYN physician.

All residency programs across the country try to get the top medical school graduates. Our program is competitive because the numbers that apply far exceeds the number of available slots. Those who finish their residency here become licensed physicians then practice wherever they want. They will have done research and papers, are highly trained, and can teach. In short, they emerge from this program as well-qualified physicians.

That is a wonderful thing to have here in Asheville.

- **Mission Children's Hospital—**

Was the hospital an immediate success?

There was some good general pediatric care in the area, and the pediatricians were doing a marvelous job. But they needed specialty care to expand their complex work for complex patients. For example, a child who had a significant need was sent to Chapel Hill or Atlanta, or someplace like that.

The hospital, as part of the safety net in the region, recognized that we needed to expand children's specialty services. Over the next decade it became Mission's Children Hospital, and now we have a true Children's Hospital here, with upwards of more than sixty pediatric specialists. I remember that when I started the hospital there were only three of us in the pediatric specialty.

And so it appears that either I have a flypaper attachment that attracts things, or else we were uncommonly lucky to have been so successful in developing the programs.

At that time in Asheville there were only a few other pediatric specialists that included Kim Masters, a child psychologist, and Will Hufstutter, a pediatric neurologist. There also were some pediatric allergists and neo-natalogists took care of the sick premature babies.

- **The Driving Force—**

But you were the driving-force behind it all, 'the boss', per se.

Yes, that was my position. Being employed as the medical director meant that I had to develop the program. I was extremely fortunate to be able to work with Linda Poss, a Nurse Administrator with Mission Hospital, whose passion was to develop a program for children, and with Lou Hammond, the Nurse Administrator for Mission's Children's and Women's services. Those two women, along with Barbra McClean who I hired, were driving forces in development of the children's hospital.

It was a little rocky at first. We were stuck on a roller-coaster, not sure which time we were up or which time we were down, and had to figure out where funding for the programs would come from. But we had tremendous support from the hospital foundation and President Bruce Thorsen, a good friend. He was a major force helping us raise funds, supporting whatever we needed, coming up with ways to obtain philanthropic donors, and so on. And Bob Burgin, Hospital CEO, was a major help in assuring development of the Children's Center.

Mission Hospital had planned to expand its inpatient part and build a new ward and a new intensive-care unit for children. There were eighteen inpatient beds, nine intensive-care beds and twenty-plus adolescent surgical beds.

Since then it has expanded the neo-natal intensive care unit to about sixty beds. So in total, the Children's Hospital inpatient wing is now comprised of about a hundred beds.

Please explain your various roles in the progression of Mission Children's Hospital from inception to now.

Progression is a good word, but evolution may be a better one. I seem to always catch the train just before it leaves the station.

As you know, I came to Asheville in 1982 from Charlotte, where there was a beginning focus on pediatric specialists in surgery and neurology that helped provide finite care and enhance general pediatrician practice. This really didn't exist here, though Asheville had wonderful general pediatricians and a fledgling pediatric floor at Mission Hospital. That was basically it.

Mission Hospital then put together a planning team of pediatricians from the community, and by the late eighties it was recognized that there was a growing need for more specialized services for children.

Through the early nineties the committee asked Mission to concentrate on developing a pediatric center for specialty care to support primary care pediatricians and primary care physicians in the area.

What were your biggest fundraising and budget challenges and obstacles?

As the growth of the children's development program at Thoms Hospital occurred, including consultations for medical genetics, it became increasingly apparent that this model of development could be utilized in meeting the other needs for specialized care in the region. Reimbursement for children's services has always lagged behind other populations needing health care. Thus we had to always turn to additional resources for funds.

We raised just over eleven-million dollars for a new outpatient center building that we turned over to the hospital. It opened six years ago. In terms of total philanthropic dollars, I would say we raised about twenty-million dollars over the past fifteen years.

I still enjoy telling meaningful stories about the joy of taking good care of our children to groups and organizations across the state and country.

And I'm still a consultant to the children's programs in development, working with the foundation to raise money, and work with the hospital on two political fronts, in Raleigh and in Washington. Those efforts take about forty percent of my time.

• Involvement of Ruth and Billy Graham—

How did Billy and Ruth Graham become involved in the hospital?

Community leaders associated with that effort enlisted Ruth and Billy Graham because they lived here, and Ruth's father was instrumental in some of the medical work that led to the formation of Mission Hospital. Ground was broken in 1993 for the new wing of the hospital that would house a pediatric care unit on a pediatric floor.

At that time it was named The Ruth and Billy Graham Children's Health Center. The Grahams had generously allowed use of their names for this unfolding program because it was dedicated to the expansion of children specialty services for WNC, and there were few specialty services in this region for pediatric patients.

I developed a pretty solid relationship with Ruth, and had some good visits with her in her home and other places. She was a very gracious person. I also had some interesting times with Billy himself. He was still on the trail at that time, but of course has since slowed way down. We can't overstate the power value of the Graham names. They attracted national attention to the program, and gave us a jump-start, in relation to what could have been.

Everett Koop, then the Surgeon General of the United States, gave the keynote speech at the groundbreaking ceremony for the new wing of the hospital in 1993.

The members of the Graham family who were present made a plaster mold of their hands. That motif has been used many times to represent how the hands of dedicated people have aided the lives of so many children.

My wife went to the ground-breaking but I could not because I was responsible for treating patients at Thoms Hospital.

Tell me about the Congressional Medal presented to the Grahams.

When Newt Gingrich was Speaker of the House of Representatives, Ruth and Billy Graham were given the Congressional Gold Medal. The Graham's graciously allowed an event to take place that would give publicity to the emerging children center.

A dinner was held that night in Washington, D.C. to which all sorts of dignitaries were invited. Paul Harvey was the master of ceremonies, and speakers included President Bill Clinton, Surgeon General Koop, and the Grahams' son Franklin.

I was the final speaker of the evening. I read the prepared remarks I wrote in about ten minutes while flying on an airplane a few weeks before. For some reason, and I think this must have been the kind of thing Lincoln had happen when he quickly wrote the Gettysburg Address, because I found the right thing to say at the right time, and in very few words. It seemed to capture the imagination of everyone in the audience, and was probably the best speech I ever gave.

It was incredible what happened as a result of my little speech: I got letters from people who heard it saying that I had captured the essence of the evening, and in less than five minutes.

What was the essence of your speech?

The essence was that experience had taught me that no matter the station of life a parent found themselves in, with rare exceptions they loved their children, and that it is incumbent upon us to recognize the people we serve by providing compassion and appropriate medical care. And I told how Billy Graham's tour of the neonatal intensive unit, where small babies cling to life, had impressed him so much that he asked what my dreams for the program were. So I told him. He said to me, "Dream your dreams because they have a way of coming true."

I concluded my speech by saying, "These are the dreams for our children: that their bodies will be healthy, their minds clear, and their spirits filled with joy."

• Opportunity Arises—

So, duty came first and kept you from that significant event.

In mid-1993, Bob Burgin, CEO of Mission Hospital, called me to ask, "What kind of person do we need to lead this program, what are the necessary qualifications?"

I answered, "There are three things to look for: find someone who understands specialty care, is familiar with the local areas and not competitive with practitioners here now, and has some sense of the national scope." Then he said to me, "I want your CV" and I replied, "Sorry, not interested, I'm happy in the program that I'm doing." A few weeks later he called again and demanded, "I want your CV!" This time I replied, "I give up, you can have it."

There was a national search going on, but by then I'd become interested in the opportunity, and the possibilities of what could happen. Eventually I was chosen to lead the program, and on January 1st of 1994 assumed the position of medical director of what was then called the Ruth and Billy Graham Children's Health Center.

It was one of those things you almost had to hold onto with both hands because that train was moving rapidly out of the station! But six months into the program we had pediatric surgery, pediatric intensive care, and pediatric cancer care.

• Growth—

Just how fast did that train go?

We continued to grow rapidly, as pediatric specialists came in, and then space became a problem. So we moved all sorts of things around in terms of revolving space in order to do the outpatient work. By late 1994 and early 1995, we had six or eight pediatric specialists, and everything was moving very rapidly.

After five years, the Ruth and Billy Graham Organization, the BGEA, had grown uncomfortable that the Graham name was used to attract attention and funds, and some people misunderstood our mission. So, we made a mutually agreeable decision in the late 1990's to remove the Graham name and simply call it Mission Children's Hospital.

We were now qualified for the National Association of Children's Hospitals and Related Institutions because we had developed resources such as outreach programs, the dental program, the Family Support Network and the Safe Kids Network, and hosted summer camps. We had specialists in quite a few areas, as well as designated nursing inpatient and outpatient programs.

That was the evolution of the hospital. I was kind of riding the crest of the wave, identifying people we should hire as specialists, working with the Mission staff overseeing development of the program, recommending where we should and shouldn't put money, doing much of the PR and fundraising, and continuing to see patients.

- **The State of Medicine Today—**

What do you think of the state of medicine in the country today, compared to 20 or 30 years ago?

Technically, medicine has greatly advanced. Technology has dramatically changed the face of how we do things. Pharmacological research and efforts have hugely increased, and both have driven up the cost of medical care. And there is a great deal of confusion and misconception that all of us in medical care know the best way to take care of people, or the best way for them to access the medical care they need.

One-on-one contact was very important in my practice. I knew my families well and they knew me, a good collaboration. But now most personal contact has been lost in the medical profession, now care is fragmented.

We are trying to get back to the concept of the 'medical home'. But I fear that as technology advances and the cost of care goes up, we will continue to have multi-tiered medical care. It is no secret that children covered by Medicaid get less care, and that care is less well-delivered than those who are in private pay insurance.

That's the nature of our system now, and I think that is unfortunate, and just not right.

Would you care to comment on the state of the health insurance industry, and the potential value of a single-payer solution?

Remember that the health insurance industry is a private business, and the bottom line is to make money, and that's the reason they exist. They gamble on benefiting from insuring at a lesser fee those people who are probably not going to be terribly ill will, and charging more to insure those people who may become terribly ill. Sadly, that person is usually on the spectrum of medical bankruptcy.

I don't think Insurance companies operate on conscience, nor should they be expected to. And, we will always have a need for private carriers, private insurance, whatever you call it.

I do believe that we need to re-vamp the system of care, and I think that all people have the right to medical care. The single-payer solution is a very appropriate way to do it, and would be the most significant system to accomplish what we are after. But that will never happen in this country. There are just too many opposing forces, and too much money to be made by those opposing forces. Sadly, money is always what drives the bottom line.

Is there a major move in this nation to return to family medicine?

The National Institute of Medicine identified the fact that there is a shortage of primary care physicians in the country, well-documented over the last decade, but now, in my opinion, a great deal of personal contact is now placed on trying to train more.

There are four types of primary care physicians by definition: those in OBGYN, family medicine and pediatrics, and internal medicine. Those four groups of physicians comprise the primary care workforce for medical care in the country, so there has been emphasis upon training more of them.

The one area that seems to be attracting fewer physicians is internal medicine; internists are spinning off into various phases of adult care medicine rather than into general internal medicine.

- **About Childhood Obesity—**

You put a major focus on childhood obesity. Tell me about that epidemic.

When I was in general pediatric practices in Charlotte in the seventies and early eighties, we seldom saw children who were obese, and we never saw a condition called Type II Diabetes in children. But those conditions are now evident in at least a third of our pre-school children, and a fourth of our elementary and high school children.

We have a raging obesity epidemic brought on by a number of factors: the movement from an active lifestyle to a sedentary lifestyle compounded by excess TV watching, and overuse of computers and electronic games.

Further compounding this are changes in school profiles that demand more academic programs rather than active interaction for children, accessibility to foods high in fat and low in caloric strength, economic situations and lifestyles of parents who both might be working, *etcetera.*

Over the last few decades this epidemic spread worldwide, and studies now show that children of this generation will live shorter lives than the previous one. It is more complicated than just getting the right kind of exercise and eating the right kind of foods, it also has to do with poverty, where people live, and many other factors.

This is something that we are becoming more involved in, more concerned about. Next month I'll be co-chairing a new task-force from the Institute of Medicine in North Carolina that will address childhood obesity.

What data concludes that for the first time, today's children will have less longevity than their parents?

This data is from the Center of Disease Control and from the National Institute of Health, developed through the American Academy of pediatrics. Almost every major scientific body has collected data with the same results.

The reason for such concern is that obesity early in life leads to kidney disease, cancer, pulmonary disease, cardiovascular disease, skeletal disease, and depression. In fact, it leads to all of the major factors of health that we can measure. It is a really critical problem.

- **Defining a Career—**

As you look back, how would you define your distinguished career that continues to this day?

The most defining part of my career medically has to be patient contact, working with children and their families. For any pediatrician of note, that has to be the highlight of their career, just to be able to do that!

I decided it was time to retire from practice at age sixty-five, and then was asked to become a Senior Fellow with 'Action for Children', an advocacy group in North Carolina. They knew that in my practice I had influenced one family and one child at a time, and now could influence the care of multiple children and multiple families at the same time by advocating better health care, better reimbursement, and better opportunities in education for those who accessed the program.

I look at what I'm doing now, and what my next steps will be. That's an evolutionary process for me, the way my mind tends to work. I see opportunities that ought to be fulfilled, and then go on to the next step. It seems those around me often say, "Hey let's do this," and I find myself in the center of being able to ignite things.

For example, I love to drive on the Blue Ridge Parkway and love hiking, so recently I thought to myself: "What is wrong with building a program, or doing some kind of initial work to get families or just children out on the trails around the parkway." We have this natural resource here, and we could teach them about nutrition and activity, and this would help with the obesity epidemic.

I met with the director of the Blue Ridge Parkway Foundation, who liked my idea. Then we met with Phil

Francis, superintendent of the Blue Ridge Parkway, who said, "Hey that's a great idea." Next we gathered a small group of people for a meeting, and from that Blue Cross and Blue Shield gave us money to hire a facilitator. We had brainstormed, and the program now known as 'Kids and Parks' was born.

Coincidentally, just this morning my wife told me that an article in the Mountain Section of this morning's local paper reported that Blue Cross and Blue Shield has given a significant grant of over $700,000 to Kids and Parks', and the program was now designed to get families and children out on the trails in National and State Parks. From that idea, the program has now gone viral: it's all over the country!

That is a perfect explanation of evolution within my own career; and how my mind is like a computer: new information in and new answers out!

- **Advice for Young Physicians—**

What advice would you give to young physicians?

If I were to teach a course in medical school now, it would be to inspire young physicians. I would hope this would be an introductory course in the first year then again as the last course in the last year. I would basically want them to know they will be treading very precious ground!

Medicine is the only area of life where people put so much trust in the hands of another, their bodies, their hopes, their dreams, their souls, their worries, their fears, their aspirations. People will show their very essence and what their needs are, so you need to wrap your head around the fact that you will be doing something nobody else in the world can do. So, never, ever deny yourself the privilege of recognizing that as a gift to you.

They should learn that technology can get in the way of understanding that we're dealing with people who need medical help. One of the things that was delightful was engaging families about their history, like asking "where did ya' come from, where did ya' grow up, when did ya' get married?" To me the history of a family was so entertaining, and furthermore, it helped you enter their lives and gain trust.

- **Feelings—**

What are your feelings when parents say thanks for helping their child?

Well, it would be a feeling of satisfaction. But I also say to them, "I may be the one who points out the right direction, but it is you who do the real work."

And who else besides your high school teacher Mr. Willis inspired the young Olson Huff?

The Reverend Harry Bentley, pastor of the Salem Baptist Church in the little community where I grew up. He preached but did not preach at you! He was constructive and supportive and kind and forward thinking.

Baptists then were not like Baptists today, and he seemed to appreciate the value of young people, and provided an atmosphere where people cared and the church was a welcoming place.

- **About Faith—**

You are an ordained elder in the Presbyterian Church; would you share some core religious beliefs?

I believe the human person is designed to have a focus outside their self. I think we need to have a center greater than us, and we need to structure our sense of being.

My life began in a religious environment that was pretty restrictive, the old hard-shell fundamental Baptist that guarantees Hellfire damnation if you act bad, play cards or drink. My parents were part of that but didn't preach to us, never told us to believe this or do that, like so many of my cousins, aunts and uncles, and of course my parents. Although I did not necessarily recognize their strengths, I sensed their concern and support. I can easily look back and see how very important their influence was.

When we moved to the farm in Indiana we again went to the Baptist church, a good place that gave me an understanding of the basic Christian principles I grew up with that seemed legitimate to accept, like Jesus is God, Jesus died for us to go to Heaven, standard stuff that was pretty much all right with me.

One of the first persons I met at the University of Kentucky was Andy Blaine, director of the Baptist Student Union that became for many of us our fraternity or sorority. He made so much sense, and it was a collegial, comforting and reassuring place to be, just a wonderful experience.

There we had noon-day devotions and all sorts of standard Christianity expressed with kindness and acceptance, and that set well with me.

I believed then that Baptists were the chosen group, but didn't have a problem with Jews or Catholics or anybody. Andy was a mentor in terms of getting people to ask questions about this. He didn't stay long, went to Oxford for his Doctorate, and then became an under-secretary of the United Nations.

In medical school the Christian Medical Society provided a resource for nurturing faith that related to the profession, and this made me to think of myself as a healer in the same respect that Jesus was a healer. I could identify with that, and again followed standard religious protocol.

Through most of my early practice experience, marriage, life, things pretty much worked out that same way. However, I then began to look more at the broadness of what it means to have a faith, what to really believe in, what the Bible says. I began to understand that much of the Bible is literature inspired by people's perception of a spirit that is guiding them, and that much of the teachings are great psychology, some of the best in the world.

It may seem strange to love your neighbor, but by the same token show anger. If you control that anger you will become a healthier person. There is tremendous psychological counseling in the Bible, and those who wrote it were not ignorant. I began to understand that there is a flow to what we believe in that can guide our relationship with others, and give us something to hold on emotionally, psychologically, socially, spiritually. That is the guiding principal that I think we ought to call God.

The gospel of John begins: "In the Beginning there was the Word and the Word was light and that light became the guiding principal of the world." That word was God.

That is paraphrasing the first chapter and first sentences. What I think that gospel means is: God begat God, God is the creator of God, and that spirit was formed from the utter void of space so we can incorporate into ourselves a belief in who we are, and that can give us an ability to impart that to others.

To me "in the beginning" is the continuation, and as spiritual human beings we are attracted to a 'light', if you will, and at the same time believe that we are not rigidly involved in a categorical framework of religious dogma so literal that it could destroy much of the world.

In my rambling words here is the evolution of my faith: I was comfortable in a structure without questions, but I now understand the whole dimension of faith is to lead one's life based upon principals portrayed through Biblical writings, and that the evolution of understanding from past generations sensitive to themselves and what they heard from one another made them sensitive enough to write the words we can live by.

- **Observations and Questions—**

Many people might wonder just how you managed to rise from childhood on a hardscrabble farm to become a successful physician, author, film producer and, most of all, family man.

For me, being able to read was important. I was an early and avid reader of stories, and was captivated by *Ivanhoe,* its romance and action, and by Hurlburt's Bible Stories, where I could imagine Goliath and David, and other examples of characters who overcame to achieve glory.

I guess I'm Horatio Alger-ish. I was a playful boy, and I didn't experience harshness from my parents or in school in Pittsburgh, Kentucky, and I had my books.

How would you respond if I said you seemed to be a happy and contented man?

I would say that you are right! In fact, Marylyn and I talked about that just last night. We were having dinner on our screened-in back deck, where in good weather we usually eat breakfast and dinner. Our view is full of beautiful trees and greenery, and we enjoy watching the birds eat from the bird-feeder. We were just finishing when we commented to each other just how pleasant it all is, and how very fortunate we are.

We certainly do not have an exotic lifestyle, nor do we have expensive tastes. We do like to travel, modestly. We were in London last fall, never been there before. I liked their class, and boy did we have a good time, it was one of the most wonderful weeks ever. I absolutely love London; it's a great city.

I'll bet that you consider yourself fortunate?

Oh gosh yes! No way on earth do I understand how I got where I am; nor do I understand the reasons I get so many awards for the different things I do. I don't understand because I don't see myself as an extra-special individual; I just see myself as being fortunate to be where I am, and being surrounded by such special people in my life.

I often think that when you get into these fortunate positions you can inspire ideas for others to fulfill. Then you and they can move on to the next idea.

You are obviously a sensitive and caring person, and you seem to rely on your instincts, both as a human being, and as a pediatrician. Am I right?

Yes. I am sensitive, especially to things around us, whether it is a butterfly on the bush, a bird in the air, blue sky or a storm, and to awareness of the dignity in people, and in all the dirt that makes us human.

That's what I was trying to capture in a one-page fantasy piece I wrote, about why it was so significant for me to observe the homeless out on the street, and then being able to translate what I saw: that people in such bad straits can be an inspiration to somebody else.

As a healer, I instinctively know that if something is true of one group of children in need then it is true of many more children. Their need becomes a personal challenge, and I challenge others to seek ways to bring their influence, resources and passion together to help as many children as possible have the best opportunity for a healthy and happy life.

Sometimes I serve as peacemaker, negotiator, facilitator, supporter and catalyst for others. I hope that I have helped make North Carolina a model for access to healthcare, services and support for children and their families.

That's all part of my nature, what I've done, what I do.

Dr. Huff with wife Marylyn and Heath Shuler (center) before he was elected to congress, and friends.

. . . with wife and two of the stars of the film, Cameron Bancroft and Aidan Mitchell.

Dr. Olson Huff often enjoys spending time with his family, and is seen in this photo hiking.

. . . with son David, and grandchildren at "Simple Things" screening preview.

. . . in his military garb.

Olson Huff and David being interviewed at the premier of their movie, "Simple Things."

Section 5: **Excerpts from Dr. Huff's extensive writings**

- ## From *The Window of Childhood*—

Dr. Huff's book *The Window of Childhood* consists of nineteen heartwarming short stories about how children tell us of love, joy, pain, death, hope, friendship and the discovery of new things. He provides a window through which children are seen as unpolished and unspoiled persons who excite response and encourage participation. The vignettes portray children as vibrant, dynamic persons. A quote from the book sums up Dr. Huff's incredible compassion for his young charges, and for all of us:

As we experience children, as we see them not as small creatures but as vibrant and dynamic persons, we can experience our own roots and begin to discover ourselves. They tell us of love, joy, pain, death, hope, and fears that are often locked deep within us.

Dr. Huff invites the reader to share in each child's vulnerability and pride, fear and hope, simplicity and complexity, and reminds us that childhood is more than a time for growing up, more than a prelude to adulthood. His books go beyond personal stories and instinctive advice and counsel for parents, they are reflections of his deep commitments to being a husband and father, and then a pediatrician. This is clearly evidenced by his dedications in book:

To Marylyn, whose gentle insistence of do it, do it has borne fruit; and to David, Stephen and Daniel, who taught me that being a pediatrician did not make me a better father, but that being a father helped me to be a better pediatrician'.

The author poignantly relates stories of real children like—
- Flora, a nine-year-old who comforted other children in the hospital with her cheerful presence. More interested in the happenings of others, she paid little attention to her own plight; and
- April, a baby with spina-bifida who permanently affected everyone who knew her, though she never walked and spoke only a few words; and
- A boy who has a special relationship with his dog, teacher, step-sister, and a newly found friend; he had been labeled as having 'behavioral problems' who develops into a fine leader.

- ## Dr. Huff's *Reflections*—

Dr. Huff presented *Reflections of a Past-President'* at the North Carolina Pediatric Society's 80th Anniversary event in August of 2011 at the Grove Park Inn Resort and Spa in Asheville:

On the wall of the study hall of my high school was a picture titled 'Looking Forward'. The artist had placed in the center of the painting a young man, resolute, eyes toward the future, his hand pushing open a gate, and his parents standing on the steps behind him waving goodbye.

In some ways, that is what we pediatricians do: look forward. We take the young, their unsure parents, their communities and their own fragile dreams and push them forward. We do so because it's not only our job, but also our calling. In that job and in that calling we discover much about our profession and ourselves. In that respect, I found the meaning of being president of the North Carolina Pediatric Society.

First, I had to look backwards, not forward. I had to lean on the legacy of those who formed the mold I was to fit: the Tayloes, Edwards, Schwartz', Williams, Princes, and a host of others whose character, passion common sense and intellect had seen to it that indeed there would be children who could look forward, and have ties that were safe, healthy and rewarding, and that their environment would be the same. The legacy they provided me was advocacy, and that defined the meaning of my presidency.

Prevention of smoking, handgun control, bike helmets, all-terrain-vehicles, child abuse, vaccines, Medicaid, adequate pay for a day's work all became the themes of advocacy that were not always easily diagnosed, and certainly never rapidly cured. Of all those, however, the most demanding one was the fight to have North Carolina adopt the new federal program designed to provide health insurance coverage for children who were just a bit above Medicaid levels of eligibility.

SCHIP brought me into the world of political maneuvering and face-to-face with the challenge of being what I was elected by my colleagues to do. By leaning on the legacy of those before me and look to what could be. I learned that diagnosing and treating ills took on new meaning. Like the Lorax who spoke for the trees, I had to speak for the children. It was in that fashion that the meaning of my term as President of the North Carolina Pediatric Society was defined.

• From His *JAMA* Column—

Following are excerpts from the column by Dr. Olson Huff in the *Journal of the American Medical Association* (JAMA) March 16, 1984 edition titled 'The Face Beyond' and sub-titled 'A Piece of My Mind':

Occasionally when my day seems such a jumble of incessant crying children, demanding problems, and lengthening hours, as to make me wonder about my choice of profession, I remember the face of a certain child, and I am renewed . . . I don't recall his name. He always sat rigidly in his wheelchair backed up against the wall, white enameled steel beds surrounding him like the bars in a prison . . . His dark eyes burned when I dared to look at him, and I knew that he needed more from me than movies. I pretended not to notice . . . That was years ago, and I don't recall his name. But like a flicker of blue sky pushing through gray clouds, my mind is occasionally stimulated by the memory of his searching eyes, and I am challenged anew: challenged to be the man whose presence can release some of the fear and hurt in the young who see me daily, and challenged to reassure them that they no longer need to search beyond my face to find one who is a friend.

• About the Doctor in *Our State*—

An article about Dr. Huff was published in *Our State* magazine's January 2005 magazine. It was written by Constance E. Richards and headlined *Doctors Now* with the sub-head *One for the Kids— Dr. Olson Huff, Asheville Pediatrician*. The following is excerpted from the article's text:

North Carolina's children have someone looking out for them. Named one of the 100 most influential citizens of Western North Carolina in the 20th century by the Asheville Citizen-Times, developmental pediatrician Dr. Olson Huff has been a stalwart advocate for the health and safety of children for than 33 years. Now his approach to wellness of children is going national with plans for a feature-length motion picture, a book, and a campaign to fund new children's outpatient and educational centers that will serve several states in the Southeast.

More than just partaking in the physical treatment of children, Huff has been instrumental and active in voicing concerns and finding solutions for those who are too small to be heard.

"It's not healthy for any of us," Huff argues. "We simply need more random play. We need to have our communities to build in places for random play—greenways, walkways and parkways for encouraging people to get out into activity that doesn't sit them in front of a TV or video game."

While the problems for children's health care nationally are still legion and the goals lofty – widespread health insurance, the best preventive care for children, developing good communications skills in children, and easing the burden of poverty through policy changes – Dr. Olson Huff is leading the uphill battle from his corner of North Carolina.

Section 6: **Chronology**

- **Career—**
- 2002-Present: Pediatric Medical Consultant to Mission Hospital and Mission Children's Hospital.
- Current: Adjunct Faculty for MAHEC, the Mountain Area Health Education Center, Asheville; Chairman of the Board, 'The Sixty-Second Parent' multi-media company.
- 1994-to-2001: Founding Medical Director and Developmental Pediatrician, Ruth and Billy Graham Children's Health Center- became Mission Children's Hospital in 1999.
- 1987-1994: Developmental Pediatrician, Founding Medical Director, Center for Childhood Development and Learning, Thoms Rehabilitation Hospital - renamed The Olson Huff Center in 1994.
- 1980-1990: Assistant Clinical Professor of Pediatrics for MAHEC.
- 1982-1987: Developmental Pediatrician for the Developmental Evaluation Center in Asheville.
- 1978-1980: Developmental Pediatric Program Consultant for Emotional and Behavioral Adjustment, Charlotte-Mecklenburg public schools.
- 1974-1979: Developmental Pediatrician, Charlotte-Mecklenburg Center for Human Development
- 1970: Certified by the American Board of Pediatrics.
- 1968-1971: Private practice for pediatrics and child development in Charlotte, N.C.
- 1957-1958: Public school teacher at Clear Spring High School, Clear Spring, Indiana.

- **Education—**
- Summer 1986: Mini-Fellowship, Medical Genetics, Wake Forest University School of Medicine.
- 1973: Studies in Special Education of Handicapped Children and Fellowship Training Developmental Pediatrics, Division for Disorders of Development and Learning, UNC Chapel Hill.
- 1967-1968: Chief Resident in Pediatrics, Charlotte Memorial Hospital, Charlotte, N.C.
- 1966-1967: Resident in Pediatrics, Charlotte Memorial Hospital.
- Summer 1963: Aviation Medicine School, Brooke Air Force Base, San Antonio, Texas.
- 1962-1963: Rotating Internship, Wilford Hall USAF Hospital, San Antonio, Texas.
- 1962: M.D. Degree, University of Louisville, Louisville, Kentucky.
- 1958: Post-Graduate Studies, History and Biology, University of Kentucky.
- 1957: B.A. Chemistry, University of Kentucky.
- Summer at Indiana University, 1955.

- **Academic Appointments—**
- Assistant Clinical Professor of Pediatrics, University of North Carolina at Chapel Hill, 1975-1992.
- Assistant Professor of Family Medicine, UNC, 1992-present.
- Assistant Professor, Dept. of Special Education, Western Carolina University, Cullowhee, 1988-1989.
- Guest Lecturer in Child Development, UNC, 1977-1978.

- **Military Service—**
- 1963-1964: Flight Surgeon for the US Air Force, stationed Takhli, Thailand, and Saigon, Viet Nam.
- 1964-1966 stationed at Pease Air Force Base in New Hampshire.

- **Honors and Recognitions—**
- Glaxco-Kline Lifetime Achievement Award, 2011.
- Jim Bernstein Community Health Achievement Award, 2011
- Founder's Award, Mission Hospital, 2009.
- Advocacy Award, Senior Section, American Academy of Pediatrics, 2009.
- Inducted into University of Kentucky's 'College of Fine Arts and Sciences Hall of Fame', 2009.
- Lifetime Achievement Award, Distinguished Service, Asheville-Buncombe Comm. Rel. Council, 2009.

- Smart Start of North Carolina Dick Arnold Volunteer Award, 2008.
- One of *Ashville Citizen-Times* '100 Most Influential Persons in Western N.C. in the 20th Century'.
- The Order of the Long Leaf Pine, one of North Carolina's highest civilian awards, 2007.
- Lewis Hine Award, National Child Labor Committee, 2007.
- AHEC Glen Wilson Award for Public Service, 2007.
- Child Abuse Prevention Services Blue-Ribbon Award, 2006.
- Health and Wellness Trust Fund Distinguished Service Award for Preventive Health, 2005.
- Advocacy Award, NC Alliance for Athletics, Health, Physical Education, Recreation and Dance, 2004.
- Citation for Outstanding Service as Pres. of NC Chapter, American Association of Pediatricians, 2003.
- Glaxo Smith Kline Child Health Recognition Award, 2002.
- David Tayloe, Sr. Community Service Award, NC Chapter of AAP.
- Leslie Anderson Leadership Award, 2001.
- North Carolina Dental Society Special Recognition Award, 1998.

- **Professional Society Memberships—**
- American Academy of Pediatrics, *Emeritus* Fellow.
- North Carolina Pediatric Society and NC Chapter of AAP.
- North Carolina Medical Society, *emeritus m*ember.
- Buncombe County, NC Medical Society, *emeritus* member.
- Senior Section AAP member.
- College of Physician Executives.
- Academy of Cerebral Palsy and Developmental Pediatrics.

- **Professional Boards—**
- Frank Porter Graham Child Development Institute.
- Advisory Board, Children First, Buncombe County.
- Advisory Board, Buncombe County Child Abuse Prevention Services.
- Advisory Board, Blue Ridge Parkway Foundation.
- Chair, Board of Directors, Healthy Kids, Healthy Parks, Blue Ridge Parkway Foundation.
- Chair, Board of Directors, North Carolina Partnership for Children.
- Governor appointee to Task Force on Integration of Early Childhood Programs in North Carolina.

- **Books Authored—**
- *The Window of Childhood:Glimpses of Wonder and Courage,* Westminster John Knox Press 1990/2001.
- *Practical Guide to Parenting Two, Three and Four Year Olds,* Book One of *The Triumphant Child Series* from 'The Sixty-Second Parent'.
- *The First 60 Days of Life: How to Enjoy Your Newborn Baby,* a part of *The Triumphant Child Series.*
- Plus numerous articles, op-ed pieces, letters to editor, *etc.*

- **Personal—**
- Born August 6, 1936 in Krypton, Kentucky.
- Married to Marylyn (Zibell), sons David, Stephen and Daniel, resides in Black Mountain, N.C.
- Ordained elder in Presbyterian Church, PCUSA.
- Hobbies: enjoys reading mystery novels, history, writing, hiking, jogging, playing with grandchildren Katie, Lydia, Benjamin and Riley.

Note: Dr. Huff plans to continue writing in his semi-retirement, including his first novel. For information about acquiring books or articles authored by Dr. Huff, please e-mail: olson@60secondparent.com

Glenis Redmond

Performance Poet

Omaha Indian Grandma Donna's translation of 'poet':
"Woman that flies with words."

Sections about Performance Poet Glenis Redmond:

1) From Those in the Know about Glenis Redmond

2) Key Biographical Highlights about the Poet

3) Comprehensive Poetry Definitions

4) **Glenis' Life Journey, in Her Own Words**

5) Selections from Glenis Redmond's Beautiful Poetry

6) Photos

Section 1: **From Those in the Know about Glenis Redmond**

- **From a United States Representative—**

Glenis Redmond, a person of passion and depth, pulls at our heartstrings, and makes us think beyond our personal bubbles. The first time I heard her recite a poem about her grandmother, I was a fan.

I appreciate and admire Glenis, and she would get my vote for 'Poet Laureate'.
  — **U.S. Rep. Patsy Keaver, Asheville, N.C.**

- **From Fifth World Women—**

I am at the feet of Glenis Redmond and the epic women's lineage she harkens from. She is a whirling dervish for creative good and a force of nature. She moves mountains and she is the mountain.   — **Debra Roberts, fifthworldwomen.com and holybeepress.com**

- **From a Senior Citizen Center Director—**

Glenis Redmond is absolutely phenomenal! The seniors were mesmerized from the first to the last spoken word.

Ms. Glenis has the unique ability to take you on an unforgettable journey that soothes the heart and touches the soul while building bridges of understanding, forgiveness and love.

Her delivery is bold, engaging and spellbinding. We will never be the same.
  — **Melanie Marie Ford, director Senior Citizen Resource Center, New Brunswick, N.J.**

- **Press Release from Loyd Artists—**

Glenis Redmond's love of words has carried her across the country for many years. Glenis logs over 35,000 miles a year bringing poetry to the masses.

This 'Road Warrior Poet', though steeped in Afro-Carolinian roots, speaks a universal tongue of love, loss, celebration, sorrow and hope. Her verse lifts family, culture and community.

She encourages others to find their voice at diverse venues, from prisons, universities, festivals, conferences, theatres to schools.

Her poems sooth, elicit and inspire others to travel their own poetic road.

- **From a *Wild Goose* Review—**

I've heard Nikki Giovanni, Lucille Clifton and Evie Shockley read their wonderful work, and I've heard the extraordinary prose of Alice Walker, Zora Neale Hurston and Toni Morrison, and now there is another name to add to the pantheon of powerful black women writers: Glenis Redmond.

I've not yet heard her 'perform' her poetry, although her credentials as a finalist in the National Poetry Slam and reputation as a performer speak highly of her stature.

I just finished her collection of Poetry 'Under the Sun', and found it brilliant and enjoyable throughout.
  — **From a review of Under the Sun published in 'Wild Goose, Winter 2008.**

- **From a Glenis Fan—**

Words jump from Glenis Redmond's tongue. They swing and strut, sigh and scream — like fireworks that sizzle, boom and fall as sparks, stirring listeners in their wake.
   — **Anonymous.**

- **From a Newspaper Review—**

Redmond doesn't read her poem so much as she declares it in full-body motion.
   — **Orlando Sentinel.**

- **The Way Her Words Draw You In—**

It's the way her words seem to draw you into a seemingly innocuous subject and singe you with the fury of intelligence scorned. It's in another league.
   — **London Time Out.**

- **From a North Carolina Poet Laureate—**

Glenis Redmond's poem 'Footnotes' closes out the new issue, and I give five-star credit to Editor George Brosi for that decision because the poem, in addition to being a stunner, is a piece that lingers in your mind long after you've closed the magazine.

Glenis, well-known as a performance poet, has been honing her poetic skills and expanding her poetic territory.
   — **Review by former NC Poet Laureate Kathleen Stripling Byer in *Appalachian Heritage*.**

Section 2: **Key Biographical Highlights about the Poet**

- **Education—**

Glenis Redmond, a longtime resident of Asheville, is a native of Greenville, S.C. and an Erskine College graduate there. She recently received a Master of Fine Arts in Poetry Degree at Warren Wilson College in Swannanoa, N.C.

The celebrated 'Performance Poet' was on the Task Force that created the first Writer-in-Residence program at the Carl Sandburg Home National Historic Site in Flat Rock, is a 2010 Hermitage Fellow, and is a Kennedy Center Teaching Artist listed in their National Register for touring performing artists.

- **Awards and Recognitions—**

The notable poet is a Cave Canem Fellow, Literary Fellowship recipient from the North Carolina Arts Council, where she is a Humanities Council trustee, and was an 18th Annual Arida Arts Symposium Honoree in 2010.

Glenis' essay, *Memory: What Hangs on Trees* will be published in *Orion Magazine*, and several of her poems were published in *Home is an Anthology of African American Poetry* in *Carolinas Hub-Bub City*.

Also in the summer of 2012, her poem titled *Carolinese,* Glenis was announced as one of the semi-finalists in the James Applewhite Poetry competition that was recommended for publication in the *North Carolina Literary Review* by the Poetry Editor*.

Glenis again was awarded the "Best WNC Poet in 2011" from the *Mt. Xpress* Hall of Fame, which she has won every year since 1999. The e-mail to her read: "Greetings and great news for you. You were voted #1 Poet by our readers for 2011! Congratulations!" Arenda

Glenis previously earned the Denny C. Plattner Poetry Award in 2008 for the *Appalachian Heritage Journal*, won a North Carolina Literary Fellowship in 2005-2006, received the William Mathews Award in 2002, won a Vermont Studio Grant in 1997, received the Carrie McCray Literary Award in 1995, and was awarded an Atlantic Center for the Arts Grant in 1995.

- **Community Involvement—**

Glenis has served on the board of the Asheville Arts Museum since 2010, the North Carolina Humanities Council since 2009, and is a member of the Associated Writing Program since 2008.

She also served the Asheville Arts Council from 2003-2006, Project STEAM from 2003-2005, and the Flat Rock Playhouse from 2004-2005.

- **Books and Writings by Glenis—**

Glenis' 2007 book of poetry is titled *Under the Sun,* and her 2004 book is titled *Backbone: Underground Epics*, published by Main Street Rag in Charlotte, N.C.

Her audio recordings include *Monumental* in 2004, *Coming Forth* produced by Whitewater Studios in 1997, *Glenis on Poetry* on National Public Radio in 2002, and *Mama's Magic* from Heron Productions in 1998.

Individual pieces by Glenis have been featured in *Meridians, The Asheville Poetry Review, Obsedian II,* and numerous other literary journals across the nation.

- **A 'Road Poet'—**

Glenis is known as a fulltime 'road poet', performing and teaching poetry across the country.

She founded 'The Asheville Poetry Slam' at the Green Door down Carolina Lane, where she found a 'tribe of poets' that answered her Afro-Carolinian call and response poetry stride-for-stride.

She was brought more alive by that movement, became a true-believer of 'words that sing and dance in the air' then twice became Individual Regional Slam champion and top-ten National finalist.

Glenis hopes to conjure poetry each time she 'speaks a poem', whether a signature piece or a newly fashioned poem. She loves poetry in all its shapes and forms.

Among Glenis' select venues in Western North Carolina include the Diana Wortham Theatre in Asheville, the Asheville WordFest and Warren Wilson College.

In South Carolina she performs at The Peace Center for the Performing Arts in Greenville, Duke University in Durham, and UNC Wilmington.

Other performance venues are throughout Florida, and in Washington, New Jersey and Hawaii.

She has also performed at the Paddington International Poetry Slam in London, England.

To contact Glenis Redmond e-mail poetica11@aol.com

Note: Samples of poems written by Glenis Redmond, including *Carolinese* that was selected for publication in the *North Carolina Literary Review* appear in Section 5.

Section 3: Comprehensive Poetry Definitions

Compiled by State Theater, New Brunswick, NJ

- **PERFORMANCE POETRY—**

Type of spoken word that includes elements of theatre and sometimes music.

- **HIP HOP POETRY—**

Poetry performed to a rhythmic beat; an element of the larger hip hop culture encompassing specific styles of music, dance, fashion, graffiti art, *etc.*

- **RAP—**

The rhythmic spoken delivery of rhymes, word-play and poetry, often with musical accompaniment; part of hip hop culture. There is some debate about whether rap should be considered poetry or music.

- **SLAM POETRY—**

Hip hop or rap poetry performed in competition.

- **RHYTHM—**

Through spoken-word poetry, poetry is written in 'free verse', and does use rhythm. The rhythm is irregular, following the shape of the verse, and helps propel the poem forward.

- **REPITITION—**

A lot of performance poetry uses repetition of words or phrases to reinforce important ideas.

- **RHYME—**

While performance poetry does not use strict rhyme schemes, it occasionally uses rhyme to emphasize a particular idea or theme.

- **FREE VERSE—**

Poetry that does not use rhyme or a regular rhythm pattern.

- **SPOKEN WORD—**

Poetry, lyrics or stories created for performance for an audience, rather than reading the poetry.

For more information on Performance Poet Glenis Redmond visit her website: www.glenisredmond.com or www.loydartists.com. Poetry Books by Glenis Redmond are available from the author by e-mailing detailed requests to poetica11@aol.com, or by ordering from bookstores or online bookstores.

Section 4: **Glenis' Life Journey, in Her Own Words**

North Carolina Hall of Fame Poet Glenis Redmond and I are chatting at a sidewalk table by the Asheville Green Sage coffee shop on a warm late-summer afternoon in the final interview for this book. The intelligence and wit of this charming woman competes with and overcomes the din of passing traffic and pedestrian chatter. Our initial meeting was a month before at beautiful Kenmure Country Club in Flat Rock where she was teaching a class to budding teachers and poets, and we connected multiple times since.

Glenis has thoughtfully shared her life journey for this book, from those first burgeoning feelings about poetry through the now. She tells her fascinating and meaningful life story through an outpouring of memories that reflect a strong yet gentle core essence.

- **The Early Years—**

Glenis, my first questions are, of course, when did you first decide to be a poet, and who inspired you?

I don't know if I ever fully came to that realization. I think it claimed me when I was twelve from an assignment in middle school then began to write poetry in my journal. A teacher said I should keep the journal fifteen minutes every day, and I discovered I was writing my feelings, my thoughts. Little did she know that I came from a pretty intense home life, and that my journal would become my best friend.

I didn't have a lot of inhibitions, because I was always involved in activities and sports. I was a cheerleader in high school, I ran track, I was junior class president and I was in theatre, so I was always an extrovert. And I was only a C-student, until my freshman year in high school. I was sitting in biology class on the first day of school and Mr. Jack Candler came in and said: "A black girl sat there where you're sitting last semester, she was a straight A student, and I believe you will be too."

That comment changed my life! I was almost reduced to tears and overwhelmed because it was the first time somebody told me that. I was always being applauded for my athleticism, my being able to dance, and my being social or gregarious, but no one had ever looked at me and said, "You are smart!" I believed him so much that I became an Honor Roll student. Because Mr. Candler cared enough and applauded everything I did that I made straight A's in his class. He was a great story-teller, and I would be spellbound. That same man who changed my life wrote my recommendation letter for college. Sadly, Mr. Candler has since passed, but his wife is still alive.

After biology class I decided I wanted to be a medical examiner like Jack Klugman, I don't know if you remember his TV series, but I thought I wanted to do that, too, but I soon found out it wasn't my calling.

The Student Government later asked me to be the commencement speaker for a graduating class at Woodmont High School, my *alma mater*. The ceremony was held at Furman University and it was like whoa! - 1000 people were there! The beautiful circle that day was that his wife and son came. She said, "I attended the ceremony just to hear you, I wasn't planning on coming." I had written a poem for Mr. Candler that my mother urged me to send to his wife, but I was too shy at first. I finally sent it, and she wrote me the sweetest note of thanks.

We lived in Italy for a while, and an elementary school teacher named Mrs. Van did important things for my growth as a person and student. She would read aloud to us for an hour every day, and I remember hearing *The Hobbit*. She also took us on field trips to Venice, Pompeii, many interesting places. That all helped set me up to become a poet. Children who are read to become curious; reading helps create neuron pathways. I was an insatiable reader, but nobody knew it because I was a C-student.

Mrs. Van did something different for us, and she saw something special in me. I wrote to her in Turkey back in the 80's to let her know I was getting married, and to invite her to the wedding. She wrote back, "I will always remember you, Glenis. We're now reading *Huckleberry Finn*."

Mark Twain was an amazing writer whose work is littered with racial slurs, including the *n* word, and Mrs. Van had no idea how to handle that, so it got very uncomfortable. I was only in fifth-grade but I said out loud: "I think we can save that by reading it in the context of how Mark Twain used it in that moment in time, but that's not an excuse to use it now."

We had a wonderful experience with the book, and she later told me, "I'll never forget the day you set the tone, Glenis." Mark Twain, Samuel Clemens, was not a bigot, of course, he was actually the opposite! I'm not into censorship, and believed that even as an eleven-year-old.

I had another inspirational professor later when I was in the Erskine College psychology department, Dr. Gorry from New York, a fast-talking Northerner who really knew the lay of the land. I was in an inter-racial relationship that offended a lot of people at Erskine when he said, "Glenis, you can't help who you fall in love with; you got to tell people that."

In the college *alma mater* song there is a line I won't sing: "Walking the hallways that my forefathers walked." I told Dr. Gorry that I couldn't sing that because my forefathers did not walk these halls. Then he said, "Your forefathers built these halls," and it blew my mind wide open. Now I could go to class with the understanding that their blood, sweat and tears are in the soil, in the brick, in the mortar, and what they did was build a path for me to walk on. I no longer would leave because I felt alienated, and he did that for me.

- **Family—**

Tell me about your mother and your siblings.

My mother, Jeanette Vivian Redmond, is the center of my universe! Just yesterday I posted her picture that I took last weekend on Facebook. I don't know if you are familiar with African-American women and their hats, but she has her church-lady hat on, and she's dressed-to-the-nines. All I can say is: they don't make them like that anymore!

My mother is so old-school she cooks from scratch, sews by hand, and is instinctively and ultimately wise, and very humble. She is just a beautiful spirit! When people are near her there's a blessing that happens; she's just that kind of woman. I'm not even one-eighth of what my mother was and is.

But a lot of the values my mother has I hold dear and try to pass on. She's a rock. She turned 75 in September 12, 2011, but don't tell her I told you that! She's a beautiful spirit, and I've learned a lot from her. I study at her feet, I mean I really do! I just study and watch and learn life lessons, hear her wisdom, feel her compassion towards everyone. And this woman does not hold grudges. I have never seen anyone else who experiences difficult things and just lets them go. I don't have that ability quite yet, but I'm studying, I'm studying. She teaches me every day.

So yeah, she's who I model myself after, but I'm more of a modern woman. I mean that my mother does not understand me being on the road six months out of the year. She doesn't understand how I read a map, she doesn't know how to. But the traveling, the performing, that's my father's side of me, the part of him that I am. I'm my mother's child and my father's daughter.

I am particularly grateful that my mother named me Glenis Gale. It has poetic and dramatic resonance. I'm named after Glynis Johns, a flamboyant Welsh actress, fitting since my daughters deem me a diva. I blame it on the name. I also bear the name of the X-1 jet that broke the sound barrier: 'Glamorous Glennis'. I find that synchronistic and fitting, as well. I was born to be a bard, and a loud one, at that.

I have four brothers and one sister. The oldest is my brother David then my sister Velinda, Willie, Errick, myself, and Jeffrey, a musician a lot like my father, with his ways and his musical talents. There are two non-denominational ministers in the family, Errick and Velinda, who has her own church in Greenville.

And your father?

My father, Johnny Clifton Redmond, passed about seven years ago, lovely person, but very deeply complicated. He grew up in the 'Jim Crow South', and went into the military to escape racism and poverty, and all of that. He was a musician and a heavy drinker, I believe to numb his emotional pain.

But my father laid down a map for us, kind of sacrificed his life so that we, his children, could have a better life. But at the time, being only twelve, I didn't know all the sacrifices being made, and what the complications were.

My dad was a blues and jazz gospel pianist who played by ear, an amazing sensitive musical soul. His mother had taught him, and he was a prodigy, playing piano at age three. That was his true love, his talent, and I think he would have liked to pursue that always. He first played at Bethlehem Baptist Church in Fountain Inn, South Carolina, and then had an opportunity in the Air Force where he led his own jazz and blues band.

He told me that one day he was playing at the military hospital where he worked and the doctors and nurses and patients that were free came to hear him, and they were all singing. A day later he got a call asking him to be in the military band. But he and my mother made the decision that he would not take the position because it would take him away from the family six months out of the year.

Do you feel a connection between your father's almost savant-like musical gifts and your poetry?

After my father passed I started looking back at our relationship very differently. I always thought there was a lot of conflict, and that my father wanted me to be something I wasn't. But after he died I realized that he was trying to protect me from the artist's life he had led for so long. We were so much alike that we could not stay in the same room, but now I finally realized my father's gift was similar to my gift. I just couldn't recognize it back then. He wanted obedience. I was an outspoken free thinker since the day I was born. We clashed.

One night back in the 90's I was on stage talking to my audience and I began to make a lot of connections with him. I started thinking, 'wow'! I wrote a poem called *Gimme the Beat* about my father that ends: "My father's the one who gave me the beat that frees my soul".

I realized then that my father was still handing me gifts: rhythm, all that music and lyricism that is poetry, and the improvisation that's in my poetry. I lived with music 24/7, as he was always playing the piano. His music is inside of me, and so my voice was and is inspired by that kind of lifestyle. I didn't realize until I was fifteen that not everybody had that kind of experience growing up.

An odd thing is if he had taken the job offered in the Air Force band, he would have had to travel six months out of the year. Well, guess who now travels six months out of the year? I do! So, I have pretty much followed in my father's footsteps artistically.

I think connections can continue even after someone has passed. Our relationship has grown and, more importantly, there has been so much more healing, so much more space. I realize that whatever happened in my family household, he was not doing anything to me personally, it was just that things were happening to him. Now I have a more expanded view, more of a birds-eye view of our daughter-father relationship. When you have children you become more forgiving of your own parents. It's a difficult job to raise kids. We all have our flaws, and it's all complicated

Having my father come to the Peace Center in Greenville unannounced while I was performing for

1,000 middle school students was very special. Afterwards he said, "Now I know what you do, you are a teacher."

That was the highest compliment my father could have paid me. His mother always valued teaching. My father passed the next year, but at least he died understanding what I did in the world.

You said your father joined the military in part to escape racism. How do you deal with that sensitive subject?

I think as a writer and poet I always must set the tone about weighted issues, not turning my head, not being in denial. If that makes someone uncomfortable, that's okay, there are some things that make us all uncomfortable, but we can go deeper as human beings from it.

Malidome Some' wrote a book called *Of Water and Spirit* that has this line: "There is a knowledge that cannot be eaten with the head." Once I heard that African proverb I believed it. I think the heart does the hard work. You can bring it in through your brain, and as a poet my heart makes sense of it.

I am what you call highly sensitive to everything, to feelings, moods, foods, environment, the land. I do protect myself because I'm in so many places.

And here's the tricky part: you got to stay open and protect yourself at the same time. My goal is to never put the wall up, and not feel that you might as well dig the grave now and go.

But yes, there are places that are still not safe, much of it caused by racism.

In your forties you begin to realize you can't pull back, that your time in life is finite, although I think the spirit is.

• Twin Daughters—

You beamed and lovingly told me about your twin daughters when we first met.

Oh yes! I am the proud mother of twin daughters! The oldest by fourteen minutes is Vivian Celeste, named after my mother, and the youngest is Maya Amber, named after Maya Angelou. Amber goes off to Queens College on Friday. I just went shopping for her and Amber; they both go by their middle names. Amber is a Creative Writing major and a Women's Study minor, and very much the poet, so I named her right. Celeste is a Visual Artist, finishing up at Appalachian State.

The twins were born on September 5th in 1989, and it seems the time has just flown by. I can't believe I have children who are twenty-one years old, but at the same time it's been a lot of work. It's probably the most rewarding and most difficult job that I ever had, raising twins. I call them my Epic Poems, my only two true epic Poems.

I became especially proud when I realized I'd passed along the poetic gene, as evidenced by Amber winning the first Word Slam for High School Students in 2007. To sit in the audience and watch my child come into her own was one of the most meaningful moments of my life.

Celeste too has her own voice. She does it however through visuals. She has a powerful eye and mind. Her concepts are subversive. She paints about the South, incorporating her dual-heritage.

My daughters have taught me a lot. I conceived them when I was twenty-seven, and that's when I came into myself artistically, or started to. A lot of women who have children say, "Oh I can't write; I don't have the time." When I was carrying the girls I began writing again.

You said your Epic Poems are also your children. Give me a capsule of what you think was the most significant role you played in their development.

It's hard to say because I'm in it, but I see myself as a mom very different than I see my own mom. I've forgotten who made the quote that says there are two types of mothers or maternal instincts: one that nurtures and is there a supply of your children's physical needs, and the other to spur your children as far as dreams are concerned, to inspire them. I took care of my children maternally and physically, but feel like another important role, one they also play for me, was to inspire them to fulfill their purpose.

- **Finding a Voice—**

When did you find your voice and your purpose?

Not when I was counseling and working 9-to-5, dragging, life was hard for me. This was down in Greenville, South Carolina where I was doing clinical counseling, drug and alcohol abuse front-line for the Care Center for the state of South Carolina. It was beautiful, admirable work, but not the work that I continued doing.

But once I started finding my voice through poetry, I started fitting a model that my daughters could look up to. It was much better to show them someone who is fully alive than someone who is half dead, dragging through life. But my focusing on poetry as a career was a controversial move to everybody within my traditional setting.

It would have been a shame if my writing life had ended before I experienced my spirit and didn't have that life force. But as soon as the twins came, the life force came back into me and gave me new purpose. I started writing again and connected with my spirit, and knew I wasn't going to be long on the track of pursuing psychology and a doctorate.

I didn't know how it all was going to change, but those two beings arrived and altered my course!

Did you write poetry in college?

I didn't write as much in college, I was more academically driven. But I was the literary editor of *The Review*. There I was not as connected with myself, but I was trying to be a good student, a good daughter, a good sister, all of that. I was very artistically inclined.

And if there was a talent show I was in it. I was crowned Miss Arrow, the first black pageant winner in Erskine's history. The only reason I did the pageant was because it was an outlet, and my fiancé at the time, my ex husband now, urged me to enter. Plus I needed what the south was not giving me, outlets as an artist.

I was always dancing, always searching for some venue where I could express myself.

Then I went to graduate school at Texas Tech University to work on a Master's degree in Child and Family Studies. But I still didn't know who I was. I was working hard in the program, but it didn't feel quite right. There was a lot of racism in west Texas. I was building character, but kept bumping up against these edges. That was very much my life, and if my writing had ended then it would have been a shame.

We moved to Richmond, where I was studying for a Ph.D in the Psychology Counseling program at Virginia Commonwealth University on a full fellowship. When I found out I was pregnant, at that moment in time, I picked the pen back up. I was twenty-seven.

One morning I was driving on Monument Avenue that is lined with statues of Confederate soldiers when I realized, "I'm on the wrong road!" It was an epiphany, literally and figuratively. I felt, "I don't belong here," so I told my major advisor, Doctor Strong, a fitting name since he was a manly man: "I don't want to do this anymore." He asked, "So, what do you want to do?" He seemed kind of offended, so I admitted to him what I hadn't admitted to anybody in a very quiet voice: "Poetry." It was like I punched him, and he said, "So, you're one of those! I have a son who's an artist, a musician."

I was writing poetry here and there, but not on a frequent basis, experimental type that I kept it in a journal. I'd been writing in a journal since I was twelve, and I look back through them sometimes. They are quite personal; a lot of it is garbage.

We had the twins now, and it was just too much to be a couple away from family and friends trying to raise two daughters. I had to take a job to make ends meet doing drug and alcohol abuse counseling. Then I started getting really sick. We didn't know what was wrong for a couple of years then found I had fibro-myalgia, a chronic illness. While I was counseling and getting sick, my boss, Pat Edwards, asked me why I hadn't applied for medical leave. I was just someone who didn't take time off, and remember that I broke down and cried, which I don't often do. So, I took an eight-week medical leave and never went back.

• The Return to Greenville—

What came next?

Next we moved back to Greenville. I found a book called *The Artist Way* and entered a poetry class held every Saturday for twelve weeks. During the last session I said that I wanted to do poetry readings, and when I returned from a break learned that my classmates had planned my first poetry reading.

Then and there I made a pact to hold five readings a month *gratis* in the local community for one year." And I did just that, for girl scouts, at churches, anywhere they would have me. It was like my own self-study of poetry.

Characterize the importance and relevance of poetry to your soul, nature and heart.

Poetry is a vehicle for me to talk about the difficult, to say the unsayable. Poet Audre Lorde wrote one of my favorite poems favorite, *The Litany for Survival*. In it she's talking to the black race, and there's one line in there that says: "We were never meant to survive."

It's the job of the poet and she did it! It's true. Now I look back at my family severed by slavery and poverty, at the many people who have not made it out yet. I live a life of luxury as a poet, but only because of those who came before me. I am walking on their shoulders.

I mean that I didn't get here by myself, and have been fortunate and blessed. I am not talking about financially or any of those things. I am talking about spiritually, and that those who came before me paved my way, but they did not survive.

I write a lot of ancestral work, I call it piece work because I come from a family of quilters and seamstresses. I don't sew, except with words and emotion and memory. I'm piecing together what has been severed, and that is what I see as my job. In the last semester of my Master's program at Warren Wilson College, I found the plantation where my family was owned on my mother's side, and that was a huge deal!

It's hard to tell my feelings about this because I'm still working through them; my thinking had been that I may never know my roots, that I may go to my grave and never know. But now that I do know, it's a whole new chapter of tilling that ground.

I wrote a 'persona poem' for my great-grandfather born in the 1850's, *What My Hands Say*. It's written in his voice, and he's talking about working the land. At the end of the poem he says: "*What if I could make more than my mark/that's suppose to speak for me."*

A friend of mine, Allan Wolf, read the poem and asked if I knew that the verse meant, in Latin, 'to turn the soil', which is what my grandfather did, he turned the soil, was what I do. I too turn the soil, a line.

So, we're not that far apart from one another, but at the same time we are worlds apart.

- **Bridging Past and Present—**

Does your mind often travel across bridges that link the past and present?

Yes! I have this fascination with my great-grandfather and great-grandmother, who were both born slaves. I live to tell their stories because how could they tell their stories? Only orally, they couldn't write them down.

In West Africa there are people called 'Griots' who keep the lineage alive, keep the stories alive. And that's what I feel my job is, too. People often describe me as only a performance poet, but I think deeper than that. I think this career is in my DNA, something I came to do, and it is a vital role. I care about our young people, and that's why I'm so passionate about going into schools to teach poetry. I think we have a lot of Griots who haven't been given their just place in life.

Once a child believes "I have a role" then something alters within them, and that is the beautiful result of the teaching work I do. I get to see their light go on, and see their realization of, "Yes, I can grow these tools."

Thankfully the people at Bethlehem Baptist church took me seriously when I was twelve; if someone died I wrote the obituary poem, if someone got married or someone was born, I wrote for that, too. They'd call my mother with a request, and then I would write down all the particulars then write a poem for the church. In the same way, I want to help the children of today.

I saw you perform a few years ago and was struck by the aura you radiate, your charisma, and the force with which you deliver insightful poetry. Do you enter 'the zone', much like Michael Jordan and other world-class athletes?

I enter a zone when I write. Being in the zone helps my poetry performance go deeper, and that helps me to honor my mother and grandmother. But it even goes deeper than that, it keeps me alive spiritually, physically too, and it pays the bills. Poetry and performance replenish my immune system, makes me want to get up in the morning. I'm completely obsessed with poetry.

Earlier you told me that that whenever you enter a port you are swept with special feelings. Can you describe them?

That's a hard one, not something I talk about much. I do write a lot about those times when I go to port cities and amazing experiences wash over me about history, ancestors, uncontrollable feelings I cannot explain that probably have nothing to do with this lifetime. It always seems to me that I've been here before.

The first time it happened was on vacation with my then husband in Charleston, South Carolina. On a carriage ride, lo and behold, my ancestors spoke to me! I had no context for it, but they started pointing the way by saying: "You need to tell this story; our story has not been told." That's when I started becoming aware that what lies in the land does not die. Just like it still exists in Charleston.

I wrote about this in my journal, and it completely altered me; I became a different person. Every time I would go to New Orleans, Bristol, Liverpool, anywhere there was a port that had something to do with the slave trade, it was like what slaves often said in the black church: "I was slain in the spirit."

I couldn't explain what was happening to me, and it wasn't until years later that I realized that the land and the ancestors were informing me that something took place here, and that something took place there. These places exist all over the world, but that's nothing new, and I'm not anything special. If you're sensitive you pick up on it. It's here in Asheville by my house, in the slave cemetery, in the Confederate cemetery. I think everybody is special in that sense. Energy never dies.

I came to accept that I am part of both the religion of my ancestors and my Christian faith, and that there is nothing I can do about it. I don't find a conflict, but I think most people would. It makes great sense to me when I'm in a black church and see African ways taking place. It happens all the time.

• Challenges—

What was the most difficult challenge you faced, what did you do about it, and what were the results?

Blane Sherer and I met at Erskine College and divorced when the children were seven. He lives in Arden and is a sleep technician for the hospital, and he is still active in their lives. The twins were only seven and it was really tough on them, still is. Though I am better for it, and we are better for it, I would never recommend divorce unless absolutely necessary.

When I got married I thought it would be forever, of course. But we grew apart, and it wasn't anybody's fault. But when your children are impacted by separation you feel like a failure; their home was taken apart because the two of you couldn't live under one roof. And that was challenging in many ways: I had to leave the life I knew and come into a new one.

So I built a new life and became a poet. Everyone thought I was crazy, and I probably was, but for the first time I was living alone, after going from my parent's home to college then from college to marriage.

How much of your poetry is manifested by challenges, such as tragedy or the sadder side of life, and how much from optimism and the 'glass half full' point-of-view?

I can't give numbers. A lot of people think my poetry is kind of 'Pollyannaish', but it really isn't. There is always some thread of sorrow running through it. My process as a writer is to not use writing as therapy, though it is therapeutic. I'm making art! And by the time the writing comes back around, a lesson emerges that makes sense.

My main messages are that I'm not going to let you down, I will not play the victim, I will always note the challenge and where I'm going, and I will always try to figure a way out. That's my stance in life, I won't move from it.

My biggest career challenge was trying to balance single-motherhood with being a fulltime touring artist. My former mother-in-law, Sara Sherer, was an active grandparent and stepped in while I was on the road to help take care of the girls. I never had to worry about the well-being of my daughters while I was away on the road. When people asked me at Q & A sessions after performances, "How do you leave your children?" I would respond that I do not leave my children; I work to help sustain their lives!

Even in the bleakest of times I find what hope there is. There have been some dark challenges, but I don't allow much pessimism, cynicism and skepticism. They don't work for me. And I believe the universe is ultimately wise.

I've noticed ever more frequently the seeming connection of all the energy in the universe. I'm not going to assign a spiritual, physical or occult explanation for this apparent phenomenon, but wonder if it resonates with you.

Yes! I live in that and count on that, that's where my faith lies, in the universe being connected. I don't always know how it is connected, but I trust there is an answer. As a matter of fact, the times I've been most challenged are when I've felt I've been the most cared for.

I have a preconception of where life should go, and that's doing a number on me, like I hear. I often hear: "No, you are not going there," when things look like they are falling apart.

So, they're actually coming together in a greater good for my being.

As I get older I'm learning to trust that more, and not suffer the demands of having to be somewhere else. I believe that you're supposed to be where you are right now, and have that experience because it enriches you for the next step on your journey. Some days it's easier to believe that than others, but it's been a constant in my life. I try to be open to the moment; I don't ever want to be dead set in my thinking.

- **Serendipity and Spirit—**

Suddenly a passerby spots Glenis, and they hug and exchange friendly conversation. I ask Hedy Fisher, an Asheville resident of 33 years and a community leader to tell me about the poet, for the record.

I met Glenis many years ago at a poetry festival then saw her perform at some Poetry Slam competitions. She ended up moving up here, rented a house from me, and ended up buying it. I call it Asheville serendipity. She's one of the best performers and poets I have come across in my life. Very few poets are at her level, in my opinion, and I'm not exaggerating! I'm happy to be a vignette in your book, and in her life.

After Hedy leaves I remark that her popping up at the precise moment we were discussing serendipity was quite a coincidence, whereupon Glenis corrects me:

No, the universe just said to you: "You're on the right track." That's what I think synchronicity is: showing us that!

Let's pick up where we left off about how things 'speak to you'.

The cosmology and the religion of my ancestors are the culture and religion of Yoruba, the tribe from West Africa, Nigeria where my family came from. The cosmic energy there is completely powerful. I was raised Christian, but when I came to Asheville I met an African drummer, I don't remember his name, who said: "I live with both sides of the spirit, from Christianity and from the roots of Africa where I come from."

When he said that I thought: "That's it, that's the soul! That's the spirit that led us here, that came with us in the transferring! If a language was taken, if food was taken, if clothing was taken, then what do people have left? What they have left is their spirit, and that spirit is incredible. I'm interested in looking at how Africa still remains in the South. I call it "The Africanization of the South."

Many people would look at it and say, "That is really southern." But a lot of things that we think are southern are actually African. Why? Well, if you bring 40,000 people in through the mouth of Charleston, that's going to change South Carolina, and anywhere else you bring that many in will alter that place. What was going on in these port cities is that the spirit came here with them!

And that spirit still exists and transcends. Something woke me to this just yesterday as I was reading a phrase in a book *Legba's Crossing: The Narratology in the African Atlanti* by Heather Russell. She speaks of *those people who are the placeless*, those that live in-between the worlds, the one of their heritage and the mainstream.

The 'placeless' are the translators for the non-traditional, and that's what I do in my work: I'm a placeless person who speaks from the tradition from which I come, which is non-traditional. I make sense out of what that is. I read signs from people that talk about reading the clouds and the trees and the wind. I'm reading the differences between people, and I try to make sense of it. That is my job.

So, a new chapter suddenly opened up in your understanding of your heritage, and yourself. Is it serendipitous that you're memorializing brand-new thoughts in this interview today? Do you know where these thoughts are going to take you, how they might evolve and perhaps influence your poetry, and your personal life?

It is serendipitous. I'm waiting to hear where the next place will be. It's like I'm in limbo right now waiting to hear, but the answer will come in due time. I have a lot to do right now with my mom and my brother and that sort of thing. I'm in a good place, but in a holding pattern. I've learned when you're in a holding pattern to just hold, or you'll get burnt out.

I have plenty to do, I'm still working, I'm pretty much still on the road. My life has been upended, so -to-speak, in some ways, but in others this is probably the most solid it's ever been. It's a paradox to live your life like that, but I'm where I'm supposed to be. I could be in Massachusetts, in Italy, in upstate New York, in Colorado, in any number of places, or I could be in all those over the next five years.

David Whyte, an amazing poet, said something like, and I'm paraphrasing: "The spirit knows before the body knows; the spirit has already gone before and prepared a place, but it takes the body a while to catch up, it takes the man and the woman a while to catch up."

So in dreaming the spirit is preparing you and will say, "Yes this is where you are going."

I already know where I am going, but I don't physically know where I am going, and it's interesting to trust that in-between-ness. I think that's a great way to allow self-growth. There's going to be growth where there's a different sort of writing that needs to occur, where a different understanding needs to take place.

- **About Racism—**

Tell me about your reaction when you hear what could be fairly construed as racist language.

If someone refers to people of color, that includes anybody with brown skin, anyone with color. But for blacks to call someone colored is a weighted issue because it's a weighted word. He or she might not have intended that, and someone other than me might take offense.

I do have places where I get sensitive, but I think it is better to address something up front than to go home and let it build and eat you alive. My best defense against racism or racist language, if I'm not taken off guard, is to handle it in my own way at that moment, and then don't carry it or internalize it.

I think what is important is to set the ground when people have preconceived stereotyped images about race. An example of one incident that influenced me to do what I do came one day I was performing at an author's conference in an elementary school. The principal walked up to me holding the hand of a little black boy and said, "I want you to meet Jamar."

The Jamar looked up and said, "You don't look like no author." I asked, "What do you think an author looks like?" His verbatim response was, "You know how he look when he be lookin' in that book." His lack of education and inability to express himself well inspired me even more to do what I love: teach! *How would you explain your personal view of your art, and your devotion to it?*

Where some people see performance poetry, other people see page poetry. I do my best to live in the wide world of poetry. After traveling the world for eighteen years doing performance poetry and competing in Poetry Slams, I hadn't yet gotten an official degree in performance, but I sure feel like I'd earned one. How? By going on stage for an audience three times every day!

But that honed skills you cannot get anywhere else, and taught me a lot about talking to an audience, and them talking back. I really believe in call and response, which is another thing that stems from my West African roots. It's a beautiful thing to allow yourself space to learn, and I recently returned to school for a Master's Degree. As a student in my forties that meant a lot, and it meant even more that the twins and I were in college together.

Some people asked why I was going back when I was already making a living with poetry. I said I am going back for me. It was about me crafting and going deeper. I think that niche was carved for me. When I started traveling there were not a lot of performance poets making a living, there were only a few of us around: Saul Williams, Roger Bonair-Agard, and mums. But I was in the right time at the right place!

I'll never forget the second showcase I signed to with the Loyds, where presenters came to buy and book entertainers for a year. I was in a Lancaster, Pennsylvania hotel and had fifteen minutes to do my thing. I did my thing and got a standing ovation. I was the only woman, the other performers were male. Turns out I became completely booked for several years.

I felt like my mother and her sister, Aunt Dot, who has since passed, were there to witness my performance. I kind of understood then that this was supposed to be; that it was not so much about me.

You obviously have tremendous recall of your work, and you call on deep emotion to perform. Do you have poet heroes? And what is the highlight of your 'slam' career?

I study my work, but not in the same way I would study someone else's. It may be mine, but I still need to practice it. I have gotten stuck, but not often. I was known in the slam circuit as someone who could recall anything. If I memorized it, it was mine. As I get older, it doesn't roll out as easy, but I still have a strong memory.

Emotion is very connected to what I do. I think performance allows you to fly; it gives you wings! I'm inspired by Lucille Clifton and Maya Angelou, women of color who wrote the type of poems that empower me. I found Maya Angelou's work as a youth, and found Lucille Clifton's work in my early thirties. When I started battling chronic illness, her work inspired and helped heal me.

I put together the first Poetry Slam in Greenville in 1995, and took the first all-women's slam team to the Nationals in Portland, Oregon where I ranked in the individual top ten. The next year I came in third in the Nationals in Middletown, Connecticut. I am proud to say this slam still exists today.

I no longer slam, but I believe in it for building stage skills and creating audiences. I was instrumental in creating the Slams in Asheville and Buncombe county schools, in association with the Asheville Area Arts Council, and coordinating with Allan Wolf, Graham Hackett and Susanne Hackett. I am proud to say it still exists today, as does the Greenville Poetry Slam.

- **Teaching Experiences—**

What were some of your other significant teaching experiences?

One particularly significant experience came while I was working at the Carl Sandburg Home National Historic Site teaching a poetry workshop and had the privilege of meeting Helga Crile Sandburg. She asked me to do a poem, and I did *Mama's Magic* for her. I was in tears, overcome by the moment. Then she did a poem for me, and my daughter Amber did a poem for her. Later Helga wrote an open letter about me:

"No one is more capable of interpreting the poems of my father, Carl Sandburg; I believe you could be an important voice for my father's works. I feel that his background as the son of a railroad worker in the CB&Q Blacksmith shop in Galesburg, Illinois, his mother as a Swedish immigrant, and you with your varied ancestry, fit together. Glenis has grace and power in her delivery, and would stir her students to a fresh understanding of my father's messages, and bring him into the present day."

I was featured at the Carl Sandburg Writer in Residency Program. As a Poet/Educator living in Asheville, aiding in the process of creating the program, and I'm pleased and honored to remain a part of it at this juncture.

I always thought there should be a Writer's Residency in the WNC region, and any budding writer visiting the Sandburg estate 'Connemara' will understand that it's an ideal location for such a venue. My chief role in this project is to act as an artist advocate, ensuring that that our literary community has a vested interest in CSWiR. Equally, I see myself as a spokesperson to ensure that the program receives not only regional and local recognition, but national attention, as well.

I feel all connected parties are like me, avid lovers of Carl Sandburg's work, and they have a determined interest in spreading his "Poet of the People" mission.

In the Writer-In-Residency Program, an author is selected by a panel of artists and community members. Once selected, the author is invited to take residence on the grounds for three weeks to devote time to writing and research.

And once while being interviewed on the *State of the Union* an NPR station in Chapel Hill, I was talking poetry with host Frank Stasio when a college student called to say that I had visited his high school and taught a poetry workshop. And, he not only remembered the workshop but read that poem on air. It was a beautiful Praise Poem.

Another memorable time came when I was working at the Omaha Indian reservation school in Nebraska. After teaching classes one day, my host asked if I wanted to sit with the elders. I sat with Grandma Donna as she translated the lessons of the students into their native tongue. I asked permission to question her and she agreed. I asked her to translate the word poetry in her language and she replied, "Woman that flies with words."

Grandma Donna has since died, and I am glad to have had that opportunity to sit with her.

• Poignant Thoughts—

As we wind down, what poignant thoughts come to mind about your poetic journey?

One of my most poignant moments in my life came when, after writing praise poems since age twelve and teaching this poetic form for thirteen years, a DNA test revealed that the lineage of my father is Nigerian. Then later when I was studying for my Master's at Warren Wilson College, I learned that Nigerians are the chief praise poets of Africa.

And finally, what advice would you give to budding and fledgling poets:

Read, read, and then read some more. Then write, write, and then write some more.

Finally, I know our readers and your fellow notables would enjoy some of your poetry. Will you please forward me some to cap off your biography in this book.

Yes I will, tomorrow.

Section 5: **Selections from Glenis Redmond's Beautiful Poetry**

Birthright

Daddy soldiered,
like many enlisted military men
lived on base in the barracks.
Lost without the fold of family
He requested weekend leave,
On a Friday in January
After pocketing his pass,
He lit down Highway 26 quick
Mid-state to Upstate South Carolina home.

Monday morning the commander
summons him about who knows what.
On a hunch he pulls out his pass,
Sinks when he reads the large letters stamped,
LEAVE DENIED.

He explains, much later.
Tells me the story in my thirties
of my weekend conception
his inadvertent AWOL,
of his planting a seed,
me defying authority ever since.

Her father Johnny Clifton Redmond receiving a military medal.

What My Hand Say

For great-grandpa, Will Rogers
born in the 1800's

My hand say, *pick, plow, push and pull,*
'cause it learned to curl itself around every tool
of work. The muscles say, *bend yourself like the sky,*
coil yourself blue around both sun and moon.

Listen, my back be lit by both. My hand
got its own eyes and can pick a field of cotton
in its sleep. Don't mind the rough bumps-
the callused touch. I work this ground

like it was my religion and my hands
never stop praying. Some folk got a green thumb,
look at my crop and you'll testify my whole hand
be covered. I can make dead wood grow.

I listen to my hand, it say, *Work.*
My hand got its own speech. It don't stutter
it say, *Work, Will.* Though it comes to mostly nothin,
this nothin is what I be working for.

Come harvest time I drive the horse
and buggy to town. Settle up.
This is where my hand loses its mind,
refuses to speak.

Dumb-struck like the white writing page.
The same hand fluent on the land,
don't have a thang to say around a pen.
The same fingers that can out work any man

wilts. What if I could turn my letters
like I turn the soil? What if I could
make more than my mark, a wavery X
that supposed to speak for me.

Published in the Hikmet Nazim Poetry Festival Chapbook, Spring 2011

Mama's Magic

My mama is magic.
Always was and always will be.
There is one phrase that constantly bubbled
From the lips of her five children,
'My momma can do it'.
We thought mama knew everything.
Believed she did, as if she were born full grown
from the Encyclopedia of Britannica.
I could tell you stories
Of how she transformed
A run-down paint-peeled shack
Into a home.
How she heated us with tin tub baths
from a kettle on the stove.
Poured it over in there like an elixir.
My mama is protection
like those quilts her mother used to make.
She tucked us in with cut out history all around us.
We found we could walk anywhere in this world
and not feel alone.
My mama never whispered the shame of poverty
in our ears.
She taught us to dance to our own shadows.
"Pay no attention to those grand parties
on the other side of the tracks.
Make your own music," she'd say
as she walked,
she cleaned
the sagging floorboards of that place.
"You'll get there."
"You'll get there."
Her broom seemed to say with every wisp.
We were my mama's favorite recipe.
She whipped us up in a big brown bowl
supported by her big brown arms.
We were homemade children.
Stitched together with homemade love.
We didn't get everything we ever wanted
but we lacked for nothing.
We looked at the stars in my mama's eyes

They told us we owned the world.
We walked like kings and queens
even on midnight trips to the outhouse.
We were under her spell.
My mama didn't study at no
Harvard or Yale.
The things she knew
you couldn't learn in no book!
Like...
How to make your life sing like
sweet potato pie sweetness
out of an open window.
How to make anybody feel at home.
How at just the right moment be silent
and with her eyes say,
"Everything's gonna be alright, child,
everything is gonna be alright."
How she tended to all our sickness.
How she raised our spirits.
How she kept flowers
living on our sagging porch
in the midst of family chaos.
My mama raised children like
it was her business in life.
Put us on her hip and kept moving,
keeping that house Pine-Sol clean.
Yeah, my mama is magic.
Always was and always will be.
Her magic?
How to stay steady and sure
in this fast paced world.
Now when people look at me
with my head held high
my back erect
and look at me with that...
"Who does she think she is?"
I just keep on
walking
with the
assurance inside.
I am Black Magic!
I am Jeanette Redmond's child

If I Ain't African

Someone tell my heart
to stop beating like a djem'be drum.
If I ain't African
someone tell my hair
to stop curling up like the continent
it is from.
If I ain't African
someone tell my lips
to stop singing a Yoruban song.
Someone speak to my hips
tell them their sway
is all wrong.
If I ain't African
how come I know the way home?
Along the Ivory Coast
feel it
in my breast of bones.
If I ain't African
how come my feet do this African dance?
How come every time
I'm in New Orleans or Charleston
I fall into a trance?
If I ain't African how come
I know things I ain't supposed to know
about the middle passage-slavery
feel it deep down
in my soul?
If I ain't African
someone tell their Gods
to stop calling on me,
Obatala, Ellegba, Elleggua,
Yemaya, Oshun
Ogun!
Tell me why I faint
every time
there is a full moon.

If I ain't African
how come I hear
Africa Africa Africa
everywhere I go?
Hear it in my heartbeat
hear it high
hear it low.
If I ain't African
someone tell my soul
to lose this violet flame
someone tell their Gods
to call another name.
someone take this drum beat
out of my heart
someone give my tongue
a new mouth
to part.
If I ain't African
someone tell my feet
to speak to my knees
to send word to my hips
to press a message on my breast
to sing a song
to my lips
to whisper in my ear
If I ain't African
If I ain't African
If I ain't African
PLEASE
tell my eyes
'Cause if I ain't Africa
I ain't livin'
and God knows
I ain't
ALIVE!

College Prep

They devote whole schools to College Prep.
Some children are primed since Preschool for it.
My College Prep was a door marked closed,
a path not paved with open study guides
for the PSAT, SAT or Guidance Counselor chats
about the ACT or boosting my 2.0 GPA.
I was a straight "C" student, completely proud of it.
I didn't know no better, but like my mama says,
When you know better, you do better.
I didn't, but my Guidance Angel did.
He appeared my freshman year
sans wings, sans wand, armed with a few words.
Mr. Candler, my first biology teacher
large jowls
large belly.
Mr. Salivation, as he talked about his favorite
subject, food.
His depiction so apt we could see that big ol' pot
of pinto beans
with a whole onion thrown over in there for
taste.
I remember how his false teeth would slip
right out of his Jerry Clower mouth.
The Mr. Candler who called all boys Hoss
and who called all girls Miss Hickey.
Mr. Candler of the Southern Swagger,
pointing his all-knowing thick finger first day of
class
at me and said, A black girl sat there last
semester,
where you're sitting. She was a straight "A"
student.
I believe you will be too.
I immediately thought, This man don't know me.
So how could he name something in me,
that sat down all my life?
He called me out. Called to that something.
It took notice and rose.
He plunked down my potential like stones.
I stepped on his every word.
This is where the door of my future
creaked open, where my honor began to roll.
This is where I knew whole-heartedly

I needed another path than the one laid leading
to vocational school, manual labor at the 3M or
Michelin plant.
This is where I silenced the echoing voices from
home and all around me
in Piedmont, in Moonville, in Greenville County.
Girl, all you need is God and a man.
God, yes. A man, yes. All, no.
Just a quick survey of the marriages I knew,
and it didn't take rocket science to figure out,
my way was not that way.
Maybe I did alter my destiny, rearrange my fated
stars.
Facing doubters and detractors
shouting She will never do well.

I paid my own way clocking twelve-hour shifts
working sunup to sundown as summer hire
at Mama's factory tape plant job on Donaldson
Road.
Nothing wrong with making an honest living.
Reeling tape on and off on 12-hour-long shifts.
I would stumble to the clock,
punch out with that annoying flicker
of artificial fluorescent light.
Loud machinery still drumming,
as I climbed in my bed to sleep
and I considered my College Prep complete.
My road future fated and stamped irrevocably
sealed
when walking off the factory floor resolved
never to return, Jack Candler humming,
You do not belong here.

At my Alma Mater or anywhere
I am feeling foreign and insufficient
I know that I'm a long way from home sitting
in the front row of the classroom
but I am just where I'm meant to be.

Published in Kakalak: A Journal of Carolina Poets, 2006

Schooled

Learning takes hold best when placed
in the body. When seed takes root, blooms!

Branches past the brain, places itself
in the heart, where knowing becomes known.

I recall the moment in 5th grade,
when Senora's voiced drenched the class

with a calming rain, beating a cadence
we could feel. Her words sounded

a sweet a foreign river to my first week
in Italy ears. How her lyrics flowed

in and out as she proclaimed
our Italian names. Michael became Michele,

Angela turned into Angelina,
Charles translated into Carlo.

When she came to Glenis, the pause
seemed to last forever. How I waited

on the word, the ebony reed of myself
stranded in her inhalation of wind.

Finally, Gladiola! It took me years
to understand the grace in the name,

an African flower striving
in unfamiliar terrain.

Like me at my college alma mater
As the whole campus sang,

Here amid the same traditions
that our fathers knew. My throat closed.

I professed to Dr. Gorry how I could not
sing this song, because my forefathers

did not walk these halls or know
these traditions. I remember
the language of his eyes aligned
me like both sun and moon,

as if to say, carry this lesson deep
in the meat of your bones:

Your forefathers built this land
with their blood, sweat and tears.

They watered and prepared this ground
upon which you stand. It is their singing

that brought you into these halls.
Honor them with your being.

Published in New Millennium, Fall, 2010

NOTES: To book a Glenis Redmond performance: www.loydartists.com
To purchase her poetry books: www.glenisredmondstore.com

Loudoun Library, 2010.

Hello. . .
© Karakein

Glenis on stage performing at
Wordfest in 2010.
© John Fletcher

Glenis Redmond often helps children, here she is shown volunteering her time at Middlesex Academy.

. . . and she devoted time to teaching children the in's and out's of poetry at an Omaha Nation Poetry Workshop.

. . . helping children find confidence in themselves and their abilities at Middlesex County (NJ) Academy Poetry Workshop.

Under The Sun.
© Daniel Perales

Laurel of Asheville.
© Daniel Perales

Family celebration when Glenis obtained her Master's:
Velinda Simmons, David Miller, Glenis, Mama Jeanette
Redmond Willie Redmond and Jeffery Redmond.
Missing: Errick Redmond.

Glenis with brother Errick.

Glenis' twin daughters Maya Amber Sherer and
Vivian Celeste Sherer.

Amber, Celeste, Brock & Glenis Redmond; Brock
is Glenis' nephew, her surrogate son.

Dr. Doug M. Orr

College President, Geographer, Teacher, Author Musician

My parents instilled in me significant qualities that have enriched my life: A sense of wonder and curiosity about places, maps and the mysteries of the cosmos; a love of music and its shared sense of community; and a deep sense of fairness and social justice about the course of human affairs. Those values abide in me still.
— **Doug Orr**

Sections about Doug Orr:

1) What Others say about Doug Orr

2) Highlights of his Life and Careers

3) **Doug's Life Journey, in His own Words**

4) Photos

5) Excerpts from writings by and about Dr. Orr

6) Chronology

Section 1: **What Others say about Doug Orr**

- **College Vice President in Awe of Doug Orr—**

Visionary by nature . . . this is what comes to mind when I ponder the success of Doug Orr. Maybe it is his musical background and creative spirit that drives his success. I have often opined that if Doug's presidency 'did not work out', he could always sing for his supper.

I suspect it is in this notion of freedom from hunger that allows for Doug's magical blend of leadership and vision. A vision without a leader and a leader without a vision is a terrible sight to behold. What makes Doug a tremendous success is his ability to do both while playing guitar, but not chewing gum at the same time.

Combined with this is great humanity and humility, and for that I am in awe of Doug Orr. The number of times he quickly passed on praise, or shared praise with others, always made a positive impression on me. This is one of the misunderstood features of good leadership, how to lead with your arms around those on both sides of you on the podium, how to share in the success. While Doug taught and mentored me with many solid traits of leadership, being a good human being is one that not many visionary leaders understand.
  — **Richard Blomgren, Vice President, Warren Wilson College**

- **Former Student: 'Dr. Orr Gracious and Welcoming'—**

I have known Dr. Orr personally for over twelve years, and have always held him in extremely high regard. As an international student from Jamaica, I started my studies at Warren Wilson College in Asheville, North Carolina in the fall of 1999. When I started school, Dr. Orr was holding the position of President of the College. As I started to get to know everyone on campus, I did not get to meet "Dr. Orr"; I got to meet Doug and his most gracious wife Darcy. Doug is the kind of person who is so generous and kind that you feel immediately at ease when talking to him. Every bit of formality that I had conjured up to speak with the President of the College melted away with his easygoing charm and grace.

Even though Warren Wilson College was comparatively small with around 900 students at the time, it was no small feat for the President to be on a first-name basis with the majority of students. I have extremely fond memories of Thursday afternoons walking to Gladfelter (the student cafeteria) for dinner as Doug and his wife Darcy led the jam session with their musical talents on the guitar and dulcimer. Everyone could partake in this wonderful community bonding activity. That's how Dr. Orr made his mark on the daily lives of all the students attending Warren Wilson College, everyone was welcome to get together and share as a community. When I told my friends that I could not only talk to the President of my College but I could listen to him and his wife play music for us, they were in disbelief. At their colleges they barely knew who the President was, much less be able to have an engaging conversation with him.

Dr. Orr is not only the most gracious and welcoming college President I have ever encountered, he is a brilliant leader and a talented fundraiser. As a student you would never hear about Dr. Orr's numerous achievements from him, you would read about it in the newspaper, online or in some prestigious journal or the other. He was the school's most ardent champion and in my opinion our biggest asset. Dr. Orr has been an inspiration to me and my entire graduating class. He has left an indelible mark on the Warren Wilson College landscape, not only as a role model for leadership but as the high water mark for all other college presidents to aspire to.
  — **Johnelle Causwell, Jacksonville, FL.**

Section 2: **Highlights of his Life and Careers**

- ### Fifteen Fruitful Years as President of Warren Wilson College—

Dr. Doug Orr retired in 2006 after serving fifteen fruitful years as the fifth president of Warren Wilson College, the independent college in Swannanoa near Asheville that is characterized by its distinctive program of liberal arts undergraduate and graduate education. The college combines academics, work and community service in a learning community committed to environmental responsibility, cross-cultural understanding and the common good, plus an 'international-experience' for every student.

Significant growth and achievement during the Orr watch was exemplified by twenty-two new facilities, including the first LEEDS Gold Certified building in the Carolinas for the arts-and-crafts style 'Doug and Darcy Orr Cottage' that houses the admissions and college advancement offices.

He also oversaw planning that doubled student enrollment, added eleven new academic majors and 17 minors, increased fulltime faculty from 38 to 62, with 94-percent holding terminal degrees.

During his presidential stint, Warren Wilson had one of the highest percentages of graduates going to the Peace Corps of any college or university in the nation. In 1998 he said in a newspaper interview: "Students generally come to Warren Wilson wanting to make a difference in the world. They're highly altruistic."

Another significant moment during Orr's tenure came in 2002 when MFA Program for Writers faculty members Richard Russo and Carl Dennis won Pulitzer Prizes in fiction and poetry, respectively.

- ### Successful Fundraising Campaigns—

Funding for the growth initiatives resulted from two highly successful capital campaigns, including the college's first comprehensive campaign that raised $25,619,144 from 5,000 contributors, the largest amount up to that time ever raised in a Western North Carolina campaign.

The Centennial Campaign funded the Shelley Mueller Pew Learning Center, the Martha Ellison Library renovation and expansion, the new Hamill Science Center and Witherspoon Science Building, Ransom Fellowship Hall, the Morris' Community Pavilion, and various college programs and student scholarships. It also helped triple the size of the college's endowment.

- ### Senior Affiliate Consultant—

Doug Orr is currently a Senior Affiliate Consultant for Performa Higher Education and serves as an Association of Governing Boards consultant, assisting independent college and university governing boards in becoming more effective, cohesive and strategic in carrying out their responsibilities. He also works with the board leadership and the president in facilitating comprehensive presidential assessments and coaching.

- ### Twenty-Three Years at UNC Charlotte—

Prior to assuming the presidency of Warren Wilson College, Dr. Orr for 23 years served as vice-chancellor and professor of geography at the University of North Carolina at Charlotte.

In 1961 Orr graduated from Davidson College, and subsequently earned an MBA in 1963 and a

Ph.D. in 1968 from UNC Chapel Hill. He was the recipient of the Honorary Doctor of Humane Letters at North Carolina State University's 2001 fall commencement, along with Governor Jim Hunt and three others.

- **Serving College Boards—**

Dr. Orr was appointed to the UNC Asheville Board of trustees by the governor in 2006 and also serves on the board of Berea College. For 25 years he was on the Johnson C. Smith University board of trustees and chaired the education committee, was board chair of North Carolina Independent Colleges and Universities, board chair of the Association of Presbyterian Colleges and Universities, and served on the AGB Presidents Advisory Council, and the Council of Independent Colleges board.

- **Award-Winning Urban Planner and Teacher in Charlotte—**

At UNC Charlotte, Orr was a principal visionary and planner of University City, an award-winning mixed-use project. He also founded WFAE-FM, Charlotte's National Public Radio Station.

- **The Orr Name Carried Forward and Honored—**

Doug Orr's name is being carried forward thanks to the Student Merit Scholarship Award initiated by the North Carolina Outward Bound School, where he served on the board and forged a partnership with Warren Wilson College, and was honored with Dr. Douglas Orr Day on April 25, 2006, as designated by the Buncombe County Board of Commissioners.

- **Awards and Recognitions—**

Among Orr's awards and recognitions are the Teacher of Excellence Award from UNC Charlotte, presented annually to the outstanding teacher on the faculty; the Paul Harris Fellow Award by Rotary International for contributions to the better understanding and friendly relations of peoples of the world; the Chairman's Award from the Greater Asheville Chamber of Commerce for Scholarship, Leadership and Citizenship; and, The Garden Clubs of America Conservation Commendation Award on Behalf of the Earth.

In 2006, Governor Mike F. Easley bestowed the Order of the Long Leaf Pine Award on Dr. Orr. It is one of North Carolina's highest civilian honors.

- **Founding 'The Swannanoa Gathering'—**

Another impressive Doug Orr initiative is The Swannanoa Gathering he founded soon after assuming the presidency of Warren Wilson College. The festival began with 75 attendees and now draws more than 1,500, and gives national and international attention to Warren Wilson College and Western North Carolina.

- **Books and Publications—**

The accomplished geographer and musician is the author of five books, and has a major new work in progress with co-author Fiona Ritchie, host of *Thistle and Shamrock* that is broadcast on 375 *NPR stations,* titled *Wayfaring Strangers: Connections of the Music of Scotland/The Scots, Irish and the Appalachians* to be published by University of North Carolina-Press. His wife Darcy is the book's art director. During his Charlotte years Doug and Darcy had performed in a band that emphasized the connection between the music of the Appalachians and the Celtic lands.

Dr. Orr's published books include the *North Carolina Atlas: Portrait for a New Century,* with co-author Alfred W. Stuart, UNC Press, 2000; *Land of the South,* Oxmore House, 1989; and *Metrolina Atlas,* UNC Press, 1970. He has also written numerous by-lined columns and op-ed pieces.

- **Doug and Darcy Orr, Musicians—**

The diverse accomplishments of Doug Orr include playing guitar and singing during regular appearances with Maggie's Fancy, his former band that played Celtic and Appalachian music and include wife Darcy as a member. Maggie is one of the most popular Celtic names and was the name of Darcy's dog that posed in typical Celtic whimsy fashion for the official band photo.

- **And an Athlete, Too—**

Doug was twice state champion tennis player at Greensboro High School where he also starred in basketball then became team captain and number one player on Davidson College's tennis team.

- **Tribute to the Orr Presidency: 'A Tough Act to Follow'—**

Dr. Orr remains identified with Warren Wilson College in action roles, and by the sheer depth of his spiritual connection. Those connections and feelings are returned to the President *Emeritus* by many within the Warren Wilson world, as evidenced by writer Ben Brown's article titled 'The Orr Presidency: A tough Act to Follow', with a sub-head 'Pity the president who succeeds Doug Orr' published in the winter 2006 alumni publication, *Owl & Spade.* Excerpts from the article:

Who would want to follow the act of a singing geographer, a CEO who shepherded a small private institution in an Appalachian Mountain Valley into a leading player, not only in higher education but also in regional business, the arts and environmental sustainability? . . . It's the future that's likely to make Doug most proud . . . Doug sees a ripening coalescence of opportunity and mission . . . He writes in a recent essay: 'In higher education there's an opportunity to reverse an alarming trend toward white-collar vocationalism that forsakes education for training and simply shapes young people to be cogs in an economic engine' . . . the disciplined student, the confident leader in Doug, are mediated by the stuff that comes from the heart. In what may be his most famous annual appearance, Doug and Darcy and recruited colleagues sing that message to an audience of freshmen and their parents. It's a performance calculated to mystify anyone braced for a stuffy president's introduction to the rigors of higher ed:

> *You've got to sing, like you don't need the money*
> *Love, like you'll never get hurt*
> *Dance, like nobody's watching*
> *It's got to come from the heart if you want it to work.*

- **From His Installation and Retirement Addresses—**

Two addresses by erudite Warren Wilson President Doug Orr stand as bookends for his notable 15-years of leadership. The first was delivered at his Inauguration Ceremony on April 15, 1992, and the second at his Commencement address to graduating seniors on May 13, 2006, which also served as his farewell to the beloved institution. Excerpts from both addresses follow:

The inauguration address titled 'Warren Wilson College and the Tree of Life' included the description of the interconnectedness of everything as believed by early inhabitants of the Appalachians, the Cherokee: *They believed that nothing in God's universe exists alone, that every drop of water, every human being, all creatures in the web of knowledge are part of an immense and evolving whole.*

Dr. Orr reaffirmed the college's commitment to learning, service and community: *Our students learn the dignity of work as a way of becoming rather than acquiring . . . gifted and deeply committed teachers affect eternity, the results of their labors ripple through humankind.*

He described teachers and students as multi-faceted renaissance people, *Just a few blossoms on the current Warren Wilson Tree of Life that include a plumber-baker, a philosopher-carpenter, a folk-art -environmental scientist, a kayaking-psychologist, a banjo-playing-English teacher, a student caucus leadership-recycling director, and a farm crew-poet.*

Among Orr's comments: *We are honored to have been designated as North Carolina's hub campus for college and university community service programs . . . and are especially proud of our students who each year collectively give 20,000 hours of service to those in need.* And he concluded: *We must share this creative wellspring of the earth adventure with one another, poised on the edge of forever, in this diverse, colorful, springtime pageant that is our Tree of Life.*

Dr. Orr's Farewell Commencement address also drew from the wisdom and culture of the Cherokees, who named the Swannanoa Valley, meaning 'Land of Beauty'. He said: *There were four universal healings held in the crucible of the arts; they were significant to the Cherokee in the literal and metaphorical sense. They believed that whenever you've stopped singing or dancing, or being enchanted by stories, or feel uncomfortable with the sweet territory of silence, you have begun to experience loss of soul and spirit.*

Then he suggested five other significant arts for meaningful living: The Art of Wonder bequeathed at birth; The Art of the Moment in our brief life journey in the long span of cosmic time; The Art of Joy that is in your birthright; The Art of Adventure that refuses to box us in and makes us dare to risk; and finally, The Art of Community that is more relevant than ever for the communities of today's fractured world. He also cited an African proverb: *Whatever action you take for or against another impacts you.*

He concluded: *Graduates of this eternal time and place plant your seeds, carry out your random acts of community building, nurture your tree of life. Go from here with a sense of wonder, breathe deeply each of God's moments given to you, never postponing the joy of the journey, fulfill the adventure of your restless soul, and go hand-in-hand with your brothers and sisters of the world community. God bless you, Warren Wilson College, and all your daughters and sons: this wild and noble birthplace of dreams; this muse to musicians, artists, scientists and teachers; this beacon of light for peace; this rhythmic sound of mother nature in the wind; this trumpet's call to justice. Godspeed to each of you on your journey.*

(Excerpts from Doug Orr's extensive writings appear in Section 5.)

Section 3: **Doug's Life Journey, in His Own Words**

As I drove up winding mountain roads for my first interview with Doug Orr, it seemed fitting that I had to journey high to meet the Notable who made so many significant contributions to the students and faculty of Warren Wilson College in Swannanoa near Asheville, where he served as president for fifteen richly productive years. After arriving at the beautiful aerie home that juts over Black Mountain and being cheerfully greeted by Darcy Orr, Doug led me onto a porch overlooking the rolling terrain. They instantly made me feel at home with warm smiles and a cup of piping-hot coffee. There were many family photos on display, so I started the discussion at the center of their universe.

Dr. Orr, please tell me about your family.

We have two daughters. The oldest is Heather Abernathy, married to David Abernathy. Heather was born on June 19 of 1965, and has two children, daughter Campbell and son Colin. Each Tuesday I pick up Colin at school and take him to his guitar lesson, and then we go out and have ice cream together.

Since graduation from the University of North Carolina years ago, Heather has been involved in fundraising, first with Blue Cross Blue Shield in Chapel Hill where she met David, and then in Seattle, Washington at the University of Washington. When David finished his doctorate, they moved to Asheville, and he was appointed to a faculty position at Warren Wilson College, while Heather continues to work for the University of Washington as East Coast representative.

Our second daughter, Holly, was born on January 20, 1970. She and her partner Jenn have a young son Quincy, and they live in Brooklyn. Believe me, I've given Holly the complete history of the Brooklyn Dodgers, and about her dad wearing a Dodgers ball cap and cheering 'them bums' on for many years. Holly is trained in city planning and geographic information systems, which is computerized mapping. She formerly worked for the City Planning Department in New York and currently is with New York University in their new Global Technology Services Program.

My brother Don is four years younger than me and four inches taller – he inherited the size in our family. He worked with Unify, a textile company and later as chairman of the board of Unify he traveled to China, Ireland, all over the globe. He's retired now in Greensboro, North Carolina, and has a passel of wonderful grandchildren.

Do you get together often as a family?

We do, and most recently it was during the Swannanoa Gathering. My wife and I stayed with Colin in a dormitory because we wanted him to have total immersion in the kids program. The other two grandchildren will be in the kids program in summer 2012. We often have a family reunion at the nearby Lake Eden Arts Festival.

It sounds like a fun learning experience for the kids.

I think one of the most precious gifts you can give a child is a sense of wonder and curiosity. My parents provided that for me, and I think it translated to my career in academia and my interest in just about everything. We try to pass that on to our grandchildren.

The youngsters make me think about the sheer wonder of the world and our presence here. And they come out with the funniest and most endearing expressions. Their parents are very creative in exposing them to the music and the artistic world. They are a joy, and we relish every minute of time with them.

- **The Young Years—**

Very nicely said, now let's go back in time and explore your earliest memories.

Well, I had a very rich experience in my pre-school years, right up through Kindergarten. My father was an attorney with the Securities and Exchange Commission in Washington D.C. and his first boss was Joe Kennedy, President Kennedy's father. The SEC had just been formed, and dad was assigned cases throughout the country. I was born in Washington D.C. and we lived in Silver Springs, Maryland.

In the ensuing years throughout the Second World War we lived in San Francisco, Miami Beach, Philadelphia, and then back to Washington. I especially have early memories of Miami Beach during the heart of World War II when there were German submarines off the coast. We'd hear explosions and there were blackouts at night. Toward the end of the war my brother Don had been born and Dad decided he had quite enough of moving a young family around the country. So he became an attorney for Burlington Industries, the world's largest textile company based in Greensboro. That is where I did all of my public schooling, other than attending kindergarten in Swarthmore, Pennsylvania.

How were the high school years for you?

I graduated from Greensboro Senior High school, the primary one in the city at that time.

My parents instilled in me significant qualities that have enriched my life: A sense of wonder and curiosity about places, maps and the mysteries of the cosmos; a love of music and its shared sense of community; and a deep sense of fairness and social justice about the course of human affairs. Those values abide in me still.

My mother introduced me to the guitar and music; her name was Charlotte, like the city where I once lived. My dad learned to play tennis on an old clay court at his house in Athens, Georgia, so he introduced me to the game. My hobbies were tennis, basketball, and music.

And then you became a champion tennis player in high school.

We had an amazing team. Our coach, Don Skakle, was a wonderful teacher and later became head coach at the University of North Carolina where he had been a great tennis player. At one point we won over sixty straight matches. My partner Jim Spence and I were state high school doubles champions two years in a row. Jim lives in Greensboro, retired from a career as a computer programmer.

Tell me about your basketball experience.

I loved basketball, which is sort of a complementary sport to tennis because of the demands of footwork and agility. I was point guard for the Greensboro 'Whirlies', the only school nickname of its kind in the country, and short for 'whirly-gig', a tornado or cyclone.

We had a fine team. In my senior year we reached the finals of the state tournament. Greensboro always had strong basketball teams because of its legendary coach. I had a few college basketball scholarship offers but when I matriculated to Davidson College I only played intra-mural basketball. I decided that giving my full attention to tennis and studies was quite enough.

Who inspired you during your high school years?

When you think back to teachers, as I'm sure most of us do, you especially appreciate them, but you usually didn't convey that at the time. Teaching high school can be a daunting job - trying to herd teenagers.

I remember a couple. One was Mrs. Garrett, an English teacher who instilled in me a love of literature. The other was a hefty football coach, Lody Glenn, who taught political science and civics. He helped me realize the importance of academics, as well as athletics. I was a bit of a casual student in high school when he thankfully woke me up, and that inspired me to start accumulating an academic record that would allow me admission to a good college. Mr. Glenn went on to become principal at Greensboro High School.

Did you have a best friend and were you a social person in high school?

Yes. Some of my closest friends were athletic related as I played on the basketball and tennis teams, and we practiced and hung out together. And I had friends in the usual clubs and organizations. Some of those friendships started in junior high school, and one in first grade.

Have any of those friendships continued through the years?

Yes, they have. In fact, Pete Wyrick, who started in the first grade with me, accompanied me all the way through college, and we maintain a friendship today. We recently had our fiftieth college reunion at Davidson, and Pete, another classmate, Darcy and I performed music after the banquet. Pete lives in Charleston with his wife now. He's retired as a highly respected book publisher and now serves in an editorial capacity.

- **An Age of Innocence—**

What jumps out at you besides what you've told me about those high school years?

It was an age of innocence in many ways. This was the 1950's and we weren't a very diverse lot because integration had not yet occurred. I took a lot for granted, but there were early awakenings. I suppose the music was an awakening because we often adopted as our music the rhythm-and-blues by exclusively black artists. We had to seek ways to hear them, both on the radio and in concert.

Later I wrote a newspaper column about how my brother and I saw Elvis Presley in 1955 when he was an unknown twenty-year old. It was at an Andy Griffith Show in Daytona Beach, Florida, and Andy had a lineup of musicians we had never heard of, such as Marty Robbins, Ferlin Huskey and Elvis Presley, who closed the show, and was just electric. I realized later why Andy didn't want to follow Elvis, even though he was the headliner. Elvis arrived on stage with just two musicians, Scotty Moore on guitar and Bill Black on bass, they had only been performing together for about a year, and they brought the house down.

For the first time we heard this young white guy 'singing black', as has been expressed. He was drawing on the music of the black gospel musicians and churches, and combining that with 'white country' and gospel.

Elvis had recording sessions at Sun Studios in Memphis, and it is often said that the first rock n' roll song was recorded there. He soon made it big-time on national television.

That music and those musicians were really important to the civil rights movement, as the rhythm-and-blues artists were being adopted by white teenagers like myself.

Sounds like you have good memories of your childhood.

Some of my best memories relate to the music and the good times we had together then, such as going to the old Greensboro Tobacco warehouse without the knowledge of my parents to hear famous R&B performers like The Drifters and Roy Hamilton.

I recall that there was a chicken-wire fence down the middle of the dance floor to separate the blacks and the whites. I had never seen anything like this, but we were there for the music, and when The Drifters and Clyde McPhatter came on, their music was so riveting and their harmonies so captivating that people were dancing like crazy.

Then the chicken-wire fence came down and there were not blacks and whites there, just kids. I later realized this was 'straw in the wind', that I was seeing music breaking down barriers, whether they were chicken-wire fences or the long-held prejudices people had carried for generations.

- ## Writing of Childhood Memories—

Teenage impressions about cross-cultural ties in music helped give you inner-strength and knowledge to always stand up for what is right, as clearly reflected in many of your later by-lined newspaper pieces.

While I was a geography professor at the University of North Carolina in Charlotte the *Charlotte Observer* asked me to write guest columns about the growing concept of regionalization and the qualities that make cities tick. During that time I helped plan University City next to the UNC campus in Charlotte.

But I also wrote personal-remembrance columns such as the one about Elvis. Another column recalled the time I met the impressive African-American mayor of Birmingham while visiting the city, and while there traced the steps of the early civil-rights pioneers. I went to the Civil-Rights Museum and became captivated by the history, and by the scars and the accomplishments during that era in Birmingham.

I continued to write op-ed pieces later in the *Asheville Citizen-Times.* A special one was about seeing Jackie Robinson play baseball for the Brooklyn Dodgers against the local Greensboro Patriots, and being there with my dad, and hearing the response from the segregated black crowd that was seeing their hero live for the first time, and how memorable and impactful that was on my young life.

I didn't fully appreciate the impact of the sounds I heard and the sights, as I was only eleven-years-old. As the civil rights era ensued, I reflected and began understanding it all much more, and I recalled an old spiritual: *What's that sound ringing in my ear? It's the sound of freedom calling!*

I understood later that when the African-American fans first saw Jackie Robinson coming to the plate that day, the ethereal sound that arose was freedom calling, just as they would later hear the sound of freedom calling from the speeches of Martin Luther King and John Lewis and others in subsequent years.

Interestingly, shortly after that time the historic sit-in by university students at the Woolworth Diner in Greensboro occurred, and that was ground-breaking for the civil rights movement, just as was Jackie Robinson's presence in minor league ballparks as the Dodgers worked their way through the South from spring training to Brooklyn's Ebbets Field to start the season.

- ## The Davidson College Years—

I applied to several colleges and universities and was accepted by Duke, UNC Chapel Hill and Wake Forest. I was pulled toward Chapel Hill because of the sports connection and I had a lot of friends going there, but I was drawn by Davidson College's commitment to smaller classes and to the liberal arts. In retrospect, it was a wise decision to attend Davidson because I later had a large-university experience at UNC Chapel Hill graduate school.

Did Davidson offer you a college scholarship for tennis or basketball?

Davidson did not offer scholarships for tennis in those days, only for basketball and football. So my parents paid my way. I played tennis and won some collegiate tennis matches and lost some. We were heavily scheduled so we might be as competitive as possible running up to our conference tournament. We played against many of the best teams in the country, like the University of Miami, most ACC teams, and some Big-10 teams that came through the South. We won our share, and let's just say I had some good losses to some outstanding college players.

I had entered Davidson in 1957 and graduated in 1961 with a degree in Business Administration. I thought I'd eventually enter the business world like my father. As I look back I wish I had majored in history or English, but it was still a valuable experience, particularly since I did eventually become a college administrator.

I received an MBA in 1968 at UNC Chapel Hill. But as I was completing that degree I began having a better sense of self in that my heart wasn't in the direction of being a business executive, but rather toward academia and teaching. So, I shifted course and decided to pursue a doctorate in either history or geography. I was able to obtain an assistantship in the Department of Geography, and three years later, in 1968, I received my doctorate.

Tell me more about Davidson.

Davidson is still small today with about 1600 students, but in those days there were just 800 of us, all male, but many years ago Davidson became co-ed, to its great benefit. I made many close friends through athletics and the tennis team, and the Sigma Alpha Epsilon fraternity. We lived in a dormitory but took our meals to the frat house.

Davidson today is truly diverse, integrated by gender, ethnic background, nationality. I treasured my time there, and it triggered, though I didn't know it then, early stirrings to eventually wind up in academia.

Who inspired you during your time at Davidson?

All of the professors were very engaged teachers, after all that is why they joined a small liberal arts college with emphasis on undergraduate teaching. The professors were mentors and friends, and they'd have you over to their houses on Sunday nights for dessert and coffee with their spouses. I greatly admired many of them for teaching, and most of all for instilling in me a sense of learning and wonderment and wanting to know more.

One of the teaching legends there was history professor Frontis Johnston, who later became dean of the faculty and interim president. He was very well-spoken and inculcated in me a love of history and how it connects to everything. Professor of geography Jim Reid resonated with me, and helped me understand why I loved geography, and why I looked at maps endlessly and day-dreamed.

My English professor taught British Literature, and that fascinated me. They were examples of what I think was across-the-board excellence in undergraduate teaching.

History and geography especially captivated me because they are both integrative sciences; that is they integrate all knowledge, one in the time dimension, and the other in the spatial dimension. For one who likes to 'graze in every pasture', as my mentor and faculty advisor in graduate school said - it appealed to me to look at all knowledge from geographical and historical perspectives.

This planted the seeds for my graduate school choice of geography, though in part it was because I was able to get an immediate graduate assistantship.

- **Geography, an Integrative Science—**

I didn't imagine it at the time, but since geography is an integrative science, you learn to put the varied pieces together to solve what seems like a jig-saw puzzle. That learning experience was helpful when I became a college administrator; in that job you have to assemble the pieces because you are flooded with a wide variety of information, personnel matters and program planning.

If I have a talent, I think it is that I can synthesize and integrate pretty well the different pieces.

What interests me about the book project we are involved in now, as well as about the atlases we authored, is that my efforts stem from that early learning at Davidson, and especially the exposure to geography that continued into graduate school.

The college tennis experience was invaluable too, not only in friendships made, but in all of the dynamics that go with athletics: physical fitness, nutrition, self-discipline and team-work that helped me throughout the years.

While a student at Davidson I taught tennis during the summer at a camp near Hendersonville, and later for the Greensboro Parks and Recreation Department. I moved from one playground to another and put nets on concrete slabs that were really basketball courts, then hit balls to kids who'd never even seen a tennis racquet before. At the summer camp I lived in a cabin supervising teenage boys, and took them camping and for excursions on the river.

Those experiences led to my love of working with kids of all ages, and that continues now, even though I am retired as an educator. That includes being a good grandparent.

• ROTC and Military Service—

I know you became an ROTC officer at Davidson. Recap that experience and your time in service.

ROTC was required then for the first two college years for all students, and it counted toward graduation credit. You could choose to continue for two more years and graduate with a commission as a second-lieutenant. In 1961 there was a draft, so unless you were pre-ministerial or pre-medicine you were going to be drafted and go in the service as an enlistee.

I completed four years of ROTC along with many of my classmates, and a few weeks after graduation entered the United States Army Transportation Corps as a Second-Lieutenant stationed in Fort Eustis, Virginia.

During the progression from Second to First Lieutenant I became a company Commander and experienced invaluable leadership training. I had men in my Company who had been in the Second World War, everywhere from the Normandy invasion to the Bataan Death March in the Philippines. I also taught a variety of courses ranging from international issues to local training courses.

One fellow company commander was an African-American career officer Carl Thomason, and we got along famously, He often came to dinner at our house; that was in 1961 and 1962 when integration still hadn't arrived through most of the South, but it had occurred within the military, and that was a great benefit to me.

Were you able to keep up with tennis during your military service?

I met some outstanding tennis players at Fort Eustis, including Norm Parry, who was ranked eleventh nationally when he played at UCLA. Others included the number-one players from North Carolina and Harvard.

The commanding general loved to play tennis in his spare time, so he recruited us to play for Fort Eustis. We played in a few tournaments. That is how I wound up playing the great Australian legend Rod Laver in the first round of a tournament in Miami in the dead of winter in 1963, the first year he won the Grand-Slam of tennis. He accomplished it again in 1968.

How did you do against Laver?

Ha-ha. I lost but somehow won three games. Let's put it this way, Rod Laver lost three games, I didn't necessarily win them. It was a wonderful experience, and he is an admirable individual and sportsman, and one of history's finest tennis players.

I stay in touch with my old tennis buddies, and sometimes we hold reunions, including a recent one at the Indian Wells tennis tournament in Palms Springs California. Some years we meet at the US Open Tennis Tournament. We share war stories, and our wins become more predominant and our losses just fade away with time.

I'll bet a reunion makes it seem like it all happened yesterday?

It does, particularly the photographs, and sharing stories. We wonder where the time went; it's been almost fifty years.

- **Famous Friends and Acquaintances—**

I understand that you are friends with Arthur Sulzberger, Jr., publisher of the New York Times, had an involved discussion with President Clinton, and have met Prince Charles and President Carter. What are your impressions of them, and some of the other famous people you've come in contact with?

Jimmy Carter was highly intellectual, but there was shyness about him that Bill Clinton certainly did not have. He is a great thinker, and impressive with his civic mindedness, but I don't think he relished politics the way that Clinton did.

I also met George Herbert Walker Bush, gave him a tour of the UNC Charlotte campus, and liked him personally. An aside is that he is first-cousin to the wife of former Warren Wilson President Ben Holden, so he agreed to speak here when he was vice-president. I dropped him a note when he retired from politics to wish him well and thank him for years of service, and he responded with a hand-written note.

William F. Buckley, Jr. was another I met in the course of my work, and I was impressed with his intellectualism and his principled conservatism, even though I was often not in agreement. His love of lively but civil discourse is missed.

Arthur Sulzberger is a friend I admire very much. I met Arthur when we both served on the North Carolina Outward Bound board, and he once gave me a tour of the New York Times board and news rooms.

- **Loving What You Do—**

It seems safe to conclude that during your working life you were paid for doing what you love and enjoy.

That is very true. I had left the professorship years before and that was a loss. On the other hand I continued my research, writing books, and made guest appearances in classes when invited by a history or geography professor. I welcomed that.

I could not teach full-time because there was just too much travel in my schedule, but Warren Wilson's values and programs really coalesced with many of my personal interests: The music, the commitment to serving others, internationalism, liberal arts, the environment.

One of my most life-shaping experiences as a new professor at UNC Charlotte was going through North Carolina Outward Bound. I tried to explain to folks later that I came to understand more about how people learn on a twenty-three-day Outward Bound course than in five years of graduate school. In graduate school you learn about a subject matter in great depth, but not necessarily about how students learn. On Outward Bound there are significant team dynamics, as well as introspection.

I learned a great deal about stretching yourself, making oneself vulnerable, being willing to try something new, not judging others or yourself harshly when you try and come up short. I was very moved by the Outward Bound experience, including our relationships with the environment, back in 1970. That instilled in me an understanding of the importance of connecting rather than competing with nature, and I incorporated that philosophy into my teaching.

When I arrived at Warren Wilson I tried to build and enhance the environmental component, including the establishment of the Environmental Leadership Center. For many years I served on the North Carolina Outward Bound Board of Directors, so it all came full circle.

Early in my tenure at Warren Wilson the Outward Bound Director John Huie, who I had known at Davidson, called on me and suggested a partnership with Warren Wilson. Outward Bound was outgrowing its office space in Morganton, and eventually we worked out an arrangement whereby its headquarters moved to Warren Wilson on property we deeded to them. We also initiated an Outdoor Leadership studies major at Warren Wilson, in partnership with North Carolina Outward Bound. I share this story because I think the Outward Bound experience had a major impact upon shaping my educational philosophy on several levels.

- **Becoming a College President—**

What was the route for you to the college presidency?

I was not planning to seek a college presidency, and I had made a career decision to go back to the professorship. I had been a fulltime professor for only a few years before I was called into the administration at UNC Charlotte as a Vice Chancellor, which in the UNC system is a Vice President. I had an eighteen year run as a Vice Chancellor, but longed to get back into teaching. I had often been invited to participate in presidential searches around the country but always declined.

One of the individuals who really shaped my life, second only to my father as a male mentor, was Dean Colvard, the first chancellor at UNC Charlotte, a native of western North Carolina from Ashe County who had first hired me. I had served as his executive assistant for a while in Charlotte.

Dean had special affinity for Warren Wilson, and in fact had been assigned to this area when he worked for the Department of Agriculture early in his career. He also was a graduate of Berea College, like Warren Wilson a work college. Without asking, he nominated me for the presidency of Warren Wilson; he had always aspired for me to be a college president.

The Presidential Search Committee at Warren Wilson contacted me, but I told Dean Colvard "I'm not planning to seek this out" and he said, "Well, just take a look at it."

I did take a first look without telling Darcy. We already had our life's game plan and built a house in Charlotte, and she was a professor at Central Piedmont Community College, teaching computer-assisted-design in the engineering department. She's both a right-brain and left-brain person, as she was an English Literature major teaching engineering CAD.

We had talked about one day retiring to Asheville because we both love the mountains, and some of my best memories growing up were here with my parents, hiking and enjoying the Blue Ridge Mountains and valleys. So, I drove up to quietly look at the college.

I had heard it was a very unique place. When I entered the campus I was stunned by the physical beauty of the setting. And I was enamored that this was the first liberal arts work college to make service-learning part of its mission, that it had a commitment to social justice and was the first in the South to permanently integrate. It also had significant international and environmental dimensions. All of the parts were there that appealed to me.

I spent a couple hours just walking around and talking with a few students. When I got home and indicated to Darcy what was afoot, we decided to take it a step at a time. I was called by the co-chair of the Search Committee a few weeks later for an interview, and then was invited to be a finalist interviewee. After a meeting with the Search Committee at an airport hotel in Charlotte, I received a call inviting me to come to the campus.

Darcy and I spent two days on campus for my nonstop interviews and I subsequently was offered the position. We did a lot of soul-searching, then said yes and never looked back. We left a lot of good friends in Charlotte but felt Warren Wilson was a good fit for us and our values. And certainly the setting is special.

• Fifteen Years Helping the College Grow—

What were the challenges you faced when you started at Warren Wilson?

The college was facing some struggles when we arrived, and the administrative work was demanding. The college had a very small enrollment but a most worthy mission. It has developed a national board of trustees and donor base, and a unique niche in American higher education. So, Warren Wilson needed to have high visibility. It entailed a good bit of effort on everyone's part to develop that, and to build new programs.

Over the course of the years we received some good publicity with feature stories in the *New York Times*, the *Los Angeles Times, USA Today* and *Time,* and that coverage continues to the present day. Recently, *Sierra Magazine* once again rated Warren Wilson as one of the greenest colleges in the country, ranking us number four nationally, one notch ahead of Stanford, which is pretty good company.

How many students were there when you started and how many students are there now?

There were 425 students when we arrived the summer of 1991. Today, if you include the MFA program, there are about 1,000 students. There are twenty-seven majors, and the degrees are BA, BS, Master of Fine Arts and Creative Writing. A second graduate program has recently been added, in education.

Looking back, we really enjoyed our fifteen years of helping the college develop and grow, working with great colleagues, and striving to put Warren-Wilson on the map nationally as eighty-percent of students come from out of state.

• A Two-Fold Career Path—

You've been immersed in diverse career paths and endeavors, and are sort of a Renaissance man, if you don't mind me saying so. Please go back and tell more about your early years in education.

Career-wise, it has really been a two-fold professional journey in that I had my cap set on being a lifetime professor. After I received my doctorate in the Department of Geography at UNC Chapel Hill I applied several places, but was particularly interested in staying in North Carolina; I'm a native Tar Heel and love the state.

The Charlotte campus had been born only a few years before, and it appeared to be an up-and-coming university, so I had a chance to be part of something in its formative, historic stages. I applied and was offered a teaching job, but at the last minute there were state budget problems, some things never change, and the funding did not go through for the position.

I got a call from the Chancellor's office indicating that they would have to delay offering the teaching position for a year or two, but that the chancellor wanted to interview me again about being his Executive Assistant. I was hired by him, and also taught one course per year.

After two years working with Chancellor Colvard I became a faculty member in the Department of Geography and taught fulltime for three years. Dean always had administrative plans for me, and invited me to come back into the administration as a Vice Chancellor for Student Affairs, and later in Advancement and Public Service.

Then you became an author; tell me about your books.

I kept my hand in teaching for a while as I embarked on book projects. The first was the only one of its kind nationally, an "urban atlas". Charlotte was growing at a considerable pace, overlapping the South Carolina line, and the idea of the 'Metrolina' ensued, which is a corruption of the term metropolitan and Carolina. It consisted of twelve counties in a compact area, with Charlotte as the centerpiece.

Many city planners and elected officials had said, "We need to get a handle on this area's growth and change to understand it better." So we hatched the idea of a thematic atlas that was not just listings of places, but with chapters on such topics as urbanization, population growth, history, cultural arts and the environment. We invited experts in each of those areas to author chapters, and we served as editors, wrote the introduction, drafted sidebars, and each wrote a major section.

It was published by the University of North Carolina press in 1970 and was the first urban atlas in the country.

Then the idea occurred to take the concept of a thematic atlas statewide, and UNC Press was again interested. We used the same format of experts writing chapters, with us as editors. We filled the atlas with maps and graphics as we had done with the Metrolina Atlas, and it was published in 1977.

Later we used the same concept for our first venture with a commercial publisher, *Southern Living Magazine's* Oxmoor House, a noted publisher of books about the South. We took our format and concept to "The Land of the South," which focused on the fifteen southern states. But first we had to define what and where is the South? Obviously the Southern phenomenon occurs more in some states than others. And Mid-Western states like Indiana and Illinois are much more southern than say, South Florida or West Texas.

And you continued writing as an author of atlases and a unique book about Appalachian music.

A few years later we started new conversations with UNC Press about an atlas for the new century for publication in 2000. We had developed at UNC Charlotte the premier cartography lab in higher education. It had started in a very rudimentary form with maps scribed with a needle pen, then worked its way to computerized mapping over a twenty-year period.

The Atlas of *North Carolina, Portrait for a New Century* was published by UNC Press in 2000 and was very well received. Through a foundation grant, a copy was placed in the hands of every legislator in North Carolina, each member of the Board of Governors of the UNC system, and every public library throughout the state. It also was given to other public and business leaders and elected officials. Later an online version of some of the chapters was maintained.

One of my closest friends, Jim Clay, co-authored with me the *Metrolina Atlas,* but sadly he died of cancer halfway through the *North Carolina Atlas* work. My colleague and co-author Al Stuart and I dedicated the book to him. Jim and I had taught together, traveled together, attended International New Town meetings together, and were able to incorporate the lessons of regional planning and the 'New Town' movement of planned communities.

Tell about your diverse teaching roles at that time.

I was teaching the courses previously mentioned, and after two years in the Chancellors Office, began fulltime teaching of courses in World Cultures, Political Geography, the South, and the Geography of Europe. Then I returned to the administration at UNC Charlotte.

A few years ago I was also asked to team teach a course twice a year at the Association of Governing Boards Institute about board development for college presidents and board chairs, and that allowed me also to keep up the teaching experience.

So over the years, even though I have not been in the formal class room day-to-day, the combination of guest appearances and public speaking allowed me to sustain the teaching.

In retirement I have increased the amount of consulting so that I work with boards of trustees and board development on-site.

- **Career Experiences That Resonate—**

Please relate other career experiences and episodes at UNC and Warren Wilson that resonate with you.

I've had the privilege of serving at two academic institutions, a public University in Charlotte, and an independent liberal arts institution in Asheville, and the striking thing about my period of time at both was that they were in their major building eras.

When I first went to Charlotte it was in an embryotic stage, had joined the UNC system only three years before, was small with no residence halls, and was under-budgeted and not well known. So my entire twenty-three years there was not only to help with the agenda of the day, but building an institution.

That was both fulfilling and demanding because you are doing two tasks: operating and building. When you build something, there are all the uncertainties ahead, setbacks, budget problems and growing pains, along with the expectations of new students and faculty that cannot always be fulfilled because you're really chasing a dream.

And of course we had big dreams, and what has happened at Charlotte has been phenomenal. When I went there in 1968, there were 2,000 students, now there are 25,000, and it is a major urban research university. So in perspective, it has been on a very fast track, but at the time had never ending growing pains.

During my first two years at Warren Wilson in the early nineties we were in the midst of another recession, although not as bad as the current one. It took us two years to sell our Charlotte home. Warren Wilson had undergone very little growth, and fundraising was difficult at first, but things turned around and we really had a fulfilling run of helping develop the institution, maturing it, growing it.

I had joined an institution with a very worthy history and mission, but there were only 425 students, and enrollment had declined. It was not that well-known, was under-budgeted, and needed a stronger presence on the national stage, new buildings and new programs. So for my entire fifteen years I was privileged but challenged to be leading an institution in a significant building mode.

It sounds like you were the right man at the right place at the right time.

In recent years there has been some leveling out, consolidation, but I just happened to be there when the college needed to grow very badly and needed new infrastructure. We recruited many talented new faculty and staff, and developed national marketing strategies. The striking thing in this professional journey is that I was repeating what I experienced at Charlotte. But I've got to say in retrospect that I wouldn't change a thing.

I often told people we were recruiting, "If you want to join an institution that is simply navigating through and managing something already in place, we're not it. We are operating an entity that is complex, but are also building for the future, and you've got to be prepared and have the patience, the wherewithal and the creativity to be part of the building process, and at the end of the day be gratified that you were a part of that journey and had a significant impact in shaping an institution."

Those were huge challenges; how did they play out?

There were plenty of challenges and wakeful nights connected with the building process. Also, when you move from a vice president or vice chancellor role to being a president, there are a whole new set of challenges that you know intellectually will be at work, but until you are there emotionally you cannot fully understand them.

I've said to new college presidents, or those looking to be a college president, that my previous experience entailed good mentors and I had seen the ins and outs of just about every kind of program, so I knew the dynamics of building an institution.

What you are never prepared for until you are fully in the president's role is that everything can eventually land on your desk, as opposed to being more compartmentalized as a vice president. When you serve as president, most of the hard, tough decisions make their way to you. The Harry Truman iconic "The buck stops here" quote is something that becomes a day-to-day reality.

College presidents are responsible to at least a dozen stakeholder groups or constituents, including students and their parents, faculty, staff, alumni, trustees, major donors, the media, the government, all on different levels. It is stimulating to have contact with those groups, but they always have expectations you cannot possibly fulfill 100 percent. You have to adjust and emotionally and temperamentally deal with it.

I know college presidents who could not weather that dynamic and took early retirement, or worse, because work demands are day and night. When you are a vice president, you work hard, long hours, but it is not 24/7 as it is when you are the CEO and responsible for everything.

So I grew into that, learned from it, understood it, but I would still sometimes wake up in the middle of the night with a list bouncing through my head, wondering whether I had satisfied someone, or if I could meet this or that expectation. Nevertheless, it is an exhilarating experience and one of life's privileges to serve as a college president.

- **Courage in Action at Warren Wilson *Circa* 1952—**

Through the late forties and into the early fifties, Warren Wilson was quietly contemplating how it might break the color barrier of segregation. One day in 1952 some students approached the administration and said, "We've met a young man through the Presbyterian Church here who lives in Swannanoa, named Alma Shippy, and he's African-American. Why can't he become a student here?" The administration's response was, "We are close to the start of school but let's take a vote of all of the boys in Sunderland Dorm, because that is where Alma would live." And by a vote of 52-to-1, remarkably, they voted to admit Alma.

Well, classes were already underway and all of the boys in Sunderland Dorm already had roommates, so consequently Alma had to have a room of his own. But to symbolize that they were all friends of Alma's, and in a way Alma's roommates, each of the boys in Sunderland took the doors off their hinges and simply had open rooms to symbolize: "We are all your roommates, Alma!"

Those were some of the heroic shoulders I was standing on at Warren Wilson. It took great courage for those students and the administration to do that in the South of 1952. In many ways it was revolutionary. This true story was shared with me by Billy Edd Wheeler, who was a student in the dorm. He became one of the finest musicians and songwriters ever to come through North Carolina, and is a good and valued friend. His compositions have sold about seventy-million records.

- **Leadership Skills—**

How did you hone your leadership skills to guide the college to such enormous success?

I've read a lot about leadership, studied leaders, tried to be one, and a biography about FDR really struck me: "He was bright enough, though not the intellectual that Woodrow Wilson or others might be, but he had a first-class temperament."

I think that a first-class temperament is an 'emotional quotient' that is as important as the intellectual quotient, and until you are in the position you cannot totally appreciate that, you will be challenged by it, and you will have setbacks. There were days when I said, "Lord, this is a tough job," but you work through it. In retrospect, it's human-nature to magnify things more than they really need to be.

And I was privileged to be a colleague to faculty who came to Warren Wilson from some of the finest universities in the country, and they are committed to undergraduate teaching while at the same time involving students in scholarship.

What are some of your special achievements?

The College, through the North Carolina Academy of Sciences, has won more top awards for undergraduate student research than any other college or university in North Carolina, and I think that is because each faculty member is undergraduate teaching oriented. Many of the new faculty are especially interested in scholarship and research, and involve students in that research.

We also had one of the highest percentages of graduates going to the Peace Corps of any college or university in the nation. And in 2002, MFA Program for Writers faculty members Richard Russo and Carl Dennis won Pulitzer Prizes in fiction and poetry. And, of course, there are many environmental recognitions.

- **More about *Wayfaring Strangers*—**

Currently, you and Fiona Ritchie are deeply occupied in completing a new book about the roots of Appalachian music, and you've invested a lot of yourselves in the project. Tell me more about it.

Wayfaring Strangers will have a sub-title something like: *The Connections of the Music of the Appalachians and the Scots-Irish.* Its origins for me go back to childhood, and in the 1960's and my love of folk music. If you were interested in the folk music of the sixties, you couldn't help but be connected to some of the great standard-bearers in the Appalachians, old-timers whose music came from Scotland and Ireland. My own ancestry is Scots-Irish, so I had that affinity.

I was always regaled by stories by my father about Scotland, who on his mother's side was a Fraser, and on his father's side an Orr, a sub-clan of MacGregor. And through college I played a lot of folk music, including the Kingston Trio, Joan Baez, and all the rest.

I met Fiona Ritchie in 1981 while I was a vice chancellor for public service and development at UNC Charlotte and one of the departments in my division was the new public radio station that I helped launch. We obtained a remaining frequency slot with the Corporation For Public Broadcasting, and it became an NPR affiliate, WFAE.

We were on the air only a few months when a young woman from Scotland walked into my office, an exchange student who asked if she could volunteer at the public radio station because they had a great tradition of public radio in Britain through BBC. The answer was, "We need all the help we can get and we would be glad to have you volunteer."

Later she asked, "Would you mind if I tried a local program of Celtic music?" I responded, "Great idea, Fiona. I'm a sixties 'folky' with Scots-Irish ancestry!"

The station manager said at the time, "We'll try it Fiona, but with that accent you probably won't make it in public radio." She loves to tell the story on herself, because one thing that has endeared Fiona to her multitude of listeners is her beautiful Scottish accent.

Her program was carried locally for two years, then we pitched it to National Public Radio, initially American Public Radio, and they took it on for a trial period of six months on twenty-five affiliate stations. Today Fiona's show is carried to a half million people in 350 affiliate stations throughout the United States, and she is occasionally heard on BBC, on Armed Forces Radio, and on United Airlines flights.

I recall that background because putting *The Thistle & Shamrock* on the air got me in touch with Celtic music more than ever. There also was a Celtic music renaissance going on among young musicians in Scotland and Ireland, and it was taking the folk music world by storm. Those musicians were touring, public radio was helping, and consequently I started playing more folk music.

I met Darcy through a music gathering in Charlotte and we formed a band we named Maggie's Fancy that played Celtic and Appalachian music. We wanted a Celtic name that had sort of a casual affinity to it, and one of the most popular Celtic names is Maggie. It was also the name of Darcy's springer spaniel. In the first band picture, in typical Celtic whimsy, Maggie is posed with the rest of the band.

So those threads were coming together, and over the years as we made our way to Warren Wilson, Fiona was having great success with *The Thistle & Shamrock*. But she moved back to Scotland to be closer to her parents, met a wonderful Australian guy, and they started a family.

- **Deciding to Write *Wayfaring Strangers*—**

In the mid-90s I broached the idea to Fiona about doing a book together: "Fiona, you have a beautiful voice, are well spoken and creative in your programs, and write extremely well. Wouldn't it be nice if both of us could leave behind a piece of ourselves, of our passion and avocation, of the music through a book?" I mentioned to her that I'd authored several books, and how this book concept sort of semi-related to geography. She responded positively, and during subsequent years we incrementally started hatching the book project. It was delayed several times because she had two young kids, but they are now in school fulltime. She also was attentive to her ailing mother in a nursing home before her mum sadly passed away.

But we were conducting research, interviewing folk icons like Pete Seeger, Jean Ritchie, Doc Watson and others, acquired a whole library of books, spent time at the Center for Migration Studies in Northern Ireland, the Library of Congress, and the book started coming together. Darcy is the art director for *Wayfaring Strangers*, as she was for a Warren Wilson publication. And she is a fine watercolor and oil painter, so she has a good eye for lay-out and design.

What is the story line behind the music in the book?

The book tells the story of Celtic music through immigrants who started in Scotland, migrated to Northern Ireland to what is called Ulster, then to America, mainly through Pennsylvania, then over generations traveled down the Great Wagon Road into the Carolinas, and finally settling in the Southern Appalachians.

They brought with them their stories and songs and fiddle tunes, and much of that was preserved through the so-called "Song Catchers" or "Song Collectors" living in our mountains. We tell the story in four major sections of the family tree of the music.

Interviewees play a large part in the book. We interviewed Jean Richie just before she suffered a stroke, then Pete Seeger who is still going strong at ninety-two, and just missed interviewing his brother Mike Seeger before he died.

You want to preserve these voices and let them relate the stories that need telling, that have universal truths.

- **Immigrants Were In All Family Trees—**

Immigrants at one time or another are part of our family tree, and that continues today. When people immigrate they bring with them their stories, their songs and their special memories.

We will tell a poignant story that was shaped in the new land and explains how the Scots-Irish had the largest influence on the music of the Appalachians, but another very important influence came from African-Americans who gave us the banjo, gourd instruments, and were involved in dance calling and some of the percussive work. And the Germans, the English, the French, and even the Cherokee, were also part of what we call a 'tapestry of Appalachian music'.

This is a story that repeats itself around the world and in other cultures, and I hope it will raise understanding and sensitivity to the experience of immigrants today as well as other centuries and generations, because our ancestors went through many of the same things that immigrants today are experiencing.

When and why did the Scotch-Irish immigrants come to the United States and settle in the South, and how did their music start to blend in a cultural immersion?

There was a period of time in the eighteenth-century when the immigration from Ulster, Northern Ireland, was at its peak. It started in force about 1716, and the impetus for it was economic and religious discrimination. Ulster was colonized with Scots by King James as a way of offsetting the ethic population. Over the years the Protestant Presbyterians, were caught in a squeeze between the English Anglicans and the Catholics. They were not landowners, but were given land to settle. And there was rent-racking, an acceleration of rent rate every year or less. It was a form of economic discrimination, along with the religious discrimination.

About that time the linen trade was in full force across the Atlantic, especially between the port of Philadelphia and Northern Ireland, so ocean routes became available, and entire Presbyterian congregations, as well as individuals, started sailing to America, and the songs they brought with them were very poignant. The leaving was often called an 'American Wake', as they left their families, their neighbors, their communities, knowing in their hearts they'd probably never see each other again. So the American Wake became a combination of song, dance, tears, laughter, and stories that went all night or all week.

A body of songs connected with the leaving resulted. A booklet by a scholar of Irish-American Folksong called '1000 Ships are Sailing' captures the trauma of leaving and the voyage, and a lot of the music. A second phase was 'the crossing' that included musicians, fiddle players, and singers. A third phase was the arrival in the new land from about 1716 through the revolutionary war in 1776, and a continuation to the 1800s.

In all, an estimated quarter-million immigrants came through the port of Philadelphia, and some went into indentured servitude to pay off the cost of the crossing. Then they settled in Pennsylvania partly because of religious tolerance by the Quakers. But the Scots always suffered from wanderlust, and in a few generations started looking for another promised land in the Carolinas, and the fourth phase commenced.

'The Great Indian Trading Path' became the 'Great Philadelphia Wagon Road' through the Shenandoah Valley into the Southern Appalachians. Predominant numbers settled in the Piedmont of the Carolinas, but many hardy ones wound up in the Appalachians where the coves and hollows became time capsules.

In the book we also examine the relationship of the black and white cultures in the mountains. The larger black population was in the coastal plain where there were plantations. Interestingly enough, the last Gaelic speaking church in North Carolina, Gaelic being old Scottish, was a black church. Blacks had settled there as slaves, but gained their freedom.

Variations of old songs from Scotland are carried on in the mountains to this day and many traditional musicians like David Holt, Shelia Kay Adams, Jean Richie, Laura Boosinger and others are the 'song-catchers' who remember and revere those who came before.

- **Environmental Concerns—**

You have strong concerns about the environment. Do you believe the universe is connected and perhaps interacts with us in different ways, and that one connection is to the world around us?

Yes. I have a deep belief in the concept of the 'tree of life', which was the title and theme of my presidential inauguration address at Warren Wilson, and is an old concept that dates back to the Torah—the Jewish Old Testament, the West Africans and the Cherokee, and is woven into the quilts of Appalachian mountaineers. They were all expressing a belief that everything on the planet is interconnected, every drop of rain, every human being. John Muir, the great Scottish naturalist and explorer, expressed "Everything we come across is somehow hitched to everything else in the universe".

Native Americans understood this very well because their lifeblood depended on not competing with but harmonizing with nature. Many other cultures also understand that. Industrialization in this country drew us away from compatibility and harmonization with the environment, until we started discovering in the early 1970's that we were losing the quality of our air, water and land, and that we must find a way to be compatible with nature. Hence the environmental sustainability movement began and now is a worldwide movement. But its roots are deep and include the tree of life concept.

An old folk song about the tree of life includes this line: "Aint'cha got the right, aint'cha got the right, to the tree of life." It means that you have the right to be connected to opportunity, to others, to get a fair shake, and that a community of kindred spirits is at work.

We are going to find out that on this little blue dot we call Earth that the tree of life concept becomes more and more paramount. Certainly the astronauts saw through the windows of their capsules just how tiny and fragile our planet is. If we don't get along and don't find a way to harmonize with each other and with our natural environment then future generations are not going to have quality of life, or even life.

I hope we continue to write about that through our poetry and songs, extending to political discourse and academic curriculum. What we are seeing today, gratifyingly, is that sustainability has become a byword in academia around the country. Warren Wilson is a leader because students come here with a passion to make a better world, to harmonize with the environment, to be good stewards. It is certainly a concept to live by, whether you are an artist, or you are in the business community, or you are an elected official or a musician or a teacher.

How have you been involved in environmental activity?

It is something I've lived by and certainly treasure. In a way, the book we are doing picks up on the family tree of the music that is part of the tree of life.

The first time I met Jane Goodall was when we taped her for some interviews for a series of programs on National Public radio called, 'An Environmental Minute'. That never came to fruition, mainly for financial reasons, but she was one of the first persons we interviewed. My impression of Jane was a complex combination of a very soft-spoken and gentle person but steel inside, evidenced by the strength and perseverance she had in Africa to save the chimpanzees, and to become a United Nations Ambassador for world for environmental causes. Her presence on campus made us redouble our environmental efforts at Warren Wilson.

Some people embrace your views and some people deny the science of global climate change. Is that accurate in your view, and do you see our country moving forward on this vital subject?

Well, I think it is both alarming and hopeful. It's easy for us as an advanced nation, along with European cultures, to tell the developing world of Africa, parts of Latin America, wherever, to slow down economic growth and therefore their economic opportunity because it is infringing on the environment.

In West Virginia, how do you tell coal miners they've got to stop mountaintop removal that will cost their jobs and affect their families for generations, even though it decimates eons of nature's work?

We have to find a way to talk with rather than at or past each other, and understand where others are coming from. I think this will continue to be a difficult challenge, internationally and nationally. We are in an economic recession with a high unemployment rate, which means it is all the harder to implement cap-and-trade and other climate-control measures.

So, what's the good news?

I am heartened by the extent young people are the 'green team', and at Warren Wilson are aware that they want the older generation to walk-the-talk about greening the planet. They come out of college and enter their communities with a strong commitment to sustainability, and a belief that sustainable enterprise can work in the business world. It doesn't have to be lose-lose, it can be win-win in terms of economic growth and sustaining our environment.

Your mantra of 'spreading the seeds and they are going to grow' is an extension of that philosophy into the greater culture, and perhaps that is where real hope lies. Is that an accurate statement?

Very much so! I'm sure if you're a teacher in the public schools you might feel like you're beating your head against the wall because of budget cutbacks, greater class sizes, and you don't always enjoy immediate feedback from students. So you've got to remind yourself to plant seeds for future generations, and you do the best you can. The Johnny Appleseed metaphor expresses about planting seeds: 'You hope as many blossom as possible, you just don't know where or when'.

My favorite quote about teaching is 'A great teacher effects eternity'. I really believe that, because the spreading of seeds has a ripple effect over lives and generations.

- **Pack Square coming alive—**

You captured memories of your early years in Asheville that are also excerpted later in this book. Do any of those moments particularly resonate with you?

Soon after I arrived here, I was befriended by Roger McGuire, who many credit as being the primary visionary for Pack Place and Pack Square, and the revitalization of downtown.

Roger, a retired executive with *Southern Living Magazine,* had moved to Asheville from Birmingham because his daughter and son-in-law lived here. He also was on the board of trustees at Warren Wilson College, and on the Presidential Search Committee that hired me, and we immediately developed a friendship. We shared a mutual love of city and regional planning, and he invited me to join the Pack Place Board. We spent a lot of time dreaming and envisioning what was to come.

During the 1920's and the aftermath of the Great Depression, Asheville had slipped into a drive-through downtown with many closed storefronts. In 1994, after the opening of Pack Place and the revitalization of Pack Square, I did an op-ed article quoting Thomas Wolfe, the famous Asheville author, about the importance of the square as the living heart of a town.

Today Asheville is a 'Paris of the South', as some say. Certainly it is on everyone's radar, as a vibrant downtown. And it really all began with that revitalization of Pack Square, and Roger's vision of Pack Place, and that of others who came along to offer new hope and a dream for Asheville, which now has one of the most attractive medium-size downtowns in the country.

What year did you go on the Pack Place board?

I joined the pack place board almost immediately after I got here in the fall of 1991 and served two terms. Later I joined the board of one of the components of Pack Place, the Diana Wortham Theatre at about the time I retired at Warren Wilson in 2006. My wife and I have been regular supporters of the theatre's Main Stage Series, and we have performed there.

I served for a while as a Vice Chair of the Pack Place board, and since have served on about ten boards. I tried to steer away from chairing any because I had a day-and-night job at Warren Wilson. But I felt it was important for the college to connect with Asheville and the area, and to be part of the revitalization. Warren Wilson has benefitted from Asheville now being so well-known across the country.

One of the first things I worked toward when I came to Warren Wilson was to work to restore our mailing address from Swannanoa to Asheville. We originally were the Asheville Farm School, and Swannanoa is a wonderful old Cherokee name, but the admission counselors had a hard time getting people to know where it was and how to pronounce it. So, we celebrate with a letterhead tagline that we are in the Swannanoa River Valley, but our mailing address is Asheville.

Among those important to the revitalization of Asheville included Roger, who brought the original dream and was willing to think outside the box while others were cautious; Julian Price, who was in elementary school with me, a visionary with great resources that he shared with community causes, and Leslie Anderson, who is a Warren Wilson board member but back then was a key city staff member. Certainly elected officials of that time also deserve credit. Sadly, Roger died in 1994 and Julian about eight years ago from cancer, but their legacies endure in this community.

Tell me about Diana Wortham and Pack.

Diana Wortham is a citizen of Asheville who supports the arts and is still active, and comes to events. She has been very generous with major gifts to Pack Place and the theatre that was named for her, but is very modest and doesn't want a lot of attention. She is one whose heart followed her vision. George Pack was an early leader in the community, and as I recall might have held elective office.

The Pack Place opening came in increments, and like many things took longer than expected. They were renovating the old library on the square and turning it into a combination of the theatre, the Art Museum, the Gem and Mineral Museum, and Health Adventure, but the grand opening really was in 1994. Wilma Dykeman, the great writer from these parts who wrote *The Tall Woman* and *The French Broad,* was the guest speaker. She once was our commencement speaker.

- **The Orr Legacy—**

Looking back over your career achievements, and they continue, what do you think will be your legacy?

I'll take a cautious stab at it but largely leave that to others. I think any academic person takes pride in his scholarship, as I do with my books. But I hope my greatest accomplishment entailed having an impact on students' young lives, not just through my own work, but from recruiting good people more talented than me in many areas, who worked diligently to make the campus a special learning community.

Do you often hear from former students?

Yes, and that is something that gives us a great deal of pride. We were just at the Black Mountain farmers market and saw a whole string of Warren Wilson graduates selling produce and working with sustainable agriculture.

We often get invitations to weddings, or see students who are musicians, or have done good work in the Peace Corps. We relish those contacts, and I suppose what we miss most in retirement is seeing students day-to-day.

I continue to help the college as needed in terms of friend-building or fund raising activity, but basically we let our successors do their job, and especially come to the campus related to music occasions.

You also continue to serve the community, as Warren Wilson students and grads are encouraged to do.

Yes. Besides the governing boards of UNC at Asheville and Berea College, I've served on the boards of Dianna Wortham Theatre and Lake Eden Arts Festival that also has programs in the schools and internationally for children, I'm on the Hub Alliance board with other community leaders who plan and envision the future of Asheville and Western North Carolina.

And I serve the National Council of the Center of Courage and Renewal which draws upon the work of Parker Palmer, the respected writer and activist whose work has been an important part of my life. I recently retired from the North Carolina Center for International Understanding board, which does a lot of good work, and we have participated in some of their International programs. It's based in Raleigh.

Tell me more about the Center.

The Center for International Understanding had its birth as the old Friendship Force, which was a homestay for families and individuals visiting other countries. When I joined the board that component was still in place, and former governor Jim Hunt had a major role in its work. One of our first experiences with the center was a homestay in Norway above the Arctic Circle with a family in a small village, along with several others from Asheville. For a variety of reasons, mainly economic, there are not many homestay trips anymore, but there are international trips. What the center works to do is establish bridges for elected and school officials to their counterparts in other countries.

A lot of work is being done with Mexico, and Darcy and I were just there, even though I had just retired from the board. The program has also taken elected officials from North Carolina to Russia, France, China, really all over the globe, but its primary emphasis is helping shape public policy regarding international programs in education and building bridges among public schools.

Sounds like you are still a very busy man.

Well, some say it is a failed retirement. But, as you know, we struggle to seek balance all of our lives. I just haven't quite found it yet. But it's a wonderful life and I'm not complaining. I do wish there were more lifetimes and more hours in the day, but we are privileged to live here, to have the friends we do, to have involvements from book writing to music to grandchildren.

The newspaper of higher education did a piece about five years ago about quality of life in academia and selected the five best destinations for Academics to retire to, and one was Asheville. Others were similar to Asheville, including Colorado Springs, Colorado and Flagstaff, Arizona. They all have rich physical beauty, but also excellent cultural arts and a diversity of people. We are fortunate to live here.

- **Founding the Swannanoa Gathering—**

You founded the Swannanoa Gathering; tell me about it.

The idea for the Swannanoa Gathering came about after Darcy and I attended a music camp in West Virginia six or seven times and were struck by how much energy, celebration, joy and sense of community there was. The Swannanoa Gathering provides instruction in various forms of traditional music and is organized around theme weeks.

It primarily came about through our love of the music. Now Darcy and I continue as the college hosts for the summer Swannanoa gathering workshops that run for five weeks. We do a welcome, meet and greet, participate and lead song circles.

When I first came to Warren Wilson I knew there was a heritage of music involvement with fine musicians like David Holt, a faculty member for five years in the late 1970's, and many others like Billy Ed Wheeler and David Wilcox, who attended Warren Wilson.

This was fertile ground for establishing a summer music camp and workshop, so the second full summer here we launched the Swannanoa Gathering.

I hired an old music friend, Jim McGill, who was a professional musician for many years and toured nationally with a duo. Jim didn't have any background in administration but he knew the music and musicians, and for the first couple of years I mentored him, then he just ran with it.

The Gathering has grown from a very modest beginning of about seventy-five students to 1500 participants in 2011, including family and youth from all over the world. There are five weeks of seven different themes, and during 'Appalachian Old-Time Music Week' alone we hosted a large international contingent of thirty individuals from other countries ranging from Australia to Norway. We've also seen an explosion in the kid's programs for those six and older, and with youth scholarships.

What has the Swannanoa Gathering meant to the college?

It has been very gratifying and certainly helped the college with its national and global visibility. The Gathering builds friendships, attracts students to enroll at the college, and even garners contributions especially targeted toward the youth scholarship program.

I come to Warren Wilson almost every Monday for a music jam-session in front of the Student Center that includes faculty, staff and students, something I initiated in the early nineties. I play the guitar, and Darcy plays the mountain dulcimer and concertina. She's now learning to play the banjo.

How did you propose to Darcy?

Interesting question. I was to attend the annual meeting of the International New Town Association in San Francisco, as I had a hand in planning a new community contiguous to UNC Charlotte. I invited Darcy to go with me. Before the meeting started we made a side trip up to Mendocino, a bucolic little village on the coast about four hours north of San Francisco, and one evening in front of a little historic college that had a picket fence around it and the Pacific Ocean in the background, I popped the question.

And she answered . . . ?

She said yes. I told her it sure would've ruined the trip if she said no.

Darcy is just great in so many ways, including helping the grandchildren with art. She's a very talented artist and musician, and has a passion for watercolor and oil painting. As we speak she's at a painting workshop. She is also the art editor for *Wayfaring Strangers.*

• Looking Inward—

What are your feelings about the politics of today?

I hope the disharmony we see in politics today doesn't translate toward discrimination against people of different backgrounds, different sexual persuasions, different ethnic groups. We should never forget that our country is a beacon to the world as a melting-pot.

We must try to assimilate people, even though we're experiencing challenges now in terms of immigration, gay rights, and equal economic opportunity for all people. This growing gap between the haves and the have-nots is one of our overriding concerns.

You obviously care very deeply about civil rights, and the division in the country today, as I do. Please summarize your feelings about those sensitive subjects.

I was inspired by the John Kennedy presidency, the idea of the Peace Corps, Civil Rights, Martin Luther King, and all those who came along to follow or lead.

We need to look at the divisiveness in our country and remind ourselves how far we've come. Yet in terms of people having equal economic opportunity, unfortunate gaps remain.

But Lord, we come a long way, especially in electing a person of color to be the nation's president.

There are other bridges to cross. I think we are approaching gender-equality, but we are not there yet as a country.

Another thorny and controversial issue is gay rights, and I'm seeing some of the same prejudices I heard during the Civil Rights movements of the sixties and seventies. We are overcoming some hurdles, but there is still too much of 'we' and 'they', of distrust of "oneness."

Finally Dr. Orr, are you an optimist and do you consider yourself fortunate?

Yes. In expressing optimism, one of the things that has impressed me about American society and the human spirit in general is the characteristic of resiliency that we saw after 9/11, and after all kinds of tragedies in this country that we thought might bring us to our knees. We've seen many individuals display that resilience, courage and spirit, and that underscores my general optimism.

But along with that is a great sense of concern with some of the directions we are headed in terms of divisiveness between the haves and the have not's. In many ways this is a fragmented and explosive time in the world, but the human spirit and its fundamental goodness are qualities I hold on to. Parker Palmer, who I mentioned earlier, recently authored a book that should be a best seller titled: *Healing the Heart of Democracy: The Courage to Create a Politics Worthy of the Human Spirit.*

That is a call to all of us.

Dr. Doug Orr at a Warren Wilson College Commencement.

Doug and Darcy performing at a Warren Wilson College Celebration event.

North Carolina Atlas publication reception with former governor Jim Hunt and former UNC President Bill Friday (left) in 2000.

On stage with Rodney Lytle as the "Brothers Blues" at the Lake Eden Arts Festival.
© 2008 R.L. Geyer

. . . with folk music legend Tom Paxton.
© 2011 R.L. Geyer

. . . performing at the 2011 Swanannoa Soltice at Diana Wortham Theatre in Asheville with Amy White and Al Petteway. Doug began this event in 2003, and also founded the Swanannoa Gathering at Warren Wilson College.
© Stephen Houseworth

'The Elvi'—
Rich Bellando, Billy Edd Wheeler and
Doug Orr strike a pre-concert pose.

. . . with daughter Heather and son-in-
law David Abernathy.
© 2011 R.L. Geyer

. . . with daughter Holly.
© 2011 R.L. Geyer

. . . with grandkids—
Quincy, Campbell, and Colin.

Section 5: **Excerpts of Writings by and about Doug Orr**

The following excerpts from the extensive writings by and about Dr. Doug Orr speak volumes as to his passion, depth of character and vision of academia, and his contributions to North Carolina, the country and the world as a geographer and analytical historian.

Equally skilled as a writer and orator, his personal and professional values are clearly reflected in his columns, books and public addresses. Although these articles were written near the close of the last century and the beginning of the new one, they proved to be prescient in many respects, and contributed greatly to ongoing debates of the day to the now. His by-lined columns were all written from in-depth experience and observations about the subject matter.

- ***The North Carolina Atlas, PORTRAIT FOR A NEW CENTURY.***

Published at the dawn of the new century in 2000 by UNC Chapel Hill and London with an introduction by then Governor Jim Hunt, this thematic *Atlas* provides an in-depth and highly accessible account of the state's physical environment, history, population and economy, and explores its government, politics, education, health, culture and outdoor recreation. The narrative traces the shifts and patterns that made North Carolina what it is today, and examines contemporary challenges in technology and globalism, and presciently forecasts where these and other trends will lead in the new century.

The 461 pages and 20 chapters of *The North Carolina Atlas* were a decade in the making. Darcy Orr was the graphics editor who designed the book's high-resolution graphics, including photographs, maps and charts. The vivid and interpretive text includes expository sidebars by guest writers Charles Kuralt of 'On the Road' television fame and Doris Betts.

Orr also enlivened his book with a heartwarming vignette about attending a 1950 Brooklyn Dodgers' game at Greensboro Memorial Stadium with his father, memorable because Jackie Robinson, who had broken baseball's color line in 1947, played second base and batted fifth. Orr wrote: *The excitement in the air was electric, as the National League champions had come to town.*

Reviews:
Our State magazine called the book: *A valuable reference source for the state's government and business leaders, news media, students, and 'Tar Heel' citizens.*

The *Fayetteville Observer* commented: *The book is not just a mountain of information. It also has a point of view, a perspective one where North Carolina has been and where it is going. It really does commend itself to a general audience.*

And from *Business North Carolina: Nowhere else can you find a single volume that tells so much about this place, from the geologic formations that created the land beneath our feet to the weather systems that rule the sky above our heads, and how those forces have made us who we are . . . A crash course in understanding a very special place and its people at a critical point in their history.*

- **Excerpts from Published Newspaper Articles by Doug Orr—**

- **Articles from a personal perspective—**

Title: ***Early Elvis: Crossing the musical divide.*** From *The Charlotte Observer*, August 16, 2002:
Excerpts: *Elvis Presley was only 20 and less than a year into professional performing when I crossed*

paths with this phenomenon who was to revolutionize American musical history. It was a warm July evening in 1955 in Daytona Beach, Florida . . . A youthful Elvis came on last, strode to the microphone, guitar draped over his shoulder and wearing a bright orange sport coat and slacks with an open-neck shirt. He assumed a wide-spread stance, a shy smile, a bod movement that seemed tuned to some internal rhythm, and immediately cut loose with the old Arthur 'Big Boy' Crudup blues song, 'That's All Right Mama' . . . His trademark stage persona was there in this raw talent: a combination of restless energy, edginess, rebellion, sexuality and sheer joy of the throbbing beat of the music, accompanied by the Elvis body language of leg twitches, jiggles, wiggles and ballooning trousers . . . there was a spontaneity to this three-piece ensemble that seemed unpackaged and unpretentious . . . The audience response was instantaneous, with an electricity that was new and honest . . . I then understood why Andy Griffith chose not to close the show. Who would want to follow that dynamic blur of pulsating rhythm and motion? . . . We teenagers of the era simply wanted unencumbered access to all of the music, black or white, and a kid from Memphis was leading a musical revolution.

Title: *Remembering Robinson, Exhibition game turned into the moment generations had longed for.*
Guest column from *The Asheville Citizen-Times,* April 2, 1998:
Excerpts: *It was an early spring day nearly 50 years ago at a baseball game in my North Carolina hometown that I witnessed the stirring of the racial liberation of the South. Although Jackie Robinson had broken baseball's color barrier in 1947, the 1948 spring exhibition schedule began his first visits to the baseball parks of the South . . . Until then, the South's African-Americans had been deprived of seeing their sports heroes firsthand . . . Robinson had exploded upon the American baseball scene and changed forever the face of baseball and American society . . . He became an instant celebrity, as well as lightning-rod for old passions of racial separation . . . As the Dodgers made their railway odyssey from one Southern city to another, attendance at the parks were overflowing, with African-American fans in segregated sections, usually making up half the crowd . . . It was at Greensboro's Memorial Field, home of the Carolina Patriots when the Dodgers rode into town . . . The crowd of 8,434 was the largest in North Carolina history, and a subsequent newspaper account reported 'another 500 clung perilously to treetops and rooftops around the outside of the stadium . . . I especially remember the fans seated down the first base and left-field lines – Jackie Robinson's people, overflowing 'the colored sections', dressed as if they had come to church. In a way, they had . . . Even before Robinson came to the on-deck circle for his at-bat a steady murmur arose from those segregated seats . . . Then number 42 emerged into view, with that characteristic pigeon-toed walk, gracefully taking practice swings. The gathering sound from the stands took on an ethereal quality, not really a cheer but rather a deep-seated stirring, as if a collective human soul was speaking with a single voice. It began to spill onto the field in a rising crescendo. Their moment, one that generations before them had longed for was occurring before their eyes . . . Robinson went 3-for-7 and fielded flawlessly . . . The crowd reaction – that haunting, resonating sound – stayed with me, although as a child of the South I could not fully comprehend its essence at the time . . . I never forgot that April day and that undefinable crown response when Jackie Robinson first made his way to the plate . . . Witnessing baseball's panorama that warm spring day with my dad, the deep-throated wail was no less than freedom's song, whose refrain extended back through time and place, as far back as the slave ships from West Africa. And its messenger, passing through the ballparks of our Southern towns, was number 42, playing second base for the Brooklyn Dodgers.*

Title: *New generation brings hope for peace in N. Ireland.*
Guest column from the *Asheville Citizen-Times,* November 9, 1998:
Excerpts: *Ordinarily, the Scottish ferry port of Stranraer would be bustling with travelers for the next -morning crossing to Belfast in Northern Ireland. However, on this October evening, a quiet vacancy prevailed, confirmed by the proprietor of our bed-and-breakfast, who lamented that since the devastating Omagh bombing a few weeks earlier, his rooms were infrequently booked, a pattern that followed other terrorist incidents be extremists on both sides of the long Irish struggle . . . My*

wife Darcy and I were en route to Belfast for a commencement ceremony for 165 Northern Ireland college students, Protestant and Catholic, who spent a year of study at 58 American colleges, including Warren Wilson and Montreat in Western North Carolina . . . I was also interested in visiting the emigration route of the Scots-Irish, the ancestral link for many of us in the Mountain and Piedmont regions of the Carolinas . . It has been a long and winding odyssey by land and sea for our Scotch-Irish ancestors, including those who eventually settled throughout the slopes and coves of the Southern Appalachians . . . Scots left a rocky terrain for the promise of good farming land and better economic opportunity . . . The paradoxes of today's Belfast became apparent – two blocks from our hotel the courthouse was surrounded by a ring of concrete barriers and a conspicuous police presence. Yet just across the street, as part of the city's River Lagan waterfront development, is a magnificent new Performing Arts Center . . . Most significantly, there is a stirring of peace in the destiny of this land or paradox and beauty. The current hard-won peace agreements and Nobel Peach Awards reflect the potential and the promise . . . For us, a harbinger of hope came that misty autumn commencement evening as we greeted Irish college students, Catholic and Protestant, from 13 campuses throughout Northern Ireland who came together to celebrate their shared experiences . . . As I watched these young people – Northern Ireland's next generation of leaders it occurred to me that their experience in reality was a program of peace, allowing the old religious and historic differences to simply fall away, like the soft Irish rain that fell outside.

- **Articles from a professional perspective—**

Title: ***Universities have vital role in urban scene.*** From *The Charlotte Observer,* October 15, 1982:
Excerpts: *It is particularly important to emphasize that the contemporary community service role of universities should not detract from but rather flow out of the fundamental teaching mission. Community internships are one example; utilizing local urban case studies in the classroom is another. Likewise, academic research can draw upon the surrounding urban area as a laboratory for applying research ideas to pressing community needs.*

- **From a Series of Guest Columns by Dr. Orr in the** *Asheville Citizen-Times*—

Title: ***Delegation returns from Burlington with a vision for Asheville.*** September 30, 1997:
Excerpts: *It should be our responsibility in Asheville though opportunities like the Intercity Visit Program and Asheville-Buncombe Vision, to be open to good and even bold ides from other places, and after scrutiny and debate, apply them as appropriate to our special time and place . . . The common thread of sustainable community development was defined as ensuring that development meets the needs of the present without compromising the ability of future generations to meet their own needs. We frequently heard 'does it withstand the test of time?' and 'what about the impact upon our children and grandchildren?' . . . Even the community dialogue comes across as sustainable, drawing on the old New England town meeting custom that is inclusive, animated, outspoken and yet basically civil – an approach that invites ongoing citizen involvement and trust.*

Title: ***Regionalism holds our future.*** February 23, 1994:
Excerpts: *The world is reorganizing itself today as the old boundaries and economic/political units are giving way to new geographic groupings. City limits have become just that, too restrictive. County lines, designed in another century, are often irrelevant, and states are too extensive to offer a coordinated community . . . Smaller regional groupings such as our WNC settings have much to gain . . . This regional phenomenon has several interesting characteristics. It is a bottom-up regional initiative. It focuses on a process of collaboration among several sectors – businesses, education, service organizations, elected officials – rather than governmental reorganization . . . The regional issues run the gamut: cultural arts distinctiveness, transportation, economic cohesiveness, land and water use, education . . . WNC regionalization efforts are usually around a particular issue, and have included the Land of the Sky Council of Governments, Carolina West, Mountain Outdoor Recreation*

Alliance, WNC Associated Communities and several others, and there is funding to establish a WNC Economic Development Commission . . . Obviously, close coordination of these initiatives will be crucial to the evolvement of a cooperative region . . . Hopefully, a regional vision is within sight.

Title: ***May our public square return.*** July 4, 1992:

Excerpts: *As we celebrate the Pack Place grand-opening festivals on July 4 we can recall Thom Wolfe's description and prophecy for Pack Square, of things past at the square, of changes, and the possibility of the heart of our town coming back again as a vibrant people-place and community living room . . . American urban society in general has witnessed a demise of public life and active public spaces over the past several decades. But it has not always been that way – in Asheville, in other parts of our country, or through the Western civilization . . . as I have traveled and studied urban settings over the years, I am struck by the fact that downtown Asheville is one of the few medium-sized cities with the ingredients for a mixed-use downtown and a public square that can be a true living room and community core, where we celebrate and focus our diversities and commonalities.*

Section 6: **Chronology**

- **Personal—**
- Dr. Doug M. Orr, born December 9, 1938, Washington, D.C.
- Spouse—Darcy Orr, married June 27, 1987.
- Children—Heather Abernathy, Advancement Officer, Univ. of Washington. Holly Orr, Global Technology Services, New York Univ. Grandchildren—Colin and Campbell Abernathy, Quincy Orr.

- **Athletics—**
- Greensboro Senior High School tennis doubles state champion twice.
- Davidson College tennis number-one player and team captain.

- **Education—**
- B.A., Davidson College, 1961, ROTC Captain.
- MBA, UNC Chapel Hill, 1963. Ph.D., UNC Chapel Hill, 1968.

- **Professional Experience—**
- Professor of Geography and Vice Chancellor, UNC Charlotte, 1968-1991.
- President, Warren Wilson College, 1991-2006.
- Consultant, Association of Governing Boards, Performa Higher Education, 2006-present.

- **Awards/Recognitions—**
- North Carolina Order of the Long Leaf Pine, awarded by the governor.
- Teacher of Excellence Award, UNC Charlotte, award to outstanding teacher on the faculty.
- Paul Harris Fellow Award by Rotary International.
- Chairman's Award, Asheville Chamber of Commerce for Exemplary Leadership, Service, Vision.
- The Garden Clubs of America Conservation Commendation Award on Behalf of the Earth.
- Doug Orr Student Merit Scholarship Award formed by North Carolina Outward Bound School.
- Dr. Douglas Orr Day, April 25, 2006, designated by Buncombe County Board of Commissioners.
- Dr. Doug and Darcy Orr Cottage, Warren Wilson College.
- Doug and Darcy Orr Music Endowment, Swannanoa Gathering

- **Selected Books/Publications—**
- *Wayfaring Strangers: Connections of the Music of Scotland/the Scots-Irish and the Appalachians,* co-author Fiona Ritchie, host on NPR, by UNC Press-in process.
- *North Carolina Atlas: Portrait for a New Century,* co-author Arthur W. Stuart, UNC Press, 2000. *Land of the South,* Oxmoor House, 1989.
- *Metrolina Atlas,* UNC Press, 1970.

- **Organizations Past and Present—**
- Board Chair, North Carolina Independent College Association.
- Board Chair, Association of Presbyterian Colleges and Universities.
- UNC Asheville Board of Trustees.
- Berea College Board of Trustees.
- Association of Governing Boards Presidents Council.
- Council of Independent Colleges Board.
- Asheville Chamber of Commerce Board.
- North Carolina Center for International Understanding Board.
- Diana Wortham Theatre Board, Asheville, N.C.
- Lake Eden Arts Festival Board
- Asheville Hub Alliance Cabinet.

Billie Ruth Sudduth

Basket-Artist and Teacher

I think my legacy is that I opened a new world for basket-makers by getting baskets off the floor and onto pedestals as art objects people want to collect like they collect glass and pottery, and that baskets are now seen in an entirely different light.
— Billie Ruth Sudduth.

Sections about Billie Ruth Sudduth:

1) From Those in the Know about Billie Ruth

2) Special Achievements and Moments

3) **Billie Ruth's Life Journey, in Her Own Words**

4) Photos

5) Chronology

Section 1: **From Those in the Know about Billie Ruth**

- **Happy owners of Billie Ruth Sudduth Baskets—**

We have gotten to know Billie Ruth over the past several years through our enjoyment of her wonderful baskets that are now prized possessions in our home. We have commissioned her to do baskets for us, and always are so pleased with her work. We visit her home studio/home and probably wear out our welcome by staying too long and talking too much, but she is always so delightful to visit and to share her experiences about her work, her family, and how she and Doug enjoy their lives. A true artist and a genuine person that we are so proud to call friend.
    — **Cathy and Phil Winstead, Cary and Banner Elk, NC.**

- **An Inspiration to Everyone—**

Billie Ruth continues to be an inspiration to everyone with whom she comes in contact. She is a truly gifted teacher to ALL students, from accomplished basket weavers (Penland) and art educators to elementary school students. She created and wrote 'Math in a Basket', incorporating the inter-connection of math, science and art which has been taught in numerous schools. Years ago, Billie Ruth made a list of her goals, even including an almost unattainable idea of becoming a North Carolina Living Treasure. She has amazingly achieved ALL those goals, and shown me and others what unlimited potential one life can have when you believe in yourself. Her positive attitude, sense of gratitude and amazement that honors and recognitions just keep coming make me smile and say "well-deserved!" It has been a delight and privilege to have been her student in basket classes, to have her teach my students, and watch her achieve national recognition. Bravo, Billie Ruth!
    — **A former Billie Ruth Sudduth Student.**

- **From a Collector—**

How can you not love someone named Billie Ruth? I stopped by her booth at an American Craft Council Show in Charlotte many years ago, not knowing that it was such an important event in my life. I had never heard of Billie Ruth, and thus did not know of her growing reputation. While in her booth admiring her baskets, I kept hearing more knowledgeable people come by speaking to her with reverence. Hearing some of these conversations made me look at her baskets more closely. I really hate to admit that I didn't buy my first basket from her: I admired her workmanship, but I grew up a Bear Bryant fan and Billie Ruth was a Roll Tide person. But I figured if she went to Alabama that she had to be special, and she was. Many craft shows later, going to many just to visit Billie Ruth and her husband Doug, I have been fortunate to collect several of her baskets. In fact, I am looking at two of them in my office as I write this. Billie Ruth would be loved by all who know her if she never made a basket, for she is a loving and giving person. How blessed we all are to know such a beautiful person.
    — **Low Harry, Preferred Power.com**

- **A Gracious Artist—**

Billie Ruth Sudduth has been a gracious artist to work with. Her exhibition at our gallery in Western North Carolina was very well received by both young and old audiences alike. The technique used in each of her baskets is both thoughtful and masterful, while her attention to form and function is part of what made her a 'North Carolina Living Treasure'
    — **David Trophia, Crimson Laurel Gallery, Bakersville, N.C.**

Section 2: **Special Achievements and Moments**

- **Honors from North Carolina, The Smithsonian and her *alma mater*—**

Billie Ruth received 'The Order of the Long Leaf Pine' from Governor Mike Easley in 1998, one of the top honors bestowed on a North Carolinian, and in 1997 became the first woman and tenth person to be named as a 'North Carolina Living Treasure' for creative excellence in the field of crafts.

The Living Treasure award included a bronze medal designed by Stephen D. LeQuire, sculptor and associate professor of art at UNC-Wilmington. She has also received an Individual Visual Artist Grant and Fellowship, and an Emerging Artist Grant from the North Carolina Arts Council.

In 1997, Billie Ruth was honored with the Smithsonian Craft Show Merit Award in Washington D.C. She has exhibited at the Smithsonian Craft Show 13 times, and is featured in *Skilled Work,* the Smithsonian publication that showcases artwork in the Renwick Gallery permanent collection. 'An Oral History with Billie Ruth Sudduth' is in the Smithsonian's Archives of American Art Oral History Program that was started in 1958 to document the history of the visual arts in the United States. A 2007 interview by Mija Riedel is in the Archives of American Art's Nanette L. Laitman Documentation Project for Craft and Decorative Arts in America. It was conducted at Billie Ruth's Bakersville studio.

In 2005, Huntingdon College President J. Cameron West honored 1967 alumna Billie Ruth with the President's Medallion for achievement while she and husband Doug, a Duke graduate, were in Montgomery, Alabama to celebrate the opening of her show titled 'Math in a Basket' at the Museum of Fine Arts. West said that her baskets were "exquisitely built, unique, at once inspired and inspirational." The citation to Billie Ruth reads in part: *Billie Ruth Sudduth has achieved much but, truth be told, achievement was never her mission. She simply seeks to make beautiful, lasting, useful art that is as much a story of the earth as a floret in the middle of a sunflower, a spiral on a seashell, or the curve of an elephant tusk.*

- **Major Media Coverage—**

Billie Ruth was featured on the CBS-TV Sunday morning show, "Handmade in America," and has appeared on several PBS-TV shows and in documentaries, as well as on Voice of America and HDTV. In the fall of 2011, she appeared with four other Western North Carolina craft artists following the PBS-TV premiere of "Give Me the Banjo" hosted by Steve Martin, and also on "Around Town" with Linda Staunch in New Bern, NC. In addition to *Smithsonian* magazine, she has been featured in *American Craft, Southern Accents, Colonial Homes, American Style, Southern Living, Home, Fiberarts,* the Philadelphia Museum of Arts *Member Magazine, Preservation, The Crafts Report,* and voluminous other publications.

- **Fibonacci's 'Nature Sequence' in Basketry—**

Billie Ruth Sudduth's unique basket-making artistry replicates the patterns found in nature, as represented by the then obscure thirteenth-century mathematician Fibonacci in his formula known as the 'Nature Sequence'. Details of this intriguing formula appear following the photo section.

Note: A chronology of Billie Ruth Sudduth's life and career, comprehensive listings of media coverage and articles, awards and recognitions, and shows and exhibitions appear in Section 5.

- ## Details of Fibonacci's Nature Sequence—

Billie Ruth's basket-making technique replicates the patterns found in nature, as represented by mathematician Fibonacci in his 'Nature Sequence' formula. Following is her explanation of the formula:

My baskets blend the historical with the present through color, pattern, surface embellishment, and form. I am inspired by the classical shapes typical of Shaker and Appalachian baskets, but I travel back over seven centuries for the most profound influence on my work: the 'Nature Sequence' developed by Leonardo of Pisa (Italy), better known by his nickname, Fibonacci (ca 1170-1250), who was considered the most outstanding mathematician of the middle ages. The 'Nature Sequence', also known as Fibonacci Numbers, is written by starting with two 1s, adding them to get 2, and then adding the next two numbers successively: the first few terms being 1,1,2,3,5,8,13,21,34,55,89, etc. After the first few Fibonacci numbers, the ratios of any two progressing numbers approximate the Golden Mean (1:1.618 or 5:8), which has been used to unify design since ancient Greece. Because Fibonacci numbers approach infinity, the design possibilities are unlimited.

Man has used the ratios in the shape of playing cards and window frames, on the piano keyboard, and in the structure of great buildings. Farmers have used Fibonacci numbers to rotate their crops, stockbrokers have used them in investments, and computer engineers use them in computer programming. I use the Fibonacci numbers in my baskets. The rhythm of the pattern seems predetermined, as if by nature. Initially, I was concerned by my inability to free form, random weave, and be more expressive in expanding the possibility of a basket. However, the sense of order gained by incorporating Fibonacci numbers in my work evolved into my style, a natural progression of balancing family and career.

As I have become more secure in my work, I have felt more comfortable with the order in what I do, and it has become the basis for the direction in which I want to continue. I want to expand the possibilities of design while maintaining function. This object called a basket should look like a basket and not be so far removed from form and function that it is not discernible as a basket.

Seneca said that 'art imitates nature'. Whether viewed as art or craft, my baskets demonstrate this. The weaving utilizes a mathematical structure of spiral growth found in nature to create baskets with a rhythmic, naturally flowing design, both visual and tactile, beckoning the viewer to touch and explore with eyes and hands. I do not separate myself from nature but through weaving affirm being part of it. Each signed and dated basket from JABOBS is hand-woven, hand-dyed and hand-shaped without the use of a mold, and consists of the finest natural materials available. No two baskets are exactly alike. European cut reed splints are used to construct the baskets.

Split oak and round reed baskets are hand-carved for the handles with a shave horse and draw knife. Henna and madder are used for the red dye and iron oxide for rich black color. Most of the baskets are brushed with a protective coating of linseed oil, crushed walnut hull stain, and other secret ingredients to seal the fibers. Great care and time are taken in the dyeing process. The dyes are color fast and light fast, but it is recommended that the baskets not be placed in windows that receive direct sunlight. Baskets are like any other fibers, in that slight fading will occur when exposed to sunlight over long periods of time. The forms are either classical Shaker Cat's Head shapes, appearing as if they are sitting on feet, or Appalachian inspired if the baskets sit flat. Most Appalachian baskets have handles and are functional, capable of holding objects. Shaker inspired baskets are more sculptural, and designed to hold interest.

Section 3: **Billie Ruth's Life Journey, in Her Own Words**

The beautiful drive from Hendersonville through the Blue Ridge Mountains to Bakersville was prelude to meeting a talented and amazing person, Billie Ruth Sudduth, who elevated basketry to an art form unique in the nation, and perhaps the world.

The trip took us past Penland School, nationally renowned for teaching crafts and where Billie Ruth has often taught, and ten-minutes later wound up a twisting mountain road to a 'JABOBS' sign: acronym for 'Just A Bunch of Baskets'. The thriving well-equipped studio is in the home of the craftsperson and her husband Doug, whose skill as an amateur photographer is evident in the exquisite photos of some of his wife's masterpieces that appear in the photo section.

After Billie Ruth greeted and welcomed us into her rustic hilltop home, I started the interview by asking about the scope of her career in basketry:

Billie Ruth, how many baskets have you woven in your career?

Well, you first asked me that on the phone, but I didn't have any idea how many until I pulled out this notebook, and now I can tell you exactly how many I've made.

I started keeping a record in 1983 when I began making baskets, so from number one it goes all the way back to exactly who bought them, when they bought them, and how much they paid for them. As of today, I am up to 10,068 baskets.

How would you describe the work ethic that motivates you to create so many baskets?

This has been my passion, but now the pressure is off because I'm not preparing to do any more craft shows. But I am preparing for other things.

The amazing thing I've discovered is that I'd rather be weaving than doing just about anything. And so, I find myself in my studio every morning until about eleven p.m. I used to work until midnight or one a.m. every day.

What other things are you doing now that you are not doing shows, or working until the wee hours?

Well let's see. I've got seven grandchildren, so I'm teaching them. Six live clear across the state, and one lives in London. I've taught three of my grandchildren to weave. And I love to plant and I love to grow things. I think if I weren't a basket maker I'd be a potter, because I love to play in mud and dirt.

Another thing that I've done in the last year or so is take charge of my health in terms of not sitting all day and making baskets. I've decided that I need to walk and get on my exercise bike.

Dr. Oz says that if you read while you're exercising then you're not exercising enough. Well, I ride hard for about twenty minutes then pick up a book then ride another twenty minutes. My goal when I got on Medicare was to be as healthy as possibly, and now I am.

- **The Early Years—**

Please tell me about your childhood and early years.

I was born in Tennessee in 1945, the youngest of five children. My mother died in 1946 and my father couldn't keep us all, so I was put up for adoption. My oldest brother Peter Hayden Prince, now deceased, was on the Pulitzer Prize committee for photography, and the editor of newspapers in Tennessee. I didn't meet him until I was 20. They all kept track of me, but I grew up thinking I had only one brother; I didn't know about the other three.

I was an only child, and my adoptive mother changed my name to Billie Ruth, her nickname because she was scared of Billy Goats. Ruth was after an aunt. So, I had two families, adopted and natural.

Something about baskets resonated with you early in life, but you didn't exactly know why.

Yes. I think it all started because my family was middle-class and didn't have silver serving pieces and pottery, not unusual in Birmingham. But my mother did have a basket to put rolls in on Sundays, and a few imports that hung on the walls, so they were always around me.

Family members were very creative, with hands that knitted, tatted, crocheted, rug-hooked, and quilted. My mother knitted my sweaters, and I thought I'd died and gone to heaven when I got to buy a store-bought sweater. Now I would kill for a hand-knitted sweater, but I didn't like them back then. My grandmother gave me a cross-stitch sampler when I was eleven that I didn't finish until ten years later because I hated needle and thread. I would scotch-tape and staple the hems of my dresses so I wouldn't have to sew them.

My biggest regret from high school was not taking more math courses. I took the language route because I hated math, and in my sophomore year failed geometry. It was horrible. I hated the teacher, yet I scored in the ninety-eighth percentile in a math achievement test. Then somebody would say "she's not applying herself."

Looking back, I don't think the teachers knew how to teach me, and it just wasn't very interesting to me at the time. But I liked sports, and was a cheerleader in the ninth grade and ruined my voice. And I liked the boys and was a social being, and a swimmer, and kind of a well-rounded person. I didn't like to just sit. Still don't.

Since my baskets have become so mathematically based, I wish I had taken calculus and higher level math, because that is how I communicate now.

But I've read and educated myself about the subject.

Then I became a mediocre student at Huntingdon College until my dad died and it appeared I would have to quit. But the dean said, "Look, you're smart and you make good grades," so I stayed, thanks mainly to scholarships, and finished on the Dean's List and in the Honor Society for Psychology.

My two years in graduate school at the University of Alabama was the time when I became a serious student and made exceptional grades.

- **Family—**

Congratulations on having seven grandchildren. Please tell me about the rest of your family.

William Douglas, everyone calls him Doug, is my husband, nine years my senior. We celebrated forty-three years of marriage last December. Mark and Chris are our sons.

Mark is a hurricane researcher for his own company based in Wilmington, North Carolina. He does a lot of unique things, especially when he's working in the eye of a hurricane. He recently got back from a rendezvous in Texas at the Bolivar Peninsula that was slammed by Hurricane Ike. He used an experimental plane to videotape the hurricane then sent it back, so he didn't actually go into the eye. He has six children, four sons and two daughters.

Chris is quite an amazing guy. He graduated from UNC, and my husband is a Duke graduate, so that was a bone of contention for quite a while. We couldn't afford to send him to Duke, but he spent a year at Carolina in the study-abroad program in England. When he graduated he was headed to Wake Forest Law School, and got a job over the summer with Bank of America, and they saw his promise and promoted him. Bottom line, he loved England and finessed a transfer to London, where the bank paid for his MBA tuition. The reason he loves London is it's a jumping-off place to hike Kilimanjaro in the summer, ski in the Alps in the winter. He's with Credit Suisse now, married to a British lady, and they have a little boy.

Tell me how you met Doug.

I was in my first year of graduate school at the University of Alabama when we met. So now when you look at my baskets you'll see they are crimson, not red, because I am a loyal Crimson Tide fan!

Doug was running a mental health center in Montgomery Alabama when I was placed there as an intern for three different agencies. The following summer I had planned to go to Martha's Vineyard in Massachusetts and be a barmaid at the Seafood Shanty, but didn't so I could stay near him.

Has Doug always been supportive of your basket weaving career?

Extremely! I couldn't have done it without his enthusiasm for what I do. It was really funny in the early days when I would get accepted into prestigious shows like the Philadelphia Museum of Art, or the Smithsonian, and we would look at each other and wonder 'Is this a fluke?'

Doug would arrange to take a vacation or a weekend to go with me to Philadelphia or Chicago for craft shows, and to be with me. Later, in 1994, we decided to move to Bakersville for my career because of Penland School and the whole Western North Carolina craft community. I call that supportive! I don't think either of us realized at first what I was creating. We knew people bought it and liked it, but we were the last people to know. When they called me to say I had been named a 'North Carolina Living Treasure' I wondered if it was a mistake, because I didn't think I was old enough. That was in 1997.

My boys also supported my efforts, though they sure missed home-cooked meals. I think the first time they really understood what it is that I do was at a ceremony at UNC-Wilmington when they saw on the marquee: "Billie Ruth Sudduth, Living Treasure."

• Alabama Experiences—

Please go back and tell me about your college experiences.

I earned a BA in psychology and sociology from Huntingdon College in 1967, mainly supported by scholarships.

I had grown up in a Methodist church that thought I hung the moon, that I could do no wrong. I secretly think that after my dad died, those scholarships that suddenly appeared were from somebody from my church, but to this day I don't know who. So, I didn't have to quit college and go home, which my mother wanted me to do to be near her. I didn't want any part of that.

After earning my B.A. degree, I spent two years at the University of Alabama earning a Master of Social Work degree.

Then I worked at the state hospital. It was segregated at the time I was there, all black, then integrated, then segregated again.

So you stayed in Alabama; then what happened?

That was in 1968, and George Wallace was the Governor's number one advisor. He had already been elected governor twice and could not serve a third term, so he got his wife Lurleen elected.

There were no American doctors in that hospital, just Cuban refugees, and only three or four of the staff were white, the rest black. I remember there was a unit in the back of the institution that housed the criminally insane. I didn't really know what I had signed on to do, but it turned out to be probably the most remarkable experience I ever had as a student.

I discovered that other people who ran mental health centers throughout the state had never been to that hospital and complained about it to my boss in the state office. His philosophy was: "Don't just complain, do something about it!"

Did you do something about it?

I wrote a paper on what the state should do, and while I was still there that summer they started visiting the hospital and saw first-hand how atrocious the conditions were. Not long after that, the state or the feds or somebody sued the mental health people in Alabama in a case called Wyatt vs. Stickney. The bottom line is it resulted in a new system where money would follow the patient, better mental health care, and more patient rights.

I was very much into that career, and next I wrote the Interstate Compact on Mental Health for Alabama. That was during my second year of graduate school under my internship with the Commissioner of Mental Health.

Congratulations on that accomplishment. How did a young woman of the south adjust so well to such a challenging environment?

Well, the University mindset was not really like most of Alabama. It's hard to explain, but the people there were and are very progressive, and their attitudes were not like they were in the rest of the state. Earlier they had tried to integrate it but that was stopped. By the time I was in graduate school the university was integrated, though not yet on a grand scale.

Back in the 1950's social work was often called communistic and liberal and whatever. But the biggest problem while I was in graduate school was not integration, as the university felt it had a handle on that, it was water pollution.

It was a very progressive environment there, as most of the faculty were from the northeast, mainly Syracuse, New York.

• Proud of the South—

What do you think of race relations in the south now?

The first time that I went home from college for the weekend with a female black student, we met my mother in Birmingham at Woolworths for lunch, and she was petrified, and sort of slinked down, like she was asking, "What are you doing?"

I think we could do another whole book on the south now. Back then most people's beliefs were based on how they were raised, but when they were offered other options it changed their views, especially in Birmingham.

I lived in Birmingham when they blew up the Baptist Church in 1963 and killed four little girls, and in college during the Selma-to-Montgomery March, and I rode the train from college back home. My family was terrified of me being on public transportation, but unless you went to a site where demonstrations were taking place, it wasn't all that bad. But there were certain areas you just didn't want to go to.

I am personally very proud of how the south has turned around on this subject.

What came next in your journey?

Because I had never been out of the south, I was the typical college graduate just itching to see the world. But then I met Doug and made the decision to go to Mobile, Alabama to work in a state psychiatric hospital so I could see him over the summer. Doug was in mental health administration his entire 38-year career, and as I said before, back then he was director of multi-county mental health programs in various parts of North Carolina.

My mother was not impressed that I was marrying Doug, so the wedding was on me, and I had relatives who offered to help.

How did you handle your mother?

All the while I had been dating Doug. This will sound terrible in the book but it's true, you just didn't live with somebody before you married, so we got married in December, 1968 during my second year in graduate school.

I had to go back to take my finals right after the wedding, so I took my books with us on our honeymoon trip through Murphy, Maggie Valley, Cherokee and Gatlinburg, which is another good story. When we got back we were broke but I had great stipends and didn't have to pay a lot for my education.

You told me you had an interesting basket story that unfolded on your honeymoon - please tell it.

On the honeymoon I had maybe five dollars left for spending money when we went through Cherokee in the December cold. There was one lone native-American sitting out front of an old shop, wrapped in a blanket with a hat on, with a bunch of baskets in front of him.

I asked him "how much is the basket?" and he answered "how much you got?" and I said "five dollars." The basket was forty or fifty dollars, but I somehow managed to buy it.

That was the second-beginning of my collecting baskets. The first had been when I was twelve on a family trip, also to Cherokee when my parents bought me a little basket. From then on I liked baskets. But I went from age twelve to age twenty-three, the year I got married, without getting another one.

I loved that first basket, I treasured it, and I kept it until the move back from Las Vegas when the moving people lost nine cartons of my baskets.

- **Fulltime Basketry—**

When did you decide to make baskets fulltime?

I have a Master's degree and in 1974 was hired as a school psychologist in Craven County. I had longevity of ten years in the County School System, and passion for the job. I loved it, but the work was very demanding. It is a small county in eastern North Carolina, and at times I was the only psychologist serving a huge population of students. I would be at one end of the county and get a call that a child would be hiding under a trailer at the other end, and I would have to respond. It is the longest geographic county in the state, and by the time I'd get there, they often had resolved the issue.

Children always have issues, and my personal opinion is that if the schools did a little bit more to intervene with some of the problems going on with the children and get the parents more involved, things would not escalate as badly.

Our teachers had huge classrooms and they couldn't be everything to everybody but it was a wonderful school system and I loved the people I worked with.

Then one year my supervisor suggested I do something fun over the summer break. She knew I had two sons and a husband, still do, but I followed her suggestion and turned to basketry.

- **A Move to Las Vegas—**

What happened next for the Sudduths?

By the mid-eighties I was really into fulltime basketry. Doug decided he wanted a hospital inpatient experience and got a job running the Southern Nevada Inpatient Mental Health Services, so we packed up the boys and moved to Las Vegas.

It was wonderful, and probably the best thing we could have done for ourselves. All of us, minus Doug, found out what we were made of in a new place with new people, new schools, new jobs.

I had already quit my career, this was 1986, but I didn't want to just sit at home in Las Vegas and not know anybody or whatever, so I went back to work out there as a school psychologist.

The difference was that in New Bern I was one of two or three in the in best of times, but in Las Vegas I was one of seventy-four, and they paid for me to further my education.

The administrators knew of my interest in basketry, and that I was already teaching basket-making in New Bern. But with this school district, you have to relate things to the curriculum, and that is how my course 'Math in a Basket' was born.

What prompted you to use math in your craft?

I had done so much with statistics and math in my job that I now approach basketry mathematically by using parallels and perpendiculars, right angles, Fibonacci numbers, all of that. I wrote up a little thing for CEU credits to teach one summer showing how a teacher could increase children's interest in math through basket-making, which evolved over time into Math in a Basket.

Did the students pick it up because of the visuals?

Yes. And another thing about basket making is that it's therapeutic. Being a psychologist I quickly realized that in teaching basket classes I was also running group-therapy sessions. Some of my earliest students will probably cringe when they hear me say that, but it's true. In the early days, the majority of my students were teachers and nurses, and I don't think you can get more stressed than they are.

You said that movers lost all of your baskets; that must have been hard.

When we moved from Las Vegas back to Wilmington in 1989, they lost my entire collection of baskets. I had been making them for about six years. I, didn't want to fly back because I wanted to see the country, so we took Amtrak from Las Vegas to North Carolina and shipped all of our furniture, and the movers lost the nine cartons with sixty or seventy baskets and some wardrobe items.

We decided to rent a condo over the summer before house-hunting, so there was a three-month time period that we were without our belongings.

We had seen the light that it was crucial for our boys to be where they could get a good college education, and we knew that North Carolina is renowned for its universities. Unfortunately, for the first year we had to pay out-of-state tuition while we re-established residency.

And the net value of your loss must have been pretty high?

Yes, but they didn't pay full value. My Baby-Grand Piano was delivered but the movers dropped it on the drive-way, and my grandmother's china cabinet came back with broken glass.

It was awful, awful.

Do you still play the piano?

Not well. But my parents' dream was for me to become a musician.

- **The First Basket—**

What first drew you to make your first basket, and what style was it?

In 1983 after I took my boss' advice and did something for fun, I signed up for a Monday night basket-making course through the community college, and it was a little bit like lifelong learning is today. But it only cost twenty dollars.

We started to make an Appalachian egg basket, and just fifteen minutes into that first class I had an epiphany and knew instantly that I loved the material and loved the process. I liked the group, the people, the social part; it was like playing music.

I've said a whole bunch of times over the years that you can see the music I make, you just can't hear it.

I never did get that accomplished in music but I now connect with it through my work, the over and the under and the rhythm, until I complete something.

I didn't finish the egg basket in class, but I went home that night and stayed up until three a.m. from the anticipation of seeing it as a finished product.

It turned out beautiful, and if I did it today, I couldn't do it any better.

Do you still have it?

The University of North Carolina in Wilmington has it on display as part of the Living Treasure thing. I offered it to the Smithsonian, which has some of my Fibonacci pieces on display, but they didn't want that particular one. But the Smithsonian did an oral history on me that is now online. They sent a person from San Francisco who spent two days interviewing and video-taping me, and now I'm in their permanent collection.

If you go to the American Art museum you can punch a button and up I pop to talk about baskets. It is really funny, because I didn't wear a lot of makeup, though I think I look pretty decent in the video. I did wear earrings a fellow craftsperson had made, and a jacket another craftsperson had woven. But when they said, "Billie Ruth, you need to powder your nose, it's a little shiny" I said, "I always shine."

I am really glad I am archived at UNC Wilmington because six of my grandchildren live there. I'm hoping that someday it will matter to them, you know, what I have done with my life.

So, music plays a significant role in your artful basket-making craft.

Weaving is my music.

It was funny when the TV program *Voice of America* came here to interview me about the sounds of basketry and I really exaggerated slushing the dye pot to create more sound. But my career is visual. I see what I do, I feel it, and that is what I love most, that I can touch it, I can caress it, and I can love it.

I also love gardening but a garden lasts only a season, especially vegetables. Weaving a basket also needs proper care, and when finished it sort of creates my own immortality. It didn't start out that way but I realized 10,000 baskets later that is what I have done.

• Still Committed to Basketry—

After 10,000 baskets and still counting, why is Billie Ruth Sudduth still committed to basketry?

Well, I think the big word is passion. I just absolutely love what I do, and I love the people that respond to my baskets. It's sort of a two-way street, and that is why I went the craft show route for most of my career, because it was important for me to know who got them.

It's like I have 10,000 relatives out there now, and I hear from many in my huge extended family. It is personal, and not just about making a living. I've become a part of these other people's environment. They don't just buy a basket of mine without seeing my personality in it.

Why do you keep such detailed records about your customers and sales?

It actually started because two boys who were not neat-freaks, and a husband who is a pack-rat. As I grew up as an only child, everything had its place and was very organized. When I married and had kids, that all went out the window.

Basketry was another way for me to find order in my life, and I also did it out of pure compulsiveness, I guess. And if I did a three inch basket then a ten-inch one, I didn't want to repeat them, so I started keeping records to prevent duplication.

• 'Baskets with a Brain'—

Certain people who saw my early Fibonacci baskets, I call them "baskets with a brain," would comment, "You've got fractals in there," and I would ask, "What are fractals?" Well, there are Archimedes and logarithmic spirals, and if I had taken calculus and higher level mathematics I would have known that. I just used fractals intuitively, but then I began to learn Archimedes and logarithmic fractals.

I never will forget a collector of mine in Atlanta at a craft show who said that "1, 1, 2, 3 are the first four numbers of the 'Fibonacci Sequence'." I asked "What's that?" because I just did them in a single spiral all the way up because it looked good, it felt good.

Then I got on the internet and this collector started sending me books on Fibonacci. He used it as a stock broker in a program that shows when market gains and losses hit the 'Golden Ratio', telling him when to buy or sell or something.

So, I educated myself about Fibonacci. In retrospect don't know how I lived without it my whole life.

Amazingly, everybody in my immediate family, my husband, me, my sons, our birthdates and wedding dates, are all Fibonacci numbers. My son was born on the first, my other son on the third, my husband on the fifth, me on the thirteenth, and we got married on the twenty-first.

Though I did Fibonacci intuitively, I got bored with the sequence of over, under, over, under, and started doing twills. That means I go over more than one at a time then come up after a while with an over one. Let's see, I will do under one, over one, under two, over three, and just keep repeating that.

I am impressed how the universe seems to collide in your world.

Yes, except that I tried it with the Virginia lottery and didn't hit a single number.

Explanations of your use of Fibonacci numbers appear elsewhere in your bio, but please expand on that.

The simplest way to understand the numbers is to first look at how beautifully a seashell spirals from its center according to the 'Nature Sequence', the 'Fibonacci numbers'. Each row as it comes out approximates the 'golden mean' of 1-to-1.618.

If you look at the cap of an acorn, or a pine cone, or a sunflower as they spiral out from the center you will see that they follow that same 'golden ratio', the numerical sequence of numbers Fibonacci figured out in the thirteenth-century while studying the reproductive cycle of rabbits, go figure, that they reproduce like this: 1 rabbit plus 1 rabbit equals 2, then 3 and 5 equals 8 then 8 and 13 equals 21 then 13 and 21 equals 34, and so on.

That's true for a pine cone or a flower petal or a ram's horn or an elephant's tusk, and now they are saying that the DNA chain and hurricanes and tornadoes and all of these spirals have this same proportion as they spiral out from the center.

The hard part for me would be relatively easy if I were a two-dimensional artist able to create things that are advanced according to this sequence. But, transferring it into a three-dimensional object like this took some figuring. On paper I could do it two-dimensionally, but I couldn't make it go three-dimensionally, so I had to figure out how to do that, and to make them zig and zag and whatever.

This is very simple but you have upset that weaving pattern and shoot it the other way. At first I thought I had to weave backwards but figured out I didn't have to. So now just about everything I create is Fibonacci based. Some are pure Fibonacci where they follow the sequence, 1 row to the left, 1 row to the right, 2 to the left, 3 to the right, 5, 13, 21, 34. Some are more subtle, like in baskets you usually buy.

In an enormous basket, rather than zigging and zagging four rows or seven rows, I pick the number five or the number eight or the number three. I'm Fibonacci driven, and in just about everything I do I use the numbers, the sequence. That put me on the map! Who knew?

- **Ninety-Percent Intuition—**

How much does intuition play into your basketry?

I think ninety percent, quite honestly. I think it came from my education, and that I probably had a better math education than I thought. Part of it comes from the visuals of it, being able to see what I am doing, and seeing that it worked.

But I also have to give maybe fifty percent to people that responded to my work. It was like I was doing subliminal advertising: they had not a clue what it was they liked about these baskets, but they were drawn to them.

I don't have any of my major pieces here. But if you go to Bakersville and look into the Crimson Laurel Gallery there are two wonderful Fibonacci pieces on display.

I'm trying to figure out if your baskets are an extension of you, or if you are an extension of your baskets.

Both. I sign and date all of them, and that was intuitive.

- ## The Feminine Form—

I'm a big fan of Dan Brown's works, 'the feminine' and all that. I could have written *The Di Vinci Code* because I know more about Fibonacci than he told in the one chapter about him. But that was the only thing in the book that he got spot-on, when he was talking about Fibonacci.

My baskets are in 'feminine form', they are 'hers' and 'shes'.

I learned at a craft show that men love to feel feminine. Men will pick up baskets with shapes like hips and waists on ladies. I'm not sure how that came about, this is not a common shape for baskets and I do not use a mold, I hand shape everything.

Do you have a picture of what you are going to do in your head, or do you make a sketch?

I have to know what I am going to do. No sketches. The only thing that I have to know is the sequence 1, 1, 2, 3, 5, 8, 13, 21, 34. But I do have to know before I start how big I want it so I won't run out of the dye. It's like wallpaper, no two dye vats are the same.

But another thing is the upside down cat-head shape. A great IQ test for little children who have a pet is to ask what pet this basket represents. The ears, head and mouth are of a cat. It not only is a cat-head shape, I take pride that these baskets sit like an actual animal on all four feet. It's really easy to make a wobbly three-something but to make one with four feet that is level - that's hard!

There's a wine basket over there, and there are all sorts of things inside. But the thing about making them for me is that from beginning to end my hands are on the material. I touch it, I create it, I shape it, there's no mold. It's all done with my hands and my vision.

Pretend like one of your best baskets is here and tell me about it.

Okay. If you look at the structure and at the zigs and the zags of what is called a Calabash Clam basket, you'd see that you could carry bricks in it because has a double-bottom. I mean it is strong but rather than randomly zigging and zagging using 4's or 7's, I purposely choose the number 5, which is a Fibonacci number, to me the most sacred of the Fibonacci numbers, in that didn't come from anywhere but my head, maybe because my husband's birthday is the 5th and I love him.

And so I love the number 5, and I weave 5 rows and change directions and go 5 the other way and back and forth.

Pure Fibonacci pieces like that one will maybe start with 1 and then zig to the left and the next row will zig to the right and the next one to the left and the next one to the right and so on.

The 'Golden Ratio' occurs between each zig and zag on even the smallest of the baskets I make.

- ## Some Key Moments—

Please give a brief stream-of-consciousness of some other key career moments.

In 1983 I had a full-time job and was a full-time mom and wife. But the only place I didn't weave was in church. I would weave on the side lines of soccer games, when my kids were in theatre I would weave while they were trying out, everywhere I could. Unfortunately I'd get home from my job at 3 or 3:30 in the afternoon, at best, when the kids were doing all of their activities then have dinner and do homework, so I really didn't get to weave until maybe 9 or 10 at night, and I would stay up until 2 or 3 in the morning then get up at 6 a.m. I didn't get much sleep.

I declared one day to my husband, I guess it was in 1985, that I wanted to quit my job and just see what I could do with my baskets. I had entered a couple of art shows and won the Juror's Choice

Award the first time at bat, amazed that somebody liked my work.

But I had the energy and the motivation, and didn't want to wait until I retired, so I quit my job. It was a little tough making ends meet and I had quite a year when Doug decided to move us to Vegas. I started back to work out there, and was a psychologist for three years.

In Las Vegas I was devoted to basketry and really in to it, and ideas were flowing. So, I entered a few art shows in the desert southwest. I did a basket show in a casino one time where they loved my work, and I felt that something was happening.

So, we came back to Wilmington in 1989, and by 1991 I was at the Smithsonian showing my work, so you know it was a good decision. They believed in me, and I believed in what I was doing.

When we returned I didn't go back to work. That was the year my older son started college and my husband calculated, "Okay second income gone and no money coming in from baskets." But they all supported me, and I couldn't have done it without that support.

One of the big things that happened to make it possible was that Domino's Pizza moved to town, and the kids could just call in their order. So I quit cooking, and they learned to use the washer and dryer.

- **A $14,000 Basket—**

How much was the most expensive Billie Ruth basket ever sold?

Well there are two ways of looking at it, the most expensive one I've ever sold myself was $6,000, and the most that a basket of mine ever went for was $14,000 at a Penland charitable auction about three years ago. It is called 'Fibonacci in Chaos', and the reason this went for so much was because two collectors got into a bidding war, not because of its significance.

People support Penland, collectors, donors, benefactors, students, and about 250 of us from all over the country donate things to the annual auction.

I'm not kidding myself that the basket was worth $14,000, but the top bidder got something really nice for what was mainly my contribution to Penland.

Tell me about the $6,000 basket that you sold.

It was actually my 10,000th basket!

This lady wanted my 10,000th basket done in Nature's Sequence, which is Fibonacci 1, 1, 2, 3, 5, 8, 13, 21, 34, and was willing to wait until I got to that number. I scampered to get a lot of smaller baskets done so I could work on hers.

Over the years I discovered that when I'm free to make what I want to make, it's going to turn out better than if you told me what you wanted. That might be tight and not well shaped and may not sit well.

I was so nervous working on her basket making sure it was right that I thought it was going to take me two years, but it turned out beautifully right off the bat.

What is the normal range of prices for your baskets?

People look at my prices and want to know how long it takes to make the baskets. I value what I make and never sell them for cheap, ever, and the prices have progressively gone up.

For example, the price is $17 for a Carolina Snowflake and $6,000 for a Nature's Sequence, the most expensive basket I do. It takes 45 minutes to make a snow flake, and seventeen dollars an hour is not a great rate of pay when you consider it takes two weeks to dye and get the color I use, and another half-day to carve a handle or sand it.

I've never calculated my per-hour, because to me that's irrelevant. Maybe two-hundred hours go into making a major basket.

I've been doing this for twenty-nine years, and it took that long to get where I am. Time isn't the primary factor; it's the art, the product.

It took me twenty of the last thirty years to realize that people are buying my baskets because of what I created, and not because they need a basket to put their eggs in.

• Baskets as Art—

Was realizing your baskets were more art than craft a Eureka moment?

Yeah! It was just really amazing when I figured that out.

But it doesn't matter. I don't mean to sound flip, but I still make what I want to make. This egg basket I'm holding is number ten-thousand-and-something, but I hadn't made an egg basket in probably twenty years. I just wanted to go back and see if I could still do it. This is the third one I've made in the last few months just because I am enjoying going back to that form.

• Teaching Basketry—

Do you still teach at the Penland School and elsewhere?

At Penland you are not a faculty member, you teach for one or two- weeks or a month at a time. When I was really into teaching I would rotate between Arrowmont School of Arts and Crafts in Gatlinburg, Tennessee, the John Campbell Folk School down in Brasstown and Penland.

I am going to be doing a one-week residency in 2013 at Spring Island, a nature preserve island retirement community in South Carolina. It's in February, so I might escape one of the snows up here.

I could pick any time between October and April, but February is our worst month and I chose to get off the mountain.

Do your new students have any prior knowledge of basketry?

I teach beginners at all levels, and the different craft schools specify how much advance experience they need. I discovered 10 years ago that I go on automatic pilot when I'm making a basket, so much so that I forget to teach something basic to somebody who has never made a basket. I realized that while teaching my grandchildren and I get a little impatient. so now I request that they have some level of experience.

Can you tell me about one of your teaching successes?

One of my students, Mary Jane Everett, has a museum exhibition in Alabama, and won a visual-artist fellowship from the state of Alabama.

An amazing thing that is different with potters and glass-blowers and in other craft medium is that you're not going to find many professional basket makers on the planet. Maybe that's one reason I have thrived and survived, because I'm one of maybe a dozen in the whole country.

How many are there in North Carolina?

None. There are a lot of basket-makers, but they either have other jobs or are hobbyists. There was another marvelous one in Winston-Salem, John Skau, but he passed away about three years ago. One reason is that it's very hard to make a living at it, and most people won't pay $3,000 for a basket.

There are plenty of baskets you can buy for ten-dollars at Pier One, and there's nothing wrong with them. Those are useful baskets you can also buy at craft fairs, but they are not art baskets.

Give me one line that sums up Billie Ruth Sudduth.

Uh, hmm . . . happy!

- **Summing Up a Career—**

Can you describe a few serendipitous moments in your basketry career?

Amazing! It really has all been a little bit unbelievable.

My baskets are in the Smithsonian collection because while I was living in Wilmington and contracting with various school systems to do re-evaluations and weaving in my garage fulltime, the State Arts Council called to tell me that the Curator of Art from the Oakland Museum was on a clipper-ship cruising the inter-coastal waterway and would stop to visit three or four local craftspeople.

I had already received an emerging artist grant from the Arts Council, so they gave him my name and he asked for slides of my work. My mantra is to never say no to opportunity, so I sent them. Then he visited me in my home studio next door to an IRS agent, and yes, it's okay to print that.

The guy comes with this group from Oakland and New Zealand, and it was love at first sight: I loved him, he loved me, he loved my work, and his birthday was my birthday, September 13. That began a friendship and two or three years later he called to say he loved the name of my business, JABOBS, for Just a Bunch of Baskets, and loved my name, Billie Ruth.

Well, he called me 'Billiebob', and said that he is the Curator in charge at the Smithsonian and wanted to commission the best basket I've ever made. Talk about nervous, it took me six months to get one to him.

That basket is still there, perpetually on view. And that has had a domino effect with other museums that now display my baskets. My basket is in the American Museum of Art, where they've also done the video on me. You can punch a button for an oral history about me. And then they did a book on their collection that featured me in it.

That was the same year I was named a Living Treasure, so I think Doug and I figured, "Hey maybe this really isn't just a fluke."

What else stands out in your mind as a significant moment or event?

The neatest thing I've ever done tied my Master's degree with my basket career when I was asked to be the Honors Day speaker at the University of Alabama School of Social Work. Can you imagine those students wondering why a basket-maker was giving the speech?

I connived with the dean of the school that I would only talk for one minute then sit down. So, I got up and said, "Congratulations, this was a wonderful university when I was here, and I was taught to be cogent, lucid and succinct, so with that I am going to wish you well."

I sat down then got back up, and then kind of followed the movie *Forrest Gump*. I love that movie; it's my life: Alabama, Crimson Tide football, integrating the university, love, chocolate, Vietnam.

I left out of my earlier comments is a very powerful thing that that happened to me in graduate school when I interviewed George Wallace for part of my master's thesis. A computer had randomly selected lawyers in Alabama for us to interview, and I got the names of the former governor and his brother. I was bound and determined that I wasn't going to be awestruck; I was going to be professional. Well, he was charismatic and it went well. I asked questions I needed to ask, but admit I was taken with his charisma, and then understood the power he had over people.

- **The Billie Ruth Impact—**

How would you describe your basket-making skill?

It's advanced, but I by no means know all of the techniques in basketry. There's a shaker basket also called a cheese basket, a simple one woven on a diagonal, and the only way I can do it is to put it on a checkered table cloth and follow the lines.

Are you still learning?

Oh yeah. Oh yeah.

What do you think will be your legacy?

I think my legacy is that I opened a new world for basket-makers by getting baskets off the floor and onto pedestals as art objects people want to collect like they collect glass and pottery, and that baskets are now seen in an entirely different light. And I did that because I took a different path and didn't hook up with galleries just for them to promote me.

The Emerging Artist Grant I got was spent on photography of my work, so I've been able to document it not only in my ledger but visually.

How many books have you published?

My first book in 1986 was *How to Make Carolina Snow Flakes,* and my second was *Math in Baskets*. Both were self-published. Then my third book, *Baskets: A Book for Makers and Collectors,* was published then translated into German, and now Shiffer Publishers has reprinted it.

Malcolm MacDonald, former head of the University of Alabama Press, is a great mentor of mine. He now lives in Weaverville. When I was approached to do a book I didn't really want to, but he said, "It will live long past you or your baskets, you do the book!"

It was painful, I mean it took me a year, because I had to gather images and write the book. As it turned out, it made Amazon's top-ten sales list on the first day it came out. It did very well; I think 25,000 copies were sold, but it's no longer in print.

The German edition was "Korbe Design". We didn't know what that meant until it got published, and then the reprints. The publisher had said, "Just send us images of your own work," so I made the reprint of the book a catalog of my baskets, with some text.

The original publisher asked me to do another book titled "100 Baskets," and I started putting it together. But then I thought, "Nope, I don't want to do this," and handed it over to somebody else.

No, I'm like Forrest Gump here: I said everything I needed to say on the subject in that first book, though I do think that "Life is like a box of chocolates; you never know what you're going to get."

- **Twists and Turns—**

It seems like your life has changed directions, thanks to your determination and drive.

There have been people who encouraged me to someday do a story of my life, because, you know from this bio that it's had quite a few unique twists and turns.

I did not realize it at the time, but my adopted mother was so afraid that my natural family would come take me away that she clung to me. Then when my dad died and she wanted me to quit college and come home and be with her and I didn't, it probably broke her heart.

Just how much of that has affected me I don't really know, but it had to be profound. It became very important for me to have a real family, to have my own children, and a husband - we've been together forty-three years now.

I think the greatest legacy my oldest brother Pete left me was a genealogy of my father's side of the family so I was able to learn a great deal about several generations of the family. I don't know much about my mother's side but it all plays a part. It can be confusing to have had two families growing up, and knowing that one is afraid of the other, and the other wants to be a part of that one.

I think the way that was resolved with me was when my adopted mother died and I no longer felt torn.

- **Several families and balance—**

It seems no matter how old one gets, conflicts and interwoven events prevail. That has really impacted you because you have your natural family, your adopted family, your family with Doug, your baskets.

You are so right. Balance for me came with my adopted family. My adoptive father was an amazing man. On his death-bed he told me to finish college before getting married. Education was important to him.

We passed his legacy to our sons and told them, "You are going to go to college whether you want to or not, and if you don't finish in four years you're going to pay for the rest of it."

You are a product of your environment, your culture, your family, what you see, your belief system. I think my having a liberal arts education plays heavily into my understanding of all that.

You have a positive outlook, are optimistic, and have a good sense of humor.

Well okay, I choose to be optimistic. But that is hard sometimes, especially when you see the news and find out they are going to do away with so many good programs, and that the NEA is going to be cut and slashed. That is scary.

Back when I was overweight, I had a bit of a health-scare that fortunately was because of a reaction to medication. Then I asked myself, "Okay, how can I quit taking my meds?" Now I don't believe in taking medicine anymore at all, yuck.

I had already quit smoking but wanted to lose some weight and get my numbers good, and I did.

You said you are an avid reader, what do you like to read?

I read every book that John Grisham wrote and by the way, he has a cousin in Bakersville. And when Dan Brown came out with *The Di Vinci Code* I read it and everything he wrote, and David Baldacci novels.

I was really fascinated with Greg Mortenson's *Three Cups of Tea* about setting up Afghani schools, and am reading *1,000 Splendid Sons*. So, I am all over the board. As a child I was at the library every week. I love biographies, they were all in an orange jacket, and I read everything about everybody. And I used to play tennis five times a week.

Then I started making baskets and I quit reading, quit cooking, quit exercising, quit doing just about everything, and really devoted the years to basketry. But it is been amazing how much I have gotten back into reading, especially while combining it with making baskets.

• A verbal studio tour—

Let me show you my studio.

Careful, don't trip here. We've got energy lights, so it'll take a second to get bright enough for you to be able to see anything. This is the shave horse, an ancient device, mainly wooden, that I sit on to carve with two draw knives. The canning pots out by the propane heater are to keep our dog from getting behind them.

I make my dye here, and the material stays in the dye vat for a week then goes to that sink where I rinse it in salt water and vinegar. That takes a week. So, it is two weeks before I can start making the basket. This is the preparation area.

The wonderful thing about this room is that in winter when the leaves are gone, I've got a clear shot of the entire Black Mountain range and can see storms coming in. I ask Doug to drive the car to the bottom of the driveway. I go outside much of the time, except for when it is hot and I have to keep the blinds closed.

This is a great atmosphere to create.

Sounds like you really love your environment.

I do, I really, really do, and I love the people up here. A whole bunch of new craft artists are moving in and starting their families, and then there are us old goats that are trying to mentor some of them, but unfortunately no basket-makers yet.

A young man that bought my booth last summer is a natural-materials basket-maker, and he had me sign the bottom of one of the pedestals because he's hoping he will have the success that I had. His name is Matt Tommey.

Is his work similar to yours?

No, no, no, no! I think I am the only person on the planet that is doing it my way. If others are doing it they are under the radar. Imitation is the sincerest form of flattery, but they haven't learned a way to uniquely make it their work.

• Give-backs to society—

Aside from your basketry, teaching and mentoring as significant as they are, what kind of give-backs do you think people owe society, and what sorts of things have you done?

I think the biggest difference between me and a lot of people is that I don't give time *per se* to an organization, but I do give time in the form of a finished basket that I give to an organization to auction or raffle off. This is probably worth a lot more than volunteering some place.

My donated baskets are used to raise money for every cause from the Food Pantry to the Hospital

Foundation, for My Meds to the American Cancer Society. And I have walked the track during the Relay for Life. That is a big passion of both me and my husband, and he delivers for Meals on Wheels, and serves on the boards of this and that and the other.

The Smithsonian and non-profit museums often come to artists for donations, and their generosity of giving to organizations so they can continue to do good work is incredible.

- **Parting thoughts—**

Thanks, Billie Ruth. Please give me parting thoughts about your future plans.

As an artist-in-residence in schools I work closely with students, though not as much now as during the early years of my career. But this is an area where many artists and crafts people are able to use their talent to teach young people.

If we don't teach the young ones then who will be the craft artists of the next generation?

I plan to keep doing what I love to do, basket-making, and this is the reason I decided to get completely healthy. And by the time I hit sixty-five, I was at a much better weight.

Lastly, it's important to repeat what I said: I used to smoke but quit maybe five or six years ago, and that was the hardest thing I ever did.

So put this in your book for your readers as my final words: "Don't ever smoke!"

Billie Ruth Sudduth working in her studio.

. . . with husband, Doug.

Sudduth Family
Thanksgiving Day 2011.

Fibonacci 21.

Fibonacci in Reverse.

Crimson Tide.

Japanese Twill Weave Cat's Head.

Section 5: **Chronology**

- **Born—**
- September 13, 1945 in Sewanee, Tennessee; grew up in Birmingham, Alabama.

- **Education—**
- Primarily self-taught as a basket-maker.
- 1963-1967. BA in Psychology and Sociology, Huntingdon College in Montgomery, Alabama.
- 1967-1969. M.S.W. at the University of Alabama in Tuscaloosa.
- 1975-1989. Graduate studies in psychology, education, special education, learning disabilities, and language at East Carolina University, University of Nevada-Las Vegas and Fresno Pacific College.

- **Employment—**
- 1983-present. Studio artist, basketry teacher and proprietor of JABOBS— Just a Bunch of Baskets.
- 1989. Left 20-year professional career to devote fulltime to basketry.
- 1983-1989. Combined and integrated the two careers, dividing a 16-hour workday between each.
- 1966-1989. Medical/psychiatric social worker or school psychologist at Duke University Medical Center, John Umstead Hospital, New Bern-Craven County Schools, Clark County School District.

- **Memberships—**
- National Basketry Organization. Charter Member.
- Piedmont Craftsmen. Exhibiting Member.
- Carolina Designer Craftsmen. Exhibiting Member.
- Southern Highland Handicraft Guild. Exhibiting Member.
- American Craft Association.

- **Basketry Teaching Experience—**
- 2009, 2002, 1999, 1997, 1996, 1993. Penland School of Crafts, Penland, N.C.
- 2008. Basketmaking as an Art Form, UNCA Center for Creative Retirement, Asheville, N.C.
- 2003,1993, 1998. John C. Campbell Folk School, Brasstown, N.C.
- 2001, 1999. Arrowmont School of Arts and Crafts, Gatlinburg, TN.
- 1999. Math in a Basket, Smithsonian Institution, Renwick Gallery/Alliance, Washington, D.C.
- 1997. Winston-Salem /Forsyth County Schools, Math in a Basket, sponsored by Piedmont Craftsmen.
- 1995. East Carolina University, School of Art, Greenville, NC. Guest Artist.
- 1991-1993. Cameron Museum of Art, Wilmington, N.C.
- 1993,1992,1991 NC Basketmaker's Association Convention: Winston-Salem, Fayetteville, Raleigh.
- 1991. Math in a Basket, New Hanover County School District, Wilmington, NC Eisenhower Grant.
- 1990. Market the Art, Secaucus, New Jersey. Sponsored by *BASKETMAKER MAGAZINE*.
- 1988-1989. Clark County School District, Las Vegas. Basketry as prof. development course, teacher re-certification.

- **Awards/Fellowships/Grants/Honors—**
- 2007 Oral History Program, Archives of American Art. Smithsonian Institution. Washington, D.C.
- 2005 Huntingdon College, Montgomery, Alabama. President's Medal for Achievement.
- 2004 Individual Visual Arts Fellowship, North Carolina Arts Council.
- 2003 UNC–Wilmington; Acquisition of Papers, University Archives, Randall Library, Wilmington, N.C.
- 2002 Alumni Achievement Award, Huntingdon College, Montgomery, Alabama.
- 1998 Award of Excellence in Fiber, Piedmont Crafts Fair, Winston Salem, N.C.
- 1998 Niche Award, Philadelphia, Pa.

- 1997 North Carolina Living Treasure Award; Wilmington, North Carolina.
- 1997 Smithsonian Craft Show Merit Award, Washington, D.C.
- 1997 Niche Award Finalist. Philadelphia, PA.
- 1994 Individual Visual Artist Grant, North Carolina Arts Council.
- 1993 Southern Arts Federation/National Endowment for the Arts Visual Artist Fellowship Finalist.
- 1990/1991 Emerging Artist Grant, Arts Council of the Lower Cape Fear/North Carolina Arts Council.

- **Collections—**
- **Columbia Museum of Art, Columbia, S.C.**
- Asheville Art Museum, Asheville, N.C.
- Montgomery Museum of Fine Arts, Montgomery, Alabama.
- Renwick Gallery, National Museum of American Art, Smithsonian Institution, Washington, D.C.
- Museum of Art and Design, New York, New York.
- Mint Museum of Craft and Design, Charlotte, N.C.
- Charles A. Wustum Museum of Fine Arts, Racine, Wisconsin.
- Louise Wells Cameron Art Museum, Wilmington, N.C.
- University of North Carolina, Wilmington , N.C.
- American Embassy, Niamey, Niger, Africa. (Art in Embassies Program).
- Lloyd Cotsen Collection, Los Angeles, CA.
- Glaxo Pharmaceuticals, Research Triangle Park, N.C.
- Bank of America, Corporate Headquarters, Charlotte, N.C.
- Thomas S. Kenan Institute for the Arts, Winston-Salem, N.C.
- Kathleen Price Bryan Family Fund, Greensboro, NC.
- Holiday Inn Corporation. Hickory, N.C.
- President Jimmy Carter. The Carter Institute, Atlanta, Georgia.

- **Writings by and About Billie Ruth—**
- 2010 *Basket Inspirations for Makers and Collectors*. Schiffer Publishers. Author.
- The Laurel of Asheville, Billie Ruth Sudduth, A North Carolina Living Treasure. November.
- 2009 *Our State,* Why We Love North Carolina. No Place Like Home essay. February.
- 2008 *Carolina Home and Garden*. Weaving a Legacy. Feature. December.
- *WNC*, Mountain Living in Western North Carolina. Photograph. Nov/Dec.
- *Family Circle*, Miracle on Oak Street. Article. December.
- *Southern Living*, A Storybook Christmas. Photograph. December.
- *Exhibit A, A Collection of Creativity from the Carolinas*. Artist profile. December
- *Asheville Citizen-Times*, Bakersville Basketmaker Appreciates Aclaim. Feature. September 21.
- *House Beautiful*, Everybody's Favorite Accessory-BASKETS! Photograph. June.
- *WNC,* Photograph. May.
- *Living in Style*, Serious Folks, Serious Art. Feature. February.
- 2007 *American Style*, Photograph. December.
- 2006 *USA Today*, Town Hangs Hope on Holiday Tree. Interview, photograph. December 5.
- *Our State*, Summer Postcards, article, photograph. June.
- *The Washington Post*, April 21, 2006. Photograph.
- *500 Baskets*, Jan Peters, Lark Books, Sterling Publishers, New York, Photographs.
- 2005 *Our State*, Living Treasures, Misti Lee, Feature. September.
- *Highland Handcrafters*, Appalachian Craftspeople, Michael Joslin. Front cover, article.
- 2004 *Smoky Mountain Living*, Billie Ruth Sudduth, Weaving Beauty from Tradition and Creativity, Feature. Vol. 4, Number 4, Fall.
- *The Nature of Craft and the Penland Experience*, Lark Books, Sterling Publishers, NY. Photograph.
- *Fiberarts Design Book VII*, Lark Books, Sterling Publishers. Photograph.
- *Our State,* The Best of Our State at Pinehurst. Photograph. Feb.-June.

- NC State Department of Transportation Highway Map. Photograph.
- *The Crafts Report*, April. Photograph.
- 2003 *Our State*, Carolina Snowflakes, Sept. 2003-Jan. 2004.
- *The Crafts Report*, Where Can You Find Craft Collectors? Article, photograph. November.
- *Craft Heritage Trails of Western North Carolina, Handmade in America*. Cover, narrative, photos.
- *Delta Sky,* Basket Cases. Feature. March.
- 2002 *Log and Timber*, Warm Woven Wishes. Feature, July/August.
- *The Crafts Report*, Billie Ruth Sudduth Pounds Out a New Line of Baskets, Feature. June.
- *Fiberarts Magazine*, Fibonacci Numbers in Basketry: 1,1,2,3,5,8,13,... Author. Jan/Feb.
- 2001 Shuttle, Spindle, & Dyepot, Photograph. Fall.
- *Washington Craft Show Program*, Front cover photograph.
- *Korb-Design*, Haupt, Bern, Switzerland. Author
- *Objects for Use: Handmade by Design*, Harry N. Abrams Inc., New York. Photograph.
- *The Washington Post*, Nation's Artisans Crafting Goods and a Good Living. Interview. April 16.
- 2000 *Beautiful Things*, Guild Publishing. Photograph.
- *Carolina Women's Press.* The Long Way Around, How 34 Women Found the Lives They Love, Photographs, Feature.
- *American Baskets*, Robert Shaw, Random House, Inc. Photographs.
- *Baskets, Tradition and Beyond*, Leier, Peters, Wallace, Guild Publishing. Photographs.
- *American Style*, A Passion for Baskets, Spring 2000, #20, 8 page feature.
- *Biltmore Estate, The 2000 Destination Guide*, Photographs, article.
- 1999 *Making the New Baskets*, Jane LaFerla, Lark Books, Sterling Publishing, New York. Photograph.
- *The Chicago Tribune*, "Crafting a New Career at Midlife", Aug. 24. Feature.
- *Shuttle, Spindle, and Dyepot*, A Conversation with the Renwick Gallery's Kenneth Trapp. Volume *XXX,* No.3, Issue 119, Summer. Photograph-Easy as Can Be: Fibonacci 1,1,2,3. Author. Front cover, feature article.
- 1998 *Skilled Work, American Craft in the Renwick Gallery,* National Museum of American Art,
- Smithsonian. Kenneth Trapp and Howard Risatti. Smithsonian Institution Press. Photos, narrative.
- *American Craft.* Photographs. June/July.
- *Math in a Basket*. Author.
- *The Craft Heritage Trails of Western North Carolina*. Handmade in America. Cover, photos, narrative.
- *Southern Accents*. Photograph. April/May.
- *American Style*. She's a Living Treasure. Spring.
- *Niche*. Photograph. Spring.
- *Smithsonian Magazine*. Photograph. February.
- *Niche*. Photograph. Winter.
- *Crafts Report*, Sudduth Named Living Treasure. Article, photograph. January.
- 1997 *Southern Living*, Crafts on the Cutting Edge. Photograph. Dec.
- *Johnson City Press*, The Golden Mean. Feature. Dec. 15.
- *Wilmington Star News*, Dream Weaver. Feature. Oct. 28.
- *American Craft*, Photograph. Aug/Sept.
- *Southern Accents*, High Art. Photograph, article. July/August.
- *American Style*, Put All Your Eggs in These Baskets. Photograph. Spring.
- 1996 *Fiberarts*, Swatches. Photograph. Nov/Dec.
- *Home.* Photographs. Nov.
- *Southern Accents*. Sept/Oct. Photograph
- *Shuttle, Spindle, & Dyepot.*, Gallery, Summer. Issue 107.
- *Our State*. Feature, August.
- *American Craft,* Gallery, April/May.
- *Fiberarts* Design Book V, Lark Books/Sterling Publishers. Photograph.
- *Fiberarts,* Swatches, Photograph. Nov./Dec.
- *Raleigh News and Observer.* Feature. Nov. 25.

- 1994-1999 *Early American Life*, America's 200 Best Craftsmen. Aug./Oct.
- *American Craft.* Portfolio.
- *The Torch*, A Monthly Newspaper for the Smithsonian Institution. Photograph. April.
- *Home.* Second Nature. Photograph, article. May.
- 1993 *The New York Times.* Review. Sunday , April 25.
- *Twill Basketry,* Lark Books/Sterling Publishers. Photographs.
- 1992 *Fort Worth Star Telegram.* Art Review. Sept. 29.
- *Members Magazine, Philadelphia Museum of Art*. Photograph. Fall.
- 1991 *Shuttle, Spindle, and Dyepot,* Feature interview. Issue 87.

- **Select Exhibitions—**
- 2010 Solo Exhibition, Ogden Museum of Southern Art, New Orleans, Louisiana.
- 2009 "Craft in America". Fuller Craft Museum, Brockton, Massachusetts.
- 2008 "Basketworks, The Cotsen Contemporary American Basket Collection. Racine Art Museum. Racine, WI.
- 2008 "Billie Ruth Sudduth – 25 Years and 10,000 (almost) Baskets Later". Solo Exhibition. Toe River Arts. Council Gallery. Spruce Pine, N.C.
- 2008-2012 "American Masters" Southern Arts Federation Seven State Tour. Invitational.
- 2007-2008 "Craft in America", Arkansas Arts Center, Little Rock Arkansas; Museum of Contemporary Craft,
- Portland, Oregon; Mingei International Museum, San Diego, California. Invitational. Book.
- 2007 "Pursuing Excellence", Blue Spiral I and the Center for Craft, Creativity, and Design, Asheville, N.C.
- Invitational. Catalog.
- 2006 "The 2006 Governor's Executive Mansion North Carolina Craft Exhibition", Raleigh, NC. April-October. Juried by invitation. Catalog.
- 2006 "2004-2005 NCAC Fellowship Recipients Exhibition", Asheville Art Museum, Asheville, North Carolina. April-July. Catalog.
- 2005 Long Beach Museum of Art, "Engaging Nature". Contemporary Baskets from the Collection of Lloyd and Margit Cotsen. Long Beach, California.
- 2005 Asheville Museum of Art, "Tradition and Beyond – The Baskets of Billie Ruth Sudduth", Asheville, North Carolina. Solo exhibit.
- 2005 Montgomery Museum of Fine Arts, "Math in a Basket." Solo exhibit. Catalog.
- 2005 "High Fiber" Renwick Gallery of the Smithsonian American Art Museum. Survey of the permanent collection in fiber. Group exhibition.
- 1994-through-2006 The Smithsonian Craft Show. Washington, D.C. Juried. Catalog.
- 2004 "The Nature of Craft and the Penland Experience", Mint Museum of Craft and Design, Charlotte, NC. Invitational. Catalog.
- 2004 "NC Craft 04: A Celebration of Penland's 75th Anniversary", Wellington B. Gray Gallery, School of Art, East Carolina University, Greenville, NC. Invitational.
- 2003, 2001, 2000, 1999, 1996, 1992, 1991. Philadelphia Museum of Art Craft Show. Juried. Catalog.
- 2002 "Baskets Now: USA" Arkansas Arts Center, Decorative Arts Museum, Little Rock, AR. Invitational.
- 2002 "Honoring Women" Handmade in America; UNCA Blowers Gallery, Asheville, NC. Invitational.
- 2001-2002 "OBJECTS FOR USE: Handmade by Design", American Craft Museum, New York; Invitational curated by Paul Smith. Book.
- 2001-2002 "Contemporary Baskets", Paris Gibson Square Museum of Art; Great Falls, MN. Invitational.
- 2001 "Southern Women of Influence", Kentucky Art and Craft Foundation, Louisville, KY. Invitational.
- 2001 "Craft is a Verb", Tampa Museum of Art. Selected objects from the American Craft Museum.
- 2003, 2001, 2000, 1999, 1994 SOFA, New York, Chicago.
- 1999 "Head, Heart, Hands", American Craft Museum, New York, Permanent Collection. 1999 "Southeastern Basket Invitational", Blue Spiral I, Asheville, N.C.
- 1999 Mint Museum of Craft & Design grand opening, Charlotte, NC. Permanent collection.
- 1998-99 "Craft is a Verb" Mississippi Museum of Art, Jackson, MS. American Craft Museum Collection.
- 1998 "Billie Ruth Sudduth - Baskets". ERL Originals. Winston-Salem, NC. Two person exhibition.

- 1997 "The Renwick at 25 - The Reinstallation of the Permanent Collection", Smithsonian Institution, National Museum of American Art, Renwick Gallery, Washington, D.C.
- 2004, 2002, 2000, 1998, 1997 "Contemporary Baskets", del Mano Gallery, LA. Invitational. Catalog.
- 1997 "Celebrating American Craft", The Museum of Decorative Art, Copenhagen, Denmark. Catalog.
- 1996 "Guests of United States", Jahresmesse Kunsthandwerk; Museum fur Kunst und Gewerbe; Hamburg, Germany. Invitational.
- 1996 "The Nature Sequence-Baskets of Billie Ruth Sudduth". St. John's Museum of Art, Wilmington, NC. Solo exhibition.
- 1995 "Accounts Southeast-Craft", Southeast Ctr. for Contemporary Art, Winston-Salem, NC. Invitational.
- 1995 "Treasures", John Michael Kohler Arts Center, Kohler, Wisconsin. Invitational.
- 1995 "Vessels - American Craftsman Series", Castle Gallery, College of New Rochelle, NY. Invitational.
- 1995 "Alabama Impact - Contemporary Artists with Alabama Ties", Mobile Museum of Art, Mobile, Al. Huntsville Museum of Art, Huntsville, AL. Invitational. Catalog.
- 1994 Festival of the Masters, Walt Disney World, Orlando, FL. Juried.
- 1993-1994 "Craft of the Carolinas". Gibbes Museum of Art, Charleston, SC; Rudolf E. Lee Gallery, Clemson University, Clemson, SC; Spirit Square for the Arts, Charlotte, NC; Green Hill Center for North Carolina Art, Greensboro, NC; Folk Art Center, Asheville, NC. (Traveling exhibition). Juried. Catalog.
- 1993 "A Celebration of American Crafts", The Philadelphia Museum of Art, Art Rental and Sales Gallery, Philadelphia, Pa. Invitational.
- 1993 "Southeastern Juried Exhibition 1993", Fine Arts Museum of the South, Mobile, AL. Catalog. Juried.
- 1993 "Spotlight '93, Southeast Crafts", Arrowmont School of Arts and Crafts, Gatlinburg. Catalog. Juried.
- 1993 "Small Expressions", Handweavers Guild of America, James and Meryl Hearst Center for the Visual Arts, Cedar Falls, Iowa. Traveled to "The Gathering", Bucknell University, Lewisburg, PA. Juried. Catalog.
- 1993 "Woven, Plaited, Twined, Coiled", Sawtooth Center, Milton Rhodes Gallery, Winston-Salem, N.C. Juried. Catalog.
- 1993 "Fiber Celebrated '93", Intermountain Weavers Conference, Nevada State Museum, Las Vegas, NV. Juried. Catalog.
- 1992 "Materials Hard and Soft", Meadows Gallery, Center for Visual Arts, Denton, TX. Juried. Catalog.
- 1992 "Spotlight '92", American Craft Council, SE Region, Hand Workshop, Richmond, VA. Juried. Catalog.
- 1992 "Fiber Invitational". Chelsea Gallery, Western Carolina University, Cullowhee. 2-person exhibition.
- 1992 Fine Arts Center, Francis Marion College, Florence, SC. Solo exhibition.
- 1991 "The Wichita National '91", The Wichita Center for the Arts, Wichita, KS. Juried. Catalog.
- 1991 "Fiber Celebrated '91", Colorado Springs Fine Arts Center, Colorado Springs, CO. Juried. Catalog.
- 1991 "34th Chautauqua National Exhibition of American Art", Chautauqua Art Association Galleries, Chautauqua, NY. Juried. Catalog.
- 1991 "Crafts National 25", Zoller Gallery, Penn State University, University Park, PA, Juried. Catalog.
- 1991 "Small Expressions", Handweavers Guild of America, Lane Community College Art Gallery, Eugene, OR. Juried. Catalog.
- 1991 "Southern Fibers '91", Student Center Gallery, North Georgia College, Dahlonega, GA. Juried.
- 1990 "Wilmington Artist VI", St. John's Museum of Art, Wilmington, NC. Juried.
- 1989 "Fiber Celebrated '89", Intermountain Weavers Conference, Salt Lake Arts Center, Salt Lake City, Utah. Juried. Catalog.

Dr. Matt Hayes, M.D., Ph.D., FACEP

Pioneer National Emergency Medical Services

"I believe my life journey so far has been almost magical. In spite of enormous handicaps, the biggest of which was myself, I managed to persevere, and perhaps when I leave this earth it will be just a tiny bit better than before."
— Dr. Matt Hayes

Sections about Matt Hayes:

1) About Dr. Hayes from His Peers

2) Highlights of His Medical Career

3) **Dr. Hayes' Life Journey, in His Own Words**

4) Photos

5) Chronology

Section 1: **About Dr. Hayes from His Peers**

- **Contribution forever relevant—**

Matt Hayes' contribution to society is notable now and will be forever relevant. His forward thinking of medical care spurred what is known today as "emergency room specialty".

Countless lives have been saved because critical care experts now manage the areas where critical care happens - there is no need for an intern to be heading the ER when crash victims with head trauma are being rushed in by ambulance and helicopter.

Matt saw the weakness in the system and, most importantly, did something to strengthen it. Matt also will become an inspiration to many St. John's University pre-med students as his picture and story will be portrayed in the Biology department of his alma mater.
— **Wally Halas,** Associate Vice President, St. John's University

- **Important role in ACEP history and development—**

Redacted from a letter to Dr. Hayes:

Thank you for your years of devotion to Emergency Medicine since its inception. Emergency Medicine faced a long, arduous road in becoming the 23rd recognized medical specialty. It is because of a small number of dedicated physicians such as yourself that our specialty gained recognition.

The American College of Emergency Physicians owes you a great deal of gratitude toward your efforts in building the first chapter in Washington. In researching the history, we found your original letters and memos coordinating committees and meetings to adopt the Constitution and by-laws necessary to form the chapter. You were also recognized as a Charter Member in the book *Twenty-Five Years on the Front Line* published in 1993 for the 25th anniversary of ACEP.

Please accept our sincerest appreciation for the important role you played in the history of the specialty and the development of the American Certified Emergency Physicians.
— **Dean Wilkerson,** JD, MBA, CAE, Executive Director of ACEP

- **Elevating status of emergency physicians—**

Matt Hayes and I worked side-by-side in Washington State to successfully elevate the status of emergency physicians in hospitals and throughout the medical community. We overcame resistance and resentment from other doctors and politicians to help lift emergency physician training and certification to its present high level of professionalism.

Matt's work and diligence were of high quality, and I greatly enjoyed working with him during those memorable pioneering years.
— **Dr. Richard Romth,** M.D., FACEP, FACS, former president of ACEP

Section 2: **Highlights of His Medical Career**

- **Hayes: First Army ER Doctor, Driving Force in Emergency Medicine Changes**

When Matt Hayes entered the Army Reserve in the 399th Combat Support Hospital, he became the first and only Emergency Room Doctor in the Army, and probably in all Armed Forces of the United States of America. Fellow Reserve Officer Col. Jim Becker, retired Director of Reserve Officers, Office of the Surgeon General of the United States, later summed up Dr. Hayes' career contributions: "For as long as he can remember, Matthew J. Hayes, M.D., Ph. D, '57, challenged the status quo, a dominant characteristic of his personality that would ultimately lead him to become a driving force behind sweeping changes in the field of Emergency Medicine."

The changes began after he helped form the American College of Emergency Physicians in 1968 to serve as a nucleus of information related to emergency services, and to provide an opportunity for physicians in emergency medicine to upgrade the caliber of services rendered, pool their knowledge and seek solutions to mutual problems. They also formed a Certification Board, developed a curriculum to educate doctors, developed Board Examinations then gained recognition from the AMA, national Medical Educators, and more. He was First Delegate to the ACEP, and served as the first president of the Washington Chapter based in Seattle.

- **Excerpt from *Reflections of an Original Emergency Room Doctor—***

Dr. Matt Hayes authored a 1675-word biographical essay in 1968, and the following excerpt provides insight into his inspiration for helping to change how Emergency Physicians are trained:

In 1966 in a major medical school affiliated teaching hospital, I approached the end of my internship and eagerly scooped up emergency room responsibilities. When a patient showed up, whether a gunshot victim or a comatose patient found on the street, the charge nurse took vital signs and then called for a doctor. After chasing her doctor for a significant amount of time, the nurse was finally put through and might find out that the attending physician was a gynecologist. In a teaching hospital, things were significantly better because there was always a crew of interns and residents physically present.

My 24-hour shift began one Saturday at noon, and several automobile accident victims and a knife-attack victim showed up. There was lot of blood smeared on the accident victims, from superficial wounds, as it turned out, while the knife-fighter was dry. But this patient had Tension Pneumothorax, a life-threatening impending disaster which was diagnosed with a careful look. On Sunday just before I was to be relieved, a somewhat tipsy member of the yacht club who had been skewered by a flagpole was brought into the ER. This was not my first ER shift, but it dramatized the core problem more than the others. There was a complete disconnect between patient needs and the training of physicians on call. The resistance and emotional venom rampant in hospitals during these formative years of emergency medicine was widespread. It is difficult for everyone involved to realize the need, both individually and collectively, to revise their thinking, but this must be done.

- **Contribution to *Emergency Department Organization and Management* Book—**

Dr. Matt Hayes contributed a lengthy chapter on education and training to *Emergency Department Organization and Management,* a book published by C.V. Mosby Company of St. Louis and edited by A.L. Jenkins in 1975 for the American College of Emergency Physicians. The royalties from book sales were used for continuing education of professionals in the field of emergency medicine.

Section 3: **Dr. Hayes' Life Journey, in His Own Words**

The home of Dr. Matt Hayes sits on a hilltop overlooking Long John Mountain in Carriage Park, a large gated community in Hendersonville, North Carolina. Just before arrival for the initial interview with the emergency physician pioneer for this book of Notables, the retired doctor had been crafting a table, one of the fruits of his intense new hobby of woodworking, while wife MaryBeth was tending to flowers in her small and well-designed garden. I begin the taped interview by asking the doctor:

Dr. Hayes, now that you are well into your retirement and have had time to reflect, how would you characterize your medical and life journeys thus far?

I believe my life journey so far has been almost magical. In spite of enormous handicaps, the biggest of which was myself, I managed to persevere. Perhaps when I leave this earth it will be just a tiny bit better than before.

Your philosophy of leaving the world a better place is noble, but in contrast with self-deprecation.

Though I did not believe in myself and am still self-hypercritical, I was blessed at every stage of my schooling with at least one teacher that believed in me and steered or pushed me in the right direction.

Imagine my personal gratification as I presented a copy of my Ph.D. thesis written in German to my eighth-grade nun, my high school registrar, and my college biology professor, who all hoped I'd make something of myself. Sister Patricia frequently said to me, "Matty, you are the most stubborn boy I have ever taught. If you could only learn to use your stubbornness to your advantage . . ." She never finished the sentence.

Did you use it?

That stubbornness got a workout later when I began to study medicine in a German University, without knowing the language. That is an example of why I've been called feisty, because I refuse to give up!

• The Early Years—

Before we journey to your experiences studying medicine in Germany, tell me about your early years.

My father left Harristown in Kilrane Conty, Wexford, Ireland to look for work, and he and a classmate found it in Wales working the coal mines. He also met my mother there. But two tragedies caused him to go to sea as a stoker, and he eventually made his way to New York. The first tragedy was when the calamitous coal mine strikes threw him out of work, and the second was the death of a classmate from a cave-in as they pilfered coal from an abandoned shaft to heat their flat in the winter.

I had two older sisters and one younger one. We grew up in the Williamsburg section of Brooklyn in an otherwise all- Italian neighborhood. My father's day job then was as superintendent of a small apartment building, and his evening job was running an elevator at Forty Wall Street, in Manhattan.

I began grade school at the local Catholic school and learned to read very well and very fast. My mother couldn't read well, and as I found out when I was in the army, she never really learned to write or spell. My father left school in the sixth grade, so he was better schooled.

While only in the second grade, I got a library card and read every fairytale in stock. On Sundays I read the newspapers out loud to my parents and an old-maid aunt who lived with us, who also couldn't read. I didn't understand what I was reading, though.

The neighborhood was noisy, charming, scary, caring, and exciting. I was one of two boys with blond hair. Everybody else had black hair and a darker Mediterranean complexion.

World War Two provided work for everybody. My father already had two jobs, but now my mother worked at night, my aunt worked during the day, as did my oldest sister, Rona. With this opportunity to save, my parents were able to put a down-payment on a house in Ozone Park, Queens. This was a big step up!

I attended Nativity Grade School in Ozone Park, run by the cheerful and friendly Ursuline sisters. I have wonderful, carefree and happy memories from these years. During class, I did all of my homework, and immediately after school hid my books under the big fir tree, in front of the church. They were safely protected in a gas-mask case. In spite of this, for most of the grades, I remained in the top three highest grades in the class. This was important in that it set me up for a difficult time in high school, since I never studied.

• Then High School—

My first high school, there would be five, was Jesuit-run Brooklyn Preparatory, the most difficult school to gain entrance to in New York City at the time. Because I was a January graduate, my class was designated to complete the full year in one semester plus summer school. This would put us on the same time-line as the rest of New York City, since January admissions were being phased out.

Very simply put, I had no schooling habits to count on, and no immediate adult to guide me. Heretofore I never did homework and barely ever studied. Everything came easy. Then there was this thing called puberty. What a shock!

For me high school was a waste of time and I played hooky whenever I could. I spent my days in the New York City Public Library, or in one of the many museums or zoos. I argued with most of my teachers when I did attend. I managed to go to five high schools with six transfers; I went to one school twice in the three years I was supposed to have spent in high school. I got special permission from Albany to take the fourth-year English and History Board of Regents exams in my third year, and was told I would be graduated if I received a grade greater than seventy-five percent. I did and thus was never a high school senior.

Were you good in science and math in high school?

You cannot be worse at math than I was. I took algebra five times and failed it four times because certain things made no sense to me, and I used to argue with my teachers. I went to summer school to repeat algebra, an hour course five days a week. It took me almost an hour traveling to get there, so I always signed up for a second course in something else just to round out the trip!

What did you do after graduation?

After graduation I had no clue what to do next. I was just seventeen-years old with only three interests: playing games and goofing around and chasing girls were my major interests. My options were to get a job, go into the military, or go to college if I were allowed in, but my grades were all over the map. For those subjects that I liked they were reasonably good, but many others were poor.

Which option did you choose?

My father didn't believe I had graduated high school and thought I was trying to pull the wool over his eyes. I somehow managed to get accepted by St. John's College, how is another story that I'll tell you later. After I graduated from summer school I started at St. John's about a month later and majored in biology, although I had never taken chemistry or physics in high school.

I had to work after classes to pay the tuition and laboratory fees because there was not enough money at home, and my father wanted me to get a job. He thought I was wasting my time in yet another school. I also secretly thought I was wasting my time too, especially since I had no plan. My peers all wanted to become teachers, lawyers, doctors and dentists, and so on. It seemed that I just wanted to hang around.

- **Rough start at St. John's University—**

Tell me the story of how you got accepted at St. John's.

During the summer of 1953, just after qualifying as a high school graduate, the registrar of the school, Dan Rood, asked why I was still hanging around. He was a fantastic guy who knew kids through and through, and had a good heart. I told him that I didn't know what to do with myself and really felt lost.

"Well," he said, "I've got to get ready for the next class of kids. You have two options: get a job, or join the army". Now that sounded so grown up to me, and I still felt like a kid. I asked him what sort of a job, to which he answered: "What can you do?"

I had no real answer. The only things I was any good at were slap-ball and climbing trees, and I was a tricky runner, hard to catch. When I told him that he said, "Then it's easy, join the Army!"

"Jeez Dan, you're no help!" I bellowed, and then he added, "You could go to college, you're smart enough." He calmed me down and said he'd call a few college registrars he knew. When I told my father about this, he wanted to know what crazy scheme I had cooked up this time, and said he wasn't going to fall for any more of my nonsense.

My sister Anne, who thought I was a smart kid but a juvenile delinquent at heart, was always trying to get me to read books above my age group. For my birthday she gave me a copy of Einstein's *General Theory of Relativity* and Voltaire's *Candide*. I read a bit into both books, but Einstein confused me and Voltaire was boring.

Mr. Rood arranged for an interview with the Registrar at St. John's College. I thought I would look smart if I brought the books Anne gave me to the interview then remembered too late that St. John's was a Catholic University and Voltaire was an anti-church French philosopher, and Einstein was probably an atheist. I was sitting on a bench and through an open door sat a priest smoking a cigarette and staring at me. I don't know about you, but at that age I didn't like it when people stared at me. I looked away once or twice, but he seemed to have fixed his gaze in my direction. I really got ticked off and made a face to annoy him.

That must have gone over real well.

The priest, Father Newman, shouted to the Registrar: "Mr. Kienle, send that young man into my office immediately!" Mr. Kienle was talking to Dan Rood on the phone and muttered, "Hayes hasn't been here for ten minutes yet and he's already in trouble." I was ushered into Newman's office and took a seat. By this time I knew that Newman was somebody important. He was the Dean! Mr. Kienle was getting my high school transcripts verbally per phone. There had been no time to prepare and mail my convoluted HS transcripts. Father Newman asked me what business I had with St. John's. I hesitated but finally blurted out that I wanted to attend school here. I cannot adequately describe the look on his face.

The Registrar entered and stared at me with a piercing look. I decided to open *Candide,* though I had no real idea what it was about. Newman asked if I had read other books like the two I was carrying and I lied, "Sure I have, tons of them." Father Newman then took one glance at my grades, threw them down on the desk and asked roughly, "Do you think you are college material?"

It was the way he asked it, challenging me, daring me! I thought, who does he think he is? I snapped back, "Of course I'm college material, why else would I be here?"

His jaw dropped and he just looked at me-puzzled. After a long silence, he asked what I intended to major in. I barely understood the question and hadn't given it much thought; I just knew that it wouldn't be algebra! "Well, I thought maybe biology." After all, I had a tank full of tropical fish at home.

He said, "I can't believe you want to major in science with your background. That's rich, and I'm going to enjoy watching you fall flat on your face and fail. It will give me a certain sense of closure to personally kick you out of St. John's; that is if I let you in." Then Father Newman laid out conditions: I had to maintain a total grade average of eighty percent for the first year or I would be asked to leave. He made out a murderous program for me. At the time, I had no idea then that most of my peers had a much easier program. I was still quite furious that this priest thought I was a dumbbell.

I am able to see now that the basic problem was I did not believe in myself, and when others seemed to believe in me, I was just too immature to take them seriously.

• Finding an after-school job—

I told my father that though I was going to go to college, he wouldn't have to pay for it, if he could get me a good part-time job. Most of my peers got jobs after school as file clerks for one of the many insurance companies in New York City, but they only paid minimum wage of eighty-five cents an hour. The best paying jobs were in construction, and I was only qualified as a common laborer.

My father got me a job in a demolition company that was doing work in a building in the heart of the financial center on Wall Street. We could only work when the building was empty at about 5:30 p.m., and finished shortly before midnight. It was brutally hard work, swinging sledgehammers to knock down inside walls, or filling wheelbarrows with debris then running them up a ramp and dumping them in a truck.

How did you hold up with that incredible schedule of college and work?

The boss took one look at me and said, "You won't last one night!" I was a skinny kid and not really muscular, but I was stubborn. I lasted until this job was finished and earned enough for tuition for that semester, but I had a hard time juggling lectures, laboratories, homework and studying while working.

I studied as best I could and prepared for the next day on the subway to Wall Street. My father always had supper ready for me, and I ate and studied in an empty office until work began. I would leave at about midnight to get home to Queens at one a.m. I was dragging the next morning when the alarm clock went off, but I never once thought of quitting. I told myself but no one else that I'd have to be broken before I gave up.

And I was earning $3.20 an hour on this job, and that went a long way in making me independent. At the end of two semesters and many part-time construction jobs where I was making tuition money, I had an average grade of just under eighty-percent; not too shabby. To my surprise, Father Newman greeted me with a big smile and asked if I could do better if I didn't have to work after school? I emphatically said yes. "Could you get on the Dean's List if you didn't have to work?" he asked. I suspected that this conversation was going in a very good direction and didn't hesitate to bellow: "With ease!"

Was your suspicion correct?

Yes! The dean was silent for a pregnant moment then explained that he was empowered to award a full scholarship, including books and lab fees, to a student who helped out in the athletic office on campus. I was almost speechless for once in my life but asked meekly, "Why not try me out on a semester by semester basis? If I don't maintain a minimum eighty-five-percent average and qualify for the Dean's List, you could stop my scholarship and kick me out!" He grinned and shook my hand. "It's a deal!" he said. "You are on your own now."

The work at the athletic office was trivial and the rest of my years at St. John's were a steady round of parties, girls, and work in construction and at the Post Office during vacation times. All this permitted me to buy an old jalopy of a car and have the most wonderful time in college that anybody ever had. I had no trouble staying on the Dean's List, and Father Newman and I became close. We both had risked and we both had won.

Did you stay in contact with Father Newman?

Many years later when the priest was quite old and I had returned from Germany with both an M.D. and a Ph.D., we met at a St. John's function, and his face lit up like a Christmas tree. He said: "I love all those initials after your name Matty, but they don't surprise me. I knew all the time that you could do anything you set your mind to. You just needed a little push, some tough love, and an opportunity". I had tears in my eyes. I never saw him again.

I managed to stay in the top twenty percent of my class, and along the way was in the Glee Club and French Club, business manager of the school newspaper, treasurer then Vice-president of my fraternity, and a member of the Chapel Players acting group. I had spent a huge amount of time on the college campus and loved every moment.

• Drafted into the Army—

What came after graduation?

I almost became a fighter pilot for the Navy, and it was a fluke that I didn't. In my senior year I went to Fort Hamilton, in Brooklyn, with a fraternity brother to take the U.S. naval flight examination, which was four days long and very difficult to pass. But Bill Foohey and I did pass and were given a slot in the next training school to be held in Pensacola Florida shortly after graduation. I was very excited that I was going to become a 'fly-boy'! But at the end of June I got notice from the Department of the Navy that the Appropriations Bill had stalled and the Flight School was canceled temporarily. I was told that it could take a month or a year. I decided not to wait, and I told them to take my name off the Flight School list.

The draft board had been alerted when I became a candidate student pilot, so when my name was removed from the list, I was drafted into the Army on July 22nd of 1957. I reported to Fort Dix, New Jersey as a recruit. The first thing they did was shave our heads then we got uniforms, including underwear, winter and summer garb, field uniforms, and more; I'd never seen so much junk. We were told to guard it all with our lives, because each missing piece would be purchased new and deducted from our pay. I earned a whopping $62 a month.

The second thing on our schedule was a battery of tests to determine what branch of the Army we would be sent to, and what we'd do there. This was not without significant consequences. For instance, if one showed an aptitude for recognizing tools and what they were used for, there was a good chance he would be assigned to the Motor Pool, and spend two years black with grease from repairing trucks, jeeps, even tanks!

I was cautious before the testing got to me. I left our recruit area and asked various soldiers about what the different assignments were like, and just what did signal and communications really do? I had been vaguely interested in that, but learned they spend a lot of time sleeping in tents away from the barracks, pull a lot of night duty, and serve units training out in the field, so yuck, that was out. But I now had an idea of what not to do.

But you had no idea of what to do at that point?

When it came time for the testing, I deliberately failed those things that might get me into some job that I would regret. I was showed a picture of a wrench and called it a hammer and said it was used to bang in nails. The communications exams were a little trickier, basically a test in Morse-Code. So, I learned the alphabet in Morse-Code and made sure I didn't choose the correct answer. And so it went.

I scored high only in reading and interpreting army regulations and documents. Because I had a college degree, the Army offered to send me to Officer Candidate School, but increase my term of service to three years instead of the obligatory two. Then upon successful completion of OCS, I would be commissioned a Second Lieutenant.

I tried to bargain and told them I would go to OCS, but only if I could stay the obligatory two years. They delayed my exit from Fort Dix, which was mainly a reception and processing fort. Everyone else in my barracks went to Texas and was scheduled to serve in Korea. This was repeated at least three times, as I kept moving to the barracks with new recruits, who then would get shipped out.

Finally, a Sergeant called me out of formation and sent me to a new barracks where I was again told that I could go to OCS if I signed up for three years, but I said, "No Thanks" and that was the end of it.

• Assigned to Fort Meade—

Where did you go from Fort Dix?

Recruits from my latest barracks all went to Fort George G. Meade in Maryland near Washington D.C., the temporary home of the Second Armored Cavalry rapid-deployment tank outfit that was on orders to go to Germany, which was a lot better than going to Korea.

It seemed that my luck, with a little push from me, was turning. I was assigned to Tank Company, not good, but headed to Germany. A short time later a Sergeant in charge of personnel at Headquarters asked if I was interested in working for him. He needed someone honest and smart enough to manage the Battalion's Payroll. In other words, he needed a Finance Clerk. It was rumored that the last clerk was caught stealing and was now in the stockade. Not hesitating I said loudly, "I'm your man!"

I was transferred to Headquarters Company and put on orders for an Army school in Fort Knox, Kentucky to take the personnel course. That was a lonely, cold eight weeks. We were told that the recruit with the highest grade on the final exam would be given a three-day pass. I was determined to get that pass and did so.

I used the three days off to visit a Trappist Monastery in nearby Louisville. Thomas Merton was a monk there and I had read several of his books. I was vaguely interested in monasticism, in particular, the mother of all monastics, the Trappists, who take a vow of silence. I put on my Class-A uniform and hitch-hiked to the monastery where I was welcomed, no questions asked, given a private room, towel and soap, and a booklet describing what is forbidden and what is allowed. It was a delightful three days.

Shortly after returning to Fort Knox, I was given transportation back to Fort Meade to join my outfit. The Second Armored Cavalry was busy preparing to board the old World War Two Liberty ships docked in Baltimore that would take us to Bremerhaven, Germany. I felt a new chapter of my life was beginning.

• Sailing to Germany—

The battalion of about 950 men was loaded onto the flat-bottomed Liberty ships that pitched and rolled wildly even in calm waters. It took six-plus days to sail from Baltimore to Bremerhaven, and the ship became a floating vomit-receptacle! I held out for three days, but after someone vomited directly on me, I joined the rest. What a trip! I secured a top bunk, so that I wouldn't be vomited on from above.

I lived in an old German barracks in Bindlach, located a few miles from Bayreuth, Germany, home of Richard Wagner and the world famous Bayreuth Festspielhaus, where once a year powerful and famous people of the western world flock to this small German town to listen to opera. I Even managed to attend one performance.

I was made a Finance Clerk and became proficient at the job. I answered to a Sergeant in Battalion Headquarters during my working hours, but a Captain, my company commander, ruled over everything else in my life in Headquarters Company.

On my first foray into the town of Bayreuth, at the Metropole Hotel, we had an amusing encounter. I was chatting up some local young ladies and the Captain approached me. I guess he wanted to show off, because he tried to impress the ladies with his German. Unfortunately, he made a fool of himself and caused all the ladies to break out in loud, raucous laughter!

He said over and over loudly above the din of laughter while pointing to me, "Er ist mein Man aber Ich bin Chef !". Translated this means: "He is my husband, but I am the boss!" He didn't like me and I didn't like him, but I was only a Private First-Class with one stripe on my shirt, and the disparity in power was huge. He was a petty man with a mean streak, an arrogant man with little education who did his best to make my life miserable. But he eventually paid the price. The Captain made sure I was frequently given after-duty extra work details. He went out of his way to find petty infractions and deal me maximum punishment.

Once, I was called AWOL, in my presence. He saw me running to get into the formation and called the formation to attention. Military rules forbid breaking into the formation when it is at attention. He then called the roll, something unusual for a noontime formation, and when I tried to answer "present" from outside the formation, he insisted that the first Sgt. mark me AWOL. For that infraction, he ordered me to paint the toilet in his private office. I couldn't disobey him, as that would have given him a real excuse to further punish me.

On the other hand, I did not want to give him the satisfaction of winning a contest of wills.

Dr. Hayes, it sounds like you enjoyed challenging military authority.

Yes, I enjoyed challenging all authority. But let me tell you what happened in this contest, though there were many more to come. The Charge of Quarters for the day relayed to me that the Captain had ordered me to paint his bathroom after my duty hours. I said I didn't know how to paint, so he called the Captain at home and he yelled, "Everyone knows how to paint!"

After I was given some white paint and a brush and was shown his bathroom, I got a brilliant idea and asked, "What should I paint?" He called the Captain again and told him that PFC Hayes, me, had asked what he should paint. I could hear the Captain screaming into the telephone through the closed door of the toilet: "Tell him to paint everything. I want it all painted. And do not call me again!"

So I eagerly went to work and painted the mirror over the sink then the windows, but not the window frames. I painted the doorknobs, the toilet seat and the enamel, all very carefully. I painted the light bulbs, the faucet handles, and the metal door lock. And I painted the sink inside and out. This took me quite a few hours, but I managed not to get any paint on the walls or the wooden trim.

The following morning everyone in the post could hear the Captain screaming. I remained busy at work and very quiet. Now, the Captain and I were at war! He was more powerful, but not bright. I was determined to give him the rope he needed to hang himself, and he finally did, but I'll save that story for later. I understood the difference between acceptable military punishment for breaking rules and regulations and personal vendetta punishment. I read and digested all the pertinent Army regulations. I knew these regulations better than the Captain.

Did you have other problems with authority in the Army?

Only as regards silly things For instance, the Army hates hair, I don't know why. The first thing they do to recruits is shave their heads. At that time there were no hairy people in the Army. One day in Bindlach, Germany, a Sergeant saw me with my cap off during my lunch hour and bellowed like a bull: "Private, get a haircut, your hairdo is against regulations!" It just so happened I had gotten a haircut the day before and told the barber to not cut anything off the top because I didn't want to stand out like a soldier when I went into town, I wanted to blend in.

So I looked up the hair grooming regulation then bought a small plastic ruler and carried it with me. The regulation stated how sideburns were to be trimmed, and how long hair on the back of the head should be, the distance between the uniform collar and the hair line etc. Curiously, there was not a word about the top of the head! From then on when I went to the barber I would get a dated receipt. Pretty soon I had a mop full of hair so high that my army cap kept popping up or falling off.

It was my delight to thoroughly befuddle one Sergeant after another. Even the officers were susceptible. Several times on any given day someone more powerful than me, and that was almost everyone, would bark, "Hayes didn't you get a haircut yet?" I would produce my receipt, hand them the ruler, and show them the regulation. You'd be amazed how many fell for this, especially after shouting, "Don't you quote regulations to me, I know Army regulations!" One would think that after many years in the Army they would know, but they did not.

• Seeking a discharge—

During the autumn of 1958 I read in the Army Regulations about an early discharge policy. There was a rumor that this was possible even in Europe. Farmers teachers, students, tax collectors and the like could get hardship discharges 90-to-120 days early. My goal became finding a school whose semester started about 90-to-120 days prior my discharge date, so I could qualify!

My luck held out when I applied for colleges in France and Germany and received their informational brochures. Heidelberg University started its summer semester close to the date I needed. But first I had to get accepted and enrolled, and then apply for a discharge in Germany, something the Army really did not want, or know how to do. Nobody at any level of command knew how to do that, nor could I find a single example in US Army Europe of it having been done, in spite of the rumor.

I realized that that this was going to be very tough. My exposure to languages amounted to high school Latin and French in college. My German was almost non-existent. So, I made a huge effort to teach myself. I bought a score of books and studied hard, but it still didn't seem to sink in. I couldn't really speak or read German, and did not understand much of the spoken language.

• Off to Heidelberg by train—

I made my way to Heidelberg by train without getting lost. Everyone in the Foreign Student Office there spoke English, and I was enrolled in the Interpreter institute of German-English at the lowest level. But for months my discharge application was stuck in USAREUR Headquarters because they didn't know how to proceed. I collected names and military telephone numbers of clerks like myself who worked there. I would frequently call and gently encourage them to finish my request.

Finally, my request for an early European discharge was processed and would be effective on time, and I now had just two more weeks to serve in the Army. When I left the Army, a crowd of friends gathered at the gate of the base and gave me a loud and cheerful goodbye! I walked out of the gate in Bindlach, Germany as a civilian. I also had orders that granted me a free trip from Europe back to the USA whenever I needed to use it.

By the way, I found out later when I returned from Heidelberg to visit the base that my company commander, the Captain I had butted heads with so often had been officially reprimanded, passed over for promotion, and left the US Army. Drastic!

It must have been extremely difficult to learn enough German to succeed at Heidelberg.

For me to study medicine in a foreign language that I could not speak was momentous, though my decision to attempt this was based on trivia, as I suspect most things in life are. I got a room above a bakery, and in April of 1959 went to lectures in the Interpreter's Institute along with young people from all over the world: Russians, Danes, Swedes, French, Italians, and others. The most interesting student was a South American who spoke a tribal language and nothing else! He couldn't understand anyone and, needless to say, nobody could understand him. But by the end of the semester, he was the star in German, and I was sorely struggling with the language because everybody wanted to speak to me in English. Observation: Avoid English speakers at all costs!

What did you do for recreation?

I often went to the University Foreigner's Club, a delightful social club right across from and below, the huge Castle, and a good place to pick up girls. I often watched chess games but hesitated to play. Oh, I had played on the Chess Team at St. John's, but I was sixth and last man on the third string-the weakest players.

There was a big-mouthed Egyptian that played regularly. He wasn't a good player, but he liked to brag. One day, he loudly insisted that I play with him. He knew I was an American and when I declined, he told his friends and the Germans present that the American was afraid of being whipped by an Egyptian. My face was red and my ears were burning. I retorted that I didn't want to play with him because he was loud and lacked manners and civility. By now a crowd had assembled around the table and I had no real choice; leave and I would be labeled a coward. I agreed to play then beat him in three moves. Something called Fool's Mate. I was told that he was an upperclassman in Medicine. There was hope for me!

I also had bought a bargain motorcycle and had a great time touring around.

- **Heading home—**

I notified the Army that I wanted to book my trip home and left England for New York at the end of August in 1959. I packed up my one suitcase and tied it onto the back of my motorcycle, gave a gorgeous Dane a ride on the pinion seat, and headed off to Paris to drop her off then continue to England.

On my way to Edinburgh, I overnighted in Stratford upon Avon. I couldn't afford to rent rooms for the nights, but had my army sleeping bag and air mattress and would sleep alongside the motorcycle. It rained like hell that night and I went scrambling around in the dark looking for shelter. I found something with a portico over it, and it turned out that I slept where William Shakespeare was buried; I had the upper berth and he had the lower! The local police who woke me in the morning were not amused.

What did you do after returning to America?

I got two jobs in construction within a few days of landing in New York City. One of them was on a skyscraper and paid really well. During my short breaks, I used to try to read the small anatomy book written in German and it was painfully slow. Unknown to me, several of the workers noticed this and wondered what I was doing. The shop steward on the job asked me and I told him I was a first year medical student in Germany. Shortly before I left the job I was given overtime work on the building for an entire weekend plus the holiday. This paid two times my hourly wage plus overtime and weekend/night differentials! I had to stay on the clock 24/7 to keep the many coke fires burning so the poured cement wouldn't freeze. I made more money this weekend than I did in three weeks.

I earned enough on that job to pay my way back to Germany and provide for myself for about a year. I decided to leave Heidelberg because it seemed that everybody spoke English. I transferred to the University of Freiburg in an area occupied by the French, after the war.

• Freiburg—

And you had more monumental challenges to overcome.

Yes. After one semester break but before I left New York, I tried to get Seaman's papers. Well, when I went to the Hall for Seamen, I asked what I needed to do and they said "You've got to get a job." So I went down to the docks in Manhattan and said, "I would like a job" and they said "You need to have papers". That was a typical Catch-22 and there didn't seem to be any way for me to break out of that.

However, there is more than one way to skin a cat. I happened to know a fellow whose job was to break up ships that were going to be scrapped. To make a long story short, he had letterheads from a ship that was still active on the registry but due to be broken. The Coast Guard still listed the ship as active. With the promise of a job for me on this official letterhead, they gave me Seamen's papers. On demand, my alias's could serve up 'Brick mason, airline steward, ordinary seaman, to get to get across the Atlantic, but I had no idea what to do as a seamen, so I just decided I would do as I was told. After all, I was a hard worker.

• Back and forth from Germany—

Reflecting back, how did you finance your travels back-and-forth from Germany during your college years there?

I acquired a Union Book from the Brick Masons Union. I was number 199 in the International Hod Carriers Common Laborers Union of America headquartered in Washington D.C. I had gotten that card through my father, who had a friend from Wextford, Ireland, who was politically active in the unions. I had never even looked at a brick up close in my life. I could pay the union dues of nine dollars a year because they were so minimal, and I kept the union book up for several years. With it I could go to any union hall in the city and ask for a job, and did that regularly during summer breaks from medical school.

And from observing aircraft and talking to people who worked on airlines, I discovered there were jump seats reserved for employees of airlines to be used to get to another airport to fill in. So, I made an airline identification card for Inter Ocean Airlines US, Inc. That employee card included my name, social security number, height and weight, and said I was a steward. I hadn't known what they called them but steward sounded pretty good, uptown sort of, and official. I told a local printer that I needed to pass this card on to my boss, that I'd pay him for a short run of fifty to get an affordable price, and promised to order many more in the future. He did the fifty, though I only needed one.

When I got to Freiburg I rented a room in a house where the occupants spoke no English. I identified a few English speaking Africans and two Americans, and avoided them at first.

In the beginning I read my small Anatomy handbook so slowly that it took days to get through just a few pages. I had another big problem; there was limited seating and numbers of available microscopes in Histology, the microscopic study of cells, and a necessary course for the first semester. The Germans dealt with overcrowding by requiring an examination prior to admission. I had three days to prepare but at this stage I didn't even own an Histology book. How to solve this insurmountable problem became an all engaging crisis endeavor.

I bought the book and got a brilliant idea: any exam in Histology is going to have at least one question on cell division called Mitosis. I had studied Mitosis during my biology courses at St. John's. I decided to gamble on knowing one very small area, thoroughly. It had the advantage of lots of pictures and few words. There were 12 questions. I could barely understand the instructions in German as I sat for the exam with about 150 other students, each competing for one of 75 places.

Indeed, one question was on Mitosis, so I filled my entire exam booklet with detailed pictures of the different stages of the process but wrote no text. I handed it in and waited but the results were not given out. Later, a list was put up on the bulletin board and I was on it! My detailed pictures proved that if given a chance, I could probably answer all the questions in detail. My risky plan had worked!

It must have been tough from there on in.

I caught the attention of course director Professor Dr. Hans Fischer, who was a terror. When he showed up in the dissection lab, one could hear a pin drop. The German students would actually shiver and stammer in his presence. Occasionally he would invite me into the hallway to smoke a cigarette; he was a chain smoker and had seen me smoking. The professor had learned English in an American detention camp after the war, and thankfully was treated well by the Americans.

After I barely passed one of his exams, he told me in very officious German: "Herr Hayes, it is my opinion that you are very clever and intelligent but very lazy. I am proud of our German Universities and will not permit you to return to the United States weak in training and lacking in knowledge and material, thereby giving the German Medical School a bad reputation. I will hold you to a higher standard than your German colleagues! Do you understand me?"

I understood him all too well. I thought about transferring to another University but was too stubborn to run away from a challenge. I thought, "If he thinks I am intelligent enough to outshine the German students then he must see something that I cannot. Therefore, I will bluff my way forward." From then on, I put in some serious hours studying.

• Amusing things along the way—

That sounds like college was pretty rigid and difficult. Please continue.

It was, but there were some amusing things along the way. My second attempt at bluffing in Histology went terribly wrong. We were given tissue specimens on a slide and asked to identify different structures and make a simple drawing. I was not prepared. Instead of studying, I had partied with a visiting fraternity brother from St. John's.

A few days later, Professor Fischer announced he was going to do something never done before in his teaching career. He displayed a paper on the projector, magnified about ten times. "This, meine Damen und Herren, is the worst example ever handed in by the laziest student in our Lab. He is sitting in the dark with us. I will not embarrass him by revealing his name. But, I want it known that I will not tolerate such childish attempts. Any repeat will have draconian results." I'm sure I had the reddest face of any student there, and was glowing in the dark. I was mortified and seriously shaken. I had already made a fool of myself in the dissection course by hyperventilating and almost passing out on the first quiz. This one had roots in my lack of understanding German.

But you persevered again, no doubt.

After these painful episodes I promised myself I would never again get caught short and embarrass myself. I joined a German fraternity back in Heidelberg, hoping it would help me speak the language. I went to meetings of the Freiburg chapter that were very helpful. I made some wonderful friends.

One of the Anatomy Assistant Lab instructors was a member of this Fraternity but had graduated and was referred to by the members as the 'old man'. He took me under his wing and laid out an exact and disciplined approach in identifying any histology slide.

These private lessons served me well for my entire career. I became so sharp in identifying tissue, healthy and pathological, that some semesters later, I became the-know-it-all at Goettingen University while taking laboratories in Pathological Histology. This made me very unpopular with the other students. I was on a roll but afraid I might lose momentum.

- **A bum-around semester—**

Did you lose momentum?

After successfully passing my Basic Sciences with a grade of B-plus, I had proven to myself that I could deal with the German Oral Examination system, I was headed for Paris.

I had promised myself a bum-around semester and registered at the Sorbonne University in Paris. Alas, I still had a mountain of a problem to climb. My peers told me that I would need all the free time between semesters to catch up on the material presented during the previous semester because it was simply too much to digest and learn. I might even consider adding an extra semester or two before declaring I was ready for the State Final Exam. Well, that obviated the bum-around semester and worse, it meant I would no longer be able to return to New York City in my semester breaks and work in construction.

I was almost out of money and should return to New York to work but would never be able to earn enough to carry me through to the State-Exam in this single semester break. I proved to myself that I had what it takes: the stubbornness and determination to pass the exams! However, self-doubt lingered; I could not get over the conviction that when my patient's life depended on me recalling and acting on stored medical knowledge that I would hesitate, maybe even fail, because I couldn't remember what I needed to do. This would haunt me.

My German fraternity brothers told me that for each semester a limited amount of money was available for needy students, provided they passed an exam with a grade of two, a B, or better. The supplicant student would choose a subject from his faculty, in my case, medicine and take an oral exam. I felt it unlikely that I would be awarded any of the money, since the German students were well prepared and foreigners simply did not compete in this arena.

However, I picked the subject and studied extra-hard, and asked to be examined in the appropriate institute. I figured I couldn't lose; even if I wasn't awarded any money, it meant that I had studied a subject that I was going to be examined in sometime in the future!

- **Choosing a feared medical subject—**

I threw my hat in the ring and picked the most feared medical subject, Pathology, the anatomical and physiological study of diseases. If I somehow scored high enough at this subject to win some money, I figured that my future finances would be more or less solved.

I was surprised at how long the exam took. I scored well and was awarded a small scholastic scholarship which paid my tuition and lab fees and gave me a stipend for books on a semester basis. I had to compete anew each semester. I even took advantage of it to print and publish my thesis for a Ph. D. after getting my M.D. Degree.

- **University change to Goettingen—**

Compared to Freiburg, in the middle of the Black Forest, Goettingen University was drab, colorless and boring, situated in the middle of Lower Saxony. The German students said of it that there was simply nothing else to do, but study. That sounded about right for me, and I loaded up on courses and soon got accustomed to long days of lectures and labs, and long evenings of study.

Had you figured out your main interest for a future practice yet?

Along the way, I became interested in Pediatric Cardiology and began my Ph.D. program and thesis. This endeavor bolstered my faith in myself. One does not need a Ph.D. to practice medicine. In fact, less than twenty percent of German doctors earn a Ph. D. But if one wants to stay in the university system and teach, then a Ph.D. and an M.D. are necessary for an appointment or promotion. I was actually thinking about remaining in the German University system and teaching! However, after spending some time as an upper-classman in several University clinics, I became convinced that I didn't want to compete in this arena. The internal politics seemed more important than competency.

It was getting close to the State Exams and I had to decide whether to stay in Goettingen or return to Freiburg. I chose Freiburg, where I could take wonderful walks along the small Dreisam River or into the Black Forest. The German professors were brutal in these exams and openly said: "Don't waste our time by showing up for the exam without a mastery of your subject." The German state exam took two-thirds of a year. Any subject matter from the 1st to the final semester was fair game. It was grueling. I have never been so frightened nor so intimidated in my life. All exams were oral, practical and thorough.

I passed my State exams with an average grade of B+.

What came next?

After my State Exams, I went back Goettingen University and completed my thesis. A funny thing happened during my exam for this. Part of the requirement is proficiency in languages, and I could choose the two languages to demonstrate this. I had two examiners. One language I had to prove fluency in, and the other only a reading familiarity. I chose French for the latter.

English was a foreign language in Germany so I chose English. But I almost outsmarted myself. The two professors who examined me in English were very fluent but my knowledge was stored in German and I had to translate that into English! This proved actually more difficult than regurgitating the material in German.

Finally I had to dig up enough money to pay for the lithography, printing and dissemination of my thesis, and again I got help from the scholarship fund.

- **From Freiburg to Madison, Wisconsin—**

Tell me about the beginning of your time in Madison.

I packed up my things in Freiburg but didn't stay for the official graduation, then drove to Rotterdam. I was almost out of money and had already booked an internship at Madison General Hospital in Madison, Wisconsin. I cried that evening in Rotterdam; I somehow knew that the finest time of my life had just ended. I can confirm that as my life winds down, this had been a marvelous, challenging and rewarding time of life, full of hope, adventure, unknowns, wonder and discovery.

My time in Madison was educational, but in a different sense. Compared to my fellow American interns, I was way out in front. I often had to translate in my head my medical knowledge from German to English, with the result that I spoke strange English. I was asked again and again where I learned to speak such good English! And when I answered "Brooklyn," the incredulous looks I received were something to behold.

Usually an intern asks a department head to consider him for a residency towards the completion of the Intern year, but I was offered, without asking, a residency in Pathology, Surgery, Radiology and Obstetrics -Gynecology about half-way through my year. Professor Hans Fischer would have been proud! As I progressed through one service after another I found a common personal thread of disappointment, namely that the individual services were too confining. I wasn't comfortable narrowing my scope to just cut-and-sew in surgery, or to just stare at films all day in Radiology and so on, so I put off all choices of a residency program. I passed the Wisconsin State Board Licensing Medical Exam with marks so high I was embarrassed. Compared to German exams, these were downright childish.

As part of our training, we interns would work in the Emergency Room, especially on weekends. I took a special liking to this duty, found it exciting, stimulating and challenging, and frightening.

If you remember my base fear of forgetting what to do when my patient's life depended on quick action, you can imagine the thrill of being in the very place this fear was likely to play out. I volunteered for extra shifts in the ER, and asked to do one of two optional weeks of training there. The chairman of the Intern Educational committee said he had never had such a request. It took months but was approved. The whole hospital talked about this weird German, English-speaking doctor who volunteered for the ER. Most physicians hated the ER, it was so unpredictable, chaotic and difficult, the opposite of the controlled, calm and prepared surgical operating theater or sedate internal medical station.

- **Choosing emergency medicine—**

Please give me an overview of how and why you chose emergency medicine for your medical career.

Okay. My internship was at Madison General Hospital in Madison Wisconsin, completed in April of 1966, and at that point I had a very odd idea of how medical emergencies were handled. The University of Wisconsin in Madison was a very impressive organization, and its medical school was well thought of in every sphere. But the routine staffing of emergency was very curious.

I had the occasion to moonlight, as we interns used to call it, in the emergency rooms of St. Mary's hospital, and also at Madison General, picking up shifts that were vacated by others, and that was an eye-opening experience.

In what way was it curious?

Basically this was the way it ran: The emergency room was a place that, for a lack of a better word, anything red, meaning bleeding, or broken was brought in from the outside by any conveyance, but usually by ambulances who drove second-hand hearses with a big red cross hand painted on it, and whose attendees were either down-and-outers, or in many cases people who had taken the job because they didn't last at their previous job.

They had no training, so they drove at breakneck speeds, loaded whoever they scooped up off the highway onto a gurney like a sack of potatoes then brought them to the emergency room. They gave no information, except the obvious comment that it was from an auto accident, or during a fight that the patient was wounded. Then they would tear out at breakneck speed to go somewhere else. Sad to say, in many cases the patient had been robbed of watches or rings and things like that.

This was poignant because inevitably the emergency staff was blamed when the patient realized they were minus their wedding or engagement ring, or a watch, or what have you, or if their wallet was lighter. That was most frustrating.

Was emergency medicine always so difficult in those days?

The staffing of the emergency rooms in a university hospital setting was good, and that was the model template for what was going on in the entire United States. It was good because you had interns who were the first line of defense, and on call 24/7. Secondly, you had residents in just about every specialty, and certainly in the major specialties such as OBGYN, surgery, internal medicine and pediatric medicine. These residents were always on call or present, so when the nurse downstairs got an accident victim or a patient with a complaint, she guessed who the appropriate person was to call on.

However, here it gets kind of flaky. One of the staff members was always on call, and as an officially licensed doctor in the state, board certified, he was in charge and most of the time he was chosen alphabetically. Now you have to imagine this, these are people with advanced degrees who were alphabetically chosen to be in charge. So Dr. Abel, who may be a gynecologist, might be called in to treat a ruptured spleen, or a pediatrician called in to see a geriatric stroke patient. It defied imagination.

- **Complex politics—**

Did you object to this and try to make changes in that selection procedure?

Well, the politics of it were very complex. In many cases, people without insurance or ability to pay just showed up at the ER. So did people who first made a call to a doctor's office and weren't exactly welcomed but were referred to the emergency room.

The medial politics got all diced up because the general surgeons wanted all things that bled, the orthopedists wanted all the bones that were broken, the pediatricians wanted all of the diaper set, etc.

The specialists didn't want to be on call for each one of these areas, so to make it easy for the entire staff the executive committee created a master list of doctors who would be all wise, who would be licensed to practice medicine and surgery, and would be able to decide what to do with the cases presented. It sounds reasonable, but in fact it was absurd; Dr. Able who was on call could say, "Sorry, I don't see pediatric or surgical patients. So and so sees those patients, call him."

How did the nurses handle all of that?

Just picture the poor nurse with somebody who is bleeding. She had to first call our fictitious Dr. Able, and might have to chase him down, and this is during the days when there were only fixed land telephones. Say she finally locates him at the country club, and when he finally comes to the phone maybe twenty minutes have passed, and he says "I don't see surgical cases, Dr. Baker sees them." Well, just where is Dr. Baker she wonders?

Next she tries to find Dr. Baker, who may not even be in town. When she does find him but he might say, "I'd come but I don't have hospital privileges there. I do see Dr. Able's patients but only at St. Mary's, not at Madison General." So she is back to square one, and this charade would play out *ad infinitum*, dealing with one doctor's excuse after another.

The University systems in all forty-eight states were so much better in that the appropriate chief resident could intervene and would either come down or order his intern to make an initial assessment. Patients in critical need of immediate care got immediate care, not put at the end of a telephone circus. This was not the case at community hospitals.

- **Dealing with problems—**

This was very clearly a big problem because the organization was simply not there. But the knowledge was there, the know-how was there, and the training was there, and that was all wonderful. But there was a glaring mismatch.

And it was an exciting place to work because you got the immediate satisfaction of seeing patients in acute situations. That didn't happen in hospital settings where the patient has been worked up and in bed with IV's already started, maybe scheduled for surgery or other treatment. That is generally not during the first couple of hours of an illness, so the doctor is not as challenged. In emergency medicine, we get to see the patient first and are challenged with making a rapid diagnosis.

This was the one arena for young, inexperienced doctors, post internship, to be exposed to the initial presentation of medical or surgical problems. I quickly developed a keen interest in the emergency service for what it was at that time, and this was a marvelous place not only to get experience but to be challenged, which was something that I generally enjoyed.

Another real problem at a later stage was the way medical knowledge was taught and then practiced. It was dealt with vertically, in that you took a specialty and drilled down vertically, getting ever smaller and exact until you became not only a specialist, but a super-specialist. These exacting, specialties are excellent, and where true knowledge and craftsmanship comes from. However, patients don't generally present with drilled down problems; they present with general things as 'belly pain'. This complaint covers everything from constipation, ruptured peptic ulcer, appendicitis, tubal pregnancy, gall bladder infection, sickle cell crisis-to name a few. In other words, the proper evaluation demands across the board thinking if you will; a horizontal approach.

Are you saying that a specialist may have limited knowledge of treatments needed to treat a patient?

Consider, post internship, a young doctor might do a three-to-four year stint in an internal medicine program, followed by another few years studying invasive cardiology. He would be magnificent if he were present in the ER when a complicated cardiac patient arrived, but less than effective for an acute abdomen, precipitous labor or fractured bones. His onetime knowledge of these areas is dated and not so easily recalled.

- **Elements of truth—**

But there are elements of truth in that, right?

Yes, there are. And here is another very curious thing: In every specialty there are emergencies but not that many. For example, ophthalmologists are certainly the best choice for ocular emergencies. However, if you take a town with five ophthalmology practices each might see some portion of all the ocular emergencies. Let's say twenty percent, since they only see patients during business hours. That leaves a much larger percentage of all ocular emergencies which will present to the ER for evaluation and treatment because he is available 24/7.

That is true with the other specialty practices, too. Now that is not saying that the emergency room doctor is going to do complicated eye surgery. He is neither qualified nor inclined to do it. But when a patient comes in with an ocular emergency, to preserve his vision the ER physician must take the right steps, start proper treatment, be timely, mobilize the surgical unit, and directly discuss the case with an ophthalmologist. That is the way it should be run, and time is of the essence.

Of course that is the definition of an emergency; if it could wait then it wouldn't be one. My point is that there are medical emergencies, though not that many in every discipline such as gynecology, obstetrics, surgery, cardiology , and others.

What if you could train a doctor post internship to evaluate and treat the finite number of emergencies in all of the specialties and sub-specialties? In other words, use a horizontal approach to training. He could be point person on the front line where the vertically trained specialists don't want to be, unless the problem is within their field. This would save lives and prevent needless, further unnecessary damage, loss of limb, or of function.

And that basically is what the goal was for people who gravitated towards the emergency field, as I did starting back in 1966.

- **An early commitment—**

So you became committed to emergency medicine very early in your career.

Yes, within a few years, at first simply because it was a good area, and also because I felt I was not yet equipped to do what I needed to do in medicine. Let me give you an example: I left Madison, Wisconsin and found myself in Washington State where I met a doctor who organized a team working fulltime in the ER's at two hospitals in Tacoma. He was hiring for his group and asked if I was interested.

At first I couldn't believe it, as my only experience had been in a university hospital in Madison, which I described earlier. The working shifts were twenty-four hours on duty and three days off. We had a call room, adjacent to the ER for privacy got meals in the hospital cafeteria. When patients showed up, we did what we could for them. We had to deal with on-call doctors who would snarl at us and didn't like being called. The nurses did their share of snarling too, I can tell you.

Basically we were just turned loose to deal with whoever came through the door. We did a lot of improvising. It wasn't ideal but it was a start.

- **Memorable medical experiences—**

You must have had many memorable experiences dealing with medical emergencies.

One frustrating and frightening experience I had within my first couple of months there was the drug overdose of a twenty-two-year-old male who was slightly blue when I got him, which means he had stopped breathing. In those days someone from the drug community would drive overdose victims to the emergency room entrance, blare the horn, flash the lights, then literally dump them out while still rolling and then take off so as not to be implicated. The man was getting bluer by the second, but I had no intubation equipment and worse, I didn't know how to use it! I had no training in intubation, because only anesthesiologists did that. My brain flashed with big red lights: "I need to learn how to control any airway!"

There was another option, to do a tracheotomy, but I had never done one, although I had fixed in my memory how to do it. This is one of those things that you don't have time to look up, so I made a neck incision, avoided all of the major blood vessels, cut an opening on the trachea, and asked the nurse for a tracheal tube and inserted it in the patient, and using an Ambu-Bag, forced air into his lungs. The patient soon began to turn a little pink. I asked the nurse for the remainder of the hook up and the rest of the paraphernalia to be connected to a breathing machine. But amazingly they were not available, and not to be found. There was a mad race to locate these missing parts.

The upshot to all of this was that the young man died. I almost cried and said when I walked out, "I am not going to put up with this; it is a blow that I will never ever forget." Then I talked to the doctor who hired me and he said, "Why don't you make up a list of equipment you think we need? And write up a protocol that all of us can use."

The idea that we were working there twenty-four hours a day and nobody had come up with that suggestion before, that nobody had seen to it that we had the necessary tools and training, slapped me hard across the face. It was incredulous. I left that shift really depressed and desperate and vowed, "This has to change!"

- **Learning leads to solutions—**

Soon, for that particular hospital and its sister hospital across town, the ability to directly and immediately intervene in respiratory failure was solved when I asked the anesthesiologists to tell us what we needed to do, and to provide the list of drugs that would sedate or temporarily paralyze a patient, and what tubes we needed for adults and infants. We learned to use a laryngoscope, pediatric and adult, either straight or curved blades, for different anatomical variants. At least now we had the correct hardware there.

The doctors in this group changed our shift times so that when we got off each morning at seven we could just walk across the hall into anesthesia, and practice. It was a wonderful experience. The anesthesiologists were glad to help, and to teach.. They permitted us to intubate the surgical patients that were lined up and ready to go to the operating room. We paralyzed then intubated them under their watchful eyes and tutelage.

That must have been a crucial learning experience.

Indeed, and they were right there should it go too slowly or awkwardly. The patients were sedated, paralyzed, and not able to breathe on their own. They were readied for surgery. We would do six or seven intubations from say seven to nine a.m. Now that ate into my sleep time, but it was worth it.

From that experience I quickly learned that with the proper training, support and teaching from the medical staff, we really could do this. That was a big bonus. At least now I if I faced a situation that went terribly wrong, I had a potent skill that could buy a lot of time.

There was nobody in charge when that young man I told you about died, and there was wide outrage in the hospital. I made sure, and so did the other doctors in the ER, that everybody knew there had been failure on every level. The equipment that was there to deal with the emergency had not been recently checked or had been misplaced or was not complete or didn't match; it was just a piece of this and a piece of that. They had gone through the motions only.

That was drastically wrong and I knew it had to change.

• Changes in the system—

What came next after that critical period?

That was the beginning, at least in Washington State, of a move to upgrade our services, but at that time in my mind's eye it was very local. In the rest of the state, even at the University of Seattle, they stayed the way they had been forever. That was about 1968.

Then in 1967, if I am not mistaken, I read a small medical journal article that said a group of physicians interested in emergency care were going to hold a meeting about it. When they planned a second meeting in Florida on the Gulf Coast to discuss the feasibility of organizing a group to formulate national standards for dealing with emergency care, I got so excited that I could hardly contain myself. I made sure to attend that meeting. There were nineteen physicians present from Virginia, Michigan, Ohio, California and Texas; I was the only one from Washington State.

This group was audacious enough to suggest that we had a nucleus big enough to change the entire landscape! Honestly, I dare to dream big, but I never dreamt that big. I would have been happy to see the design of organized courses result from the meeting, but these fellows wanted to organize and control all emergency services at the local level so they dare not be offered unless expertly performed.

At first I shook my head in disbelief at this giant headache, believing that it was not going to happen, at least not immediately. I had an idea about what our local politics were, and I could hear the screams from everybody three- thousand miles away at this suggestion, but that was only one part.

Number two, we were going to change medical school curricula. That seemed preposterous to me because those peacocks were locked into a vertical oriented knowledge system and were not going to yield an inch; every one of them wanted to hold onto their turf. I thought this was a pipe dream.

Number three was to recommend starting a residency program for emergency medicine, post medical school and internship. But first they would have to deal with the overriding national organization that enforces standards for post medical graduate school training, including internships and residencies. It just all sounded too good to be true. Then at the end of this meeting someone said, "By the way, we have to do something about ambulance services too, it is our weakest link!"

The amazing thing that became apparent from the small talk was that all of our problems were basically the same. I now had an inkling of what doctors from small and big hospitals from many states faced. I could have told any one of their stories and they could have told me my story. We all had the same worries and concerns, we all had the same experiences and we all had the same thought: "This can't go on like this, we have to change it." It was really uncanny; you have never seen more unanimity from a bunch of disparate doctors than this.

What was the net result for you?

Because I was from the northwest they said, "Hayes, we're putting you down to cover Washington State, Idaho and Oregon, and since California is engaged in internecine fighting, please take Northern California, and British Columbia didn't show up but is interested." I was now to be supposedly responsible for all of these states and I said, "You've got to be joking." They were not joking.

When I got back into the plane I hyperventilated all the way back to Tacoma, and when I got off of the plane my fingers were tingling and my lips were numb and I wondered, "How am I going to do this?, it is impossible."

- **Curious help in the beginning—**

Very quickly after that we identified our problem: vertical medical school teaching might be excellent for specialty training but we needed horizontal training so we could identify, isolate and catalog emergencies in all of the specialties. We said to the medical schools, "You need to teach this as part of the individual specialties."

We had curious help in the beginning. It was noted before that the blue signs with a big blue H on the highways guided the unknowing public to a hospital, presumably prepared for an emergency in one shape or another. But, small hospitals were often closed at night or on weekends, and in even more cases only had one general practitioner to take care of this or that, but could not take care of someone scraped-up, broken-up, from the highway and brought to the hospital. Help came from the Department of Transportation that sent someone to Seattle to talk with me and several other doctors. They had also met with doctors in Virginia and Michigan. "What is your sense of this?" he asked.

"I think it is absurd, and that the DOT is liable," I said. "I am not a lawyer, but if you put a sign directing the public to the hospital and you do it willy-nilly and there nobody is there when someone shows up with a heart attack, there is an issue of liability. He said "Exactly! that's exactly what I think too."

We batted this around a little bit, and he went back to Washington, DC and in short order the DOT started reviewing who gets a blue sign directing people from the highways to the hospitals, and whether there should be strings attached to that. This caught the attention of hospital administrators nationwide. There was nothing finer than that, as far as we were concerned, because now all hospital administrators from the small Hill-Burton, seventy-five bed hospitals all the way up to University hospitals understood that the Department of Transportation was looking at the signs that directed traffic to their hospital.

Also, the Department of Army Research Projects Administration was also interested in this movement. DARPA had its fingers in many pies, but one of the many things they were keenly interested in was mobilization on a State and nationwide basis. As a fledgling state national organization, we showed big on their radar. DARPA had money, political clout and were investing in things like ship-to-shore radios for emergencies, and isolated, reserved special radio frequencies on land. They were aiming at mobilization-coordination during a nuclear strike or a hurricane etc.

But their plans were conflicted and not workable. We suggested laying out a template to codify a standardized emergency plan where we would have community emergency response teams, not by whoever happened to be there that day, but by people that actually can do it, the emergency doctors. We planned to unify it all, and also include the ambulance industry. DARPA was impressed, and agreed it should be done on a State and National basis, which of course didn't exist at that time. DOT and DARPA not only encouraged us, but gave us future names to use. And that was the very heady beginning of emergency medicine in 1967 and 1968.

- **Dealing with ambulance services—**

In Washington State the ambulance service was particularly bad in the three or four different communities I worked in. In a word, they were atrocious. Routinely there were accidents with victims who then became victims a second time because of dangerous practices and unsafe driving in ill equipped vehicles. Some even leaked carbon monoxide in a rusted-out rear compartment.

I testified to the State Senate and House about what was needed to upgrade ambulance services, that had no quality control. The State routinely granted licenses to ambulances almost the way they did for taxis, conferring an operating medallion when they qualified. But the medallion owner could keep it forever or sell it to somebody else, and many unsavory characters owned these things. I was up against a lot of resistance, a lot of foot dragging, a lot of local politics that I didn't quite understand, and I wasn't making very much headway. But the broken ambulance service itself came to my rescue.

One man called an ambulance in the outskirts of Bellingham where there were two services that were rivals. Well, one just drove up and parked while the other came screaming around the corner. The driver saw his competitor going to get the patient, so he drove up on the sidewalk, knocked over trash barrels then onto the lawn, and tried to run into the house to get the patient first. Well, the first driver, not to be outdone, jumped out of his ambulance with a pistol, threatened the other driver, and actually fired a shot in the air.

As chance would have it, a reporter, who was perhaps an ambulance chaser, was on the scene and the story hit the newspapers. At my next meeting in Olympia, Washington before the Senate Health and Welfare Committee, I had copies of that newspaper article and said: "In case you haven't read the *Bellingham Herald*, this is what our ambulance service is like."

That was all I needed, and the ambulance laws were changed in Washington. Ambulances were licensed pending qualifying by examinations and approved by the County Emergency Services Administration.

That was a significant change to the system; how did it work out?

Fantastic! The two ambulance services lost their ability to transfer patients unless they had further training and passed exams. We were very busy finishing course material and formulating a syllabus. This was a brand new concept that was immediately criticized by an organization that everybody looks at as being very benign, the American Red Cross. We threatened to steal their thunder!

Explain that, please.

The American Red Cross taught the public something called resuscitation. It was pure hokum, nonsensical physical actions that had no basis in reality, physiology, or medical research. For example, they taught rescuers to put drowning-victims on their backs, tie their arms back then flop them like a bird. They did all sorts of silly things, lots of busy work, but it was proven futile, dangerous and wrong, and moreover it never worked. They insisted that they knew better because they wrote the book on it. Those drowning-victims are probably dead because the book was written wrong.

We started doing mouth-to-mouth resuscitation and chest compressions and already planned to teach tracheal intubation to be done in the field. The American Red Cross for at least two years, maybe longer, still put out their little booklets on how to deal with a person who wasn't breathing, that was flat out a guaranteed failure. They continued to train people and give them a certificate in emergency management.

- **Repeated across the country—**

Was your Washington State ambulance program the first one?

My experience in reforming ambulance service in Washington State was close to being the first. The first EMT course given in Washington was in Skagit Valley hospital, a small hospital that my group provided coverage for. Nationally, we each formed an emergency medical services organization in our own state.

I started it in Washington State and it grew in Michigan and Virginia and so on. This began to really take hold only two years after our group was founded, and it soon spread to the West and East coasts and was quickly repeated across the United States.

We had to tackle training the ambulance personnel, and we offered courses and wrote up a syllabus of requirements. Along with a half-dozen other doctors, I taught the first courses to emergency medical technicians, or, EMT's. We coined that term, as there was no such thing at that time as an Emergency Medical Technician. About half-dozen participants passed the examination and were certified to staff ambulances. In short order, I would say a year or so, the first medical emergency booklet was approved, refined and added to over time.

I am unsure if Virginia or Washington State or Michigan can actually claim prime position for giving the first emergency services training, I never looked into that. But this was never a race to be first, this was a race to get it right, and on solid footing.

Eight or nine months after that initial meeting in Florida, we held board meetings in Michigan and formalized the organization with by-laws and so on. We called it the American College of Emergency Physicians, which actually had been the name of the organization previously formed in Western Florida. We had enough signatures to draw up the various goals for physicians. It is not often that a simple thought, very simple, becomes earth-moving, in my experience.

Earth-moving is quite a characterization.

These were simple thoughts that germinated and grew, but within a year and a half of forming the American College of Emergency Physicians we were still basically unknown, though we were doing good work. If you can, picture an organization calling itself national that is hardly known in most of the United States. In fact, we were known among select physicians interested in the deal, and we were known by DARPA and the DOT, but we didn't have any deep penetration.

- **Emergency Department Nurses Association—**

This emergency area was really taking root. What came next?

Here is a key thought that came next, but I don't remember from which doctor: "We need to bring the nurses to our side!"

There was silence until another doctor piped up and said, "That is the best idea I've heard ever" then added, "Wait a minute, we'll form a group and sponsor it: The Emergency Department Nurses Association!" That is how EDNA was formed. The American College of Emergency Physicians organized and supported it.

You can imagine in any community, big or small, the first emergency contact you will have is with an ambulance driver and the second one is with a nurse. The nurse examines you, gets vital information like current medications etc. She shows empathy, control and confidence. The D in EDNA is very important, because an emergency room belongs and exists for whom: perhaps to the administration. However, a department inserted into the structure of the hospital and staff of physicians is less subject to the whim or politics of either. It can suggest its own operating rules, and its own qualification rules.

One couldn't show up at a hospital executive committee meeting without departmental privileges, but you could show up at a general meeting after all of the decisions were made. So who was responsible for the emergency rooms? It used to be said that because a lot of bleeding is encountered, the surgeons should be responsible; but there are heart attacks, diabetic comas, head injuries, tubal pregnancies and so on, and they don't quite fit into that mold. The problem was at the core of practicing medicine.

How was this resolved?

We demanded that hospitals change their by-laws, and they now include a fully staffed Emergency Department whose chief would have the same privileges as the chiefs in anesthesia, surgery, pediatrics, internal medicine, OBGYN and so on.

Medical staffs did not like it very much, and the surgeons and the orthopedists resisted it, but we would not work as a group in a hospital that did not have, or be willing to create, an Emergency Department. Nor we would work in their emergency rooms. Without physician staffing, physically present that is, 24/7, the hospital could lose its highway blue H sign!

Once we had our department, the nurses were spurred to say, "We want special education to work in that department, the physicians are getting special education, we need it too." We had ignited them to upgrade their skills and to take more courses to work in the emergency. They didn't want to be taken off the floor in pediatrics or some other place and be sent to the emergency not knowing anything. They wanted to have the necessary nursing skills, and they also eventually wanted pay for doing this Saturday and Sunday night work and so forth. I was told that in those days it was not unusual to punish a nurse who skirted some rule or other, by assigning her to the emergency room for a month or so.

- **The first EDNA meeting—**

We hosted the nurses at our meeting. It promised to be so big that the only convention sites in the country that could handle a combined ACEP with the nurses was in Vegas. The first meeting of EDNA was held in Las Vegas in 1970, and about 700 or 800 nurses showed up. A lot of them were interested in forming the nucleus, and by golly, they were well organized and immediately organized themselves. We gave them a bit of a template to work from and they took it and ran with it and never looked back. They organized themselves faster than we ever could, and then blazed right across the hospitals in the United States.

Has the Department of Nurses Association been successful?

Wildly so, yes! Nurses no longer work in the Emergency Department unless they have taken and passed the necessary courses. EDNA really took off and then broke from ACEP because they had issues that were not germane to us and these prolonged our national meetings. We had also had physician issues that were also not a concern to the nurses. Today, I understand that they have changed their name but not their mission.

Was it a mutual parting of the ways?

Oh yes. They simply outgrew us. Initially they needed us to organize their meetings, and they trained side by side with us, asking what they needed from a nurse's standpoint and so on. But it became obvious that nurses needed to train other nurses, not doctors training nurses, although we did work together. Their issues were not the same as ours, and that was a healthy difference.

- **Solving the ambulance problem—**

Were the ambulance problems resolved at this point?

We were still running up against the ambulance problems. We were training these guys in the emergency medical emergency services, let's call them civilians, but then they would leave and we'd have to train another crew, but then they left. It was becoming taxing to train people who would not stay around, and the community was losing its resources as quickly as it was getting them.

This was happening all over, training lots of people who then went on to greener pastures. It had become a significant problem.

What was your solution?

We held another board meeting in Michigan where we discussed trying to stabilize ambulance services. Illinois had a police department that usually showed up at the scene of a shooting or wherever there was bloody trauma, including on highways. That state had police ambulances.

But firemen had a few things in their favor, and number one was they already were organized very well locally and on a national scale. This was in addition to being seen as more benign by the public.

This discussion is obviously igniting meaningful memories from your career. Tell me more about the firemen.

The firemen operate on a national scale through The Fire Chiefs of America. On a state scale, the chiefs already had effective organizations, and they were already talking to each other. If the volunteer firemen want to be certified in their state, they have to follow regulations established by the chiefs. A little known fact is that firemen train all the time, and after about five years the overwhelming odds are that a fireman will become a lifer, good for thirty years.

When the fire chiefs shared that statistic with us, it was music to our ears, because we now had a group that was already basically trained and stable, committed to long term service. As a bonus, they didn't carry guns, something that spooked their potential victims.

So we started at the national level then worked down into their brother/sister organizations from state to state. We asked, "How would you like it if we trained your firemen?" and they all answered, "We'd love it." This endeavor went as fast with the firemen as it had with the nurses.

- **Two simple ideas that took off—**

So those were two simple ideas that took off with the speed of light, almost. I mean we were breathless, after successfully organizing the nurses then the fire chiefs. And the public loved it that both the nurses and firemen were now better organized to take care of them during emergencies, with trained emergency doctors to serve patients on the receiving end.

DARPA came in and started installing radios so we could talk to the fire wagons that they now had. In no time at all, EKG's were transmitted from the field to the Emergency Department electronically. And by the way, the EMT trucks you see on the road now were basically designed and equipped and approved and all of the rest of it through the American College of Emergency Physicians. We gave them guidance as to how fast they should drive, when it was appropriate to put on the siren and the lights etc.- not just to go on a coffee & donut run.

Was there pretty unanimous acceptance of all this change?

There was a really beautiful meeting of the minds in many hospitals. And EMTs, and later Paramedics, were now especially well-trained by our courses, and then they trained each other, and maybe administered exams and studied the syllabus, all with our approval. We sort of functioned as quality-control, away from the nitty-gritty day-to-day operations. Even the approvals were done on a statewide basis, so we've moved out of that. We continue today to serve as a resource and to evaluate if what they are doing is effective or not.

We looked at this marriage of services then asked, "What does an EMT or a paramedic do on slow days when things aren't happening and he wants to keep his skills fresh?" The answer was he should go to the emergency department and work side by side with a nurse who will be glad to have an extra pair of hands; and he wisely will bring donuts to her for that hands-on training. To help her, he will lift patients and generally be helpful with everything, like taking blood pressures, and he will carefully watch what is happening. Then the trainee watches and learns from the doctor whenever he intervenes.

- **No community too small—**

We put this thing together so that one hand washes the other and shakes the other, and we literally developed a community of service. No community in the United States is too small to have this if they have a hospital and a fire department, even a volunteer one. And, they all have a model that can be approved to send their people to get training and become certified. It will operate anywhere, though maybe not as good as in the middle of Boston, but certainly up to a high standard, otherwise they are not allowed to operate at all.

A word comes to mind that seems to describe what helped you accomplish all this: synergy.

Yes, synergy, yes indeed. And some of it, I have to admit just happened. We never foresaw it all working and meshing this closely together, but it soon became obvious that it was going to happen. It was contagious because of the inherent good it derived from everybody to help everybody.

- **Capsulizing a career—**

You were a pioneer in the organization and training of emergency physicians and nurses, firemen and ambulance services, all significant contributions to medicine and our society. Tell me more history of your work in these areas.

This was not done on a linear timeline. One of my early battle cries was, "We emergency doctors need to be trained, and not only that, we need to be qualified and certified." But the question arose: who was going to do it? This was a contentious issue for physicians that practiced in the so-called emergency rooms prior to them earning departmental status. We wondered how to present this to medical schools, and if they would they buy into it. The short answer was no, no, then no again; they wouldn't buy it and probably wouldn't even listen to us.

Did you find a way forward?

The American College of Emergency Physicians decided to have board examinations, which meant that if you passed the exams you would be board-certified. But this seemed like an organization awarding its janitors a Ph.D., it wouldn't mean very much, and this was an obvious problem. We had to find a higher organization that could engage with university medical graduates and post-graduates able to add credibility to our examination. There existed an over-arching group called something like "University Association of Medical Examiners". This national group of medical educators approved or not, medical specialty examinations. Pretty much all the medical specialties submitted their proposed curricula and examinations to it for critique and endorsement.

Then up stepped a medical school in Ohio that now would offer medical graduates a two-year course in Emergency Medicine, and that was the beginning, the crack in the wall. That was followed within a year by several more medical schools, and over the years their numbers have increased. Interestingly, one of the premier teaching institutions in America, namely Massachusetts General Hospital, does not offer this program to this day. They apparently have, I say tongue-in-cheek, internecine rivalries much too strong to permit encroaching on the fields of surgery and cardiology and others. But for the rest of us, Ohio became the model.

So now the emergency physicians had residencies, and we were graduating young doctors who could be certified, provided they passed the Board exam. The examination was quite difficult, and one didn't progress to the practical part until he passed the written. The first practical examinations employed actors and actresses to help, and this was ingenious, to say the least.

- **Grandfathering in—**

I have to diverge a little bit here. While we, in ACEP were still at the talking stage about all of this I opened my big mouth and addressed the problem of grandfathering in.

There then was a motion on the floor to do just that: grandfather in all current practitioners in the emergency medicine, meaning us, the old guys.

I wasn't so old at the time, but that just stuck in my throat because it seemed to me to be a do as I say thing, not do as I do. We would be diminishing the very standards we were arguing so passionately for. So I gave an impassioned speech on the floor of the national ACEP meeting saying that I didn't think that it would be right to grandfather us in because it would cheapen the value of the credentialing, because we had insisted that nurses, EMT's and paramedics pass credentialing exams while exempting ourselves!

They agreed. For my big mouth, I now had to pass this ding-dong examination myself, and that wasn't easy. The failure rate among us 'retreads', as we called each other, was over seventy-five percent! I had to take part-one twice and part-two twice. No good deed goes unpunished!

Man, it was tough!

Who established the curriculum?

Well, the way things worked was that the ACEP suggested the exam material, and it was formulated by the doctors, since we were the pioneers and nobody else knew what was really going on in the emergency rooms. We collected information on cases, and whatever else we needed from many emergency departments and that became the emphasis for the examination. There was no sense in examining things one is never going to see, esoteric things that lead to, "Gotcha, you didn't know that!" We used things that would actually be dealt with, including minutia that was important to making critical diagnoses in any of the specialties that I mentioned before.

ACEP had outside help from people who regularly create medical exams, and the final one was presented to universities with medical post-graduates for approval. If it looked sufficiently professional and appropriate then it was approved, and if not, suggestions were made. Our organization then presented and proctored the examination in-house. But if it was approved by a higher organization they conferred the specialty status. They not only conferred it in ACEP, but also in the medical schools, so the entire circle was completed.

The doctors had various and sundry backgrounds then became specialists in emergency medicine. The loop was now closed. From point of contact in the field, to the Emergency Department, the patient could now expect professional, accredited medical attention. Not only that, but these critical skills were regularly updated and refreshed. The nurses were doing it, the EMTs followed and ACEP required certain numbers of post-graduate continuing medical education courses to remain an active member.

In addition, the very critical areas of disturbances of cardiac rhythms and trauma had their own certificates, ACLS for Advanced Cardiac Life Support, and ATLS for Advanced Trauma Life Support. These demanded laboratory work, and the certificates were gained only by exams that became obsolete after a given amount of time and would need to be renewed. Control for this was given to the hospital administration and the staff physicians.

I was and am very proud about of it all, especially that we did not exonerate ourselves from the specialty examination and on-going medical education.

How different was that exam then than it is today?

That was in 1975, and it remains quite difficult. I understand there is still a high failure rate, which tells me the examination is appropriate. Remember, I took four of them and it took me twice to pass each part and I am not accustomed to failing examinations!

The author of the book titled Emergency Medicine that we all still use is quite sick but still alive, at the time of this writing. He also had to take part-two twice himself. He joked with me at the time, " I told them I wrote the book" "I even offered them a bribe but they turned me down."

I looked at him and said, "Now I don't feel so alone." I already had grey hair at that time, and here I was taking the exam a second time.

- **Hands-on through the years—**

What was your hand- on involvement with the organization through the years?

I spent a lot of time in organizing. I founded and inaugurated the ACEP College for Emergency Physicians Washington Chapter. The administration in the beginning, you have to understand, was extremely important. Without a structure and a responsible and dependable group, nothing would progress. I spent most of my efforts early-on forming, steering and managing the fledgling.

Our group had to entice just about every specialty in organized medicine to advise and where necessary to train us in every critical pathway in their respective field. This was unprecedented and in many cases stubbornly resisted. As an example, we scheduled workshops with plastic surgeons to outline best practices when repairing faces and eye lids, noses and lips on patients who had gone through the windshield.

There are so many types of procedures that require lots of little tricks, nuggets of information about doing it just so, for the best results.

Wasn't that about the time you were recruited back into the Army reserve?

Yes. Against all odds, I was recruited back into the Army Reserve as a commissioned officer. As a Major, my rank equaled that of the Executive Officer of my old unit, and in a few months as a Lieutenant Colonel, it equaled that of the Battalion Commanding Officer.

I was in a specialty where we tend to move around a lot, and found myself at an Army Reserve General Hospital in Texas. While there, I was promoted to Colonel. It was unbelievable to me that I now outranked everyone in the Second Armored Cavalry battalion, the unit I had served with as a PFC in Germany. I found that it is much easier to serve in the Army as a Colonel than as a Private.

I was activated when hostilities broke out in Bosnia and sent to Heidelberg, Germany and was put in charge of Emergency Services at the military hospital there. This was located where I had once occupied student-digs. But that was only for just a few months; then I found myself back in Texas.

- **A critique of current health care—**

Returning to a question about civilian medicine, what is your opinion of health care today?

I see health care in the United States at a precipice. Just as farming became agri-business, medicine is poised to be transmuted into a mongrelized service that will primarily serve big conglomerate business. I do not say this lightly, but the national voice has even been hijacked.

I note that the nation says it needs affordable health insurance. Of course it does not! The nation needs universal, affordable health services. Insurance companies bring nothing to this table! They merely serve as the man in the middle gaming the providers and the patients alike as they look to their bottom line.

Big Pharmacy is another threat. Today they shamelessly serve and enrich themselves only. Their main goal seems to be to gouge the public.

I point to an article published in late April 2011 in *Science Magazine* that was a scathing report on medicine by a physician in California. He basically hit the nail on the head when he wrote: "Medicine is going to have to go through an earth-shaking change if it is to survive and complete its mission."

Today it seems that mission is being defined more and more to satisfy fancy new treatments which have dubious value, and when all is said and done, is a triumph of technology, ignoring the human patient.

Can you give me some examples?

Examples might include some of the new genetically modified proteins and various treatment modalities that are often used to extend life for perhaps as little as three or six months that are marketed for as much as 90 or 100,000 dollars per month. They count on the gullible and desperate patients and their families to pressure health personnel to "pull out all the stops" and use this new research. The side effects can be horrific and the end results are often simply comparable to no treatment, or an insignificant gain of living in misery for some days or weeks.

In these cases, it is not the human that is being treated; rather it is the triumph of the pharmaceutical industry exploiting the emotionally-charged end of life scenario.

I take it that the situations you speak of are tied to the quality of life of the patient.

Yes. There is a marked difference between prolonging life and prolonging death. On the one hand, when a patient is critically ill with absolutely no chance of recovering, to extend the death process for as long as a week to keep that patient in a twilight zone, basically screaming to die, just for the satisfaction of the family or edification and bottom line of an institution is wrong-headed and cruel. On the other, to aggressively support a fading life which has promise of living is every physician's primary goal.

In my opinion, it is callous and uncaring to ignore a patient who is trying to die and force him to endure a tube in every orifice, to be hooked up to every type of mechanical device imaginable. Some orifices are even manmade, such as those in the chest cavity, the abdomen and elsewhere. It is absolutely inhumane and amounts to torture.

Families facing the demise of a loved one are seldom capable of making rational decisions. Family members often feel better knowing that everything was done that could be done, a heady price paid to assuage familial grief and guilt feelings.

- **Playing God?—**

How do you respond to the often made charge that any doctor who lets a patient die is playing God?

God does not come into this. If He did, He would certainly condemn it. People are welcome to whatever belief they have as long as it applies to them, but not when they are making decisions for others who cannot object to this well-intentioned torture. And it is torture!

That leads me to ask if you think meaningful physician-patient relationships still exist.

I am obviously dating myself when I say that the physician-patient relationship is overwhelmingly different than from my early days of caring for patients.

I made a pact with my patient to be directly responsible for them, and they were responsible for taking my advice. The patient did not make demands of me, and I didn't make demands of him. Today's physicians and patients are bombarded by print and TV/radio with wonder cures. These are shamelessly hawked like soap detergents. The art of practicing, the personal touch that discovers and molds what is best for a particular patient is all but dead.

Have the demonstrable positive effects of patient-physician loyalty disintegrated because of the Internet age, the thirty-second sound-bite mentality, and a litigious society?

Yes, and it is absolutely corrosive. A funny historical aside happened to me when I was in my internship at Madison, Wisconsin and was approached by an insurance salesman who frequently hung around the hospital. I understood that he had a duck blind and offered this to the staff. I had never shot at anything but somehow thought I might like it. I didn't like it, and I didn't go a second time; it was killing, and I didn't like that at all.

Anyway, he was selling malpractice insurance and I didn't know really what that was, as there is no such insurance in Germany. He offered me a policy for one million dollars in coverage, and in those days that was in the realm of the Rockefellers. The cost was twenty-nine dollars for the year!

When I asked, tongue-in-cheek, "Don't you have a better policy?" his eyes lit up and he said, "Yes, we have one for three million, but that'll cost you forty-two dollars." I thought I owed him something for the duck boat and blind, so I went for the deluxe package. There was never any chance I would be sued, and nobody in the medical community knew of anybody who had been. So, he got forty-two dollars for use of the boat and duck blind.

Malpractice insurance has soared since then.

My last three million dollar malpractice insurance policy prior to retiring cost me about 14,000 dollars. For emergency departments today, my guess is that insurance coverage easily accounts for twenty-five percent of the overhead.

- **Experiences over the years—**

Looking back at your extensive career, what amusing or strange experiences come to mind?

One cute story came was when I was in my last position in West Texas when a little old lady came in by ambulance. The driver said she complained of chest pain, so she was rushed in, and since we monitor the EMS net, we knew she was coming and were ready. The patient was pale and still had chest pain and shortness of breath.

She was put on the gurney and placed on a cardiac monitor. In an eye blink, we watched the reading go from a normal cardiac rhythm to ventricular-fibrillation, a deadly rhythm. When I put the paddles on her to get the reading, her eyes rolled and her head fell back. I cranked up the electric current on the defibrillator while my nurse appropriately gave her a thump on the chest with her fist. That is the very first thing to do, and in some cases the mechanical energy will cause the heart to stop racing for a second and return to a normal heartbeat. The electrical current gives a nasty shock but resets the cardiac Pacemaker. By this time, the other electrodes had been placed on her chest.

The woman gained consciousness and gave me and the nurse very cross looks. Then she said, "Nurse, I don't know why you hit me, I've never done anything to you, why are you so mean?" She then turned to me and said, "And you, you're the doctor? I don't know what you did to me, but don't ever do that to me again!"

How did you keep from laughing?

We didn't. And when we explained that we had saved her life, she wasn't so sure about that. At any rate, she lived to walk out of the hospital on her own.

- **Crediting teachers—**

You've mentioned some people you admire, is there anyone else you'd like to acknowledge for guiding you?

I think most of my teachers because they taught me to believe in myself. At every stage from grade school through medical school I attracted somebody who saw my potential and pushed me to apply myself. They believed in me when I did not believe in myself. They said that, I was intelligent and stubborn but lazy. At some point I turned my stubbornness into an attribute.

Have you had major disappointments that you care to share?

I think personal disappointments come with the territory of being one of the pioneers in emergency medicine. One was that this made me an outlier and a maverick, when I had a deep need to be accepted by my peers. But I take great pleasure in knowing I always tried to do the right thing and especially that my patients benefitted.

Is it fair to deduce that as a pioneer you were destined to make mistakes through the necessities of trial and error, but then moved forward the best way you could with the results?

Yes, that is true. There is no way to change the establishment other than taking them on frontally, head first, and that was often cantankerous and unfriendly. I wanted to change the way hospitals operated but the establishment wanted to preserve the status quo.

I was trampling on some of the biggest egos around, doing it with no background other than the fact that I was convinced I was right. But we all know that in human endeavors, most people who believe they are right are not.

- **Opinions about current medicine—**

How would you evaluate the state of medical practice today?

If medicine is not co-opted by the insurance and pharmaceutical industries, I foresee advances in genetics occurring at the same time as advances in computers and nanotechnology, and that eventually will radically change the entire practice and scope of medicine.

I believe we are standing before a paradigm shift that will re-define what medical practice is. There will be a dizzying array of new specialties, and ever more adventurous treatments. Life expectancy will increase dramatically even as individuals do their utmost to self-destruct. It will be an exciting time and I feel a little sad that I will miss it.

What is your primary advice to new emergency physicians now that it is valued highly in the medical profession?

Going through medical school, the professors always emphasized study and mastery of anatomy, physiology, biochemistry, pathology, and so on. I can re-iterate that a solid background of these basic sciences is as important as the clinical subjects. It is the foundation from which the ED doc should approach every patient.

With these tools you do not have to rely on your memory for a long laundry list of diseases, it either makes sense to you or it doesn't. You need to see the problem at its most basic level and, if you can master that, you are well equipped to get into esoteric presentations of various critical system failures.

Obviously, the Internet, and data retrieval and storage, have made a big difference in every discipline, and certainly in medical disciplines with all their complexities. The Internet can be a wonderful resource, but it can also be misused or misinterpreted in value.

What is your judgment of the massive information flow in medicine, and particularly in emergency medicine?

I wouldn't want to study medicine today. I think I would be terribly distracted by the overabundance of information. In a sense, the knowledge-nuggets are hidden in a plethora of noise. There is too much said, too many opinions, too many beliefs, and little said about listening to what you need to know. Medical information should be spelled out precisely and be at one's fingertips, not hidden away on some electronic device.

Especially in the Emergency, the patient must be carefully but quickly scrutinized and appraised. All of the information the doctor needs can be found on the patient. Once the practitioner has a good sense of what's going on, then referring to an adjunctive device can be quite helpful.

- **State of emergency care today—**

What is your opinion about the state of Emergency Medical care in the state and nation today?

Emergency Medical care is overburdened by those who have no or little medical insurance, thereby threatening to blunt an otherwise sharp instrument. This problem has no solution under today's broken system of selecting and paying for medical costs. On the positive side, full-time specialty trained emergency doctors and nurses are not only common, they are welcomed, supported and respected.

What do you think about the current and future for health insurance?

Before addressing the current and future of health insurance, a quick look at its past is enlightening. When I was an intern, purchasing health insurance had no effect on a patient's obligation to pay his doctor. There was a complete separation between an insurance company and the medical profession. This was a healthy market. The Patient had a contract with the doctor; the insurance company made a contract with the patient. They were parallel tracks. The patient paid the doctor. Whether he was reimbursed and how much he was reimbursed by his insurance company was between them.

General surgery had become much safer and popular, and big ticket items such as gastrectomies, or gall bladder removal, saw for the first time significant fees such as $400-to-$500. Some patients used to spend the medical insurance checks and stiff the surgeons. Apparently this was often enough to cause the surgeons as a group to appeal to the insurance companies to pay them directly. And thus, as I understand it, third-party insurance payments began. It is the reason we stare at disaster today!

Visit any big city in the world and look around in the most expensive areas and you will inevitably find insurance companies occupying enormous buildings. This show of wealth and power will grow and threaten all of us, if we do not address the mammoth transfer of wealth going on now between society and health insurers. Please note that one does not need insurance to purchase food, autos, haircuts, massages, and the like.

- **Comments and opinions—**

How do you feel about mandated health insurance coverage?

It is fundamentally wrong. We do not need insurance! We need affordable health access. The demand for health services can only grow; it is virtually limitless. Human nature readily spends 'other people's money' with abandon. For example, an individual who is parsimonious to the extreme will demand the latest and greatest medical aids, devices, treatments etc. that are not necessary but can 'be justified'.

Businesses line up to advertise and saturate the airwaves with these 'helpful' things and promise to do the billing and authorization process to boot. Insurance companies are the middle man in these transactions which can become nightmarishly and unnecessarily complex. This complexity is artificially created to create a need for 'experts' to guide the poor consumer through the red tape. Hence they create a need in an attempt to justify their busy dealings and manipulations.

The plan to prevent bankrupting our treasury and preventing the unlimited growth of insurance companies and all that entails could be surprisingly simple.

Tap your knowledge base of health care just a bit more and give some more comments and opinions.

Okay, here goes: healthcare is basically a three-legged stool, and all three are necessary to succeed.

Health care is defined in our Declaration of Independence as an inalienable right, as in life, liberty and the pursuit of happiness. But it is not thinkable that can be accomplished in a diseased or crippled body. So it is my contention that healthcare is a right! To secure this right we need a Single Payer, a Single Tariff Book, and a Single Electronic Medical Record, and that must be open-source-based.

The country needs the Single Payer for all health costs, and I'll say it up front: the government! It also needs the Single Tariff Book that lists allowances for all medical procedures, devices, treatments, and so on. And finally, there should be only one Electronic Medical Record based on Open-Source Software that will stabilize the other two legs.

Notice the absence of Insurance companies. Should the very well-off decide to purchase a gold-plated medical policy, then that becomes a private decision between them and an insurance company. This will get insurance companies out from the middle to where they belong: responsible only to their customers. As it is now, the insurance companies promise their customers pie in the sky and pay the providers or deny the providers, insinuating themselves between the patient's needs and their doctors' medical judgments. Their motivation is profit and profit only.

• Most satisfying accomplishment and reward—

As you look back over your long and successful career in emergency medicine, what comes to the forefront as your most satisfying accomplishment and reward?

The personal material successes I enjoyed in medicine were not really significant when measured by any current or common yardstick. I made such little money that I could not afford to attend many of the American College of Emergency Physician meetings; the air fare, hotel and fees being beyond my budget.

In the beginning, I frequently worked seventy-plus hours per week just to keep my head above water. I was never elected or appointed to an influential medico-political office, perhaps because I was too busy making ends meet.

Be that as it may, my most significant accomplishment and reward are of a different kind: that I always tried to do the right thing for my patient. I struggled lifelong to do what was sound, sensible and necessary; the things that simply had to be done!

You are signaled out by your peers as a pioneer in your chosen discipline. That must be very satisfying.

Pioneers by definition break the mold; they stir the pot. They question and challenge the established beliefs and practices and thereby they are outsiders. This is not a comfortable mantel to wear. Dare I say that one needs to be very stubborn to continue to wear it in spite of the drawbacks?

Sometime in my mid-life I came to believe that all of life is a competition, namely that one competes fiercely or not with himself. Everything else is insignificant. Edmund Hillary didn't conquer Mount Everest, he conquered himself!

- **Enjoying fruits of a dream—**

Are you enjoying your retirement?

At the very end of my career in my final medical position, I came to professionally enjoy the fruits of my dream. I took up a post at a teaching hospital that had an emergency department, well organized and supported by the staff and community so thoroughly that it didn't seem real. The remuneration was also exceptional, and that permitted me to accumulate a modest retirement nest egg.

My wife MaryBeth and I decided to retire in Ireland and built a stone cottage in Killorglin, County Kerry. The Celtic tiger was roaring and we enjoyed a lovely eight years before deciding to come home. I thought a lot about what I would do when I retired. MB and I loved to hike, or hill walk, as they call it in Ireland. And, we certainly did a lot hill walking in the Slieve Mish and the McGillicuddy Reeks. But I needed something to challenge myself with-something difficult.

And what challenge did you accept?

The most difficult thing that I could think of that was also feasible was building cabinets and furniture. I had never built anything, and my knowledge of tools went no further than hammer, and screwdriver.! But, after reading books and WoodWorking journals for about two years, I took the plunge, had an outbuilding constructed and populated it with a variety of tools as saws, shapers, jointers, routers, planers, and more.

With nobody to teach me, hold my hand or advise me; with great trepidation, I began to learn how to use the tools. It was the most difficult and scariest thing I have ever done in my life. But, I was adamant and reminded myself that if I could learn medicine in German, then I could learn woodworking in English.

It sounds like you are deeply into your new avocation.

The nicest thing about woodworking is that it is open-ended, meaning that the sky is the limit as to how refined or advanced one can take it. But it also had breadth, everything from wood turning to marquetry. As my skills improved, I dared make items for neighbors and friends and gave them away.

MaryBeth and I decided to return home and to locate in Western North Carolina and take advantage of the area's richness in wood crafts, and the almost inexhaustible opportunities to hike or 'hill walk'. We built a small home in Hendersonville with a small woodworking shop located on the lower level. Since returning home, some of my projects include a table housing a modern sink, a craftsman-style queen- sized bed, linen cabinet, and an Arts and Crafts style bookcase. My current project is a fold-down top notebook computer desk. MaryBeth has a list long enough to keep me busy for a long time. I predict a lot of sawdust in my future.

- **Final thoughts—**

What would be your final thoughts and hopes after these reflections about your life and career?

I would very much like to express a debt of gratitude to Dr. Richard Romfh. During the formative years in Washington State, his was the voice of quiet reason; a necessary foil against my almost manic drive and activities.

It is my fervent hope to someday reach a rebel like myself and give him/her a chance to challenge himself. To help fulfill that wish, MaryBeth and I endowed a small scholarship at my alma mater, St. John's University in New York City. The scholarship is called The Spirit of Inquiry.

My final thoughts would emphasize some things I said at the beginning of our interviews, that my life journey has been almost magical, and despite enormous handicaps I managed to persevere. And as I said, most importantly, perhaps when I leave this earth it will be just a tiny bit better than before.

Section 4: **Photos**

...Making sawdust

Perhaps 1mm less?

Complete family gathering: Matt, Mary Beth & MeToo

...At home in Hendersonville

HAYES MATHEW J A1701
087-28-6220
97-08-17
COL MC

Official Army Picture

Section 5: **Chronology**

- **Personal—**
- Dr. Matthew J. Hayes
- Born March 7, 1936, Williamsburg, Brooklyn, NY
- Wife MaryBeth

- **Education—**
- 1941, Trinity Grade school, Brooklyn
- 1945, Transferred to Nativity grade school, Woodhaven, Queens, NY, graduated January 1950
- 1950-1953, Attended five high schools, graduated in third year
- 1953, St. John's University on scholarship, biology major-philosophy minor, graduated 1957, BSC
- 1959, Language School, Heidelberg University, Germany
- 1960-1964, University of Freiburg, Germany, Medical Degree
- 1965, University of Goettingen, Germany, Ph. D.
- 1965, Completed Internship, Madison General Hospital, Madison, Wisconsin

- **Military—**
- 1957-1959, U.S. Army Reserve, two-year active service in Germany, E-4
  — Three-months, Reserve Hospital, Bosnia
  — Promoted to PFC 1958, Promoted to Spec. 4th Class 1959
- 1959-1963, Mandatory USAR (Army Reserve)
- 1977, Re-entered USAR as Major
- 1978, Promoted to Lieutenant-Colonel
- 1992, Promoted to Colonel
- 1996, Army Commendation Medal for Meritorious Service as Emergency Room Chief, US Army Hospital, Heidelberg, Germany
- 1997, Retired from the USAR after 27 years of service

- **Employment—**
- August 1960, High-steel construction union laborer; evening job destruction firm on Wall Street, NYC

- **Career—**
- 1964-retirement: Emergency Physician

- **Recognitions—**
- Founding member, American College of Emergency Physicians
- St. John's University Founders Society, with wife MaryBeth

- **Hobbies—**
- Hiking in the mountains; woodworking-creating furniture in craftsman style

Joe Epley

Global Public Relations Leader

"I took the view that if something wasn't right for an ethnic segment of our society then it wasn't right for the PRSA membership, and that we should hold our conferences only where local governments treat all people with respect and dignity."
— Joe Epley

Sections about Joe Epley:

1) Testimonials from Those in the Know

2) Highlights from Joe's Career

3) Excerpts from Articles about Joe

4) **Joe's Life Journey, in His Own Words**

5) Photos

6) Chronology

Section 1: **Testimonials from Those in the Know**

- **Joe Epley, a catalyst for change—**

Joe's achievements before coming to Polk County included founding and growing the most prestigious public relations firm between New York City and Miami. His numerous awards that include the Order of the Long Leaf Pine from the State of North Carolina will be best covered elsewhere in this book.

My association with Joe began with the Polk County Economic Development Commission, which he chaired for two terms. He brought new enthusiasm and effective organization to this body. Joe founded the Foothills Economic Partnership, a coordinating and information-sharing group of representatives from county entities and leadership.

Joe is or has been on the boards of the Blue Ridge Parkeway Foundation, Upstairs Art Space in Tryon and the Pavillion, an internationally renowned addiction treatment facility, and is currently on the board of Thermal Belt Outreach Ministry where he led the search for a new director and refocusing of its vital mission. He served as chair of the Visioning Committee that led to formulation of Polk County's Comprehensive Plan, which will guide county policy for years to come.

He is an extremely effective leader who guides with efficiency and dignity and is a catalyst for change. His steadfast loyalty to friends and causes is a quality enhanced by his career in Special Forces. I am proud to call Joe my friend.
    — **Ambrose Mills**, Chair, Polk County Economic & Tourism Development Comm.; US Army Lt. Col.-ret.

- **A rare individual and role model—**

Joe is one of those rare individuals who understands the world longitudinally, i.e., with both a thorough knowledge of history and a profound vision for the future, as well as latitudinally, i.e., his cosmopolitan worldview that has helped him to empathetically communicate and reach understanding with those having diverse cultural and ideological perspectives. These traits have contributed to Joe's professional leadership, as well as to his greatness as a human being. He is the ideal role model whom public relations practitioners should seek to emulate.
    — **Dr. Dean Kruckeberg**, APR, Fellow PRSA; Professor, Department of Communication Studies; Executive Director, Center for Global Public Relations, University of North Carolina, Charlotte.

- **Remarkable in American and International PR—**

Joe Epley is quite a remarkable personality in the American and international PR and communications community. As a professional, he is a man of vision and integrity with envious political intuition and insight. We met in the beginning of the 1990s at the time of amazing transformation of the former USSR when the emerging new Russian State created the opening to a market economy, democratic political system and freedom of information

At that time, Joe became president of the Public Relations Society of America, and he was very helpful to us in founding Russian Public Relations Association, and he can be referred to as the number one foreign contributor to establishing PR in Russia in business and education.

He is a great presenter, and former students at MGIMO, the Foreign Ministry Institute in Moscow, remember his lectures on business communication which helped them to find their way and build successful careers in PR.

To just add a personal touch to his profile, let me say that Joe is a man of his word, committed to his friends and always willing to help. He is a self-made man who started from scratch and accomplished much in business. He is an outstanding American and a distinguished citizen of North Carolina.

> — **Alexander Borisov,** Founder-President of Russian Public Relations Association, scholar, diplomat, Professor of International Studies.

- **A pioneer in globalization of PR—**

Joe has been a pioneer in the globalization of public relations - well before it was 'cool'. In the late 1980s, Joe travelled to international destinations, especially to the Soviet Union, to spread the 'public relations gospel' of the importance of two-way communication to build and maintain mutual understanding and cooperation.

> — **John Paluzek, APR,** Former President, Public Relations Society of America; Gold Anvil winner; Chair of Global Alliance, Ketchum Sr. VP

- **Respected around the world—**

Joe is not just a big name in his home state of North Carolina; he is respected around the world for professionalism and integrity in his chosen profession of public relations. We are contemporaries and have known each other and worked together for many years. He has been a prime mover in taking our craft from its earlier role as publicity to becoming a central professional discipline behind most successful organizations as they learned that policies, ethics and strategies were as important as products and services.

Joe has added wise counsel and expert guidance to many large and small enterprises to help them be more effective, more successful, more stable, and, above all, better corporate citizens. He is a hero to many in my corner of the world, the United Kingdom and many parts of the globe, for he is so generous with his time and his help to so many, particularly the younger professionals with whom he works.

> — **Roger Haywood,** Chief Executive *Issues Managers*, UK corporate strategist; Fellow, Institute of Marketing; Past President British Public Relations Institute; Chair, WORLDCOM PR Group.

- **About Joe Epley's Historical Novel: *A Passel of Hate*—**

Joe Epley has used his retirement wisely by opting to be involved in numerous important community activities, and by authoring in 2011 an intriguing 349-page historical novel titled *A Passel of Hate* (ISBN-10: 1461075939, ISBN-13: 9781461075936). Following is text from the back cover that provides a clear view of the novel's content:

In the Carolinas, the American War for Independence is a civil war with many families and neighbors split in their loyalties. When infamous Tory raider Rance Miller brings his murderous terror campaign to the Western Carolinas, Jacob Godley and his youngest brother join the Liberty Men to exact revenge – but three other brothers serve the Loyalists as their respective forces converge on Kings Mountain.

Gripping, visceral, and full of intensity, Joe Epley's novel is as historically fascinating as it is emotionally satisfying. Surrounding the Loyalists forces, the Liberty Men charge the hill with deadly enthusiasm. When the savage fighting ends with a decisive and tide-turning triumph for the American side, Jacob's victory is bittersweet as his four brothers perished in the battle. Afterwards, Jacob is driven by hatred as he tracks Rance Miller through the Carolina backcountry to seek revenge he so desperately needs.

Brutal in its depiction of the harrowing nature of war and the price paid by our revolutionary ancestors, A Passel of Hate and its breakneck pacing forge a relentless adventure full of bravery, horrific violence, and first-rate historical-action entertainment.

Section 2: **Highlights from Joe's Career**

- **Earning the Gold Anvil—**

In 2008, the Public Relations Society of America presented its former President Joe Epley with the Gold Anvil, its top award. Following are excerpts from the recommendation by former Counselors Academy chair Davis Young, APR, of Cleveland, OH that detail his lifelong adherence to doing what is right:

Joe Epley has distinguished himself over many years as a sophisticated and ethical professional, as well as a deeply committed leader of PRSA nationally. Several years ago, the editor of the Encyclopedia of Public Relations asked me to write a profile about Joe and I focused on three specific areas where he made important contributions to our field: 1) Doing what's right, 2) Vision, and 3) Unique contribution of helping to introduce public relations to Russia.

While Joe was president of PRSA in 1991, many African-American members said they would not attend the national PRSA conference in Phoenix because the State of Arizona had decided not to celebrate Martin Luther King Day. Moving it to another city would have cost PRSA about $500,000 in contractual penalties. Nevertheless Joe said "We cannot have a conference at a location in which many of our members would not participate on moral grounds."

His solution was to call a special meeting that included the PRSA board, representatives of chapters in Arizona, members of PRSA's cultural diversity committee, and other trusted advisers. Joe and several nationally prominent PRSA members assisted in waging an election which made Arizona the first to establish a Martin Luther King Day by popular vote. The theme of the conference was "What's Right?" and Joe said, "Our focus has to change from building awareness to building relationships, from educating to persuading. We do that by paying as much if not more attention to personal, corporate and product reputation as we do to promoting products and ideas."

Joe has not avoided controversial clients, rather presents them with constructive alternatives to achieve the same type of win-win result as he did for PRSA in Arizona. For instance, he convinced a major chemical company to open its gates not only to neighbors, but also to the Sierra Club for scrutiny so they could see what the company was doing to protect the environment. This tactic, now employed widely, was largely unacceptable when Joe first used it. His result was public support for a client at a critical time. As Joe has said, "We can build awareness, but it won't be worth a hill of beans if everyone in an organization's management doesn't embrace the basic principles of ethical conduct in business and corporate responsibility in society."

His vision from the early days of the Information Highway was to promote use of the Internet. He saw how the Internet would affect business, including public relations. Joe has always been an early adopter of new technology. His monograph on hourly billing practices and daily time sheets became a standard reference for counselors for many years. He also foresaw the downside of technology, saying: "The world is drowning in an ocean of information overload, awash with messages that conflict, obscure, deceive, inform, educate, promote, motivate or just trivialize. Navigating that sea of information clutter is our job. We must shape our messages to take advantage of the tools, not let the tools rule our communication."

Joe's work in introducing public relations into the former Soviet Union included leading the PRSA drive to supply textbooks and curricula to the Russians for their first course in western-style public relations. He made multiple trips to Russia to give hands-on support and mentoring guidance, and set up internships in this country for Russian practitioners. He also personally mentored practitioners in several other countries. The Russian PR Association bestowed lifetime membership on Joe on its tenth anniversary in 2001. *(Author's note: Russia honored him again in 2011).*

Through this work, and also by helping to found and chair the WORLDCOM Public Relations Group, the world's largest consortium of independent PR counseling firms with operations in 35 countries, he has truly been an important global ambassador and role model for the way the business of public relations should be practiced.

- ### 'Godfather of Public Relations' set the bar for Carolinas PR—

The *Charlotte Observer* once described Joe Epley as an icon and the man who set the bar for Carolinas Public Relations, a reputation earned though consistent sound advice and quality services that enhanced the reputation of many high profile organizations. Joe is widely respected for working quietly behind the scenes while keeping his clients and their goals in the forefront.

Accredited in PR and member of the Public Relations Society of America's prestigious College of Fellows, Joe achieved an international reputation for his ethical no-nonsense approach in applying PR techniques to management challenges. PR executives in Russia described him as 'the Godfather of Public Relations'.

After a decade as news reporter and editor with television stations in Asheville and Charlotte, Joe established Epley Associates Public Relations, a consulting firm that quickly became one of the more prominent and respected independent agencies in the Southeastern United States. With Joe as CEO, the firm achieved a regional and global reach. Joe sold the company in 2005.

- ### North Carolina Public Relations Hall of Fame—

The School of Journalism and Mass Communication at the University of North Carolina at Chapel Hill issued the following release upon induction of Joe into the UNC School of Journalism Public Relations Hall of Fame in 1991:

Joe S. Epley is a native of Forest City and was educated at US Army Schools and at Charlotte College, now the University of North Carolina at Charlotte. In 1968, he founded Epley Associates Inc., which has grown into one of the largest public relations firms in the Southern United States. His honors include five presidential citations for leadership from the Public Relations Society of America (PRSA) from 1986 through 1990, and the 1981 Infinity Award from the Charlotte Public Relations Society.

Epley's importance in the development of public relations includes his role as founding member of the WORLDCOM Group, and an international network of independent public relations firms organized in 1988. He also served as vice president from 1986 to 1988 for IPR-North America, a group of 28 independent public relations firms in the United States that were members of the worldwide International Public Relations Group of Companies. In addition, he has served in a number of capacities for PRSA, including treasurer in 1989. He is now president of the 15,000-member national organization. He also had a pivotal role in the development of the Charlotte Chapter of PRSA, as a founding board member and president, and served in all officer ranks. He is on the executive committee of the NC Citizens for Business and Industry, the equivalent of the state chamber of commerce.

Epley wrote two professional monographs for the Counselors Academy. He also was peer reviewer for two professional books: "Strategic Public Relations Counseling" and "When You are the Headline."

- ### Awards and Recognitions—

The global public relations leader has earned many distinctive awards and recognitions, including:
- *The Gold Anvil, the PRSA's highest award for lifetime achievement;*
- *University of North Carolina School of Journalism Public Relations Hall of Fame;*
- *Defense Information School Alumni Hall of Fame;*
- *Infinity Award, Charlotte Public Relations Society's highest recognition for outstanding achievements and contributions to the profession;*
- *Order of the Long Leaf Pine, one of North Carolina's highest awards for individual achievement.*

• **More on Epley's view of ethics in PR—**

Following are excerpts from a 1993 speech he made at the Defense Information School in Fort Benjamin Harrison, Indiana, just after Gulf War One. He did major research on ethics, one of his prime areas of expertise in PRSA, for the talk to several hundred Public Affairs students. He then became the first Army and first enlisted person to be inducted into the DINFOS Hall of Fame. His comments were based on a survey that sampled opinions from students and faculty at the Defense Information School, Public Affairs personnel in the military, news reporters in 50 cities near military installations, and senior civilian public relations practitioners located throughout the United States who distinguished themselves in the practice.

Some have called ethics and the military an oxymoron, yet the United States military community is a mirror of the civilian community when it comes to morals and integrity. And while those outside the public affairs and major command roles don't fully understand the importance of building understanding with the media and the nation, most do understand the difference between ethical and unethical communications.

Ray Heibert, a journalism professor from the University of Maryland, wrote: "We have just witnessed in the war in the Persian Gulf either history's most impressive use of military weapons, or history's most thorough use of words and images as weapons of war, or both." It is his thesis that mass communication is today an essential part of modern warfare, and that public relations is a primary weapon of war. He said, "Both sides attempted to manage the words and images of the battle." I disagree with Professor Heibert's thesis that public relations is a weapon of war. Public relations, as practiced in the Western world by those who believe in the ethics of truthful and non-deceptive communications, is not a weapon, it is a means of building understanding. Communication as a weapon is called psychological operations. Deceptive communications is not public relations!

Your reputation will be enhanced once journalists and the general public understand the difference between public affairs and psychological operations. If the military and political leadership use public affairs personnel to engage knowingly in deceptive practices, your mission will become extremely difficult, for few will believe anything you say.

Professor Heibert is right when he says public relations is an essential part of modern warfare. It is my contention that it is the process by which the public understands the military and government actions through honest and ethical communications. Without the trust that ethical communications creates, the public will lose faith with the military and the government. This was demonstrated during the waning years of the Vietnam War.

I also agree with Professor Heibert's contention that with the great advances in technology, information flow has greatly increased. Battlefield commanders do not have the luxury of isolation from the media or from the American people. In fact, with improvements in technology, reporters can record and transmit live via satellites from anywhere under any conditions with equipment carried in a briefcase. News reports will be coming faster as the events unfold and with little time to reflect on what is being reported. Real-time communication opens new ethical dilemmas for journalists and public affairs people. In fluid situations, you will not have much time to ponder the issues. Action must be instinctive, and it must be right!

It should be noted that those public affairs people who are members of the Public Relations Society of America obligate themselves to abide by its Code.

As Winston Churchill said, "Never give in, except to convictions of honor and good sense!"

Section 3: **Excerpts from Articles about Joe**

- *Izvestia,* **one of Russia's most prominent newspapers—**

The following is an excerpt from the Russian-to-English translation of an article about Joe in the December 24, 2001 edition of the *Izvestia* newspaper in Moscow:

Question: What is your attitude in the use of compromising materials against competitors during PR campaigns?

Answer: With us, the war of compromising materials I call the 'pissing contest'. Both sides are the losers. It is the extreme measure one better not resort to if the situation is not critical.

Question: In connection with the September 11 events in the United States, how do you respond to terror in the information field?

Answer: Public relations rely on mutual understanding. Terrorists are incapable of understanding because they perceive the world lopsidedly. At the same time, disseminating this information increases fear, mistrust and suspicion. That is why a high-powered information campaign is on in the US, aimed at preventing the incitement of hatred toward Arabs, and Muslims in general. In addition, given that many companies have very strongly suffered through terrorist acts, it is necessary to restore confidence in business as a whole.

Question: Must, in your view, the PR business companies help their opposite numbers from power entities?

Answer: The US power structures have very powerful PR departments. An information department has been part of the US Defense Department since the time of World War II. It is one of the most powerful subdivisions in the country. I know what I am talking about since I received my first PR education precisely at a course established under that department. The propaganda subdivisions of military departments are quite capable of coping on their own. At the same time, US PR officials have never refused support to government entities. For instance, 15 years ago, New York had a negative image because of the rampant crime. Foreign tourists were simply afraid to visit the city. Local PR agencies united into a conglomerate and helped the city administration solve the problem. If military entities require assistance from PR firms, they will get it.

- *Business: North Carolina—*

Following are some excerpts from a February 1990 *Business North Carolina* article titled 'Epley reaches top of the flack stack':

After the Charlotte Public Relations Society gave a "Best Little Whorehouse in Charlotte" party a few years ago, it was Joe Epley who gave the members a good scolding

. . . Epley is the non-nonsense president of one of the largest agencies in the Southeast. He doesn't disclose revenues, but he employs 39 in Charlotte and Raleigh offices, and his clients include Philip Morris USA and Burroughs Wellcome Co., maker of the Aids drug AZT. His specialties include government relations, issue management and marketing

. . . "to work for Epley you must sign a public relations code and complete an accreditation process"

. . . "If there is respect for the practice of PR, it's because of him," says Bill Ballenger, vice president of Carolina Public Relations/Marketing in Charlotte

. . . Epley defines PR as creating an understanding between a company and the public. That can be tough. One of his clients is Chem-Nuclear Systems Inc., under contract with the state to build a low-level radioactive waste-disposal facility.

- ### *North Carolina* magazine—

An August 1991 profile in the magazine *North Carolina,* billed as "The Voice of Business, Industry and the Professions since 1943," was titled 'Joe Epley, Born to Communicate'. Excerpts from that article follow:

"Dubbed *Mr. Public Relations by The Business Journal, Joe Epley is a self-made and largely self-educated man, a former Green Beret who prefers wilderness and whitewater canoeing to more genteel, low-risk recreations*

. . . *"I can be outgoing when I have to be," he says, "but it is not a natural thing. Obviously, I'm not too introverted or I wouldn't be where I am today," chuckles Epley, a balding, bearded 6'1"bear of a man*

. . . *"Some people played golf; I jumped out of airplanes," quipped Epley, who spent 14 of his 22 years in the military in Special Forces. But he quit parachuting – at his wife's insistence – after he broke a thumb on a jump*

. . . *As an outspoken individualist, Joe Epley defies the stereotype of the glad-handing, backslapping PR person*

. . . . *"Public relations is a management function," Epley explains, "because it deals with the heart and soul and philosophy of an organization*

. . . *Friends and business associates have no trouble identifying Joe Epley's strengths: candor, sincerity, tenaciousness, immense credibility with reporters and CEO's alike, attention to detail, and a knack for finding, training, keeping and motivating a first-rate staff.*

- ### *Greater Charlotte Biz*—

And the media plaudits continued in a profile that was published in *Greater Charlotte Biz* titled: *A commitment to excellence and ethics puts Epley Associates at the top of its game.* The lengthy article went on to report:

In 1998, Epley Associates celebrated its 30th anniversary, and to honor that achievement Governor Jim Hunt said: "Joe has set the bar high for ethical and professional practice of public relations in our state."

Section 4: **Joe's Life Journey, in His Own Words**

Joe Epley became a personal friend when I moved to Western North Carolina in 2005. Then in 2011 when the idea for this book was born, and following in-depth research into Joe's impressive career accomplishments and inspiring professional persona, he became the first of the twelve Notables to be interviewed. We met at a coffee shop in downtown Tryon for the first of multiple sessions, where trying to tape-record amid neighbor chatting with neighbor was a challenge we managed to overcome. I started - where else? – asking Joe about his early childhood and family:

Joe, what is your first childhood memory?

My first memory? Gosh, I guess it was when I was a little kid running around half naked in the neighborhood and flattening pennies on the railroad track.

I'll try not to picture that. Where did you live?

I grew up in Forest City, North Carolina. We moved out into the country when I was about eleven.

Do you have siblings?

I have one brother and one sister. My brother Wayne is two years younger and my sister Catherine is six years younger. My mother had a knack for taking care of others, so we have an extended family of brothers and sisters. While they aren't blood kin, they are just as close.

And what kind of numbers are you talking about and where do they live?

The oldest lives in Dallas, Texas, and an older cousin, who is more like a brother and closer to my family than his own, lives in Summerset, Kentucky. Another younger one about the same age as my sister lives in Lexington, North Carolina.

Are you in touch with all of them?

Yeah, we have family reunions every few years.

How did you feel about your parents welcoming in strays, as you called them?

I've always thought that my folks were very good down-to-earth people. They didn't put on airs, and didn't care for anybody that did. My father was a truck driver and mother was a homemaker. She worked for a while in a floral shop just to have something to do after all the kids left home. Both of them were very devoted to their church, they believed in people treating other people right. The whole family thing was basically to treat people honestly and with respect.

- **An early lesson—**

It sounds like they set wonderful examples for their kids.

I remember when I was five or six years old, we lived near an African-American neighborhood.. One day my mother heard me call out the N-word to a black woman walking nearby. Mother yanked me away, carried me inside the house and washed my mouth out with soap. She said we are all born the way God wants us to be and have no right to insult anybody, whoever they are, no matter what color they are, or anything else.

She marched me to house of the woman who might have heard me, knocked on her door and said, "My son has something to tell you!" I was scared to death but managed to apologize. That was an important lesson.

- **Wife and children—**

Tell me about your wife and children.

I met my wife when I was on assignment for WLOS-TV and Dorcas was a student at the old Asheville-Biltmore Junior College. We will celebrate our fifty-third anniversary in June of 2012. It's been a good marriage. We had ups and downs like anyone else, but things always worked out. My wife is a lot more tolerant than me, which makes her a wonderful person. Without her, I would not have achieved the success I did.

She came into the business about ten years after I started it and took over the administrative and financial ends, which she enjoyed. Unlike a lot of husband-wife teams in business, Dorcas didn't try to be the boss, and actually was more of an advocate for the employees than for management. Everybody really loved her.

We have two children. Our daughter Meredith works in the marketing department in Greenville Memorial Hospital in South Carolina. She is a graduate of Western North Carolina University, and has a Masters in English Literature from UNC Charlotte.

Our son Stewart is in the moving business in Charlotte. He's a year and a half younger than his sister, and has two children of his own who live in West Virginia. He had a live-in friend for a while, but when she moved on, her children decided to stay with Stewart, so he raised them as his own.

Meredith has two children: Katie, who has degrees in Comparative Religion from the College of Charleston, and in Nursing from the Medical University of South Carolina in Charleston; and Peter, who graduated in 2012 from the American College for Building Arts, a school that focuses on construction, contracting and restoration of historical buildings, in addition to Liberal Arts studies.

- **Hobbies and interests—**

What were and are now your hobbies and interests?

I developed a lifelong fondness for science fiction as a teenager. I remember back in the 1950s reading about a one-world society with devices that allow you to receive messages in any language then interpret them and communicate back effectively; and about traveling to the moon, robots that can do multiple chores, laser weapons, and computers that think. Today, many of those fantasies have become reality, and the most significant of the dreams of yesteryear is that our big blue marble has indeed become a global village.

I also have enjoyed the outdoors and especially whitewater and wilderness canoeing. I did eight major expeditions into the northern Canadian sub-Arctic wilderness.

- **Pursuing Public Relations—**

When did you decide to pursue a career in public relations?

I decided to be a journalist at age twelve. Fate put me into the Army after high school, and fortunately I got into the Defense Information School where we learned more than just newspaper writing. I learned to make speeches to civic groups, how to stage special events, and so on.

I joined the Special Forces in the Army Reserves and studied psychological warfare, and learned about theories of mass persuasion and manipulative communication. I still wanted to be a reporter, so I worked in TV as a reporter and editor for ten years. I soon realized that I was not learning anything new, and that I was just a contemporary historian who was not making things happen. So I made a career change to PR.

What was your first job in public relations?

My first PR job had been in Army Information, but more as a writer and photographer than a planner and advisor. After returning to civilian life, I became a television journalist for ten years, and also did freelance work. I was promoted to editor but found the job boring, not intellectually challenging.

Then a friend offered me a retainer comparable to my salary at the time, with a year's contract. Within a few days I signed up two more accounts, and thirty years later two of them were still active clients.

How would you evaluate the public relations profession then and today?

When I started my firm in 1968 there were not many people in the PR profession, and the practitioners were almost all former journalists who focused primarily on media and media relations. Most folks didn't know what I did; even my wife couldn't explain it to her mother.

Now, many colleges and universities provide a solid foundation for students planning to enter the profession. The pool is more aggressive and talented, but far too many practitioners look at their work as a job and not as a profession. PR pros must be involved in community affairs, learn how to network, and lead through building consensus, think strategically and take a long view of issues. They should maintain their convictions but also have the insight to know when to stop arguing an issue with a client or boss.

And of course these days one must understand how to use the persuasive power of computers and technology that have revolutionized how we communicate and think, and the practitioner must be able to write and speak coherently and compellingly.

I personally told every new employee through the years: "When you stop learning, you must leave the firm."

Do you feel the PR industry treats men and women equally; and how so in comparison with other occupations?

I don't believe gender is much of a factor anymore; talent and ability dictate how one is treated and advances. Failure or success is primarily the result of your own talent and abilities now, and excuses are cop-outs.

I don't believe in cop-outs.

• Values in the profession—

Reflecting back on your early life again for a moment, it seems that being forced to apologize for using a racial slur, though you were too young to understand it then, obviously made a huge impression on you. I'll bet that inspired you to make minority rights a centerpiece of your PR career.

Well, you can see how it could. I don't know if it was a conscious bridge, it was just that I grew up with a set of entrenched values. It's not that you say, "Hey, I'm going to have this attitude or that attitude," it's just something deep inside you that seems natural; that you should be fair and respectful to all people, treat people right.

A lot of people talk the talk, but you walked the walk during your career. Give an example that fits this discussion.

As I was preparing to become president of the Public Relations Society of America in late 1990, I heard several members of both races say they would not attend the 1991 conference in Phoenix because the

Arizona legislature refused to honor Martin Luther King day, a holiday recognized in all other states. They said that in good conscience they could not go to an area that failed to recognize diversity or the work done to bring equality.

PRSA did not have a high percentage of African-American members, but I got to know those who were leaders in the profession. We in PRSA were trying hard to diversify the profession with African-Americans, Hispanics and Asians. If we canceled the scheduled conference in Phoenix because the Arizona Legislature wouldn't legalize the holiday, it could have cost the organization several hundred thousand dollars in penalties for yanking a contracted event. We asked leaders within the minority community about this and they said: "Don't worry about changing the conference, we just won't go, and we won't think badly of the PRSA because we understand the financial situation."

My board and I took the view if something wasn't right for an ethnic segment of our society then it wasn't right for the membership, and that we should hold the conference only where local governments treat all people with respect and dignity.

What happened then?

I hadn't officially taken over the PRSA presidency when I scheduled an emergency meeting of my board of directors in Chicago just before the New Year to make this a win-win solution. We held it with the Chair and Vice Chair of the PRSA Diversity Committee, leaders of our chapters in Arizona, my board of directors, and other influential leaders within our profession who had a high degree of political savvy and cultural sensitivity. All paid their own travel expenses.

One man I was particularly close to was the late Bob Stone, who was number two at Hill and Knowlton, the country's largest PR firm, and was my personal PR counselor for my new role in PRSA.

Another was a retired Army general and information officer. He really impressed me by taking the exam to become Accredited in Public Relations while most of the members who had it made thought, "Who needs an APR, and who cares?" The General was an African-American who got an APR to set an example for others but didn't stay in public relations very long because he got a high-paying job in another field and moved on.

Our group also included Denise Gray, an African-American practitioner with AT&T, who later became Vice President of Public Relations for the Ford foundation.

Especially helpful was Davis Young, a close friend who I succeeded as chair of the PRSA Counselors Academy. He and I came to the same conclusion: we should solve this dilemma in a meaningful way so that people can understand what we are doing and why we are doing it. Davis was the 1991 national conference co-chair and had selected "What's Right" as the theme before this crisis developed.

During a meeting at the Chicago O'Hare airport, we discussed calls from the mayor of Phoenix asking us to not pull the conference. I asked the mayor, "How can we still have the conference when we have members who are offended by your state's lack of respect for Martin Luther King?" The Mayor said "That was the State, it wasn't Phoenix."

The Mayor was doing what he had to do and I appreciated that, but the conference theme was already set and we were determined to do what was right. We decided that instead of running away from the problem, we would confront it straight on and bring the issue to the forefront in Phoenix and the state of Arizona.

We went a step further by having PRSA take the lead to organize and help guide our Arizona PRSA members on ways to more effectively address the issue. I called some of the most talented political consultant friends from around the county and asked, "Will you volunteer for a PRSA Taskforce and help make a major difference in Arizona life?"

They said yes. Then we put together with our Arizona members a campaign that led to Arizona becoming the only state in the nation to have a Martin Luther King holiday approved by a state-wide public referendum.

Although the election had yet occurred, the momentum was under way. In November of 1991, we held the largest PRSA conference ever, with some 2000 members and guests in attendance. There was no boycott by our minority members. In fact, the crisis was resolved in a way that brought greater understanding to ethnic and cultural diversity to our members and to the state of Arizona.

- **Russian Public Relations Association—**

When and how did you become involved in Russian PR?

It started at the 1990 PRSA National Conference in New York when word got to me that a man in the Russian Consulate at the United Nations wanted to talk to us about starting a study of public relations in the Soviet Union. I asked Jerry Dalton, who I succeeded in office as president of PRSA, to join us for the meeting. I had no idea what to expect. We met with Alexander Borisov, a forward-thinking Dean of the Department of International Communications of MGIMO, a prestigious school run by the Foreign Ministry and considered to be the Georgetown University of Russia.

He said that to have a free market economy in the Soviet Union, it had to begin with two-way communications, something that was not taught or encouraged under the Communist regime. He wanted us to help in setting up a course of study in the western style of public relations.

It sounds like you had a real dilemma on your hands.

He was a delightful fellow, and after chatting for about an hour I said, "Okay, I'll get some textbooks together and send them to you." I contacted some academic and other friends, and within a couple of weeks we put together two big boxes of public relations textbooks and delivered them to the Soviet Consulate in New York for shipment to Moscow at their expense.

A month later I received a fax from Borisov requesting advice about the curriculum they developed. It was a good curriculum. I faxed copies to four or five academic friends and to the Chair of PRSA's Educators' Section. I asked all, "What do you think?" Some tweaked it a little bit; all were impressed with the Russian's first effort to teach our profession. I faxed their suggestions back to Borisov,

- **Growing friendship—**

In late spring of 1991 I was asked to speak at a European PR Conference in Barcelona Spain. When I got there, I learned that Borisov had been invited to speak about changes in the Soviet Union and the introduction of public relations there. During that time our friendship grew even more.

He offered to drive me around Barcelona the next day but I said, "No, I have to go back to the States in the morning." Then at 10:30 p.m. as we were finishing up a banquet, he arranged with the local Russian consulate for a Mercedes with a burly driver who I am sure was KGB. He drove us all over Barcelona, including where the summer Olympic Games were held that year.

Borisov and I agreed that he would come back to the States and I would go to Russia to help build more mutual support and understanding for the profession and between our two countries.

It was terribly hard to communicate between our two countries in 1991, as there were only ninety telephone lines from the West into Russia, and all went to Moscow, but we managed to talk on the phone frequently. I arranged for him to take a two-week tour visiting PRSA chapters in ten American cities to give him a better idea of the diversity and extensiveness of the profession in the U.S. It would also give our practitioners a better understanding what was happening with the introduction of PR to our Cold War adversary. PRSA covered his airfare within our country, and I recruited friends in each city visited to provide ground transportation and a place to stay. It was a hectic two weeks for Borisov, who talked to local PRSA chapters, did newspaper and TV interviews, and attended a lot of meet-and-greet receptions. He was treated as a major celebrity.

Did he come to North Carolina?

Midway in the tour, I brought him to Charlotte on a Friday. I remember two events.

One was a visit to an elementary school that my firm had adopted. On arrival, he was surprised to see a marquee outside the school that read, "Welcome Professor Borisov." He was overwhelmed by the warm hospitality. All of the school's sixth-graders cheered him. Throughout the auditorium, hand-drawn posters about Russia were posted on the walls. Borisov talked for thirty minutes about his country's elementary schools then answered questions, some quite astute. But when one student asked him if he favored Mr. Gorbachev or Mr. Yeltsin in the upcoming elections in the new Russia, he just smiled and evaded the answer. At noon that day, Borisov spoke about the development of PR in Russia to the Charlotte PRSA Chapter, which had changed the date of its monthly meeting to accommodate him. There was a full house at the event. He also did a major interview with *Charlotte News.*

The weekend was purely social. He stayed at our home, and we drove him through the mountains along the Blue Ridge Parkway to the top of Mount Mitchell. It was quality time, and we really got to know each other better, and that solidified a friendship that continues strong today.

From Charlotte he went out west to San Francisco, Los Angeles then to Phoenix, where he became the first Russian to attend a PRSA National Conference. He received a standing ovation from 2,000 members when introduced. Several other foreign PR representatives from former Iron Curtain countries were in attendance, including a friend who founded the Hungarian Public Relations Association and served many years as its president.

In late November I took a delegation of six PRSA leaders, including four spouses, to Moscow for a week-long visit that was graciously hosted by Borisov and his colleagues during the waning days of the old Soviet Union. At that time, public relations was not practiced or taught in Russia outside of Moscow.

I lectured at MGIMO, which is an acronym for long Russian words I cannot pronounce, but essentially means the University for International Affairs. My biggest surprise there was that I didn't need an interpreter when lecturing to MGIMO students. All the courses in the International Communications Department were all taught in English. It was a very prestigious school students in which every student had to pass a rigorous examination just to get in, and once accepted, had to master two foreign languages in order to graduate. We also learned that the USSR was a diverse multi-cultural society, with 110 recognized languages spoken throughout the Republics.

• Getting PR off the ground in Russia —

Was that trip successful in getting PR off the ground in Russia?

We attended one of the first meetings of the newly-formed Russian PR Association, only about twenty people in attendance. Most of didn't know what the hell PR was, but they knew it was needed for the emerging business freedoms in their country. There was an eagerness to learn, even by men approaching middle age.

The Russians paid our expenses once we were in the country, and put us in a hotel right behind the Foreign Ministry reserved previously for the political leadership of the Republics of the Soviet Union when they came to Moscow. It was small hotel and nobody on the staff knew English. We found out later that MGIMO had offered to teach the staff English if they would provide us rooms and meals for a week. The Russian economy then was very weak, but most Russians were adept at bartering.

Did you also train the Russians in PR here?

While there, several of us conducted lectures, and all provided advice where appropriate. One of the things that we often talked about, even at our first get-together, was how to train students who had no mentors to teach them the practical applications of public relations theories learned in the classroom. This was a brand new profession for them.

Fortunately, I knew a lot of people in PR management around the U.S, so it didn't take many calls to get eight young Russians placed in internships. Most went to small or mid-sized PR firms. The hosts agreed to train the Russians for four to six months, and provide them with living expenses and a small stipend. By U.S. law, we couldn't pay them a salary.

It was really an eye-opener for the students to be exposed to stuff that we here take for granted. There were few luxuries in Russia in those days, and little variety in basic commodities such as housing, clothing and food. Some students were overwhelmed by having to make choices among a dozen brands for the same type of commodity.

It was much different in Russia than it is today.

Did the Russian students speak English, or did they need a translator?

One of the requirements for internship was that the student had to speak and write in English. The lady who came to us had taught herself English, but her first languages after her native Russian were Hindi, Urdu and French. I asked, "Why in the world did you take Hindi as a foreign language?" and she answered, "I didn't choose it. When I took the aptitude test at the university, those with the best aptitude were assigned the hardest languages."

We had four Russian interns working in our office at various times, two for extended periods of time. A couple of the first groups of interns that came to the U.S. were professors teaching public relations courses, and that gave them some practical experience.

Does the Russian Association have a substantial membership today?

At the start of 2012, The Russian Public Relations Association had more than 600 members and was no longer Moscow-centric. More important than numbers are the quality and skills of PR practitioners and educators today. Today, more than 200 universities and institutes in Russia teaching public relations, and some offer Master's Degrees.

There are large and small PR firms, but most of the big firms are in Moscow and many focus on government relations. During the 1990s and early 2000s, many of them began to practice political PR because that was where the money was.

I have talked to practitioners and leaders in PR firms over there, and am impressed with the sophistication they exhibit. More and more Russian corporations are conscious about their public image now, and even smaller companies are beginning to engage public relations firms to help with marketing and other issues.

Are they combining their advertising and PR into one agency, or are they separate agencies?

Yes, there is integrated marketing offered. Some agencies work in all disciplines; others specialize in certain areas, pretty much like in this country but not yet as extensive as in this country where the profession is much older.

You must have been gratified that you were invited back to Russia for the twentieth anniversary.

I was, and humbled. The invitation also covered all my expenses. The last time I was there was two weeks after 9/11, more than ten years ago.

- **Crisis-Problem Management—**

One of the most sought-after PR consultants is the crisis-problem management specialist. Since that is one of your specialties, please explain a problem you faced, your proposed solution, and the results.

A situation occurred many years ago when the first Superfund sites were being labeled by the federal government throughout the nation. Our client was then called Sodyeco, the largest manufacturer of dispersed dyes in the country, located in Mecklenburg County between Charlotte and Mount Holly. It was on a thousand-acre site where blue dye was made for about eighty percent of the blue jeans produced in the United States.

Superfund sites were major hazardous waste storage sites that the Environmental Protection Agency deemed as a public threat. They would come in, cleanup the site and force the owners to foot the bill.

When the EPA was developing Superfund sites, we became aware that our client was going to be one of two sites in North Carolina. The selection of sites had some political considerations as well as the technical reasons. But our client was a responsible manufacturer and did not feel it should have the stigma of being named as a Superfund site. The company had done a lot of work in cleaning up its problems created by past practices that had been standard in the chemical industry.

The client asked us, "What do we do? We don't want our neighbors, customers and employee families to think badly of us, and the public needs to know that we operate in a responsible manner." We designed a two-pronged approach to addressing the issue. The first was for the client to work quietly with the EPA and our Congressional delegation to hopefully get Sodyeco de-listed and keep the company name out of the headlines. The second approach was to develop and implement an aggressive community relations program that would build greater understanding about what this company manufactured, and how it was working diligently to protect the environment.

As with most chemical companies in that era, and this is in the 1970s and early 1980s, the gates were closed to all outsiders. Nobody knew what was going on inside the company, except that they had put in some scrubbers to stop air pollution that smelled like rotten eggs all the time. We decided to do several things, including being open about every spill that occurred on site. The company had one of the most modern wastewater treatment facilities on the Catawba River. We invited groups of about a dozen neighbors to tour the plant for on-site orientations to demonstrate the company's progressive program of protecting the area from pollutants. Next, we began inviting various political leaders like city council members, mayors, county commissioners, state legislators, and even Governor Jim Hunt, for one-on-one visits.

We also invited selected news reporters for one-on-one visits, and while our intent was not to generate news, a couple of good articles came out of that. Later when a Superfund story ran on the wire, reporters would already have background knowledge about the company, its record, and its environmental philosophy, rather than having to be educated near deadline. We even invited environmentalists like the Sierra Club, heresy for the chemical industry in those days, to visit the site. Whenever a public announcement by the EPA was made naming the company as a Superfund site, we had employees, their families and neighbors, the local political leadership, the media and customers get immediate communications from the company CEO explaining what happened, the company's commitment to a clean environment, and why it should be classified a Superfund site.

Most visitors were impressed with the company's aggressive environmental protection activities and its belief that pollution-prevention pays good dividends. For example, when it installed scrubbers to collect sulfur that previously would have been lost in the atmosphere, it saved more than five-million dollars in operational costs per year.

These actions mitigated criticism of company operations. When the Superfund site was announced, I went to the *Charlotte Observer* to present statements explaining why the company should not be on the list to an environmental reporter who had written extensively about the company in the past. He said, "You guys have already cleaned up your mess." The headline that followed stated that North Carolina had two Superfund sites, but it did not include our company's name. The second paragraph of the story identified our client as one of the sites, and the third paragraph was our statement. While all the elements of the story were in the article, you couldn't have asked for better coverage and placement!

Letters to employee families provided key messages so family members could better inform their neighbors, their hair dresser, their barber, their service station guy and others about key company message points. We did away with the old theory that you didn't want others to talk about the company. People are going to gossip regardless, so give them the facts to help correct unwanted rumors.

About six months after the Superfund news broke, Governor Hunt visited the plant with a gaggle of reporters and TV crews. He said, "While most companies finagle their way out of meeting the requirements, Sodyeco does it the right way."

- **Enlightened management, lawyers—**

Joe, most of my former PR clients seeking crisis management were reluctant to reveal all the facts, until I explained that it's integral to know the full story in order to devise an Action Plan to control the message before it controls them. Our job as PR strategists is to make a situation better or neutralize it, never make it worse, right?

Prior to the 1990s, few organizations were able to effectively manage crisis communications before things got out of control. But as management became more attuned to the importance of public sentiment, greater efforts went into keeping the public informed. They usually knew what they wanted to say, but often did not know how they should explain the crisis or problem, or they didn't have the resources to do an effective communications program.

Of course, some companies today still botch the obvious or, as in the case of BP's gulf oil spill, the CEO continually put his foot in his mouth, thereby destroying public confidence in the company. After the dismissal of the CEO, BP seems to have been doing a much better job of getting its message across and restoring credibility.

Like firemen, we are usually brought in after the barn is already on fire. Some of the time, however, we have a chance to do remedial work and preventative action beforehand, as we did with Sodyeco. When you let a situation get out of hand in the public arena, it is very difficult to turn around a negative image that has been fixed in the public mind.

The biggest problem, particularly before the mid-1990s, was the lawyer who felt it best not to say anything that might be used in a court of law. However, the legal profession has since come around big time to embrace PR. In fact, now some of our best promoters are law firms that bring us in to help handle situations. We work very much in tandem as equal partners. Lawyers at the table figure out the legal aspects about what should be done, and we focus on doing what's right in the court of public opinion. That teamwork produces the best results for the client.

- **A crisis handled—**

Give an example of how you handled a crisis for a client.

The Sodyeco case study was one of the best. Another good example of a crisis client of Epley Associates involved a trucking company that was one of the largest liquid chemical haulers in the country. It faced a situation where two employees had died while cleaning the inside of a tank trailer. Another company man had been killed the same way about six months before in another part of the system. All had violated company safety policies.

Shortly after the tragedy, the company's Charlotte facility was raided by federal agents and charged with clean water violations. I think the raid was staged partly so the new District Attorney could get a headline, and that much effort certainly didn't justify the extent of slanted coverage and bad publicity that our client received. Although the fatal accidents had nothing to do with the clean water violation, the media made it appear that there was a pattern of wrong doing by our client.

The company's competitors cut the headlines from the newspapers and mailed them to customers around the country. The trucking company lost ten percent of its business almost overnight from customers who said they didn't want anything to do with our client whether they were right or wrong.

The company president and his lawyers came to my office to discuss the situation. I said, "I'm not concerned as much about the press as I am about getting your business back, we can deal with the media in a timely fashion, but we must set priorities on our actions." I advised the president to get on a plane the next day and visit the top five customer CEOs in person and explain what happened, and what the company was doing about it. I suggested that the Executive Vice President go to the next five customers, and then don't stop until they had visited their next top twenty-five customers.

In just one day, personal one-on-one messages were delivered by senior officials to customers that represented about ninety percent of the company's business. The situation was too critical to leave to phone calls or letters, or to delay even one more day. E-mail wasn't big in those days, but even if it was, I would insist on in-person meetings because face to face dialog is always far more effective than communication through any other medium.

The company's lawyer interrupted my comments and said to the client "You've got to be careful about what you say because we may have some litigation coming up." The trucking company's replied, "If we don't get the business back, it doesn't matter what happens in a trial." Then the CEO addressed the deaths of his employees by saying, "I never in all my life want to again tell a wife or child their husband or father is dead. It is just not right!" Then he asked, "How can we make employees understand basic safety"?

You had a lot to absorb and then deal with. What was your plan of action?

First, we had to learn more about the company's business and how they did things. All employees signed releases that said they understood the safety rules, so why didn't they follow those rules?

I sent two young practitioners fresh out of college to find out how safety was communicated. One was a lady born with a silver spoon in her mouth who went to Principia College; the other was a guy who just graduated from North Carolina State. We put them at different truck terminals as wash-rack operator trainees, a job that required no education and was not high paying. In fact, it was a dirty job that had high risks when rules were not followed.

After they spent two days on the job, I asked what they learned. They said that the employees who cleaned the tanks are dumb, most didn't finish high school, and they didn't read or have high comprehension levels. There was little potential for these people, and it was a low paying job that was so nasty and dirty that nobody else wanted it.

We found out that the training was different in both locations, and differed from company policy. We surmised that there was no uniformity in operations throughout the company. Written communication alone would not solve the problem, so we suggested something simple: training videos that teach each phase of the job, including showing how to hook up a hose to the back of a trailer, and how to put on a safety harness when going into a tank to clean it out. The company agreed and we produced four ten-minute videos.

We used the CEO in each video to state bluntly to the employees "If anyone tells you to do something that is unsafe or harmful to the environment, you are authorized to call me direct. My phone number is …."

The CEO made it clear that the manager at each location was accountable for ensuring their employees abided by the video instructions, and all safety and environmental regulations were followed religiously.

On the environmental front, we did media training for the top brass, developed fact sheets, and insisted the company provide better training and oversight for environmental protection.

A simple solution, but did it work?

An interesting thing happened after the safety and training director tried to get us to video short cuts on the job instead of show what company safety and operational policies required. We complained to the CEO that training instructions had be match corporate policy and there should be no conflicts. The safety and training director argued that his was the best and that we should not be so rigid. The company lawyer almost fell out of his chair, and the safety guy was fired on the spot.

As a result of the program we produced, there were fewer accidents, improved supervision, better employee morale and less turnover, all positive factors that improved the bottom line. The company was able to sell some of the training videos to other bulk carriers and recoup some of the production costs.

This is the kind of attention to detail that you have to do in a business to maintain credibility. It also demonstrated what senior managers can accomplish when they put the public good above shaving a few pennies in operational cost at the expense of sound safety and training practice and policy.

How did you apply your strategic public relations knowledge and intuition into growing a client business that was failing because of not retaining or gaining enough customers? Give an example of your Action Plan and the results.

Well, it's always a mixture. The greatest success in PR comes when you deal with CEOs or senior executives who have extensive decision-making power. I tried to avoid working with marketing directors, except in cases of pure marketing engagements.

Some of them are very good, don't get me wrong, but at many companies they are here today and gone tomorrow; they want immediate gratification, they do not think long term, and they look for something for nothing. Since many cannot make a decision on their own, they try to lead you down the Primrose Path to make you think they can.

I personally didn't invest a lot of time and energy following marketing managers' agendas because time is too often wasted by not getting the full picture. Yet for marketing accounts, they do become your bosses. I believe in public relations as a management function.

- **Another client example—**

Can you give me an example of a tough client?

I remember an assignment to help prevent the State Legislature from passing a law that would give auto rate-making authority solely to the North Carolina Insurance Commissioner. The Commissioner wanted to cut rates far below the level where companies could cover their losses. We represented a group of insurance companies that had about eighty percent of the Property Casualty Insurance in the state.

So you became a lobbyist?

No, we didn't lobby in the legal sense. One problem was that the industry had too many lobbyists, but no coordination. We were able to bring them together to focus more effectively on issues for common good of the various entities in the industry. We coordinated with lobbyists to influence public opinion, and to get editorial opinion strong enough to influence the decisions of legislators supporting the Commissioner's bill. Instead of being in competition with the lobbyists who worked directly with the legislators, we worked as collaborators to develop and implement winning strategies.

If the bill had passed, about half of the companies, if not all, would have pulled out of North Carolina and consumers would not have been able to buy a car in the state because nobody would lend money to those without collision insurance.

What was the bottom line?

We formed the North Carolina Insurance News Service to serve as the public relations arm for Property and Casualty Insurance Carriers in North Carolina. For the next twenty five years, we educated the public about auto and home insurance issues that impacted policy holders. We aggressively supported stronger DUI legislation, and sponsored a statewide reward program for information leading to the arrest of arsonists.

Did you have a favorite client or two through your almost four-decade career?

I don't know that I had just one, most were good, responsible organizations run by conscientious executives. One of the things I pride myself on is that our major clients stayed with us for years. I mentioned the Insurance News Service. Then there was Carolina Health Care System that started out as Charlotte Memorial Hospital, Philip Morris and Sodyeco, all with tenures lasting more than twenty years.

One of the most fun clients was one of our first, Carowinds. I developed the initial written concept for the park and created its name. From its concept through the next twenty years, we continued to represent the park through several ownership and management changes. Then Paramount bought the park, and they had their own ways of doing things.

- **Handling difficult clients—**

Give me some input on how you handled difficult clients.

I was fortunate to not have many difficult clients. The problem clients were those who were dishonest, procrastinators or cheats that didn't want to pay for services received. If I suspected a client of dishonesty, I severed the relationship. If they didn't pay their bills, I became hardnosed, and usually we parted ways as I took the necessary action to collect. I don't think I averaged one bad client situation a year in either category. The procrastinator is the most difficult to handle. These are honest folks who have a difficult time making a decision. In most cases, we got them to move by explaining in detail the impact on their reputation by failing to act.

The best way of handling a difficult client is to do enough up front investigation with them before signing on. I remember once I was asked to work for PTL during one of many newspaper exposes on the life of Jim and Tammy Baker. I refused the account, which would have been in the six figures, because Baker's reputation was saying one thing and doing another. Eventually his antics caught up with him and a lot of people were hurt.

Another potential client objected to a clause in our contract that required the client to pay for collection costs if a bill was unpaid for more than ninety days. I told him that if he couldn't pay his bills within ninety days, I didn't want to work with him, and didn't.

- **Planning and rapid-response time—**

Tell me about the importance of planning and rapid-response time in dealing with crises.

For best results you've got to plan, but you also must be able to move as fast as circumstances demand. Let me give you a case study example:

Let me go back to working with Carowinds and their emergency communication plan that we developed for them. Every year, the park held a crisis-simulation drill with emergency first responders for things like fires, ride accidents with multiple casualties and that sort of thing. We told management they should also use the drills to train employees on how to deal with the media when they show up for breaking situations. Theme parks survive on repeat business, and if parents don't feel their children will be safe in a park, business drops off. Effective public communications during a crisis for the park industry is critical to ease public anxiety and maintain public confidence.

A real-time emergency scenario was staged when the park was closed. Only employees, local fire departments, EMTs, and some others knew about it. Park employees were trained to cope with disasters and multiple casualties. It was also a perfect opportunity to help implement procedures in the emergency communications plan, because it is more difficult to cope with the media when you are in the midst of chaos and people are hurt.

There is little time to deal with reporters during an emergency situation, but they can't be ignored. So our staff played the role of hard nosed reporters during these exercises. Department heads and security personnel in particular were taught to respectfully but firmly keep reporters from interfering with emergency operations, and in getting essential factual information to the media as fast as possible.

Our people came in and acted as news reporters, some as obnoxious reporters who demand to get their way, some with video cameras, all trying to get information from employee regardless of the person's duty. Afterwards, we reviewed all of this on video with senior management and department heads so everybody could see the impact of certain behaviors and understand that although they may be up to their butts in alligators, they still have to present a positive image showing that they are on top of situation. They must act with a delicate balance of keeping the public informed while addressing pressing needs of patron and employee safety. Split-second decisions often have to be made.

What was the result of this massive effort?

Two or three weeks after one of these annual drills on a Sunday afternoon about five o'clock, some teenage boys were in the woods about a half-mile from the park shooting an AK-47 assault rifle into the air. A bullet came down into the park and killed a sixteen-year old girl in the swimming pool. The bullet then lodged into another little girl's body, but fortunately she was not killed. No one knew where the shot had come from.

Immediate concerns were getting aid to those hurt and getting everyone else to safety. The park was quickly evacuated. Through the local media, parents who expected to pick up their children at a later hour were informed of what happened, and an appeal was made to others to avoid the area until the crisis was resolved. Park employees stayed with patrons whose transportation had not arrived to help calm their fears and ensure their safety.

Even though the park was full at the time, the general manager was out of town, the public relations director was off that day, and I was attending a conference in the western U.S. To complicate the matter, CNN had a crew covering the televangelist Jim Baker scandal just down the street from Carowinds.

Department heads usually rotated duty as the officer in charge on weekends. Thanks to good advance planning and training, they handled the situation brilliantly. In fact, the way they handled evacuating the park by working with the media, and keeping up a flow of information drew praise in a *Charlotte Observer* editorial. Without those real-time drills, it would be doubtful the managers on duty could have handled such a tragic and chaotic situation with the skill that they did.

The second team made the best out of a terrible situation without misleading anybody.

Right, they reacted quickly and in a way that demonstrated they weren't trying to hide anything. Their priority task though, was caring for the casualties and, as well as other patrons in the park. As a result, the public retained high confidence levels in park management, and park attendance did not suffer.

- **About famous cases—**

You previously mentioned the BP oil spill, can you please give brief responses to the PR surrounding some other well-known crises, starting with the Exxon Valdez oil spill.

You can't make a silk purse out of a sow's ear, but I think Exxon could have done better communications than it did. Disasters caused by negligence often makes matters worse and leads to potential civil and criminal litigation. I believe that Exxon had too many lawyers and not enough community relations and PR folks involved in working the court of public opinion. That's my perception.

Was that because Exxon didn't have a plan to control the message?

It didn't seem like it had a plan. Keep in mind you can have the greatest contingency plans in the world, but if they are not implemented quickly by competent people, the plans are useless. Many large corporations have emergency plans, but few spend the money or take the time to have managers practice implementing the plans. You can't wait until the world is falling down around you to look up the plan to see what is done next. Real-time training sessions with strong critiques must be staged frequently for contingency communication plans to be effective.

The Tylenol scam?

Good, fast thinking, excellent PR execution on the part of senior management. Again, there was a CEO who had an intuitive feel for doing the right thing for the public good.

Disgraced Congressman Anthony Weiner?

Self-destructive and arrogant. And as the immortal Forrest Gump's mama would say, "Stupid is as stupid does."

The Barack Obama 2008 presidential campaign?

Excellent, well executed. But the opposition party four years later accused him of not delivering on expectations.

Lady Gaga?

That isn't PR. She has created a sensational image that is outlandish, and is in the same category as people like Sid Vicious, or whatever his name was, and other so-called stars who think that being ridiculous draws loyal fans. I pay little attention to inconsequential people whose life centers on hype.

What aspects of the person out front, the spokesperson, are necessary to make sure the client's image stays healthy, and do you think each one of these folks needs a PR tutorial?

An organization's spokesperson should put the public good in the forefront of his or her thinking, work from known facts, and not be intimidated by selfish interests of other managers or demanding media. Spokespersons must communicate candidly with the media and public. Yet, they still must protect the interest of their organization. In most cases that is not a conflict, although some narrow-minded executives and advisors don't see it that way. It takes practice to walk that narrow tight rope.

It may not be necessary for a media-savvy spokesperson to have a PR advisor, but it is advisable to have one. Executives today seem to understand the key principles of molding public opinion better than management in years past. However, it still helps to have PR counselors working with you and to provide objective thinking, and to evaluate the public impact of the organization's messages.

Some executives and public figures still have a hard time understanding that in today's world of 24/7 media, you can't hide unpleasant, illegal or immoral conduct for long. Credibility for the individual executive and organizations are strengthened by candid, truthful and timely communication.

- **Influences—**

Who influenced you the most in your business, your particular business?

One was a fellow named Pat Hall, the truest entrepreneur I ever met. Pat was a self-made man who made millions by buying used textile machinery in the 1940s and 1950s then selling them to other countries. After that, he got into commercial real estate and put together huge land deals that brought both the Westinghouse turbine plant and the big Philip Morris cigarette factory to the Charlotte area.

He thought big, and taught me that it only costs ten to twenty percent more to go first class but you get a hundred percent more in return, that anything worth doing is worth doing right, and that you don't take short cuts if you want to have good results.

Pat put together the Carowinds project, and that is how I really got started in business. When I told him I was leaving TV to start my own business, he said, "Why don't you come down here?" At that time I was considering working out of my home to see how things would go.

My first big project came when he told me about an idea to build a theme park that would be in two separate states, and asked me to help bring his concept to reality.

He was a great entrepreneur and creative thinker, but not a good manager. Pat ran the park for the first two years before it was sold. He offered me a full-time job that I refused. I helped him with PR, but then he hired his own people, we drifted apart, but continued as friends and stayed in contact.

Another important influence on my success was one of the great pioneers in public relations, Chet Burger who told me that the amount of a fee charged was not an issue with clients who felt they were getting value from what I provided. He added, "But if they don't perceive value, any fee is too much."

- **The Philip Morris project—**

What came next for you?

Pat Hall and I started working together again when Philip Morris was looking for a plant site in the area. Pat was putting together the land to lure the company to Cabarrus County, just north of Charlotte. I was hired by Philip Morris to assess community attitudes and heritage.

Cabarrus was a one-industry county at that time: textile giant Cannon Mills. After the local Chamber leadership invited Philip Morris to the area, Cannon said publicly they didn't want Philip Morris or its 2,000 union jobs. The local chamber leaders put together petitions with 50,000 names that said they wanted Philip Morris to come. My job was to evaluate the true feelings within the community to help the company make its decision; it did not want to locate where it was not welcome.

I was an intelligence gatherer, seeing and interpreting what was going on in the community. Until a decision was made by the company, I was not to take any actions that might influence the situation one way or the other.

So you weren't involved in promoting Phillip Morris, per se.

Not at that point. They wanted me to find out for sure just how welcome they would be. I knew the editor of the paper, a State senator and the mayor, and was able to get a lot of good information. We started active work when the announcement was to be made. Knowing that there would be a lot of people coming out for the event, including the Governor, Congressman and Secretary of Commerce, we were charged with planning and staging a spectacular announcement.

What year are we talking about?

1978. The only property close to the site big enough for the expected crowds was the fairgrounds.

However, a big windstorm had blown some of the roof off Exhibition Hall and they hadn't fixed it yet. The only way we could stage the event there was to rent a circus tent, and after some searching, I found one in Virginia that could hold five thousand people.

I asked the manager of the fairgrounds how long it would take to get a roof on the Exhibition Hall, and he said about a month and would cost four thousand dollars. I asked, "What if we paid for that roof, could you get it up in two weeks?" He answered quickly, "Heck yeah."

I called the client in New York and said, "Here are our options: not only is the roof going to cost less than a big tent, but if it is raining we won't have to worry about mud and water coming under the tent, and secondly we are doing something good for the community."

That was a no-brainer, they put the roof up, and we gained more goodwill in the community for the client. Media came from throughout the region for what was then the biggest industrial announcement ever made in the state, about a half-billion dollar investment! In addition, we had to coordinate dinners and stage a private breakfast for VIPs and locals who would become close friends of the company.

This was the biggest announcement I was ever involved in, nearly everybody in my firm worked the event, and a few extras were called in to help achieve all of the client's objectives.

- **A question of conscience—**

This question of conscience stems from my experience with Phillip Morris. I served on a committee of fifteen people from all corners of New Jersey charged with assessing the population's attitudes towards tobacco. Although I recognize the First Amendment right to free speech, I had to wrestle with my conscience about helping promote tobacco in any way. How do you feel about tobacco advertising?

As long as a product is legal it should have the same commercial free speech rights as political free speech. I believe wholeheartedly that if tobacco is as harmful as people say it is then it should be outlawed completely. We were not involved in promoting product.

We worked on tobacco-grower relations, community and media relations, and promoting art exhibits in Charlotte and at the Art Museum in Raleigh. We were involved with tax issues and preventing restrictive anti-smoking regulations.

How much did the tobacco industry contribute to the financial health of the area with jobs and for vendors?

Tobacco in North Carolina, until about ten years ago, provided the state's number-one manufacturing revenue, followed by furniture and textiles. It was also the state's largest cash crop by far.

The Southern Piedmont of North Carolina did not grow tobacco, and it had no tradition in tobacco, unlike that of the Northern Piedmont and Eastern North Carolina. But, the community embraced the company and appreciated its proactive community relations activities.

At its peak, Philip Morris employed 2,500 people in manufacturing jobs at the Cabarrus plant, not counting jobs they brought in for construction and vendors and all of that. When the textile industry started dying out, tax revenue from the Philip Morris plant was a lifesaver for Cabarrus County and the city of Concord.

- **Professional disappointments—**

Briefly tell me your biggest professional disappointment, if you care to.

I have been very fortunate in that disappointments have been few, but there have been some. I think the biggest disappointments were clients who talked a big game then didn't do what they were supposed to do. There were plenty of those in political campaigns where the candidate wants to run for office, so you lay out a plan that includes some things that nobody can do for them, but they refuse to put in the energy to work at winning public support.

Then there were the occasional potential clients who wanted to use deceptive communications. We would have no part of that.

It was also disappointing to have an occasional employee who could not quite meet our professional performance standards. We had a rigorous selection process for new employees, regardless of their experience level. Despite this screening process, there were a few during our four decades who couldn't adequately perform and I had to let them go. I felt I had failed as well for not being more diligent.

Fortunately, disappointments were few and far between.

• A friend chats about Joe—

Ambrose Mills, a friend of Joe's who wrote a testimonial about him for this book, stops by to say hello, and I ask him to join our discussion and ask: Ambrose, what kind of guy is Joe Epley?

Joe Epley is a great guy! He's got tons of stories and he's got a lot of accomplishments, and I am happy to call him my good friend. I've known him for six years.

What did you do or what do you do in your career?

Well I was an infantry reservist. I served twenty-seven years in the military and retired as a Lieutenant Colonel. In business, I worked for a client of Joe's at one time, Sodyeco, but I didn't know him then.

Joe, Ambrose seems like a very good friend.

Oh yes. Ambrose succeeded me as chairman of the Economic Development Commission here in the county and did a ten times better job than I. He was also instrumental in leading the effort to secure the Alexander Ford property on Green River for the Overmountain Historic National Victory Trail. This is a significant historical site, and was the last camping place for the overmountain men on their trek to defeat Britain's loyalist army at Kings Mountain.

• Another Case History—

Joe, please cite another interesting sample Case History from your memory archives.

One of our most enjoyable assignments was Contractors Service and Rentals Company, CSR for short, that operated nine branches in the two Carolinas where they sold, serviced and rented construction equipment. They wanted to improve their community relations exposure through making a monetary gift to the North Carolina State Zoo then being established near Asheville.

But rather than just a corporate monetary gift, I suggested they purchase an animal for the zoo, which we could then tie in to promotional activities. The zoo's management was ecstatic when I told them CSR would buy them an elephant. We acquired a baby elephant, the zoo's first, and got the zoo to name it C'sar, which was very fitting because the company's logo was CSR.

Our action-plan included a big media event the day the elephant arrived. We gave C'sar an elephant -size Styrofoam hardhat that bore his name, photographed him with the state Secretary of Natural Resources and the zoo's CEO, and those photos were published in most of the newspapers in the state.

A year later, we held a gala birthday party for C'sar at the zoo that featured a birthday cake made of peanuts. All of the employees' children were invited to attend and were served ice-cream and real cake, as were members of the media and state officials. Six TV stations and several newspapers covered the event, and our photographer distributed photos to all of the newspapers and magazines in the state, as well as to national trade publications.

We got Pulitzer Prize-winning cartoonist Gene Payne of the *Charlotte Observer* to draw a cartoon of C'sar wearing his hardhat, and then put the logo on thousands of tee-shirts for sale at the Zoo and client retail locations. A shirt was given to every employee and child under eighteen. Every CSR store had a hundred-pound bag of peanuts for customers and employees to munch on, and 10,000 bumper stickers in corporate colors that read "See C'sar at the NC Zoo" were produced and distributed throughout the state.

The results were terrific: for three years, my client gained significant marketing recognition for its donation of the baby elephant to the zoo. C'sar became a good marketing mascot, as well as catalyst for the company's first major formal employee relations program.

Our campaign brought thousands of people to the zoo; it was a win-win for all with minimal investment.

• Where PR is heading—

From your vantage-point as elder-statesman, where do you think the PR discipline is heading in the 21st century?

I believe public relations practitioners, whether working for not-for-profits, in corporations or in consulting firms large and small, have great opportunities in this ever-changing world. But they have to work at being more than just creative writers or event planners.

The days of the corporate journalist have basically vanished; now there is a growing demand for the practitioner to serve as a principal advisor to senior management whether externally or internally.

What is your advice to young practitioners, and college graduates who are majoring in public relations?

The successful public relations practitioner will be a strategic thinker who understands the complexity of business, the intricacies of local and global politics, the instability and flexibility of public attitudes, communications technology, and opportunities in the making. European and North American public relations firms will engage in more partnerships and joint ventures, and these efforts will not be restricted to just large multi-national firms.

To be successful, PR practitioners of the future should have solid foundations in psychology, to understand motivation and belief; political science, to understand how the government works; anthropology, to understand changes and the importance of cultural adaptation; sociology, to be able to precisely estimate tendencies in development of a society; in interaction of people; and in economics, to understand business and financial factors that affect commerce. They also need to know the basic communication skills of writing and using traditional and social media. And of course, they meet the demands of clients who expect us to walk on water.

I am confident the PR profession will continue to grow and prosper in the global marketplace. We who shape public perceptions of our discipline must continue to demonstrate aggressive leadership to change for the better how we do business here and around the world. We need new strategies to better train new professionals, and to ensure that we equip our firms in the most effective way to meet client needs in an expanding global environment.

People should realize that all PR is not the same, and that there is no set formula for solving problems. General PR practitioners must be able to use effectively new trends in social media, get media placement, and understand issues management and government relations. Those who specialize in specific disciplines must also have the flexibility to adapt to changing situations.

I believe more practitioners will go into niche fields, but everyone in the profession needs to understand the significant differences between marketing and management PR, and understand the role of a consultant versus that of an internal staff member. To succeed, the practitioner must demonstrate talent, initiative, and the objective thinking that makes them an integral part of any management team. It is a good idea to seek out a mentor to help direct and guide your career. But most of all, they must think strategically and have a broad understanding of changing factors that affect their employer's organization.

- **The current phase—**

You seem to be enjoying yourself now, free of the pressure of running your own business. Is that right?

I entered the current phase in my life in 2005 when I sold the firm and moved to the Tryon area to retire, but you can't just turn off a life style. I continue to do some consulting and am active in a number of community activities. I tell folks that I can't get a grasp on the retirement gig; I suspect it is just a frame of mind.

For as long as I can remember, I have wanted to write a novel but never quite got around to it. So, I stopped procrastinating and wrote a historical novel about the western Carolinas during the American Revolutionary War titled *A Passel of Hate*. Now I'm into doing a second book about the same era.

- **The Epley legacy—**

Aside from your contributions to establishing diversity and high ethical standards within the public relations profession, what would you consider to be the primary elements of your legacy?

I would like for it to be for a commitment to lifelong learning. I've never received a college diploma but have always been an ardent supporter of education, and of advancing the public relations discipline through strong educational and professional development. I tell young college students that getting a degree is just the first phase of one's education. When you decide to stop learning it's time to quit, for you no longer will be proving yourself useful to others and yourself.

In 2003 to commemorate the thirty-fifth anniversary of the founding of Epley Associates Public Relations, a Scholarship Foundation was established in my honor. The annual scholarship goes to exceptional students preparing for a career in PR through endowments at three universities in North Carolina, including Appalachian State, North Carolina State, and the University of North Carolina at Charlotte. It is registered as a non-profit charity by the Internal Revenue Service.

I have been honored by UNC-Charlotte where students who meet certain criteria are awarded the Epley Certificate in International Public Relations. I also serve as an advisor to the Center for Global Public Relations, and am on the Board of Advisors for the College of Liberal Arts and Sciences at UNC-Charlotte.

And, that I built my career and company through long days of hard work and never resting an inquisitive mind.

Portrait of Joe Epley in front of a Lady Justice Gagged poster was made by the Charlotte Observer. Epley commissioned the poster as part of a national PR campaign to build awareness and support for commercial free speech.
Photo courtesy The Charlotte Observer

World travelers, Joe and his wife, Dorcas, enjoy a sunrise at Uluru (Ayers Rock) in the heart of Australia's outback in 2004.

In Budapest in 1998, Roger Haywood, former chair of the British Public Relations Institute confers with Epley and Hubert Wisse of the Netherlands at a Worldcom Public Relations Group conference in Budapest, Hungary.

The Epley Philosophy: "Deceit, deception, selfishness nor hypocrisy have a place in ethical public relations."

Jeffery Julian, the 2008 president of the Public Relations Society of America, presents PRSA's prestigious Gold Anvil award to Epley at the Society's international conference in Detroit.

In September, 2001, Sergei Belenkov, President of the Russian Public Relations Association, presents a lifetime membership to Joe Epley in recognition for his role in establishing the Association in 1991. Joe's Moscow trip to receive the award was delayed two weeks by the 9/11 attack in New York.

One of the first documentary television programs produced by Joe Epley was on the gridiron career of football great Charlie Choo-Choo Justice, shown here reviewing game film with Epley at WLOS-TV in Asheville in 1962. Looking on is the late Bob Phelps, a popular TV personality in the 1950s and 60s.

Joe Epley speaks at the 20th anniversary celebration conference for the Russian Public Relations Society in Moscow in December 2012. Alexander Borisov, the founding president of RPRA is seated on the right.

During the 1980s and early 90s, Joe made nearly a dozen deep wilderness canoe trips into Canada's arctic and sub-arctic wildernesses. Here he holds a wolf pup caught on the Thelon River in the Barrens of the Northwest Territories.

Section 6: **Chronology**

- 1938 Born, Forest City, NC
- 1956 Graduated, Cool Springs High School, Forest City, NC
- 1956 Entered Active Army
- 1959 Employed as news reporter/photographer – WLOS TV, Asheville
- 1959 Married Dorcas Starnes of Asheville
- 1963 Moved to Charlotte as news reporter/editor for WBTV
- 1963 Joined National Guard Special Forces, earned the Green Beret
- 1968 Began Epley Associates Public Relations firm in Charlotte. CEO until 2005 retirement
- 1968 Transfer from National Guard 20th Special Forces to Army Reserve 11th Special Forces
- 1973 Accredited by the Public Relations Society of America
- 1978 Retired from US Army Reserve as Master Sergeant
- 1980 President, Charlotte Chapter, PRSA
- 1981 Awarded Charlotte PR Society Infinity Award for exceptional professional achievement
- 1981 President, Executives Association of Greater Charlotte
- 1983-1988 Board of Directors, Charlotte Chamber of Commerce
- 1985-2003 Board of Directors, North Carolina Citizens for Business and Industry
- 1986-1988 Chair, America's Group-International Public Relations Group of Companies
- 1986 Chair, PRSA Counselor's Academy
- 1987-2006 Board of Visitors, Johnson C. Smith University
- 1988 Co-founded the Worldcom Public Relations Group
- 1989 Named Tar Heel of the Week by Raleigh News and Observer
- 1989-2001 Board of Advisors, N.C. Outward Bound School
- 1990 Began helping introduce PR education and professional standards to the Soviet Union
- 1991 President, Public Relations Society of America
- 1992 University of North Carolina School of Journalism Public Relations Hall of Fame
- 1992 President, PRSA Foundation
- 1993 Alumni Hall of Fame, Defense Information School
- 1996 President, PRSA Foundation
- 1997-2003 Board of Directors, Charlotte World Affairs Council
- 1998-1999 Chair, Worldcom PR Group for North and South America
- 1999-2005 Board of Advisors, Charlotte area Salvation Army
- 1999- current Board of Directors, The Marketing Alliance (publicly traded national insurance brokerage)
- 2000-2002 Global chair, Worldcom Public Relations Group
- 2001 Awarded life time membership in Russian Public Relations Association
- 2003-2008 President's Council, Central Piedmont Community College
- 2004 Awarded North Carolina's Order of the long Leaf Pine
- 2004-2010 Member Polk County Economic Development Commission
- 2005 Sold Epley Associates and retired, moved fulltime to Tryon, NC
- 2005-2011 Board of Directors, Pavilion
- 2006 Chair, PRSA College of Fellows
- 2006-2012 Trustee, Blue Ridge Parkway Foundation
- 2006 Board of Advisors –Center for Global Public Relations
- 2007-2013 Board of Advisors, UNC-Charlotte College of Liberal Arts and Sciences
- 2007-2008 Chair-Polk County Visioning Committee
- 2008 Awarded Gold Anvil by PRSA for Lifetime Achievement
- 2008-2009 Chair, Polk County Economic Development Commission
- 2010 Board of directors Thermal Belt Outreach Ministry
- 2011 Published historical novel: "*A Passel of Hate*"

● ● ●

Richard Ritter

Studio Glass Artist and Volunteer Fireman

35 years ago, I wanted to get to know my neighbors, and the local Volunteer Fire Department was a good fit. I have enjoyed community service and helping people. Glass blowing and fire fighting have lots in common. It's important to keep a cool head, to respect the heat and get the job done!
— Richard Ritter.

Sections about Glass Artist Richard Ritter:

1) From Those in the Know about Ritter & His Glass Art

2) Highlights of His Life and Career

3) **Richard's Life Journey, in His Own Words**

4) Photos

5) Shows and Exhibitions

6) Chronology

Section 1: **From Those in the Know about Ritter & His Glass Art**

- **Art Professor: 'Ritter is a Pioneer in the Studio Glass Movement'—**

Although he is best known to his neighbors in Bakersville as a tireless community volunteer and former chief of the fire department, Richard Ritter is recognized worldwide as a master of the art of glass.

Ritter's art is the expression of his intimate knowledge of his medium. A meticulous technician, he mixes and melts his own colors of glass rather than relying on the palette available from industry. During his early investigations of glass working he devised a rudimentary method of making slices of patterned glass cane known as murrinis, a decorative device known in ancient Egypt and Rome and familiar today in the *millefiori* paperweights of Italy.

Now in his fifth decade as an artist in glass, he is in utter control of the 'murrini process', capable of creating images that range from photographic realism to grotesque fantasy. Suspending these richly patterned canes within a crystal matrix, Ritter plays incisive images against broad strokes of color applied hot from the furnace. When the glass has cooled, he may use the processes of cutting and polishing to open a window deep into the glass matrix; sandblasting and electroforming often provide a counterpoint on the surface.

Modeled images that echo Ritter's background as a jeweler also appear. The work is many layered, and marked by a unique and unsurpassed richness.

A student at Penland School of Crafts in 1971 and later an artist in residence there, he married Jan Williams, an artist in residence in flat glass at the school who had been his student and assistant. In 1980 the couple settled in Young Cove, a few miles from Penland School. In the farmhouse there they brought up their three children, and there they live and create their work today.

Ritter frequently teaches at Penland, where his generosity in sharing his knowledge with a new generation of artists has been recognized by a scholarship endowed in his name.

Richard Ritter is a pioneer in the Studio Glass Movement in the United States and one of its masters. As artist, teacher and community volunteer he would be honored wherever he chose to live. Western North Carolina is proud to claim him as our own.
   — **Joan Falconer Byrd,** Professor of Art, Western Carolina University.

- **Three Ritter Children Reflect about their Artist Dad—**

The Ritter children, William, Kaete Syed and Richie, each wrote about their father in a Western Carolina University 2009 publication titled "40 Years in Glass". That publication promoted the Fine Art Museum's partnership with the Toe River Arts Council in presenting "A dramatic exhibition featuring the extraordinary Richard Ritter". Excerpts from the Ritter children:

William: *I've grown up the son of a master artist. I cut 'murrinis' and pulled cane for my allowance without thought of the great privileges of my unique upbringing. I was 'dragged' to galleries around the country when I would rather be down by the creek catching frogs. Mine was a childhood full of exposure to pottery, glass and painting. After taking art classes at WCU, I began to understand the incredible skill and craftsmanship of my father's work—he is a creative genius. I am very proud of my father for this—the art that is his life's work. But, if you ask me, his greatest legacy is an unswerving dedication to community, family and friends . . . behind a very, very talented and hardworking artist is a good gardener and great neighbor.*

Kaete: *My father's murrinis were the magic treasure of my childhood. Murrinis filled my pockets; were buried in boxes imagined to be a Dragon's hoard of jewels . . . they were as natural a part of the world as the air I breathed or the flowers I gathered . . . they became more cherished as I learned it was an ancient art, all too rarely practiced. I carry one with me always – a piece of home, of family, of tradition, wherever I go.*

Richie: *I grew up surrounded by glass. It was and still is part of my life on a daily basis. As soon as I arrived home on the school bus, I would run up to the studio to open doors on the furnace or glory hole. As I was given more essential jobs I remember the thrill of being trusted to carry the pipe and reheat the piece. There is a kind special, intricate dance that occurs as the piece comes to life before our eyes. Each piece is special, and seeing older works is like visiting old friends. They link to emotions and memories that I will always cherish.*

- ## Jan Ritter Explains the Signature Richard Ritter Process—

Jan Ritter, a glass artist in her own right, explains the meaning of the esoteric term murrini that is the signature of her husband Richard's studio glass art and is frequently referred to in this biography:

A murrini can be defined as a slice off of a piece of long glass cane that has an image created that runs the entire internal length of the cane. Richard would always describe to his students that making a murrini is like making a jelly roll. You start with layers of cake and jelly, roll them up and slice the cake to reveal the spiral within. The Italians made fantastic murrinis with images of flowers that they called '*millefiori*' which means "a thousand flowers". The term *millefiori* just doesn't describe images of people, animals, or abstract shapes. So, in the contemporary glass world, we use the term murrini.

Richard hired me to work with him in his studio at Penland in 1974, and my first job was cutting murrini on the diamond saw. Within a few weeks, he was busy creating a "family portrait murrini" that included images of his father, mother, and sister Kathy. This one murrini took him six months to create, and was made up of thousands of tiny colored glass threads. There was a lot of work to be done in mixing up the raw materials and coloring oxides to melt the colors, and pulling the threads. The culmination of all of that work was when we actually fused the murrini at 1100 degrees Fahrenheit in an annealler, attached them to a hot blow pipe and pulled the cane. That year, Richard also had the idea that it would be fun to fuse a glass bowl in a ceramic mold that would hold 1000 murrini slices. It wasn't long before I became pretty good at cutting murrini.

In the next few years, Richard made a lot of murrini, and I got the idea to take one sample of each murrini and stash it in a jar so that someday he would have a collection. Most often he would use every last slice in his pieces, so he had no permanent record of each individual cane, whether it was an image of a fish or a butterfly, or an abstract pattern. After two years, I had quite a collection in that jar, but one day he discovered it - "What's this?" he asked as he shook the jar. He walked over to the annealing oven, poured out all of the murrinis, and used them all together in his next piece. Believe me from then on I stashed them where he wouldn't find them. Today we are truly thankful that I kept samples of the murrinis over the years. They create a history of his art in many small glass murrini slices. And believe it or not, after all these years I am still cutting those murrinis!

Author's Note: Wikipedia defines *millefiori* as a glasswork technique that produces distinctive decorative patterns on glassware, and interprets the term as a combination of the Italian *mille* for thousand and *fiori* for flowers. Apsley Pellatt in his book *Curiosities of Glass Making* first used the term *millefiori,* which appeared in the Oxford Dictionary in 1849; they were called mosaic beads before then. While the use of this technique long precedes the term *millefiori,* it is now frequently associated with Venetian glassware. The technique has been applied to polymer clays and other materials. Polymer clay is quite pliable and does not need to be heated and reheated to fuse it.

Section 2: **Highlights of His Life and Career**

- **Named a 'North Carolina Living Treasure' in 2011—**

Richard Ritter's unique career began in earnest in 1969 and the honors keep rolling in, as the studio glass art master was designated a "North Carolina Living Treasure" in 2011 by the Museum of World Cultures of UNC Wilmington. Established in 1986, this statewide award honors craftsmen who have consistently grown in their art over decades of work.

- **Honored with the Governor's Award for Volunteer Service—**

The Mitchell County resident was honored in 1998 with the North Carolina Governor's Award for Volunteer Service for his efforts as Chief of Bakersville Volunteer Fire and Rescue during a devastating flood in his district. Richard began that volunteer service in 1982 and continues to serve today.

- **An Honorary Doctor of Fine Arts—**

In 2000, Ritter was named an Honorary Doctor of Fine Arts by the Center for Creative Studies School of Art and Design in Detroit, Michigan. He is a graduate of the Art School of the Society of Arts and Crafts, which is in the College for Creative Studies, where he majored in Crafts, Advertising and Design.

- **Grants from 1972 through 2001—**

In 2000-200l, the studio glass artist received a North Carolina Artist Fellowship Grant, in 1984 the National Endowment for the Arts Fellowship Grant, and in 1972 both the National Endowment for the Arts Penland Residency Grant, and the Louis C. Tiffany Grant for Penland School of Crafts Residency Grant. Ritter served on the Board of Directors for the Penland School of Crafts from 1992-through-2000, and also the North Carolina State Arts Council from 2007 to 2011.

- **Media Exposure—**

Ritter was featured in the cover story titled 'Richard Ritter-Thinking in the Language of Glass' by Joan Falconer Byrd, professor of art at Western Carolina University in Cullowhee, in the August 1998 edition of *American Craft Magazine.* Her knowledge-based testimonial to him is featured in Section 1 of this biography, in which she gives personal evaluations of his skill, talent and dedication to studio glass art.

Richard was also featured in articles titled 'Blown Away: International Glass of the 21st-Century' in the Flint Institute of Arts publication; 'Voices of Contemporary Glass, the Heineman Collection' in the Corning Glass publication; and '40 Years in Glass' in a Western Carolina University publication.

- **A Major Installation—**

Ritter's studio glass art has been featured in a permanent Installation at the Novi Public Library in Novi, Michigan since 2010. The Installation features 16 solid glass apples in homage to the orchard that once covered the site in Richard's boyhood. Comprehensive lists of his teaching experience, and Select Retrospectives, Permanent Collections and Exhibitions appear in Section 5.

Section 3: **Richard's Life Journey, in His Own Words**

After a lengthy drive from Hendersonville through the picturesque Blue Ridge Mountains of North Carolina and over winding country roads, I arrive at the Ritter home and studio tucked on a hillside overlooking a sprawling garden in Bakersville. Jan Ritter is put-at-ease welcoming, and moments later Richard, the Notable biography subject for today, emerges from his studio with daughter Kaete. The studio glass artist seems the modern version of a sixties craftsman, complete with pony-tail.

I begin the interview with Jan as the proud and willing co-spokesperson for the Ritter clan, to nodding approval from her husband and Kaete:

- **Family and Home—**

Jan, tell me about your children.

Richie was born in September 1978, Kaete in November 1981, and William was born in February 1987. Richie works for Western Carolina University on software for the IT Department. Over the years Richie has been a real asset in the studio, and became one of Richard's most valuable apprentices during his twenties. Kaete is a sculptor with a passion for iron; she and her husband Zishan Syed are expecting their first child this spring. William is a musician with plans to further his education in Appalachian Studies in the fall. All of our children have grown up working beside us in the studio and each has made unique contributions to our work.

Richard, please describe what got you here and tell me about your wonderful garden.

Our home is kind of a throwback to where we came from. She grew up on a hundred-acre farm in Bucks County, Pennsylvania, and I grew up on a little twenty-two acre farm in Novi, Michigan, so we both know and like farming. We've both worked the earth, and that is pretty much what our garden is all about - we want to know where the things we eat are grown.

So, what is growing in your garden right now?

Sweet potatoes, potatoes, all kinds of beans, cucumbers and soy beans – this is the first time I've grown soy beans, sunflowers, and lots of Japanese beetles.

I see corn right behind the sunflowers.

Yeah, early corn and late corn, and we have raspberries, broccoli, beans, peas, squash, and lots of dill to go with our cucumbers beyond that orange fence. Of course, the raspberries are taking over one side, and we've got a blueberry patch there.

Richard, how long have you been in this house?

Since June of 1981. I'm from the Land of Lakes, so I have a pond up there stocked with bluegills and trout. And if you ever need a place to stay, we have a cabin a mile down the road, pre-Civil War, with a trout pond in the front. Our mountain home was built in 1902 and I rebuilt it in the 1980s. My dad built three houses when I was growing up. He was a tool and die-maker, so the 'hands thing' is in the family I guess.

- **Studio Glass Art—**

Tell me about your evolution to studio glass art.

Over the years I've had many apprentices or assistants. I hesitate to call all of them apprentices because some were more skilled than I am. There were times I had two or three, but lately we've scaled down to just Jan and me.

Richard, can we tour your studio?

Sure, follow me. This is what is called a hot shop, in other words, where we work with hot glass. When I started glassblowing, there were no furnaces or equipment commercially available, so you had to build your own. We built all of the equipment in here, pretty much.

So this is the original equipment from when you first moved in here?

Actually, I built one furnace and Jan built the other, and we've rebuilt them a few times in the past 35 years. But that was out of necessity because small scale furnaces for glass studios were not commercially available.

I think it's a shame that most artists making glass these days have no idea how to build equipment. All of these annealing ovens I built and have used for almost forty years.

So you basically start from scratch by building your furnaces. Sounds like you have a unique hands-on approach to your art.

Yes, unique to the people that worked in the first twenty-five years of the Studio Glass Movement. I continue to make my own glass from the raw materials, too. In other words, I use my own 'cake mix'; I do not buy commercial glass. My batch consists of silica, soda, lime, barium, and a few other ingredients.

• Learning and teaching—

I take it that all of your products are from your own custom-made glass? How did you learn what must be a complex process?

Yes it is. I trace it back to art school where we were taught how to mix our own paints, and how to make our own canvases. But art programs rarely teach that anymore.

Which art school?

I graduated from the Art School of the Society of Arts and Crafts in Detroit, Michigan in 1969. I later was awarded an Honorary Doctor of Fine Arts from my *alma mater*. It was an honor to be the first craftsman awarded a Doctoral Degree by CCS.

The Studio glass movement had started in the early sixties, and the Society of Arts and Crafts built its shop in 1969, and I had the good fortune to be a part of that. My experience at the school prepared me for a lifetime of work in the arts. I am genuinely thankful for my education there.

Where else have you taught?

I have given workshops in hot glass all over the U.S. in the past forty years, The Toledo Art Museum, Tulane University, The University of Illinois, Urbana, and Western Carolina University, to name a few. I have also taught at the Sheridan College of Art in Toronto.

How many years have you taught at Penland, and do you still teach?

Since 1972, I have taught fourteen summer sessions in Glass, and eight Concentration Sessions in Glass at the school.

I first went to Penland as a student in 1971 back when I just started in glass, and when I became a resident artist at Penland I helped to build the program. I didn't study glass at art school; I graduated as an advertising illustrator, and did that for six years. In fact, I was a figure illustrator, but the need for that died immediately after I graduated. I really didn't like it anyway; there were just too many bosses.

Jan, do the Ritters have any shows coming up soon?

Richard is part of a group assembled by Habitat Galleries in Royal Oak Michigan that puts together artists to show their work at "Sculpture, Object, Function Art". There is a good show coming up in Santa Fe, New Mexico. An assemblage of galleries from all over the country often comes together to show the work of ten to fifteen artists they each represent.

How many pieces will Richard display, and can you describe them in art-speak?

Richard will have five pieces at this show. He's been working on three of them in small-scale sculpture: a green apple, a red apple, and a yellow pear, all solid glass pieces.

- **Unique work—**

I'm no expert, of course, but the Richard Ritter studio glass method seems unique.

What makes Richard's work unique is the *murrini,* which is what he uses to get imagery in his glass.

That is an esoteric term that we explained in the introductory pages, but please tell us more about it.

They were known back then as *millefiories, which is* Italian for "a thousand flowers". But that didn't apply for a portrait, so in the contemporary glass movement we use the word murrinis.

Neither word is right or wrong in this business, but we like murrinis better because we think it covers all images from realistic to abstract in cane.

Look at this dragonfly; could you consider it to be a flower?

We make our own images; everything is made from scratch; that is our work.

Richard, about how long would it take for you to make one of these pieces?

Well, making all the parts are the problem. It's hard to say because you don't know exactly; there are a lot of processes involved.

In addition to working the piece hot, you need to 'cold work' the piece: you will grind, sand-blast, and acid etch the piece of glass, and on it goes.

It's pretty hard to keep an accurate record of time, but I am not a record keeper anyway, as Jan will tell you.

- **No labels—**

When someone asks you what you do, what is your short answer? Are you a glass sculptor?

I generally say I'm a glass artist, but lately I drop off the word glass. Labels do not mean a lot to me. Oops....or maybe they do?

When I started in glass it was functional, but I soon realized that sculptural forms better suited my imagery. I made things for people to actually use for about ten years, but when you realize I've been doing this for forty years then that doesn't seem so long, right?

Back then it was more about the "process of making' with the glass, and using murrini and cane was an exciting surface element. But then form became more important to me than making each piece just a vessel.

When I was in jewelry, I did a lot of production work, and a lot of commissions. I found that very hard to keep doing over and over again, so I totally got away from that.

I wouldn't take any work on commission when I went into glass, and I still don't take it if there are a lot of strings attached

How would you describe your craft to an uninitiated observer like me?

I have to go back to when I first was trained as a painter and an illustrator because images always had important meaning for me. I got into the glass movement because it was brand new and exciting. I really liked the material and what I could do with it to make glass images. What other material can be so fluid and instantly solid within seconds?

Of course command of the material didn't all come that fast or easily. I can show you my very first piece, and then go on in chronological order to today. It is really personal to try to describe the journey of coming up with an idea, and then working at it for two to three years to get it right.

Describe the beautiful glass piece you are holding.

The original drawing for this core piece doesn't look anything like how it turned out, because when I finished it I had gotten beyond what I had imagined. I think glass art is my way of presenting images. I'm not an artist who is trying to change the world or anything; I just love to do beautiful things with glass.

Did you have an epiphany, or did you gradually decide to become a studio glass artist?

I think the decision moment happened when I first worked with glass.

Can you describe that?

When I was at art school, I took every painting class I could. You signed up for fifteen hours but could take as many hours as you wanted for the same tuition, so I took painting, I took sculpture, I took ceramics, I took jewelry. In fact, my second major was in jewelry. The college is right across from the Detroit Museum, an incredible resource for an art student.

But I left school with only a half-semester to graduation to take a great job with an advertising agency. I worked for two different agencies for a total of six years.

When did you start with glass art?

In 1968 I became disenchanted with advertising, decided to go back to finish my education and went back to Arts and Crafts to study Jewelry.

- **Back to school—**

How did you make a living after you lost your job?

I went around for a couple of weeks looking for jobs, but every place I went looked just like the place I had just left, so I went back to finish school, determined to finish what I started. After graduation, I didn't want to do advertising again.

I knew the director of the school and told him I was going back into jewelry. He said "Okay, that's great," and then added, "Oh by the way, we need somebody to teach advertising, and if you agree to teach a few courses that will cover your tuition."

I was going to go back to school full-time because part time would have taken forever, so I taught advertising.

So you couldn't get away from advertising after all.

Nope. I felt a little guilty about not liking advertising but teaching it. Four of my students received scholarships that year; three changed over to Fine Art, so let's just say that the advertising department was not real happy with me.

My art education made it possible to do whatever I wanted to do in glass, because I also had the ability to use a wide variety of processes and materials.

What came next for you?

After graduation, I was hired to teach jewelry at Arts and Crafts as a junior professor, but it was only a part time position for nine dollars an hour, and other than my first wife having some income as a museum art historian, we were struggling.

There was school in Birmingham, Michigan just outside of Detroit called the Bloomfield Art Association, an upscale area that had an art center for adult education students with evening courses for kids, and some courses that could be used for college credit. I went there to teach jewelry because they were paying fifteen dollars an hour. So I was busy teaching jewelry at two schools and making my own jewelry to sell.

When I took the teaching job at the arts center, I said on my resume that I'd done glass before. Well, I actually had just one semester helping build the glass shop at Arts and Crafts, and I only gathered glass eleven times, and that is not really a full semester's worth. Anyway, they asked if I could build them a glass shop and I said sure, so I built it then started a program there.

- **The Mark Peiser Influence—**

Soon I began selling pieces to galleries in New York and Birmingham. I was also showing jewelry and glass at The America House Gallery in *Birmingham, Michigan*, and that's where I first saw Mark Peiser's work, and how I found out about Penland and its summer programs.

I called Mark and said "I'd love to come down and take a class". The class was full, but Mark said that he would make space for me. As I was using simple murrini in my pieces, Mark encouraged me to stay on and take the next session in glass at Penland which was taught by Dick Marquis. Dick Marquis is probably the most renowned *murrini* maker in the United States, and he had just come back from studying glass in Italy on a Fulbright Scholarship.

I told Bill Brown, the Director at that time, that I'd like to stay at Penland but I had spent all of my savings to take Peiser's session. Bill Brown asked me what I could do to help the studio, and I agreed to repair the annealing ovens in exchange for tuition, room and board to attend Dick's class.

I got to stay, and have literally pretty much stayed since then. That was in 1971. I will be forever thankful that Bill Brown gave me the opportunity that changed my life.

How influential has Mark Peiser been to you and your career?

Very influential! Mark is one of the main reasons I make my own glass. Mark mixes his own glass, and I went to him to learn a little about it. Later on he helped me develop my first batch of glass and taught me how to do my own colors, and I've grown from that. He got me started, but basically it wasn't so much the skill stuff, but his philosophy of "Just go ahead and do it!"

When I went back to Michigan, I taught glass again that year at the Bloomfield Art Association. I had to work all summer long then throw away what I was making in order to show the students how to make new things. And as Jan well knows, there was no market for glass.

How did you sell your pieces?

For the first three years I went to art fairs. Of course the fairs weren't at everybody's back door like they are now. Many of the other exhibiting artists purchased those early pieces of glass; those folks were a wonderful support system.

- **Progression as an artist—**

Describe your progression through the years as a glass artist, the different phases or stages you went through, and your philosophy about it all.

Penland School and its Director Bill Brown had a philosophy that extended well beyond the arts community. This was a school that taught the crafts to people from all walks of life. Penland was and is a life changing alternative to the university system. The reason the dining hall tables there are round is literally because Bill Brown preferred to sit with all of us, there was no pecking order, and everybody was considered equal. I loved it.

It sounds like Penland is a very creative and friendly school.

It is and was, especially during that fertile seventies contemporary craft movement. And, Bill Brown deservedly received the Governor's Award from the State for his work.

Jan, what do you think about the Governor's Award and his work at the school?

That was justly deserved recognition for Bill and for Penland. We were invited to go to the awards ceremony and celebration at the Governor's mansion. We had worked hard to help get Bill nominated. We sent letters to artists, art professors and teachers around the country, and many wrote wonderful endorsement letters for him. Over the years, Bill Brown's philosophy spread with all of its former teachers and students throughout the university systems all around the world.

Richard, I take it that the movement was fueled by Bill's philosophy.

Yes, he didn't separate the students, and just did whatever he could do for each artist. And he relied on everyone to share their knowledge, enjoy the beautiful environment at Penland, eat great food, have fun, and grow artistically.

For many years Mark and I would get together to hire teachers for the summer, drawing them from many areas around the country.

There were no tricks, you taught everything you knew to anybody that wanted to learn. You didn't keep anything secret, you shared everything. I've always believed that when you teach at Penland you are going to learn something yourself.

- **Growing quickly—**

How did the glass movement progress after those early years?

The glass movement doesn't sound like it happened quickly because it is now fifty-years-old, but it did. By the eighties it was really off and running.

As a glass artist and Richard's partner and wife, how do you see the movement, Jan?

As the movement grew the artists grew in their ability to make really technically proficient glass, with colors and detail in their objects, imagery, things they couldn't imagine before, that you couldn't even imagine when you started.

In the early years, many artists melted glass bottles to work with. With everyone sharing what they knew with others working in the field, the information grew exponentially.

Richard, how difficult is it to become proficient at making glass art?

I really consider myself self-taught as far as the glass goes, and that's both a good and bad thing. It probably took me eight years to discover what some kids now can do in eight weeks or eight months.

But I see some limitations in that they sort of get in a rut a little early, no matter how much data they have. I think the findings and discoveries back then led us in directions where some people won't go now because they can simply buy glass in a plastic baggie and then melt it.

We still make our own glass, and I make my own colors.

Explain the advantage of doing all that in your studio.

Okay, let's say I want to do a bright red. I might not be able to find the red to buy, or a yellow or a pink. Making your own color is like painting, though there are wonderful painters that just use color tubes. I just prefer to have my own pallet. Out of necessity, we created our own unique formulas for our crystal and colored glasses in the early days. A few of us still do to this day.

- **Glass artists in the early years—**

Who were some of your contemporaries through the years?

There weren't many out there in those early years. Two early teachers and innovators were Dominick Labino and Harvey Littleton. These were the pioneers, and the next generation was not far behind them.

Dominick was an inventor, the master of the technical part, making the furnaces and formulas to make glass blowing possible on a small scale so that an individual artist could be technician, artist, and designer. Harvey was the artist and teacher who gathered the students together. He was an incredible promoter for the studio glass movement. Together they worked to give this creative movement its start.

Then those students spread out and built their own small studios.

I read that Harvey's father was director of research and development for Corning Glassworks but wanted his son to go into physics. But Harvey opted to work with glass and became a legend in glass -blowing and sculpture.

Harvey Littleton is a true artist. In fact the studio glass movement will be celebrating its fiftieth year in glass at the Toledo Art Museum where it all started in 1962.

Jan, how widespread is studio glass art in this area?

There are over twenty-five hot glass studios in Western North Carolina, including two energy efficient glass studios offering residencies. One is called the Energy Exchange of Mitchell and Yancey Counties, and the other is the Green Energy Park in Jackson County.

There are some within universities around the country, but glass studios tend to cluster around schools, like they are situated around Penland.

Richard, do glass artists often get together in clubs or groups?

The Glass Arts Society started at Penland, and Jan and I did its first newsletter. The second annual meeting was in my studio at Penland. The first twenty years, the Glass Art Society existed primarily for artists and students. In later years, collectors, museums and galleries joined as well.

Jan, how would you describe your husband's involvement in the glass arts community?

Richard and I wanted to live near to Penland School and its extended family of artists. It has been wonderful to have friends nearby struggling with the same issues we are in the studio. It's hard to describe Richard's philosophy. He has been incredibly proud to be a part of the studio glass movement, and he is still amazed by what new ideas are being expressed.

It sounds to me like you are private artists and persons, and comfortable with your lifestyle choices.

Yes, yes! It has never been about the fame and fortune for Richard or me. It has been a joy working with glass, raising a family and working the farm.

- **The complexities of the art—**

Please try to explain the processes Richard uses, and show some samples of your husband's work.

You really do need to see the murrinis or none of this will make sense. Kaete is going to the house to get some. And here is an August 1998 *American Craft,* the premier craft magazine in the country, that features Richard on the cover. It has an article inside with his description of murrinis.

Thanks, Kaete. This one is a very simple *murrini.* This little circular image is very minimal imagery, hand-blown glass piece that Richard did in 1970. At his studio in Michigan, he melted down scrap glass from the Blenko factory in West Virginia in his furnace. This piece has a silver nitrate background, a metallic substance with threads laid on top of it.

Those first murrinis were nothing more than little circles of color. Over the next forty years, Richard's murrinis have become increasingly more complex.

And this is the glass cane we work with. If you cut off a tiny slice with a diamond saw, the slice is called a murrini. On this cane you can see the flowers go all the way through the length of the cane, so if you slice off a piece, you still have that image again and again and again.

The process of Richard's work is to make the murrini first, and that takes a lot of time.

Richard, I read that this process was actually first done by early Romans, right?

I believe the earliest murrini pieces were found in Egypt.

When you are designing a piece, do you work from a sketch of what you are going to do, or do you lay out the pieces in sequence, or what?

All of the things you just said.

The dragonfly murrini we showed you was actually from a drawing my son William did when he was twelve-years-old.

The family portrait murrini that was used on that piece over there took me eight months to build, with thousands of rods of colored glass.

Jan please tell me about Kaete's sculpture, and start by describing in layman's terms the black metal chair next to you. I'll ask her more about her art later.

Generally Kaete is a metal sculptor and does blacksmithing. She did this particular piece as a learning process about how to form flat steel into a work of art. She calls it the "Red Queen's Chair".

She recently exhibited it at the Toe River Arts Council and a little girl actually sat in it. That was really fun.

- **Involved in the community—**

Richard, after you moved to Bakersville in 1981 you immediately became an important part of the community. Tell me what motivated you and how you began your community service.

I wanted to get to know my neighbors, and I also wanted to join the Volunteer Fire department. As a kid I always wanted to be a fireman.

I just liked the whole idea of community service because I've always liked to help people, and I always react really well to stress. If something is going on that needs my help, I just step in and just do it. And I'm not afraid of fire, I like to fight it.

Three of our neighbors were firemen and they just asked if I'd like to join. I was from Michigan, and occasionally around the fire hall I heard words about "Yankee's" and "Damn Yankee's", all in good fun.

I wondered what the difference really was until they explained that "The Yankees went home!" I have tremendous respect for my neighbors. It has been an honor to live in Young Cove among such honest, hardworking and caring families. They have been so good to us.

You've served continuously since 1981 - when did you become fire chief, and what has been your most memorable firefighting experience?

I was chief during the big flood in 1998. The flood destroyed fifty-two bridges and wiped out about twenty-five homes in our Fire District in Mitchell County. Our District covers about six miles each way from the fire department building located in downtown Bakersville.

That was a very difficult situation for residents and businesses affected by the flood, and we were glad to help them.

Are you often called on to fight fires elsewhere?

We'll go anywhere in the county to work with other fire departments. We are so rural and so small that we have to do that.

Our thirty-member fire and rescue crew includes ten women, more than most others. In fact, we were the first fire department in the county to have a woman member.

Before becoming chief did you serve as assistant chief?

I served nine years as assistant chief then two years as chief then as assistant chief again. We don't have a fire department where people stay in those positions for years and years. We are all volunteers.

- **Flood and fire—**

Richard, describe the impact on your lives and on the area because of the flood of 1998.

We were busy twelve hours every day for eight weeks during the flood, and I couldn't work in my studio for all that time. I was in the same fix as so many of my neighbors and friends, my bridge had washed away so I had no way to get propane up to our home and studio to run my furnaces.

We met with the county emergency management more than I wanted to, but then we would go out and try and help people with their problems.

During the actual flooding we rescued people at great risk to the members on our department. People were without fuel, electricity and medical supplies. Everything just broke down.

What were some of your observations of that event, Jan?

The flood was in January, so when people had no heat or electricity, and no transportation, it was a matter of taking all of the needed services to them.

More than a foot of snow fell within a week of the flood, roads were completely destroyed, and hundreds of trees fell. There were miles of frozen mud everywhere, basements full of water, and great holes where bridges had stood.

Several years later we had a terrible fire in the jail here that was really awful.

Were there deaths from the jail fire?

Eight people died right here in our little town. There were twenty prisoners in the jail at the time of the fire, and the eight were trapped in an upstairs cell.

I managed to resuscitate one man who was dragged out of the fire. Initially, I assumed he was gone because I couldn't find a pulse, and he was completely blackened from the dense smoke.

Fortunately when I opened up his airway he took a gulp of air, and then he was fully revived on the way to the hospital.

I didn't have an air pack, so I really had no business going into the jail in the first place. I went in a few times anyway, but only to a certain level where other firefighters could hand me someone to drag out of the jail onto the street. I will never forget it.

Do you know how that fire started?

It was not determined how it started but we truly believed it was arson. The State after all these years has finally admitted that it was arson.

What vintage was the building that housed the jail?

It was built in the 1950's. The jail was in the back of the old courthouse in town. If you wanted to film a movie that needed to show a very old jail then that would have been it. But it has since been torn down.

What your role in the fire department after the flood and fire?

I scaled myself back down a bit. It really had effect on me to know that so many people were lost in the fire, and to have seen eight bodies lying there on the sidewalk because the police wouldn't let us cover them. They thought it might destroy the crime scene, or something. Finally, the firefighters prevailed and we covered the dead. It is a painful memory.

Did your Fire and Rescue service for so many years have both a mental and physical effect on you?

Yes. I have seen a lot of deaths. In the years before the seat belt law was adopted, so many people died in car wrecks. In thirty-seven years of responding, I have witnessed neighbors and friends suffering some of their darkest moments. Suicides, farm accidents, plane wrecks, and drowning have been some of the most difficult.

When you face horrible things like that do you feel adrenaline kicking in?

Yes.

Jan, how does Richard deal with such horror?

It's a lot like glass-blowing, sometimes it gets really tough and hot, but Richard just keeps at it until it's done. He has this ability to stay calm in a crisis.

Richard, tell me about the volunteer award you received in 1998.

Oh, you mean The Governor's Award for Volunteering. I was nominated by the Mitchell County Commissioners because I spent weeks working as a volunteer during the flood.

I was involved for eight weeks during the flood, but I have served for thirty years with the fire department, and still do.

What else are you involved in locally, or in the county?

I have loved volunteering for Penland for forty years. I've been a student, teacher and resident artist at Penland, and I was a board member for eight years and served on the executive board. I also helped to coach soccer locally for fifteen years. I just finished up eight years on the North Carolina State Arts Council, a wonderful experience.

- **Jan, Studio Glass Artist—**

Jan, give me a summary of your studio glass art career.

I began glassblowing at the Philadelphia College of Art in 1972 and came to Penland in 1974. That is where I met Richard. We were married in 1977 and had children right away, and they were always my primary focus when they were growing up.

Is that how you see it, Kaete?

Yes, but I think she worked a lot more in glass than she remembers when we were little.

How about it, Jan?

Through all the years of child rearing, I never stopped working in the glass studio, and have always assisted Richard with his work. I am a support system for him and always had my hands in glass. It has been a wonderful shared experience with him for thirty-four years. He assists me with my work as well. My work is very different from Richard's work.

How would you describe that difference?

This is one of my pieces. It's a blown glass bowl with etching of children; very different than Richard would do.

When I have a commission, I work from pictures of the collector's children in their environment. Then I create the design of the piece using imagery of their children's pets and toys.

In one family the children were involved in the Nutcracker Suite, so I created a bowl with that theme. That is the kind of thing I do.

Richard, do you and Jan work as a team, or separately but in the same milieu?

I'd say separately. But she will sometimes make a comment when we are working on a piece. I will critique her work as well.

Can you ballpark how many pieces you've created in your career?

Jan has recorded all of the pieces that I have made since we moved to the farm here in Bakersville in

1981 and that numbers around 1000 in thirty-one years. In the early years, I didn't keep many records.

Do you keep a record, Jan?

Some of Richard's series were so complicated technically that he was only able to make ten a year. Some series he was able to make forty a year.

Does that sound about right to you, Richard?

Yes, I decided early in my career that I didn't want to do production work.

Jan please describe the piece I'm pointing at in 'art-speak'.

In art speak, that is a solid glass sculpture composed of three parts with a surface covered with floral themes. The one I'm holding has leaves and flowers of different colors and different patterns.

Can you expand on that description, Richard?

These pieces are actually from my 'Floral Core' series. In the past, the imagery on my pieces was more abstract.

- **What crystal means—**

How has your view of your art changed over the years, Richard?

It is pretty obvious that in the beginning I was just trying to blow glass, period. But as I went along making pieces, I discovered just what crystal means to me, and began using different layers of crystal in my work.

Just so you know, crystal is clear glass with no color. The only color in this crystal I'm holding comes from the murrinis I put inside. What drew me to crystal was that I was after a different look. It is hard to describe these things because some of them are just intuitive. But I like what happens when colored and opal glasses interact in my pieces.

Glass is very hard, what happens when you melt it?

When it is hot it becomes like honey and you can readily smooth it, cut it, and manipulate it. You do this off-hand, and we use tools as extensions of our hands and fingers. You form it on a metal pipe then re-heat it in what is called a glory hole.

Jan that sounds like it could be dangerous. Is it?

The tools are designed so that you work just out of range of the heat off of the piece. We can use wet newspaper, or a product called a 'Gott Steamer' to form and shape the piece without getting burned.

Richard, have you burned yourself often?

Not too often. Most of my burns are from when I am teaching.

How about you, Jan?

Very rarely; you do it once and you really don't want to do it again.

Richard, what happens when you make a mistake with a piece? Are you able to recover it?

Yes, usually if it is not too extensive I can fix it. I've been doing this for so long that thankfully I don't make too many mistakes.

Bite your tongue.

Yeah, I know. I was talking about how few mistakes I make just the other day then asked out loud "Now it's going to happen, right?"

- **Showing the glass art—**

What shows are you doing these days?

Since 2009, all or part of my 'Fortieth Year in Glass Retrospective' has been touring. I continue to work with major glass galleries and to show at SOFA Chicago each year.

How much time did you devote to your career in your early days?

That furnace would never be turned off. We worked seven days a week.

So you worked maybe fifty to sixty hours a week back then. What about now?

We worked even more than that when we started. Now it's more like thirty hours a week, but we are also a lot more efficient now.

- **Kaete's art—**

Kaete, please describe your art.

Well, probably because of Dad I am really into a lot of different mediums, and my favorites are working with clay, steel, and glass. Since I am working out of Pittsburgh for now, before I head back to school in Boston, I do not have access to this fabulous and amazing giant studio, so I do small pieces, mostly jewelry.

Whenever I come home, I try to do larger pieces. But I am less abstract than my dad and tend to make usable things. So a lot of my early blacksmithing work was to make kitchen tools, like spatulas forged out of diamond plate and rebar.

What do you think you are going to end up doing?

Oh boy, I am still figuring that out.

How do you look at your parent's art?

It's funny, but to me it is all completely normal, growing up around the studio and Penland School.

See all the crazy *murrinis* on this table? Well, they are really gorgeous, but I used to just carry them around just for fun.

Now you fully appreciate the skill and hard work that goes into studio glass are.

Yes, and if you think about how much work it takes just to make one face in glass, it is unbelievable! And when I was a kid I would just think "Oh, I should bury one in the garden".

You planned to grow one.

Yes! But growing up around the shop was all invaluable and has had an incredibly huge effect on me.

Now whenever I do my own artist statement, I always say that I am the child of two artists who made a great impact on my life.

Jan, you've been extremely helpful with your analysis of Richard's art, and your own. Thanks.

I guess you know that some artists are not terribly verbal, it's so much easier to make art than to talk about it

Quite the contrary, you have both told the story well! Richard, what comes next?

I married a younger woman and now she won't let me retire. But she does keep me going.

- **Positive Impacts on students—**

Richard, do you think you've had a significant positive impact on your students through the years?

Yeah, I think so. I've always had so much fun teaching, and students have been my best resource for finding apprentices to work in my own studio. I have enjoyed following their careers as the years go by, and I count some of them as my dearest friends.

Who do you especially remember, Jan?

The apprentices that worked for us for extended periods of time, and who have kept in touch over the years. Most have gone on to do very interesting things. Some of them, not many, also do murrini, despite it being so time consuming.

Richard had a student from Japan who recently earned a Master's Degree in Australia. She sent photos of her graduate school glass piece that was all *murrini,* a very nice and beautiful piece. We were both really excited about that.

Finally Richard, what is the most important message you give to your students?

The main thing I tell my students is for them not to be afraid to move on, and to do the things they love, even though sometimes their creations won't be appreciated.

Richard and his wife Jan Williams working in his studio in Young Cove near Bakersville, North Carolina in 2009.

Richard and Jan, studio glass artists, in the comfort of their Bakersville home.

. . . doing a glass-blowing demonstration for students at the Bloomfield Art Association in Birmingham Michigan in 1971. Richard built this second glass-blowing facility in the state in 1970.

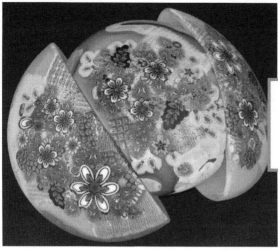

'Floral Core Series 136' made in 2008, the final piece of this series of 136 solid glass sculptures with floral murrini imagery blown between 2001 and 2008.

Detail shot of 'Floral Core Series 136' showing murrinis of flowers, leaves and abstract patterns.

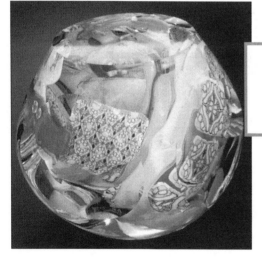

'Untitled Solid Glass Sculpture'. One of Richard's Triolet Series pieces made at his studio in Young Cove in 1988. There were about 75 pieces in this series.

'Mandala Series 31', blown in 1998. This vessel is etched and copper electro-formed on the surface, one of 30 'Mandala Series' pieces from 1996-1998.

An early murrini vessel blown in 1973- 'Blown Vessel with bug murrinis'. Richard made this at Penland School of Crafts when he was an artist in residence.

'Grail Series 12', solid glass sculpture with etched and copper electroformed band. 1993

'Kaete Portrait Vessel' created in 1974 at Penland. This features the first 'cold stack' portrait murrini that Richard made. The portrait is of long-time friend Kaete Shaw.

'The Fruit's Quadrille' – 2011: Four solid glass fruits with murrinis and lattacino with etched glass and steel bases.

Richard Ritter, Chief of Bakersville Volunteer Fire and Rescue, at a house fire investigation near Red Hill in 1997. Richard has served for over 30 years.

Living Treasure Medallion.

Jan assists Richard at the bench in his studio.

Section 5: **Shows and Exhibitions**

- **Retrospective Public Exhibitions—**
- Nov. 2011-April 2012, Richard Ritter—North Carolina Living Treasure, Cameron Art Museum, Wilmington, NC
- Travelling Exhibitions -
  Richard Ritter-A Life in Glass, the Ogden Museum of Southern Art, New Orleans, Louisiana
  Richard Ritter-40 Years in Glass, the Greenhill Center for North Carolina Art, Greensboro NC
  Richard Ritter-40 Years in Glass, the Fine Art Museum of Western Carolina University
- 2009, Richard Ritter-40 Years in Glass, Toe River Arts Council, Spruce Pine NC.
  Original show included 80 pieces of Richard's work spanning 40 years.
- 2000, Richard Ritter-Suspended Expressions, Visions in Glass, University of Michigan at Dearborn.
- 1999, Richard Ritter-30 Years in Glass, Christian Brothers University, Memphis, Tennessee
- 1990, Richard Ritter-A 20 Year Retrospective, the University of Michigan at Dearborn
- 1984, Richard Ritter-A 15 Year Survey, Center for Creative Studies, Detroit, Michigan

- **Other Selected Public Exhibitions—**
- First solo Exhibition of Glass and Metalwork, America House Gallery, Birmingham, Michigan, 1969
- In addition to Retrospective Public Exhibitions, over 40 solo exhibitions in galleries throughout North America
- Exhibited in over 300 Public Gallery and Museum Exhibitions 1969-current (exhibitions follow):
- Habitat Galleries Annual International Invitational Exhibitions, Michigan, 1974-2011
- Habitat Galleries Annual International Glass Invitational Exhibitions, Florida, 1984-2010
- Tradition Innovation-American Masterpiece of Southern Craft-Traditional Art, Travelling Exhibition, 2008-2010
- Blown Away, International Glass of the 21st Century, Flint Institute of the Arts, Flint, Michigan, 2009
- The Italian Influence in Glass, Bergstrom-Mahler Museum, Neenah, Wisconsin, 2009
- Voices of Contemporary Glass: The Heineman Collection, Corning Museum of Glass, 2008
- The Nature of Craft and the Penland Experience, 75th Anniversary of Penland School of Crafts Mint Museum of Craft and Design, Charlotte North Carolina, 2005
- White House Collection of American Crafts, Travelling Exhibition, 1995-2004
- The Italian Influence in Contemporary Glass, Corning Museum of Glass, 2004
- Art Glass of this Century, Museum of Fine Arts, St. Petersburg, Florida, 1999
- By Our Hands-Handmade in America, Travelling Exhibition, 1998
- A Passion for Glass: The Aviva and Jack Robinson Studio Glass Collection, Detroit Institute of the Arts, 1998
- International Contemporary Glass Exhibition, Hsinchu Cultural Center, Taiwan, 1997
- The First Ten Years of Contemporary Glass, Glasmuseum, Ebeltoft, Denmark, 1996
- Himsinche Cultural Center International Glass Exhibition, Taiwan, 1995
- North Carolina Glass, Ebeltof Museum, Ebeltof, Denmark, 1995
- Form and Light, Contemporary Glass from the Permanent Collection, American Craft Museum, New York, 1994
- Glass America, Heller Gallery, New York City 1978, 1984, 1987, 1993
- Tiffany to Ben Tre: A Century of Glass, Milwaukee Art Museum, Milwaukee, Wisconsin, 1993
- Cristalomancia Art Contemporaneo en Vidrio, Rufino Tamayo Museum, Mexico City, 1992
- Thousands of Flowers, American Millefiori Glass, the Museum of American Glass, Wheaton Village, NJ, 1992
- New Art Forms- Sculpture Objects Function Art (SOFA) Chicago, Annual Exhibitions, 1987-2011
- 25 Years of Studio Art Glass, Corning Museum of Glass, Corning, New York, 1987
- World Glass Now, Hokkaido Museum of Modern Art, Sapporo, Japan, 1982

- American Glass Art, Evolution and Revolution, Morris Museum of Arts and Sciences, Morristown, NJ, 1982
- American Glass Now, Yamaha Corporation, Tokyo, Japan, 1979
- Americans in Glass, Leigh Yawkey Woodson Art Museum, Wausau, Wisconsin, 1978
- Corning Museum of Glass Bicentennial Exhibition, Corning, New York, 1976
- Contemporary Art Glass, Lever House, New York City, 1976
- North Carolina Glass, Western Carolina University, Cullowhee, NC, 1974, 1976, 1980, 1982, 1984, 1986
- National Glass Show, Bloomfield Art Association, Birmingham, Michigan, 1971

- **Selected Museums and Public Collections—**
- Asheville Art Museum, Asheville, NC
- Aviva and Jack A. Robinson Studio Glass Collection, Detroit Institute of the Arts
- Bergstom-Mahler Museum, Neenah, Wisconsin
- Blowing Rock Art and History Museum, Blowing Rock, NC
- Carnegie Museum of Art, Pittsburgh, Pennsylvania
- Charles A. Wustum Museum of Fine Arts, Racine, Wisconsin
- Chrysler Museum, Norfolk, Virginia
- Christian Brothers University Art Collection, Memphis, Tennessee
- Cleveland Museum of Art, Cleveland, Ohio
- Corning Museum of Glass, Corning, New York
- Detroit Institute of the Arts
- Fine Art Museum, Western Carolina University, Cullowhee, NC
- Glashaus Lobmeyr, Vienna, Austria
- Hickory Museum of Art, Hickory, NC
- High Museum of Art, Atlanta, Georgia
- Hunter Museum, Chattanooga, Tennessee
- J.B. Speed Museum, Louisville, Kentucky
- Krannert Art Museum, University of Illinois, Urbana
- Los Angeles County Museum of Art
- The Lowe Art Museum, University of Miami,
- The Milwaukee Art Museum, Milwaukee, Wisconsin
- The Mint Museum of Craft and Design, Charlotte, NC
- The Montreal Museum of Fine Art, Montreal, Canada
- The Museum of American Glass, Millville, New Jersey
- The Museum of Art and Design, New York City
- The Museum of Fine Arts, Boston, Massachusetts
- The Museum of Glass, Tacoma, Washington
- Museum Jan van der Togt, Amstelveen, Netherlands
- The Novi Public Library, Novi, Michigan
- Ogden Museum of Southern Art, New Orleans, Louisiana
- Presbyterian Hospital, Charlotte, NC
- Racine Art Museum, Racine, Wisconsin
- The Smithsonian American Art Museum, Washington, DC
- Southern Highland Craft Guild, Folk Art Museum, Asheville, NC
- St. Louis Art Museum, St. Louis, Missouri
- The University of Iowa Hospitals and Clinics, Iowa City, Iowa
- The University of Michigan at Dearborn, Permanent Art Collection, Dearborn, Michigan
- The Vice President's Residence, Washington, DC
- The White House Permanent Art Collection, Washington, DC
- Zanesville Art Center, Zanesville, Ohio

Section 6: **Chronology**

- **Personal—**
- Richard Ritter Born 1940, Detroit, Michigan
- Wife—Jan
- Daughter—Kaete
- Sons—Richie and William

- **Education—**
- Graduate of the Art School of the Society of Arts and Crafts, Detroit, Michigan, 1969
- Honorary Doctor of Fine Arts, Center for Creative Studies School of Art and Design, Detroit
- Artist in Residence at Penland School of Crafts, North Carolina, 1972-1976

- **Honors—**
- North Carolina Living Treasure, 2011
- National Endowment for the Arts Fellowship Grant, 1984
- North Carolina Artist Fellowship Grant, 2000-2001
- North Carolina Governor's Award for Volunteer Service, 1998
- North Carolina Arts Council by appointment of the Governor, 2007-2011

- **Teaching—**
- Shared knowledge of glass with students in craft schools and universities throughout the United States.
- Connection with Penland School of Crafts continues, has taught 22 workshops in glassblowing.
- Richard Ritter Scholarship established in his honor at Penland School.
- Also taught workshops for: Society of Arts and Crafts, Detroit; Sheridan College of Art, Toronto, Canada; Archie Bray Foundation, Helena Montana; Newcomb College at Tulane University, New Orleans, Louisiana; Western Carolina University, Cullowhee, North Carolina; Toledo Museum of Art, Toledo, Ohio; Bloomfield Art Association, Birmingham Michigan; University of Illinois at Champaign, Urbana, Illinois; California State University, San Luis Obispo, California;

● ● ●

Julyan Davis

Internationally Exhibited Southern Realist Painter

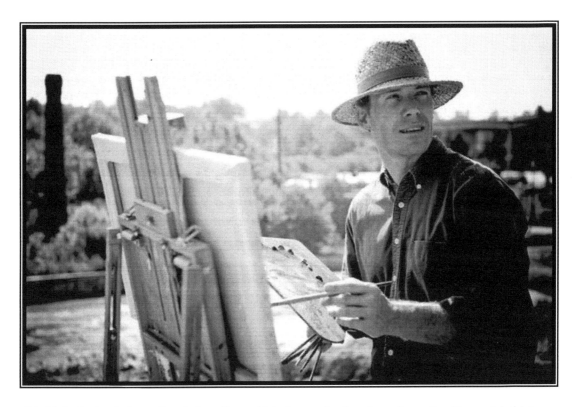

"British Artist Julyan Davis has found his home in the American South . . . his history with the region reads like a romance. A delightful guide, Davis traveled halfway across the world to remind the American South of its own inherent beauty."
— **From Deborah Walden's Article 'Julyan Davis, Southern Art', May 2011,** *Nashville Arts Magazine.*

Sections about Julyan Davis:

1) Testimonials and Letter-Critique-Response

2) Excerpts from Magazine Articles about His Art

3) **Julyan's Life Journey, in His Own Words**

4) Photos

5) Chronology

Section 1: **Testimonials and Letter-Critique-Response**

- **Fellow artist: 'Julyan is the premier landscape painter in the region'** —

When I had my first show at Blue Spiral 1, I sensed I was a perceived as a threat by some of the regular artists there. Julyan Davis and Daniel Nevins, on the other hand, came right up to me and took me under their wings.

Julyan had me over for a party, and emailed me the day after to thank me for my attendance - one classy guy, I thought. I soon learned that Julyan is not just a supreme gentleman, but also a genuinely nice, sweet man. Keep in mind, he's way ahead of me career-wise, and there's nothing I can do to help him.

As an artist, it goes without saying that Julyan is the premier landscape painter of the region. His landscapes, especially the more domesticated, forlorn landscapes are deeply moody and psychological. But it's Julyan's figurative, narrative work that I believe is what is greatest about him.

The figurative work has hitherto been greatly under-appreciated and under-represented, something that I hope will change after his show at the Greenville Museum. Piercingly wistful and relentlessly probing, these works are Julyan at his best. 'Banks of the Ohio' is among the few finest works of art I have seen come out of Asheville.

— **Taiyo la Paix,** painter, Weaverville www.taiyopaix.com

- **Vision Gallery owner: 'Julyan's compositions give a sense of place - the South'** —

I usually feel very inadequate when pressed to write about an artist, and, it's difficult to write something unique about art and artists, as it often feels like it's all been said. But with Julyan, I think I can take a stab.

From my desk at my gallery I can stare straight ahead at one his paintings - a laundromat interior, and frankly it's hanging where it is so I can see it whenever I look up. In a better world art-market-wise, it would probably go home with me, but in this sour economy I really need to sell, not buy. So I'm using how I feel about this painting in order to write about his work in general. It's written from the gut, and not academically, as you will see.

Julyan Davis has a way of taking an often overlooked and sometimes downright ugly scene, whether it's an interior or a landscape, and painting it using his rather somber palette, to render it absolutely riveting. His interiors, from laundromats to abandoned houses or commercial buildings, at first glance appear frozen in time. Yet before you know it, you have been pulled slowly into the painting, noticing an interior door, a shaft of light from a barely visible window, and you are dying to know what lurks in the areas beyond your view. It no longer feels frozen in the least. You half expect that you could turn away, then back, and maybe catch a glimpse of a fleeting figure. Or maybe a door that you remembered as being closed is now cracked open, maybe even enough to give you a hint of what used "be" in those spaces.

His landscape paintings are pretty empty for the most part yet don't convey a sense of loneliness at all. The compositions are just enough to give you a sense of place, of weather and perhaps time of year, without any added color or details to detract from being in that place at that time. He captures on canvas, how it would you now it would feel to be in that very landscape in the flesh.

Julyan says he is compelled to paint the disappearing aspects of the South, and thankfully it seems to me that he does so without making them nostalgic in the least. They are what they are, and perhaps this gives them a somewhat raw feel emotionally, however once you relate to one of his paintings I daresay you wouldn't have it any other way. Once a fan of his work, you won't think to wonder *why* he paints "*what*" he does, but rather you will be thankful that such a gifted painter chose 'that particlar subject' to paint.

— **Lee Dellinger**, Vision Gallery www.twogalleries.net

• Constance Vlahoulis: 'Like a memory, one can walk into his paintings' —

When I was asked by author Jack Prather who I thought was an important local living artist, Julyan Davis immediately came to mind. Although the Asheville area has dozens of artists who have reached the upper levels of the art world, Julyan's work conveys a sense of place in a way that is unlike most. Like a memory, one can walk into his paintings, as they evoke feelings of the viewer that become part of the work.

My friend and colleague, Wendy Outland, who was manager of Blue Spiral 1 for many years, recalls her first meeting with Julyan at the gallery. "He was charming and professional, with a genuine modesty that, given the high quality of his work, was refreshing. The paintings he brought in were more subtle early on; but if you looked closely, you were likely to discover something unexpected in what had initially appeared to be a typical landscape. It's a skill Julyan has expertly honed over the years."

What I appreciate so much is that Julyan has made himself accessible to all levels of local artists. Be it his well-written blog, instruction, or an entertaining lecture, his generous spirit comes through loud and clear, yet in a way that makes others feel so comfortable. Those who know him, realize how fortunate Asheville is to have this true master in our mist. And now, readers will get to know him too.

— **Constance Vlahoulis**, The Conn-Artist Studios & Art Gallery

• A Letter-critique-response —

I had always wondered why other artists' paintings of Charleston did not move me. Having studied yours, I realized that a more poetic synthesis was needed, something which started with eyesight but went so much farther. In any case, I just wanted to tell you how thoroughly captivated I was with your hard-and-fast poetry. You own the South as much as any native.

— **Brett Busang**, painter and author, Memphis TN.

(P.S: Jack. you've inspired me to finish my novel about John Sloan and Robert Henri, and one about Memphis, as well. Brett.)

Julyan Davis came to this country from England where he was, as I understand, already established. But because the imagery and folklore of the South appealed to him he stayed, and has created a body of work that should be the envy of us all. Native New Yorkers ignore the local genius, as it were, because it's been there all the time. They don't notice it, but outsiders do. And it is from them that we get "our" New York City.

For Davis, the American South started off as myth, but has become, in his hands, the hard, but poetic, reality for which most painters strive, but few actually realize. He is a case-hardened realist - by which I mean that, no matter how many small liberties he takes with the evidence ("the fact", as Edward Hopper called it), the truth that emerges from his light-filled, but conceptually rooted, canvases is the sort of truth only a novel or poem can adequately address. It didn't surprise me to learn that Davis had initially been attracted to Southern folklore. The South has made many negative contributions to our culture, but has redeemed itself with storytelling. Davis understood that from the git-go and got right on it.

Over the years, however, his emphatic attention has drifted (if that's the word) to such physical realities as not only anchor a mailbox to the spur of a dusty road or the foundation of a house to its native soil, but to the mythologies that permeate man-made phenomena. And in the South, every physical reality is front-loaded with myth and story. That mailbox is not just a mailbox, but might bear some heartbreaking communication somebody's overlooked for years. That hill-clinging house may have been the scene of a grisly encounter that someone sitting on a porch years later will tell to some outsider who'll formalize it into a short story.

Yet, for Davis, the physical reality is often enough. His love of architecture translates into an almost supernatural sense of the significant detail (bad word, that), which expresses the heft of the place as well as its often-sorry condition. Like all great realists, Davis is attracted to character - the character time will stamp on things that are ultimately perishable. These things are here now, he seems to say, but we must acknowledge that they won't last forever. Davis' South is haunted by what is as well as what ain't. No landscape is merely empty, no house is without its baggage, and no street is actually safe. There is a kind of paradox - and disturbing harmony - between the strange fruit of a road-bend or mountaintop and its stunning realization. It's as if Davis knows something we don't and wishes to tell us the news.

He most certainly knows a lot about painting. From a purely formal standpoint, his work is irresistible. The marvelous compression of his imagery is not "real", but a result of "putting in and taking away". He never loses sight of the essentials and embellishes them as any good storyteller would. He understands optical color, but doesn't totally rely on it. Take a photograph of something and watch its intensity fade - assuming it's not a great photograph. Davis takes his subject in hand and wrestles it to the ground. I can feel the struggle, even if the result is serenely beautiful (another bad word, but I must use it). Painters who rely on tricks of observation and showy brushwork give us the sort of wall decoration that fades when the lights are turned out - or when dinner-party guests are in excellent form and upstage all the furniture.

Davis' work, while richly textured and sometimes "quirkily" painted, compels us to sit and stare. It makes us more observant than we actually are. And it introduces us to a dimension that is both familiar and hyper-real. I'm happily uncomfortable in Davis' world, which gives me something I have never seen inside of a presumably accessible slice of reality. Davis is clearly a student of realist painting, but he doesn't need for us to know it. That could also be said of Eakins, Hopper and Andrew Wyeth. Davis' genius consists of his ability to transform reality just enough for us to see both its surface textures and its underlying menace, melancholy, brute strength or what have you. His work is about familiar things, but in his hands these things shift a bit. A kind of dimensional crack appears and we are asked to slip inside of it. Those of us who do are exponentially rewarded; those who don't have their vacation pictures.

Section 2: **Excerpts from Magazine Articles about His Art**

- **From a May 2011 article in *Nashville Arts Magazine*—**

Following are excerpts from the article written by Deborah Walden titled *"Julyan Davis, Southern Art"*:

British artist Julyan Davis has found his home in the American South. His history with the region reads like a romance. The American South took hold of his imagination . . . Davis was so captivated by Carl Carmer's book, Alabama, that he packed up his paints and moved there . . . Davis' art has continued to grow over his two decades stateside . . . He says, "I like exploring abstract shapes and flat qualities. I try to take two extremes of what influences me and bring them together. That's how each artist finds their own unique style." . . . A technical virtuoso as a painter, he is able to anchor large regions of strong line and shape into naturalistic images. His paintings at times have a photographic quality. And sometimes his landscapes are so simplified, so boiled down, that they are like whispers or suggestions of a place. They are always beautiful, and they always seem to hint at a human presence . . . "I like faded, slightly haunted-feeling spaces," he says . . . A delightful guide, Davis traveled hallway across the world to remind the American South of its own inherent beauty.

- **From the Holiday 2007 *Garden & Gun, 21st-Century Southern America*—**

Following are excerpts from the article by Randall Curb, *"Refined Oils—British expat Julyan Davis makes his home and his art in Asheville, North Carolina"*: Julyan quickly established his central artistic vision of the South – and hoopskirts and honeysuckle were no part in it . . . "I've always had empathy," he says, "with the constrained characters of old ballads, and in a way my empty landscapes are haunted by such ghosts . . . "It's about that pull created between the beauty I see in the color, light, and pattern of something, and the objective fact that it would be considered by many to be negligible or even ugly" . . . I was astonished by the range of styles in which he was proficient . . . Moving inexorably but never reflexively from classical realism in landscapes, still life, and the occasional portrait, to a freer, ore personally gratifying technique has been Julyan's real education as an artist . . . Julyan is an astute and imaginative colorist . . . "I want a painting to look like a painting," he says . . . Asheville seems a perfect fit for Julyan. It's surrounded by 'deep Southernness', with inherent old traditions and values. "But it's also," he says," an oasis from some of those past values. There are many 'refugees' from the rest of the South here – people who didn't fit back in Georgia or Tennessee, who bring much energy to a less judgmental future and yet have an attractive affection for the homes and life left behind" . . . Then the challenge in his words is "finding a new way to capture a familiar effect, a new kind of mark, say one that is both ugly and beautiful, or that conveys only paint at one moment and the world observed at the next. This is what keeps me going."

- **From Volume 23 May 2011 *Legends Magazine*—**

Following are excerpts from the article in *Legends Magazine: In the fall of 2010, British-born painter Julyan Davis was invited to paint the wilderness areas Of Kiawah Island. As a landscape painter, he has traveled the world from Russia to Alaska. He is best known for his paintings of the South, where he has lived for over twenty years, and Deer Isle, Maine, where he spends his summers.*

And from Artist's Notes: "It is important to find tension in a painting. There is a quote by French mathematician and philosopher Blaise Pascal that can be applied to painting. He says, in effect, to achieve greatness, one must find the middle point between two extremes in oneself. In other words, a unique voice is to be found from all our influences that seem most personal, and most in juxtaposition. It helps to find a seemingly insurmountable problem. In my case, I suppose I'm trying to marry Turner and Cezanne. I can't give up the luminosity and mystery of the 19th-century landscapists, but I love the flatness and sculptural solidarity of Modernism. I want my cake and eat it too. French painter Pierre Bonard is a big influence on my work. His color of course, but also the very playful way he can direct your eye around a canvas. If he doesn't want you to see the cat in the corner of the room for a while, then you won't see it for a while.

- **From the article 'Uncommon Ground' by Alli Marshall *Our State*, June 2009—**

Excerpts follow sub-head 'Asheville Painter Julyan Davis lends a fresh eye to the landscapes of the South':

At first glance, Julyan Davis's work could be described as photorealism. From across the room his Southern-themed canvases look more like sun-drenched photographs than paintings. But Davis believes his work defies that description. "Maybe from a distance it's very realistic, but as you get close up it falls into blocks of color and very definite lines," he says. Look closely at 'Washerteria' and the realistic effect gives way to a Cubist-inspired flattening of planes. The same is true for many of Davis's paintings: saturated slices of Americana - a motel sign, a Laundromat, a motor court pool in winter – reveal an eerie beauty. "It's not that I go around looking for Americana," he says. But in many ways, Americana found him.

- **A brief about Notable Julyan Davis—**

Julyan Davis is an English-born artist who moved to the United States more than two decades ago and now lives in the Montford District of Asheville, North Carolina.

He received his art training at the Byam shaw School of Art in London. After completing his B.A. in painting and printmaking, he traveled to the American South on a painting trip that was also fueled by an interest in the history of Demopolis, Alabama and its settling by Bonapartist exiles.

His work is exhibited from New York to Europe, and is in many public and private art collections. Recent acquisitions include from the Greenville County Museum of Art where his work was shown solo then exhibited along with work by Andrew Wyeth and Jasper Johns. Others include the Gibbes Museum in Charleston, South Carolina, the Morris Museum in Augusta, Georgia, and the North Carolina Governor's Museum and Western Residence.

Julyan's Greenville Museum show in May 2012 will feature work based on his interpretation of traditional American ballads throughout the contemporary South.

Section 3: Julyan's Life Journey, in His Own Words

I arrive in the Montford District of Asheville at the quaint historic home of artist Julyan Davis and meet a much younger British Southern art painter than expected. Julyan, who turned 46 last year, on September 11th of 2011, guides me into a dimly-lit dining room filled with many of his impressive paintings. We engage in friendly conversation before diving into his life and career for this book of Notable biographies. But first the Brit serves tea, of course.

Julyan, I'd like to start the interview by asking about your very first memory?

My first memory, gosh, that is a tricky question. I recall at age four or five being in a Spanish restaurant in London. Wherever we went, my parents took pen and paper for me, and I remember doing a drawing of a Flamenco guitarist who was performing.

- **Early Thoughts about an Art Career—**

When did the desire to become a professional artist begin to emerge?

I was definitely one of these artists who picked up a pen very early on, or a pencil, or whatever. I think it was sort of known from the get-go that I was going to be an artist.

I always thought of myself as being academically quite studious as a young boy, but I realize now that I was a bit more of a hellion than I originally thought.

I preferred art, but I was not too strong in the sciences, or very interested in mathematics. I remember my parents, when I was about nine, had to take me out of school because I was one of a small group of troublemakers who were playing truant and generally causing mischief. They put me into a Jesuit boarding school to shape me up, which it did, and effectively. I became much more successful as a student, generally, but through it all, art was always my strong point. And English.

Where did you live?

All through my childhood we moved around a good bit. My mother used to renovate houses, and my father was a barrister, a lawyer in London. My mother is still alive, her name is Suzy Davis, and my late father was Timothy.

I was born at my grandparent's home. They owned and ran a little prep school in the southwest of England (the school closed the year after I was born, but they kept the property) and I developed strong ties to that part of the country. We often visited them in Somerset, near Cornwall. The one place that stayed the same was where my grandparents lived.

What came next?

My father took a job as a magistrate in Hong Kong during the last two years of my high school, and we all went out there. The English system narrows the focus of your education, and you take many exams in many subjects by the age of sixteen, and then three subjects for the last two years of high school. My choices, in Hong Kong, were in history, English and art.

A formative experience and a great lesson was when I took the art exam. It was sent back to England to be judged, and I got a D, and basically failed the exam. I was furious, I pitched a fit.

Oh, I have this image of myself as a docile, extremely shy near-sighted teenager, but every now and then people remind me that I did things like I did that day- throwing the furniture off a rooftop cafeteria. I stormed out of the school.

- **A lesson from rejection—**

How big a lesson was it?

It was a big lesson in dealing with rejection. I took the exam a second time and got an A, but the previous experience still rankled me. On top of that, I had great trouble getting into a foundation course. I tried three or four places but they all rejected me; but I managed to find a place at the last minute. That course lasted a year.

In the same way, I had several choices for colleges for my degree, but was rejected by them all. Two art schools in London, one in Cornwall and one in the cold, wintery north of England. They all said, "Not interested".

The lesson was excellent preparation for when I left art school. I had to either accept that those people were right, I was not qualified, or choose to disagree and just believe in myself. To have learned this early proved invaluable, I have known many artists who struggled with rejection throughout their careers. After that, I was never rankled by rejection.

Did they give you an analysis of why they rejected you?

They probably did give me an analysis, I don't really recall. I will say in retrospect that they may have been right! I don't know if my work was that strong.

So, you felt there were elements of correctness in their evaluation?

Well yeah, absolutely. When I am teaching, I often tell students that I got pieces of good advice but ignored them. I just decided that I was going to be an artist, and that there was no option to not to be an artist.

Julyan, every artist and writer struggles, especially at the beginning of their careers.

There is a common bond between successful people who have gone through that and come out better for it, not worse. I know exactly what you are implying with your question: that every writer or artist struggles until they become a success.

- **Influenced by Music—**

What were some of the major influences on you as a child?

My father was an avid 'Americanophile' with a great interest in folk music, so I grew up listening to as much American folk music as Scottish and Irish folk music. This influenced my painting, particularly here in the South.

Did you have favorite music during your childhood?

Well, the earliest stuff was by people like Burl Ives, *The Wayfaring Stranger* and all the other albums he did.

I met Burl Ives and told him he was my favorite singer when I was a kid growing up in Brooklyn, and that his song about a dog always made me teary.

Old Blue, oh yeah, that is a very sad song.

Julyan, I just wanted to share that memory with you.

I am glad you did. I had a great stack of records and discovered the Blues and Appalachian music, Bluegrass, and all of that. Early on it was the American folk music I loved most. In fact, my father's dream was to move to Santa Fe, New Mexico because Burl Ives lived there.

- **Reading and Writing—**

I understand that your father was also a writer, and that you have writing in your veins.

My father actually considered joining a law firm in Santa Fe, but he never got to move to the States. He was leaning towards moving to the American west, so I grew up with that idea, and I guess that led to my interest in Southern literature. *To Kill a Mockingbird* by Harper Lee was required reading in high school back then, and that book got me interested in Eudora Welty and Flannery O'Connor and that whole lot of writers.

Later we went on a trip to the States to the Grand Canyon and hiked all around Utah and Arizona, and that certainly made an impression on me. That trip came after I finished art school in Bristol, and at that time my father was an established crime fiction writer. I have his books over there, *Kid Glove Charlie* ,*The Gentleman from Chicago, The Cook General.*

His real name was Timothy Francis Davis, but he wrote under the name John Cashman, who was a notorious nineteenth century forger.

When did he write the books?

He wrote them during his thirties, from the 1970's into the early 1980's. They were fictional novels based on real-life Victorian criminals. *The Gentleman from Chicago* was based on a poisoner who started in London and moved to Chicago, and some people think he may have been 'Jack the Ripper'. *The Cook General* is a famous case of a maid who murdered the lady she was working for, rather gruesome. *Kid Glove Charlie* was about a fabulous character, Charles Peace, a fearless burglar who even went to Scotland Yard dressed as a woman to give misleading evidence against himself.

What came next in your pursuit of art, and are you also writing?

I had attended the Byam Shaw School of Art in London for three years and received a degree in fine art and printmaking. The school no longer exists. It has been incorporated into the University of London. When I came out of the art school I tried my hand at being an artist.

At the same time, this was in 1987, I had found an original copy from the thirties of Carl Carmer's book *Stars Fell in Alabama*. It made me think about doing some writing. I saved enough money to travel to Alabama, via the New York Public Library and the Library of Congress for research, and began playing at being a writer. I had no firm idea, it was just sort of just an image, you know. For me, that period of time was romantic and had a comic aspect to it. That is how I was drawn to the South.

I'm currently working on a couple of books, one a sort of reflection upon the South and my career as an artist here, the other a comic novel set here in Asheville.

- **Living in an art and cultural community—**

You own this house that you've been living in for six years in a very quaint section of Asheville, which is well-known as an art and cultural community. Tell me the history of why you picked this house.

I had been living near Highlands in Scaly Mountain, North Carolina, and that was wonderful but very secluded. I would come up to Asheville a lot, and so I decided to get a condo here.

As it turned out, condo living didn't really suit me: nobody wanted to take responsibility for anything, and a result the place starting falling to pieces almost immediately. So, I started looking for a house.

Well, you seem to have a Type-A personality, so that couldn't work.

No. So I found the closest neighborhood of residential streets to downtown in the Montford Disrict, and started looking around. I stumbled upon this house which was larger than I wanted. But the decision was really made for me when I discovered that the previous owner was Peggy Seeger, half-sister to Pete Seeger. Her parents had been very influential collectors of folk music, and she had known folks like the Lomaxes, Woody Guthrie, Josh White and Leadbelly. I was familiar with Peggy's career. She had lived in England for many years, and had been married to the Scottish folk singer and song writer Ewan MacColl, who wrote *The First Time Ever I Saw Your Face* for her.

You light up when you speak about Pete Seeger.

Yes, I recently read an interesting article about Pete Seeger in *The New Yorker* magazine that mentioned he lived out in the woods, and there wasn't a single stick around the place, as he would collect all the kindling for firewood. It made me remember when I lived in Scaly Mountain and had that same kind of self-sufficient lifestyle.

• Teaching and helping—

Switching gears, you said you taught art, and taught an apprentice for a year. Tell me more.

Teaching has been very intermittent for me, and I've never done it large-scale for financial reasons. It is very cost-ineffective, unless you take it on full-time. I don't have the full qualifications to teach at the university level because they require a Master's Degree now.

Do you help younger struggling artists?

I've done that, and one particular case especially appealed to me when I was living between Highlands and Asheville. There was this little frame shop in Franklin that did all of my framing, and they were showing work by a very talented young artist in his last year in high school who I took interest in and helped. He was my apprentice for a year. Unfortunately he learned that at least some galleries are unnerved by a lack of the expected qualifications. Based on his work, they were all ready to take him on until they discovered his age and lack of an official degree. Then they lost their nerve. He is now in art school, but at least not an overpriced one. We stay in touch. He is a great young man.

I have a couple of folks I teach periodically now. The first to approach me was the terrific blues singer, Chuck Beattie. He brought a portrait he was working on to show me, and I chatted with him about approaches he could take. We have become fast friends since. The second is a man half his age, Sandusky Parris, a part-time student. He and I were asked to paint at a charity event. Sandusky liked what I did and took me up on an invitation to drop by the studio anytime. We also have become good friends.

Both these folks are enthusiastic and interested, and often act like my guardian angels. Chuck paints for pleasure, Sandusky would make more of it. His fairly remarkable achievements for a thirty-two-year-old suggest to me that he is close to being able to support his art. Both gents kindly pay their way at the odd lunch, or in Sandusky's case, fixing pretty much any mechanical obstacle that strays into my path!

• Similar landscapes—

I am struck by the similarity of the landscape in England and in the American South.

I had done many paintings of the English landscape, and when I came over here the landscape was the main thing that appealed to me about the South. I made the transition, I will say as a footnote, during the first few years I lived in the United States. Most of my early sales of paintings to people in the South were of very traditional English landscapes.

Tell me about your studio.

The studio suffices for now as a space, and I am still teaching and offering advice to local artists. It is currently filling up with my paintings scheduled for the Greenville Museum in May 2012.

- **Techniques and subjects—**

How would you describe your technique, and what subjects do you produce on canvas now?

Right now I am painting mainly urban, lived-in places. The majority of paintings are of buildings, and recently a lot of interiors or of some human presence, and set in the South and in the Southeast.

All of that work has a sort of haunted presence, a sense of something having taken place, a kind of narrative going on, a mood.

I am no art critic, but I said basically that same thing to my wife last night.

Parallel to that my work explores the music that first influenced me, as I mentioned earlier. In art school my work was about folk music, sea shanties, mainly.

In the last three years I have come back to painting the figure. I have two current bodies of work: the empty places and the narrative paintings based on the music.

How would you describe your evolution as an artist and your artwork?

I really labor to make sure a painting is definitely seen as a painting. My work has been described as looking very realistic from a distance, but up-close as very abstract.

I love all forms of painting. I began by learning all the traditional techniques, and I've done abstract, expressionist and photo-realistic paintings.

You are considered a prolific artist, Julyan. How many paintings have produced professionally, how many are in galleries, and how many have you sold, ballpark?

I have done perhaps 1500 paintings total during my career, I've sold nearly all of those. At the moment my work is represented in galleries in London, Charleston, Atlanta, Nashville, Morehead City, two in Maine, and one here in Asheville.

Where are the Maine galleries?

In Stonington, on Deer Isle, and in Portland.

- **Influences of other artists—**

What twentieth-century artists do you admire?

That is a good question. There are a a great many painters I like, rather than particular works that have altered my path. It is their approach and the way they have chosen to work that I find influential. I like Francis Bacon, Balthus, Matisse, Bonnavld, even De Kooning

What painters are you closest to in the history of art?

I definitely have strong ties to the precursors to my type of work. I paint observational things of America, both outdoors and interiors, and like many before me, I have a slight melancholy in my paintings.

That strikes me about that painting of a mansion on your dining room wall.

That piece is titled *Antebellum Mansion*, and the location is in Alabama.

I studied your realistic painting of a living room and wondered if you put a certain curve on the lampshade to show it was a painting and not a photo.

Yes, absolutely.

The one thing in writing as well as in painting is to have a tension between all manner of things. You can have a beautiful subject that is painted in a very ugly fashion, and that is a very interesting tension; and you can have an ugly thing painted very exquisitely, and that is another kind of tension.

In all of this there is like a push-pull between old and new painting all the time, so inch-to-inch you go between twentieth-century and nineteenth-century painting, and that is what I work towards.

Subject matter determines the technique, so mine has always been to see how far I can go, and that is my work.

- **Other influential artists—**

Who are the artists that influenced you the most, and who do you admire the most both past and present?

It would be Velazquez first. When you step up to his work, it dissolves into pure paint. Rembrandt is the painter I should put probably first, he covered everything as a great draftsman, a great landscape painter, a great figure painter, a great portrait painter. He painted every aspect of his life, and in so many media, like print-making, painting, drawing, everything, but for some reason he remains a close second for me.

Bonnard is a favorite, one of the latter post-impressionist painters. I love his color.

Now, what contemporary artists do you like, or perhaps emulate?

I don't really watch many contemporary painters in that way. I try in a way not to study them too closely. But I do follow writers, and it's funny that you should ask me that question about contemporary artists. That was a very big thing when I was in art school, and particularly now. They say to go to every exhibition of every artist, but I think it can stop you from exploring things.

I understand you are going to have a show in May 2012 at the Greenville County Museum of Art in South Carolina. That museum has a large collection of Andrew Wyeths. How do you judge him as an artist?

A lot of the art world looks down on Andrew Wyeth; they think he is a bit too sentimental. I went to the museum on the Olson Farm where he painted up in Maine, and that is when I realized that Wyeth had been a really big influence on me when I was a teenager. I just hadn't thought about it before; hadn't made that connection.

But Wyeth was the only painter I'd ever looked at who did sort of deteriorated rooms, and interiors. And I was interested in that even before art school. I'd done paintings of my grandparent's school which was falling down, and so that is where the interiors come from, and from that Wyeth influence. I am very pleased they are hanging my show alongside their huge Wyeth collection.

- **View of the universe—**

Julyan, do you feel a connection with the universe, as so many people say they do these days?

Well, let me try, and if my answer is not sufficient then you can further explain what you mean.

There are no insufficient answers to that question; a connection to the universe is a personal feeling or experience.

Okay, I will answer in terms of my life at this point. I certainly feel that I've lived an immensely fortunate life and am fulfilled. I feel if I was told tomorrow that I had some terminal illness that I've achieved quite enough. When I was young I wanted all kinds of accolades from certain places, but not when I became a true artist. I feel I have found my place in the world, in the universe.

- **Facing adversity—**

You said you feel fortunate. Expand on that a bit.

I feel lucky, as though my life has been remarkable. I also feel that the difficult things have all been necessary parts of my life.

All those up and down experiences chiseled and forged you into the man you are now, right?

Yes, yes! I have made mistakes in my life, and there are things I regret, but it is important to keep trying to improve oneself.

You've accomplished a great deal for someone in his mid-forties, though maybe not all you wanted to.

I agree on both counts. There's certainly room for improvement.

- **Giving Back—**

What is your attitude about giving back to the community, and to society?

A lot of people tend to put artists on some kind of moral pedestal, particularly if they suffered for their art. I don't. There is nothing morally wrong with inflicting your opinions upon the world, but rarely is there anything morally courageous about it.

There may have been a time when a painter could risk his life with the subject of a painting, but not anymore, at least not in the Western World. If an artist suffers, it is their choice to do so.

These thoughts have always bothered me. A lot of artists feel guilt for being in such an ephemeral craft. What use are we in the real world? How are we contributing other than by producing a luxury? Expensive, flat, furniture, in my case! We artists are always being asked to donate paintings to auctions for good causes, and we almost always do. There are no tax benefits other than the value of the materials, but the gesture is not as grand as it might seem, as we might give away an old set-aside painting or something like that.

What I do consider an accomplishment came about when I moved to America and was introduced to the concept of tithing- to give away ten-percent of one's yearly income. This became a tradition- checks were written each Christmas morning, not for religious organizations, but for varied charities. Doctors without Borders and the Carter Center received the lion's share. At the time, because I was earning a lot, it did not seem a hardship, more a pleasure. Only now, when times are much harder, does it seem an achievement and something to hold on to.

For me, this was a kind of relief. I could be the selfish artist, driven to do his best work, and the work I was best at, and each Christmas just pass on with pleasure the brave and difficult real work to absolute professionals.

There is a row of books on my shelves that have personal dedications and notes of thanks from

President Jimmy Carter to my ex-wife Madeleine and I. They are prized possessions. I can only strive to be able to affect others at that level again. It is the most important lesson I can teach my son.

Most if not all of your twelve notables, Jack, are driven folk. It seems we have all learned that philanthropy is sweet absolution for our greedy obsession with self-advancement.

- **The spiritual Julyan—**

Do you consider yourself a spiritual person?

On the spiritual or bigger picture of life, I was raised Catholic but am definitely a lapsed Catholic, and I have not been to church for many years. But now that I have a young child, I am very much aware of trying to give him some sense of meaning of the bigger picture. And I am very aware that religion gives you, particularly at an earlier age, the gift of faith.

The greatest gift of religion is that it allows you to be agnostic. If you have no religion from day one, you are never given that luxury. You have to know faith to doubt it, or to say "I don't know." As for atheism, you are born with that. I don't really want my son to grow up with no kind of religion.

I was writing an essay about all that when a friend of mine showed me a sign he had picked up on the side of the road in Alabama, a piece of classic folk art that read "Gob is goob". The person who made the sign had accidently reversed the two d's.

Now I think that the saying "Gob is goob" is kind of my religion.

I don't really believe in an afterlife, or that God is going to step in and help you, but I absolutely believe in those aspects of mankind that are supernatural, and in goodness.

Sounds like you've thought a lot about this subject.

Yes, I have. There was a spiritual response provoked by the threat of Darwinism. It said something like, "I'll take everything you are saying into consideration, but there are three things you are not covering about man."

If I am remembering correctly, the argument referred to design, which is man's creative ability to create- in architecture, art, writing; and the second was to the scientific mind- the capacity to think in terms of mathematics and physics and such abstract subjects. The last was our unnatural (according to Darwin's view of nature) capacity to give selfless love, to give to something outside your family, or to die for a total stranger, that kind of thing.

- **Work ethic—**

You must possess a strong work ethic to have produced so many paintings by age forty-five. How much of a work day do you put in these days?

I paint about six to seven hours a day now, but I used to do a great deal more. I've been putting a lot of focus into it, and it seems stronger than ever, which is good, and now I can work more quickly.

I was working very long hours when I was doing very detailed, almost photographic realism. So things have gotten lighter work-wise in that respect, which as how it should be.

Roughly, I work six days, but I used to work every day of the week. I still get sort of a weird kick out of working on Christmas day or the Fourth of July or on my birthday, a special day when I shouldn't be working but can choose to paint something entirely frivolous, like a fun project in the back of my mind.

Do you ever wake up in the middle of the night and head for your easel, sort of like I do with writing?

No I don't, but that is a good question. I am someone who tries to always paint by natural light. It was a problem finding a studio in Asheville with enough natural light.

- **'Art-speak' explanations—**

Explain In 'art-speak' why your work is stronger now, and why natural light is so important to an artist.

Well, in terms of the work being stronger, I mean I am not having to labor over things as much, I am far quicker at finding my subjects, and a lot of my subject matter is really gaining respect in the world of art. And I push myself in terms of trying to do work that is unlike anything out there region.

A lot of artists work by electric light, and many do not demand as much light as I do. But if you do a painting by electric light at night when you look at it in daylight it can be a very unpleasant shock.

Also, a painting could be hung in a stairwell or next to a large window, so I figure if it looks good in direct sunlight, it will look good everywhere.

Does painting in natural light allow you to give a more realistic portrayal of your subject?

Not particularly, it is really just the quality of the colors. If you paint under electric light, that yellow light will affect all of the colors when they are seen in natural light, which is a bluer light.

How is the appreciation of your work within the community of artists manifesting itself?

Just two days ago I got a very nice email from an established artist who said he was looking at the Charleston gallery website and saw my work, then proceeded to go to all my websites. He actually said he should put his brushes away, which he meant as a compliment, and he also said that I seem to leave no stone unturned. Then he assured me that I was a more Southern painter than any Southerner he knew of.

His critique must have buoyed your spirits.

It did. Although it came at a time where I feel my work is getting a lot of critical notice and the value in it has gone up, this is still a dificult economy and words like this are a great help.

Explain what's going on with your work now.

The work is selling at good prices, but only in a few, strong markets. The regional art market generally consists of middle-class buyers rather than the wealthiest collectors, and therefore, with this economy, the buying public has diminished.

- **His own worst critic—**

Are you your own worst critic?

I think I am my most critical critic, yes.

On my blog I wrote a thing about how to effectively destroy a painting when it is beyond salvage and only tying up your time. I wrote that you must not kick it, or punch it because canvas is quite resilient and you will hurt your knuckles.

My advice was to "Just step back, breath, reverse the brush in your hand, put a small hole through the center of the canvas, go get a drink, then put the canvas away, calm down, and start on something else."

You have a unique perspective. For example, you've said that awards and prizes are unimportant, but now as you enter your middle years, the end of your beginning years, however you label them, acceptance means more. Right?

Not more, no, less. But it is still important. So is a sense of humor. For example, I was painting with two guys on the Outer Banks recently, and sharing jokes and funny stories about the nuts and bolts of the business. I told a story. An artist asked me "Where do you show in ......?" I replied, "I show at ACS Gallery." "Oh, yeah? I haven't heard of it. What does ACS stand for?" "Air Conditioned Storage."

And a lot of dark humor, too. Our favorite question from Sunday painters attending workshops, "Mr. Davis, what kind of pliers do you recommend for opening tubes of paint that have dried shut."

What discourages you?

The number one discouraging thing at the moment for me is that art has gotten rather dumbed down. The galleries enjoyed a boom through the nineties and got lackadaisical about educating the public.

Many artists also got lazy, and the quality of their work dropped off, pretty much because anything they painted got sold. There needs to be a level of competition for art to be of high quality.

The galleries could sell anything then, so an awful lot of Sunday painters joined galleries that said, "Come aboard." And that became a very big bone of contention with professional artists.

So, art purchasers were then less discerning and relatively uneducated about how to judge what was the better art.

Exactly, and that is very discouraging to my peers and myself. Now many galleries are in this position where they have access to good art, but they don't really have the tools to sell it.

Are you saying that some of the people selling art don't understand it themselves?

Oh they get it, but they are not comfortable saying "This painting is an investment" or that "This artist is better than that artist." One of the reasons I recently had to raise my prices, was simply to draw attention to my experience and achievements compared to new, younger artists. My peers tell me my prices are still too low for where I am in my career.

• Overcoming negatives—

So, you are overcoming the negatives through self-promotion, raising prices and therefore perceived value, and elevating your reputation via museum showings.

That is all true and very well put. In that respect for instance, the work I am doing now is better than ever because I realize I've got to paint completely unique things that almost force people to look, that draws people's attention, that requires the gallery to explain it, and to an extent that justifies the new pricing.

Where are you now in technique and choice of subject matter?

I started focusing on interiors and it seems people are responding, so that is basically what has become a large part of where I am heading subject-wise.

My work, as I said, started off as very traditional, but part of it was modernist, inspired by the post-impressionists, and all sorts of painters from The New York School of Painting in the fifties who did very 'painterly' work that was rejuvenated by Abstract Expressionism.

I kept that sort of painting under the bed, though every now and again I would re-introduce it, but it never became popular with the public.

What came next for you?

I had this second body of work, and that played quite an important part in my career.

I don't know if this story should be in the book but it is interesting as an overview. I was doing a crazy amount of work painting seven days a week producing sort of nineteenth-century type landscape paintings, big, heroic canvases showing Maine and the landscapes of Western North Carolina and parts of the south.

It was a lot of work, but they were priced reasonably and sold as fast as I could paint them. They allowed me to keep experimenting at home.

I had a big show at a gallery that had always sold well. The owner told a local paper that my kind of art paid for them to show the real art exhibited upstairs. They published this negative quote. That was enough for me.

The next year they gave me another one-man show, and I gave them all of the work I had done for myself of the same subject matter, but this time it was very brightly colored expressionist paintings. The public was not amused. It was sort of like when Bob Dylan switched to an electric guitar. It was not popular.

But that was something I had to do as an artist, and it totally revitalized my work. Financially it was a big blow, as I had made 150,000 dollars the year before but that year made only a third of that amount.

Because I had changed my work across the board, and every gallery received the new work, a number of galleries said, "You know this is not what we want, but we prefer your older paintings."

Do you take a lot of risks like that?

Artists take risks, unintentional or not! There is mythology in art that artists always start traditionally then loosen up. Well, they do loosen up, but that is just a pleasant side effect of ageing!

• Painterly realism—

How would you respond to a critic asking "What word or phrase would describe your work?"

I would say my work is 'painterly realism'.

In other words it looks realistic.

That is what I would call it, realistic, but 'painterly' is the art-speak term I would use. It is important to get that clear, so let me put it another way. Some people say my paintings look photographic at a distance.

Most artists hate the word photographic, but that is the best word because at a distance they do look photographic. But when you get close, they dissolve into abstract paintings, and that is really the best definition of painterly realism.

It works on a double level, and that is what satisfies a painterly painter who wants this strange double thing going on when you look at the painting. It could look like a distant hill, and at the same time like two pieces of paint laid over each other.

• Goals for the future—

Do you have set goals for the future, or do you just sort of let things happen?

Those are very good questions. Short-term, it looks like I am going to be pushing more and more towards the sort of work that I first painted when I came to America, of overlooked, abandoned places. That has been the main direction in my work, but my art does reflect my life, too.

I don't how this is going to market, but I am enjoying working on a smaller scale just doing pure landscapes in places like Maine and South Carolina, and from my recent trip to Kiawah. This is all being done on a small level, very painterly, almost abstract.

Does that fill a part of your inner sense of you want to be alone, to be private, to be sequestered?

I have certain landscapes I visit often. They show no sign of man and they give me that sense of peace. There's a tiny island I have painted again and again up in Maine. On my last trip Finn's (my son) mother suggested we paddle over to it. — She was always very good at pushing me to try new things. The interior of the island was littered with shells, old lobster shells, all manner of things dropped by seagulls, all this below the trees shrouded in moss. It was a magical place. I did several quite abstract paintings based just on the memory of this.

- **Confidence going forward—**

Are you confident about your art career in the future?

I think I have confidence in my art, and that probably helps me with rejection and those sorts of things; but finding new ideas and handling problems is one area where I am unfailingly confident.

That aspect of your nature probably helps you accept critique.

That is so true.

Thanks for being so forthright. The goal is to portray the inner essence of each Notable, including Julyan Davis.

This has been very interesting for me because so many changes have happened in my life in what seems like a short time, but this project of yours has caused me to stand back and take stock of my life and career.

After a long period of financial success I am now just like every artist who faces the trials of this economy. But I also am able to begin another chapter in my career as an artist, and I feel better than I have in years about my work and where it can go.

So, after all is said and done, things are looking up for you.

Yes, I really believe they are.

Section 4: **Photos of Julyan Davis' Paintings**

'She looked east, she looked west' (Barbara Allen) Oil on canvas 36x38" 2012

Shady Grove Oil on carved Oak 2002. The traditional music of the Appalachians provided Davis with an emotional tie to the landscape of WNC

Bank Interior, Newbern 2003
Oil on canvas 30x24"

Middlecreek, Winter 1999
Oil on canvas 40x30"
Davis was known for capturing the waterfalls of WNC, particularly those often undiscovered.

Deer Isle, Maine 2000
Oil on canvas 40x30"
Davis bveing a realist painter, and still approaches any new subject with this kind of deference, before familiarity allows him to experiment.

Abandoned Mansion Hale County, Alabama
36x38" 2007
Davis has found his own slant on a part of the South celebrated by photographers Walker Evans and Willian Christenberry.

Green House, Newbern, Alabama.
Oil on canvas 24x30" 2004

Washerteria Oil on canvas 20x36" 2003
Davis' urban scenes show the unexpected beauty in the mundane.

Corner store, Montford Avenue. Oil on canvas 30x72" 2006
Davis lives in Asheville's historic Montford district.

- ## The Artist Explains His Art—

Julyan Davis' Statement for the Greenville Art Museum Show—

The traditional folksong of the Appalachians is close to my heart. I inherited an enthusiasm for such music from my father. With its Celtic origins, it has provided my connection to the Southern landscape since my arrival here twenty three years ago. The songs of this region provide me with an old, familiar narrative and a human history that connects to my own background. Some artists are happy to record every alien vista and strange culture travel can provide, but I have found this old tie important in placing me in this new land.

For many years I painted scenes; landscapes and urban views, old buildings and interiors, with not a figure in sight. Despite this, they were often described as being haunted by a human presence, and as places that somehow told a story. In these new works the figure has entered the scene. Why this return to sentiment? - because the introduction of these figures do add just that, sentiment. My empty views are more dispassionate, journalistic even. They owe a lot to the tone of such photographers as Christenberry, Eggleston, Sternfeld. If anything, these paintings owe more to the medium of film. They want to tell a story, but in a single, evocative image.

These stories are old, but one only has to pick up a newspaper to see they remain fully contemporary. Lovers still fall prey to despair and suicide, or end up in the crime report. These are paintings set very much in the present, but nothing taking place in them is new.

The South wears its passion on its sleeve. It possesses what is referred to as a 'culture of honor', which is a gift to any artist, writer or musician. As in the Scottish Border Country, where 'Barbara Allen' originated many hundreds of years ago, people here take things personally. This makes life compelling. 'Hamlet' would be a play diminished if the hero had just sought therapy instead of revenge. These paintings are about people who are, in Shakespeare's words, 'passion's slave(s)'.

The fact I was given an introduction this winter to the upstate area called the 'Dark Corner' was the happiest coincidence. It provided me with the perfect title for this continuing body of work, and a renewed connection to that particular part of the Blue Ridge - I lived for several years outside Highlands, North Carolina.

With its fiery independence and clannish loyalties, South Carolina's 'Dark Corner' typifies exactly the culture that has kept this music alive for centuries, and acted again and again upon the passion it evokes. And what a name! That was a gift, because these paintings are all about the dark corners to which our hearts can take us.

When I painted the Southern Highlands there was always in my mind this music, full of myth and romance that had long ago been the vanguard from my own country. The characters in this collection of paintings are the ghosts conjured from such landscape.

Section 5: **Chronology**

- **Personal—**
- Born: September 11th, 1965 in Chard, Somerset, England.
- Relocated to the United States 1991—(Tuscaloosa, Alabama)
- Moved to Highlands, North Carolina. 1995
- Primary residence in Asheville, North Carolina since 2005.

- **Education—**
- 1981-1983 Attended South Island School, Hong Kong.
- 1984-1985 Filton College, Bristol. (Art Foundation Course)
- 1985-1988 Byam Shaw School of Art, London. (B.A. Painting and Printmaking)

- **Selected Shows—**
- 2012 — Greenville Museum of Art, Greenville, SC.
- 2012 — Hickory Museum of Art, Hickory, NC.
- 2012 — Helena Fox Fine Art, Charleston, SC
- 2011 — The Bascom, Highlands, NC.
- 2011 — Kiawah Island, SC.
- 2010/7 — Mason Murer Gallery, Atlanta, GA.
- 2009 — George Billis Gallery, New York, NY.
- 2009 — Tinney Contemporary, Nashville, TN
- 2009 — Mauger Modern. Scope Fair. London, Amsterdam, Miami
- 2009 — Greenhut Galleries, Portland, Maine
- 2008 — Mauger Modern Art, Bath, UK
- 2009/8 — Carolina Galleries, Charleston, SC.
- 2007/4 — Blue Spiral 1 Gallery, Asheville, NC.
- 2005 — Carolina Galleries, Charleston, SC.
- 2004/3 — Watson Gallery, Maine.
- 2004 — The Fine Arts Center, Highlands, NC.
- 2004 — John Tucker Fine Art, Savannah, GA.
- 2002 — Birmingham Museum of Art, Birmingham, AL.
- 2001 — Southern Vermont Arts Center, Manchester, VT.
- 1998 — Francis Kyle Gallery, London.
- 1997 — Entergy Building, New Orleans, LA.
- 1995 — First Street Gallery, New York, NY.
- 1995 — Atlantic Gallery, Washington, DC.
- 1994 — Mistral Gallery, London.
- 1993 — Gadsden Arts Center, Gadsden, AL.
- 1988 — Poole Art Center, Poole, Dorset.

- **Selected Collections—**
- Greenville Museum of Art, Greenville, SC.
- Morris Museum, Augusta, GA.
- Gibbes Museum of Art, Charleston, SC.
- Governor's Mansion, Raleigh, NC
- Governor's Western Residence, Asheville, NC
- Bascom Fine Art Center, Highlands, NC.
- Sloss Furnaces National Historic Monument, Birmingham, AL.

- Birmingham Southern College, Birmingham, AL.
- University of Montevallo, Montevallo, AL.
- Samford University, Birmingham, AL
- B.F. Goodrich Corp. Charlotte, NC.
- Mission Hospitals, Asheville, NC.
- National Bank of Commerce
- Amsouth Bank
- Compass Bank
- Banker's Club, Cincinnati, Ohio.
- Skyline Club, Indianapolis, IN.
- Retirement Systems of Alabama, Montgomery, AL.
- Byam Shaw Permanent Collection, London.

- **Reviews and Publications—**
- Nashville Arts Magazine 2011
- Legends Magazine 2011
- Our State Magazine (NC) 2009
- Carolina Home and Garden 2009
- Garden and Gun Magazine 2007
- Carolina Arts Magazine 2005
- Museum and Galleries Guide 2001/1999
- Asheville Citizen-Times 2001
- Birmingham News 2001
- Bangor Daily News 2000
- Savannah Morning Post 2000
- Times-Picayune 1996
- Memphis Commercial Appeal 1994

● ● ●

Final Quotes from the Twelve Notables

"Western North Carolina received a huge boost when Jack Prather and his family came to our mountains to live. It is rare that someone recognizes regular folks in the mountains, much less writes a book about them. He has put in writing the lore of the mountain folks." - **Judge Harry C. Martin**

"To be included with this incredibly talented and accomplished group of individuals is both an honor beyond compare and a very humbling experience." - **Dr. Olson Huff.**

"It is an honor to be included among this group of North Carolinians. I appreciate the time Jack Prather took to get a thorough and complete interview." - **David Holt**

"I am honored to be in the company of such a notable group of kindred spirits whose many and varied good works I have admired over the years, and appreciate Jack Prather's thoughtful authorship. I'm sure the other honorees share my sentiment that we only symbolize the notable contributions beyond measure of fellow citizens who day-in and day-out enhance the quality of life of Western North Carolina and make this a special place to live." - **Doug Orr**

"As I continue to age I still think of myself as a 'boy from Canton' and proud of the summers I worked in the huge Champion Paper Mill that dominated our hometown. The only 'notables' I knew while growing up were the Labor Day Celebration Beauty Queen and the high school football coach. I am humbled to join this illustrious group of Western North Carolina's gifted citizens. Finding myself amongst these genuine form givers, I feel a bit like a lost ball in high weeds but am honored to bring my treasured Haywood County roots to the pages of this book." - **Rev. Dr. Dan Matthews**

"Jack Prather's Zeitgeist intuitiveness is laser-like as he gets to the heart of each notable. Herein he showcases struggle, beauty and success. His genius is in his ability to capture and hold stories that resonate and will be carried out into the greater world, not just for now, but for generations to come." - **Glenis Redmond**

"Jack Prather has assembled an eclectic group of notables to write about. He has pursued this project with passion and 'heart'. I look forward to reading about this interesting group of people from all over Western North Carolina." - **Billie Ruth Sudduth**

"It's an honor to be included in this book, and summoned at this point in my career to be interviewed so thoroughly by the author. Jack Prather's particular slant on our varied lives: his inquiry into how each of us has affected others through our own careers, has been a great reminder of what, finally, we will hope to achieve in our lives. Jack's book came along at the same time I became a father. It's a gift to get this clear view of what matters in the end." - **Julyan Davis**

"When Jack first asked about including me in his book, I took his inquiry in stride. Then I found myself telling stuff that had remained for years my private domain. The interviews not only challenged me, but gave me personal release and a sense of relief that comes with sharing one's shortcomings and failures. Just as accomplishments are inevitably exaggerated and unevenly attributed, we all agonize about our screw-ups while most folks around us don't give them the time of day. They have their own lives to live and their own stories to tell." - **Captain Ray West**

"Little did I know over 40 years ago that a trip to North Carolina to take a class at Penland School of Crafts would settle me here in the mountains for the rest of my life. Like each of the Notables, I am proud to be included among this diverse group of creative and inventive individuals. Thanks to Jack for the opportunity!" - **Richard Ritter**

"I thoroughly enjoyed taking this stroll along my life's path with Jack Prather. It was not only pleasurable, it solidly reinforced my belief that simple acts of kindness and encouragement from teachers at every level can have profound effects. I salute my teachers, who transformed a very mixed up youth into a meaningful member of society. In a sense, it doesn't really matter where one has been; it matters where he is going. Jack has a keen ear and sympathetic approach, and the ability to make what seemed like an impossible task, an easy one." - **Dr. Matt Hayes**

"Western North Carolina is home to many people who have worked unselfishly through their lives to better the lives of thousands. Prather has done an exceptional job of capturing the lives of the more notable ones. I am both honored and humbled to have been included with such an august group of outstanding citizens." - **Joe Epley**

Author Bio—

Jack J. Prather is a multiple award-winning former journalist and public relations strategist, and the author of six books. In 2005, he and wife Pam moved to Hendersonville, North Carolina from New Jersey, after a two-year interlude at Smith Mountain Lake, Virginia.

Twelve Notables in Western North Carolina from Future Now Publishing (FNP) is potentially the launch of a new series of biographies about North Carolinians who have made their mark anywhere in the region, state, nation or world.

A portion of the proceeds from the sale of Jack's books are dedicated to a new Young Writers' Scholarship Fund that he founded.

Prather has written two mystery thriller novels, *The Day of the Knights* (PublishAmerica 2007) and *Investigative Reporter* (Future Now Publishing 2011).

The author's *Speaking Up in Poetry & Prose* (PublishAmerica 2007) consists of fifty pieces about social, political, religious and life issues of importance to all Americans. The book was featured for several years at the Carl Sandburg Home National Historic Site in Flat Rock, where his poem *Sandburg Homage* was on display.

Jack founded The Prather Strategic Public Relations Group in 1978, and FNP in 1986 when he wrote *The PR Bluebook* (S-W Press 1986). That was followed in 1991 by *The Power of PR,* a two-hour video produced by WSUS Channel-8 TV, then a second guidebook titled *All PR is Local* (Amazon-Booksurge 2004).

Diverse clients Jack served during his career as a PR strategist and crisis manager included two U.S. Congressmen, two state legislators, Warner Bros. Jungle Habitat, Space Farms Zoo and Museums, Playboy Resorts Inc., and conference centers, ski areas, healthcare entities, and legal, realty, accounting and financial firms.

Jack was *the* PR consultant to Ames Rubber Corporation, winner of the 1993 Malcolm Baldrige National Total Quality Award presented by President Bill Clinton and the late Secretary of Labor Ron Brown in Washington D.C. Prather's several professional honors include The Communicator 'Award of Distinction' in 1996.

As a young journalist, he earned six New Jersey Press Association writing and editing awards, including Best Column in All Divisions. He later won prizes for magazine articles, op-ed pieces ghost-written for clients, and for poetry.

Member of North Carolina Writers Network, Author's Den, Book Tour, The Book Marketing Network, The Read WNC, The National Read.